Why Do You Need this New Edition?

If you're wondering why you should buy this new edition of *Writing and Reading across the Curriculum, Brief Edition*, here are five good reasons!

1. **A completely new unit on marriage and family** in America (Sociology, Ch. 5), with readings by well-known writers like Stephanie Coontz, Andrew Sullivan, William Bennett, and Alix Kates Shulman explores the changing roles (and expectations) of women as "wives," gay marriage, and "the radical idea" of marrying for love.

2. **A completely new unit on sleep** (Biology, Ch. 8) focuses on the science of sleep, why adolescents and college students are chronically shortchanged, and why school should start later, including a study from the National Sleep Foundation.

3. **New readings** in Ch. 7, What's Happening at the Mall?, examine the history of American shopping malls and their role in contemporary American culture, and a new reading in the widely admired unit on Obedience to Authority (Ch. 6) looks at today's "uncivil disobedience."

4. **New models and examples** in Chs. 1–4 offer enhanced guidance on academic writing.

5. **And a new appendix, "A Guide to Avoiding Plagiarism,"** available in all Longman revisions, helps you understand how to use source material appropriately in your college writing.

Writing and Reading Across the Curriculum

BRIEF EDITION

Third Edition

Laurence Behrens
University of California
Santa Barbara

Leonard J. Rosen
Bentley College

PEARSON
Longman

New York • San Francisco • Boston
London • Toronto • Sydney • Tokyo • Singapore • Madrid
Mexico City • Munich • Paris • Cape Town • Hong Kong • Montreal

Senior Vice President and Publisher: Joseph Opiela
Executive Editor: Suzanne Phelps Chambers
Senior Sponsoring Editor: Virginia L. Blanford
Senior Supplements Editor: Donna Campion
Senior Marketing Manager: Sandra McGuire
Production Manager: Savoula Amanatidis
Project Coordination and Text Design: Elm Street Publishing Services
Electronic Page Makeup: Integra Software Services, Pvt. Ltd.
Cover Design Manager: Wendy Ann Fredericks
Photo Researcher: Julie Tesser
Senior Manufacturing Buyer: Alfred C. Dorsey
Printer and Binder: Courier Corporation—Stoughton
Cover Printer: Courier Corporation—Stoughton

For permission to use copyrighted material, grateful acknowledgment is made to the copyright holders on pp. 509–512, which are hereby made part of this copyright page.

Library of Congress Cataloging-in-Publication Data
Behrens, Laurence.
    Writing and reading across the curriculum, brief edition/Laurence Behrens, Leonard J. Rosen.—Brief ed., 3rd ed.
        p. cm.
    Includes index.
    ISBN-13: 978-0-205-62229-0
        1. College readers. 2. Interdisciplinary approach in education—Problems, exercises, etc.
    3. English language—Rhetoric—Problems, exercises, etc. 4. Academic writing—Problems, exercises, etc. I. Rosen, Leonard J. II. Title.
PE1417.B3965 2008
808'.0427—dc22

                                                                                        2007050116

Please visit us at www.pearsonhighered.com

ISBN-13: 978-0-205-62229-0
ISBN-10: 0-205-62229-1

2 3 4 5 6 7 8 9 10—CS—11 10 09

Contents

Chapter 2
Critical Reading and Critique   25

Chapter 3
Synthesis 51

Chapter 4
Analysis   98

PART II
AN ANTHOLOGY OF READINGS   119

SOCIOLOGY
Chapter 5
Marriage and Family in America   121

PSYCHOLOGY
Chapter 6

Obedience to Authority   204

AMERICAN STUDIES
Chapter 7
What's Happening at the Mall?   264

BUSINESS
Chapter 9
New and Improved: Six Decades of Advertising   406

Preface

Writing and Reading Across the Curriculum: Brief Edition was created for those who find the standard edition appealing and useful but who also find its length impractical. The present text offers five of the most popular anthology chapters, somewhat abridged, from the longer edition. The rhetoric section preceding the anthology of readings has been abbreviated to cover those writing types for which *Writing and Reading Across the Curriculum (WRAC)* is best known: the *summary,* the *critique,* the *synthesis,* and the *analysis.* The *Brief Edition* does not include the longer text's chapters on introductions, conclusions, and theses. Many instructors, however, already supplement their course reader with a handbook that provides ample coverage of these topics, as well as coverage of research and documentation.

STRUCTURE

Like the longer text, *Writing and Reading Across the Curriculum: Brief Edition* is divided into two parts. The first part introduces the strategies of summary, critique, synthesis, and analysis. We take students step-by-step through the process of writing papers based on source material, explaining and demonstrating how summaries, critiques, syntheses, and analyses can be generated from the kinds of readings students will encounter later in the book—and throughout their academic careers. The second part of the text consists of five subject chapters drawn from both academic and professional disciplines. Each subject is not only interesting in its own right but is representative of the kinds of topics typically studied during the course of an undergraduate education. We also believe that students and teachers will discover connections among the thematic chapters of this edition that further enhance opportunities for writing, discussion, and inquiry.

FOCUS ON ARGUMENTATION

Part I of *Writing and Reading Across the Curriculum: Brief Edition* is designed to prepare students for college-level assignments across the disciplines. This edition continues the standard edition's strengthened emphasis on the writing process and on argument, in particular. We emphasize the following:

- **The Elements of Argument: Claim, Support, Assumption.** This section adapts the Toulmin approach to argument to the kinds of readings that students will encounter in Part II of the text.
- **Developing and Organizing the Support for Your Arguments.** This section helps students to mine source materials for facts, expert opinions, and examples that will support their arguments.
- **Annotated Student Argument Paper.** A sample student paper highlights and discusses argumentative strategies that a student writer uses in drafting and developing a paper.

PART I: NEW AND CONTINUING APPARATUS, TOPICS, READINGS, AND STUDENT PAPERS

Throughout Part I, we include boxed material that emphasizes the practical applications of writing summaries, syntheses, and critiques. We also provide brief exercises so that students can practice reading and writing critically in a controlled environment, with specially chosen selections, as they work through the instructional materials.

Chapter 1: Summary

Students are taken through the process of writing a summary of Barbara Graham's "The Future of Love: Kiss Romance Goodbye, It's Time for the Real Thing." We demonstrate how to annotate a source and divide it into sections, how to develop a thesis, and how to write and smoothly join section summaries.

Chapter 2: Critical Reading and Critique

Chapter 2 offers a model critique on "We Are Not Created Equal in Every Way" by Joan Ryan, an op-ed piece that takes a strong view of parents who push their children, at an early age, to become professional dancers and athletes. As in earlier editions, the critique section follows a set of guidelines for practicing critical reading.

Chapter 3: Synthesis

Chapter 3 provides an argument synthesis, "Keeping Volunteerism Voluntary," along with summaries and excerpts of several source materials for that paper. The argument synthesizes opinion pieces by various advocates and opponents of national service. The chapter concludes with a new example comparison-contrast synthesis, framed as a response to an exam question on World War I and World War II.

Chapter 4: Analysis

The analysis chapter opens with brief, competing analyses of *The Wizard of Oz* that demonstrate how, employing different analytical principles (one psychoanalytic and the other political), two writers can read very different meanings into the classic movie. Following an example analysis by Marie Winn that examines excessive television viewing as an addiction ("The Plug-In Drug"), we present a student example of analysis: an application of a theory by sociologist Randall Collins to living conditions in a college dormitory. We explain how to locate principles useful for conducting analyses, and we show how to write analyses themselves. Throughout Part II in the anthology, students will find ample occasions to practice this essential skill.

PART II: THEMATIC CHAPTERS

Part II of *Writing and Reading Across the Curriculum: Brief Edition* provides students with opportunities to practice the skills of summary, synthesis, critique, and analysis they have learned in Part I. Two of the chapters in this section—"Marriage and Family in America" and "To Sleep"—are new to this edition.

Chapter 5: Marriage and Family in America

Definitions of marriage and family, husband and wife, mother and father are changing before our eyes. A once-stable (or so we thought) institution seems under attack—an unusually fertile context in which to offer a new chapter on "Marriage and Family in America." The chapter pivots on the work of marriage scholars like historian Stephanie Coontz and sociologist David Popenoe. Other selections, such as those by Hope Edelman and Eric Bartels, offer personal, often charged accounts of marriage from the inside. Students will follow the debate over gay marriage; they will also examine two ongoing controversies concerning working mothers versus stay-at-home mothers (often referred to as "the Mommy Wars") and the so-called "stalled revolution"—the feminist complaint that, in an age of working women, men have not shouldered their share of household work. We've selected readings that will challenge student assumptions and produce writing informed not only by the provocative and sometimes emotionally raw views of chapter authors but also by their own personal experiences. For each of our students has direct experience with marriage and family—some positive, some not; and each, we believe, can bring the authority of that experience to bear in mature, college-level writing.

Chapter 6: Obedience to Authority

The Obedience chapter continues to build on the profoundly disturbing Milgram experiments. Other selections in this chapter, such as Philip Zimbardo's account of his Stanford prison experiment and Solomon Asch's "Opinions and Social Pressure," have provided additional perspectives on the significance of the obedience phenomenon. This edition adds two new selections. In "Uncivil Disobedience," James J. Lopach and Jean A. Luckowski closely examine radical environmental groups and others who engage in planned disobedience. They find that such groups and individuals often fail to meet the standards of such former practitioners of civil disobedience as Socrates, Gandhi, and Martin Luther King, Jr.

Chapter 7: What's Happening at the Mall?

In this chapter we gather the work of historians, an urban planner, a geographer, a sociologist, a theologian, an American studies scholar, and cultural critics to investigate a fixture on the American landscape: the shopping mall. Malls are not only ubiquitous (48,695 of them as of 2005), they stand at the confluence of streams in American myth, race, class, business, gender, law, and design. As James Farrell, one of the authors in this chapter, puts it: Malls are "a place where we answer important questions: What does it mean to be human? What are people for? What is the meaning of things? Why do we work? What do we work for?" What's happening at the mall, it turns out, is far from obvious. New to this edition: historian Kenneth Jackson's "A Brief History of Malls"; theologian Jon Pahl's exploration of "The Mall as Sacred Space"; and cultural commentator Virginia Postrel's "The Mall as Setting for Authentic Life." The selections gathered here will challenge students' commonplace views of malls. With this chapter we have tried to make the ordinary a bit strange (malls as religious centers?) and in the process provide ample occasion for thoughtful writing.

Chapter 8: To Sleep

Sleep is the most common and, until recently, one of the least understood of human behaviors. Annually, tens of millions of dollars fund basic research on sleep; but experts do not yet know precisely *why* we sleep. This new chapter gathers the work of biologists, neurologists, psychologists, and journalists who specialize in science writing to investigate what one author in this chapter terms a "state so familiar yet so strange." Students will read an overview of sleep and an introduction to the physiology of sleep before moving on to the principal focus of the chapter: the sleep of adolescents—particularly, of college-age adolescents. Various researchers report on the state of adolescent sleep (generally insufficient) and the causes and consequences of and potential solutions to adolescent sleep debt. Quite aside from providing an insight into the science of sleep, this chapter serves a practical function: to educate college students on the mechanics and dangers of sleep debt. Even for those not intending a career in the sciences, learning what happens cognitively and physically when we deprive ourselves of sleep should make for fascinating reading—and create ample opportunities to practice college-level writing.

Chapter 9: New and Improved: Six Decades of Advertising

The centerpiece of this chapter is a portfolio of forty-two full-page advertisements for cigarettes, liquor and beer, automobiles, food, and beauty and cleaning products that have appeared in popular American and British magazines since the mid-1940s. Advertisements are key indicators not only of our consumerism but also of our changing cultural values, and our less variable human psychology. Students will find the advertising chapter ideal for practicing their analysis skills. Prior to the portfolio, we offer several analytic tools that students can use to discern how advertisements operate: how they attempt to manipulate us, how they reveal our values and our sometimes hidden drives. The first article identifies the fifteen basic appeals of advertising; the next two consider the textual and graphic elements of the marketer's craft. A fascinating view of how marketers have presented five product categories over sixty years, this chapter will help students see themselves, culturally speaking, as products of a particular time and place. The chapter remains substantially the same as in the previous edition, with the exception of a new ad for Camel cigarettes replacing the old Virginia Slims ad.

SUPPLEMENTS

The *Instructor's Manual* for *Writing and Reading Across the Curriculum, Brief Edition*, Third Edition, provides sample syllabi and course calendars, chapter summaries, classroom ideas for writing assignments, introductions to each set of readings, and answers to questions included in the text.

In addition, Pearson's **MyCompLab** provides a rich array of resources for students in first-year composition, including writing tutorials, extensive practice opportunities in grammar and usage, and guidance in research and avoiding plagiarism. A new release for Fall 2008 will allow you to write and revise your papers; use interactive tutorials and exercises for grammar, writing, and research; create a study plan and track your progress; do peer review; see instructors' comments; get help with your papers from Smarthinking's e-tutors; and create an e-portfolio of your work. To see more, go to *mycomplab.com.* MyCompLab is available packaged at no additional cost with most Longman texts for composition.

ACKNOWLEDGMENTS

We have benefited over the years from the suggestions and insights of many teachers—and students—across the country. We would especially like to thank these reviewers: David Elias, Eastern Kentucky University; Kathy Ford, Lake Land College; Daven M. Kari, Vanguard University; Lindsay Lewan, Arapahoe Community College; Jolie Martin, San Francisco State Univerisity; Kathy Mendt, Front Range Community College–Larimer Campus; RoseAnn Morgan, Middlesex County College; David Moton, Bakersfield College; Thomas Pfau, Bellevue Community College; Amy Rybak, Bowling Green State University; Horacio Sierra, University of Florida; and Deron Walker, California Baptist University.

We would also like to thank the following reviewers for their help in the preparation of past editions: James Allen, College of DuPage; Chris Anson, North Carolina State University; Phillip Arrington, Eastern Michigan University; Anne Bailey, Southeastern Louisiana University; Carolyn Baker, San Antonio College; Bob Brannan, Johnson County Community College; Joy Bashore, Central Virginia Community College; Nancy Blattner, Southeast Missouri State University; Mary Bly, University of California, Davis; Paul Buczkowski, Eastern Michigan University; Jennifer Bullis, Whatcom Community College; Paige Byam, Northern Kentucky University; Susan Callendar, Sinclair Community College; Anne Carr, Southeast Community College; Jeff Carroll, University of Hawaii; Joseph Rocky Colavito, Northwestern State University; Michael Colonnese, Methodist College; James A. Cornette, Christopher Newport University; Timothy Corrigan, Temple University; Kathryn J. Dawson, Ball State University; Cathy Powers Dice, University of Memphis; Kathleen Dooley, Tidewater Community College; Judith Eastman, Orange Coast College; David Elias, Eastern Kentucky University; Susan Boyd English, Kirkwood Community College; Kathy Evertz, University of Wyoming; Bill Gholson, Southern Oregon University; Karen Gordon, Elgin Community College; Deborah Gutschera, College of DuPage; Lila M. Harper, Central Washington University; M. Todd Harper, University of Louisville; Kip Harvigsen, Ricks College;

Michael Hogan, Southeast Missouri State University; Sandra M. Jensen, Lane Community College; Anita Johnson, Whatcom Community College; Mark Jones, University of Florida; Jane Kaufman, University of Akron; Rodney Keller, Ricks College; Walt Klarner, Johnson County Community College; Jeffery Klausman, Whatcom Community College; Alison Kuehner, Ohlone College; William B. Lalicker, West Chester University; Dawn Leonard, Charleston Southern University; Clifford L. Lewis, University of Massachusetts Lowell; Signee Lynch, Whatcom Community College; Krista L. May, Texas A&M University; Stella Nesanovich, McNeese State University; Roark Mulligan, Christopher Newport University; Joan Mullin, University of Toledo; Susie Paul, Auburn University at Montgomery; Aaron Race, Southern Illinois University–Carbondale; Nancy Redmond, Long Beach City College; Deborah Reese, University of Texas at Arlington; Priscilla Riggle, Bowling Green State University; Jeanette Riley, University of New Mexico; Robert Rongner, Whatcom Community College; Sarah C. Ross, Southeastern Louisiana University; Raul Sanchez, University of Utah; Rebecca Shapiro, Westminster College; Mary Sheldon, Washburn University; Philip Sipiora, University of Southern Florida; Joyce Smoot, Virginia Tech; Bonnie A. Spears, Chaffey College; Bonnie Startt, Tidewater Community College; R. E. Stratton, University of Alaska–Fairbanks; Katherine M. Thomas, Southeast Community College; Victor Villanueva, Washington State University; Jackie Wheeler, Arizona State University; Pat Stephens Williams, Southern Illinois University at Carbondale; and Kristin Woolever, Northeastern University.

We gratefully acknowledge the work of Michael Behrens, who made significant contributions to the "Marriage and Family in America" chapter.

A special thanks to Suzanne Phelps Chambers, Rebecca Gilpin, Beth Keister, and Martha Beyerlein for helping shepherd the manuscript through the editorial and production process. And our continued gratitude to Joe Opiela, longtime friend, supporter, and publisher. Our former editor Ginny Blanford has moved to other projects, and we thank her for her able stewardship of our books over the years.

LAURENCE BEHRENS
LEONARD J. ROSEN

A Note to the Student

Your sociology professor asks you to write a paper on attitudes toward the homeless population of an urban area near your campus. You are expected to consult books, articles, Web sites, and other online sources on the subject, and you are also encouraged to conduct surveys and interviews.

Your professor is making a number of assumptions about your capabilities. Among them:

- that you can research and assess the value of relevant sources;
- that you can comprehend college-level material, both print and electronic;
- that you can use theories and principles learned from one set of sources as tools to investigate other sources (or events, people, places, or things);
- that you can synthesize separate but related sources;
- that you can intelligently respond to such material.

In fact, these same assumptions underlie practically all college writing assignments. Your professors will expect you to demonstrate that you can read and understand not only textbooks but also critical articles and books, primary sources, Internet sources, online academic databases, CD-ROMs, and other material related to a particular subject of study. For example: For a paper on the progress of the Human Genome Project, you would probably look to articles and Internet sources for the most recent information. Using an online database, you would find articles on the subject in such print journals as *Nature, Journal of the American Medical Association,* and *Bioscience,* as well as leading newspapers and magazines. A Web search engine might lead you to a useful site called "A New Gene Map of the Human Genome" <http://www.ncbi.nlm.nih.gov/genemap99/> and the site of the "Sequencing" section of the U.S. Department of Energy Joint Genome Institute <http://www.jgi/doe/gov/sequencing/index/html>. You would be expected to assess the relevance of such sources to your topic and to draw from them the information and ideas you need. It's even possible that the final product of your research and reading may not be a conventional paper at all, but rather a Web site you create that explains the science behind the Human Genome Project, explores a particular controversy about the project, or describes the future benefits geneticists hope to derive from the project.

You might, for a different class, be assigned a research paper on the films of director Martin Scorsese. To get started, you might consult your film studies textbook, biographical sources on Scorsese, and anthologies of criticism. Instructor and peer feedback on a first draft might lead you to articles in both popular magazines (such as *Time*) and scholarly journals (such as *Literature/Film Quarterly*), a CD-ROM database (such as *Film Index International*), and relevant Web sites (such as the "Internet Movie Database" <http://us.imdb.com>).

These two example assignments are very different, of course; but the skills you need to work with them are the same. You must be able to research relevant sources. You must be able to read and comprehend these sources. You must be able to perceive the relationships among several pieces of source material. And you must be able to apply your own critical judgments to these various materials.

Writing and Reading Across the Curriculum: Brief Edition provides you with the opportunity to practice the essential college-level skills we have just outlined and the forms of writing associated with them, namely:

- the *summary*
- the *critique*
- the *synthesis*
- the *analysis*

Each chapter of Part II of this text represents a subject from a particular area of the academic curriculum: Sociology, Psychology, American Studies, Biology, and Business. These chapters, dealing with such topics as "Marriage and Family in America," "Obedience to Authority," and "What's Happening at the Mall?," illustrate the types of material you will study in your other courses.

Questions following the readings will allow you to practice typical college writing assignments. Review Questions help you recall key points of content. Discussion and Writing Suggestions ask you for personal, sometimes imaginative, responses to the readings. Synthesis Activities at the end of each chapter allow you to practice assignments of the type that are covered in detail in Part I of this book. For instance, you may be asked to *summarize* the Milgram experiment and the reactions to it, or to *compare and contrast* a controlled experiment with a real-life (or fictional) situation. Finally, Research Activities ask you to go beyond the readings in this text in order to conduct your own independent research on these subjects.

In this book, you'll find articles and essays written by physicians, literary critics, sociologists, psychologists, political scientists, journalists, and specialists from other fields. Our aim is that you become familiar with the various subjects and styles of academic writing and that you come to appreciate the interrelatedness of knowledge. Political scientists and dramatists, as well as psychologists, can throw light on how and why we respond as we do to authority figures. Human activity and human behavior are classified into separate subjects only for convenience. The novel you read in your literature course may be able to shed some light upon an assigned article for your economics course—and vice versa.

We hope, therefore, that your writing course will serve as a kind of bridge to your other courses and that as a result of this work you will become more skillful at perceiving relationships among diverse topics. Because it involves such critical and widely applicable skills, your writing course may well turn out to be one of the most valuable—and one of the most interesting—of your academic career.

LAURENCE BEHRENS
LEONARD J. ROSEN

How to Write Summaries, Critiques, Syntheses, and Analyses

Summary

WHAT IS A SUMMARY?

The best way to demonstrate that you understand the information and the ideas in any piece of writing is to compose an accurate and clearly written summary of that piece. By a *summary* we mean a *brief restatement, in your own words, of the content of a passage* (a group of paragraphs, a chapter, an article, a book). This restatement should focus on the *central idea* of the passage. The briefest of summaries (one or two sentences) will do no more than this. A longer, more complete summary will indicate, in condensed form, the main points in the passage that support or explain the central idea. It will reflect the order in which these points are presented and the emphasis given to them. It may even include some important examples from the passage. But it will not include minor details. It will not repeat points simply for the purpose of emphasis. And it will not contain any of your own opinions or conclusions. A good summary, therefore, has three central qualities: *brevity, completeness,* and *objectivity.*

CAN A SUMMARY BE OBJECTIVE?

Of course, the last quality mentioned above, objectivity, might be difficult to achieve in a summary. By definition, writing a summary requires you to select some aspects of the original and leave out others. Since deciding what to select and what to leave out calls for your personal judgment, your summary really is a work of interpretation. And, certainly, your interpretation of a passage may differ from another person's. One factor affecting the nature and quality of your interpretation is your *prior knowledge* of the subject. For example, if you're attempting to summarize an anthropological article and you're a novice in that field, then your summary of the article will likely differ from that of your professor, who has spent 20 years studying this particular area and whose judgment about what is more or less significant is undoubtedly more reliable than your own. By the same token, your personal or professional *frame of reference* may also affect your interpretation. A union representative and a management representative attempting to summarize the latest management offer would probably come up with two very different accounts. Still, we believe that in most cases it's possible to produce a reasonably objective summary of a passage if you make a conscious, good-faith effort to be unbiased and to prevent your own feelings on the subject from coloring your account of the author's text.

USING THE SUMMARY

In some quarters, the summary has a bad reputation—and with reason. Summaries often are provided by writers as substitutes for analyses. As students, many of us have summarized books that we were supposed to *review critically*. All the same, the summary does have a place in respectable college work. First, writing a summary is an excellent way to understand what you read. This in itself is an important goal of academic study. If you don't understand your source material, chances are you won't be able to refer to it usefully in a paper. Summaries help you understand what you read because they force you to put the text into your own words. Practice with writing summaries also develops your general writing habits, since a good summary, like any other piece of good writing, is clear, coherent, and accurate.

WHERE DO WE FIND WRITTEN SUMMARIES?

Here are just a few of the types of writing that involve summary:

Academic Writing

- **Critique papers.** Summarize material in order to critique it.
- **Synthesis papers.** Summarize to show relationships between sources.
- **Analysis papers.** Summarize theoretical perspectives before applying them.
- **Research papers.** Note-taking and reporting research require summary.
- **Literature reviews.** Overviews of work presented in brief summaries.
- **Argument papers.** Summarize evidence and opposing arguments.
- **Essay exams.** Demonstrate understanding of course materials through summary.

Workplace Writing

- **Policy briefs.** Condense complex public policy.
- **Business plans.** Summarize costs, relevant environmental impacts, and other important matters.
- **Memos, letters, and reports.** Summarize procedures, meetings, product assessments, expenditures, and more.
- **Medical charts.** Record patient data in summarized form.
- **Legal briefs.** Summarize relevant facts and arguments of cases.

Second, summaries are useful to your readers. Let's say you're writing a paper about the McCarthy era in the United States, and in part of that paper you want to discuss Arthur Miller's *Crucible* as a dramatic treatment of the subject. A summary of the plot would be helpful to a reader who hasn't seen or read—or who doesn't remember—the play. Or perhaps you're writing a paper about the politics of recent American military interventions. If your reader isn't likely to be familiar with American actions in Kosovo and Afghanistan, it would be a good idea to summarize these events at some early point in the paper. In many cases (an exam, for instance), you can use a summary to demonstrate your knowledge of what your professor already knows; when writing a paper, you can use a summary to inform your professor about some relatively unfamiliar source.

Third, summaries are required frequently in college-level writing. For example, on a psychology midterm, you may be asked to explain Carl Jung's theory of the collective unconscious and to show how it differs from Sigmund Freud's theory of the personal unconscious. You may have read about this theory in your textbook or in a supplementary article, or your instructor may have outlined it in her lecture. You can best demonstrate your understanding of Jung's theory by summarizing it. Then you'll proceed to contrast it with Freud's theory—which, of course, you must also summarize.

THE READING PROCESS

It may seem to you that being able to tell (or retell) in summary form exactly what a passage says is a skill that ought to be taken for granted in anyone who can read at high school level. Unfortunately, this is not so: For all kinds of reasons, people don't always read carefully. In fact, it's probably safe to say that usually they don't. Either they read so inattentively that they skip over words, phrases, or even whole sentences, or, if they do see the words in front of them, they see them without registering their significance.

When a reader fails to pick up the meaning and implications of a sentence or two, usually there's no real harm done. (An exception: You could lose credit on an exam or paper because you failed to read or to realize the significance of a crucial direction by your instructor.) But over longer stretches— the paragraph, the section, the article, or the chapter—inattentive or haphazard reading interferes with your goals as a reader: to perceive the shape of the argument, to grasp the central idea, to determine the main points that compose it, to relate the parts of the whole, and to note key examples. This kind of reading takes a lot more energy and determination than casual reading. But, in the long run, it's an energy-saving method because it enables you to retain the content of the material and to draw upon that content in your own responses. In other words, it allows you to develop an accurate and coherent written discussion that goes beyond summary.

CRITICAL READING FOR SUMMARY

- *Examine the context.* Note the credentials, occupation, and publications of the author. Identify the source in which the piece originally appeared. This information helps illuminate the author's perspective on the topic he or she is addressing.
- *Note the title and subtitle.* Some titles are straightforward, whereas the meanings of others become clearer as you read. In either case, titles typically identify the topic being addressed and often reveal the author's attitude toward that topic.
- *Identify the main point.* Whether a piece of writing contains a thesis statement in the first few paragraphs or builds its main point without stating it up front, look at the entire piece to arrive at an understanding of the overall point being made.
- *Identify the subordinate points.* Notice the smaller subpoints that make up the main point, and make sure you understand how they relate to the main point. If a particular subpoint doesn't clearly relate to the main point you've identified, you may need to modify your understanding of the main point.
- *Break the reading into sections.* Notice which paragraph(s) make up a piece's introduction, body, and conclusion. Break up the body paragraphs into sections that address the writer's various subpoints.
- *Distinguish between points, examples, and counterarguments.* Critical reading requires careful attention to what a writer is *doing* as well as what he or she is *saying.* When a writer quotes someone else, or relays an example of something, ask yourself why this is being done. What point is the example supporting? Is another source being quoted as support for a point, or as a counterargument that the writer sets out to address?
- *Watch for transitions within and between paragraphs.* In order to follow the logic of a piece of writing, as well as to distinguish between points, examples, and counterarguments, pay attention to the transitional words and phrases writers use. Transitions function like road signs, preparing the reader for what's next.
- *Read actively and recursively.* Don't treat reading as a passive, linear progression through a text. Instead, read as though you are engaged in a dialogue with the writer: Ask questions of the text as you read, make notes in the margin, underline key ideas in pencil, put question or exclamation marks next to passages that confuse or excite you. Go back to earlier points once you finish a reading, stop during your reading to recap what's come so far, and move back and forth through a text.

HOW TO WRITE SUMMARIES

Every article you read will present a unique challenge as you work to summarize it. As you'll discover, saying in a few words what has taken someone else a great many can be difficult. But like any other skill, the ability to summarize improves with practice. Here are a few pointers to get you started. They represent possible stages, or steps, in the process of writing a summary. These pointers are not meant to be ironclad rules; rather, they are designed to encourage habits of thinking that will allow you to vary your technique as the situation demands.

GUIDELINES FOR WRITING SUMMARIES

- *Read the passage carefully.* Determine its structure. Identify the author's purpose in writing. (This will help you distinguish between more important and less important information.) Make a note in the margin when you get confused or when you think something is important; highlight or underline points sparingly, if at all.
- *Reread.* This time divide the passage into sections or stages of thought. The author's use of paragraphing will often be a useful guide. *Label,* on the passage itself, each section or stage of thought. *Underline* key ideas and terms. Write notes in the margin.
- *Write one-sentence summaries,* on a separate sheet of paper, of each stage of thought.
- *Write a thesis—a one- or two-sentence summary of the entire passage.* The thesis should express the central idea of the passage, as you have determined it from the preceding steps. You may find it useful to follow the approach of most newspaper stories—naming the *what, who, why, where, when,* and *how* of the matter. For persuasive passages, summarize in a sentence the author's conclusion. For descriptive passages, indicate the subject of the description and its key feature(s). Note: In some cases, *a suitable thesis may already be in the original passage.* If so, you may want to quote it directly in your summary.
- *Write the first draft of your summary* by (1) combining the thesis with your list of one-sentence summaries or (2) combining the thesis with one-sentence summaries *plus* significant details from the passage. In either case, eliminate repetition and less important information. Disregard minor details or generalize them (e.g., Bill Clinton and George W. Bush might be generalized as "recent presidents"). Use as few words as possible to convey the main ideas.
- *Check your summary against the original passage* and make whatever adjustments are necessary for accuracy and completeness.

(continued)

> • *Revise your summary,* inserting transitional words and phrases where necessary to ensure coherence. Check for style. *Avoid a series of short, choppy sentences.* Combine sentences for a smooth, logical flow of ideas. Check for grammatical correctness, punctuation, and spelling.

DEMONSTRATION: SUMMARY

To demonstrate these points at work, let's go through the process of summarizing a passage of expository material—that is, writing that is meant to inform and/or persuade. Read the following selection carefully. Try to identify its parts and understand how they work together to create an overall point.

The Future of Love: Kiss Romance Goodbye, It's Time for the Real Thing
Barbara Graham

Author of the satire Women Who Run with Poodles: Myths and Tips for Honoring Your Mood Swings *(Avon, 1994), Barbara Graham has written articles for* Vogue, Self, Common Boundary, *and other publications. She regularly contributes articles to the* Utne Reader, *from which this essay was taken.**

1   Freud and his psychoanalytic descendants are no doubt correct in their assessment that the search for ideal love—for that one perfect soulmate—is the futile wish of not fully developed selves. But it also seems true that the longing for a profound, all-consuming erotic connection (and the heightened state of awareness that goes with it) is in our very wiring. The yearning for fulfillment through love seems to be to our psychic structure what food and water are to our cells.

2   Just consider the stories and myths that have shaped our consciousness: Beauty and the Beast, Snow White and her handsome prince, Cinderella and Prince Charming, Fred and Ginger, Barbie and Ken. (Note that, with the exception of the last two couples, all of these lovers are said to have lived happily ever after—even though we never get details of their lives after the weddings, after children and gravity and loss have exacted their price.) Still, it's not just these

---

* Barbara Graham, "The Future of Love: Kiss Romance Goodbye, It's Time for the Real Thing," *Utne Reader* Jan.–Feb. 1997: 20–23.

lucky fairy tale characters who have captured our collective imag
tragic twosomes we cut our teeth on—Romeo and Juliet, Tristan a.
Launcelot and Guinevere, Heathcliff and Cathy, Rhett and Scarlett—a.
more compelling role models. Their love is simply too powerful and anarci.
too shattering and exquisite, to be bound by anything so conventional as marriage or a long-term domestic arrangement.

3   If recent divorce and remarriage statistics are any indication, we're not as
astute as the doomed lovers. Instead of drinking poison and putting an end to
our love affairs while the heat is still turned up full blast, we expect our marriages and relationships to be long-running fairy tales. When they're not, instead
of examining our expectations, we switch partners and reinvent the fantasy,
hoping that this time we'll get it right. It's easy to see why: Despite all the talk
of family values, we're constantly bombarded by visions of perfect romance. All
you have to do is turn on the radio or TV or open any magazine and check out
the perfume and lingerie ads. "Our culture is deeply regressed," says Florence
Falk, a New York City psychotherapist. "Everywhere we turn, we're faced with
glamorized, idealized versions of love. It's as if the culture wants us to stay
trapped in the fantasy and does everything possible to encourage and expand
that fantasy." Trying to forge an authentic relationship amidst all the romantic
hype, she adds, makes what is already a tough proposition even harder.

4   What's most unusual about our culture is our feverish devotion to the belief
that romantic love and marriage should be synonymous. Starting with George
and Martha, continuing through Ozzie and Harriet right up to the present day,
we have tirelessly tried to formalize, rationalize, legalize, legitimize, politicize
and sanitize rapture. This may have something to do with our puritanical roots,
as well as our tendency toward oversimplification. In any event, this attempt to
satisfy all of our contradictory desires under the marital umbrella must be put in
historical context in order to be properly understood.

5   "Personal intimacy is actually quite a new idea in human history and was
never part of the marriage ideal before the 20th century," says John Welwood,
a Northern California–based psychologist and author, most recently, of *Love and
Awakening.* "Most couples throughout history managed to live together their
whole lives without ever having a conversation about what was going on within
or between them. As long as family and society prescribed the rules of marriage,
individuals never had to develop any consciousness in this area."

6   In short, marriage was designed to serve the economic and social needs of
families, communities, and religious institutions, and had little or nothing to do
with love. Nor was it expected to satisfy lust.

7   In *Myths to Live By,* Joseph Campbell explains how the sages of ancient India
viewed the relationship between marriage and passion. They concluded that
there are five degrees of love, he writes, "through which a worshiper is increased
in the service and knowledge of his God." The first degree has to do with the
relationship of the worshiper to the divine. The next three degrees of love, in
order of importance, are friendship, the parent/child relationship, and marriage.
The fifth and highest form is passionate, illicit love. "In marriage, it is declared,
one is still possessed of reason," Campbell adds. "The seizure of passionate love

can be, in such a context, only illicit, breaking in upon the order of one's duti-ful life in virtue as a devastating storm."

8   No wonder we're having problems. The pressures we place on our tender unions are unprecedented. Even our biochemistry seems to militate against long-term sexual relationships. Dr. Helen Fisher, an anthropologist at Rutgers University and author of *Anatomy of Love*, believes that human pair-bonds orig-inally evolved according to "the ancient blueprint of serial monogamy and clan-destine adultery" and are originally meant to last around four years—at least long enough to raise a single dependent child through toddlerhood. The so-called seven-year-itch may be the remains of a four-year reproductive cycle, Fisher suggests.

9   Increasingly, Fisher and other researchers are coming to view what we call love as a series of complex biochemical events governed by hormones and enzymes. "People cling to the idea that romantic love is a mystery, but it's also a chemical experience," Fisher says, explaining that there are three distinct mating emotions and each is supported in the brain by the release of different chemicals. Lust, an emotion triggered by changing levels of testosterone in men and women, is associated with our basic sexual drive. Infatuation depends on the changing levels of dopamine, norepinephrine, and phenylethylamine (PEA), also called the "chemicals of love." They are natural—addictive—amphetaminelike chemicals that stimulate euphoria and make us want to stay up all night sharing our secrets. After infatuation and the dizzying highs asso-ciated with it have peaked—usually within a year or two—this brain chemistry reduces, and a new chemical system made up of oxytocin, vasopressin, and maybe the endorphins kicks in and supports a steadier, quieter, more nurturing intimacy. In the end, regardless of whether biochemistry accounts for cause or effect in love, it may help to explain why some people—those most responsive to the release of the attachment chemicals—are able to sustain a long-term partnership, while thrillseekers who feel depressed without regular hits of dopamine and PEA are likely to jump from one liaison to the next in order to maintain a buzz.

10   But even if our biochemistry suggests that there should be term limits on love, the heart is a stubborn muscle and, for better or worse, most of us contin-ue to yearn for a relationship that will endure. As a group, Generation Xers—many of whom are children of divorce—are more determined than any other demographic group to have a different kind of marriage than their parents and to avoid divorce, says Howard Markman, author of *Fighting for Your Marriage*. What's more, lesbians and gay men who once opposed marriage and all of its heterosexual, patriarchal implications now seek to reframe marriage as a more flexible, less repressive arrangement. And, according to the U.S. National Center for Health Statistics, in one out of an estimated seven weddings, either the bride or the groom—or both—are tying the knot for at least the third time—nearly twice as many as in 1970. There are many reasons for this, from the surge in the divorce rate that began in the '70s, to our ever-increasing life span. Even so, the fact that we're still trying to get love right—knowing all we know about the ephemeral nature of passion, in a time when the stigmas

once associated with being divorced or single have all but disappeared—says something about our powerful need to connect.

11   And, judging from the army of psychologists, therapists, clergy, and other experts who can be found dispensing guidance on the subject, the effort to save—or reinvent, depending on who's doing the talking—love and marriage has become a multimillion dollar industry. The advice spans the spectrum. There's everything from *Rules*, by Ellen Fein and Sherrie Schneider, a popular new book which gives 90's women 50's-style tips on how to catch and keep their man, to Harville Hendrix's *Getting the Love You Want*, and other guides to "conscious love." But regardless of perspective, this much is clear: Never before have our most intimate thoughts and actions been so thoroughly dissected, analyzed, scrutinized and medicalized. Now, people who fall madly in love over and over are called romance addicts. Their disease, modeled on alcoholism and other chemical dependencies, is considered "progressive and fatal."

12   Not everyone believes the attempt to deconstruct love is a good thing. The late philosopher Christopher Lasch wrote in his final book, *Women and the Common Life:* "The exposure of sexual life to scientific scrutiny contributed to the rationalization, not the liberation, of emotional life." His daughter, Elisabeth Lasch-Quinn, an historian at Syracuse University and the editor of the book, agrees. She contends that the progressive demystification of passionate life since Freud has promoted an asexual, dispassionate and utilitarian form of love. Moreover, like her father, she believes that the national malaise about romance can be attributed to insidious therapeutic modes of social control—a series of mechanisms that have reduced the citizen to a consumer of expertise. "We have fragmented life in such a way," she says, "as to take passion out of our experience."

13   Admittedly, it's a stretch to picture a lovesick 12th-century French troubadour in a 12-step program for romance addicts. Still, we can't overlook the fact that our society's past efforts to fuse together those historically odd bedfellows— passionate love and marriage—have failed miserably. And though it's impossible to know whether all the attention currently being showered on relationships is the last gasp of a dying social order—marriage—or the first glimmer of a new paradigm for relating to one another, it's obvious that something radically different is needed.

Read, Reread, Highlight

Let's consider our recommended pointers for writing a summary.

As you reread the passage, note in the margins of the essay important points, shifts in thought, and questions you may have. Consider the essay's significance as a whole and its stages of thought. What does it say? How is it organized? How does each part of the passage fit into the whole? What do all these points add up to?

Here is how the first few paragraphs of Graham's article might look after you had marked the main ideas, by highlighting and by marginal notations.

Freud and his psychoanalytic descendants are no doubt correct in their assessment that the search for ideal love—for that one perfect soulmate—is the futile wish of not fully developed selves. But it also seems true that the longing for a profound, all-consuming erotic connection (and the heightened state of awareness that goes with it) is in our very wiring. The yearning for fulfillment through love seems to be to our psychic structure what food and water are to our cells.

psychic importance of love

Just consider the stories and myths that have shaped our consciousness: Beauty and the Beast, Snow White and her handsome prince, Cinderella and Prince Charming, Fred and Ginger, Barbie and Ken. (Note that, with the exception of the last two couples, all of these lovers are said to have lived happily ever after—even though we never get details of their lives after the weddings, after children and gravity and loss have exacted their price.) Still, it's not just these lucky fairy tale characters who have captured our collective imagination. The tragic twosomes we cut our teeth on—Romeo and Juliet, Tristan and Iseult, Launcelot and Guinevere, Heathcliff and Cathy, Rhett and Scarlett—are even more compelling role models. Their love is simply too powerful and anarchic, too shattering and exquisite, to be bound by anything so conventional as marriage or a long-term domestic arrangement. If recent divorce and remarriage statistics are any indication, we're not as astute as the doomed lovers. Instead of drinking poison and putting an end to our love affairs while the heat is still turned up full blast, we expect our marriages and relationships to be long-running fairy tales. When they're not, instead of examining our expectations, we switch partners and reinvent the fantasy, hoping that this time we'll get it right. It's easy to see why: Despite all the talk of family values, we're constantly bombarded by visions of perfect romance. All you have to do is turn on the radio or TV or open any magazine and check out the perfume and lingerie ads. "Our culture is deeply regressed," says Florence Falk, a New York City psychotherapist. "Everywhere we turn, we're faced with glamorized, idealized versions of love. It's as if the culture wants us to stay trapped in the fantasy and does everything possible to encourage and expand that fantasy." Trying to forge an authentic relationship amidst all the romantic hype, she adds, makes what is already a tough proposition even harder.

fictional, sometimes tragic examples of ideal love

difficulty of having a real relationship in a culture that glamorizes ideal love

What's most unusual about our culture is our feverish devotion to the belief that romantic love and marriage should be synonymous. Starting with George and Martha, continuing through Ozzie and Harriet right up to the present day, we have tirelessly tried to formalize, rationalize, legalize, legitimize, politicize and sanitize rapture. This may have something to do with our puritanical roots, as well as our tendency toward oversimplification. In any event, this attempt to satisfy all of our contradictory

contradictions of ideal love and marriage

desires under the marital umbrella must be put in historical context in order to be properly understood.

"personal intimacy" never considered part of marriage before 20th century

"Personal intimacy is actually quite a new idea in human history and was never part of the marriage ideal before the 20th century," says John Welwood, a Northern California–based psychologist and author, most recently, of *Love and Awakening*. "Most couples throughout history managed to live together their whole lives without ever having a conversation about what was going on within or between them. As long as family and society prescribed the rules of marriage, individuals never had to develop any consciousness in this area."

In short, marriage was designed to serve the economic and social needs of families, communities, and religious institutions, and had little or nothing to do with love. Nor was it expected to satisfy lust.

Divide Selection into Stages of Thought

When a selection doesn't contain sections with thematic headings, as is the case with "The Future of Love," how do you determine where one stage of thought ends and the next one begins? Assuming that what you have read is coherent and unified, this should not be difficult. (When a selection is unified, all of its parts pertain to the main subject; when a selection is coherent, the parts follow one another in logical order.) Look, particularly, for transitional sentences at the beginning of paragraphs. Such sentences generally work in one or both of the following ways: (1) they summarize what has come before; (2) they set the stage for what is to follow.

For example, look at the sentence that opens paragraph 10: "But even if our biochemistry suggests that there should be term limits on love, the heart is a stubborn muscle and, for better or worse, most of us continue to yearn for a relationship that will endure." Notice how the first part of this sentence restates the main idea of the preceding section. The second part of the transitional sentence announces the topic of the upcoming section: three paragraphs devoted to the efforts people make to attain, save, or reinvent romantic relationships.

Each section of an article generally takes several paragraphs to develop. Between paragraphs, and almost certainly between sections of an article, you will usually find transitions that help you understand what you have just read and what you are about to read. For articles that have no subheadings, try writing your own section headings in the margins as you take notes. Then proceed with your summary.

The sections of Graham's article may be described as follows:

> **Section 1:** *Introduction*--a yearning for "fulfill-
> ment through love" pervades our culture, and that
> yearning is shaped by myths and romantic fan-
> tasies (paragraphs 1-3).

Section 2: *Marriage and love*--we expect passionate love to lead to happy, lifelong marriage. This is a relatively new and unique practice in human history (paragraphs 4-7).

Section 3: *Biochemistry and love*--love has a biochemical component, which complicates our abilities to sustain long-term relationships (paragraphs 8-9).

Section 4: *Marriage and love revisited*--many people are currently trying to preserve and/or reinvent marriage and love (paragraphs 10-12).

Section 5: *Conclusion*--the fusion of passionate love with the institution of marriage hasn't worked very well, and we need something "radically different" to replace it (paragraph 13).

Write a One- or Two-Sentence Summary of Each Stage of Thought

The purpose of this step is to wean you from the language of the original passage, so that you are not tied to it when writing the summary. Here are one-sentence summaries for each stage of thought in "The Future of Love" article's five sections:

Section 1: Introduction—a yearning for "fulfillment through love" pervades our culture, and that yearning is shaped by myths and romantic fantasies (paragraphs 1–3).

Most members of American culture crave romantic love, but we have unreal expectations based upon idealized images of love we learn from fantasies and fairy tales.

Section 2: Marriage and love—we expect passionate love to lead to happy, lifelong marriage. This is a relatively new and unique practice in human history (paragraphs 4–7).

We expect the passionate love of fairy tales to lead to "happily ever after" in the institution of marriage, and when this fails, we move on and try it again. Ironically, the idea that marriage should be based on love--rather than upon social

and economic concerns--is a relatively recent
practice in Western history.

Section 3: Biochemistry and love—love has a biochemical component,
which complicates our abilities to sustain long-term relationships (paragraphs 8–9).

Biochemists are discovering that love and lust
have hormonal causes, and their evidence suggests
that our biological makeup predisposes us to seek
the excitement of short-term relationships.

Section 4: Marriage and love revisited—many people are currently trying
to preserve and/or reinvent marriage and love (paragraphs 10–12).

Despite all the difficulties, we spend a lot of
time analyzing the elements of relationships in
order to preserve or perhaps reinvent marriage.
We clearly want to make it work.

Section 5: Conclusion—the fusion of passionate love with the institution of
marriage hasn't worked very well, and we need something "radically different" to replace it (paragraph 13).

Because confining passionate love to the institution of marriage hasn't worked very well, we need
to revise our model for human relationships.

Write a Thesis: A One- or Two-Sentence Summary of the Entire Passage

The thesis is the most general statement of a summary (or any other type of
academic writing). It is the statement that announces the paper's subject and
the claim that you or—in the case of a summary—another author will be
making about that subject. Every paragraph of a paper illuminates the thesis
by providing supporting detail or explanation. The relationship of these paragraphs to the thesis is analogous to the relationship of the sentences within
a paragraph to the topic sentence. Both the thesis and the topic sentences are
general statements (the thesis being the more general) that are followed by
systematically arranged details.

To ensure clarity for the reader, *the first sentence of your summary should begin
with the author's thesis, regardless of where it appears in the article itself.* Authors
may locate their thesis at the beginning of their work, in which case the thesis
operates as a general principle from which details of the presentation follow.
This is called a *deductive* organization: thesis first, supporting details second.
Alternately, an author may locate his or her thesis at the end of the work, in
which case the author begins with specific details and builds toward a more

general conclusion, or thesis. This is called an *inductive* organization—an example of which you see in "The Future of Love."

A thesis consists of a subject and an assertion about that subject. How can we go about fashioning an adequate thesis for a summary of "The Future of Love"? Probably no two proposed thesis statements for this article would be worded identically, but it is fair to say that any reasonable thesis will indicate that the subject is the current state of love and marriage in American society. How does Graham view the topic? What *is* the current state of love and marriage, in her view? Looking back over our section summaries, Graham's focus on the illusions of fairy tales and myths, the difference between marriage in the present day and its earlier incarnations, and the problems of divorce and "romance addiction" suggests that she does not view the current state of affairs in an altogether positive light. Does she make a statement anywhere that pulls all this together? Her conclusion, in paragraph 13, contains her main idea: "our society's past efforts to fuse together those historically odd bedfellows—passionate love and marriage—have failed miserably." Moreover, in the next sentence, she says, "it's obvious that something radically different is needed." Further evidence of Graham's main point can be found in the complete title of the essay: "The Future of Love: Kiss Romance Goodbye, It's Time for the Real Thing." Mindful of Graham's subject and the assertion she makes about it, we can write a thesis statement *in our own words* and arrive at the following:

> The contemporary institution of marriage is in trouble, and this may be due to our unrealistic expectations that passionate love leads to lasting union; it may be time to develop a new model for love and relationships.

To clarify for our readers the fact that this idea is Graham's and not ours, we'll qualify the thesis as follows:

> In her article "The Future of Love: Kiss Romance Goodbye, It's Time for the Real Thing," Barbara Graham describes how our unrealistic expectations that passionate love leads to lasting union may be partly causing the troubled state of marriage today; thus she suggests we develop a new model for love and relationships.

The first sentence of a summary is crucially important, for it orients readers by letting them know what to expect in the coming paragraphs. In the example above, the sentence refers directly to an article, its author, and the thesis for the upcoming summary. The author and title reference also could be indicated in the summary's title (if this were a freestanding summary), in which case their mention could be dropped from the thesis. And lest you become frustrated too quickly, keep in mind that writing an acceptable thesis for a summary takes time. In this case, it took three drafts, or roughly seven minutes to compose one sentence and another few minutes of fine-tuning after a draft of the entire summary was completed. The thesis needed revision because, as indicated below, the first draft was too vague and incomplete; the second draft was more specific and complete, but left out the author's point about correcting the problem; the third draft was more complete, but was cumbersome.

Draft 1: Barbara Graham argues that our attempts to confine passionate love to the institution of marriage have failed.
(Too vague—the problem isn't clear enough)

Draft 2: Barbara Graham ~~argues that our attempts to confine passionate love to the institution of marriage have failed.~~ describes how the contemporary institution of marriage is in trouble, and this may be due, she thinks, to our unrealistic expectations that passionate love will lead to lasting union.
(Incomplete—what about her call for a change?)

Draft 3: In her article "The Future of Love: Kiss Romance Goodbye, It's Time for the Real Thing," Barbara Graham describes how ~~the contemporary institution of marriage is in trouble, and this may be due, she thinks, to~~ our unrealistic expectations that passionate love will lead to lasting union may be causing the troubles in the contemporary institution of marriage today, so she argues that perhaps it's time to develop a new model for love and relationships.
(Wordy)

Final: In her article "The Future of Love: Kiss Romance Goodbye, It's Time for the Real Thing," Barbara Graham describes how our unrealistic expectations that passionate love leads to a lasting union may be partly causing the troubled state of ~~in the contemporary institution of~~ marriage today; thus she suggests we develop a new model for love and relationships.
(Add 'partly.' Cut out wordiness. Replace 'so' with 'thus')

Write the First Draft of the Summary

Let's consider two possible summaries of the example passage: (1) a short summary, combining a thesis with one-sentence section summaries, and (2) a longer summary, combining thesis, one-sentence section summaries, and some carefully chosen details. Again, realize that you are reading final versions; each of the following summaries is the result of at least two full drafts.

Summary 1: Combine Thesis Sentence with One-Sentence Section Summaries

> In her article "The Future of Love: Kiss Romance Goodbye, It's Time for the Real Thing," Barbara Graham describes how our unrealistic expectations that passionate love leads to lasting union may be partly causing the troubled state of marriage today; thus she suggests we develop a new model for love and relationships. The existing model, and our craving for romantic love, is based heavily upon idealized images of love we learn from fantasies and fairy tales.
>
> We expect the passionate love of fairy tales to lead to "happily ever after" in the institution of marriage, and when this fails, we move on and try it again. Ironically, the idea that marriage should be based on love--rather than upon social and economic concerns--is a relatively recent practice in Western history. While the romantic marriage ideal doesn't fit with tradition, biological evidence is mounting against it as well. Biochemists are discovering that love and lust have hormonal causes, and their evidence suggests that our biological makeup predisposes us to seek the excitement of short-term relationships.
>
> Nonetheless, despite all the difficulties, we spend a lot of time analyzing the elements of relationships in order to preserve or perhaps reinvent marriage. We clearly want to make it work. Because confining passionate love to the institution of marriage hasn't worked very well, Graham ends by suggesting that we ought to revise our model for human relationships.

Discussion

This summary consists essentially of a restatement of Graham's thesis plus the section summaries, altered or expanded a little for stylistic purposes. The first sentence encompasses the summary of Section 1 and is followed by the summaries of Sections 2, 3, 4, and 5. Notice the insertion of a transitional sentence (highlighted) between the summaries of Sections 2 and 3, helping to link the ideas more coherently.

Summary 2: Combine Thesis Sentence, Section Summaries, and Carefully Chosen Details

The thesis and one-sentence section summaries also can be used as the outline for a more detailed summary. However, most of the details in the passage won't be necessary in a summary. It isn't necessary even in a longer summary of this passage to discuss all of Graham's examples—specific romantic fairy tales, ancient Indian views of love and passion, the specific hormones involved with love and lust, or the examples of experts who examine and write about contemporary relationships. It would be appropriate, though, to mention one example of fairy tale romance, to refer to the historical information on marriage as an economic institution, and to explain some of the biological findings about love's chemical basis.

None of these details appeared in the first summary, but in a longer summary, a few carefully selected details might be desirable for clarity. How do you decide which details to include? First, since the idea that love and marriage are not necessarily compatible is the main point of the essay, it makes sense to cite some of the most persuasive evidence supporting this idea. For example, you could mention that for most of Western history, marriage was meant "to serve the economic and social needs of families, communities, and religious institutions," not the emotional and sexual needs of individuals. Further, you might explain the biochemists' argument that serial monogamy based on mutual interests and clandestine adultery—not lifelong, love-based marriage—are the forms of relationships best serving human evolution.

You won't always know which details to include and which to exclude. Developing good judgment in comprehending and summarizing texts is largely a matter of reading skill and prior knowledge (see page 3). Consider the analogy of the seasoned mechanic who can pinpoint an engine problem by simply listening to a characteristic sound that to a less experienced person is just noise. Or consider the chess player who can plot three separate winning strategies from a board position that to a novice looks like a hopeless jumble. In the same way, the more practiced a reader you are, the more knowledgeable you become about the subject, and the better able you will be to make critical distinctions between elements of greater and lesser importance. In the meantime, read as carefully as you can and use your own best judgment as to how to present your material.

Here's one version of a completed summary, with carefully chosen details. Note that we have highlighted phrases and sentences added to the original, briefer summary.

> In her article "The Future of Love: Kiss Romance Goodbye, It's Time for the Real Thing," Barbara Graham describes how our unrealistic expectations that passionate love leads to lasting union may

be partly causing the troubled state of marriage today; thus she suggests we develop a new model for love and relationships.

(Thesis)

Most members of American culture crave romantic love, but we have unreal expectations based upon idealized images of love we learn from fantasies and fairy tales such as "Beauty and the Beast" and "Cinderella." Tragedies such as Romeo and Juliet teach us about the all-consuming nature of "true love," and these stories are tragic precisely because the lovers never get to fulfill what we've been taught is the ideal: living happily ever after, in wedded bliss. The idea that romantic love should be confined to marriage is perhaps the biggest fantasy to which we subscribe. When we are unable to make this fantasy real--and it seems that this is often the case--we end that marriage and move on to the next one. The twentieth century is actually the first century in Western history in which so much was asked of marriage. In earlier eras, marriage was designed to meet social and economic purposes, rather than fulfill individual emotional and sexual desires.

(Section 1, ¶s 1–3)

(Section 2, ¶s 4–7)

Casting further doubt on the effectiveness of the current model of marriage, biochemists are discovering how hormones and enzymes influence feelings of love and lust. It turns out that the "chemistry" a person newly in love often feels for another has a basis in fact, as those early feelings of excitement and contentment are biochemical in nature. When people jump from one relationship to the next, they may be seeking that chemical "rush." Further, these biochemical discoveries fit with principles of evolutionary survival, because short-term relationships--and even adulterous affairs--help to more quickly propagate the species.

(Section 3, ¶s 8–9)

Nonetheless, despite such historical and biological imperatives, we don't seem interested in abandoning the pursuit of love and marriage. In order to preserve or perhaps reinvent marriage, we spend a lot of time scrutinizing and dissecting the dynamics of relationships. Self-help books on the subject of love and relationships fill bookstore shelves and top best-seller lists.

(Section 4, ¶s 10–12)

(Section 5, ¶ 13)

While some argue that such scrutiny ruins rather than reinvigorates love, perhaps our efforts to understand relationships can help us to invent some kind of revised model for human relationships--since trying to confine passionate love to the institution of marriage clearly hasn't worked very well.

Discussion

The final two of our suggested steps for writing summaries are (1) to check your summary against the original passage, making sure that you have included all the important ideas, and (2) to revise so that the summary reads smoothly and coherently.

The structure of this summary generally reflects the structure of the original—with one notable departure. As we noted earlier, Graham uses an inductive approach, stating her thesis at the end of the essay. The summary, however, states the thesis right away, then proceeds deductively to develop that thesis.

Compared to the first, briefer summary, this effort mentions fairy tales and tragedy, develops the point about traditional versus contemporary versions of marriage, explains the biochemical/evolutionary point, and refers specifically to self-help books and their role in the issue.

How long should a summary be? This depends on the length of the original passage. A good rule of thumb is that a summary should be no longer than one-fourth of the original passage. Of course, if you were summarizing an entire chapter or even an entire book, it would have to be much shorter than that. The summary above is about one-fourth the length of the original passage. Although it shouldn't be very much longer, you have seen (page 18) that it could be quite a bit shorter.

The length as well as the content of the summary also depends on its *purpose*. Let's suppose you decided to use Graham's piece in a paper that dealt with the biochemical processes of love and lust. In this case, you might summarize *only* Graham's discussion of Fisher's findings, and perhaps the point Graham makes about how biochemical discoveries complicate marriage. If, instead, you were writing a paper in which you argued against attempts to redefine marriage, you would likely give less attention to the material on biochemistry. To help support your view, you might summarize Graham's points in paragraph 10 about the persistent desire for lasting union found among members of Generation X and evidenced in the high numbers of marriages and remarriages. Thus, depending on your purpose, you would summarize either selected portions of a source or an entire source, as we will see more fully in the chapter on synthesis.

Individual and Collaborative Summary Practice

Turn to Chapter 6 and read Solomon A. Asch's article "Opinions and Social Pressure" (pages 206–212). Follow the steps for writing summaries outlined above—read, underline, and divide into stages of thought. Write down a one- or two-sentence summary of each stage of thought in Asch's article. Then, gather in groups of three or four classmates, and compare your summary sentences. Discuss the differences in your sentences, and come to some consensus about the divisions in Asch's stages of thought—and the ways in which to best sum these up.

As a group, write a one- or two-sentence thesis statement summing up the entire passage. You could go even further, and, using your individual summary sentences—or the versions of these your group revised—put together a brief summary of Asch's article, modeled upon the brief summary of Graham's essay on page 18.

AVOIDING PLAGIARISM

Plagiarism is generally defined as the attempt to pass off the work of another as one's own. Whether born out of calculation or desperation, plagiarism is the least tolerated offense in the academic world. The fact that most plagiarism is unintentional—arising from ignorance of conventions rather than deceitfulness—makes no difference to many professors.

The ease of cutting and pasting whole blocks of text from Web sources into one's own paper makes it tempting for some to take the easy way out and avoid doing their own research and writing. But apart from the serious ethical issues involved, the same technology that makes such acts possible also makes it possible for instructors to detect them. Software marketed to instructors allows them to conduct Web searches, using suspicious phrases as keywords. The results often provide irrefutable evidence of plagiarism.

Of course, plagiarism is not confined to students. Recent years have seen a number of high-profile cases—some of them reaching the front pages of newspapers—of well-known scholars who were shown to have copied passages from sources into their own book manuscripts, without proper attribution. In some cases, the scholars maintained that these appropriations were simply a matter of carelessness, and that in the press and volume of work, they had lost track of which words were theirs and which were the words of their sources. But such excuses sounded hollow: These careless acts inevitably embarrassed the scholars professionally, disappointed their many admirers, and tarnished their otherwise fine work and reputations.

You can avoid plagiarism and charges of plagiarism by following the basic rules provided on page 24 and in the Appendix (pages 497–506).

Following is a passage of text, along with several student versions of the ideas represented. (The passage is from Richard Rovere's article on Senator Joseph P. McCarthy, titled "The Most Gifted and Successful Demagogue This Country Has Ever Known.")

> McCarthy never seemed to believe in himself or in anything he had said. He knew that Communists were not in charge of American foreign policy. He knew that they weren't running the United States Army. He knew that he had spent five years looking for Communists in the government and that—although some must certainly have been there, since Communists had turned up in practically every other major government in the world—he hadn't come up with even one.*

One student wrote the following version of this passage:

> McCarthy never believed in himself or in anything he had said. He knew that Communists were not in charge of American foreign policy and weren't running the United States Army. He knew that he had spent five years looking for Communists in the government, and although there must certainly have been some there, since Communists were in practically every other major government in the world, he hadn't come up with even one.

Clearly, this is intentional plagiarism. The student has copied the original passage almost word for word.

Here is another version of the same passage:

> McCarthy knew that Communists were not running foreign policy or the Army. He also knew that although there must have been some Communists in the government, he hadn't found a single one, even though he had spent five years looking.

This student has attempted to put the ideas into her own words, but both the wording and the sentence structure still are so heavily dependent on the original passage that even if it *were* cited, most professors would consider it plagiarism.

In the following version, the student has sufficiently changed the wording and sentence structure, and she uses a *signal phrase* (a phrase used to introduce a quotation or paraphrase, signaling to the reader that the words to follow come from someone else) to properly credit the information to Rovere, so that there is no question of plagiarism:

> According to Richard Rovere, McCarthy was fully aware that Communists were running neither the

---

* Richard Rovere, "The Most Gifted and Successful Demagogue This Country Has Ever Known," *New York Times Magazine* 30 Apr. 1967.

> government nor the Army. He also knew that he
> hadn't found a single Communist in government,
> even after a lengthy search. (192)

And although this is not a matter of plagiarism, as noted above, it's essential to quote accurately. You are not permitted to change any part of a quotation or to omit any part of it without using brackets or ellipses.

RULES FOR AVOIDING PLAGIARISM

- Cite *all* quoted material and *all* summarized and paraphrased material, unless the information is common knowledge (e.g., the Civil War was fought from 1861 to 1865).
- Make sure that both the *wording* and the *sentence structure* of your summaries and paraphrases are substantially your own.

Appendix

See the Appendix (pp. 499–508) for additional information on citing sources and integrating quoted, paraphrased, and summarized material into your own work.

Critical Reading and Critique

CRITICAL READING

When writing papers in college, you are often called on to respond critically to source materials. Critical reading requires the abilities to both summarize and evaluate a presentation. As you have seen in Chapter 1, a *summary* is a brief restatement in your own words of the content of a passage. An *evaluation*, however, is a more difficult matter.

In your college work, you read to gain and *use* new information; but as sources are not equally valid or equally useful, you must learn to distinguish critically among them by evaluating them.

There is no ready-made formula for determining validity. Critical reading and its written equivalent—the *critique*—require discernment, sensitivity, imagination, knowledge of the subject, and above all, willingness to become involved in what you read. These skills cannot be taken for granted and are developed only through repeated practice. You must begin somewhere, though, and we recommend that you start by posing two broad categories of questions about passages, articles, and books that you read: (1) To what extent does the author succeed in his or her purpose? (2) To what extent do you agree with the author?

Question 1: To What Extent Does the Author Succeed in His or Her Purpose?

All critical reading *begins with an accurate summary.* Thus before attempting an evaluation, you must be able to locate an author's thesis and identify the selection's content and structure. You must understand the author's *purpose.* Authors write to inform, to persuade, and to entertain. A given piece may be primarily *informative* (a summary of the research on cloning), primarily *persuasive* (an argument on why the government must do something to alleviate homelessness), or primarily *entertaining* (a play about the frustrations of young lovers). Or it may be all three (as in John Steinbeck's novel *The Grapes of Wrath,* about migrant workers during the Great Depression). Sometimes, authors are not fully conscious of their purpose. Sometimes their purpose changes as they write. Also, multiple purposes can overlap: An essay may need to inform the reader about an issue in order to make a persuasive point. But if the finished piece is coherent, it will have a primary reason for having been written, and it should be apparent that the author is attempting primarily to inform, persuade, or entertain a particular audience. To identify this primary reason—this purpose—is your first job as a critical reader. Your next job is

---

WHERE DO WE FIND WRITTEN CRITIQUES?

Here are just a few types of writing that involve critique:

Academic Writing

- **Research papers.** Critique sources in order to establish their usefulness.
- **Position papers.** Stake out a position by critiquing other positions.
- **Book reviews.** Combine summary with critique.
- **Essay exams.** Demonstrate understanding of course material by critiquing it.

Workplace Writing

- **Legal briefs and legal arguments.** Critique previous arguments made by opposing counsel.
- **Business plans and proposals.** Critique other less cost-effective, efficient, or reasonable approaches.
- **Policy briefs.** Communicate failings of policies and legislation through critique.

---

to determine how successful the author has been. As a critical reader, you bring different criteria, or standards of judgment, to bear when you read pieces intended to inform, persuade, or entertain.

Writing to Inform

A piece intended to inform will provide definitions, describe or report on a process, recount a story, give historical background, and/or provide facts and figures. An informational piece responds to questions such as the following:

What (or who) is _____?

How does _____ work?

What is the controversy or problem about?

What happened?

How and why did it happen?

What were the results?

What are the arguments for and against _____?

To the extent that an author answers these and related questions and the answers are a matter of verifiable record (you could check for accuracy if you had the time and inclination), the selection is intended to inform. Having determined this, you can organize your response by considering three other criteria: accuracy, significance, and fair interpretation of information.

Evaluating Informative Writing

Accuracy of Information. If you are going to use any of the information presented, you must be satisfied that it is trustworthy. One of your responsibilities as a critical reader, then, is to find out if it is accurate. This means you should check facts against other sources. Government publications are often good resources for verifying facts about political legislation, population data, crime statistics, and the like. You can also search key terms in library databases and on the Web. Since material on the Web is essentially "self-published," however, you must be especially vigilant in assessing its legitimacy. A wealth of useful information is now available on the Internet— but there is also a tremendous amount of misinformation, distorted "facts," and unsupported opinion.

Significance of Information. One useful question that you can put to a reading is "So what?" In the case of selections that attempt to inform, you may reasonably wonder whether the information makes a difference. What can the person who is reading gain from this information? How is knowledge advanced by the publication of this material? Is the information of importance to you or to others in a particular audience? Why or why not?

Fair Interpretation of Information. At times you will read reports, the sole purpose of which is to relate raw data or information. In these cases, you will build your response on Question 1, introduced on page 25: To what extent does the author succeed in his or her purpose? More frequently, once an author has presented information, he or she will attempt to evaluate or interpret it—which is only reasonable, since information that has not been evaluated or interpreted is of little use. One of your tasks as a critical reader is to make a distinction between the author's presentation of facts and figures and his or her attempts to evaluate them. Watch for shifts from straightforward descriptions of factual information ("20% of the population") to assertions about what this information means ("a *mere* 20% of the population"), what its implications are, and so on. Pay attention to whether the logic with which the author connects interpretation with facts is sound. You may find that the information is valuable but the interpretation is not. Perhaps the author's conclusions are not justified. Could you offer a contrary explanation for the same facts? Does more information need to be gathered before firm conclusions can be drawn? Why?

Writing to Persuade

Writing is frequently intended to persuade—that is, to influence the reader's thinking. To make a persuasive case, the writer must begin with an assertion that is arguable, some statement about which reasonable people could disagree. Such an assertion, when it serves as the essential organizing principle of the article or book, is called a *thesis*. Here are two examples:

> Because they do not speak English, many children in this affluent land are being denied their fundamental right to equal educational opportunity.

> Bilingual education, which has been stridently promoted by a small group of activists with their own agenda, is detrimental to the very students it is supposed to serve.

Thesis statements such as these—and the subsequent assertions used to help support them—represent conclusions that authors have drawn as a result of researching and thinking about an issue. You go through the same process yourself when you write persuasive papers or critiques. And just as you are entitled to critically evaluate the assertions of authors you read, so your professors—and other students—are entitled to evaluate *your* assertions, whether they be encountered as written arguments or as comments made in class discussion.

Keep in mind that writers organize arguments by arranging evidence to support one conclusion and oppose (or dismiss) another. You can assess the validity of the argument and the conclusion by determining whether the author has (1) clearly defined key terms, (2) used information fairly, (3) argued logically and not fallaciously (see pages 32–36).

EXERCISE 2.1

Informative and Persuasive Thesis Statements

With a partner from your class, identify at least one informative and one persuasive thesis statement from two passages of your own choosing. Photocopy these passages and highlight the statements you have selected.

As an alternative, and also working with a partner, write one informative and one persuasive thesis statement for *three* of the topics listed in the last paragraph of this exercise. For example, for the topic of prayer in schools, your informative thesis statement could read this way:

> Both advocates and opponents of school prayer frame their position as a matter of freedom.

Your persuasive thesis statement might be worded as follows:

> As long as schools don't dictate what kinds of prayers students should say, then school prayer should be allowed and even encouraged.

Don't worry about taking a position that you agree with or feel you could support. The exercise doesn't require that you write an essay at this point. The topics:

school prayer

gun control

stem cell research

grammar instruction in English class

violent lyrics in music

teaching computer skills in primary schools

curfews in college dormitories

course registration procedures

Evaluating Persuasive Writing

Read the argument that follows on the nation's troubled "star" system for producing elite athletes and dancers. We will illustrate our discussion on defining terms, using information fairly, and arguing logically by referring to Joan Ryan's argument. The example critique that follows these illustrations will be based on this same argument.

We Are Not Created Equal in Every Way
Joan Ryan

In an opinion piece for The San Francisco Chronicle *(December 12, 2000), columnist and reporter Joan Ryan takes a stand on whether the San Francisco Ballet School did or did not discriminate against 8-year-old Fredrika Keefer when it declined to admit her on the grounds that she had the wrong body type to be a successful ballerina. Keefer's mother subsequently sued the ballet school for discrimination, claiming that the rejection had caused her daughter confusion and humiliation. Ryan examines the question of setting admissions standards and also the problems some parents create by pushing their young children to meet these standards.*

1   Fredrika Keefer is an 8-year-old girl who likes to dance, just like her mother and grandmother before her. She relishes playing the lead role of Clara in the Pacific Dance Theater's "Petite Nutcracker." So perhaps she is not as shy as many fourth-graders. But I wonder how she feels about her body being a topic of public discussion.

2   Fredrika and her mother filed suit because, as her mother puts it, she "did not have the right body type to be accepted" by the San Francisco Ballet School. "My daughter is very sophisticated, so she understands why we're doing this," Krissy Keefer said. "And the other kids think she's a celebrity."

3   There is no question Keefer raises a powerful point in her complaint. The values placed on an unnaturally thin body for female performers drives some

dancers to potentially fatal eating disorders. But that isn't exactly the issue here. This is: Does the San Francisco Ballet School have the right to give preference to leaner body types in selecting 300 students from this year's 1,400 applicants?

4   Yes, for the same reason UC Berkeley can reject students based on mental prowess and a fashion modeling school can reject students based on comeliness. Every institution has standards that weed out those who are less likely to succeed. I know this flies in the face of American ideals. But the reality is that all men and women are not created equal.

5   Like it or not, the ethereal, elongated body that can float on air is part of the look and feel of classical ballet. You and I might think ballet would be just as pleasing with larger bodies. But most of those who practice the art disagree, which is their right. This doesn't mean that women with different body types cannot become professional dancers. They just have to find a different type of dance—jazz, tap, modern— just as athletes have to find sports that fit certain body types. A tall, blocky man, for example, could not be a jockey but he could play baseball.

6   Having written extensively about the damaging pressures on young female gymnasts and figure skaters, I understand Keefer's concerns about body type. But for me, the more disturbing issue in this story isn't about weight but age.

7   The San Francisco Ballet School is very clear and open about the fact it is strictly a training ground for professional dancers. "We are not a recreation department," said a ballet spokeswoman.

8   In other words, children at age 8 are already training for adult careers. By age 12 or 13, the children are training so much that they either begin homeschooling or attend a school that accommodates the training schedule. The child has thrown all her eggs into this one little basket at an age when most kids can barely decide what to wear to school in the morning. And the child knows the parents are paying lots of money for this great opportunity.

9   The ballet school usually has a psychologist to counsel the students, but at the moment there is not one on staff. And the parents are given no training by the school on the pitfalls their daughters might encounter as they climb the ballet ladder: weight issues, physical ailments, social isolation, psychological pressure.

10   Just as in elite gymnastics and figure skating, these children are in the netherland of the law. They are neither hobbyists nor professionals. There is no safety net for them, no arm of government that makes sure that the adults in their lives watch out for their best interests.

11   Keefer said she would drop her lawsuit if the school accepted her daughter. The San Francisco Ballet School offers the best training in the Bay Area, she said. Fredrika, however, has said she is quite happy dancing where she is. Still, the mother gets to decide what's best for her daughter's dancing career. The child is clearly too young to make such a decision. Yet, in the skewed logic of elite athletics and dancing, she is not too young to pay the price for it.

Critical Reading Practice

Look back at the Critical Reading for Summary box on page 6 of Chapter 1. Use each of the guidelines listed there to examine the essay by Ryan. Note in the margins of the selection, or on a separate sheet of paper, the essay's main point, subpoints, and use of examples.

Persuasive Strategies

Clearly Defined Terms. The validity of an argument depends to some degree on how carefully an author has defined key terms. Take the assertion, for example, that American society must be grounded in "family values." Just what do people who use this phrase mean by it? The validity of their argument depends on whether they and their readers agree on a definition of "family values"—as well as what it means to be "grounded in" family values. If an author writes that in the recent past "America's elites accepted as a matter of course that a free society can sustain itself only through virtue and temperance in the people" (Charles Murray, "The Coming White Underclass," *Wall Street Journal,* October 20, 1993), readers need to know what, exactly, the author means by "elites" and by "virtue and temperance" before they can assess the validity of the argument. In such cases, the success of the argument—its ability to persuade—hinges on the definition of a term. So, in responding to an argument, be sure you (and the author) are clear on what exactly is being argued. Unless you are, no informed response is possible.

Ryan uses several terms important for understanding her argument. The primary one is the "body type" that the San Francisco Ballet School uses as an application standard. Ryan defines this type (paragraph 5) as "the elongated body that can float on air." Leaving other terms undefined, she writes that the ballet school's use of body type as a standard "flies in the face of American ideals" (paragraph 4). Exactly *which* ideals she leaves for the reader to define: These might include fair play, equality of access, or the belief that decisions ought to be based on talent, not appearance. The reader cannot be sure. When she reports that a spokeswoman for the school stated that "We are not a recreation department," Ryan assumes the reader will understand the reference. The mission of a recreation department is to give *all* participants equal access. In a youth recreation league, children of all abilities would get to play in a baseball game. In a league for elite athletes, in which winning was a priority, coaches would permit only the most talented children to play.

When writing a paper, you will need to decide, like Ryan, which terms to define and which you can assume the reader will define in the same way you do. As the writer of a critique, you should identify and discuss any undefined or ambiguous term that might give rise to confusion.

Fair Use of Information. Information is used as evidence in support of arguments. When you encounter such evidence, ask yourself two questions: (1) "Is the information accurate and up-to-date?" At least a portion of an argument becomes invalid if the information used to support it is inaccurate or out-of-date. (2) "Has the author cited *representative* information?" The evidence used in an argument must be presented in a spirit of fair play. An author is less than ethical when he presents only evidence favoring his views even though he is well aware that contrary evidence exists. For instance, it would be dishonest to argue that an economic recession is imminent and to cite only indicators of economic downturn while ignoring and failing to cite contrary (positive) evidence.

As you have seen, "We Are Not Created Equal in Every Way" is not an information-heavy essay. The success of the piece turns on the author's use of logic, not facts and figures. In this case, the reader has every reason to trust that Ryan has presented the facts accurately: An 8-year-old girl has been denied admission to a prestigious ballet school. The mother of the girl has sued the school.

Logical Argumentation: Avoiding Logical Fallacies

At some point, you will need to respond to the logic of the argument itself. To be convincing, an argument should be governed by principles of *logic*—clear and orderly thinking. This does *not* mean that an argument should not be biased. A biased argument—that is, an argument weighted toward one point of view and against others, which is in fact the nature of argument—may be valid as long as it is logically sound.

Several examples of faulty thinking and logical fallacies to watch for follow.

Emotionally Loaded Terms. Writers sometimes attempt to sway readers by using emotionally charged words—words with positive connotations to sway readers to their own point of view (e.g., "family values") or words with negative connotations to sway readers away from the opposing point of view. The fact that an author uses emotionally loaded terms does not necessarily invalidate the argument. Emotional appeals are perfectly legitimate and time-honored modes of persuasion. But in academic writing, which is grounded in logical argumentation, they should not be the *only* means of persuasion. You should be sensitive to *how* emotionally loaded terms are being used. In particular, are they being used deceptively or to hide the essential facts?

Ryan appeals to our desire to protect children in "We Are Not Created Equal in Every Way." She writes of "disturbing issue[s]," lack of a "safety net for" young people on the star track to elite performance and an absence of adults "watch[ing] out for [the children's] best interests." Ryan understands that no reader wants to see a child abused; and while she does not use the word *abuse* in her essay, she implies that parents who push young children too hard to succeed commit abuse. That implication is enough to engage the sympathies of the reader. As someone evaluating the essay, you should be alert to this appeal to your emotions and then judge if the appeal is fair and convincing. Above all, you should not let an emotional appeal blind you to shortcomings of logic, ambiguously defined terms, or a misuse of facts.

Ad Hominem **Argument.** In an *ad hominem* argument, the writer rejects opposing views by attacking the person who holds them. By calling opponents names, an author avoids the issue. Consider this excerpt from a political speech:

> I could more easily accept my opponent's plan to increase revenues by collecting on delinquent tax bills if he had paid more than a hundred dollars in state taxes in each of the past three years. But the fact is, he's a millionaire with a millionaire's tax shelters. This man hasn't paid a wooden nickel for the state services he and his family depend on. So I ask you: Is *he* the one to be talking about taxes to *us?*

It could well be that the opponent has paid virtually no state taxes for three years; but this fact has nothing to do with, and is a ploy to divert attention from, the merits of a specific proposal for increasing revenues. The proposal is lost in the attack against the man himself, an attack that violates the principles of logic. Writers (and speakers) should make their points by citing evidence in support of their views and by challenging contrary evidence.

Does Ryan attack Fredrika Keefer's mother in this essay? You be the judge. Here are lines referring directly or indirectly to Krissy Keefer. Is Ryan criticizing the mother, directly or indirectly? Cite specific words and phrases to support your conclusion:

> Fredrika and her mother filed suit because, as her mother puts it, she "did not have the right body type to be accepted" by the San Francisco Ballet School. "My daughter is very sophisticated, so she understands why we're doing this," Krissy Keefer said. "And the other kids think she's a celebrity."
>
> There is no question Keefer raises a powerful point in her complaint.
>
> Keefer said she would drop her lawsuit if the school accepted her daughter. The San Francisco Ballet School offers the best training in the Bay Area, she said. Fredrika, however, has said she is quite happy dancing where she is. Still, the mother gets to decide what's best for her daughter's dancing career. The child is clearly too young to make such a decision. Yet, in the skewed logic of elite athletics and dancing, she is not too young to pay the price for it.

Faulty Cause and Effect. The fact that one event precedes another in time does not mean that the first event has caused the second. An example: Fish begin dying by the thousands in a lake near your hometown. An environmental group immediately cites chemical dumping by several manufacturing plants as the cause. But other causes are possible: A disease might

---

TONE

Tone refers to the overall emotional effect produced by the writer's choice of language. Writers might use especially emphatic words to create a tone: A film reviewer might refer to a "magnificent performance" or a columnist might criticize "sleazeball politics."

These are extreme examples of tone; but tone can be more subtle, particularly if the writer makes a special effort *not* to inject emotion into the writing. As we've indicated above in the section on emotionally loaded terms, the fact that a writer's tone is highly emotional does not necessarily mean that the writer's argument is invalid. Conversely, a neutral tone does not ensure an argument's validity.

Note that many instructors discourage student writing that projects a highly emotional tone, considering it inappropriate for academic or preprofessional work. (One sure sign of emotion: the exclamation mark, which should be used sparingly.)

---

have affected the fish; the growth of algae might have contributed to the deaths; or acid rain might be a factor. The origins of an event are usually complex and are not always traceable to a single cause. So you must carefully examine cause-and-effect reasoning when you find a writer using it. In Latin, this fallacy is known as *post hoc, ergo propter hoc* ("after this, therefore because of this").

The debate over the San Francisco Ballet School's refusal to admit Fredrika Keefer involves a question of cause and effect. Fredrika Keefer's rejection by the ballet school is caused by the school's insistence that its students have an "ethereal, elongated body." Certainly if the school changes that standard, the outcome changes: Fredrika Keefer is admitted.

Ryan also uses cause-and-effect logic in the essay to suggest that Fredrika Keefer's mother, and by extension all parent managers, can cause their children harm by pushing them too hard in their training. At the end of the essay, Ryan writes that Fredrika is too young "to decide what's best for her . . . dancing career" but that "she is not too young to pay the price for" the decisions her mother makes to promote that career. The "price" Fredrika pays will be "caused" by her mother's (poor) decisions.

Either/Or Reasoning. Either/or reasoning also results from an unwillingness to recognize complexity. If in analyzing a problem an author artificially restricts the range of possible solutions by offering only two courses of action, subsequently rejecting the one that he opposes, then he cannot logically argue that the remaining course of action, which he favors, is therefore the only one that makes sense. Usually, several other options (at the very least) are possible. For whatever reason, the author has chosen to overlook them. As an example, suppose you are reading a selection on genetic engineering and the author builds an argument on the basis of the following:

> Research in gene splicing is at a crossroads: Either scientists will be carefully monitored by civil authorities and their efforts limited to acceptable applications, such as disease control; or, lacking regulatory guidelines, scientists will set their own ethical standards and begin programs in embryonic manipulation that, however well intended, exceed the proper limits of human knowledge.

Certainly, other possibilities for genetic engineering exist beyond the two mentioned here. But the author limits debate by establishing an either/or choice. Such limitation is artificial and does not allow for complexity. As a critical reader, be on the alert for either/or reasoning.

Hasty Generalization. Writers are guilty of hasty generalization when they draw their conclusions from too little evidence or from unrepresentative evidence. To argue that scientists should not proceed with the human genome project because a recent editorial urged that the project be abandoned is to make a hasty generalization. This lone editorial may be unrepresentative of the views of most individuals—both scientists and laypeople—who have studied and written about the matter. To argue that one should never obey authority because Stanley Milgram's Yale University experiments in the 1960s show the dangers of obedience is to ignore the fact that Milgram's experiments were concerned primarily with obedience to *immoral* authority. Thus, the experimental situation was unrepresentative of most routine demands for obedience—for example, to obey a parental rule or to comply with a summons for jury duty—and a conclusion about the malevolence of all authority would be a hasty generalization.

False Analogy. Comparing one person, event, or issue to another may be illuminating, but it may also be confusing or misleading. Differences between the two may be more significant than the similarities, and conclusions drawn from one may not necessarily apply to the other. A writer who argues that it is reasonable to quarantine people with AIDS because quarantine has been effective in preventing the spread of smallpox is assuming an analogy between AIDS and smallpox that is not valid (because of the differences between the two diseases).

Ryan compares the San Francisco Ballet School's setting an admissions standard to both a university's and a modeling school's setting standards. Are the analogies apt? Certainly one can draw a parallel between the standards used by the ballet school and a modeling school: Both emphasize a candidate's appearance, among other qualities. Are the admissions standards to a university based on appearance? In principle, no. At least that's not a criterion any college admissions office would post on its Web site. A critical reader might therefore want to object that one of Ryan's analogies is faulty.

Ryan attempts to advance her argument by making another comparison:

> [The rejection of a candidate because she does not have a body suited to classical ballet] doesn't mean that women with different body types cannot become professional dancers. They just have to find a different type of dance—jazz, tap, modern—just as athletes have to find sports that fit certain body types. A tall, blocky man, for example, could not be a jockey but he could play baseball.

The words "just as" signal an attempt to advance the argument by making an analogy. What do you think? Is the analogy sufficiently similar to Fredrika Keefer's situation to persuade you?

Begging the Question. To beg the question is to assume as a proven fact the very thesis being argued. To assert, for example, that America is not in decline because it is as strong and prosperous as ever is not to prove anything: It is merely to repeat the claim in different words. This fallacy is also known as *circular reasoning*.

When Ryan writes that "There is no safety net for [children placed into elite training programs], no arm of government that makes sure that the adults in their lives watch out for their best interests," she assumes that there should be such a safety net. But, as you will read in the sample critique, this is a point that must be argued, not assumed. Is such intervention wise? Under what circumstances, for instance, would authorities intervene in a family? Would authorities have the legal standing to get involved if there were no clear evidence of physical abuse? Ryan is not necessarily wrong in desiring "safety nets" for young, elite athletes and dancers; but she assumes a point that she should be arguing.

Non Sequitur. *Non sequitur* is Latin for "it does not follow"; the term is used to describe a conclusion that does not logically follow from a premise. "Since minorities have made such great strides in the past few decades," a writer may argue, "we no longer need affirmative action programs." Aside from the fact that the premise itself is arguable (*have* minorities made such great strides?), it does not follow that because minorities *may* have made great strides, there is no further need for affirmative action programs.

Oversimplification. Be alert for writers who offer easy solutions to complicated problems. "America's economy will be strong again if we all 'buy American,'" a politician may argue. But the problems of America's economy are complex and cannot be solved by a slogan or a simple change in buying habits. Likewise, a writer who argues that we should ban genetic engineering assumes that simple solutions ("just say 'no'") will be sufficient to deal with the complex moral dilemmas raised by this new technology.

Understanding Logical Fallacies

Make a list of the nine logical fallacies discussed in the last section. Briefly define each one in your own words. Then, in a group of three or four class-mates, review your definitions and the examples we've provided for each logical fallacy. Collaborate with your group to find or invent examples for each of the fallacies. Compare your examples with those generated by the other groups in your class.

Writing to Entertain

Authors write not only to inform and persuade but also to entertain. One response to entertainment is a hearty laugh, but it is possible to entertain without encouraging laughter: A good book or play or poem may prompt you to reflect, grow wistful, become elated, get angry. Laughter is only one of many possible reactions. As with a response to an informative piece or an argument, your response to an essay, poem, story, play, novel, or film should be precisely stated and carefully developed. Ask yourself some of the following questions (you won't have space to explore all of them, but try to consider some of the most important): Did I care for the portrayal of a certain character? Did that character (or a group of characters united by occupation, age, ethnicity, etc.) seem overly sentimental, for example, or heroic? Did his adversaries seem too villainous or stupid? Were the situations believable? Was the action interesting or merely formulaic? Was the theme developed subtly or powerfully, or did the work come across as preachy or shrill? Did the action at the end of the work follow plausibly from what had come before? Was the language fresh and incisive or stale and predictable? Explain as specifically as possible what elements of the work seemed effective or inef-fective and why. Offer an overall assessment, elaborating on your views.

Question 2: To What Extent Do You Agree with the Author?

When formulating a critical response to a source, try to distinguish your eval-uation of the author's purpose and success at achieving that purpose from your agreement or disagreement with the author's views. The distinction allows you to respond to a piece of writing on its merits. As an unbiased, evenhanded critic, you evaluate an author's clarity of presentation, use of evidence, and adherence to principles of logic. To what extent has the author succeeded in achieving his or her purpose? Still withholding judgment, offer your assessment and give the author (in effect) a grade. Significantly, your assessment of the presentation may not coincide with your views of the author's conclusions: You may agree with an author entirely but feel that the presentation is superficial; you may find the author's logic and use of evidence to be rock solid but at the same time may resist certain conclusions.

A critical evaluation works well when it is conducted in two parts. After evaluating the author's purpose and design for achieving that purpose, respond to the author's main assertions. In doing so, you'll want to identify points of agreement and disagreement and also evaluate assumptions.

Identify Points of Agreement and Disagreement

Be precise in identifying points of agreement and disagreement with an author. You should state as clearly as possible what *you* believe, and an effective way of doing this is to define your position in relation to that presented in the piece. Whether you agree enthusiastically, disagree, or agree with reservations, you can organize your reactions in two parts: (1) summarize the author's position; and (2) state your own position and elaborate on your reasons for holding it. The elaboration, in effect, becomes an argument itself, and this is true regardless of the position you take. An opinion is effective when you support it by supplying evidence from your reading (which should be properly cited), your observation, or your personal experience. Without such evidence, opinions cannot be authoritative. "I thought the article on inflation was lousy." Or: "It was terrific." Why? "I just thought so, that's all." This opinion is worthless because the criticism is imprecise: The critic has taken neither the time to read the article carefully nor the time to explore his or her own reactions carefully.

EXERCISE 2.4

Exploring Your Viewpoints—in Three Paragraphs

Go to a Web site that presents short persuasive essays on current social issues, such as reason.com, opinion-pages.org, drudgereport.com, or Speakout.com. Or go to an Internet search engine and type in a social issue together with the word "articles," "editorials," or "opinion," and see what you find. Locate a selection on a topic of interest that takes a clear, argumentative position. Print out the selection on which you choose to focus. Write one paragraph summarizing the author's key argument. Write two paragraphs articulating your agreement or disagreement with the author. (Devote each paragraph to a *single* point of agreement or disagreement.) Be sure to explain why you think or feel the way you do and, wherever possible, cite relevant evidence—from your reading, experience, or observation.

Explore the Reasons for Agreement and Disagreement: Evaluate Assumptions

One way of elaborating your reactions to a reading is to explore the underlying *reasons* for agreement and disagreement. Your reactions are based largely on assumptions that you hold and how these assumptions compare with the author's. An *assumption* is a fundamental statement about the world and its operations that you take to be true. A writer's assumptions may be explicitly stated; but just as often, assumptions are implicit and you will have to "ferret them out"—that is, to infer them. Consider an example:

> *In vitro* fertilization and embryo transfer are brought about outside the
> bodies of the couple through actions of third parties whose compe-
> tence and technical activity determine the success of the procedure.
> Such fertilization entrusts the life and identity of the embryo into the
> power of doctors and biologists and establishes the domination of tech-
> nology over the origin and destiny of the human person. Such a rela-
> tionship of domination is in itself contrary to the dignity and equality
> that must be common to parents and children.*

This paragraph is quoted from the February 1987 Vatican document on artificial
procreation. Then Cardinal Joseph Ratzinger (and now Pope Benedict XVI),
principal author of the document, makes an implicit assumption in this paragraph: No good can come of the domination of technology over conception. The
use of technology to bring about conception is morally wrong. Yet thousands of
childless couples, Roman Catholics included, have rejected this assumption in
favor of its opposite: Conception technology is an aid to the barren couple; far
from creating a relationship of unequals, the technology brings children into the
world who will be welcomed with joy and love.

Assumptions provide the foundation on which entire presentations are
built. If you find an author's assumptions invalid—that is, not supported
by factual evidence—or if you disagree with value-based assumptions
underlying an author's positions, you may well disagree with conclusions
that follow from these assumptions. The author of a book on developing
nations may include a section outlining the resources and time that will be
required to industrialize a particular country and so upgrade its general
welfare. Her assumption—that industrialization in that particular country
will ensure or even affect the general welfare—may or may not be valid. If
you do not share the assumption, in your eyes the rationale for the entire
book may be undermined.

How do you determine the validity of assumptions once you have identified
them? In the absence of more scientific criteria, you may determine validity by
how well the author's assumptions stack up against your own experience,
observations, reading, and values. A caution, however: The overall value of an
article or book may depend only to a small degree on the validity of the author's
assumptions. For instance, a sociologist may do a fine job of gathering statistical
data about the incidence of crime in urban areas along the eastern seaboard. The
sociologist also might be a Marxist, and you may disagree with the subsequent
analysis of the data. Yet you may still find the data extremely valuable for your
own work.

Readers will want to examine two assumptions at the heart of Ryan's
essay on Fredrika Keefer and the San Francisco Ballet School's refusal to
admit her. First, Ryan assumes that setting a standard for admission based
on a candidate's appearance is equivalent to setting a standard based on

---

* From the Vatican document *Instruction on Respect for Human Life in Its Origin and on the Dignity
of Procreation,* given at Rome, from the Congregation for the Doctrine of the Faith, 22 Feb. 1987,
as presented in *Origins: N.C. Documentary Service* 16.40 (19 Mar. 1987): 707.

a candidate's "mental prowess," the admissions standard (presumably) used by universities. An appearance-based standard, Ryan writes, will "weed out those who are less likely to succeed" in professional ballet. The writer of the critique that follows agrees with Ryan's assumption. But you may not. You may assume, by contrast, that standards based on appearance are arbitrary while those based on intellectual ability rest on documented talent (SAT scores or high school transcripts, for instance). Ryan makes a second assumption: that there is an appropriate and inappropriate way to raise children. She does not state these (appropriate) ways explicitly, but that does not keep Ryan from using them to judge Krissy Keefer harshly. You may disagree with Ryan and find a reason to cheer Krissy Keefer's defense of her daughter's rights. That's your decision. What you must do as a critical reader is recognize assumptions whether they are stated openly or not. You should spell them out and then accept or reject them. Ultimately, your agreement or disagreement with an author will rest on your agreement or disagreement with the author's assumptions.

CRITIQUE

In Chapter 1 we focused on summary—the condensed presentation of ideas from another source. Summary is key to much of academic writing because it relies so heavily on the works of others for support of claims. It's not going too far to say that summarizing is the critical thinking skill from which a majority of academic writing builds. However, most academic thinking and writing do not stop at summary; usually we use summary to restate our understanding of things we see or read. Then we put that summary to use. In academic writing, one typical use of summary is as a prelude to critique.

A *critique* is a *formalized, critical reading of a passage.* It also is a personal response, but writing a critique is considerably more rigorous than saying that a movie is "great," or a book is "fascinating," or "I didn't like it." These are all responses, and, as such, they're a valid, even essential, part of your understanding of what you see and read. But such responses don't illuminate the subject for anyone—even you—if you haven't explained how you arrived at your conclusions.

Your task in writing a critique is to turn your critical reading of a passage into a systematic evaluation in order to deepen your reader's (and your own) understanding of that passage. Among other things, you're interested in determining what an author says, how well the points are made, what assumptions underlie the argument, what issues are overlooked, and what implications can be drawn from such an analysis. Critiques, positive or negative, should include a fair and accurate summary of the passage; they may draw on and cite information and ideas from other sources (your reading or your personal experience and observations); and they should also include a statement of your own assumptions. It is important to remember that you bring to bear an entire set of assumptions about the world. Stated or not, these assumptions underlie every evaluative comment you make; you therefore

---

GUIDELINES FOR WRITING CRITIQUES

- *Introduce.* Introduce both the passage under analysis and the author. State the author's main argument and the point(s) you intend to make about it.

  Provide background material to help your readers understand the relevance or appeal of the passage. This background material might include one or more of the following: an explanation of why the subject is of current interest; a reference to a possible controversy surrounding the subject of the passage or the passage itself; biographical information about the author; an account of the circumstances under which the passage was written; or a reference to the intended audience of the passage.
- *Summarize.* Summarize the author's main points, making sure to state the author's purpose for writing.
- *Assess the presentation.* Evaluate the validity of the author's presentation, as distinct from your points of agreement or disagreement. Comment on the author's success in achieving his or her purpose by reviewing three or four specific points. You might base your review on one (or more) of the following criteria:

  Is the information accurate?

  Is the information significant?

  Has the author defined terms clearly?

  Has the author used and interpreted information fairly?

  Has the author argued logically?

- *Respond to the presentation.* Now it is your turn to respond to the author's views. With which views do you agree? With which do you disagree? Discuss your reasons for agreement and disagreement, when possible, tying these reasons to assumptions—both the author's and your own. Where necessary, draw upon outside sources to support your ideas.
- *Conclude.* State your conclusions about the overall validity of the piece—your assessment of the author's success at achieving his or her aims and your reactions to the author's views. Remind the reader of the weaknesses and strengths of the passage.

---

have an obligation, both to the reader and to yourself, to clarify your standards by making your assumptions explicit. Not only do your readers stand to gain by your forthrightness, but you do as well: In the process of writing a critical assessment, you are forced to examine your own knowledge, beliefs, and assumptions. Ultimately, the critique is a way of learning about yourself—yet another example of the ways in which writing is useful as a tool for critical thinking.

How to Write Critiques

You may find it useful to organize your critiques into five sections: introduction, summary, assessment of the presentation (on its own terms), your response to the presentation, and conclusion.

The box on page 41 offers some guidelines for writing critiques. They do not constitute a rigid formula. Thousands of authors write critiques that do not follow the structure outlined here. Until you are more confident and practiced in writing critiques, however, we suggest you follow these guidelines. They are meant not to restrict you, but rather to provide a workable sequence for writing critiques.

DEMONSTRATION: CRITIQUE

The critique that follows is based on Joan Ryan's "We Are Not Created Equal in Every Way," which appeared in *The San Francisco Chronicle* as an op-ed piece on December 12, 2000 (see pages 29–30), and which we have to some extent already begun to examine. In this formal critique, you will see that it is possible to agree with an author's main point, at least provisionally, but disagree with other elements of the argument. Critiquing a different selection, you could just as easily accept the author's facts and figures but reject the conclusion he draws from them. As long as you carefully articulate the author's assumptions and your own, explaining in some detail your agreement and disagreement, the critique is yours to take in whatever direction you see fit.

Let's summarize the preceding sections by returning to the core questions that guide critical reading. You will see how, when applied to Joan Ryan's argument, they help to set up a critique.

To What Extent Does the Author Succeed in His or Her Purpose?

To answer this question, you will need to know the author's purpose. Joan Ryan's "We Are Not Created Equal in Every Way" is an argument—actually, *two* related arguments. She wants readers to accept her view that (1) a school of performing arts has the right to set admissions standards according to criteria it believes will ensure the professional success of its graduates; and (2) parents may damage their children by pushing them too hard to meet the standards set by these schools.

By supporting a ballet school's right to set admission standards based on appearance, Ryan supports the star system that produces our elite athletes and performers. At the same time, she disapproves of parents who risk their children's safety and welfare by pushing them through this system. Ryan both defends the system and attacks it. Her ambivalence on the issue keeps the argument from fully succeeding.

To What Extent Do You Agree with the Author? Evaluate Assumptions.

Ryan's views on the debate surrounding Fredrika Keefer's rejection from the San Francisco School of Ballet rest on the assumption that the school has the right to set its own admissions standards—even if we find those standards harsh. All private institutions, she claims, have that right. The writer of the critique that follows agrees with Ryan, although you have seen previously how it is possible to disagree.

Ryan's second argument concerns the wisdom of subjecting an 8-year-old to the rigors of professional training. Ryan disapproves. The writer of the critique, while sympathetic to Ryan's concerns, states that as a practical and even as a legal matter it would be nearly impossible to prevent parents such as Krissy Keefer from doing exactly as they pleased in the name of helping their children. In our culture, parents have the right (short of outright abuse) to raise children however they see fit.

Finally, the writer of the critique notes a certain ambivalence in Ryan's essay: her support of the ballet school's admission standards on the one hand and her distaste of parent managers like Krissy Keefer on the other. The writer does not find evidence of a weak argument in Ryan's mixed message but rather a sign of confusion in the broader culture: We love our young stars but we condemn parents for pushing children to the breaking point in the name of stardom.

The selections you will be likely to critique are those, like Ryan's, that argue a specific position. Indeed, every argument you read is an invitation to agree or disagree. It remains only for you to speak up and justify your position.

Format note: The model critique that follows is single spaced in order to reduce the number of pages in this textbook. To conform to Modern Language Association (MLA) format, your paper should be double spaced.

MODEL CRITIQUE

Ralston 1

Eric Ralston
Professor Reilly
Writing 2
11 January 2008

A Critique of "We Are Not Created Equal
in Every Way" by Joan Ryan

1   Most freshmen know how it feels to apply to a
school and be rejected. Each year, college admissions
offices mail thousands of thin letters that begin:
"Thank you for your application. The competition this
year was unusually strong. . . ." We know that we
will not get into every college on our list or pass

every test or win the starring role after every audi-
tion, but we believe that we deserve the chance to try.
And we can tolerate rejection if we know that we compete
on a level playing field. But when that field seems to
arbitrarily favor some candidates over others, we take
offense. At least that's when an ambitious mother took
offense, bringing to court a suit that claimed her
eight-year-old daughter, Fredrika Keefer, was denied
admission to the prestigious San Francisco Ballet
School because she had the wrong "body type" (A29).

2   In an opinion piece for the San Francisco
Chronicle (12 December 2000), Joan Ryan asks: "Does
[a ballet school] have the right to give preference
to leaner body types?" Her answer is a firm "yes."
Ryan argues that institutions have the right to set
whatever standards they want to ensure that those
they admit meet the physical or intellectual requirements for professional success. But she also believes
that some parents push their children too hard to
meet those standards. Ryan offers a questionable
approach to protecting children from the possible
abuses of such parents. Overall, however, she raises
timely issues in discussing the star system that
produces our world-class athletes and performers. The
sometimes conflicting concerns she expresses reflect
contradictions and tensions in our larger culture.

3   The issue Ryan discusses is a particularly sensitive one because the child's mother charged the ballet
school with discrimination. As a society we have made
great strides over the past few decades in combating
some of the more blatant forms of discrimination--
racial, ethnic, and sexual. But is it possible, is it
desirable, to eliminate all efforts to distinguish one
person from another? When is a standard that permits
some (but not all) people entry to an institution discriminatory and when is it a necessary part of doing
business? Ryan believes that schools discriminate all
the time, and rightly so when candidates for admission
fail to meet the stated criteria for academic or professional success. That UC Berkeley does not accept
every applicant is discriminating, not discriminatory.
Ryan recognizes the difference.

4   She maintains, correctly, that the San Francisco
Ballet School, like any other private institution, has
the right to set standards by which it will accept or
reject applicants. Rejection is a part of life, she

Ralston 3

writes, expressing the view that gives her essay its
title: "We Are Not Created Equal in Every Way." And
because we are not created equal, not everyone will
be admitted to his or her number one school or get a
turn on stage. That's the inevitable consequence of
setting standards: Some people will meet them and
gain admission, others won't. Ryan quotes the
spokesperson who explained that the San Francisco
Ballet School is "'not a recreation department'"
(A29). In other words, a professional ballet school,
like a university, is within its rights to reject
applicants with body types unsuited to its view of
success in professional ballet. The standard may be
cruel and to some even arbitrary, but it is understandable. To put the matter bluntly, candidates
with unsuitable body types, however talented or
otherwise attractive, are less likely to succeed in
professional ballet than those with "classical" proportions. Female dancers, for example, must regularly
be lifted and carried, as if effortlessly, by their
male counterparts--a feat that is difficult enough
even with "leaner body types." Ryan points out that
candidates without the ideal body type for ballet are
not barred from professional dance: "[t]hey just have
to find a different type of dance . . . just as athletes have to find sports that fit certain body
types" (A29).

5   The San Francisco Ballet School is <u>not</u> saying
that people of a certain skin color or religious
belief are not welcome. That <u>would</u> be discriminatory
and wrong. But the standard concerning body type
cuts across <u>all</u> people, rich or poor, black or
white, Protestant or Jew, male or female. Such a
broad standard could be termed an equal opportunity
standard: If it can be used to distinguish among
all people equally, it is discriminating, not
discriminatory.

6   Ryan's parallel concern in this essay is the damage
done to children by parents who push them at an early
age to meet the high standards set by professional
training programs. Children placed onto such star
tracks attend special schools (or receive home school-
ing) in order to accommodate intense training schedules
that sometimes lead to physical or psychological
injuries. In healthy families, we might expect parents
to protect children from such dangers. But parents

who manage what they view as their children's "careers" may be too single minded to realize that their actions may place Johnny and Susie at risk.

7   Ryan disapproves of a star track system that puts children into professional training at a young age. In pursuing a career in dance, for instance, a young "child has thrown all her eggs into this one little basket at an age when most kids can barely decide what to wear to school in the morning" (A29). The law makes no provision for protecting such elite performers in training, writes Ryan: "There is no safety net for them, no arm of government that makes sure that the adults in their lives watch out for their best interests" (A29).

8   Like the rest of us, Ryan assumes there are appropriate and inappropriate ways to raise children. While she does not explicitly share her preferred approach, she is very clear about what does not work: pushing children like Fredrika Keefer into professional ballet school. When Ryan points out that "no arm of government" looks out for children like Keefer, she implies the need for a Department of Youth Services to supervise parent managers. That is not a good idea.

9   There is no sure way to tell when a parent's managing of a child's dance or athletic schedule is abusive or constructive. Intense dedication is necessary for would-be elite athletes and performers to succeed, and such dedication often begins in childhood. Since young children are not equipped to organize their lives in pursuit of a single goal, parents step in to help. That's what the parents of Tiger Woods did on recognizing his talents:

> [H]is father . . . [started] him very early. . . . [Tiger] was on the Mike Douglas show hitting golf balls when he was three years old. I mean, this is a prodigy type thing. This is like Mozart writing his first symphony when he was six, that sort of thing, and he did show unique ability right from the beginning. And his life has been channeled into being a pro. His father has devoted his life to bringing him to this point. His father hasn't worked full-time since 1988. That's what it's been all about. (Feinstein)

10   Ryan would point out, correctly, that for every Tiger Woods or Michelle Kwan there are many child-athletes and performing artists who fall short of their goals. They may later regret the single-minded focus that robbed them of their childhood, but there is no way to know before committing a child to years of dedicated practice if he or she will become the next Tiger or an embittered also-ran. We simply do not have the wisdom to intervene in a parent manager's training program for her child. And Joan Ryan is not going to find an "arm of government" to intervene in the child rearing of Fredrika Keefer, however much she may "pay the price for" (A29) her mother's enthusiasm.

11   The tension in Ryan's essay over high standards and the intense preparation to meet them mirrors a tension in the larger culture. On the one hand, Ryan persuasively argues that elite institutions like the San Francisco Ballet School have the right to set standards for admission. At such institutions, high standards give us high levels of achievement—dancers, for instance, who "can float on air" (A29). We cheer brilliant performers like Tiger Woods and Michelle Kwan who started on their roads to success while still children. The star system produces stars. On the other hand, Ryan condemns parents who buy into the star system by pushing their children into professional training programs that demand a single-minded focus. We are horrified to learn that Macaulay Culkin of the <u>Home Alone</u> movies never really had a childhood (Peterson). Of course Culkin and others like him didn't have childhoods: They were too busy practicing their lines or their jumps and spins. If Ryan defends high standards in one breath and criticizes parents in the next for pushing children to achieve these standards, she is only reflecting a confusion in the larger culture: We love our stars, but we cannot have our stars without a star system that demands total (and often damaging) dedication from our youngest and most vulnerable citizens. That parents can be the agent of this damage is especially troubling.

12   Joan Ryan is right to focus on the parents of would-be stars, and she is right to remind us that young children pressured to perform at the highest levels can suffer physically and psychologically.

Ralston 6

Perhaps it was better for Fredrika Keefer the child (as opposed to Fredrika Keefer the future professional dancer) that she was not admitted to the San Francisco School of Ballet. For Keefer's sake and that of other child performers, we should pay attention to the dangers of the star system and support these children when we can. But without clear evidence of legally actionable neglect or abuse, we cannot interfere with parent managers, however much we may disagree with their decisions. We may be legitimately concerned, as is Ryan, that such a parent is driving her child to become not the next Tiger Woods but the next admission to a psychiatric ward. In a free society, for better or for worse, parents have the right to guide (or misguide) the lives of their children. All the rest of us can do is watch--and hope for the best.

[New Page]

Ralston 7

Works Cited

Feinstein, John. "Year of the Tiger." Interview with Jim Lehrer. Online News Hour. 14 Apr. 1997. 28 Jan. 2006 <http://www.pbs.org/newshour/bb/ sports/tiger_4-14.html>.

Peterson, Paul. Interview with Gary James. 28 Jan. 2006 <http://www.classicbands.com/ PaulPetersonInterview.html>.

Ryan, Joan. "We Are Not Created Equal in Every Way." San Francisco Chronicle 12 Dec. 2000: A29.

EXERCISE 2.5

Informal Critique of Sample Essay

Before reading the discussion of this model critique, write your own informal response to the critique. What are its strengths and weaknesses? To what extent does the critique follow the general Guidelines for Writing Critiques that we outlined on page 41? To the extent it varies from the guidelines, speculate on why. Jot down some ideas for a critique that takes a different approach to Ryan's essay.

CRITICAL READING FOR CRITIQUE

- *Use the tips from Critical Reading for Summary on page 6.* Remember to examine the context; note the title and subtitle; identify the main point; identify the subpoints; break the reading into sections; distinguish between points, examples, and counterarguments; watch for transitions within and between paragraphs; and read actively.
- *Establish the writer's primary purpose in writing.* Is the piece primarily meant to inform, persuade, or entertain?
- *Evaluate informative writing. Use these criteria (among others):*

  Accuracy of information

  Significance of information

  Fair interpretation of information

- *Evaluate persuasive writing. Use these criteria (among others):*

  Clear definition of terms

  Fair use and interpretation of information

  Logical reasoning

- *Evaluate writing that entertains. Use these criteria (among others):*

  Interesting characters

  Believable action, plot, and situations

  Communication of theme

  Use of language

- *Decide whether you agree or disagree with the writer's ideas, position, or message.* Once you have determined the extent to which an author has achieved his or her purpose, clarify your position in relation to the writer's.

Discussion

- Paragraph 1 of the model critique introduces the issue to be reviewed. It provides brief background information and sets a general context that explains why the topic of fair (and unfair) competition is important.
- Paragraph 2 introduces the author and the essay and summarizes the author's main claims. The paragraph ends (see the final three sentences) with the writer's overall assessment of the essay.
- Paragraph 3 sets a specific context for evaluating Ryan's first claim concerning admissions standards. The writer summarizes Ryan's position by making a distinction between the terms *discriminating* and *discriminatory.*

- Paragraph 4 evaluates Ryan's first claim, that the ballet school has the right to set admission standards. The writer supports Ryan's position.

- Paragraph 5 continues the evaluation of Ryan's first claim. Again, the writer of the critique supports Ryan, returning to the distinction between *discriminating* and *discriminatory*.

- Paragraphs 6–7 summarize Ryan's second claim, that parents can damage their children by pushing them too hard through professional training programs at too early an age.

- Paragraphs 8–10 evaluate Ryan's second claim. In paragraph 8 the writer states that Ryan makes a mistake in implying that a government agency should safeguard the interests of children like Fredrika Keefer. Paragraphs 9–10 present a logic for disagreeing with Ryan on this point.

- Paragraph 11 evaluates the essay as a whole. Ryan defends the right of schools in the star system to set high standards but objects when parents push young children into this system. This "tension" in the essay reflects a confusion in the larger culture.

- Paragraph 12 concludes the critique. The writer offers qualified support of Ryan's position, agreeing that children caught in the star system can suffer. The writer also states that there is not much we can do about the problem, except watch and hope for the best.

Practice Critique

Select either of the following articles in Part II of this book:

"A Marriage Agreement," Alix Kates Shulman (pages 178–183)

"The Mall as Sacred Space," Jon Pahl (pages 294–299)

Write a critique of the selected article, following the directions in this chapter for determining the author's purpose in writing the piece and for assessing the author's success in achieving that purpose.

For a somewhat more challenging assignment, try writing a critique of the following article:

"Disobedience as a Psychological and Moral Problem," Erich Fromm (pages 245–250)

Before writing your critique, consider the earlier discussions of evaluating writing in this chapter. Examine the author's use of information and persuasive strategies. Review the logical fallacies and identify any of these in the selection you've chosen to critique. First work out your ideas informally, perhaps producing a working outline. Then write a rough draft of your critique. Review the article—the subject of your critique—and revise your rough draft at least once before considering it finished.

Synthesis 3

WHAT IS A SYNTHESIS?

A *synthesis* is a written discussion that draws on two or more sources. It follows that your ability to write syntheses depends on your ability to infer relationships among sources—essays, articles, fiction, and also nonwritten sources, such as lectures, interviews, visual media, and observations. This process is nothing new for you, since you infer relationships all the time—say, between something you've read in the newspaper and something you've seen for yourself, or between the teaching styles of your favorite and least favorite instructors. In fact, if you've written research papers, you've already written syntheses. In a *synthesis*, you make explicit the relationships that you have inferred among separate sources.

The skills you've already learned and practiced in the previous two chapters will be vital in writing syntheses. Clearly, before you're in a position to draw relationships between two or more sources, you must understand what those sources say; in other words, you must be able to *summarize* those sources. Readers will frequently benefit from at least partial summaries of sources in your synthesis essays. At the same time, you must go beyond summary to make judgments—judgments based, of course, on your *critical reading* of your sources: what conclusions you've drawn about the quality and validity of these sources, whether you agree or disagree with the points made in your sources, and why you agree or disagree.

Further, you must go beyond the critique of individual sources to determine the relationships among them. Is the information in source B, for example, an extended illustration of the generalizations in source A? Would it be useful to compare and contrast source C with source B? Having read and considered sources A, B, and C, can you infer something else— in other words, D (not a source, but your own idea)?

Because a synthesis is based on two or more sources, you will need to be selective when choosing information from each. It would be neither possible nor desirable, for instance, to discuss in a ten-page paper on the American Civil War every point that the authors of two books make about their subject. What you as a writer must do is select from each source the ideas and information that best allow you to achieve your purpose.

PURPOSE

Your purpose in reading source materials and then in drawing on them to write your own material is often reflected in the wording of an assignment. For instance, consider the following assignments on the Civil War:

WHERE DO WE FIND WRITTEN SYNTHESES?

Here are just a few of the types of writing that involve synthesis:

Academic Writing

- **Analysis papers.** Synthesize and apply several related theoretical approaches.
- **Research papers.** Synthesize multiple sources.
- **Argument papers.** Synthesize different points into a coherent claim or position.
- **Essay exams.** Demonstrate understanding of course material through comparing and contrasting theories, viewpoints, or approaches in a particular field.

Workplace Writing

- **Newspaper and magazine articles.** Synthesize primary and secondary sources.
- **Position papers and policy briefs.** Compare and contrast solutions for solving problems.
- **Business plans.** Synthesize ideas and proposals into one coherent plan.
- **Memos and letters.** Synthesize multiple ideas, events, and proposals into concise form.
- **Web sites.** Synthesize information from various sources to present in Web pages and related links.

American History: Evaluate the author's treatment of the origins of the Civil War.

Economics: Argue the following proposition, in light of your readings: "The Civil War was fought not for reasons of moral principle but for reasons of economic necessity."

Government: Prepare a report on the effects of the Civil War on Southern politics at the state level between 1870 and 1917.

Mass Communications: Discuss how the use of photography during the Civil War may have affected the perceptions of the war by Northerners living in industrial cities.

Literature: Select two twentieth-century Southern writers whose work you believe was influenced by the divisive effects of the Civil War. Discuss the ways this influence is apparent in a novel or a group of short stories written by each author. The works should not be *about* the Civil War.

Applied Technology: Compare and contrast the technology of warfare available in the 1860s with the technology available a century earlier.

Each of these assignments creates for you a particular purpose for writing. Having located sources relevant to your topic, you would select for possible use in a paper only those parts that helped you in fulfilling this purpose. And how you used those parts—how you related them to other material from other sources—would also depend on your purpose. For instance, if you were working on the government assignment, you might possibly draw on the same source as another student working on the literature assignment by referring to Robert Penn Warren's novel *All the King's Men,* about Louisiana politics in the early part of the twentieth century. But because the purposes of these assignments are different, you and the other student would make different uses of this source. Those same parts or aspects of the novel that you find worthy of detailed analysis might be mentioned only in passing—or not at all—by the other student.

USING YOUR SOURCES

Your purpose determines not only what parts of your sources you will use but also how you will relate them to one another. Since the very essence of synthesis is the combining of information and ideas, you must have some basis on which to combine them. *Some relationships among the material in your sources must make them worth synthesizing.* It follows that the better able you are to discover such relationships, the better able you will be to use your sources in writing syntheses. Notice that the mass communications assignment requires you to draw a *cause-and-effect* relationship between photographs of the war and Northerners' perceptions of the war. The applied technology assignment requires you to *compare and contrast* state-of-the-art weapons technology in the eighteenth and nineteenth centuries. The economics assignment requires you to *argue* a proposition. In each case, *your purpose will determine how you relate your source materials to one another.*

Consider some other examples. You may be asked on an exam question or in instructions for a paper to *describe* two or three approaches to prison reform during the past decade. You may be asked to *compare and contrast* one country's approach to imprisonment with another's. You may be asked to *develop an argument* of your own on this subject, based on your reading. Sometimes (when you are not given a specific assignment) you determine your own purpose: You are interested in exploring a particular subject; you are interested in making a case for one approach or another. In any event, your purpose shapes your essay. Your purpose determines which sources you research, which ones you use, which parts of them you use, at which points in your paper you use them, and in what manner you relate them to one another.

TYPES OF SYNTHESES: ARGUMENT AND EXPLANATORY

In this chapter we categorize syntheses into two main types: *argument* and *explanatory*. The easiest way to recognize the difference between these two types may be to consider the difference between a newspaper article and an editorial on the same subject. For the most part, we'd say that the main purpose of the newspaper article is to convey *information,* and the main purpose of the editorial is to convey *opinion* or *interpretation.* Of course, this distinction is much too simplified: Newspaper articles often convey opinion or bias, sometimes subtly, sometimes openly; and editorials often convey unbiased information, along with opinion. But as a practical matter, we can generally agree on the distinction between a newspaper article that primarily conveys information and an editorial that primarily conveys opinion. You should be able to observe this distinction in the selections shown here as Explanation and Argument.

Explanation: News Article from The New York Times

Private Gets 3 Years for Iraq Prison Abuse
By David S. Cloud

September 28, 2005

1 Pfc. Lynndie R. England, a 22-year-old clerk in the Army who was photographed with naked Iraqi detainees at Abu Ghraib prison, was sentenced on Tuesday to three years in prison and a dishonorable discharge for her role in the scandal.

2 After the sentence was announced, Private England hung her head and cried briefly before hugging her mother, one of the few signs of emotion she showed in the six-day trial.

3 She had been found guilty on Monday of one count of conspiracy to maltreat prisoners, four counts of maltreatment and one count of committing an indecent act.

4 She made no comment on Tuesday as she was led out of the courthouse in handcuffs and leg shackles.

5 Earlier in the day, though, she took the stand and apologized for abusing the prisoners, saying her conduct was influenced by Specialist Charles A. Graner Jr., her boyfriend at the time.

6 She said she was "embarrassed" when photographs showing her posing next to naked detainees became public in 2004.

7 "I was used by Private Graner," she said. "I didn't realize it at the time."

8 Specialist Graner was reduced in rank after he was convicted in January as ringleader of the abuse.

9 Often groping for words and staring downward, Private England directed her apology to the detainees and to any American troops and their families who might have been injured or killed as a result of the insurgency in Iraq gaining strength.

10   Prosecutors argued on Tuesday that the anti-American feeling generated in Arab and Muslim countries by the Abu Ghraib scandal justified sentencing Private England to four to six years in prison and dishonorably discharging her from the Army. The charges the jury found her guilty of on Monday carried a maximum penalty of nine years. . . .

Argument: *Editorial from the* Boston Globe

Military Abuse

September 28, 2005

1   The court-martial conviction Monday of reservist Lynndie England for her role in the abuse of Iraqi prisoners at Abu Ghraib should fool no one that the Pentagon is taking seriously the mistreatment of Iraqis, especially after the release last Friday of a report on torture by members of the 82d Airborne Division stationed near Fallujah. . . .

2   If the [new] allegations are found credible, they further demolish the contention by officials that the abuse first reported at Abu Ghraib in 2004 was an isolated case of a few bad apples. Pentagon brass also tried to explain away the activities of England's unit as the actions of relatively untrained reservists. It is less easy to dismiss as a fluke such abuse when it occurs at the hands of the 82d Airborne, a thoroughly trained and highly decorated division.

3   The new charges, along with other accusations of abuse that have emerged since Abu Ghraib, including 28 suspicious detainee deaths, provide strong evidence that both reservist and active duty troops throughout Iraq were confused about their responsibility to treat detainees as prisoners of war under the terms of the Geneva Conventions. . . . Congress should have long since created a special commission, as proposed in a bill by Senator Carl Levin of Michigan, to investigate the issue of prisoner abuse. . . .

4   A truly independent inquiry, along the lines of the one done by the 9/11 commission, could trace accountability for prisoner abuse through statements and policies by ranking civilian and military officials in the Bush administration. Accountability for the shame of prisoner torture and abuse should not stop with Lynndie England and her cohort.

We'll say, for the sake of convenience, that the newspaper article provides an *explanation* of England's sentence and that editorial provides an *argument* for investigating responsibility *beyond* England. As a further example of the distinction between explanation and argument, read the following paragraph:

> Researchers now use recombinant DNA technology to analyze genetic changes. With this technology, they cut and splice DNA from different species, then insert the modified molecules into bacteria or other types

of cells that engage in rapid replication and cell division. The cells copy the foreign DNA right along with their own. In short order, huge populations produce useful quantities of recombinant DNA molecules. The new technology also is the basis of genetic engineering, by which genes are isolated, modified, and inserted back into the same organism or into a different one.*

Now read this paragraph:

Many in the life sciences field would have us believe that the new gene splicing technologies are irrepressible and irreversible and that any attempt to oppose their introduction is both futile and retrogressive. They never stop to even consider the possibility that the new genetic science might be used in a wholly different manner than is currently being proposed. The fact is, the corporate agenda is only one of two potential paths into the Biotech Century. It is possible that the growing number of anti-eugenic activists around the world might be able to ignite a global debate around alternative uses of the new science—approaches that are less invasive, more sustainable and humane and that conserve and protect the genetic rights of future generations.[†]

Both of these passages deal with the topic of biotechnology, but the two take quite different approaches. The first passage came from a biology textbook, while the second appeared in a magazine article. As we might expect from a textbook on the broad subject of biology, the first passage is explanatory and informative; it defines and explains some of the key concepts of biotechnology without taking a position or providing commentary about the implications of the technology. Magazine articles often present information in the same ways; however, many magazine articles take specific positions, as we see in the second passage. This passage is argumentative or persuasive. Its primary purpose is to convey a point of view regarding the topic of biotechnology.

While each of these excerpts presents a clear instance of writing that is either explanatory or argumentative, it is important to note that the sources for these excerpts—the textbook chapter and the magazine article—contain elements of *both* explanation and argument. The textbook writers, while they refrain from taking a particular position, do note the controversies surrounding biotechnology and genetic engineering. They might even subtly reveal a certain bias in favor of one side of the issue, through their word choice and tone, and perhaps through devoting more space and attention to one point of view. Explanatory and argumentative writing are not mutually exclusive. The overlap in the categories of explanation and

---

* Cecie Starr and Ralph Taggart, "Recombinant DNA and Genetic Engineering," *Biology: The Unity and Diversity of Life* (New York: Wadsworth, 1998).

[†] Jeremy Rifkin, "The Ultimate Therapy: Commercial Eugenics on the Eve of the Biotech Century," *Tikkun* May–June 1998: 35.

argument is also found in the magazine article: In order to make his case against genetic engineering, the writer has to explain certain elements of the issue. Yet, even while these categories overlap to a certain extent, the second passage clearly has argument as its primary purpose, whereas the first passage is primarily explanatory.

In Chapter 2 we noted that the primary purpose in a piece of writing may be informative, persuasive, or entertaining (or some combination of the three). Some scholars of writing argue that all writing is essentially persuasive, and even without entering into that complex argument, we've just seen how the varying purposes in writing do overlap. In order to persuade others of a particular position, we typically also must inform them about it; conversely, a primarily informative piece of writing also must work to persuade the reader that its claims are truthful. Both informative and persuasive writing often include entertaining elements, and writing intended primarily to entertain also typically contains information and persuasion. For practical purposes, however, it is possible—and useful—to identify the *primary* purpose in a piece of writing as informative/explanatory, persuasive/argumentative, or entertaining. Entertainment as a primary purpose is the one least often practiced in purely academic writing—perhaps to your disappointment!—but information and persuasion are ubiquitous. So, while recognizing the overlap between these categories, we distinguish in this chapter between two types of synthesis writing: explanatory (or informative), and argument (or persuasive). Just as distinguishing the primary purpose in a piece of writing helps you to critically read and evaluate it, distinguishing the primary purpose in your own writing helps you to make the appropriate choices regarding your approach.

We'll first present some guidelines for writing syntheses in general and then focus on the argument synthesis. Toward the end of the chapter, we'll discuss the explanatory synthesis.

HOW TO WRITE SYNTHESES

Although writing syntheses can't be reduced to a lockstep method, it should help you to follow the guidelines listed in the box on pages 58–59.

THE ARGUMENT SYNTHESIS

It's likely that most of the papers you'll be writing in the next few years will be focused on developing support for particular positions or claims, so we'll consider the argument synthesis first and in more detail. An argument synthesis is *persuasive* in purpose. An example: *Welfare reform has largely succeeded* (or *failed*). Writers working with the same source material might conceive of and support other, opposite theses. So the thesis for an argument synthesis is a claim about which reasonable people could disagree. It is a claim with which—given the right arguments—your audience might

---

GUIDELINES FOR WRITING SYNTHESES

- *Consider your purpose in writing.* What are you trying to accomplish in your paper? How will this purpose shape the way you approach your sources?
- *Select and carefully read your sources,* according to your purpose. Then reread the passages, mentally summarizing each. Identify those aspects or parts of your sources that will help you fulfill your purpose. When rereading, *label* or *underline* the sources for main ideas, key terms, and any details you want to use in the synthesis.
- *Take notes on your reading.* In addition to labeling or underlining key points in the readings, you might write brief one- or two-sentence summaries of each source. This will help you in formulating your thesis statement, and in choosing and organizing your sources later.
- *Formulate a thesis.* Your thesis is the main idea that you want to present in your synthesis. It should be expressed as a complete sentence. You might do some predrafting about the ideas discussed in the readings in order to help you work out a thesis. If you've written one-sentence summaries of the readings, looking these over will help you to brainstorm connections between readings and to devise a thesis.

    When you write your synthesis drafts, you will need to consider where your thesis fits in your paper. Sometimes the thesis is the first sentence, but more often it is *the final sentence of the first paragraph.* If you are writing an *inductively arranged* synthesis (see page 68), the thesis sentence may not appear until the final paragraphs.
- *Decide how you will use your source material.* How will the information and the ideas in the passages help you fulfill your purpose?
- *Develop an organizational plan,* according to your thesis. How will you arrange your material? It is not necessary to prepare a formal

---

be persuaded to agree. The strategy of your argument synthesis is therefore to find and use convincing *support* for your *claim.*

The Elements of Argument: Claim, Support, and Assumption

Let's consider the terminology we've just used. One way of looking at an argument is to see it as an interplay of three essential elements: claim, support, and assumption. A *claim* is a proposition or conclusion that you are outline. But you should have some plan that will indicate the order in which you will present your material and that will indicate the relationships among your sources.

- *Draft the topic sentences for the main sections.* This is an optional step, but you may find it a helpful transition from organizational plan to first draft.
- *Write the first draft* of your synthesis, following your organizational plan. Be flexible with your plan, however. Frequently, you will use an outline to get started. As you write, you may discover new ideas and make room for them by adjusting the outline. When this happens, reread your work frequently, making sure that your thesis still accounts for what follows and that what follows still logically supports your thesis.
- *Document your sources.* You must do this by crediting them within the body of the synthesis—citing the author's last name and page number from which the point was taken and by providing full citation information in a list of "Works Cited" at the end. Don't open yourself to charges of plagiarism! (See pages 22–24 and the Appendix at the end of this book.)
- *Revise your synthesis,* inserting transitional words and phrases where necessary. Make sure that the synthesis reads smoothly, logically, and clearly from beginning to end. Check for grammatical correctness, punctuation, and spelling.

Note: The writing of syntheses is a recursive process, and you should accept a certain amount of backtracking and reformulating as inevitable. For instance, in developing an organizational plan (Step 6 of the procedure), you may discover a gap in your presentation that will send you scrambling for another source—back to Step 2. You may find that formulating a thesis and making inferences among sources occur simultaneously; indeed, inferences are often made before a thesis is formulated. Our recommendations for writing syntheses will give you a structure; they will get you started. But be flexible in your approach; expect discontinuity and, if possible, be assured that through backtracking and reformulating you will eventually produce a coherent, well-crafted paper.

trying to prove. You prove this claim by using *support* in the form of fact or expert opinion. Linking your supporting evidence to your claim is your *assumption* about the subject. This assumption, also called a *warrant,* is—as we've discussed in Chapter 2—an underlying belief or principle about some aspect of the world and how it operates. By nature, assumptions (which are often unstated) tend to be more general than either claims or supporting evidence.

For example, here are the essential elements of an argument advocating parental restriction of television viewing for their high school children:

Claim
High school students should be restricted to no more than two hours of TV viewing per day.

Support
An important new study and the testimony of educational specialists reveal that students who watch more than two hours of TV a night have, on average, lower grades than those who watch less TV.

Assumption
Excessive TV viewing adversely affects academic performance.

As another example, let's consider an argumentative claim on the topic of what some call computer-mediated communication (CMC).

CMC threatens to undermine human intimacy, connection, and ultimately community.

Here are the elements of this argument:

Support
- While the Internet presents us with increased opportunities to meet people, these meetings are limited by geographical distance.
- People are spending increasing amounts of time in cyberspace: In 1998, the average Internet user spent over four hours per week online, a figure that has nearly doubled recently.
- College health officials report that excessive Internet usage threatens many college students' academic and psychological well-being.
- New kinds of relationships fostered on the Internet often pose challenges to pre-existing relationships.

Assumptions

- The communication skills used and the connections formed during Internet contact fundamentally differ from those used and formed during face-to-face contact.
- "Real" connection and a sense of community are sustained by face-to-face contact, not by Internet interactions.

For the most part, arguments should be constructed logically so that assumptions link evidence (supporting facts and expert opinions) to claims. As we'll see, however, logic is only one component of effective arguments.

EXERCISE `3.1`

Practicing Claim, Support, and Assumption

Devise two sets of claims with support and assumptions for each. First, in response to the example immediately above on computer-mediated communication and relationships, devise a one-sentence claim addressing the positive impact (or potentially positive impact) of CMC on relationships—whether you personally agree with the claim or not. Then list the support on which such a claim might rest, and the assumption that underlies these. Second, write a claim that states your own position on any debatable topic you choose. Again, devise statements of support and relevant assumptions.

DEMONSTRATION: DEVELOPING AN ARGUMENT SYNTHESIS—VOLUNTEERING IN AMERICA

To demonstrate how to plan and draft an argument synthesis, let's consider another subject. If you were taking an economics or sociology course, you might at some point consider the phenomenon of volunteerism, the extent to which Americans volunteer—that is, give away their time freely—for causes they deem worthy. In a market economy, why would people agree to forgo wages in exchange for their labor? Are there other kinds of compensation for people who volunteer? Is peer pressure involved? Can a spirit of volunteerism be taught or encouraged? And, in light of the articles that follow and the example argument based on them, can the government—which has the constitutional right to compel military service—*compel* citizens to serve their communities (rendering their service something other than an act of volunteering)?

Suppose, in preparing to write a short paper on volunteering, you located the following sources:

- "A New Start for National Service," John McCain and Evan Bayh
- "Calls for National Service," Landrum, Eberly, and Sherraden
- "Politics and National Service: A Virus Attacks the Volunteer Sector," Bruce Chapman

Read these sources (which follow) carefully, noting as you do the kinds of information and ideas you could draw upon to develop an *argument synthesis*. Note: To save space and for the purpose of demonstration, two of the three passages are excerpts only. In preparing your paper, naturally you would draw upon entire articles and book chapters from which the extracts were taken. And you would draw upon more articles than these in your search for materials in support of your argument (as the writer of the example paper has done on pages 71–79). But these three sources set the poles of the debate. The discussion of how these passages can form the basis of an argument synthesis resumes on page 67.

A New Start for National Service
John McCain and Evan Bayh

John McCain (R-AZ) and Evan Bayh (D-IN) are U.S. senators. This op-ed piece appeared in the New York Times *on November 6, 2001, a few weeks after the terrorist attacks of September 11.**

1   Since Sept. 11, Americans have found a new spirit of national unity and purpose. Forty years ago, at the height of the cold war, President John F. Kennedy challenged Americans to enter into public service. Today, confronted with a challenge no less daunting than the cold war, Americans again are eager for ways to serve at home and abroad. Government should make it easier for them to do so.

2   That is why we are introducing legislation to revamp national service programs and dramatically expand opportunities for public service.

3   Many tasks lie ahead, both new and old. On the home front, there are new security and civil defense requirements, like increased police and border patrol needs. We will charge the Corporation for National Service, the federal office that oversees national volunteer programs, with the task of assembling a plan that would put civilians to work to assist the Office of Homeland Security. The military will need new recruits to confront the challenges abroad, so our bill will also improve benefits for our servicemembers.

---

* "A New Start for National Service" by John McCain and Evan Bayh, *The New York Times*, November 6, 2001. Copyright © 2001 by The New York Times Company. Reprinted by permission.

4   At the same time, because the society we defend needs increased services, from promoting literacy to caring for the elderly, we expand AmeriCorps and senior service programs to enlarge our national army of volunteers.

5   AmeriCorps' achievements have been impressive: thousands of homes have been built, hundreds of thousands of seniors given the care they need to live independently and millions of children tutored.

6   Since its inception in 1993, nearly 250,000 Americans have served stints of one or two years in AmeriCorps. But for all its concrete achievements, AmeriCorps has been too small to rouse the nation's imagination. Under our bill, 250,000 volunteers each year would be able to answer the call—with half of them assisting in civil defense needs and half continuing the good work of AmeriCorps.

7   We must also ask our nation's colleges to promote service more aggressively. Currently, many colleges devote only a small fraction of federal work-study funds to community service, while the majority of federal resources are used to fill low-skill positions. This was not Congress's vision when it passed the Higher Education Act of 1965. Under our bill, universities will be required to promote student involvement in community activities more vigorously.

8   And for those who might consider serving their country in the armed forces, the benefits must keep pace with the times. While the volunteer military has been successful, our armed forces continue to suffer from significant recruitment challenges.

9   Our legislation encourages more young Americans to serve in the military by allowing the Defense Department to create a new, shorter-term enlistment option. This "18-18-18" plan would offer an $18,000 bonus—in addition to regular pay—for 18 months of active duty and 18 months of reserve duty. And we would significantly improve education payments made to service members under current law.

10   Public service is a virtue, and national service should one day be a rite of passage for young Americans. This is the right moment to issue a new call to service and give a new generation a way to claim the rewards and responsibilities of active citizenship.

Calls for National Service
Roger Landrum, Donald J. Eberly, and Michael W. Sherraden

The passage that follows introduces the work of William James, a Harvard philosopher whose speech "The Moral Equivalent of War" (1906) helped set an agenda for the national service movement. The essay appears in a collection of scholarly commentaries on national service, edited by Sherraden and Eberly.

1   The first major call for a national service in the United States was by the social philosopher and psychologist William James. James' seminal essay "The Moral Equivalent of War" was given as a major address at Stanford University in 1906

and first published in 1910. The essay proposed national service as a pragmatic means by which a democratic nation could maintain social cohesiveness apart from the external threat of war. In his extraordinarily vivid language, James attacked a view he considered ingrained in Western civilization from Alexander the Great through Theodore Roosevelt: that war's "dreadful hammer is the welder of men into cohesive states, and nowhere but in such states can human nature adequately develop its capacity." James wasn't any easier on pacifists, suggesting that the "duties, penalties, and sanctions pictured in the utopias they paint are all too weak and tame to substitute for war's disciplinary function." The most promising line of conciliation between militarists and pacifists, James thought, was some "moral equivalent of war."

> Men now are proud of belonging to a conquering nation, and without a murmur they lay down their persons and their wealth, if by so doing they may fight off subjugation. But who can be sure that other aspects of one's country may not, with time and education and suggestion enough, come to be regarded with similarly effective feelings of pride and shame? Why should men not someday feel that it is worth a blood-tax to belong to a collectivity superior in any ideal respect? Why should they not blush with indignant shame if the community that owns them is vile in any way whatsoever?
>
> Individuals, daily more numerous, now feel this civic passion. It is only a question of blowing on the spark till the whole population gets incandescent, and on the ruins of the old morals of military honor, until a stable system of morals of civic honor builds itself up. What the whole community comes to believe in grasps the individual as in a vise. The war function has grasped us so far; but constructive interests may someday seem no less imperative, and impose on the individual a hardly lighter burden.
>
> If now—and this is my idea—there were, instead of military conscription, a conscription of the whole youthful population to form for a certain number of years a part of the army enlisted against *Nature,* the injustice would tend to be evened out, and numerous other goods to the commonwealth would follow. . . .
>
> Such a conscription, with the state of public opinion that would have required it, and the many moral fruits it would bear, would preserve in the midst of a pacific civilization the manly virtues which the military party is so afraid of seeing disappear in peace.[1]

James argued that a permanently successful peace economy cannot be a simple pleasure economy. He proposed a conscription of the youthful population of the United States into national service to provide a new sense of "civic discipline" outside the context of war. James also believed that national service would benefit young people. They would experience "self-forgetfulness" rather than "self-seeking." No one would be "flung out of employment to degenerate because there is no immediate work for them to do." None would "remain blind, as the luxurious classes now are blind, to man's relations to the globe he lives on." The childishness would be "knocked out of them." The moral equivalent of war would cultivate in youth "toughness without callousness, healthier sympathies and soberer ideas, ideals of hardihood and discipline, and civic temper."

2   The logic and rhetoric of James' call for national service have an antique ring today. James was clearly thinking only of young men and the image of Ivy League undergraduates seemed to be at the center of his thinking. He didn't consider the issue of constitutional limits on involuntary servitude. His recommendation of conscription was softened only by the concepts of collectivity and social sanctions: "What the whole community comes to believe in grasps the individual as in a vise." He said nothing of cost and organization. Of course, there were half as many young people in those days, only 15 percent of them in high school, and a vastly different organization of the work force. Still, James succeeded in embedding a phrase, "the moral equivalent of war," in the national consciousness; he raised the fundamental issue of proper socialization of youth in the context of a democracy at peace; and he planted the idea of national service.

Note

  1. William James, "The Moral Equivalent of War," *International Conciliation*, no. 27 (Washington, D.C.: Carnegie Endowment for International Peace, 1910), pp. 8–20.

Politics and National Service: A Virus Attacks the Volunteer Sector
Bruce Chapman

Bruce Chapman, former U.S. Ambassador to the UN organizations in Vienna and former senior fellow at the Hudson Institute, currently serves as president of the Discovery Institute of Seattle, Washington, a public policy center for studying national and international affairs. An early proponent of the all-volunteer army who dedicated many years to public service (as secretary of state for the State of Washington, former director of the U.S. Census Bureau, and as aide to President Reagan), Chapman argues that volunteerism, "true service," is "corrupted" when it is in any way coerced or induced—through government programs, for instance, that pay stipends. The excerpted selection that follows appears in a collection of essays, National Service: Pro & Con *(1990).*

1 Proposals for government-operated national service, like influenza, flare up from time to time, depress the resistance of the body politic, run their course, and seem to disappear, only to mutate and afflict public life anew. Unfortunately, another epidemic may be on the way. The disease metaphor comes to mind not as an aspersion on the advocates of national service because, with good-natured patience, persistence, and seemingly relentless political invention, they mean well, but from the frustration of constantly combating the changing strains of a statist idea that one thought had been eliminated in the early 1970s, along with smallpox.

2   Why does the national service virus keep coming back? Perhaps because its romance is so easy to catch, commanding a nostalgic imagination and evoking times when Americans were eager to sacrifice for their country. Claiming to derive inspiration from both military experience and the social gospel—if we

could only get America's wastrel youth into at least a psychic uniform we might be able to teach self-discipline again and revive the spirit of giving—it hearkens back to William James's call for a "moral equivalent of war." But at the end of the twentieth century should we be looking to war for moral guidance?

3   True service is one of the glories of our civilization in the West, especially in the great independent (or volunteer) sector of American society. Inspiration for service in the West comes from the Bible in parable and admonition and is constantly restated in the long historical tradition of Judeo-Christian faith. Personal service is a freewill offering to God. This is very different from performance of an obligation to government, which is a tax on time or money.

4   True service, then, has a spiritual basis, even for some outside the Judeo-Christian tradition per se. Fulfillment of an obligation to government, in contrast, has a contractual basis unless it is founded on an outright commitment to a coercive utopianism. Either way, it is not true service. Nor can enrollment in a government-funded self-improvement project or acceptance of a government job be called true service. Indeed, when coercion or inducements are provided, as in the various national service schemes, the spirit of service is to that degree corrupted.

5   In practice the service in a federal program of national service would be contaminated by governmental determination of goals, bureaucratization of procedures, and, inevitably, government insistence on further regulating the independent sector with which it contracted. National service would tend to demoralize those citizens who volunteer without expectation of financial reward and stigmatize the honest labor of people whose fields were invaded by stipened and vouchered volunteers.

6   Government intervention is always a potential threat to the voluntary sector. When totalitarians have come to power in other Western countries, they have sought to absorb this sector, conferring official sponsorship on certain organizations and scorning others, thereby inculcating in the citizenry the government's valuation even on use of free time. Although in the United States totalitarianism is not a current danger to our liberal democracy, coercive utopianism is always a legitimate concern.

7   Alexis de Tocqueville saw in our own early history that the genius of voluntary association was America's superior answer to the leadership energy provided in other societies by aristocracies. But government, he warned, may seek to direct the voluntary sector in the same way it erroneously seeks to control industrial undertakings:

> Once it leaves the sphere of politics to launch out on this new task, it will, even without intending this, exercise an intolerable tyranny. For a government can only dictate precise rules. It imposes the sentiments and ideas which it favors, and it is never easy to tell the difference between its advice and its commands.[1]

Note

1. Alexis de Tocqueville, *Democracy in America*, vol. 2, book 2, chap. 5, J. P. Mayer (New York: Doubleday, 1969).

Consider Your Purpose

Your specific purpose in writing an argument synthesis is crucial. What, exactly, you want to do will affect your claim, the evidence you select to support your claim, and the way you organize the evidence. Your purpose may be clear to you before you begin research, may emerge during the course of research, or may not emerge until after you have completed your research. Of course, the sooner your purpose is clear to you, the fewer wasted motions you will make. On the other hand, the more you approach research as an exploratory process, the likelier that your conclusions will emerge from the sources themselves, rather than from preconceived ideas.

Let's say that while reading these sources, your own encounters with a service organization (perhaps you help schoolchildren improve their literacy skills) have influenced your thinking on the subject. You find yourself impressed that so many people at the literacy center volunteer without being compelled to do so. You observe that giving time freely adds to the pleasures of volunteering, and to its significance as well. Meanwhile, perhaps your school is considering a service "requirement"— that is, a mandate that all students perform a given number of community service hours in order to graduate. The juxtaposition of "compelled" service with freely given service sparks in you an idea for a source-based paper.

On the one hand, you can understand and even sympathize with the viewpoints of educators who believe that while they have students in their clutches (so to speak), they have an opportunity to pass on an ethic of service. To students who would not volunteer time on their own, setting a graduation requirement makes sense. On the other hand, it seems to you that forced volunteerism, a contradiction in terms if ever there was one, defeats the essential quality of volunteering: that it is time given freely. The donation of time to meet the needs of others is an act of selflessness that brings you profound satisfaction. Your purpose in writing, then, emerges from these kinds of responses to the source material.

Making a Claim: Formulate a Thesis

As we indicated in the introduction to this chapter, one useful way of approaching an argument is to see it as making a *claim*. A claim is a proposition, a conclusion that you are trying to prove or demonstrate. If your purpose is to demonstrate that the state should not compel people to serve their communities, then that is the claim at the heart of your argument. The claim is generally expressed in one-sentence form as a *thesis*. You draw *support* from your sources as you argue logically for your claim.

Of course, not every piece of information in a source is useful for supporting a claim. By the same token, you may draw support for your claim from sources that make entirely different claims. You may use as support for your own claim, for example, a sentiment expressed in William James's "On the

Moral Equivalent of War," that values such as selfless concern for the common good, learned through service, are desirable. Yet while James called for "a conscription of the whole youthful population" to nonmilitary service projects, you may believe that service should be voluntary. Still, you could cite James and comment, where you think appropriate, on where you and he diverge.

Similarly, you might use one source as part of a *counterargument*—an argument opposite to your own—so that you can demonstrate its weaknesses and, in the process, strengthen your own claim. On the other hand, the author of one of your sources may be so convincing in supporting a claim that you adopt it yourself, either partially or entirely. The point is that *the argument is in your hands*: You must devise it yourself and use your sources in ways that will support the claim expressed in your thesis.

You may not want to divulge your thesis until the end of the paper, to draw the reader along toward your conclusion, allowing the thesis to flow naturally out of the argument and the evidence on which it is based. If you do this, you are working *inductively*. Or you may wish to be more direct and *begin* with your thesis, following the thesis statement with evidence to support it. If you do this, you are working *deductively*. In academic papers, deductive arguments are far more common than inductive arguments.

Based on your own experience and reactions to reading sources, you may find yourself agreeing with Bruce Chapman's argument that compelled or monetarily induced service "corrupts" the experience of service. At the same time, you may find yourself unwilling to take Chapman's extreme stance that even modest stipends such as the ones earned while working for AmeriCorps and other government programs constitute "corruption." While you believe that government programs encouraging service are beneficial, you certainly don't want to see the federal government create a nonmilitary version of compulsory national service. After a few tries, you develop the following thesis:

> The impulse to expand service through volunteer
> programs like AmeriCorps, VISTA, and the Peace
> Corps is understandable, even praiseworthy. But
> as volunteerism grows and gains public support,
> we should resist letting its successes become an
> argument for <u>compulsory</u> national service.

Decide How You Will Use Your Source Material

Your claim commits you to (1) discussing the benefits of service in government-sponsored programs like AmeriCorps and VISTA, and (2) arguing that, benefits notwithstanding, there are compelling reasons not to make national service compulsory. The sources (some provided here, some located elsewhere) offer information and ideas—that is, evidence—that will allow you to support your claim. (You might draw on one universally available source, the U.S.

Constitution, not included in the materials here.) The selection by Senators McCain and Bayh provides pro-service arguments, while the essay by Bruce Chapman provides a negative one. Roger Landrum, Donald Eberly, and Michael Sherraden provide a philosophical and historical foundation for the synthesis. (Note that other sources not included in this chapter will be cited in the example paper.)

Develop an Organizational Plan

Having established your overall purpose and your claim, having developed a thesis (which may change as you write and revise the paper), and having decided how to use your source materials, how do you logically organize your essay? In many cases, including this one, a well-written thesis will suggest an overall organization. Thus, the first part of your argument synthesis will define volunteerism and set a broad context regarding its pervasiveness and history, along with mention of a possible early attempt to make national service compulsory. The second part will argue that national service should *not* be made compulsory. Sorting through your material and categorizing it by topic and subtopic, you might arrive at the following outline:

```
   I. Introduction. Pervasiveness of volunteerism
      in America. Use Bureau of Labor Statistics
      data.

  II. The desire to "make more of a good thing."
      The McCain/Bayh "Call to Service Act."
      Thesis.

 III. Intellectual history of service:
      A. Recent history. Refer to William James.
         State that service need not be military.

      B. Ancient history. Refer to Plato. State
         that citizens owe the State an obligation.

  IV. Can the U.S. government compel citizens to
      service?
      A. Military service: Yes. Right granted by
         U.S. Constitution.

      B. Transition: military vs. civilian.

      C. Civilian service: No.
         1. Logical reason: public service is not
            analogous to military service.
         2. Legal reason: U.S. Constitution
            (Amendment XIII) forbids involuntary
            servitude.
```

      3. Moral reason: compelled or induced ser-
         vice (that is, with money) "corrupts"
         spirit of service.
        a. Concede point that "less pure" forms
          of service that pay stipends, such as
          AmeriCorps and VISTA, are beneficial.
        b. But state forcefully that compulsory
          (as opposed to minimally compensated)
          service does corrupt the spirit of
          service.

V. Conclusion:
    A. Government should expand opportunities to
       serve <u>voluntarily</u> (even with pay).
    B. It should resist the impulse to compel
       young people to serve.

Formulate an Argument Strategy

The argument represented by this outline will build not only on evidence drawn from sources but also on the writer's assumptions. Consider the bare-bones logic of the argument:

Voluntary service, paid or unpaid, promotes good citizenship and benefits the community. (*assumption*)

People who have worked in volunteer programs have made significant contributions to community and public life. (*support*)

We should support programs that foster volunteerism. (*claim*)

    The crucial point about which reasonable people will disagree is the *assumption* that unpaid *and* paid volunteer service promotes good citizenship. One source author, Bruce Chapman, makes a partial and extreme form of this assumption when he writes that financially rewarded service is "corrupted" (see page 66). A less extreme assumption—the one guiding the model paper—is possible: Citizenship can be learned in a minimally paid environment such as AmeriCorps. The writer of the model paper agrees with Chapman, however, about another assumption: that service should never be compelled.

    Writers can accept or partially accept an opposing assumption by making a *concession*, in the process establishing themselves as reasonable and willing to compromise (see page 86). In our example, the writer does exactly this (see paragraph 10 in the sample synthesis that follows) and then uses as *supporting evidence* facts from a report that many paid veterans of government-sponsored teaching programs learn about citizenship and continue to teach after their contracted time is up. By raising potential objections and making concessions, the writer blunts the effectiveness of *counterarguments*.

The *claim* of the example argument about service is primarily a claim about *policy*, about actions that should (or should not) be taken. An argument can also concern a claim about *facts* (Does X exist? Does X lead to Y? How can we define X?) or a claim about *value* (What is X worth?). You have seen that the present argument rests on an assumed definition of "service." Depending on how you define the term, you will agree—or not—with the writer. Among the source authors, Bruce Chapman defines service one way (it is neither rewarded with money nor compelled), while Senators McCain and Bayh define it another (as work done with or without minimal pay to help others and reinforce core values). As you read the following paper, watch how these opposing views are woven into the argument.

A well-reasoned argument will involve a claim primarily about fact, value, *or* policy. Secondary arguments are sometimes needed, as in the present example, to help make a case.

Draft and Revise Your Synthesis

The final draft of a completed synthesis, based on the above outline, follows. **Thesis, transitions, and topic sentences are highlighted;** Modern Language Association (MLA) documentation style is used throughout.

A cautionary note: When writing syntheses, it is all too easy to become careless in properly crediting your sources. Before drafting your paper, please review the section on "Avoiding Plagiarism" in Chapter 1 (pages 22–24).

Format note: The model synthesis that follows is single spaced in order to reduce the number of pages in this textbook. To conform to Modern Language Association (MLA) format, your paper should be double spaced.

MODEL SYNTHESIS

(Thesis and topic sentences are highlighted.)

Kikuchi 1

Michael Kikuchi
Professor Carcich
English 3
31 January 2008

Keeping Volunteerism Voluntary

1   The spirit of volunteerism flourishes in America. In 2002-2003, 28.8 percent of Americans, 16 and older, some 63.8 million, freely gave time to their communities (Bureau, "Volunteering"). Prompted by a desire to serve others without thought of personal gain, more than one-quarter of us donate 52 hours a year, more than one full work-week, to building shelters, coaching Little League, caring for the elderly, teaching literacy, and countless other community

Kikuchi 2

minded pursuits (Bureau, "Volunteering"; "Table 1").
Not included in these numbers are the many tens of
thousands who donate time through less "pure" volunteer programs run by the government, such as
AmeriCorps, VISTA (Volunteers in Service to America),
and the Peace Corps, all of which pay recruits a small
stipend. Volunteerism is so pervasive that it seems
bred into the American character. A former director of
the U.S. Census Bureau observes that "Alexis de
Tocqueville saw in [America's] early history that the
genius of voluntary association was [the country's]
superior answer to the leadership energy provided in
other societies by aristocracies" (Chapman 134).

2   Advocates claim that volunteerism builds character, teaches citizenship, and addresses unfulfilled
national needs (Gorham 22). But if only one American
in four volunteers, a percentage that surely could be
improved, and if volunteerism is such a boon to communities, it is little wonder that from time to time
politicians propose to make more of a good thing.
In this spirit, in November 2001 Senators John McCain
(R-AZ) and Evan Bayh (D-IN) introduced Bill S1274, the
"Call to Service Act," which would dramatically
increase the opportunities to serve in government-
sponsored volunteer programs. "Public service is a
virtue," write the senators in a New York Times op-ed
piece not quite two months after the horrors of
September 11, 2001. "[N]ational service should one day
be a rite of passage for young Americans." The senators believe that this "is the right moment to issue a
new call to service and give a new generation a way to
claim the rewards and responsibilities of active citizenship" (A31). The impulse to expand service through
volunteer programs like AmeriCorps, VISTA, and the
Peace Corps is understandable, even praiseworthy. But
as volunteerism grows and gains public support, we
should resist letting its successes become an argument
for compulsory national service.

3   Senators McCain and Bayh do not call for compulsory service. Nonetheless, one can hear an echo of
the word "compulsory" in their claim that "national
service should one day be a rite of passage for young
Americans." The word "should" suggests nothing if not
obligation, and the word "all" is clearly implied.
It's not a stretch to imagine the senators and others
at some point endorsing a program of compulsory service, an idea that has been around for nearly a century.

In 1906, the philosopher William James called for
"a conscription of the whole youthful population"
to on-military projects that would improve character
(14). James, whom many consider the intellectual
father of national service, admired the discipline
and sacrifice of soldiers but thought it absurd that
such "[m]artial virtues" as "intrepidity, contempt
of softness, surrender of private interest, [and]
obedience to command" should be developed only in
the service of war. He imagined a "reign of peace"
in which these qualities would "remain the rock
upon which" peaceful states might be built (16).
In a famous passage of his talk at Stanford
University, which he titled "The Moral Equivalent
of War," James urges on youth a hard (but non-
military) service:

> To coal and iron mines, to freight trains,
> to fishing fleets in December, to dishwash-
> ing, clothes-washing, and window washing,
> to road-building and tunnel-making, to
> foundries and stoke-holes, and to the
> frames of skyscrapers, would our gilded
> youths be drafted off, according to their
> choice, to get the childishness knocked out
> of them, and to come back into society with
> healthier sympathies and soberer ideas.
> They would have paid their blood-tax, done
> their own part in the immemorial human war-
> fare against nature; they would tread the
> earth more proudly, the women would value
> them more highly, they would be better
> fathers and teachers of the following
> generation. (17)

James's "gilded youths" were the (male) students
of elite colleges. In the early twentieth century,
there were not nearly as many young people as today,
both in absolute terms and in college (Landrum,
Eberly, and Sherraden 23-25), and so the logistics
of compulsory national service may have seemed
manageable. A century later we might regard his
proposal as impractical or even illegal, but at the
time he struck an important chord. His vision of
learning the virtues and disciplines of citizenship
through a non-military regimen in peace time
(a "moral equivalent of war") entered our national
vocabulary and remains a part of it today (Landrum,
Eberly, and Sherraden 27).

4   The question of what sort of service, or obligation, citizens owe a country is as old as the first
gathering of peoples into a collective for mutual
safety and comfort. In one of his famous dialogues,
Plato records a conversation between Socrates, whom
Athens had imprisoned and condemned to death for
corrupting the city's youth with his teachings, and
a friend who urges that he escape and save himself.
Socrates argues that if he has accepted and enjoyed
the privileges of citizenship, then he must also
accept the judgment of the State, even if that judgment calls for his execution:

> [A]fter having brought you into the world,
> and nurtured and educated you, and given you
> and every other citizen a share in every good
> that we [that is, the State] had to give, we
> further proclaim and give the right to every
> Athenian, that if he does not like us when he
> has come of age and has seen the ways of the
> city, and made our acquaintance, he may go
> where he pleases and take his goods with him;
> and none of us laws will forbid him or inter-
> fere with him. Any of you who does not like
> us and the city, and who wants to go to a
> colony or to any other city, may go where he
> likes, and take his goods with him. But he
> who has experience of the manner in which we
> order justice and administer the State, and
> still remains, has entered into an implied
> contract that he will do as we command him.
> (qtd. in Plato)

Citizens obligate themselves to the State when they
accept its bounties and protections. But how is that
obligation to be paid? Some twenty-four hundred years
after Socrates accepted his fate and drank his cup of
hemlock, Americans pay their obligations to the government through taxes, jury duty, and obedience to
laws passed by elected representatives.

5   Can the government compel us to do more? Can it
compel us, for instance, to military or non-military
service? The U.S. Constitution grants Congress the
right to raise armies (Article 1, Section 8, Clause 14).
The way Congress chooses to do this, however, reflects
the needs of a particular time. During World War II and
the Vietnam War, the government implemented a military
draft. Today, for reasons of professionalism and morale,

Kikuchi 5

the Department of Defense prefers an all-volunteer army
to an army of conscripts. The Chairman of the Joint
Chiefs of Staff was reported to have said that the
"country doesn't need a draft because the all-volunteer
force works--in fact, the United States has the most
effective military in the world precisely because it is
all-volunteer" (Rhem 150). Former Defense Secretary
Rumsfeld saw distinct disadvantages to the draft:
"[P]eople are involuntarily forced to serve, some for
less than they could earn on the outside. . . . Troops
are 'churned' through training, serve the minimum
amount of time and leave--thus causing more money to be
spent to churn more draftees through the system" (qtd.
in Rhem).

6   Clearly the State has a constitutional right to
compel young people into military service in times of
military need, whether it chooses to exercise that
right through an all-volunteer or a conscripted army.
Does the State have an equivalent right to press
citizens into non-military service? For example,
because our libraries are understaffed, our parks ill-
kept, and our youth reading below grade level, should
the State compel citizens into service for the common
good? No--for logical, legal, and moral reasons.

7   Military need is not logically equivalent to
non-military need, primarily because non-military
needs are typically met through the normal operations of representative government and the market
economy. When the State identifies work to be done
for the common good, it taxes citizens and directs
its employees to perform that work. Alternately, it
may put out bids and pay contractors to perform the
work. This is how highways and libraries get built. If
the State does not adequately perform these basic
functions, it fails in its responsibilities. The
remedy to this failure should not be the drafting of
America's youth into national service for one or two
years. The State could not honestly or reasonably call
for universal service as a means of upgrading the
moral character of youth when its real need is to
plug holes in its own leaky ship. Such disingenuous
arguments would only call attention to the State's
failures. If the State lacks the money or competence
to do its work, then citizens should overhaul the
system by electing a new, more efficient administration. If necessary, the legislature could raise

taxes. But it should not make a bogus public "need" into an occasion to compel public service.

8   Nor does the State have a legal basis on which to press its citizens into national service. While the Constitution grants Congress the authority to raise armies, it expressly forbids forced service: "Neither slavery nor involuntary servitude, except as a punishment for crime whereof the party shall have been duly convicted, shall exist within the United States, or any place subject to their jurisdiction" (Amendment XIII). A program for compulsory national service, however noble its aims, would never withstand a legal challenge.

9   But even if advocates could circumvent the logical and legal obstacles to compulsory national service, they could not on moral grounds compel youth to serve against their will. Advocates argue, persuasively, that volunteerism builds character and promotes citizenship (Gorham 18). And, in fact, volunteer service does foster selflessness, a concern for community, and an appreciation of country (McCain and Bayh; Gergen; James; Patterson). Still, the essential quality of volunteerism is that it is time given freely. "True service," writes Bruce Chapman, "has a spiritual basis [rooted in the Judeo-Christian tradition]. . . . Fulfillment of an obligation to government, in contrast, has a contractual basis." Chapman argues that "performance of an obligation to government . . . is a tax on time or money." The spirit of service is "corrupted" when it is compelled or encouraged with stipends (140-141).

10   One need not agree, however, that volunteer pro- grams that pay youth in room and board, health care, and tuition vouchers "corrupt" the spirit of giving. Chapman makes an extreme argument that ignores the financial realities of many young people. Were they to get no compensation, many would forgo volunteering and the possibility of learning from programs that encour- age civic participation and patriotism. That would be a shame, for the members of AmeriCorps, the Peace Corps, and VISTA, all of whom are paid a small stipend, grow as individuals and as citizens, learning life-long lessons. David Gergen vividly makes this point:

Voluntary service when young often changes
people for life. They learn to give their fair

Kikuchi 7

share. Some 60 percent of alumni from Teach
for America, a marvelous program, now work
full time in education, and many others remain
deeply involved in social change. Mark Levine,
for example, has started two community-owned
credit unions in Washington Heights, NY, for
recent immigrants. Alumni of City Year,
another terrific program, vote at twice the
rates of their peers. Or think of the Peace
Corps alumni. Six now serve in the House
of Representatives, one (Christopher Dodd)
in the Senate. (60)

Unquestionably, national programs for volunteers
can benefit both the individuals serving and the
communities served. For example, AmeriCorps sets
goals lofty enough to ensure that all involved will
benefit. The Corps helps communities when it places
members in projects designed to have a positive
educational, social, and environmental impact.
Communities are also strengthened when culturally
and racially diverse people work side by side to
achieve project goals. Additionally, AmeriCorps
seeks through its programming and its job and
educational benefits to improve the lives of members
(Corporation). Both communities and individuals gain
from AmeriCorps' efforts.

11   Still, as Chapman points out, volunteerism that
is compelled in any way, that turns the impulse to
serve into an obligation, would be a corruption. If
the State instituted obligatory non-military service
for the "good" of the individual (and recall that
it could not reasonably or honestly do so for the
social "needs" of the State), the act of service
would no longer be rooted in generosity. And it is
the spirit of generosity, of one person's freely
giving to another, that underlies all the good
that volunteering achieves. Convert the essential
generous impulse to an obligation, and the very
logic for compelling service--to teach civic
values--disappears. The State could no more expect
the veterans of obligatory service to have learned
the values of good citizenship or to feel special
affection for the country than we could expect a
child whose parents order him to "make friends with
Johnny" to have learned anything useful about

Kikuchi 8

friendship or to feel a special kinship with Johnny. Affection, citizenship, and patriotism don't work that way. They are freely given, or they are coerced. And if coerced, they are corrupt. Compelled allegiance is a form of bullying that teaches nothing so much as resentment.

12   Without any inducement other than the good it would do their communities and their own hearts, 63.8 million Americans--more than one quarter of the country--volunteer. Could more people volunteer, specifically more young people? Yes, especially in light of the finding that young people in their early twenties volunteer the least, relative to all other age groups (Bureau, "Table 1"). The McCain/Bayh "Call to Service Act" deserves enthusiastic support, as does any government effort to encourage service by people younger than 25. Those who learn to serve while young turn out to be more involved with their communities over the course of their lives (Gergen; Corporation), and such involvement can only benefit us all. Reasonable inducements such as tuition vouchers, minimal pay, health care, and room and board can give young people the safety net they need to experiment with serving others and in that way discover their own wellsprings of generosity.

13   So let's support McCain/Bayh and every such effort to encourage service. Ideally, enough programs will be in place one day to offer all high school and college graduates the option of serving their communities. "[T]oo often," writes Richard North Patterson, "we offer young people a vision of community which extends to the nearest shopping mall." Government-sponsored programs for service can make us better than that, and we should promote volunteerism wherever and whenever we can. But we must guard against using the success of these programs as a pretext for establishing mandatory national or community service. Such a mandate would fail legal and logical tests and, most importantly, a moral test: Volunteerism is built on choice. To command someone to do good works, to make good works obligatory, is to poison the very essence of service.

[New Page]

Works Cited

Bureau of Labor Statistics. "Table 1: Volunteers by
    Selected Characteristics, September 2003." 17
    Dec. 2003. 17 Jan. 2008 <http://www.bls.gov/
    news.release/volun.t01.htm>.

---. "Volunteering in the United States, 2003." 18
    Dec. 2003. 17 Jan. 2008 <http://www.bls.gov/
    news.release/volun.nr0.htm>.

Chapman, Bruce. "Politics and National Service:
    A Virus Attacks the Volunteer Sector."
    National Service: Pro & Con. Ed. Williamson
    M. Evers. Stanford, CA: Hoover Institution P, 1990.
    133-44.

"Constitution of the United States of America." The New
    York Public Library Desk Reference. New York:
    Webster's New World, 1989.

Corporation for National and Community Service.
    "AmeriCorps Mission." Americorps: Getting Things
    Done. Program Directory, Spring/Summer 1995.
    Microfiche Y2N.21/29 10AM3. Washington, DC: GPO,
    1995.

Gergen, David. "A Time to Heed the Call." U.S. News &
    World Report 24 Dec. 2001: 60.

Gorham, Eric B. "National Service, Political
    Socialization, and Citizenship." National
    Service, Citizenship, and Political Education.
    Albany: SUNY P, 1992. 5-30.

James, William. "The Moral Equivalent of War."
    International Conciliation 27 (Washington, DC:
    Carnegie Endowment for International Peace,
    1910): 8-20.

Landrum, Roger, Donald J. Eberly, and Michael W.
    Sherraden. "Calls for National Service." National
    Service, Social, Economic and Military Impacts.
    Ed. Michael W. Sherraden and Donald J. Eberly.
    New York: Pergamon, 1982. 21-38.

McCain, John, and Evan Bayh. "A New Start for National
    Service." New York Times 6 Nov. 2001: A31.

Patterson, Richard North. "Keeping Alive the Spirit of
    National Service." Boston Globe 1 Aug. 1999: A27.

Plato. "Crito." Classic Literature Online Library.
    Trans. Benjamin Jowett. 17 July 2008 <http://
    www.greece.com/library/plato/crito_04.html>.

Rhem, Kathleen T. "Rumsfeld: No Need for Draft."
    American Forces Information Service 7 Jan. 2004.
    17 July 2008 <http://www.dod.gov/news/Jan2003/
    n01072003_200301074.html>.

Discussion

The writer of this argument synthesis on compulsory national service attempts to support a *claim*—one that favors national service but insists on keeping it voluntary—by offering *support* in the form of facts (rates of volunteerism from the Bureau of Labor Statistics) and opinions (testimony of experts). However, since the writer's claim rests on a definition of "true service," its effectiveness depends partially upon the extent to which we, as readers, agree with the *assumptions* underlying that definition. (See our discussion of assumptions in Chapter 2, pages 38–40.) An assumption (sometimes called a *warrant*) is a generalization or principle about how the world works or should work—a fundamental statement of belief about facts or values. In this particular case, the underlying assumption is that "true service" to a community must be voluntary, never required. The writer makes this assumption explicit. Though you are under no obligation to do so, stating assumptions explicitly will clarify your arguments to readers.

Assumptions often are deeply rooted in people's psyches, sometimes deriving from lifelong experiences and observations and not easily changed, even by the most logical of arguments. People who learned the spirit of volunteerism early in life, perhaps through "required" activities in religious or public school, might not accept the support offered for the claim that required service would be illogical, illegal, and "corrupted." But others might well be persuaded and might agree that programs to expand opportunities for national service should be supported, though service itself should never be compelled. A discussion of the model argument's paragraphs, along with the argument strategy for each, follows. Note that the paper devotes at least one paragraph to developing every section of the outline on pages 69–70. Note also that the writer avoids plagiarism by careful attribution and quotation of sources.

- **Paragraph 1:** The writer uses statistics to establish that a culture of volunteerism is alive and well in America.

  Argument strategy: In this opening paragraph, the writer sets up the general topic—volunteerism in America—and establishes that Americans volunteer in impressive numbers. The writer uses information from the Bureau of Labor Statistics, as well as the reference to volunteerism in early America, to anticipate and deflect possible criticism from those who might say: "So few of us volunteer that we should require national service in order to promote citizenship and to build character."

- **Paragraph 2:** Here the writer sets a context for and introduces the McCain/Bayh proposal to expand national service. The writer then presents the thesis.

  Argument strategy: This paragraph moves in one direction with an inspiring call to service by Senators McCain and Bayh and then takes a sharp, contrasting turn to the thesis. The first part of the thesis, "as volunteerism grows and gains public support," clearly follows from (and summarizes) the first part of paragraph 2. The transition "But" signals the contrast, which sets up the warning. A contrast generates interest by creating tension, in this case prompting readers to wonder: "Why *should* we resist compulsory service?"

- **Paragraphs 3 and 4:** In these paragraphs, the writer discusses the intellectual history of service: first, the writing of William James in the early years of the past century, and next, Plato's account of a dialogue between Socrates and a student. The writer quotes both authors at length and then discusses their relevance to the issue at the center of this essay: service to the greater community.

  Argument strategy: At this point, the writer is *preparing* to offer reasons for accepting the claim that we must resist compulsory service. The goal of paragraphs 3 and 4 is to set a deep historical context for the essay by establishing service as a significant cultural norm in America and, more broadly, by showing that the notion of obligation to the State is fundamental to civil societies. The end of paragraph 4 makes a transition to modern-day America and begins to move from the preparation for argument to argument.

- **Paragraph 5:** This paragraph opens with a question and sets up a key distinction in the essay between military and non-military service. After raising the distinction, the writer devotes the paragraph to establishing the right of the American government to draft citizens into the army. High-ranking military administrators are quoted to the effect that the all-volunteer army is a better fighting force than earlier, conscripted armies.

  Argument strategy: This paragraph begins moving the reader into the argument by introducing and discussing the first part of the distinction just presented: military service. The writer establishes that compelled military service is constitutional and in keeping with the historical obligations that citizens owe the State. But even here, in a case in which the State has the clear authority to conscript people, the writer quotes military officials to the effect that voluntary service is superior to compulsory service. The reader will find this strong preference for volunteerism continued and developed in the second part of the synthesis devoted to non-military service.

- **Paragraph 6:** This transitional paragraph raises the core question on which the argument hangs: Does the State have the right, as it does in military matters, to press citizens into non-military, national service? The writer answers the question in the final sentence of this paragraph and, in so doing, forecasts the discussion to follow.

  Argument strategy: Here the writer sets up the second part of the essay, where reasons for accepting the claim will be presented. Up to this point, the writer has established that (1) volunteers can build character through service, (2) citizens owe a debt to the State, and (3) the State can legally collect on that debt by drafting citizens into the army in time of war. In this transition paragraph, the writer poses the question that will take the rest of the paper to answer. The question becomes an invitation to read.

- **Paragraphs 7–9:** In each of these three paragraphs, the writer answers—in the negative—the question posed in paragraph 6. The State does *not* have the right to press citizens into national service. Paragraph 7 offers a logical reason: that military and non-military service are not equivalent. Paragraph 8 offers a legal reason: that the Constitution prohibits "involuntary servitude." Paragraph 9 offers a moral reason: that coerced or compelled service is "corrupted."

    Argument strategy: These paragraphs lay out the main reasons for accepting the claim that we should resist letting the successes of volunteerism become an argument for compulsory national service. The writer argues on multiple grounds—logical, legal, and moral—in an effort to build a strong case.

- **Paragraph 10:** Here the writer concedes a problem with the view (expressed by Chapman) in paragraph 9 that service that is either compelled or financially rewarded is corrupted. Allowing that this extreme position does not take into account the financial needs of young people, the writer endorses an alternate view, that minimal payment for service is legitimate. To support this more moderate position, the writer quotes David Gergen at length and also refers to the AmeriCorps mission statement.

    Argument strategy: With this concession, the writer backs off an extreme view. The tactic makes the writer look both reasonable and realistic just prior to arguing very firmly, in the next paragraph, against compulsory service.

- **Paragraph 11:** Here the writer endorses one of Chapman's strongly held positions: Forced service is not service at all and corrupts the spirit of volunteerism.

    Argument strategy: Here is the emotional core of the argument. The writer has previously argued that for logical (paragraph 7) and legal (paragraph 8) reasons, compulsory service must be rejected. The writer devotes three paragraphs to developing moral reasons. In paragraph 11, the writer uses an analogy for the first time: Compelling service is equivalent to compelling a child to like someone. Neither works. The value of service rests on the offering of oneself freely to those in need.

- **Paragraphs 12–13:** The writer concludes by restating the claim—in two paragraphs.

    Argument strategy: These concluding paragraphs parallel the two-part structure of the thesis: Part 1 (paragraph 12), that volunteerism has many benefits and deserves support; Part 2 (paragraph 13), that we must resist any effort to make service compulsory.

Other approaches to an argument synthesis would be possible, based on the available sources. One could agree with Bruce Chapman and adopt the extreme view against both compulsory and paid service. Such an argument would make no concessions of the sort found in paragraph 10 of the model synthesis. Another approach would be to argue that young people must be taught the value of service before they take these values on themselves, and that the best way to teach an ethic of service is to require a year or two of "compulsory volunteering." That which is required, goes the logic of this argument, eventually becomes second nature. We might make a parallel case about teaching kids to read. Kids may not enjoy practicing 30 minutes every night, but eventually they come to realize the joys and benefits of reading, which last a lifetime. Still another argument might be to focus on the extent to which Americans meet (or fail to meet) their obligations to the larger community. This would be a glass-half-full/half-empty argument, beginning with the statistic that one-quarter of Americans regularly volunteer. The half-full argument would praise current efforts and, perhaps, suggest policies for ensuring continued success. The half-empty argument would cite the statistic with alarm, claim that we have a problem of shockingly low volunteer rates, and then propose a solution. Whatever your approach to the subject, in first *critically examining* the various sources and then *synthesizing* them to support a position about which you feel strongly, you are engaging in the kind of critical thinking that is essential to success in a good deal of academic and professional work.

DEVELOPING AND ORGANIZING SUPPORT FOR YOUR ARGUMENTS

- *Summarize, paraphrase, and quote supporting evidence.* Draw upon the facts, ideas, and language in your sources.
- *Provide various types of evidence and motivational appeal.*
- *Use climactic order.* Save the most important evidence in support of your argument for the *end* where it will have the most impact. Use the next most important evidence *first*.
- *Use logical or conventional order.* Use a form of organization appropriate to the topic, such as problem/solution; sides of a controversy; comparison/contrast; or a form of organization appropriate to the academic or professional discipline, such as a report of an experiment or a business plan.
- *Present and respond to counterarguments.* Anticipate and respond to arguments against your position.
- *Use concession.* Concede that one or more arguments against your position have some validity; re-assert, nonetheless, that your argument is the stronger one.

DEVELOPING AND ORGANIZING THE SUPPORT FOR YOUR ARGUMENTS

Experienced writers seem to have an intuitive sense of how to develop and present supporting evidence for their claims; this sense is developed through much hard work and practice. Less experienced writers wonder what to say first, and having decided on that, wonder what to say next. There is no single method of presentation. But the techniques of even the most experienced writers often boil down to a few tried and tested arrangements.

As we've seen in the model synthesis in this chapter, the key to devising effective arguments is to find and use those kinds of support that most persuasively strengthen your claim. Some writers categorize support into two broad types: *evidence* and *motivational appeals*. Evidence, in the form of facts, statistics, and expert testimony, helps make the appeal to reason. Motivational appeals—appeals grounded in emotion and upon the authority of the speaker—are employed to get people to change their minds, to agree with the writer or speaker, or to decide upon a plan of activity.

Following are some of the most common principles for using and organizing support for your claims.

Summarize, Paraphrase, and Quote Supporting Evidence

In most of the papers and reports you will write in college and the professional world, evidence and motivational appeals derive from summarizing, paraphrasing, and quoting material in the sources that either have been provided to you or that you have independently researched. For example, in paragraph 10 of the model argument synthesis, you will find a block quotation from David Gergen used to make the point that minimally paid volunteer programs can provide lifelong lessons. You will also find two other block quotations in the argument and a number of brief quotations woven into sentences throughout. In addition, you will find summaries and a paraphrase. In each case, the writer is careful to cite sources.

Provide Various Types of Evidence and Motivational Appeals

Keep in mind the appeals to both reason and emotion. The appeal to reason is based on evidence that consists of a combination of *facts*, *statistics*, and *expert testimony*. In the model synthesis, the writer uses all of these varieties of evidence: facts (from David Gergen's article on how "[v]oluntary service . . . often changes people for life"); statistics (the incidence of volunteering in the United States); and testimony (from Eric Gorham, Bruce Chapman, David Gergen, Roger Landrum, Donald Rumsfeld, and William James). The model synthesis makes an appeal to emotion by engaging the reader's self-interest: Certainly if the federal government were to institute compulsory national service, the lives of readers would be touched. More explicitly, paragraph 11 makes a moral argument against compulsory service. Through analogy (compelling citizens to service is equivalent to ordering a child to like someone), the writer attempts to claim the reader's sympathy and respect for common sense. In effect, the writer says, responsible parents would never do such a thing; responsible governments shouldn't either. (Of course, readers could reject the analogy and the assumption about good parenting on which it rests. Some parents might very well push their children into friendships and believe themselves justified in doing so.)

Use Climactic Order

Climactic order is an arrangement of examples or evidence in order of anticipated impact on the reader, least to greatest. Organize by climactic order when you plan to offer a number of categories or elements of support for your claim. Recognize that some elements will be more important—and likely more persuasive—than others. The basic principle here is that you should *save the most important evidence for the end*, since whatever you have said last is what readers are likely to most remember. A secondary principle is that whatever you say first is what they are *next* most likely to remember. Therefore, when you have several reasons in support of your claim, an effective argument strategy is to present the second most important, then one or more additional reasons, and finally, the most important reason. Paragraphs 7–11 of the model synthesis do exactly this.

Use Logical or Conventional Order

Using logical or conventional order means that you use as a template a pre-established pattern or plan for arguing your case.

- One common pattern is describing or arguing a *problem/solution*. Using this pattern, you begin with an introduction in which you typically define the problem, then perhaps explain its origins, then offer one or more solutions, then conclude.
- Another common pattern is presenting *two sides of a controversy*. Using this pattern, you introduce the controversy and (if an argument synthesis) your own point of view or claim, then explain the other side's arguments, providing reasons why your point of view should prevail.
- A third common pattern is *comparison-and-contrast*. In fact, this pattern is so important that we will discuss it separately in the next section.
- The order in which you present elements of an argument is sometimes dictated by the conventions of the discipline in which you are writing. For example, lab reports and experiments in the

sciences and social sciences often follow this pattern: *Opening* or *Introduction, Methods and Materials* [of the experiment or study], *Results, Discussion.* Legal arguments often follow the so-called IRAC format: *Issue, Rule, Application, Conclusion.*

Present and Respond to Counterarguments

When developing arguments on a controversial topic, you can effectively use *counterargument* to help support your claims. When you use counterargument, you present an argument *against* your claim, but then show that this argument is weak or flawed. The advantage of this technique is that you demonstrate that you are aware of the other side of the argument and that you are prepared to answer it.

Here is how a counterargument typically is developed:

   I. Introduction and claim

  II. Main opposing argument

 III. Refutation of opposing argument

 IV. Main positive argument

Use Concession

Concession is a variation of counterargument. As in counterargument, you present the opposing (or otherwise objectionable) viewpoint, but instead of demolishing that argument, you *concede* that it does have some validity and even some appeal, although your own argument is the stronger one. This concession bolsters your own standing as a fair-minded person who is not blind to the virtues of the other side. See paragraphs 9 and 10 of the model synthesis for one version of the concession argument. You'll find that instead of making an opposing argument, the writer produces a supporting argument but views one part of it as flawed. The writer rejects that section (the extreme position that *any* form of compensation corrupts the spirit of volunteerism) and endorses the remaining sections. In terms of overall argument strategy, the result—the reader sees the writer as being reasonable—is the same as it would be if the writer had used the more standard concession in which an opposing argument is viewed as having some merit. Here is an outline for a more typical concession argument:

   I. Introduction and claim

  II. Important opposing argument

 III. Concession that this argument has some validity

 IV. Positive argument(s)

Sometimes, when you are developing a counterargument or concession argument, you may become convinced of the validity of the opposing point of view and change your own views. Don't be afraid of this happening. Writing is a tool for learning. To change your mind because of new evidence is a sign of flexibility and maturity, and your writing can only be the better for it.

THE COMPARISON-AND-CONTRAST SYNTHESIS

A particularly important type of argument synthesis is built on patterns of comparison and contrast. Techniques of comparison and contrast enable you to examine two subjects (or sources) in terms of one another. When you compare, you consider *similarities*. When you contrast, you consider *differences*. By comparing and contrasting, you perform a multifaceted analysis that often suggests subtleties that otherwise might not have come to your (or your reader's) attention.

To organize a comparison-and-contrast argument, you must carefully read sources in order to discover *significant criteria for analysis*. A *criterion* is a specific point to which both of your authors refer and about which they may agree or disagree. (For example, in a comparative report on compact cars, criteria for *comparison and contrast* might be road handling, fuel economy, and comfort of ride.) The best criteria are those that allow you not only to account for obvious similarities and differences—those concerning the main aspects of your sources or subjects—but also to plumb deeper, exploring subtle yet significant comparisons and contrasts among details or subcomponents, which you can then relate to your overall thesis.

Note that comparison-and-contrast is frequently not an end in itself, but serves some larger purpose. Thus, a comparison-and-contrast synthesis may be a component of a longer paper that is essentially a critique, an explanatory synthesis, an argument synthesis, or an analysis.

Organizing Comparison-and-Contrast Syntheses

Two basic approaches to organizing a comparison-and-contrast synthesis are available: organization by *source* and organization by *criteria*.

Organizing by Source or Subject

You can organize a comparative synthesis by first summarizing each of your sources or subjects, and then discussing significant similarities and differences between them. Having read the summaries and become familiar with the distinguishing features of each source, your readers will most likely be able to appreciate the more obvious similarities and differences. In the discussion, your task is to focus on both the obvious and subtle comparisons and contrasts, focusing on the most significant—that is, on those that most clearly support your thesis.

Organization by source or subject is best saved for passages that can be briefly summarized. If the summary of your source or subject becomes too long, your readers might forget the points you made in the first summary as they are reading the second. A comparison-and-contrast synthesis organized by source or subject might proceed like this:

    I. Introduce the paper; lead to thesis.

    II. Summarize source/subject A by discussing its significant features.

    III. Summarize source/subject B by discussing its significant features.

    IV. Write a paragraph (or two) in which you discuss the significant points of comparison and contrast between sources or subjects A and B. Alternatively, begin comparison-contrast in Section III upon introducing source or subject B.

End with a conclusion in which you summarize your points and, perhaps, raise and respond to pertinent questions.

Organizing by Criteria

Instead of summarizing entire sources one at a time with the intention of comparing them later, you could discuss two sources simultaneously, examining the views of each author point by point (criterion by criterion), comparing and contrasting these views in the process. The criterion approach is best used when you have a number of points to discuss or when passages or subjects are long and/or complex. A comparison-and-contrast synthesis organized by criteria might look like this:

    I. Introduce the paper; lead to thesis.

    II. Criterion 1

        A. Discuss what author #1 says about this point. Or present situation #1 in light of this point.

        B. Discuss what author #2 says about this point, comparing and contrasting #2's treatment of the point with #1's. Or present situation #2 in light of this point and explain its differences from situation #1.

    III. Criterion 2

        A. Discuss what author #1 says about this point. Or present situation #1 in light of this point.

        B. Discuss what author #2 says about this point, comparing and contrasting #2's treatment of the point with #1's. Or present situation #2 in light of this point and explain its differences from situation #1.

And so on. Proceed criterion by criterion until you have completed your discussion. Be sure to arrange criteria with a clear method; knowing how the discussion of one criterion leads to the next will ensure smooth transitions throughout your paper. End by summarizing your key points and, perhaps, raising and responding to pertinent questions.

However you organize your comparison-and-contrast synthesis, keep in mind that comparing and contrasting are not ends in themselves. Your discussion should point somewhere: to a conclusion, an answer to "So what—why bother to compare and contrast in the first place?" If your discussion is part of a larger synthesis, point to and support the larger claim. If you write a stand-alone comparison-and-contrast, though, you must by the final paragraph answer the "Why bother?" question. The model comparison-and-contrast synthesis that follows does exactly this.

EXERCISE **3.2**

Comparing and Contrasting

Refer back to two of the readings on the compulsory national service controversy: Bruce Chapman's "Politics and National Service: A Virus Attacks the Volunteer Sector" (pages 65–66) and Senators McCain and Bayh's "A New Start For National Service" (pages 62–63). Identify at least two significant criteria that you can use for a comparative analysis—two specific points to which both readings refer and about which they agree or disagree. Then imagine you are preparing to write a short comparison-and-contrast paper and devise two outlines: the first organized by source, and the second organized by criteria.

A Case for Comparison-and-Contrast: World War I and World War II

We'll see how these principles can be applied to a response to a final examination question in a course on modern history. Imagine that having attended classes involving lecture and discussion, and having read excerpts from such texts as John Keegan's *The First World War* and Tony Judt's *Postwar: A History of Europe Since 1945*, students were presented with the following examination question:

> Based on your reading to date, compare and contrast the two World Wars in light of any four or five criteria you think significant. Once you have called careful attention to both similarities and differences, conclude with an observation. What have you learned? What can your comparative analysis teach us?

Comparison-and-Contrast (Organized by Criteria)

Here is a plan for a response, essentially a comparison-contrast synthesis, organized by *criteria*. The thesis—and the *claim*—follows:

```
Thesis: In terms of the impact on cities and civilian
populations, the military aspects of the two wars in
Europe, and their aftermaths, the differences between
World War I and World War II considerably outweigh
the similarities.
```

   I. Introduction. World Wars I and II were the most devastating conflicts in history. <u>Thesis</u>

  II. Summary of main similarities: causes, countries involved, battlegrounds, global scope.

 III. First major difference: Physical impact of war.
   A. WWI was fought mainly in rural battlegrounds.
   B. In WWII cities were destroyed.

 IV. Second major difference: Effect on civilians.
   A. WWI fighting primarily involved soldiers.
   B. WWII involved not only military but also massive non-combatant casualties: civilian populations were displaced, forced into slave labor, and exterminated.

  V. Third major difference: Combat operations.
   A. World War I, in its long middle phase, was characterized by trench warfare.
   B. During the middle phase of World War II, there was no major military action in Nazi-occupied Western Europe.

 VI. Fourth major difference: Aftermath.
   A. Harsh war terms imposed on defeated Germany contributed significantly to the rise of Hitler and World War II.
   B. Victorious allies helped rebuild West Germany after World War II, but allowed Soviets to take over Eastern Europe.

VII. Conclusion. Since the end of World War II, wars have been far smaller in scope and destructiveness, and warfare has expanded to involve stateless combatants committed to acts of terror.

Following is a comparison-and-contrast synthesis by criteria, written according to the preceding plan. (Thesis and topic sentences are highlighted.)

MODEL EXAM RESPONSE
(Thesis and topic sentences are highlighted.)

1   World War I (1914–18) and World War II (1939–45) were the most catastrophic and destructive conflicts in human history. For those who believed in the steady but inevitable progress of civilization, it was impossible to imagine that two wars in the first half of the twentieth century could reach levels of

barbarity and horror that would outstrip those of any previous era. Historians estimate that more than 22 million people, soldiers and civilians, died in World War I; they estimate that between 40 and 50 million died in World War II. In many ways, these two conflicts were similar: they were fought on many of the same European and Russian battlegrounds, with more or less the same countries on opposing sides. Even many of the same people were involved: Winston Churchill and Adolf Hitler figured in both wars. And the main outcome in each case was the same: total defeat for Germany. However, in terms of the impact on cities and civilian populations, the military aspects of the two wars in Europe, and their aftermaths, the differences between World Wars I and II considerably outweigh the similarities.

2   The similarities are clear enough. In fact, many historians regard World War II as a continuation—after an intermission of about twenty years—of World War I. One of the main causes of each war was Germany's dissatisfaction and frustration with what it perceived as its diminished place in the world. Hitler launched World War II partly out of revenge for Germany's humiliating defeat in World War I. In each conflict Germany and its allies (the Central Powers in WWI, the Axis in WWII) went to war against France, Great Britain, Russia (the Soviet Union in WWII), and eventually, the United States. Though neither conflict literally included the entire world, the participation of countries not only in Europe, but also in the Middle East, the Far East, and the Western hemisphere made both of these conflicts global in scope. And as indicated earlier, the number of casualties in each war was unprecedented in history, partly because modern technology had enabled the creation of deadlier weapons—including tanks, heavy artillery, and aircraft—than had ever been used in warfare.

3   Despite these similarities, the differences between the two world wars are considerably more significant. One of the most noticeable differences was the physical impact of each war in Europe and Russia—the western and eastern fronts. The physical destruction of World War I was confined largely to the battlefield. The combat took place almost entirely in the rural areas of Europe and Russia. No major cities were destroyed in the first war;

cathedrals, museums, government buildings, urban houses and apartments were left untouched. During the second war, in contrast, almost no city or town of any size emerged unscathed. Rotterdam, Warsaw, London, Minsk, and--when the Allies began their counterattack--almost every major city in Germany and Japan, including Berlin and Tokyo, were flattened. Of course, the physical devastation of the cities created millions of refugees, a phenomenon never experienced in World War I.

4   The fact that World War II was fought in the cities as well as on the battlefields meant that the second war had a much greater impact on civilians than did the first war. With few exceptions, the civilians in Europe during WWI were not driven from their homes, forced into slave labor, starved, tortured, or systematically exterminated. But all of these crimes happened routinely during WWII. The Nazi occupation of Europe meant that the civilian population of France, Belgium, Norway, the Netherlands and other conquered lands, along with the industries, railroads, and farms of these countries, were put into the service of the Third Reich. Millions of people from conquered Europe--those who were not sent directly to the death camps--were forcibly transported to Germany and put to work in support of the war effort.

5   During both wars, the Germans were fighting on two fronts--the western front in Europe and the eastern front in Russia. But while both wars were characterized by intense military activity during their initial and final phases, the middle and longest phases--at least in Europe--differed considerably. The middle phase of the First World War was characterized by trench warfare, a relatively static form of military activity in which fronts seldom moved, or moved only a few hundred yards at a time, even after major battles. By contrast, in the years between the German conquest of most of Europe by early 1941 and the Allied invasion of Normandy in mid-1944, there was no major fighting in Nazi-occupied Western Europe. (The land battles then shifted to North Africa and the Soviet Union.)

6   And of course, the two world wars differed in their aftermaths. The most significant consequence of World War I was that the humiliating and costly war

reparations imposed on the defeated Germany by the terms of the 1919 Treaty of Versailles made possible the rise of Hitler and thus led directly to World War II. In contrast, after the end of the Second World War in 1945, the Allies helped rebuild West Germany (the portion of a divided Germany which it controlled), transformed the new country into a democracy, and helped make it into one of the most thriving economies of the world. But perhaps the most significant difference in the aftermath of each war involved Russia. That country, in a considerably weakened state, pulled out of World War I a year before hostilities ended so that it could consolidate its 1917 Revolution. Russia then withdrew into itself and took no significant part in European affairs until the Nazi invasion of the Soviet Union in 1941. In contrast, it was the Red Army in World War II that was most responsible for the crushing defeat of Germany. In recognition of its efforts and of its enormous sacrifices, the Allies allowed the Soviet Union to take control of the countries of Eastern Europe after the war, leading to fifty years of totalitarian rule--and the Cold War.

7   While the two world wars that devastated much of Europe were similar in that, at least according to some historians, they were the same war interrupted by two decades, and similar in that combatants killed more efficiently than armies throughout history ever had, the differences between the wars were significant. In terms of the physical impact of the fighting, the impact on civilians, the action on the battlefield at mid-war, and the aftermaths, World Wars I and II differed in ways that matter to us decades later. Recently, the wars in Iraq, Afghanistan, and Bosnia have involved an alliance of nations pitted against single nations; but we have not seen, since the two world wars, grand alliances moving vast armies across continents. The destruction implied by such action is almost unthinkable today. Warfare is changing, and "stateless" combatants like Hamas and Al Qaeda wreak destruction of their own. But we may never see, one hopes, the devastation that follows when multiple nations on opposing sides of a conflict throw millions of soldiers--and civilians--into harm's way.

Discussion

The general strategy of this argument is an organization by *criteria*. The writer argues that although the two world wars of the first part of the twentieth century exhibited some similarities, the differences between the two conflicts were more significant. Note that the writer's thesis doesn't merely establish these significant differences; it enumerates them in a way that anticipates both the content and the structure of the response to follow.

In argument terms, the *claim* the writer makes is the conclusion that the two global conflicts were significantly different, if superficially similar. The *assumption* is that careful attention to the impact of the wars upon cities and civilian populations and to the consequences of the Allied victories are keys to understanding the differences between them. The *support* comes in the form of particular historical facts regarding the level of casualties, the scope of destruction, the theaters of conflict, the events following the conclusions of the wars, and so on.

- **Paragraph 1:** The writer begins by commenting on the unprecedented level of destruction of World Wars I and II and concludes with the thesis summarizing the key similarities and differences.

- **Paragraph 2:** The writer summarizes the key similarities in the two wars: the wars' causes, their combatants, their global scope, the level of destructiveness made possible by modern weaponry.

- **Paragraph 3:** The writer discusses the first of the key differences: the fact that the battlegrounds of World War I were largely rural, but in World War II cities were targeted and destroyed.

- **Paragraph 4:** The writer discusses the second of the key differences: the impact on civilians. In World War I, civilians were generally spared from the direct effects of combat; in World War II, civilians were targeted by the Nazis for systematic displacement and destruction.

- **Paragraph 5:** The writer discusses the third key difference: Combat operations during the middle phase of World War I were characterized by static trench warfare. During World War II, in contrast, there were no major combat operations in Nazi-occupied Western Europe during the middle phase of the conflict.

- **Paragraph 6:** The writer focuses on the fourth key difference: the aftermath of the two wars. After World War I, the victors imposed harsh conditions on defeated Germany, leading to the rise of Hitler and the Second World War. After World War II, the Allies helped Germany rebuild and thrive. However, the Soviet victory in 1945 led to its postwar domination of Eastern Europe.

- **Paragraph 7:** In the conclusion, the writer sums up the key similarities and differences just covered, but makes some additional comments about the course of more recent wars since World War II. In this way, the writer responds to the question posed in the latter part of the assignment: "What have you learned? What can your comparative analysis teach us?"

Avoid Common Fallacies in Developing and Using Support

In Chapter 2, in the section on Critical Reading, we considered some of the criteria that, as a reader, you may use for evaluating informative and persuasive writing (see pages 26–36). We discussed how you can assess the accuracy, the significance, and the author's interpretation of the information presented. We also considered the importance in good argument of clearly defined key terms and the pitfalls of emotionally loaded language. Finally, we saw how to recognize such logical fallacies as either/or reasoning, faulty cause-and-effect reasoning, hasty generalization, and false analogy. As a writer, no less than as a critical reader, be aware of these common problems and try to avoid them.

Be aware, also, of your responsibility to cite source materials appropriately. When you quote a source, double- and triple-check that you have done so accurately. When you summarize or paraphrase, take care to use your own language and sentence structures (though you can, of course, also quote within these forms). When you refer to someone else's idea—even if you are not quoting, summarizing, or paraphrasing—give the source credit. By being ethical about the use of sources, you uphold the highest standards of the academic community.

THE EXPLANATORY SYNTHESIS

Some of the papers you write in college will be more or less explanatory (as opposed to argumentative) in nature. An explanation helps readers understand a topic. Writers explain when they divide a subject into its component parts and present them to the reader in a clear and orderly fashion. Explanations may entail descriptions that re-create in words some object, place, emotion, event, sequence of events, or state of affairs. As a student reporter, you may need to explain an event—to relate when, where, and how it took place. In a science lab, you would observe the conditions and results of an experiment and record them for review by others. In a political science course, you might review research on a particular subject—say, the complexities underlying the debate over gay marriage—and then present the results of your research to your professor and the members of your class.

Your job in writing an explanatory synthesis—or in writing the explanatory portion of an argument synthesis—is not to argue a particular point, but rather *to present the facts in a reasonably objective manner*. Of course, explanatory papers, like other academic papers, should be based on a thesis. But the purpose of a thesis in an explanatory paper is less to advance a particular opinion than to focus the various facts contained in the paper.

The explanatory synthesis is fairly modest in purpose. It emphasizes the materials in the sources themselves, not the writer's interpretation of them. Because your reader is not always in a position to read your sources, this kind of synthesis, if done well, can be very informative. But the main characteristic of the explanatory synthesis is that it is designed more to *inform* than to *persuade*. As the writer of an explanatory synthesis, you remain, for the most part, a detached observer.

Practice Explanatory Synthesis

Write an explanatory synthesis on volunteerism using the sources presented earlier in this chapter (pages 62–66), the sources referred to in the sample paper (pages 71–79) but not included in this chapter, and any other sources you might find on the topic. Use the following guidelines:

- **Consider your purpose.** Your purpose in this paper is to present the relevant facts about volunteerism in a reasonably objective manner. You yourself should not take a position on which types of volunteer efforts are most worthy of support; your responsibility, rather, is to report objectively on the opposing sides of the debate (as represented in your sources) as well as on the essential facts about the state of volunteering in America today.

- **Select and carefully read your sources.** Draw upon the same sources that the writer of the argument synthesis used. You may use some or all of these sources; feel free to enhance your discussion by discovering additional sources through research.

- **Formulate a thesis.** Design your thesis primarily to *inform* rather than to *persuade.* Example: "A tradition of volunteering runs deep in American history and informs the wide variety of volunteer efforts one finds on the local and national levels today."

- **Decide how you will use your source material.** Locate facts and ideas from the readings that will help you to support your thesis.

- **Develop an organizational plan.** Devise an outline that will enable you to present your material effectively. A thesis will often imply an organizational plan. For example, the sample thesis above commits you to (1) recounting the history of volunteerism in America, (2) categorizing the types of volunteer efforts one finds today, and (3) drawing a relation between efforts today (both locally and nationally) and efforts undertaken earlier in American history. This order might offer the most logical structure for your discussion; but during the composing process, you might decide on a different order—which may require you to modify your original thesis.

- **Draft clear, organizing statements for the main sections.** Expand each major point of your outline into a statement that distills the main idea(s) of the paragraph(s) it will organize. Give every paragraph within a section a clear topic sentence.

- **Write and revise your synthesis; document your sources.** See the model argument paper on volunteerism for an example synthesis with carefully documented sources.

SUMMARY

In this chapter, we've considered two main types of synthesis: the *argument synthesis* and the *explanatory synthesis*. Although for ease of comprehension we've placed them into separate categories, these types are not, of course, mutually exclusive. Both argument syntheses and explanatory syntheses often involve elements of one another. Which format you choose will depend upon your *purpose* and the method that you decide is best suited to achieve this purpose.

If your main purpose is to help your audience understand a particular subject, and in particular to help them understand the essential elements or significance of this subject, then you will be composing an explanatory synthesis. If your main purpose, on the other hand, is to persuade your audience to agree with your viewpoint on a subject, or to change their minds, or to decide upon a particular course of action, then you will be composing an argument synthesis. If one effective technique for making your case is to establish similarities or differences between your subject and another one, then you will compose a comparison-and-contrast synthesis—which may well be just *part* of a larger synthesis.

In planning and drafting these syntheses, you can draw upon a variety of strategies: supporting your claims by summarizing, paraphrasing, and quoting from your sources; and choosing from among formats such as climactic or conventional order, counterargument, and concession that will best help you achieve your purpose.

The strategies of synthesis you've practiced in this chapter will be important in composing a research paper, the successful execution of which involves all of the skills in summary, critique, and synthesis that we've discussed so far.

4 Analysis

WHAT IS AN ANALYSIS?

An *analysis* is an argument in which you study the parts of something to understand how it works, what it means, or why it might be significant. The writer of an analysis uses an analytical tool: a *principle* or *definition* on the basis of which an object, an event, or a behavior can be divided into parts and examined. Here are excerpts from two analyses of L. Frank Baum's *The Wizard of Oz*:

> At the dawn of adolescence, the very time she should start to distance herself from Aunt Em and Uncle Henry, the surrogate parents who raised her on their Kansas farm, Dorothy Gale experiences a hurtful reawakening of her fear that these loved ones will be rudely ripped from her, especially her Aunt (Em—M for Mother!). [Harvey Greenberg, *The Movies on Your Mind* (New York: Dutton, 1975).]

> [*The Wizard of Oz*] was originally written as a political allegory about grass-roots protest. It may seem harder to believe than Emerald City, but the Tin Woodsman is the industrial worker, the Scarecrow [is] the struggling farmer, and the Wizard is the president, who is powerful only as long as he succeeds in deceiving the people. [Peter Dreier, "Oz Was Almost Reality," *Cleveland Plain Dealer* 3 Sept. 1989.]

As these paragraphs suggest, what you discover through an analysis depends entirely on the principle or definition you use to make your insights. Is *The Wizard of Oz* the story of a girl's psychological development, or is it a story about politics? The answer is *both*. In the first example, psychiatrist Harvey Greenberg applies the principles of his profession and, not surprisingly, sees *The Wizard of Oz* in psychological terms. In the second example, a newspaper reporter applies the political theories of Karl Marx and, again not surprisingly, discovers a story about politics.

Different as they are, these analyses share an important quality: Each is the result of a specific principle or definition used as a tool to divide an object into parts to see what it means and how it works. The writer's choice of analytical tool simultaneously creates and limits the possibilities for analysis. Thus, working with the principles of Freud, Harvey Greenberg sees *The Wizard of Oz* in psychological, not political, terms; working with the theories of Karl Marx, Peter Dreier understands the movie in terms of the economic relationships among characters. It's as if the writer of an analysis who adopts one analytical tool puts on a pair of glasses and sees an object in a specific way. Another writer, using a different tool (and a different pair of glasses), sees the object differently.

WHERE DO WE FIND WRITTEN ANALYSES?

Here are just a few types of writing that involve analysis:

Academic Writing

- **Experimental and lab reports.** Analyze the meaning or implications of the study results in the Discussion section.
- **Research papers.** Analyze information in sources; apply theories to material being reported.
- **Process analysis.** Break down the steps or stages involved in completing a process.
- **Literary analysis.** Analyze characterization, plot, imagery, or other elements in works of literature.
- **Essay exams.** Demonstrate understanding of course material by analyzing data using course concepts.

Workplace Writing

- **Grant proposals.** Analyze the issues you seek funding for in order to address them.
- **Reviews of the arts.** Employ dramatic or literary analysis to assess artistic works.
- **Business plans.** Break down and analyze capital outlays, expenditures, profits, materials, and the like.
- **Medical charts.** Perform analytical thinking and writing in relation to patient symptoms and possible options.
- **Legal briefs.** Break down and analyze facts of cases and elements of legal precedents; apply legal rulings and precedents to new situations.
- **Case studies.** Describe and analyze the particulars of a specific medical, social service, advertising, or business case.

You might protest: Are there as many analyses of *The Wizard of Oz* as there are people to read it? Yes, or at least as many analyses as there are analytical tools. This does not mean that all analyses are equally valid or useful. The writer must convince the reader. In creating an essay of analysis, the writer must organize a series of related insights, using the analytical tool to examine first one part and then another of the object being studied. To read Harvey Greenberg's essay on *The Wizard of Oz* is to find paragraph after paragraph of related insights—first about Aunt Em, then the Wicked Witch, then Toto, and then the Wizard. All these insights point to Greenberg's single conclusion: that "Dorothy's 'trip' is a marvelous metaphor for the psychological journey every adolescent must make." Without Greenberg's analysis, we probably would not have thought about the movie as a psychological journey. This is precisely the power of an analysis: its ability to reveal objects or events in ways we would not otherwise have considered.

The writer's challenge is to convince readers that (1) the analytical tool being applied is legitimate and well matched to the object being studied; and (2) the analytical tool is being used systematically to divide the object into parts and to make a coherent, meaningful statement about these parts and the object as a whole.

DEMONSTRATION: ANALYSIS

Two examples of analyses follow. The first was written by a professional writer. The second was written by a student, in response to an assignment in his sociology class. Each analysis illustrates the two defining features of analysis just discussed: a statement of an analytical principle or definition, and the use of that principle or definition in closely examining an object, behavior, or event. As you read, try to identify these features. An exercise with questions for discussion follows each example.

The Plug-In Drug
Marie Winn

The following analysis of television viewing as an addictive behavior appeared originally in Marie Winn's 2002 book, The Plug-In Drug: Television, Computers, and Family Life. *A writer and media critic, Winn has been interested in the effect of television on both individuals and the larger culture. In this passage, she carefully defines the term* addiction *and then applies it systematically to the behavior under study.*

1   The word "addiction" is often used loosely and wryly in conversation. People will refer to themselves as "mystery-book addicts" or "cookie addicts." E. B. White wrote of his annual surge of interest in gardening: "We are hooked and are making an attempt to kick the habit." Yet nobody really believes that reading mysteries or ordering seeds by catalogue is serious enough to be compared with addictions to heroin or alcohol. In these cases the word "addiction" is used jokingly to denote a tendency to overindulge in some pleasurable activity.

2   People often refer to being "hooked on TV." Does this, too, fall into the lighthearted category of cookie eating and other pleasures that people pursue with unusual intensity? Or is there a kind of television viewing that falls into the more serious category of destructive addiction?

3   Not unlike drugs or alcohol, the television experience allows the participant to blot out the real world and enter into a pleasurable and passive mental state. To be sure, other experiences, notably reading, also provide a temporary respite from reality. But it's much easier to stop reading and return to reality than to stop watching television. The entry into another world offered by reading includes an easily accessible return ticket. The entry via television does not. In this way television viewing, for those vulnerable to addiction, is more like drinking or taking drugs—once you start it's hard to stop.

4   Just as alcoholics are only vaguely aware of their addiction, feeling that they control their drinking more than they really do ("I can cut it out any time I want—I just like to have three or four drinks before dinner"), many people overestimate their control over television watching. Even as they put off other activities to spend hour after hour watching television, they feel they could easily resume living in a different, less passive style. But somehow or other while the television set is present in their homes, it just stays on. With television's easy gratifications available, those other activities seem to take too much effort.

5   A heavy viewer (a college English instructor) observes:

> I find television almost irresistible. When the set is on, I cannot ignore it. I can't turn it off. I feel sapped, will-less, enervated. As I reach out to turn off the set, the strength goes out of my arms. So I sit there for hours and hours.

6   Self-confessed television addicts often feel they "ought" to do other things— but the fact that they don't read and don't plant their garden or sew or crochet or play games or have conversations means that those activities are no longer as desirable as television viewing. In a way, the lives of heavy viewers are as unbalanced by their television "habit" as drug addicts' or alcoholics' lives. They are living in a holding pattern, as it were, passing up the activities that lead to growth or development or a sense of accomplishment. This is one reason people talk about their television viewing so ruefully, so apologetically. They are aware that it is an unproductive experience, that by any human measure almost any other endeavor is more worthwhile.

7   It is the adverse effect of television viewing on the lives of so many people that makes it feel like a serious addiction. The television habit distorts the sense of time. It renders other experiences vague and curiously unreal while taking on a greater reality for itself. It weakens relationships by reducing and sometimes eliminating normal opportunities for talking, for communicating.

8   And yet television does not satisfy, else why would the viewer continue to watch hour after hour, day after day? "The measure of health," wrote the psychiatrist Lawrence Kubie, "is flexibility . . . and especially the freedom to cease when sated." But heavy television viewers can never be sated with their television experiences. These do not provide the true nourishment that satiation requires, and thus they find that they cannot stop watching.

EXERCISE **4.1**

Reading Critically: Winn

In analyses, an author first presents the analytical principle in full and then systematically applies parts of the principle to the object or phenomenon under study. In her brief analysis of television viewing, Marie Winn pursues an alternate, though equally effective, strategy by *distributing* parts of her analytical principle across the essay. Locate where Winn defines key elements of addiction. Locate where she uses each element as an analytical lens to examine television viewing as a form of addiction.

What function does paragraph 4 play in the analysis?

In the first two paragraphs, how does Winn create a funnel-like effect that draws readers into the heart of her analysis?

Recall a few television programs that genuinely moved you, educated you, humored you, or stirred you to worthwhile reflection or action. To what extent does Winn's analysis describe your positive experiences as a television viewer? (Consider how Winn might argue that from within an addicted state, a person may feel "humored, moved or educated" but is in fact—from a sober outsider's point of view—deluded.) If Winn's analysis of television viewing as an addiction does *not* account for your experience, does it follow that her analysis is flawed? Explain.

The Coming Apart of a Dorm Society
Edward Peselman

Edward Peselman wrote the following paper as a first-semester sophomore, in response to the following assignment from his sociology professor:

> *Read Chapter 3, "The Paradoxes of Power," in Randall Collins's* Sociological Insight: An Introduction to Non-Obvious Sociology *(2nd ed., 1992). Use any of Collins's observations to examine the sociology of power in a group with which you are familiar. Write for readers much like yourself: freshmen or sophomores who have taken one course in sociology. Your object in this paper is to use Collins as a way of learning something "nonobvious" about a group to which you belong or have belonged.*

Format notes: The model analysis that follows is single spaced in order to reduce the number of pages in this textbook. To conform to American Psychological Association format, your paper should be double spaced. The citations are in APA format (see pp. 518–519).

MODEL ANALYSIS

Coming Apart 1

The Coming Apart of a Dorm Society
Edward Peselman
Sociology of Everyday Life
Murray State University
Murray, Kentucky
23 March 2008

Center information horizontally and vertically on the page.

The Coming Apart of a Dorm Society

1   During my first year of college, I lived in a
dormitory, like most freshmen on campus. We inhabi-
tants of the dorm came from different cultural and
economic backgrounds. Not surprisingly, we brought
with us many of the traits found in people outside of
college. Like many on the outside, we in the dorm
sought personal power at the expense of others. The
gaining and maintaining of power can be an ugly business, and I saw people hurt and in turn hurt others
all for the sake of securing a place in the dorm's
prized social order. Not until one of us challenged
that order did I realize how fragile it was.

2   Randall Collins, a sociologist at the University
of California, Riverside, defines the exercise of
power as the attempt "to make something happen in
society" (1992, p. 61). A society can be understood
as something as large and complex as "American
society"; something more sharply defined—such as a
corporate or organizational society; or something
smaller still—a dorm society like my own, consisting
of six 18-year-old men who lived at one end of a
dormitory floor in an all male dorm.

3   In my freshman year, my society was a tiny but
distinctive social group in which people exercised
power. I lived with two roommates, Dozer and Reggie.
Dozer was an emotionally unstable, excitable individual
who vented his energy through anger. His insecurity
and moodiness contributed to his difficulty in making
friends. Reggie was a friendly, happy-go-lucky sort
who seldom displayed emotions other than contentedness.
He was shy when encountering new people, but when
placed in a socially comfortable situation he would
talk for hours.

4   Eric and Marc lived across the hall from us and
therefore spent a considerable amount of time in our
room. Eric could be cynical and was often blunt: He
seldom hesitated when sharing his frank and sometimes
unflattering opinions. He commanded a grudging
respect in the dorm. Marc could be very moody and,
sometimes, was violent. His temper and stubborn
streak made him particularly susceptible to conflict.
The final member of our miniature society was
Benjamin, cheerful yet insecure. Benjamin had certain
characteristics which many considered effeminate, and
he was often teased about his sexuality—which in turn
made him insecure. He was naturally friendly but,

Coming Apart 3

because of the abuse he took, he largely kept to himself. He would join us occasionally for a pizza or late-night television.

5   Together, we formed an independent social structure. Going out to parties together, playing cards, watching television, playing ball: These were the activities through which we got to know each other and through which we established the basic pecking order of our community. Much like a colony of baboons, we established a hierarchy based on power relationships. According to Collins, what a powerful person wishes to happen must be achieved by controlling others. Collins's observation can help to define who had how much power in our social group. In the dorm, Marc and Eric clearly had the most power. Everyone feared them and agreed to do pretty much what they wanted. Through violent words or threats of violence, they got their way. I was next in line: I wouldn't dare to manipulate Marc or Eric, but the others I could manage through occasional quips. Reggie, then Dozer, and finally Benjamin.

6   Up and down the pecking order, we exercised control through macho taunts and challenges. Collins writes that "individuals who manage to be powerful and get their own way must do so by going along with the laws of social organization, not by contradicting them" (p. 61). Until mid-year, our dorm motto could have read: "You win through rudeness and intimidation." Eric gained power with his frequent and brutal assessments of everyone's behavior. Marc gained power with his temper—which, when lost, made everyone run for cover. Those who were not rude and intimidating drifted to the bottom of our social world. Reggie was quiet and unemotional, which allowed us to take advantage of him because we knew he would back down if pressed in an argument. Yet Reggie understood that on a "power scale" he stood above Dozer and often shared in the group's tactics to get Dozer's food (his parents were forever sending him care packages). Dozer, in turn, seldom missed opportunities to take swipes at Benjamin, with references to his sexuality. From the very first week of school, Benjamin could never--and never wanted to--compete against Eric's bluntness or Marc's temper. Still, Benjamin hung out with us. He lived in our corner of the dorm, and he wanted to be friendly. But

Coming Apart 4

everyone, including Benjamin, understood that he occupied the lowest spot in the order.

7 That is, until he left mid-semester. *According to Collins, "any social arrangement works because people avoid questioning it most of the time" (p. 74). *The inverse of this principle is as follows: When a social arrangement is questioned, that arrangement can fall apart. The more fragile the arrangement (the flimsier the values on which it is based), the more quickly it will crumble. For the entire first semester, no one questioned our rude, macho rules and because of them we pigeonholed Benjamin as a wimp. In our dorm society, gentle men had no power. To say the least, ours was not a compassionate community. From a distance of one year, I am shocked to have been a member of it. Nonetheless, we had created a mini-society that somehow served our needs.

8 At the beginning of the second semester, we found Benjamin packing up his room. Marc, who was walking down the hall, stopped by and said something like: "Hey buddy, the kitchen get too hot for you?" I was there, and I saw Benjamin turn around and say: "Do you practice at being such a _____, or does it come naturally? I've never met anybody who felt so good about making other people feel lousy. You'd better get yourself a job in the army or in the prison system, because no one else is going to put up with your _____." Marc said something in a raised voice. I stepped between them, and Benjamin said: "Get out." I was cheering.

9 Benjamin moved into an off-campus apartment with his girlfriend. This astonished us, first because of his effeminate manner (we didn't know he had a girlfriend) and second because none of the rest of us had been seeing girls much (though we talked about it constantly). Here was Benjamin, the gentlest among us, and he blew a hole in our macho society. Our social order never really recovered, which suggests its flimsy values. People in the dorm mostly went their own ways during the second semester. I'm not surprised, and I was more than a little grateful. Like most people in the dorm, save for Eric and Marc, I both got my lumps and I gave them, and I never felt good about either. Like Benjamin, I wanted to fit in with my new social surroundings. Unlike him,

                                                    Coming Apart 5
I didn't have the courage to challenge the unfairness
of what I saw.

10   By chance, six of us were thrown together into a
dorm and were expected, on the basis of proximity
alone, to develop a friendship. What we did was sink
to the lowest possible denominator. Lacking any real
basis for friendship, we allowed the forceful, macho
personalities of Marc and Eric to set the rules,
which for one semester we all subscribed to—even
those who suffered.

11   The macho rudeness couldn't last, and I'm glad
it was Benjamin who brought us down. By leaving, he
showed a different and a superior kind of power.
I doubt he was reading Randall Collins at the time,
but he somehow had come to Collins's same insight: As
long as he played by the rules of our group, he suffered because those rules placed him far down in the
dorm's pecking order. Even by participating in pleasant activities, like going out for pizza, Benjamin
supported a social system that ridiculed him. Some
systems are so oppressive and small minded that they
can't be changed from the inside. They've got to be
torn down. Benjamin had to move, and in moving he
made me (at least) question the basis of my dorm
friendships.

[New Page]

                                                    Coming Apart 6
                            Reference
Collins, R. (1992). *Sociological insight: An intro-
    duction to non-obvious sociology* (2nd ed.).
    New York: Oxford University Press.

EXERCISE 4.2

Reading Critically: Peselman

What is the function of paragraph 1? Though Peselman does not use the word
sociology, what signals does he give that this will be a paper that examines the
social interactions of a group? Peselman introduces Collins in paragraph 2.
Why? What does Peselman accomplish in paragraphs 3–4? How does his use

of Collins in paragraph 5 logically follow the presentation in paragraphs 3–4? The actual analysis in this paper takes place in paragraphs 5–11. Point to where Peselman draws on the work of Randall Collins, and explain how he uses Collins to gain insight into dorm life.

HOW TO WRITE ANALYSES

Consider Your Purpose

Whether you are assigned a topic to write on or are left to your own devices, you inevitably face this question: What is my idea? Like every paper, an analysis has at its heart an idea you want to convey. For Edward Peselman, it was the idea that a social order based on flimsy values is not strong enough to sustain a direct challenge to its power, and thus will fall apart eventually. From beginning to end, Peselman advances this one idea: first, by introducing readers to the dorm society he will analyze; next, by introducing principles of analysis (from Randall Collins); and finally, by examining his dorm relationships in light of these principles. The entire set of analytical insights coheres as a paper because the insights are *related* and point to Peselman's single idea.

Peselman's paper offers a good example of the personal uses to which analysis can be put. Notice that he gravitated toward events in his life that confused him and about which he wanted some clarity. Such topics can be especially fruitful for analysis because you know the particulars well and can provide readers with details; you view the topic with some puzzlement; and, through the application of your analytical tool, you may come to understand it. When you select topics to analyze from your experience, you provide yourself with a motivation to write and learn. When you are motivated in this way, you spark the interest of readers.

Using Randall Collins as a guide, Edward Peselman returns again and again to the events of his freshman year in the dormitory. We sense that Peselman himself wants to know what happened in that dorm. He writes, "I saw people hurt and in turn hurt others all for the sake of securing a place in the dorm's prized social order." Peselman does not approve of what happened, and the analysis he launches is meant to help him understand.

Locate an Analytical Principle

When you are given an assignment that asks for analysis, use two specific reading strategies to identify principles and definitions in source materials.

- **Look for a sentence that makes a general statement about the way something works.** The statement may strike you as a rule or a law. The line that Edward Peselman quotes from Randall Collins has this quality:

"[A]ny social arrangement works because people avoid questioning it most of the time." Such statements are generalizations—conclusions to sometimes complicated and extensive arguments. You can use these conclusions to guide your own analyses as long as you are aware that for some audiences, you will need to re-create and defend the arguments that resulted in these conclusions.

- **Look for statements that take this form: "X" can be defined as (or "X" consists of) the following: A, B, and C.** The specific elements of the definition—A, B, and C—are what you use to identify and analyze parts of the object being studied. You've seen an example of this approach in Marie Winn's multipart definition of addiction, which she uses to analyze television viewing. As a reader looking for definitions suitable for conducting an analysis, you might come across Winn's definition of addiction and then use it for your own purposes, perhaps to analyze the playing of video games as an addiction.

Essential to any analysis is the validity of the principle or definition being applied, the analytical tool. Make yourself aware, both as writer and reader, of a tool's strengths and limitations. Pose these questions of the analytical principles and definitions you use: Are they accurate? Are they well accepted? Do *you* accept them? What are the arguments against them? What are their limitations? Since every principle or definition used in an analysis is the end product of an argument, you are entitled—even obligated—to challenge it. If the analytical tool is flawed, then the analysis that follows from it will be flawed also.

Following is a page from Collins's *Sociological Insight*; Edward Peselman uses a key sentence from this extract as an analytical tool in his essay on power relations in his dorm (see page 105). Notice that Peselman underlines the sentence he will use in his analysis.

1 Try this experiment some time. When you are talking to someone, make them explain everything they say that isn't completely clear. The result, you will discover, is a series of uninterrupted interruptions:

A: Hi, how are you doing?
B: What do you mean when you say "how"?
A: You know. What's happening with you?
B: What do you mean, "happening"?
A: Happening, you know, what's going on.
B: I'm sorry. Could you explain what you mean by "what"?
A: What do you mean, what do I mean? Do you want to talk to me or not?

2   It is obvious that this sort of questioning could go on endlessly, at any rate if the listener doesn't get very angry and punch you in the mouth. But it illustrates two important points. First, virtually everything can be called into question. We are able to get along with other people not because everything is clearly spelled out, but because we are willing to take most things people say without explanation.

Harold Garfinkel, who actually performed this sort of experiment, points out that there is an infinite regress of assumptions that go into any act of social communication. Moreover, some expressions are simply not explainable in words at all. A word like "you," or "here," or "now" is what Garfinkel calls "indexical." You have to know what it means already; it can't be explained.

3 "What do you mean by 'you'?"

4 "I mean *you, you!*" About all that can be done here is point your finger.

5 The second point is that people get mad when they are pressed to explain things that they ordinarily take for granted. This is because they very quickly see that explanations could go on forever and the questions will never be answered. If you really demanded a full explanation of everything you hear, you could stop the conversation from ever getting past its first sentence. The real significance of this for a sociological understanding of the way the world is put together is not the anger, however. It is the fact that people try to avoid these sorts of situations. They tacitly recognize that we have to avoid these endless lines of questioning. Sometimes small children will start asking an endless series of "whys," but adults discourage this.

6 In sum, any social arrangement works because <u>people avoid questioning it most of the time.</u> That does not mean that people do not get into arguments or disputes about just what ought to be done from time to time. But to have a dispute already implies there is a considerable area of agreement. An office manager may dispute with a clerk over just how to take care of some business letter, but they at any rate know more or less what they are disputing about. They do not get off into a . . . series of questions over just what is meant by everything that is said. You could very quickly dissolve the organization into nothingness if you followed that route: there would be no communication at all, even about what the disagreement is over.

7 Social organization is possible because people maintain a certain level of focus. If they focus on one thing, even if only to disagree about it, they are taking many other things for granted, thereby reinforcing their social reality.

The statement that Peselman has underlined—"any social arrangement works because people avoid questioning it most of the time"—is the end result of an argument that takes Collins several paragraphs to develop. Peselman agrees with the conclusion and uses it in paragraph 7 of his analysis. Observe that for his own purposes Peselman does *not* reconstruct Collins's argument. He selects *only* Collins's conclusion and then imports that into his analysis, which concerns an entirely different subject. Once he identifies in Collins a principle he can use in his analysis, he converts the principle into questions that he then directs to his topic: life in his freshman dorm. Two questions follow directly from Collins's insight:

1. What was the social arrangement in the dorm?
2. How was this social arrangement questioned?

Peselman clearly defines his dormitory's social arrangement in paragraphs 3–6 (with the help of another principle borrowed from Collins). Beginning with paragraph 7, he explores how one member of his dorm questioned that arrangement:

> That is, until he left mid-semester. According to Collins, "any social arrangement works because people avoid questioning it most of the time" (p. 74). The inverse of this principle is as follows: When a social arrangement is questioned, that arrangement can fall apart. The more fragile the arrangement (the flimsier the values on which it is based), the more quickly it will crumble. For the entire first semester, no one questioned our rude, macho rules and because of them we pigeon-holed Benjamin as a wimp. In our dorm society, gentle men had no power. To say the least, ours was not a compassionate community. From a distance of one year, I am shocked to have been a member of it. Nonetheless, we had created a mini-society that somehow served our needs.

Formulate a Thesis

An analysis is a two-part argument. The first part states and establishes the writer's agreement with a certain principle or definition.

Part One of the Argument

This first argument essentially takes this form:

Claim #1: Principle "X" (or definition "X") is valuable.

Principle "X" can be a theory as encompassing and abstract as the statement that *myths are the enemy of truth.* Principle "X" can be as modest as the definition of a term—for instance, *addiction* or *comfort.* As you move from one subject area to another, the principles and definitions you use for analysis will change, as these assignments illustrate:

Sociology: *Write a paper in which you place yourself in American society by locating both your absolute position and relative rank on each single criterion of social stratification used by Lenski & Lenski. For each criterion, state whether you have attained your social position by yourself or if you have "inherited" that status from your parents.*

Literature: *Apply principles of Jungian psychology to Hawthorne's "Young Goodman Brown." In your reading of the story, apply Jung's principles of the* shadow, persona, *and* anima.

Physics: *Use Newton's second law* (F = ma) *to analyze the acceleration of a fixed pulley, from which two weights hang:* m₁ *(.45 kg) and* m₂ *(.90 kg). Explain in a paragraph the principle of Newton's law and your method of applying it to solve the problem. Assume your reader is not comfortable with mathematical explanations: do not use equations in your paragraph.*

Finance: *Using Guidford C. Babcock's "Concept of Sustainable Growth"* [Financial Analysis 26 (May–June 1970): 108–14], *analyze the stock price appreciation of the XYZ Corporation, figures for which are attached.*

The analytical tools to be applied in these assignments change from discipline to discipline. Writing in response to the sociology assignment, you would use sociological principles developed by Lenski and Lenski. In your literature class, you would use principles of Jungian psychology;

GUIDELINES FOR WRITING ANALYSIS

Unless you are asked to follow a specialized format, especially in the sciences or the social sciences, you can present your analysis as a paper by following the guidelines below. As you move from one class to another, from discipline to discipline, the principles and definitions you use as the basis for your analyses will change, but the following basic components of analysis will remain the same:

- *Create a context for your analysis.* Introduce and summarize for readers the object, event, or behavior to be analyzed. Present a strong case about why an analysis is needed: Give yourself a motivation to write, and give readers a motivation to read. Consider setting out a problem, puzzle, or question to be investigated.
- *Introduce and summarize the key definition or principle* that will form the basis of your analysis. Plan to devote an early part of your analysis to arguing for the validity of this principle or definition *if* your audience is not likely to understand it or if they are likely to think that the principle or definition is *not* valuable.
- *Analyze your topic.* Systematically apply elements of this definition or principle to parts of the activity or object under study. You can do this by posing specific questions, based on your analytic principle or definition, about the object. Discuss what you find part by part (organized perhaps by question), in clearly defined sections of the essay.
- *Conclude by stating clearly what is significant about your analysis.* When considering your analytical paper as a whole, what new or interesting insights have you made concerning the object under study? To what extent has your application of the definition or principle helped you to explain how the object works, what it might mean, or why it is significant?

in physics, Newton's second law; and in finance, a particular writer's concept of "sustainable growth." But whatever discipline you are working in, the first part of your analysis will clearly state which (and whose) principles and definitions you are applying. For audiences unfamiliar with these principles, you will need to explain them; if you anticipate objections, you will need to argue that they are legitimate principles capable of helping you as you conduct an analysis.

Part Two of the Argument

In the second part of an analysis, you *apply* specific parts of your principle or definition to the topic at hand. Regardless of how it is worded, this second argument in an analysis can be rephrased to take this form:.

> **Claim #2:** By applying Principle (or definition) "X," we can understand *(topic)* as *(conclusion based on analysis)*.

This is your thesis, the main idea of your analytical paper. Fill in the first blank with the specific object, event, or behavior you are examining. Fill in the second blank with your conclusion about the meaning or significance of this object, based on the insights made during your analysis. Mary Winn completes the second claim of her analysis this way:

> By applying my multipart definition, we can understand *television viewing* as *an addiction*.

Develop an Organizational Plan

You will benefit enormously in the writing of a first draft if you plan out the logic of your analysis. Turn key elements of your analytical principle or definition into questions and then develop the paragraph-by-paragraph logic of the paper.

Turning Key Elements of a Principle or Definition into Questions

Prepare for an analysis by developing questions based on the definition or principle you are going to apply, and then by directing these questions to the activity or object to be studied. The method is straightforward: State as clearly as possible the principle or definition to be applied. Divide the principle or definition into its parts and, using each part, develop a question. For example, Marie Winn develops a multipart definition of addiction, each part of which is readily turned into a question that she directs at a specific behavior: television viewing. Her analysis of television viewing can be understood as *responses* to each of her analytical questions. Note that in her brief analysis, Winn does not first define addiction and then analyze television viewing. Rather, *as* she defines aspects of addiction, she analyzes television viewing.

Developing the Paragraph-by-Paragraph Logic of Your Paper

The following paragraph from Edward Peselman's essay illustrates the typical logic of a paragraph in an analytical essay:

> Up and down the pecking order, we exercised control through macho taunts and challenges. Collins writes that "individuals who manage to be powerful and get their own way must do so by going along with the laws of social organization, not by contradicting them" (p. 61). Until mid-year, our dorm motto could have read: "You win through rudeness and intimidation." Eric gained power with his frequent and brutal assessments of everyone's behavior. Marc gained power with his temper—which, when lost, made everyone run for cover. Those who were not rude and intimidating drifted to the bottom of our social world. Reggie was quiet and unemotional, which allowed us to take advantage of him because we knew he would back down if pressed in an argument. Yet Reggie understood that on a "power scale" he stood above Dozer and often shared in the group's tactics to get Dozer's food (his parents were forever sending him care packages). Dozer, in turn, seldom missed opportunities to take swipes at Benjamin, with references to his sexuality. From the very first week of school, Benjamin could never—and never wanted to—compete against Eric's bluntness or Marc's temper. Still, Benjamin hung out with us. He lived in our corner of the dorm, and he wanted to be friendly. But everyone, including Benjamin, understood that he occupied the lowest spot in the order.

We see in this example paragraph the typical logic of analysis:

- *The writer introduces a specific analytical tool.* Peselman quotes a line from Randall Collins:

  > "[I]ndividuals who manage to be powerful and get their own way must do so by going along with the laws of social organization, not by contradicting them."

- *The writer applies this analytical tool to the object being examined.* Peselman states his dorm's law of social organization:

> Until mid-year, our dorm motto could have read:
> "You win through rudeness and intimidation."

- *The writer uses the tool to identify and then examine the meaning of parts of the object.* Peselman shows how each member (the "parts") of his dorm society conforms to the laws of "social organization":

> Eric gained power with his frequent and brutal
> assessments of everyone's behavior. Marc gained
> power with his temper—which, when lost, made
> everyone run for cover. Those who were not rude
> and intimidating drifted to the bottom of our
> social world. . . .

An analytical paper takes shape when a writer creates a series of such paragraphs and then links them with an overall logic. Here is the logical organization of Edward Peselman's paper:

- Paragraph 1: Introduction states a problem—provides a motivation to write and to read.
- Paragraph 2: Randall Collins is introduced—the author whose work will provide principles for analysis.
- Paragraphs 3–4: Background information is provided—the cast of characters in the dorm.
- Paragraphs 5–9: The analysis proceeds—specific parts of dorm life are identified and found significant, using principles from Collins.
- Paragraphs 10–11: Summary and conclusion are provided—the freshman dorm society disintegrated for reasons set out in the analysis. A larger point is made: Some oppressive systems must be torn down.

Draft and Revise Your Analysis

You will usually need at least two drafts to produce a paper that presents your idea clearly. The biggest changes in your paper will typically come between your first and second drafts. No paper that you write, including an analysis, will be complete until you revise and refine your single compelling idea: your analytical conclusion about what the object, event, or behavior being examined means or how it is significant. You revise and refine by evaluating your first draft, bringing to it many of the same questions you pose when evaluating any piece of writing, including these:

- Are the facts accurate?
- Are my opinions supported by evidence?
- Are the opinions of others authoritative?
- Are my assumptions clearly stated?

- Are key terms clearly defined?
- Is the presentation logical?
- Are all parts of the presentation well developed?
- Are significant opposing points of view presented?

Address these same questions on the first draft of your analysis, and you will have solid information to guide your revision.

Write an Analysis, Not a Summary

The most common error made in writing analyses—which is *fatal* to the form—is to present readers with a summary only. For analyses to succeed, you must *apply* a principle or definition and reach a conclusion about the object, event, or behavior you are examining. By definition, a summary (see Chapter 1) includes none of your own conclusions. Summary is naturally a part of analysis; you will need to summarize the object or activity being examined and, depending on the audience's needs, summarize the principle or definition being applied. But in an analysis, you must take the next step and share insights that suggest the meaning or significance of some object, event, or behavior.

Make Your Analysis Systematic

Analyses should give the reader the sense of a systematic, purposeful examination. Marie Winn's analysis illustrates the point: She sets out specific elements of addictive behavior in separate paragraphs and then uses each, within its paragraph, to analyze television viewing. Winn is systematic in her method, and we are never in doubt about her purpose.

Imagine another analysis in which a writer lays out four elements of a definition but then applies only two, without explaining the logic for omitting the others. Or imagine an analysis in which the writer offers a principle for analysis but directs it to only a half or a third of the object being discussed, without providing a rationale for doing so. In both cases, the writer would be failing to deliver on a promise basic to analyses: Once a principle or definition is presented, it should be thoroughly and systematically applied.

Answer the "So What?" Question

An analysis should make readers *want* to read. It should give readers a sense of getting to the heart of the matter, that what is important in the object or activity under analysis is being laid bare and discussed in revealing ways. If when rereading the first draft of your analysis, you cannot imagine readers saying, "I never thought of ____ this way," then something may be seriously wrong. Reread closely to determine why the paper might leave readers flat and exhausted, as opposed to feeling that they have gained new and important insights. Closely reexamine your own motivations for writing. Have *you* learned anything significant through the analysis? If not, neither will readers, and they will turn away. If you have gained important insights through your analysis, communicate them clearly. At some point, pull together your related insights and say, in effect: "Here's how it all adds up."

Attribute Sources Appropriately

In an analysis you work with one or two sources and apply insights from those to some object or phenomenon you want to understand more thoroughly. Because you are not synthesizing a great many sources, and because the strength of an analysis derives mostly from *your* application of a principle or definition, the opportunities for not appropriately citing sources are diminished. Take special care to cite and quote, as necessary, the one or two sources you use throughout the analysis.

CRITICAL READING FOR ANALYSIS

- *Read to get a sense of the whole in relation to its parts.* Whether you are clarifying for yourself a principle or definition to be used in an analysis, or are reading a text that you will analyze, understand how parts function to create the whole. If a definition or principle consists of parts, use these to organize sections of your analysis. If your goal is to analyze a text, be aware of its structure: Note the title and subtitle; identify the main point and subordinate points and where they are located; break the material into sections.

- *Read to discover relationships within the object being analyzed.* Watch for patterns. When you find them, be alert—for you create an occasion to analyze, to use a principle or definition as a guide in discussing what the pattern may mean.

   In fiction, a pattern might involve responses of characters to events or to each other, recurrence of certain words or phrasings, images, themes, or turns of plot, to name a few.

   In poetry, a pattern might involve rhyme schemes, rhythm, imagery, figurative or literal language, and more.

Your challenge as a reader is first to see a pattern (perhaps using a guiding principle or definition to do so) and then to locate other instances of that pattern. Reading carefully in this way prepares you to conduct an analysis.

ANALYSIS: A TOOL FOR UNDERSTANDING

As this chapter has demonstrated, analysis involves applying principles as a way to probe and understand. With incisive principles guiding your analysis, you will be able to pose questions, observe patterns and relationships, and derive meaning. Do not forget that this meaning will be one of several possible meanings. Someone else, possibly you, using different analytical tools could observe the same phenomena and arrive at very different conclusions regarding meaning or significance. We end the chapter, therefore, as we began it: with the two brief analyses of *The Wizard of Oz*. The conclusions expressed in one look nothing like the conclusions expressed in the other, save for the fact that both seek to interpret the same movie. And yet we can say that both are useful, both reveal meaning:

> At the dawn of adolescence, the very time she should start to distance herself from Aunt Em and Uncle Henry, the surrogate parents who raised her on their Kansas farm, Dorothy Gale experiences a hurtful reawakening of her fear that these loved ones will be rudely ripped from her, especially her Aunt (Em—M for Mother!). [Harvey Greenberg, *The Movies on Your Mind* (New York: Dutton, 1975).]

> [*The Wizard of Oz*] was originally written as a political allegory about grass-roots protest. It may seem harder to believe than Emerald City, but the Tin Woodsman is the industrial worker, the Scarecrow [is] the struggling farmer, and the Wizard is the president, who is powerful only as long as he succeeds in deceiving the people. [Peter Dreier, "Oz Was Almost Reality," *Cleveland Plain Dealer* 3 Sept. 1989.]

You have seen in this chapter how it is possible for two writers, analyzing the same object or phenomenon but applying different analytical principles, to reach vastly different conclusions about what the object or phenomenon may mean or why it is significant. *The Wizard of Oz* is both an inquiry into the psychology of adolescence and a political allegory. What else the classic film may be awaits revealing with the systematic application of other analytical tools. The insights you gain as a writer of analyses depend entirely on your choice of tools and the subtlety with which you apply them.

An Anthology
of Readings

Marriage and Family in America

Between 40 and 50% of all American marriages will fail. An even higher percentage of second marriages will end in divorce. Failed marriages of young couples have become cynically known as "Starter Marriages." Cohabitation is on the rise, and more people than ever before are choosing to stay single. A survey released by the U.S. Census Bureau in October 2006 found that domiciles led by married couples were now in the minority—just 49.7% of all households. Yet marriage continues to fascinate and inspire us—as it has every known culture throughout human history. The wedding industry generates over $60 billion a year in expenses ranging from embossed invitations to rented tuxedos to $10,000 video shoots. Newsstands are choked with bridal magazines. Tabloids splash celebrity weddings across their covers; and most Hollywood comedies still end with the prospect of a wedding. Everybody, it seems, plans on getting married. According to one set of statistics, 85% of Americans will marry at some point in their lives, and 99% say they plan to do so.

Why? What is it about the marital state that is so universally appealing? Why do we continue to wed, despite the fact that most of us, through personal experience, have experienced or witnessed divorce? For some young people, marriage is simply another fact of life—perhaps part of a dimly glimpsed future, along with 401(k) plans, 9-to-5 jobs, and other pillars of adulthood. Others may see the institution in more specific terms—for instance, a teenage girl obsessing over the color of her future bridesmaids' dresses and the merits of white versus pink roses for the centerpieces.

Whether marriage fuels our childhood fantasies or fulfills (or frustrates) our expectations as adults, very few of us can describe what it means to be married—if it ever occurred to us to do so. Doesn't this seem odd? After all, most people have no trouble describing "friendship" as a form of human relationship or "employment" or "citizenship." Yet marriage, an institution to which nearly all of us aspire, and a condition in which most of us will spend many years of our lives, resists easy interpretation. If pressed, most of us would probably characterize the marriage relationship as primarily romantic. The most idealistic and starry-eyed of us, who see marriage as a way for soul mates to pledge unending devotion to one another, dwell at one end of this spectrum. Others, aware that love can be fickle and ephemeral, sense that marriage must be about other things: maturity and commitment, an indication that one has "settled down," perhaps even a rite of passage to adulthood. (Yes, you are marrying someone you love, but you loved at 20 and didn't marry. What changed? *You* did.)

Sociologists Maria Kefalas and Kathryn Edin have demonstrated how, among poorer Americans, marriage has become a luxury item, to be purchased only when a couple has "arrived" financially, last on a "to-do" list, behind a home mortgage and new furniture. And at least some of us suspect that marriage involves pragmatic considerations of a social, political, or even avaricious nature. As they say, it's just as easy to fall in love with and marry a rich girl (or guy) as a poor one.

As the selections in this chapter will show, these conflicting and tangled motives for marrying are no accident. The very meaning of marriage has been changing over the centuries, an evolution that can be traced to broad cultural, intellectual, and economic trends. If anything, these changes seem to be accelerating. (To borrow from Hemingway—the changes seem to be happening slowly, and all at once.) But what significance can we draw from this evolution? Conservative cultural commentators point to the muddled state of contemporary marriage as proof that our society has taken a wrong turn. Yet a wrong turn from what—some historical, universally acclaimed ideal of marriage? As marriage historian Stephanie Coontz notes:

> Everyone agrees that marriage isn't what it used to be, and everyone is quite right. But most of what "everyone knows" about what matrimony used to be and just how it has changed is wrong.

With Coontz's observation as our starting point, this chapter examines the state of marriage and family in contemporary America. Historians, sociologists, anthropologists, political scientists, legal scholars, political activists, and journalists have studied marriage from their various perspectives; and they have offered observations about its impact on our culture, our lives, and indeed our very sense of who we are. Some call marriage a vital public institution that must be safeguarded for the civic good (we allude, here, to the debate over gay marriage). Others view marriage as a private concern between two consenting adults. Some venerate marriage as the ultimate partnership between the sexes. Others charge that marriage forces men and women into rigid—and unequal—gender roles.

The selections in this chapter reveal an institution in flux, the mutable nature of which forces Americans to create their own definitions—not just of marriage and family, but also of what it means to be a wife, a husband, a mother, and a father. The viewpoint in these selections ranges from the scholarly to the personal. A common theme, as you will notice, revolves around the female half of the marriage equation. Debates over the role of women, both in families and in society as a whole, underlie the most contentious debates regarding modern marriages and families. We will examine two of these disputes—working versus stay-at-home mothers, and the continued gender divide between women and men over the subject of child care and housework. As you read the selections, think about your own experiences with marriage and family. You may not be married yourself, or have even thought much about marriage; but certainly you have witnessed the marriages of family members and of friends. Ask yourself whether the viewpoint being expressed in the selections squares with your own observations and your own beliefs on the subject.

The chapter opens with two opposing perspectives, written 29 years apart by one woman, Terry Martin Hekker, on the subject of stay-at-home mothers. Taken together, these two essays paint a stark portrait of marital disillusionment and personal despair that you are unlikely to forget any time soon. The next group of selections provides historical, sociological, and anthropological views of marriage throughout history and different cultures. In the first, historian Stephanie Coontz describes the horror with which many societies treated the "Radical Idea of Marrying for Love"—an idea most of us now take for granted. In the next selection, "The State of Our Unions," marriage researchers David Popenoe and Barbara Dafoe Whitehead use national marriage statistics to argue that the institution of marriage now faces its gravest crisis. In contrast, sociologists Mary Ann Schwartz and BarBara Marliene Scott debunk five common "myths" about marriage, asking: "Were the 'good old days' really that good for all marriages and families?"

The next two selections take on the contentious topic of gay marriage, as debated by two prominent cultural commentators. First, Andrew Sullivan argues why conservatives ought to support gay marriage. Then, conservative commentator William Bennett charges that opening marriage to homosexuals would destroy the institution itself.

The chapter next turns to an extended examination of two ongoing debates regarding marriage: working mothers versus stay-at-home mothers (often referred to as the "Mommy Wars" or "the opt-out debate") and the "stalled revolution"—the feminist complaint that, in an age of working women, men still refuse to shoulder their share of the housework or child care. In the first of these perspectives, *New York Times* writer Louise Story reports that an increasing number of women at elite Ivy League colleges say they plan to stop working—at least for a number of years—when they have children. Story's article prompted a number of heated responses, including the next selection, Karen Stabiner's "What Yale Women Want, and Why It Is Misguided." Stabiner accuses the Ivy Leaguers of a "startling combination of naiveté and privilege."

Following these are two selections detailing another skirmish on the marital front: housework. According to recent research, the amount of time men spend on housework has not changed in 40 years. While an increasing number of women have joined the workforce, often earning more than their husbands, women still do the bulk of the cooking, laundry, and childrearing. Naturally, this state of affairs has occasioned anger and bitterness among wives. Is this a private issue among spouses or a more systemic, feminist one? In "A Marriage Agreement," written in 1970, feminist Alix Kates Shulman proposes a dramatic solution to hold men to their side of the equal-housework bargain.

The next two selections, by Hope Edelman and Eric Bartels, offer personal perspectives on married life that range across several of the issues raised by previous selections. Their writings provide a raw, honest look at the daily reality of married life.

These selections on marriage are intended to be provocative—to cause you to think about what marriage and family mean to you. After all, if you are like 85% of Americans, one day you too will be married.

The Satisfactions of Housewifery and Motherhood/Paradise Lost (Domestic Division)
Terry Martin Hekker

We begin with a matched set of op-ed columns written nearly 30 years apart for the New York Times *by the same author. At the time her December 20, 1977, column "The Satisfactions of Housewifery and Motherhood" was published, Terry Martin Hekker was a housewife living in South Nyack, New York, who had been married 22 years to her husband, John Hekker, a lawyer and South Nyack village judge. The column deals with Hekker's experiences as a "stay-at-home" mom at a time—the late 1970s—when many women were opting to enter the workforce rather than stay home to raise their children. As a result of the extraordinary response to Hekker's column—some of which she describes in her follow-up 2006 piece, "Paradise Lost"—she expanded the essay into a book,* Ever Since Adam and Eve, *published by William Morrow in 1979. "Paradise Lost" was published on January 1, 2006. Like her first column, it aroused much comment in op-ed pieces and blogs around the nation.*

(1977)

1   My son lied about it on his college application. My husband mutters it under his breath when asked. And I had grown reluctant to mention it myself.

2   The problem is my occupation. But the statistics on women that have come out since the Houston conference have given me a new outlook. I have ceased thinking of myself as obsolete and begun to see myself as I really am—an endangered species. Like the whooping crane and the snow leopard, I deserve attentive nurturing and perhaps a distinctive metal tag on my foot. Because I'm one of the last of the dying breed of human females designated, "Occupation: Housewife."

3   I know it's nothing to crow about. I realize that when people discuss their professions at parties I am more of a pariah than a hooker or a loan shark is. I have been castigated, humiliated and scorned. In an age of do-your-own-thing, it's clear no one meant me. I've been told (patiently and a little louder than necessary, as one does with a small child) that I am an anachronism (except that they avoid such a big word). I have been made to feel so outmoded that I wouldn't be surprised to discover that, like a carton of yogurt, I have an expiration date stamped on my bottom.

4   I once treasured a small hope that history might vindicate me. After all, nursing was once just such a shameful occupation, suitable for only the lowest women. But I abandoned any thought that my occupation would ever become fashionable again, just as I had to stop counting on full-figured women coming back into style. I'm a hundred years too late on both counts.

5   Now, however, thanks to all these new statistics, I see a brighter future for myself. Today, fewer than 16 percent of American families have a full-time housewife-mother. Comparing that with previous figures, at the rate it's going I calculate I am less than eight years away from being the last housewife in the country. And then I intend to be impossible.

6   I shall demand enormous fees to go on talk shows, and will charge for my autograph. Anthropologists will study my feeding and nesting habits through field glasses and keep notebooks detailing my every move. That is, if no one gets the bright idea that I'm so unique that I must be put behind sealed glass like the Book of Kells. In any event, I can expect to be a celebrity and to be pampered. I cannot, though, expect to get even.

7   There's no getting even for years of being regarded as stupid or lazy, or both. For years of being considered unproductive (unless you count five children, which no one does). For years of being viewed as a parasite, living off a man (except by my husband whose opinion doesn't seem to matter). For years of fetching other women's children after they'd thrown up in the lunchroom, because I have nothing better to do, or probably there is nothing I do better, while their mothers have "careers." (Is clerking in a drug store a bona fide career?) For years of caring for five children and a big house and constantly being asked when I'm going to work.

8   I come from a long line of women, most of them more Edith Bunker* than Betty Friedan,[†] who never knew they were unfulfilled. I can't testify that they were happy, but they *were* cheerful. And if they lacked "meaningful relationships," they cherished relations who meant something. They took pride in a clean, comfortable home and satisfaction in serving a good meal because no one had explained to them that the only work worth doing is that for which you get paid.

9   They enjoyed rearing their children because no one ever told them that little children belonged in church basements and their mothers belonged somewhere else. They lived, very frugally, on their husbands' paychecks because they didn't realize that it's more important to have a bigger house and a second car than it is to rear your own children. And they were so incredibly ignorant that they died never suspecting they'd been failures.

10   That won't hold true for me. I don't yet perceive myself as a failure, but it's not for want of being told I am.

11   The other day, years of condescension prompted me to fib in order to test a theory. At a party where most of the guests were business associates of my husband, a Ms. Putdown asked me who I was. I told her I was Jack Hekker's wife. That had a galvanizing effect on her. She took my hand and asked if that was all I thought of myself—just someone's wife? I wasn't going to let her in on the five children but when she persisted I mentioned them but told her that they weren't mine, that they belonged to my dead sister. And then I basked in the glow of her warm approval.

---

* Edith Bunker (wife of Archie Bunker) was a character in the 1970s sitcom *All in the Family*; in the first few years of the series, she was a traditional stay-at-home housewife.

[†] Betty Friedan (1921–2006) was an author and activist; her 1963 book *The Feminine Mystique*, documenting the stifling and vaguely dissatisfied lot of the mid-20th century traditional housewife, launched the "second wave" feminist revolution.

12 It's an absolute truth that whereas you are considered ignorant to stay home to rear *your* children, it is quite heroic to do so for someone else's children. Being a housekeeper is acceptable (even to the Social Security office) as long as it's not *your* house you're keeping. And treating a husband with attentive devotion is altogether correct as long as he's not *your* husband.

13 Sometimes I feel like Alice in Wonderland. But lately, mostly, I feel like an endangered species.

Paradise Lost (Domestic Division)

(2006)

1 A while back, at a baby shower for a niece, I overheard the expectant mother being asked if she intended to return to work after the baby was born. The answer, which rocked me, was, "Yes, because I don't want to end up like Aunt Terry."

2 That would be me.

3 In the continuing case of Full-Time Homemaker vs. Working Mother, I offer myself as Exhibit A. Because more than a quarter-century ago I wrote an Op-Ed article for *The New York Times* on the satisfaction of being a full-time housewife in the new age of the liberated woman. I wrote it from my heart, thoroughly convinced that homemaking and raising my children was the most challenging and rewarding job I could ever want.

4 "I come from a long line of women," I wrote, "most of them more Edith Bunker than Betty Friedan, who never knew they were unfulfilled. I can't testify that they were happy, but they were cheerful. They took pride in a clean, comfortable home and satisfaction in serving a good meal because no one had explained that the only work worth doing is that for which you get paid."

5 I wasn't advocating that mothers forgo careers to stay home with their children; I was simply defending my choice as a valid one. The mantra of the age may have been "Do your own thing," but as a full-time homemaker, that didn't seem to mean me.

6 The column morphed into a book titled *Ever Since Adam and Eve*, followed by a national tour on which I, however briefly, became the authority on homemaking as a viable choice for women. I ultimately told my story on *Today* and to Dinah Shore, Charlie Rose and even to Oprah, when she was the host of a local TV show in Baltimore.

7 In subsequent years I lectured on the rewards of homemaking and housewifery. While others tried to make the case that women like me were parasites and little more than legalized prostitutes, I spoke to rapt audiences about the importance of being there for your children as they grew up, of the satisfactions of "making a home," preparing family meals and supporting your hard-working husband.

8 So I was predictably stunned and devastated when, on our 40th wedding anniversary, my husband presented me with a divorce. I knew our first anniversary

would be paper, but never expected the 40th would be papers, 16 of them meticulously detailing my faults and flaws, the reason our marriage, according to him, was over.

9   We had been married by a bishop with a blessing from the pope in a country church filled with honeysuckle and hope. Five children and six grandchildren later we were divorced by a third-rate judge in a suburban courthouse reeking of dust and despair.

10   Our long marriage had its full share of love, complications, illnesses, joy and stress. Near the end we were in a dismal period, with my husband in treatment for alcoholism. And although I had made more than my share of mistakes, I never expected to be served with divorce papers. I was stunned to find myself, at this stage of life, marooned. And it was small comfort that I wasn't alone. There were many other confused women of my age and circumstance who'd been married just as long, sharing my situation.

11   I was in my teens when I first read Dickens's *Great Expectations*, with the tale of Miss Haversham, who, stood up by her groom-to-be, spent decades in her yellowing wedding gown, sitting at her cobweb-covered bridal banquet table, consumed with plotting revenge. I felt then that to be left waiting at the altar with a church full of people must be the most crushing thing that could happen to a woman.

12   I was wrong. No jilted bride could feel as embarrassed and humiliated as a woman in her 60's discarded by her husband. I was confused and scared, and the pain of being tossed aside by the love of my life made bitterness unavoidable. In those first few bewildering months, as I staggered and wailed through my life, I made Miss Haversham look like a good sport.

13   Sitting around my kitchen with two friends who had also been dumped by their husbands, I figured out that among the three of us we'd been married 110 years. We'd been faithful wives, good mothers, cooks and housekeepers who'd married in the 50's, when "dress for success" meant a wedding gown and "wife" was a tenured position.

14   Turns out we had a lot in common with our outdated kitchen appliances. Like them we were serviceable, low maintenance, front loading, self-cleaning and (relatively) frost free. Also like them we had warranties that had run out. Our husbands sought sleeker models with features we lacked who could execute tasks we'd either never learned or couldn't perform without laughing.

15   Like most loyal wives of our generation, we'd contemplated eventual widowhood but never thought we'd end up divorced. And "divorced" doesn't begin to describe the pain of this process. "Canceled" is more like it. It began with my credit cards, then my health insurance and checkbook, until, finally, like a used postage stamp, I felt canceled too.

16   I faced frightening losses and was overwhelmed by the injustice of it all. He got to take his girlfriend to Cancun, while I got to sell my engagement ring to pay the roofer. When I filed my first nonjoint tax return, it triggered the shocking notification that I had become eligible for food stamps.

17   The judge had awarded me alimony that was less than I was used to getting for household expenses, and now I had to use that money to pay bills I'd never seen before: mortgage, taxes, insurance and car payments. And that princely sum

was awarded for only four years, the judge suggesting that I go for job training when I turned 67. Not only was I unprepared for divorce itself, I was utterly lacking in skills to deal with the brutal aftermath.

18   I read about the young mothers of today—educated, employed, self-sufficient—who drop out of the work force when they have children, and I worry and wonder. Perhaps it is the right choice for them. Maybe they'll be fine. But the fragility of modern marriage suggests that at least half of them may not be.

19   Regrettably, women whose husbands are devoted to their families and are good providers must nevertheless face the specter of future abandonment. Surely the seeds of this wariness must have been planted, even if they can't believe it could ever happen to them. Many have witnessed their own mothers jettisoned by their own fathers and seen divorced friends trying to rear children with marginal financial and emotional support.

20   These young mothers are often torn between wanting to be home with their children and the statistical possibility of future calamity, aware that one of the most poverty-stricken groups in today's society are divorced older women. The feminine and sexual revolutions of the last few decades have had their shining victories, but have they, in the end, made things any easier for mothers?

21   I cringe when I think of that line from my Op-Ed article about the long line of women I'd come from and belonged to who were able to find fulfillment as homemakers "because no one had explained" to us "that the only work worth doing is that for which you get paid." For a divorced mother, the harsh reality is that the work for which you do get paid is the only work that will keep you afloat.

22   These days couples face complex negotiations over work, family, child care and housekeeping. I see my children dealing with these issues in their marriages, and I understand the stresses and frustrations. It becomes evident that where traditional marriage through the centuries had been a partnership based on mutual dependency, modern marriage demands greater self-sufficiency.

23   While today's young women know from the start they'll face thorny decisions regarding careers, marriage and children, those of us who married in the 50's anticipated lives similar to our mothers' and grandmothers'. Then we watched with bewilderment as all the rules changed, and the goal posts were moved.

24   If I had it to do over again, I'd still marry the man I married and have my children: they are my treasure and a powerful support system for me and for one another. But I would have used the years after my youngest started school to further my education. I could have amassed two doctorates using the time and energy I gave to charitable and community causes and been better able to support myself.

25   But in a lucky twist, my community involvement had resulted in my being appointed to fill a vacancy on our Village Board. I had been serving as titular deputy mayor of my hometown (Nyack, N.Y.) when my husband left me. Several weeks later the mayor chose not to run again because of failing health, and I was elected to succeed him, becoming the first female mayor.

26   I held office for six years, a challenging, full-time job that paid a whopping annual salary of $8,000. But it consumed me and gave me someplace to go every

day and most nights, and as such it saved my sanity. Now, mostly retired except for some part-time work, I am kept on my toes by 12 amazing grandchildren.

27   My anachronistic book was written while I was in a successful marriage that I expected would go on forever. Sadly, it now has little relevance for modern women, except perhaps as a cautionary tale: never its intended purpose. So I couldn't imagine writing a sequel. But my friend Elaine did come up with a perfect title: "Disregard First Book."

Discussion and Writing Suggestions

1. Hekker discovered that events have a way of reversing our most cherished beliefs. To what extent, based on your own life and on your observations of others, does Hekker's sadder-but-wiser experience appear to be universal? Can one—should one—prepare for such reversals in life? What is gained, and what is lost, by such preparation?

2. In her 1977 column, Hekker writes that traditional mothers "lived, very frugally, on their husbands' paychecks because they didn't realize that it's more important to have a bigger house and a second car than it is to rear your own children." Based on your own observations of working mothers, to what extent do you feel that Hekker's suggestion that most mothers choose to work in order to maintain an affluent lifestyle is fair and/or accurate?

3. In her 2006 column, Hekker writes, "It becomes evident that where traditional marriage through the centuries had been a partnership based on mutual dependency, modern marriage demands greater self-sufficiency." Assuming the truth of this statement, which type of marriage would you prefer—traditional or modern? Why?

4. In 2006, notwithstanding her divorce and the bitter lessons learned, Hekker maintained that she would still have stayed at home with her children until the youngest was school-age. Presumably that choice in 2006, as in the 1970s, would have involved some sacrifice of money and/or career goals. Assume that you faced this same choice. That is, assume that you are married, have a career you care about, yet also want to raise a family. Based on your values regarding childrearing, would you stay at home until the youngest is school-age? What financial and career sacrifices would you be willing to make in order to maintain this arrangement? Describe your ideal child-care arrangement.

5. In her 2006 column, Hekker writes, "Women whose husbands are devoted to their families and are good providers must nevertheless face the specter of future abandonment." To what extent do you agree with this statement? Assuming it is true, would you want to live in this way—either being a suspicious woman or an implicitly distrusted man?

6. To what extent do you feel that the self-confident Hekker of the 1977 column got her comeuppance? To what extent do you feel that she deserves your sympathy and support? On a blog site in response to the 2006 column, one poster criticized Hekker as self-pitying and bitter. Do you agree with this assessment? Describe your own reaction upon reading the paragraphs beginning, "So I was predictably stunned and devastated when, on our 40th wedding anniversary, my husband presented me with a divorce."

The Radical Idea of Marrying for Love
Stephanie Coontz

One of the bedrock assumptions of modern marriage is the once-radical idea that newlyweds must be in love. Marriage and love have existed through the ages, of course. But according to historian Stephanie Coontz, only in the relatively recent past, beginning in the eighteenth century, did the political and economic institution of marriage take on romantic associations. Reminding us through historical and cultural examples that many people were (and still are) horrified by the idea of marrying for love, and loving the one we marry, Coontz traces the intellectual development of this subversive notion back to the Enlightenment. She then hints at the long-term consequences it held for the institution of marriage.

Stephanie Coontz teaches history and family studies at Evergreen State College in Olympia, Washington, and has written numerous books on marriage and family in America, including The Way We Never Were: American Families and the Nostalgia Trap *(1992) and* The Way We Really Are: Coming to Terms with America's Changing Families *(1998). The following selection first appeared in* Marriage: A History: From Obedience to Intimacy, or How Love Conquered Marriage *(2005).*

1 George Bernard Shaw described marriage as an institution that brings together two people "under the influence of the most violent, most insane, most delusive, and most transient of passions. They are required to swear that they will remain in that excited, abnormal, and exhausting condition continuously until death do them part."

2 Shaw's comment was amusing when he wrote it at the beginning of the twentieth century, and it still makes us smile today, because it pokes fun at the unrealistic expectations that spring from a dearly held cultural ideal—that marriage should be based on intense, profound love and a couple should maintain their ardor until death do them part. But for thousands of years the joke would have fallen flat.

3 For most of history it was inconceivable that people would choose their mates on the basis of something as fragile and irrational as love and then focus all their sexual, intimate, and altruistic desires on the resulting marriage. In fact, many historians, sociologists, and anthropologists used to think romantic love was a

recent Western invention. This is not true. People have always fallen in love, and throughout the ages many couples have loved each other deeply.

4   But only rarely in history has love been seen as the main reason for getting married. When someone did advocate such a strange belief, it was no laughing matter. Instead, it was considered a serious threat to social order.

5   In some cultures and times, true love was actually thought to be incompatible with marriage. Plato believed love was a wonderful emotion that led men to behave honorably. But the Greek philosopher was referring not to the love of women, "such as the meaner men feel," but to the love of one man for another.

6   Other societies considered it good if love developed after marriage or thought love should be factored in along with the more serious considerations involved in choosing a mate. But even when past societies did welcome or encourage married love, they kept it on a short leash. Couples were not to put their feelings for each other above more important commitments, such as their ties to parents, siblings, cousins, neighbors, or God.

7   In ancient India, falling in love before marriage was seen as a disruptive, almost antisocial act. The Greeks thought lovesickness was a type of insanity, a view that was adopted by medieval commentators in Europe. In the Middle Ages the French defined love as a "derangement of the mind" that could be cured by sexual intercourse, either with the loved one or with a different partner. This cure assumed, as Oscar Wilde once put it, that the quickest way to conquer yearning and temptation was to yield immediately and move on to more important matters.

8   In China, excessive love between husband and wife was seen as a threat to the solidarity of the extended family. Parents could force a son to divorce his wife if her behavior or work habits didn't please them, whether or not he loved her. They could also require him to take a concubine if his wife did not produce a son. If a son's romantic attachment to his wife rivaled his parents' claims on the couple's time and labor, the parents might even send her back to her parents. In the Chinese language the term *love* did not traditionally apply to feelings between husband and wife. It was used to describe an illicit, socially disapproved relationship. In the 1920s a group of intellectuals invented a new word for love between spouses because they thought such a radical new idea required its own special label.

9   In Europe, during the twelfth and thirteenth centuries, adultery became idealized as the highest form of love among the aristocracy. According to the Countess of Champagne, it was impossible for true love to "exert its powers between two people who are married to each other."

10   In twelfth-century France, Andreas Capellanus, chaplain to Countess Marie of Troyes, wrote a treatise on the principles of courtly love. The first rule was that "marriage is no real excuse for not loving." But he meant loving someone outside the marriage. As late as the eighteenth century the French essayist Montaigne wrote that any man who was in love with his wife was a man so dull that no one else could love him.

11   Courtly love probably loomed larger in literature than in real life. But for centuries, noblemen and kings fell in love with courtesans rather than the

wives they married for political reasons. Queens and noblewomen had to be more discreet than their husbands, but they too looked beyond marriage for love and intimacy.

12   This sharp distinction between love and marriage was common among the lower and middle classes as well. Many of the songs and stories popular among peasants in medieval Europe mocked married love.

13   The most famous love affair of the Middle Ages was that of Peter Abelard, a well-known theologian in France, and Héloïse, the brilliant niece of a fellow churchman at Notre Dame. The two eloped without marrying, and she bore him a child. In an attempt to save his career but still placate Héloïse's furious uncle, Abelard proposed they marry in secret. This would mean that Héloïse would not be living in sin, while Abelard could still pursue his church ambitions. But Héloïse resisted the idea, arguing that marriage would not only harm his career but also undermine their love.

"Nothing Is More Impure Than to Love One's Wife as if She Were a Mistress"

14   Even in societies that esteemed married love, couples were expected to keep it under strict control. In many cultures, public displays of love between husband and wife were considered unseemly. A Roman was expelled from the Senate because he had kissed his wife in front of his daughter. Plutarch conceded that the punishment was somewhat extreme but pointed out that everyone knew that it was "disgraceful" to kiss one's wife in front of others.

15   Some Greek and Roman philosophers even said that a man who loved his wife with "excessive" ardor was "an adulterer." Many centuries later Catholic and Protestant theologians argued that husbands and wives who loved each other too much were committing the sin of idolatry. Theologians chided wives who used endearing nicknames for their husbands, because such familiarity on a wife's part undermined the husband's authority and the awe that his wife should feel for him. Although medieval Muslim thinkers were more approving of sexual passion between husband and wife than were Christian theologians, they also insisted that too much intimacy between husband and wife weakened a believer's devotion to God. And, like their European counterparts, secular writers in the Islamic world believed that love thrived best outside marriage.

16   Many cultures still frown on placing love at the center of marriage. In Africa, the Fulbe people of northern Cameroon do not see love as a legitimate emotion, especially within marriage. One observer reports that in conversations with their neighbors, Fulbe women "vehemently deny emotional attachment to a husband." In many peasant and working-class communities, too much love between husband and wife is seen as disruptive because it encourages the couple to withdraw from the wider web of dependence that makes the society work.

17   As a result, men and women often relate to each other in public, even after marriage, through the conventions of a war between the sexes, disguising the fondness they may really feel. They describe their marital behavior, no matter how exemplary it may actually be, in terms of convenience, compulsion, or self-interest rather than love or sentiment. In Cockney rhyming slang, the term for *wife* is *trouble and strife*.

18   Whether it is valued or not, love is rarely seen as the main ingredient for marital success. Among the Taita of Kenya, recognition and approval of married love are widespread. An eighty-year-old man recalled that his fourth wife "was the wife of my heart. . . . I could look at her and no words would pass, just a smile." In this society, where men often take several wives, women speak wistfully about how wonderful it is to be a "love wife." But only a small percentage of Taita women experience this luxury, because a Taita man normally marries a love wife only after he has accumulated a few more practical wives.

19   In many cultures, love has been seen as a desirable outcome of marriage but not as a good reason for getting married in the first place. The Hindu tradition celebrates love and sexuality in marriage, but love and sexual attraction are not considered valid reasons for marriage. "First we marry, then we'll fall in love" is the formula. As recently as 1975, a survey of college students in the Indian state of Karnataka found that only 18 percent "strongly" approved of marriages made on the basis of love, while 32 percent completely disapproved.

20   Similarly, in early modern Europe most people believed that love developed after marriage. Moralists of the sixteenth and seventeenth centuries argued that if a husband and wife each had a good character, they would probably come to love each other. But they insisted that youths be guided by their families in choosing spouses who were worth learning to love. It was up to parents and other relatives to make sure that the woman had a dowry or the man had a good yearly income. Such capital, it was thought, would certainly help love flower.

"[I]t Made Me Really Sick, Just as I Have Formerly Been When in Love with My Wife"

21   I don't believe that people of the past had more control over their hearts than we do today or that they were incapable of the deep love so many individuals now hope to achieve in marriage. But love in marriage was seen as a bonus, not as a necessity. The great Roman statesman Cicero exchanged many loving letters with his wife, Terentia, during their thirty-year marriage. But that didn't stop him from divorcing her when she was no longer able to support him in the style to which he had become accustomed.

22   Sometimes people didn't have to make such hard choices. In seventeenth-century America, Anne Bradstreet was the favorite child of an indulgent father who gave her the kind of education usually reserved for elite boys. He later arranged her marriage to a cherished childhood friend who eventually became the governor of Massachusetts. Combining love, duty, material security, and marriage was not the strain for her that it was for many men and women of that era. Anne wrote love poems to her husband that completely ignored the injunction of Puritan ministers not to place one's spouse too high in one's affections. "If ever two were one," she wrote him, "then surely we; if ever man were loved by wife, then thee. . . . I prize thy love more than whole mines of gold, or all the riches that the East doth hold; my love is such that rivers cannot quench, nor ought but love from thee, give recompense."

23   The famous seventeenth-century English diarist Samuel Pepys chose to marry for love rather than profit. But he was not as lucky as Anne. After hearing a

particularly stirring piece of music, Pepys recorded that it "did wrap up my soul so that it made me really sick, just as I have formerly been when in love with my wife." Pepys would later disinherit a nephew for marrying under the influence of so strong yet transient an emotion.

24   There were always youngsters who resisted the pressures of parents, kin, and neighbors to marry for practical reasons rather than love, but most accepted or even welcomed the interference of parents and others in arranging their marriages. A common saying in early modern Europe was "He who marries for love has good nights and bad days." Nowadays a bitter wife or husband might ask, "Whatever possessed me to think I loved you enough to marry you?" Through most of the past, he or she was more likely to have asked, "Whatever possessed me to marry you just because I loved you?"

"Happily Ever After"

25 Through most of the past, individuals hoped to find love, or at least "tranquil affection," in marriage. But nowhere did they have the same recipe for marital happiness that prevails in most contemporary Western countries. Today there is general agreement on what it takes for a couple to live "happily ever after." First, they must love each other deeply and choose each other unswayed by outside pressure. From then on, each must make the partner the top priority in life, putting that relationship above any and all competing ties. A husband and wife, we believe, owe their highest obligations and deepest loyalties to each other and the children they raise. Parents and in-laws should not be allowed to interfere in the marriage. Married couples should be best friends, sharing their most intimate feelings and secrets. They should express affection openly but also talk candidly about problems. And of course they should be sexually faithful to each other.

26   This package of expectations about love, marriage, and sex, however, is extremely rare. When we look at the historical record around the world, the customs of modern America and Western Europe appear exotic and exceptional.

27   Leo Tolstoy once remarked that all happy families are alike, while every unhappy family is unhappy in its own way. But the more I study the history of marriage, the more I think the opposite is true. Most unhappy marriages in history share common patterns, leaving their tear-stained—and sometimes bloodstained—records across the ages. But each happy, successful marriage seems to be happy in its own way. And for most of human history, successful marriages have not been happy in *our* way.

28   A woman in ancient China might bring one or more of her sisters to her husband's home as backup wives. Eskimo couples often had cospousal arrangements, in which each partner had sexual relations with the other's spouse. In Tibet and parts of India, Kashmir, and Nepal, a woman may be married to two or more brothers, all of whom share sexual access to her.

29   In modern America, such practices are the stuff of trash TV: "I caught my sister in bed with my husband"; "My parents brought their lovers into our home"; "My wife slept with my brother"; "It broke my heart to share my husband with another woman." In other cultures, individuals often find such practices normal and comforting. The children of Eskimo cospouses felt that

they shared a special bond, and society viewed them as siblings. Among Tibetan brothers who share the same wife, sexual jealousy is rare.

30 In some cultures, cowives see one another as allies rather than rivals. In Botswana, women add an interesting wrinkle to the old European saying "Woman's work is never done." There they say: "Without cowives, a woman's work is never done." A researcher who worked with the Cheyenne Indians of the United States in the 1930s and 1940s told of a chief who tried to get rid of two of his three wives. All three women defied him, saying that if he sent two of them away, he would have to give away the third as well.

31 Even when societies celebrated the love between husband and wife as a pleasant by-product of marriage, people rarely had a high regard for marital intimacy. Chinese commentators on marriage discouraged a wife from confiding in her husband or telling him about her day. A good wife did not bother her husband with news of her own activities and feelings but treated him "like a guest," no matter how long they had been married. A husband who demonstrated open affection for his wife, even at home, was seen as having a weak character.

32 In the early eighteenth century, American lovers often said they looked for "candor" in each other. But they were not talking about the soul-baring intimacy idealized by modern Americans, and they certainly did not believe that couples should talk frankly about their grievances. Instead candor meant fairness, kindliness, and good temper. People wanted a spouse who did *not* pry too deeply. The ideal mate, wrote U.S. President John Adams in his diary, was willing "to palliate faults and Mistakes, to put the best Construction upon Words and Action, and to forgive Injuries."

33 Modern marital advice books invariably tell husbands and wives to put each other first. But in many societies, marriage ranks very low in the hierarchy of meaningful relationships. People's strongest loyalties and emotional connections may be reserved for members of their birth families. On the North American plains in the 1930s, a Kiowa Indian woman commented to a researcher that "a woman can always get another husband, but she has only one brother." In China it was said that "you have only one family, but you can always get another wife." In Christian texts prior to the seventeenth century, the word *love* usually referred to feelings toward God or neighbors rather than toward a spouse.

34 In Confucian philosophy, the two strongest relationships in family life are between father and son and between elder brother and younger brother, not between husband and wife. In thirteenth-century China the bond between father and son was so much stronger than the bond between husband and wife that legal commentators insisted a couple do nothing if the patriarch of the household raped his son's wife. In one case, although the judge was sure that a woman's rape accusation against her father-in-law was true, he ordered the young man to give up his sentimental desire "to grow old together" with his wife. Loyalty to parents was paramount, and therefore the son should send his wife back to her own father, who could then marry her to someone else. Sons were sometimes ordered beaten for siding with their wives against their father. No wonder that for 1,700 years women in one Chinese province guarded a secret language that they used to commiserate with each other about the griefs of marriage.

35   In many societies of the past, sexual loyalty was not a high priority. The expectation of mutual fidelity is a rather recent invention. Numerous cultures have allowed husbands to seek sexual gratification outside marriage. Less frequently, but often enough to challenge common preconceptions, wives have also been allowed to do this without threatening the marriage. In a study of 109 societies, anthropologists found that only 48 forbade extramarital sex to both husbands and wives.

36   When a woman has sex with someone other than her husband and he doesn't object, anthropologists have traditionally called it wife loaning. When a man does it, they call it male privilege. But in some societies the choice to switch partners rests with the woman. Among the Dogon of West Africa, young married women publicly pursued extramarital relationships with the encouragement of their mothers. Among the Rukuba of Nigeria, a wife can take a lover at the time of her first marriage. This relationship is so embedded in accepted custom that the lover has the right, later in life, to ask his former mistress to marry her daughter to his son.

37   Among the Eskimo of northern Alaska, as I noted earlier, husbands and wives, with mutual consent, established comarriages with other couples. Some anthropologists believe cospouse relationships were a more socially acceptable outlet for sexual attraction than was marriage itself. Expressing open jealousy about the sexual relationships involved was considered boorish.

38   Such different notions of marital rights and obligations made divorce and remarriage less emotionally volatile for the Eskimo than it is for most modern Americans. In fact, the Eskimo believed that a remarried person's partner had an obligation to allow the former spouse, as well as any children of that union, the right to fish, hunt, and gather in the new spouse's territory.

39   Several small-scale societies in South America have sexual and marital norms that are especially startling for Europeans and North Americans. In these groups, people believe that any man who has sex with a woman during her pregnancy contributes part of his biological substance to the child. The husband is recognized as the primary father, but the woman's lover or lovers also have paternal responsibilities, including the obligation to share food with the woman and her child in the future. During the 1990s researchers taking life histories of elderly Bari women in Venezuela found that most had taken lovers during at least one of their pregnancies. Their husbands were usually aware and did not object. When a woman gave birth, she would name all the men she had slept with since learning she was pregnant, and a woman attending the birth would tell each of these men: "You have a child."

40   In Europe and the United States today such an arrangement would be a sure-fire recipe for jealousy, bitter breakups, and very mixed-up kids. But among the Bari people this practice was in the best interests of the child. The secondary fathers were expected to provide the child with fish and game, with the result that a child with a secondary father was twice as likely to live to the age of fifteen as a brother or sister without such a father.

41   Few other societies have incorporated extramarital relationships so successfully into marriage and child rearing. But all these examples of differing marital and sexual norms make it difficult to claim there is some universal model for the success or happiness of a marriage.

42   About two centuries ago Western Europe and North America developed a whole set of new values about the way to organize marriage and sexuality, and many of these values are now spreading across the globe. In this Western model, people expect marriage to satisfy more of their psychological and social needs than ever before. Marriage is supposed to be free of the coercion, violence, and gender inequalities that were tolerated in the past. Individuals want marriage to meet most of their needs for intimacy and affection and all their needs for sex.

43   Never before in history had societies thought that such a set of high expectations about marriage was either realistic or desirable. Although many Europeans and Americans found tremendous joy in building their relationships around these values, the adoption of these unprecedented goals for marriage had unanticipated and revolutionary consequences that have since come to threaten the stability of the entire institution.

. . .

44   [B]y the beginning of the seventeenth century a distinctive marriage system had taken root in Western Europe, with a combination of features that together not only made it different from marriage anywhere else in the world but also made it capable of very rapid transformation. Strict divorce laws made it difficult to end a marriage, but this was coupled with more individual freedom to choose or refuse a partner. Concubinage had no legal status. Couples tended to marry later and to be closer to each other in age. And upon marriage a couple typically established an independent household.

45   During the eighteenth century the spread of the market economy and the advent of the Enlightenment wrought profound changes in record time. By the end of the 1700s personal choice of partners had replaced arranged marriage as a social ideal, and individuals were encouraged to marry for love. For the first time in five thousand years, marriage came to be seen as a private relationship between two individuals rather than one link in a larger system of political and economic alliances. The measure of a successful marriage was no longer how big a financial settlement was involved, how many useful in-laws were acquired, or how many children were produced, but how well a family met the emotional needs of its individual members. Where once marriage had been seen as the fundamental unit of work and politics, it was now viewed as a place of refuge from work, politics, and community obligations.

46   The image of husbands and wives was also transformed during the eighteenth century. The husband, once the supervisor of the family labor force, came to be seen as the person who, by himself, provided for the family. The wife's role was redefined to focus on her emotional and moral contributions to family life rather than her economic inputs. The husband was the family's economic motor, and the wife its sentimental core.

47   Two seismic social changes spurred these changes in marriage norms. First, the spread of wage labor made young people less dependent on their parents for a start in life. A man didn't have to delay marriage until he inherited land or took over a business from his father. A woman could more readily earn her own dowry. As day labor replaced apprenticeships and provided alternatives to domestic service, young workers were no longer obliged to live in a master's home for several years. They could marry as soon as they were able to earn sufficient wages.

48   Second, the freedoms afforded by the market economy had their parallel in new political and philosophical ideas. Starting in the mid-seventeenth century, some political theorists began to challenge the ideas of absolutism. Such ideas gained more adherents during the eighteenth-century Enlightenment, when influential thinkers across Europe championed individual rights and insisted that social relationships, including those between men and women, be organized on the basis of reason and justice rather than force. Believing the pursuit of happiness to be a legitimate goal, they advocated marrying for love rather than wealth or status. Historian Jeffrey Watts writes that although the sixteenth-century Reformation had already "enhanced the dignity of married life by denying the superiority of celibacy," the eighteenth-century Enlightenment "exalted marriage even further by making love the most important criterion in choosing a spouse."

49   The Enlightenment also fostered a more secular view of social institutions than had prevailed in the sixteenth and seventeenth centuries. Marriage came to be seen as a private contract that ought not be too closely regulated by church or state. After the late eighteenth century, according to one U.S. legal historian, marriage was increasingly defined as a private agreement with public consequences, rather than as a public institution whose roles and duties were rigidly determined by the family's place in the social hierarchy.

50   The new norms of the love-based, intimate marriage did not fall into place all at once but were adopted at different rates in various regions and social groups. In England, the celebration of the love match reached a fever pitch as early as the 1760s and 1770s, while the French were still commenting on the novelty of "marriage by fascination" in the mid-1800s. Many working-class families did not adopt the new norms of marital intimacy until the twentieth century.

51   But there was a clear tipping point during the eighteenth century. In England, a new sentimentalization of wives and mothers pushed older anti-female diatribes to the margins of polite society. Idealization of marriage reached such heights that the meaning of the word *spinster* began to change. Originally an honorable term reserved for a woman who spun yarn, by the 1600s it had come to mean any woman who was not married. In the 1700s the word took on a negative connotation for the first time, the flip side of the new reverence accorded to wives.

52   In France, the propertied classes might still view marriage as "a kind of joint-stock affair," in the words of one disapproving Englishwoman, but the common people more and more frequently talked about marriage as the route to "happiness" and "peace." One study found that before the 1760s fewer than 10 percent of French couples seeking annulments argued that a marriage should be based on emotional attachment to be fully valid, but by the 1770s more than 40 percent thought so.

53   Romantic ideals spread in America too. In the two decades after the American Revolution, New Englanders began to change their description of an ideal mate, adding companionship and cooperation to their traditional expectations of thrift and industriousness.

54   These innovations spread even to Russia, where Tsar Peter the Great under-took westernizing the country's army, navy, bureaucracy, and marriage customs all at once. In 1724 he outlawed forced marriages, requiring bride and groom to swear that each had consented freely to the match. Russian authors extolled "the bewitchment and sweet tyranny of love."

55   The court records of Neuchâtel, in what is now Switzerland, reveal the sea change that occurred in the legal norms of marriage. In the sixteenth and seventeenth centuries, judges had followed medieval custom in forcing indi-viduals to honor betrothals and marriage contracts that had been properly made, even if one or both parties no longer wanted the match. In the eighteenth century, by contrast, judges routinely released people from unwanted marriage contracts and engagements, so long as the couple had no children. It was no longer possible for a man to force a woman to keep a marriage promise.

56   In contrast to the stories of knightly chivalry that had dominated secular literature in the Middle Ages, late eighteenth-century and early nineteenth-century novels depicted ordinary lives. Authors and audiences alike were fascinated by domestic scenes and family relations that had held no interest for medieval writers. Many popular works about love and marriage were syrupy love stories or melodramatic tales of betrayals. But in the hands of more sophisticated writers, such as Jane Austen, clever satires of arranged marriages and the financial aspects of courtship were transformed into great literature.

57   One result of these changes was a growing rejection of the legitimacy of domestic violence. By the nineteenth century, male wife-beaters rather than female "scolds" had become the main target of village shaming rituals in much of Europe. Meanwhile, middle- and upper-class writers condemned wife beating as a "lower-class" vice in which no "respectable" man would indulge.

58   Especially momentous for relations between husband and wife was the weakening of the political model upon which marriage had long been based. Until the late seventeenth century the family was thought of as a miniature monarchy, with the husband king over his dependents. As long as political absolutism remained unchallenged in society as a whole, so did the hierar-chy of traditional marriage. But the new political ideals fostered by the Glorious Revolution in England in 1688 and the even more far-reaching revolutions in America and France in the last quarter of the eighteenth century dealt a series of cataclysmic blows to the traditional justification of patriarchal authority.

59   In the late seventeenth century John Locke argued that governmental authority was simply a contract between ruler and ruled and that if a ruler exceeded the authority his subjects granted him, he could be replaced. In 1698 he suggested that marriage too could be seen as a contract between equals. Locke still believed that men would normally rule their families because of their greater strength and ability, but another English writer, Mary Astell, pushed Locke's theories to what she thought was their logical con-clusion, "If Absolute Sovereignty be not necessary in a State," Astell asked,

"how comes it to be so in a Family?" She answered that not only was absolutism unnecessary within marriage, but it was actually "more mischievous in Families than in kingdomes," by exactly the same amount as "100,000 tyrants are worse than one."

60   During the eighteenth century people began to focus more on the mutual obligations required in marriage. Rejecting analogies between the absolute rights of a husband and the absolute rights of a king, they argued that marital order should be based on love and reason, not on a husband's arbitrary will. The French writer the Marquis de Condorcet and the British author Mary Wollstonecraft went so far as to call for complete equality within marriage.

61   Only a small minority of thinkers, even in "enlightened" circles, endorsed equality between the sexes. Jean Jacques Rousseau, one of the most enthusiastic proponents of romantic love and harmonious marriage, also wrote that a woman should be trained to "docility . . . for she will always be in subjection to a man, or to man's judgment, and she will never be free to set her own opinion above his." The German philosopher J. G. Fichte argued in 1795 that a woman could be "free and independent only as long as she had no husband." Perhaps, he opined, a woman might be eligible to run for office if she promised not to marry. "But no rational woman can give such a promise, nor can the state rationally accept it. For woman is destined to love, and . . . when she loves, it is her duty to marry."

62   In the heady atmosphere of the American and French revolutions of 1776 and 1789, however, many individuals dared draw conclusions that anticipated feminist demands for marital reform and women's rights of the early twentieth century. And even before that, skeptics warned that making love and companionship the core of marriage would open a Pandora's box.

The Revolutionary Implications of the Love Match

63 The people who pioneered the new ideas about love and marriage were not, by and large, trying to create anything like the egalitarian partnerships that modern Westerners associate with companionship, intimacy, and "true love." Their aim was to make marriage more secure by getting rid of the cynicism that accompanied mercenary marriage and encouraging couples to place each other first in their affections and loyalties.

64   But basing marriage on love and companionship represented a break with thousands of years of tradition. Many contemporaries immediately recognized the dangers this entailed. They worried that the unprecedented idea of basing marriage on love would produce rampant individualism.

65   Critics of the love match argued—prematurely, as it turns out, but correctly—that the values of free choice and egalitarianism could easily spin out of control. If the choice of a marriage partner was a personal decision, conservatives asked, what would prevent young people, especially women, from choosing unwisely? If people were encouraged to expect marriage to be the best and happiest experience of their lives, what would hold a marriage together if things went "for worse" rather than "for better"?

66   If wives and husbands were intimates, wouldn't women demand to share decisions equally? If women possessed the same faculties of reason as men, why would they confine themselves to domesticity? Would men still financially support women and children if they lost control over their wives' and children's labor and could not even discipline them properly? If parents, church, and state no longer dictated people's private lives, how could society make sure the right people married and had children or stop the wrong ones from doing so?

67   Conservatives warned that "the pursuit of happiness," claimed as a right in the American Declaration of Independence, would undermine the social and moral order. Preachers declared that parishioners who placed their husbands or wives before God in their hierarchy of loyalty and emotion were running the risk of becoming "idolaters." In 1774 a writer in England's *Lady Magazine* commented tartly that "the idea of matrimony" was not "for men and women to be always taken up with each other" or to seek personal self-fulfillment in their love. The purpose of marriage was to get people "to discharge the duties of civil society, to govern their families with prudence and to educate their children with discretion."

68   There was a widespread fear that the pursuit of personal happiness could undermine self-discipline. One scholar argues that this fear explains the extraordinary panic about masturbation that swept the United States and Europe at the end of the eighteenth century and produced thousands of tracts against "the solitary vice" in the nineteenth. The threat of female masturbation particularly repelled and fascinated eighteenth-century social critics. To some it seemed a short step from two people neglecting their social duties because they were "taken up with each other" to one person pleasuring herself without fulfilling a duty to anyone else at all.

69   As it turned out, it took another hundred years for the contradictions that gave rise to these fears to pose a serious threat to the stability of the new system of marriage.

Review Questions

1. What are the two main reasons, according to Coontz, that the norms about the relationship between love and marriage began to change in the eighteenth century?

2. According to Coontz, what was the aim of people who championed the "love match" model of marriage in the eighteenth century?

3. What did a conservative writer in a 1774 issue of England's *Lady Magazine* claim was the purpose of marriage?

4. Describe the two values that critics of the "love match" feared could lead to widespread individualism. Cite at least one feared consequence of each value.

Discussion and Writing Suggestions

1. Reread the excerpt from Barbara Graham's "The Future of Love: Kiss Romance Goodbye, It's Time for the Real Thing" (presented as a basis for summary practice) in Chapter 1, pages 8–11. Compare and contrast Graham's history of the intertwining of love and marriage with Stephanie Coontz's in "The Radical Idea of Marrying for Love."

2. Coontz begins the selection with a cynical observation of marriage by George Bernard Shaw: that marriage brings together two people "under the influence of the most violent, most insane, most delusive, and most transient of passions. They are required to swear that they will remain in that excited, abnormal, and exhausting condition until death do them part." To what extent—before your reading of this selection—would you (or others you know) have subscribed to the assumptions about marriage that are the object of Shaw's scorn? To what extent do you think that Shaw is overstating the case? Explain.

3. Coontz notes that only a "small minority" of the Enlightenment thinkers who called for greater equality within marriage actually endorsed equality between the sexes. Is there a difference between equality within marriage and equality between the sexes? Is it contradictory to believe in one but not the other? Explain your answer.

4. Coontz writes that with the advent of the love-based marriage, "The measure of a successful marriage was no longer how big a financial settlement was involved, how many useful in-laws were acquired, or how many children were produced, but how well a family met the emotional needs of its individual members." To what degree would you agree that this statement describes the reality of modern marriages? Do you feel that issues such as money, number of offspring, and in-laws can or should be separated from the "emotional needs" of husband and wife? If possible, when stating your opinion, cite specific examples of marriages you have known about or witnessed.

5. Critics of the love match argued that allowing people to choose their mates would also allow them to choose badly. But presumably some arranged marriages also resulted in bad matches. Do you feel that one sort of bad match is worse than the other? And what does a "bad match" mean, exactly?

6. In her historical and cultural survey of attitudes toward love in marriage, Coontz notes that many cultures have believed that married people should "love" one another. But these cultures have also differentiated married love from romantic love, which they felt was transitory and fleeting. Do you see any distinction(s) between married love and romantic love?

The State of Our Unions
David Popenoe and Barbara Dafoe Whitehead

At the end of the previous selection, Stephanie Coontz hinted at the consequences that the rise of the "love match" would have for the institution of marriage. So how is marriage faring? In the following selection, the codirectors of the National Marriage Project at Rutgers State University warn that the institutions of marriage and family are in a state of crisis. David Popenoe is a professor of sociology at Rutgers University in New Brunswick, New Jersey. An expert in the study of marriage and family life, he has written or edited ten books, most recently War Over the Family *(2005). Barbara Dafoe Whitehead lectures and writes on the well-being of families and children for scholarly and popular audiences. She is the author of* The Divorce Culture: Rethinking Our Commitment to Marriage and Family *(1997). The following selection combines sections of Popenoe and Whitehead's 2002 and 2005 reports on marriage, presented here in three parts: Marriage, Divorce, and Unmarried Cohabitation. The earlier report appeared in* USA Today Magazine *in July 2002. The later report appears on the National Marriage Project Web site at <http://marriage.rutgers.edu/Publications/SOOO/TEXTSOOU2005.htm>.*

1   Each year, the National Marriage Project at Rutgers University publishes an assessment of the health of marriage and marital relationships in America entitled "The State of Our Unions." It is based on a thorough review and evaluation of the latest statistics and research findings about marriage, family, and courtship trends, plus our own special surveys.

2   Americans haven't given up on marriage as a cherished ideal. Indeed, most continue to prize and value it as an important life goal, and the vast majority (an estimated 85%) will marry at least once in a lifetime. Almost all couples enter marriage with a strong desire and determination for a life-long, loving partnership, and this desire may even be increasing among the young. Since the 1980s, the percentage of high school seniors who say that having a good marriage is extremely important to them as a life goal has gone up, though only slightly.

. . .

Marriage

3   Key Finding: Marriage trends in recent decades indicate that Americans have become less likely to marry, and the most recent data show that the marriage rate in the United States continues to decline. Of those who do marry, there has been a moderate drop since the 1970s in the percentage of couples who consider their marriages to be "very happy," but in the past decade this trend has swung in a positive direction.

4   Americans have become less likely to marry. This is reflected in a decline of nearly 50 percent, from 1970 to 2004, in the annual number of marriages per 1,000 unmarried adult women (Figure 1). Some of this decline—it is not clear just how much—results from the delaying of first marriages until older ages: the median age at first marriage went from 20 for females and 23 for males in 1960 to about 26 and 27, respectively, in 2004. Other factors accounting for the decline are the growth of unmarried cohabitation and a small decrease in the tendency of divorced persons to remarry.

FIGURE 1   Number of Marriages per 1,000 Unmarried Women Age 15 and Older, by Year, United States[a]

Year	Number[b]
1960	73.5
1970	76.5
1975	66.9
1980	61.4
1985	56.2
1990	54.5
1995	50.8
2000	46.5
2004	39.9

a. We have used the number of marriages per 1,000 unmarried women age 15 and older, rather than the Crude Marriage Rate of marriages per 1,000 population to help avoid the problem of compositional changes in the population, that is, changes which stem merely from there being more or less people in the marriageable ages. Even this more refined measure is somewhat susceptible to compositional changes.
b. Per 1,000 unmarried women age 14 and older.

Source: U.S. Department of the Census, Statistical Abstract of the United States, 2001, Page 87, Table 117; and Statistical Abstract of the United States, 1986, Page 79, Table 124. Figure for 2004 was obtained using data from the Current Population Surveys, March 2004 Supplement, as well as Births, Marriages, Divorces, and Deaths: Provisional Data for 2004, National Vital Statistics Report 53:21, June 26, 2005, Table 3. (http://www.cdc.gov/nchs/data/nvsr/nvsr53/nvsr53_21.pdf) The CPS, March Supplement, is based on a sample of the U.S. population, rather than an actual count such as those available from the decennial census. See sampling and weighting notes at http://www.bis.census.gov:80/cps/ads/2002/ssampwgt.htm

5   The decline also reflects some increase in lifelong singlehood, though the actual amount cannot be known until current young and middle-aged adults pass through the life course.

6   The percentage of adults in the population who are currently married has also diminished. Since 1960, the decline of those married among all persons age 15 and older has been 14 percentage points—and over 29 points among black females (Figure 2). It should be noted that these data include both people who have never married and those who have married and then divorced. (For some economic implications of the decline of marriage, see the accompanying box: "The Surprising Economic Benefits of Marriage.")

7   In order partially to control for a decline in married adults simply due to delayed first marriages, we have looked at changes in the percentage of persons age 35 through 44 who were married (Figure 3). Since 1960, there has been a drop of 22 percentage points for married men and 20 points for married women.

8   Marriage trends in the age range of 35 to 44 are suggestive of lifelong singlehood. In times past and still today, virtually all persons who were going to marry during their lifetimes had married by age 45. More than 90 percent of women have married eventually in every generation for which records exist, going back to the mid-1800s. By 1960, 94 percent of women then alive had been married at least once by age 45—probably an historical high point.[1] For the generation of 1995, assuming a continuation of then current marriage rates,

---

[1] Andrew J. Cherlin, *Marriage, Divorce, and Remarriage* (Cambridge, MA: Harvard University Press, 1992): 10; Michael R. Haines, "Long-Term Marriage Patterns in the United States from Colonial Times to the Present," *The History of the Family* 1-1 (1996): 15–39.

FIGURE 2 Percentage of All Persons Age 15 and Older Who Were Married, by Sex and Race, 1960–2004 United States[a]			
Year	Total Males	Black Males	White Males
1960	69.3	60.9	70.2
1970	66.7	56.9	68
1980	63.2	48.8	65
1990	60.7	45.1	62.8
2000	57.9	42.8	60
2004[b]	55.1	38.1	57.4

a. Includes races other than Black and White.
b. In 2003, the U.S. Census Bureau expanded its racial categories to permit respondents to identify themselves as belonging to more than one race. This means that racial data computations beginning in 2004 may not be strictly comparable to those in prior years.

Source: U.S. Bureau of the Census, Current Population Reports, Series P20-506; America's Families and Living Arrangements: March 2000 and earlier reports; and data calculated from the Current Population Surveys, March 2004 Supplement.

several demographers projected that 88 percent of women and 82 percent of men would ever marry.[2] If and when these figures are recalculated for the early years of the 21st century, the percentage of women and men ever marrying will almost certainly be lower.

9   It is important to note that the decline in marriage does not mean that people are giving up on living together with a sexual partner. On the contrary, with the incidence of unmarried cohabitation increasing rapidly, marriage is

FIGURE 3 Percentage of Persons Age 35 through 44 Who Were Married, by Sex, 1960–2004, United States		
Year	Males	Females
1960	88.0	87.4
1970	89.3	86.9
1980	84.2	81.4
1990	74.1	73.0
2000	69.0	71.6
2004	65.7	67.3

Source: U.S. Bureau of the Census, Statistical Abstract of the United States, 1961, Page 34, Table 27; Statistical Abstract of the United States, 1971, Page 32, Table 38; Statistical Abstract of the United States, 1981, Page 38, Table 49; and U.S. Bureau of the Census, General Population Characteristics, 1990, Page 45, Table 34; and Statistical Abstract of the United States, 2001, Page 48, Table 51; internet tables (http://www.census.gov/population/socdemo/hh-fam/cps2003/tabA1-all.pdf) and data calculated from the Current Population Surveys, March 2004 Supplement. Figure for 2004 was obtained using data from the Current Population Surveys rather than data from the census. The CPS, March Supplement, is based on a sample of the U.S. population, rather than an actual count such as those available from the decennial census. See sampling and weighting notes at http://www.bls.census.gov:80/cps/ads/2002/ssampwgt.htm

[2] Robert Schoen and Nicola Standish, "The Retrenchment of Marriage: Results from Marital Status Life Tables for the United States, 1995." *Population and Development Review* 27-3 (2001): 553–563.

FIGURE 4   Percentage of Married Persons Age 18 and Older Who Said Their Marriages Were "Very Happy," by Period, United States

Period	Men	Women
1973–1976	69.6	68.6
1977–1981	68.3	64.2
1982–1986	62.9	61.7
1987–1991	66.4	59.6
1993–1996	63.2	59.7
1998–2002	64.6	60.3

Source: The General Social Survey, conducted by the National Opinion Research Center of the University of Chicago. The trend for both men and women is statistically significant ($p < .01$ on a two-tailed test).

giving ground to unwed unions. Most people now live together before they marry for the first time. An even higher percentage of those divorced who subsequently remarry live together first. And a growing number of persons, both young and old, are living together with no plans for eventual marriage.

10   There is a common belief that, although a smaller percentage of Americans are now marrying than was the case a few decades ago, those who marry have marriages of higher quality. It seems reasonable that if divorce removes poor marriages from the pool of married couples and cohabitation "trial marriages" deter some bad marriages from forming, the remaining marriages on average should be happier. The best available evidence on the topic, however, does not support these assumptions. Since 1973, the General Social Survey periodically has asked representative samples of married Americans to rate their marriages

THE SURPRISING ECONOMIC BENEFITS OF MARRIAGE

When thinking of the many benefits of marriage, the economic aspects are often overlooked. Yet the economic benefits of marriage are substantial, both for individuals and for society as a whole. Marriage is a wealth generating institution. Married couples create more economic assets on average than do otherwise similar singles or cohabiting couples. A 1992 study of retirement data concluded that "individuals who are not continuously married have significantly lower wealth than those who remain married throughout their lives." Compared to those continuously married, those who never married have a reduction in wealth of 75% and those who divorced and didn't remarry have a reduction of 73%.[a]

One might think that the explanation for why marriage generates economic assets is because those people who are more likely to be wealth creators are also more likely to marry and stay married. And this is certainly true, but only in part. The institution of marriage itself provides a wealth-generation bonus. It does this through providing economies of scale (two can live more cheaply than one), and as implicitly a long-term personal contract it encourages economic specialization. Working as a couple, individuals can develop those skills in which they excel, leaving others to their partner.

Also, married couples save and invest more for the future, and they can act as a small insurance pool against life uncertainties such as illness and job loss.[b] Probably because of marital social norms that encourage healthy, productive behavior, men tend to become more economically productive after marriage; they earn between 10 and 40% more than do single men with similar education and job histories.[c] All of these benefits are independent of the fact that married couples receive more work-related and government-provided support, and also more help and support from their extended families (two sets of in-laws) and friends.[d]

Beyond the economic advantages of marriage for the married couples themselves, marriage has a tremendous economic impact on society. It is a major contributor to family income levels and inequality. After more than doubling between 1947 and 1977, the growth of median family income has slowed over the past 20 years, increasing by just 9.6%. A big reason is that married couples, who fare better economically than their single counterparts, have been a rapidly decreasing proportion of total families. In this same 20 year period, and largely because of changes in family structure, family income inequality has increased significantly.[e]

Research has shown consistently that both divorce and unmarried childbearing increase child poverty. In recent years the majority of children who grow up outside of married families have experienced at least one year of dire poverty.[f] According to one study, if family structure had not changed between 1960 and 1998, the black child poverty rate in 1998 would have been 28.4% rather than 45.6%, and the white child poverty rate would have been 11.4% rather than 15.4%.[g] The rise in child poverty, of course, generates significant public costs in health and welfare programs.

Marriages that end in divorce also are very costly to the public. One researcher determined that a single divorce costs state and federal governments about $30,000, based on such things as the higher use of food stamps and public housing as well as increased bankruptcies and juvenile delinquency. The nation's 1.4 million divorces in 2002 are estimated to have cost the taxpayers more than $30 billion.[h]

Notes

a. Janet Wilmoth and Gregor Koso, "Does Marital History Matter? Marital Status and Wealth Outcomes Among Preretirement Adults," *Journal of Marriage and the Family* 64:254–68, 2002.

(continued)

b. Thomas A. Hirschl, Joyce Altobelli, and Mark R. Rank, "Does Marriage Increase the Odds of Affluence? Exploring the Life Course Probabilities," *Journal of Marriage and the Family* 65-4 (2003): 927–938; Joseph Lupton and James P. Smith, "Marriage, Assets and Savings," in Shoshana A. Grossbard-Schectman (ed.) *Marriage and the Economy* (Cambridge: Cambridge University Press, 2003): 129–152.

c. Jeffrey S. Gray and Michael J. Vanderhart, "The Determination of Wages: Does Marriage Matter?," in Linda Waite, et al. (eds.) *The Ties that Bind: Perspectives on Marriage and Cohabitation* (New York: Aldine de Gruyter, 2000): 356–367; S. Korenman and D. Neumark, "Does Marriage Really Make Men More Productive?" *Journal of Human Resources* 26-2 (1991): 282–307; K. Daniel, "The Marriage Premium," in M. Tomassi and K. Ierulli (eds.) *The New Economics of Human Behavior* (Cambridge: Cambridge University Press, 1995) 113–125.

d. Lingxin Hao, "Family Structure, Private Transfers, and the Economic Well-Being of Families with Children," *Social Forces* 75 (1996): 269–292.

e. U.S. Bureau of the Census, Current Population Reports, P60-203, *Measuring 50 Years of Economic Change Using the March Current Population Survey,* U.S. Government Printing Office, Washington, DC, 1998; John Iceland, "Why Poverty Remains High: The Role of Income Growth, Economic Inequality, and Changes in Family Structure, 1949–1999," *Demography* 40-3:499–519, 2003.

f. Mark R. Rank and Thomas A. Hirschl, "The Economic Risk of Childhood in America: Estimating the Probability of Poverty Across the Formative Years," *Journal of Marriage and the Family* 61:1058–1067, 1999.

g. Adam Thomas and Isabel Sawhill, "For Richer or For Poorer: Marriage as an Antipoverty Strategy," *Journal of Policy Analysis and Management* 21:4, 2002.

h. David Schramm, "The Costly Consequences of Divorce in Utah: The Impact on Couples, Community, and Government," Logan, UT: Utah State University, 2003. Unpublished preliminary report.

as either "very happy," "pretty happy," or "not too happy."[3] As Figure 4 indicates, the percentage of both men and women saying "very happy" has declined moderately over the past 25 years.[4] This trend, however, is now heading in a positive direction.

Divorce

11 Key Finding: The American divorce rate today is nearly twice that of 1960, but has declined slightly since hitting the highest point in our history in the early 1980s. For the average couple marrying in recent years, the lifetime probability of divorce or separation remains between 40 and 50 percent.

---

[3] Conducted by the National Opinion Research Center of the University of Chicago, this is a nationally representative study of the English-speaking, non-institutionalized population of the United States age 18 and over.

[4] Using a different data set that compared marriages in 1980 with marriages in 1992, equated in terms of marital duration, Stacy J. Rogers and Paul Amato found similarly that the 1992 marriages had less marital interaction, more marital conflict, and more marital problems. "Is Marital Quality Declining? The Evidence from Two Generations," *Social Forces* 75 (1997): 1089.

FIGURE 5   Number of Divorces per 1,000 Married Women Age 15 and Older, by Year, United States[a]

Year	Divorces
1960	9.2
1965	10.6
1970	14.9
1975	20.3
1980	22.6
1985	21.7
1990	20.9
1995	19.8
2000	18.8
2004	17.7

a. We have used the number of divorces per 1,000 married women age 15 and older, rather than the Crude Divorce Rate of divorces per 1,000 population to help avoid the problem of compositional changes in the population. Even this more refined measure is somewhat susceptible to compositional changes.

Source: Statistical Abstract of the United States, 2001, Page 87, Table 117; National Vital Statistics Reports, August 22, 2001; California Current Population Survey Report: 2000, Table 3, March 2001; Births, Marriages, Divorces, and Deaths: Provisional Data for 2004, National Vital Statistics Report 53:21, June 26, 2005, Table 3, (http://www.cdc.gov/nchs/data/nvsr/nvsr53/nvsr53_21.pdf) and calculations by the National Marriage Project for the U.S. [not including] California, Georgia, Hawaii, Indiana, Louisiana and Oklahoma using the Current Population Surveys, 2004.

12   The increase in divorce, shown by the trend reported in Figure 5, probably has elicited more concern and discussion than any other family-related trend in the United States. Although the long-term trend in divorce has been upward since colonial times, the divorce rate was level for about two decades after World War II during the period of high fertility known as the baby boom. By the middle of the 1960s, however, the incidence of divorce started to increase and it more than doubled over the next fifteen years to reach an historical high point in the early 1980s. Since then the divorce rate has modestly declined, a trend described by many experts as "leveling off at a high level." The decline apparently represents a slight increase in marital stability.[5] Two probable reasons for this are an increase in the age at which people marry for the first time, and a higher educational level of those marrying, both of which are associated with greater marital stability.[6]

13   Although a majority of divorced persons eventually remarry, the growth of divorce has led to a steep increase in the percentage of all adults who are currently divorced (Figure 6). This percentage, which was only 1.8 percent for males and 2.6 percent for females in 1960, quadrupled by the year 2000. The percentage of divorce is higher for females than for males primarily because divorced men are more likely to remarry than divorced women. Also, among those who do remarry, men generally do so sooner than women.

---

[5] Joshua R. Goldstein, "The Leveling of Divorce in the United States," *Demography* 36 (1999): 409–414.

[6] Tim B. Heaton, "Factors Contributing to Increased Marital Stability in the United States," *Journal of Family Issues* 23 (2002): 392–409.

FIGURE 6   Percentage of All Persons Age 15 and Older Who Were Divorced, by Sex and Race, 1960–2004, United States

		Males			Females	
Year	Total	Blacks	Whites	Total	Blacks	Whites
1960	1.8	2	1.8	2.6	4.3	2.5
1970	2.2	3.1	2.1	3.5	4.4	3.4
1980	4.8	6.3	4.7	6.6	8.7	6.4
1990	6.8	8.1	6.8	8.9	11.2	8.6
2000	8.3	9.5	8.4	10.2	11.8	10.2
2004[a]	8.2	9.1	8.3	10.9	12.9	10.9

a. In 2003, the U.S. Census Bureau expanded its racial categories to permit respondents to identify themselves as belonging to more than one race. This means that racial data computations beginning in 2004 may not be strictly comparable to those of prior years.

Source: U.S. Bureau of the Census, Current Population Reports, Series P20-537; America's Families and Living Arrangements: March 2000 and earlier reports; and Current Population Surveys, March 2004 supplement, raw data.

14   Overall, the chances remain very high—estimated between 40 and 50 percent—that a marriage started in recent years will end in either divorce or separation before one partner dies.[7] (But see the accompanying box: "Your Chances of Divorce May Be Much Lower Than You Think.") The likelihood of divorce has varied considerably among different segments of the American population, being higher for Blacks than for Whites, for instance, and higher in the West than in other parts of the country. But these variations have been diminishing. The trend toward a greater similarity of divorce rates between Whites and Blacks is largely attributable to the fact that fewer blacks are marrying.[8] Divorce rates in the South and Midwest have come to resemble those in the West, for reasons that are not well understood, leaving only the Eastern Seaboard and the Central Plains with significantly lower divorce.

15   At the same time, there has been little change in such traditionally large divorce rate differences as between those who marry when they are teenagers compared to those who marry after age 21, high-school drop outs versus college graduates, and the non-religious compared to the religiously committed. Teenagers, high-school drop outs, and the non-religious who marry have considerably higher divorce rates.[9]

Unmarried Cohabitation

16 Key Finding: The number of unmarried couples has increased dramatically over the past four decades, and the increase is continuing. Most younger Americans

---

[7] Robert Schoen and Nicola Standish, "The Retrenchment of Marriage: Results from Marital Status Life Tables for the United States, 1995," *Population and Development Review* 27-3 (2001): 553–563; R. Kelly Raley and Larry Bumpass, "The Topography of the Divorce Plateau: Levels and Trends in Union Stability in the United States after 1980," *Demographic Research* 8-8 (2003): 245–259.

[8] Jay D. Teachman, "Stability across Cohorts in Divorce Risk Factors," *Demography* 39-2 (2002): 331–351.

[9] Raley and Bumpass, 2003.

YOUR CHANCES OF DIVORCE MAY BE MUCH LOWER THAN YOU THINK

By now almost everyone has heard that the national divorce rate is close to 50% of all marriages. This is true, but the rate must be interpreted with caution and several important caveats. For many people, the actual chances of divorce are far below 50/50.

The background characteristics of people entering a marriage have major implications for their risk of divorce. Here are some percentage point decreases in the risk of divorce or separation *during the first ten years of marriage*, according to various personal and social factors:[a]

Factors	Percent Decrease in Risk of Divorce
Annual income over $50,000 (vs. under $25,000)	−30
Having a baby seven months or more after marriage (vs. before marriage)	−24
Marrying over 25 years of age (vs. under 18)	−24
Own family of origin intact (vs. divorced parents)	−14
Religious affiliation (vs. none)	−14
Some college (vs. high-school dropout)	−13

So if you are a reasonably well-educated person with a decent income, come from an intact family and are religious, and marry after age twenty-five without having a baby first, your chances of divorce are very low indeed.

Also, it should be realized that the "close to 50%" divorce rate refers to the percentage of marriages entered into during a particular year that are projected to end in divorce or separation before one spouse dies. Such projections assume that the divorce and death rates occurring that year will continue indefinitely into the future—an assumption that is useful more as an indicator of the instability of marriages in the recent past than as a predictor of future events. In fact, the divorce rate has been dropping, slowly, since reaching a peak around 1980, and the rate could be lower (or higher) in the future than it is today.[b]

Notes

a. Matthew D. Bramlett and William D. Mosher, *Cohabitation, Marriage, Divorce and Remarriage in the United States,* National Center for Health Statistics, Vital and Health Statistics, 23 (22), 2002. The risks are calculated for women only.

b. Rose M. Kreider and Jason M. Fields, "Number, Timing and Duration of Marriages and Divorces, 1996," *Current Population Reports,* P70-80, Washington, DC: U.S. Census Bureau, 2002.

> **FIGURE 7   Number, in Thousands, of Cohabiting, Unmarried, Adult Couples of the Opposite Sex, by Year, United States**
>
> | Year | Number |
> | --- | --- |
> | 1960 | 439 |
> | 1970 | 523 |
> | 1980 | 1,589 |
> | 1990 | 2,856 |
> | 2000 | 4,736 |
> | 2004 | 5,080 |

Source: U.S. Bureau of the Census, Current Population Reports, Series P20-537; America's Families and Living Arrangements: March 2000; and U.S. Bureau of the Census, Population Division, Current Population Survey, 2004 Annual Social and Economic Supplement (http://www.census.gov/population/socdemo/hh-fam/cps2004).

now spend some time living together outside of marriage, and unmarried cohabitation commonly precedes marriage.

17   Between 1960 and 2004, as indicated in Figure 7, the number of unmarried couples in America increased by nearly 1200 percent. Unmarried cohabitation—the status of couples who are sexual partners, not married to each other, and sharing a household—is particularly common among the young. It is estimated that about a quarter of unmarried women age 25 to 39 are currently living with a partner and an additional quarter have lived with a partner at some time in the past. Over half of all first marriages are now preceded by living together, compared to virtually none 50 years ago.[10]

18   For many, cohabitation is a prelude to marriage, for others, simply an alternative to living alone, and for a small but growing number, it is considered an alternative to marriage. Cohabitation is more common among those of lower educational and income levels. Recent data show that among women in the 19 to 44 age range, 60 percent of high-school dropouts have cohabited compared to 37 percent of college graduates.[11] Cohabitation is also more common among those who are less religious than their peers, those who have been divorced, and those who have experienced parental divorce, fatherlessness, or high levels of marital discord during childhood. A growing percentage of cohabiting couple households, now over 40 percent, contain children.

19   The belief that living together before marriage is a useful way "to find out whether you really get along," and thus avoid a bad marriage and an eventual divorce, is now widespread among young people. But the available data on the effects of cohabitation fail to confirm this belief. In fact, a substantial body of evidence indicates that those who live together before marriage are more likely to break up after marriage. This evidence is controversial, however, because it is

---

[10] Larry Bumpass and Hsien-Hen Lu, "Trends in Cohabitation and Implications for Children's Family Contexts in the U. S.," *Population Studies* 54 (2000) 29–41.

[11] Bumpass and Lu, 2000.

difficult to distinguish the "selection effect" from the "experience of cohabitation effect." The selection effect refers to the fact that people who cohabit before marriage have different characteristics from those who do not, and it may be these characteristics, and not the experience of cohabitation, that leads to marital instability. There is some empirical support for both positions. Also, a recent study based on a nationally representative sample of women concluded that premarital cohabitation (and premarital sex), when limited to a woman's future husband, is not associated with an elevated risk of marital disruption.[12] What can be said for certain is that no evidence has yet been found that those who cohabit before marriage have stronger marriages than those who do not.[13]

Conclusions

20 As a **stage in the life course of adults,** marriage is shrinking. Americans are living longer, marrying later, exiting marriages more quickly, and choosing to live together before marriage, after marriage, in between marriages, and as an alternative to marriage. A small but growing percentage, an estimated 15% [as of 2002], will never marry, compared to about five percent during the 1950s. As a consequence, marriage gradually is giving way to partnered and unpartnered singlehood, with or without children. Since 1960, the percentage of persons age 35 through 44 who were married has dropped from 88% to 66% for men and 87% to 67% for women.

21 As an **institution,** marriage has lost much of its legal, social, economic, and religious meaning and authority. The marital relationship once consisted of an economic bond of mutual dependency, a social bond supported by the extended family and larger community, and a spiritual bond upheld by religious doctrine, observance, and faith. Today, there are many marriages that have none of these elements. The older ideal of marriage as a permanent contractual union, strongly supported by society and designed for procreation and childrearing, is giving way to a new reality of it as a purely individual contract between two adults. Moreover, marriage is also quietly losing its place in the language and in popular culture. Unmarried people now tend to speak inclusively about "relationships" and "intimate partners." In the entertainment industry—including films, television, and music—marriage is often neglected or discredited.

22 If these have been the main changes, what, then, has marriage become in 21st-century America? First, let us not forget that many of the marriage-related trends of recent decades have been positive. The legal, sexual, and financial emancipation of women has become a reality as never before in history. With few restrictions on divorce, a married woman who is seriously abused by her

[12] Jay Teachman, "Premarital Sex, Premarital Cohabitation, and the Risk of Subsequent Marital Disruption among Women," *Journal of Marriage and the Family* 65 (2003): 444–455.

[13] For a full review of the research on cohabitation see: Pamela J. Smock, "Cohabitation in the United States," *Annual Review of Sociology* 26 (2000); and David Popenoe and Barbara Dafoe Whitehead, *Should We Live Together? What Young Adults Need to Know About Cohabitation Before Marriage—A Comprehensive Review of Recent Research,* 2nd Edition (New Brunswick, NJ: The National Marriage Project, Rutgers University, 2002).

husband can get out of the relationship, which she previously might have been stuck in for life. Due to great tolerance of family diversity, adults and children who through no fault of their own end up in nontraditional families are not marked for life by social stigma. Moreover, based on a companionship of equals, many marriages today may be more emotionally satisfying than ever before.

23   We have described the new marriage system as "emotionally deep, but socially shallow." For most Americans, marriage is a "couples relationship" designed primarily to meet the sexual and emotional needs of the spouses. Increasingly, happiness in marriage is measured by each partner's sense of psychological well-being, rather than the more-traditional measures of getting ahead economically, boosting children up to a higher rung on the educational ladder than the parents, or following religious teachings on marriage. People tend to be puzzled or put off by the idea that marriage has purposes or benefits that extend beyond fulfilling individual adult needs for intimacy and satisfaction. Eight out of 10 of the young adults in our survey agreed that "marriage is nobody's business, but that of the two people involved."

24   It is a sign of the times that the overwhelming majority (94%) of never-married singles in our survey agreed that "when you marry, you want your spouse to be your soul mate, first and foremost." This perspective, surely encouraged not only by the changing nature of marriage, but by the concern about divorce and therefore the seeming necessity of finding the one right person, is something that most people in the older generation would probably consider surprising. In times past, people married to start a new family, and therefore they looked for a competent and reliable mate to share life's tasks. To the degree that a soul mate was even considered, it was more likely to have been thought of as the end result of a lifetime of effort put into making a marriage work, not something you start out with.

25   Of course, having a soul mate as a marriage partner would be wonderful. In many ways, it is reassuring that today's young people are looking for a marriage that is both meaningful and lasting. Yet, there is a danger that the soul mate expectation sets a standard so high it will be hard to live up to. Also, if people believe that there is just one soul mate waiting somewhere out there for them, as most of today's youths in fact do according to our survey, doesn't it seem more likely that a marriage partner will be dropped when the going gets rough? Isn't it easier to say, "I must have picked the wrong person"? In other words, perhaps we have developed a standard for marriage that tends to destabilize the institution.

26   There are some hopeful signs in the recent statistics that may bode well for the future of marriage. The divorce rate has slowly been dropping since the early 1980s. Since the early 1990s, the teen birthrate has decreased by about 20%, with some indications that teenagers have become sexually more conservative. Overall, the percentage of unwed births has remained at its current level for the past five years. Indeed, due to fewer divorces and stabilized unwed births, the percentage of children living in single-parent families dropped slightly in the past few years, after having increased rapidly and continuously since 1960.

27   Moreover, one can see glimmers of hope here and there on the cultural scene. There are stirrings of a grassroots "marriage movement." Churches in several

hundred communities have joined together to establish a common set of pre-marital counseling standards and practices for engaged couples. Marriage education has emerged as a prominent theme among some family therapists, family life educators, schoolteachers, and clergy. In several states, legislatures have passed bills promoting marriage education in the schools and even seeking ways to cut the divorce rate, mainly through educational means. More books are being published with the theme of how to have a good marriage, and seemingly fewer with the theme of divorcing to achieve personal liberation. Questions are being raised more forcefully by members of Congress, on both sides of the aisle, about the "family values" of the entertainment industry. These positive trends bear watching and are encouraging, but it is too soon to tell whether they will persist or result in the revitalization of this critical social institution.

Review Questions

1. What factors significantly reduce the incidence of divorce, according to Popenoe and Whitehead?

2. According to Popenoe and Whitehead, which two factors are most likely responsible for the slight increase in marital stability (i.e., a decline in the divorce rate) since the early 1980s?

3. The data show that the percentage of divorced females is higher than that of males. Why?

4. Popenoe and Whitehead suggest that it might it be erroneous to claim that, based on recent data, people who live together before marriage are more likely to experience marital instability. Explain.

Discussion and Writing Suggestions

1. Popenoe and Whitehead's key finding is that "Marriage trends in recent decades indicate that Americans have become less likely to marry, and . . . that the marriage rate in the United States continues to decline." To what extent does this finding square with your own observations and impressions of contemporary marriage? How do you account for the declining marriage rate?

2. Popenoe and Whitehead assert that, despite the conventional wisdom among many young people that living together before marriage is a useful way to discover whether a couple is really compatible, and therefore to avoid a bad marriage and eventual divorce, "No evidence has yet been found that those who cohabit before marriage have stronger marriages than those who do not." In light of this assertion, have your opinions about whether or not people should live together before marriage changed? Explain your answer.

3. Noting that 94% of never-married singles agreed with the statement that "when you marry, you want your spouse to be your soul mate, first and foremost," Popenoe and Whitehead worry that this "soul mate expectation" sets up an unrealistically high standard for marriage. How do you define "soul mate"? Do you agree that expecting a spouse to be a soul mate can destabilize the institution of marriage?

4. Popenoe and Whitehead claim that, as an institution, marriage has lost much of its "legal, social, economic, and religious meaning and authority," and that marriage is becoming devalued in popular culture. Contrast these statements with the multitudes of bridal magazines on sale at every newsstand and the breathless attention with which tabloids follow celebrity marriages. To what extent does such evidence of our culture's fascination with marriage contradict Popenoe and Whitehead's thesis? Explain your answer.

Debunking Myths about Marriages and Families
Mary Ann Schwartz and BarBara Marliene Scott

While the previous selection relied on data to gauge the current state of the institutions of marriage and family, many people use a simpler method—their sense of what a family should be, and how current families measure up to that ideal. For example, many people assume that the nuclear family—defined as a family consisting of a father, mother, and their children—is the most basic and traditional form of family. But are such assumptions valid? In the following selection, two sociologists deconstruct five common myths about marriages and families. Mary Ann Schwartz is professor of sociology and women's studies and former chair of the sociology department at Northeastern Illinois University, where she cofounded the Women's Studies Program. BarBara Marliene Scott is professor of sociology and women's studies and coordinator of African and African American studies at Northeastern Illinois University. This selection is excerpted from their book Marriages and Families: Diversity and Change *(2000).*

1 Take a few minutes to think about the "traditional family." If you are like most people, your vision of the traditional family is similar to or the same as your more general view of families. Therefore, you probably describe the traditional family in terms of some combination of the following traits:

• Members loved and respected one another and worked together for the good of the family.
• Grandparents were an integral and respected part of the family.
• Mothers stayed home and were happy, nurturant, and always available to their children.
• Fathers worked and brought home the paycheck.
• Children were seen and not heard, mischievous but not "bad," and were responsible and learned a work ethic.

2   These images of past family life are still widely held and have a powerful influence on people's perceptions and evaluations of today's families. The problem, however, is that these are mostly mythical images of the past based on many different kinds of marriages and families that never coexisted in the same time and place. A leading authority on U.S. family history, Stephanie Coontz (1992), argues in her book *The Way We Never Were* that much of today's political and social debate about family values and the "real" family is based on an idealized vision of a past that never actually existed. Coontz further argues that this idealized and selective set of remembrances of families of yesteryear in turn determines much of our contemporary view of traditional family life.

. . .

3   Our memory of past family life is often clouded by myths. A **myth** is a false, fictitious, imaginary, or exaggerated belief about someone or something. Myths are generally assumed to be true and often provide the justification or rationale for social behaviors, beliefs, and institutions. And, in fact, most myths do contain some elements of truth. As we will see, however, different myths contain different degrees of truth.

4   Some family myths have a positive effect in the sense that they often bond individual family members together in familial solidarity. When they create unrealistic expectations about what families can or should be and do, however, myths can be dangerous. Many of the myths that most Americans hold today about traditional families or families of the past are white middle-class myths. This is true because the mass media, controlled primarily by white middle-class men, tend to project a primarily white middle-class experience as a universal trend or fact. Such myths, then, distort the diverse experiences of other familial groups in this country, both presently and in the past, and they do not even describe most white middle-class families accurately. We now take a closer look at five of the most popular myths and stereotypes about the family that are directly applicable to current debates about family life and gender roles: (1) the universal nuclear family, (2) the self-reliant traditional family, (3) the naturalness of different spheres for wives and husbands, (4) the unstable African American family, and (5) the idealized nuclear family of the 1950s.

Myth 1: The Universal Nuclear Family

5   While some form of marriage and family is found in all human societies, the idea that there is a universal, or single, marriage and family pattern blinds us to the historical reality and legitimacy of diverse marriage and family arrangements. The reality is that marriages and families vary in organization, membership, life cycles, emotional environments, ideologies, social and kinship networks, and economic and other functions. Although it is certainly true that a woman and man (egg and sperm) must unite to produce a child, social kinship ties or living arrangements, however, do not automatically flow from such biological unions. For example, although some cultures have weddings and cultural notions about monogamy and permanence, other cultures lack one or more of these characteristics. In some cultures, mating and childbirth occur outside of legal marriage and sometimes without couples living together. In other cultures, wives, husbands, and children live in separate residences.

Myth 2: The Self-Reliant Traditional Family

6 The myth of the self-reliant family assumes that, in the past, families were held together by hard work, family loyalty, and a fierce determination not to be beholden to anyone, especially the state. It is popularly believed that such families never asked for handouts; rather, they stood on their own feet even in times of crisis. Unlike some families today, who watch the mail for their government checks, families of yesteryear did not accept or expect "charity." Any help they may have received came from other family members.

7   This tendency to overestimate the self-reliance of earlier families ignores the fact that external support for families has been the rule, and not the exception, in U.S. family history. Although public assistance has become less local and more impersonal over the past two centuries, U.S. families have always depended to some degree on other institutions. For example, colonial families made extensive use of the collective work of others, such as African American slaves and Native Americans, whose husbandry and collective land use provided for the abundant game, plants, and berries colonial families consumed to survive. Early families were also dependent on a large network of neighbors, churches, courts, government officials, and legislative bodies for their sustenance. For example, the elderly, ill, and orphaned dependents were often taken care of by people who were not family members, and public officials often gave money to facilitate such care. Immigrant, African American, and native-born white workers could not have survived in the past without sharing and receiving assistance beyond family networks. Moreover, middle-class as well as working-class families were dependent on fraternal and mutual aid organizations to assist them in times of need.

Myth 3: The Naturalness of Different Spheres for Wives and Husbands

8 This myth dates to the mid-nineteenth century, when economic changes led to the development of separate spheres for women and men. Prior to this, men shared in child rearing. They were expected to be at least as involved in child rearing as mothers. Fatherhood meant much more than simply inseminating. It was understood as a well-defined set of domestic skills, including provisioning, hospitality, and child rearing (Gillis, 1999). With industrialization, wives and mothers became the caregivers and moral guardians of the family, while husbands and fathers provided economic support and protection and represented their families to the outside world. Thereafter, this arrangement was viewed as natural, and alternative forms were believed to be destructive to family harmony. Thus, today's family problems are seen as stemming from a self-defeating attempt to equalize women's and men's roles in the family. It is assumed that the move away from a traditional gendered division of labor to a more egalitarian ideal denies women's and men's differing needs and abilities and thus destabilizes family relations. Those who hold to this myth advocate a return to traditional gender roles in the family and a clear and firm boundary between the family and the outside world. As we shall see later on, however, the notions of separate spheres and ideal family form are far from natural and have not always existed.

Myth 4: The Unstable African American Family

9   Although many critics of today's families believe that the collapse of the family affects all racial and ethnic groups, they frequently single out African American families as the least stable and functional. According to sociologist Ronald Taylor (1994), myths and misconceptions about the nature and quality of African American family life are pervasive and deeply entrenched in American popular thought. Although there are far fewer systematic studies of black families than of white families, African American families have been the subject of far more sweeping generalizations and myths. The most pervasive myth, the myth of the collapse of the African American family, is fueled by racist stereotypes and media exaggerations and distortions that overlook the diversity of African American family life. No more is there one black family type than there is one white family type.

10   Nonetheless, this myth draws on some very real trends that affect a segment of the African American community. . . . Early in this decade, almost two-thirds of African American babies were born to unmarried couples, a trend especially evident among lower-income and less educated African Americans. In addition, there has been a major increase in the number of African American one-parent families. Although these trends have occurred among white families as well, their impact on black families has been much more substantial, resulting in increasingly different marital and family experiences for these two groups (Taylor, 1994).

11   Based on middle-class standards, these trends seem to support the myth of an unstable, disorganized family structure in part of the African American community. And, indeed, among some individuals and families, long-term and concentrated poverty and despair, racism, social contempt, police brutality, and political and governmental neglect have taken their toll and are often manifested in the behaviors just described. To generalize these behaviors to the entire African American community, however, is inaccurate and misleading. Moreover, to attribute these behaviors, when they do occur, to a deteriorating, immoral family life-style and a lack of middle-class family values ignores historical, social, and political factors, such as a history of servitude, legal discrimination, enforced segregation and exclusion, **institutional racism**—the systematic discrimination against a racial group by the institutions within society—and structural shifts in the economy and related trends that have created new and deeper disparities in the structure and quality of family life between blacks and whites in this society. In addition, such claims serve to perpetuate the myth that one particular family arrangement is a workable model for all families in modern society.

. . .

Myth 5: The Idealized Nuclear Family of the 1950s

12   During the 1950s, millions of Americans came to accept an image of the family as a middle-class institution consisting of a wise father who worked outside the home; a mother whose major responsibility was to take care of her husband, children, and home; and children who were well behaved and obedient. This

image, depicted in a number of 1950s family sitcoms, such as "Leave It to Beaver," "Father Knows Best," "The Donna Reed Show," and "The Adventures of Ozzie and Harriet," is said to represent the epitome of traditional family structure and values. Many critics today see the movement away from this model as evidence of the decline in the viability of the family, as well as a source of many family problems.

13   It is true that, compared with the 1990s, the 1950s were characterized by younger ages at marriage, higher birthrates, and lower divorce and premarital pregnancy rates. To present the 1950s as representing "typical" or "normal" family patterns, however, is misleading. Indeed, the divorce rates have increased since the 1950s, but this trend started in the nineteenth century, with more marital breakups in each succeeding generation. Today's trends of low marriage, high divorce, and low fertility are actually consistent with long-term historical trends in marriage and family life. Recent changes in marriage and family life are considered deviant only because the marriage rates for the postwar generation represented an all-time high for the United States. This generation married young, moved to the suburbs, and had three or more children. The fact is that this pattern was deviant in that it departed significantly from earlier twentieth-century trends in marriage and family life. According to some, if the 1940s and 1950s had not happened, marriage and family life today would appear normal (Skolnick and Skolnick, 1999). Although some people worry that young people today are delaying marriage to unusually late ages, . . . the median age at first marriage in the late 1990s [was] 24.8 for women and 27.1 for men, the highest levels since these data were first recorded in 1890, [which] more closely approximates the 1890 average than it does the 1950s average of 20.3 for women and 22.8 for men. The earlier age at marriage in the 1950s was a reaction to the hardships and sacrifices brought about by the depression and World War II. Thus, marriage and family life became synonymous with the "good life." Furthermore, images of the good life were now broadcast into living rooms across the country via the powerful new medium of television. Even then, however, there were signs that all was not well. Public opinion polls taken during the 1950s suggested that approximately 20 percent of all couples considered themselves unhappy in marriage, and another 20 percent reported only "medium happiness" (quoted in Mintz and Kellogg, 1988:194).

14   Connected to the myth of the idealized nuclear family is the myth that families have been essentially the same over the centuries, until recently when they began to disintegrate. The fact is that families have never been static, they have always changed: When the world around them changes, families change in response. The idea of the traditional family of old is itself relative. According to John Gillis (1999), we are in the habit of updating our notion of the traditional family so that the location of the golden age of the family constantly changes. For example, for the Victorians, the traditional family was rooted in a time period prior to industrialization and urbanization; for those who came of age during World War I, the traditional family was associated with the Victorians themselves; and today, most people think of the 1950s and 1960s as the epitome of traditional marriage and family life.

15   This discussion of mythical versus real families underscores the fact that not all families are the same; there is not now and never has been a single model of the family. Families and their experiences are indeed different; however, difference does not connote better or worse. The experiences of a poor family are certainly not the same as those of a rich family; the experiences of a young family with young children are little like those of either a child-free family or an older family whose children have "left the nest." Even within families the experiences of older members are different from those of younger members, and the experiences of females and males are different. Certainly the experiences of Latina/o, Native American, Asian American, and black families are not the same as those of white families, regardless of class. Nor are lesbian and gay family experiences the same as heterosexual family experiences. Families are products of their historical context, and at any given historical period families occupy different territories and have varied experiences, given the differential influence of the society's race, class, and gender systems.

Review Questions

1. Based on your reading of Schwartz and Scott, offer an example of the way in which U.S. families have historically relied on institutions outside of marriage.

2. What economic change led to wives and mothers becoming the primary caregivers of children?

3. According to Schwartz and Scott, those who believe that family gender roles should return to a more traditional standard are basing their views on a myth. What is that myth?

4. Why did people marry at younger ages in the 1950s, according to Schwartz and Scott?

Discussion and Writing Suggestions

1. Schwartz and Scott's "Myth 2" concerns the "self-reliant traditional family" (see page 158). To what extent do you see evidence that American politicians use this myth to advance a political agenda, attack the positions of opponents, or argue for or against changes in the law? (Consider, for example, the extent to which politicians invoke the "self-reliant traditional family" in debates over health care, welfare, or relief from natural disasters.)

2. Politicians and conservative commentators often blame a "breakdown of the family" for many of the ills facing society. Schwartz and Scott claim that the universal nuclear family is a myth—and, thus, logically speaking, no "breakdown" could have occurred. How might the public's general acceptance that the traditional family is a myth be used to shape public policy intended to help American families?

3. Schwartz and Scott argue that the marriage patterns of the 1950s were an anomaly, not the norm, in American marriage trends. Does this observation invalidate for you the 1950s family model of "a wise father who worked outside the home; a mother whose major responsibility was to take care of her husband, children, and home; and children who were well behaved and obedient"? If you were designing your own ideal family model, which elements of the 1950s family would you keep, and which would you jettison?

4. In the section dealing with African-American families, Schwartz and Scott label as a myth the belief that "one particular family arrangement is a workable model for all families in modern society." From your experience of your own family, or families you have known, describe a nonnuclear family arrangement that you have witnessed—for example, a family in which a grandparent lived with the family. Did you feel this arrangement was successful? Explain why or why not.

A DEBATE ON GAY MARRIAGE

There are few more hot-button topics in American politics today than gay marriage. In the Defense of Marriage Act of 1996, the federal government defined marriage as the legal union of a man as husband and a woman as wife. Similar legislation has been passed in 38 states. In November 2003, however, the Massachusetts Supreme Court ruled that denying marriage licenses to gay couples violated the state's Equal Protection Clause. The following year, the city of San Francisco began issuing marriage licenses to gay couples. Hundreds of same-sex couples were legally married in the aftermath of these rulings. Responding in outrage, many conservative state legislatures rushed to pass or reaffirm laws banning gay marriage. In July 2006, court rulings in New York, Nebraska, and Washington limited marriage to unions between a man and a woman.

For Gay Marriage
Andrew Sullivan

The debate over gay marriage highlights a vast cultural divide that typically hinges on core beliefs regarding the nature of marriage itself. In the following selection from Andrew Sullivan's book Virtually Normal: An Argument about Homosexuality *(1995), Sullivan articulates a vision of marriage as a public contract that should be available to any two citizens. Andrew Sullivan is a former editor of the* New Republic *magazine who writes on a wide range of political and social topics, including gay and lesbian issues. He lives in Washington, D.C.*

1 Marriage is not simply a private contract; it is a social and public recognition of a private commitment. As such, it is the highest public recognition of personal

integrity. Denying it to homosexuals is the most public affront possible to their public equality.

2   This point may be the hardest for many heterosexuals to accept. Even those tolerant of homosexuals may find this institution so wedded to the notion of heterosexual commitment that to extend it would be to undo its very essence. And there may be religious reasons for resisting this that, within certain traditions, are unanswerable. But I am not here discussing what churches do in their private affairs. I am discussing what the allegedly neutral liberal state should do in public matters. For liberals, the case for homosexual marriage is overwhelming. As a classic public institution, it should be available to any two citizens.

3   Some might argue that marriage is by definition between a man and a woman; and it is difficult to argue with a definition. But if marriage is articulated beyond this circular fiat, then the argument for its exclusivity to one man and one woman disappears. The center of the public contract is an emotional, financial, and psychological bond between two people; in this respect, heterosexuals and homosexuals are identical. The heterosexuality of marriage is intrinsic only if it is understood to be intrinsically procreative; but that definition has long been abandoned in Western society. No civil marriage license is granted on the condition that the couple bear children; and the marriage is no less legal and no less defensible if it remains childless. In the contemporary West, marriage has become a way in which the state recognizes an emotional commitment by two people to each other for life. And within that definition, there is no public way, if one believes in equal rights under the law, in which it should legally be denied homosexuals.

4   Of course, no public sanctioning of a contract should be given to people who cannot actually fulfill it. The state rightly, for example, withholds marriage from minors, or from one adult and a minor, since at least one party is unable to understand or live up to the contract. And the state has also rightly barred close family relatives from marriage because familial emotional ties are too strong and powerful to enable a marriage contract to be entered into freely by two autonomous, independent individuals, and because incest poses a uniquely dangerous threat to the trust and responsibility that the family needs to survive. But do homosexuals fall into a similar category? History and experience strongly suggest they don't. Of course, marriage is characterized by a kind of commitment that is rare—and perhaps declining—even among heterosexuals. But it isn't necessary to prove that homosexuals or lesbians are less—or more—able to form long-term relationships than straights for it to be clear that at least *some* are. Moreover, giving these people an equal right to affirm their commitment doesn't reduce the incentive for heterosexuals to do the same.

5   In some ways, the marriage issue is exactly parallel to the issue of the military. Few people deny that many homosexuals are capable of the sacrifice, the commitment, and the responsibilities of marriage. And indeed, for many homosexuals and lesbians, these responsibilities are already enjoined—as they have been enjoined for centuries. The issue is whether these identical relationships should be denied equal legal standing, not by virtue of anything to do with the relationships themselves but by virtue of the internal, involuntary nature of the homosexuals involved. Clearly, for liberals, the answer to this is clear. Such a denial is a classic case of unequal protection of the laws.

6   But perhaps surprisingly, . . . one of the strongest arguments for gay marriage is a conservative one. It's perhaps best illustrated by a comparison with the alternative often offered by liberals and liberationists to legal gay marriage, the concept of "domestic partnership." Several cities in the United States have domestic partnership laws, which allow relationships that do not fit into the category of heterosexual marriage to be registered with the city and qualify for benefits that had previously been reserved for heterosexual married couples. In these cities, a variety of interpersonal arrangements qualify for health insurance, bereavement leave, insurance, annuity and pension rights, housing rights (such as rent-control apartments), adoption, and inheritance rights. Eventually, the aim is to include federal income tax and veterans' benefits as well. Homosexuals are not the only beneficiaries; heterosexual "live-togethers" also qualify.

7   The conservative's worries start with the ease of the relationship. To be sure, potential domestic partners have to prove financial interdependence, shared living arrangements, and a commitment to mutual caring. But they don't need to have a sexual relationship or even closely mirror old-style marriage. In principle, an elderly woman and her live-in nurse could qualify, or a pair of frat buddies. Left as it is, the concept of domestic partnership could open a Pandora's box of litigation and subjective judicial decision making about who qualifies. You either are or you're not married; it's not a complex question. Whether you are in a domestic partnership is not so clear.

8   More important for conservatives, the concept of domestic partnership chips away at the prestige of traditional relationships and undermines the priority we give them. Society, after all, has good reasons to extend legal advantages to heterosexuals who choose the formal sanction of marriage over simply living together. They make a deeper commitment to one another and to society; in exchange, society extends certain benefits to them. Marriage provides an anchor, if an arbitrary and often weak one, in the maelstrom of sex and relationships to which we are all prone. It provides a mechanism for emotional stability and economic security. We rig the law in its favor not because we disparage all forms of relationship other than the nuclear family, but because we recognize that not to promote marriage would be to ask too much of human virtue.

9   For conservatives, these are vital concerns. There are virtually no conservative arguments either for preferring no social incentives for gay relationships or for preferring a second-class relationship, such as domestic partnership, which really does provide an incentive for the decline of traditional marriage. Nor, if conservatives are concerned by the collapse of stable family life, should they be dismayed by the possibility of gay parents. There is no evidence that shows any deleterious impact on a child brought up by two homosexual parents, and considerable evidence that such a parental structure is clearly preferable to single parents (gay or straight) or no effective parents at all, which, alas, is the choice many children now face. Conservatives should not balk at the apparent radicalism of the change involved, either. The introduction of gay marriage would not be some sort of leap in the dark, a massive societal risk. Homosexual marriages have always existed, in a variety of forms; they have just been euphemized. Increasingly they exist in every sense but the legal one. As it has

become more acceptable for homosexuals to acknowledge their loves and commitments publicly, more and more have committed themselves to one another for life in full view of their families and friends. A law institutionalizing gay marriage would merely reinforce a healthy trend. Burkean conservatives should warm to the idea.

10   It would also be an unqualified social good for homosexuals. It provides role models for young gay people, who, after the exhilaration of coming out can easily lapse into short-term relationships and insecurity with no tangible goal in sight. My own guess is that most homosexuals would embrace such a goal with as much (if not more) commitment as heterosexuals. Even in our society as it is, many lesbian and gay male relationships are virtual textbooks of monogamous commitment; and for many, "in sickness and in health" has become a vocation rather than a vow. Legal gay marriage could also help bridge the gulf often found between homosexuals and their parents. It could bring the essence of gay life— a gay couple—into the heart of the traditional family in a way the family can most understand and the gay offspring can most easily acknowledge. It could do more to heal the gay-straight rift than any amount of gay rights legislation.

11   More important, perhaps, as gay marriage sank into the subtle background consciousness of a culture, its influence would be felt quietly but deeply among gay children. For them, at last, there would be some kind of future; some older faces to apply to their unfolding lives, some language in which their identity could be properly discussed, some rubric by which it could be explained—not in terms of sex, or sexual practices, or bars, or subterranean activity, but in terms of their future life stories, their potential loves, their eventual chance at some kind of constructive happiness. They would be able to feel by the intimation of myriad examples that in this respect their emotional orientation was not merely about pleasure, or sin, or shame, or otherness (although it might always be involved in many of those things), but about the ability to love and be loved as complete, imperfect human beings. Until gay marriage is legalized, this fundamental element of personal dignity will be denied a whole segment of humanity. No other change can achieve it.

12   Any heterosexual man who takes a few moments to consider what his life would be like if he were never allowed a formal institution to cement his relationships will see the truth of what I am saying. Imagine life without a recognized family; imagine dating without even the possibility of marriage. Any heterosexual woman who can imagine being told at a young age that her attraction to men was wrong, that her loves and crushes were illicit, that her destiny was singlehood and shame, will also appreciate the point. Gay marriage is not a radical step; it is a profoundly humanizing, traditionalizing step. It is the first step in any resolution of the homosexual question—more important than any other institution, since it is the most central institution to the nature of the problem, which is to say, the emotional and sexual bond between one human being and another. If nothing else were done at all, and gay marriage were legalized, 90 percent of the political work necessary to achieve gay and lesbian equality would have been achieved. It is ultimately the only reform that truly matters.

13   So long as conservatives recognize, as they do, that homosexuals exist and that they have equivalent emotional needs and temptations as heterosexuals,

then there is no conservative reason to oppose homosexual marriage and many conservative reasons to support it. So long as liberals recognize, as they do, that citizens deserve equal treatment under the law, then there is no liberal reason to oppose it and many liberal reasons to be in favor of it. So long as intelligent people understand that homosexuals are emotionally and sexually attracted to the same sex as heterosexuals are to the other sex, then there is no human reason on earth why it should be granted to one group and not the other.

Review Questions

1. According to Sullivan, what definition of marriage prohibits any public way for marriage to be legally denied to homosexuals "if one believes in equal rights under the law"?

2. Which two classes of people, according to Sullivan, does the state believe cannot fulfill the contract of marriage?

3. Summarize Sullivan's "conservative" arguments preferring gay marriage to "domestic partnership."

4. How does Sullivan believe that gay marriage will "bridge the gulf" that is often found between homosexuals and their parents?

Discussion and Writing Suggestions

1. Write a critique of Sullivan's argument in favor of gay marriage. To what extent do you agree, for example, that "the marriage issue [for gays] is exactly parallel to the issue of the military"? Or that "[l]egal gay marriage could . . . help bridge the gulf often found between homosexuals and their parents"? Follow the principles discussed in Chapter 2.

2. Sullivan makes the surprising case that conservatives should support, rather than oppose, gay marriage because marriage is a fundamentally conservative institution (more conservative, for instance, than domestic partnership). To what extent do you agree with his reasoning?

3. Imagine for a moment, as Sullivan suggests, that you belong to a class of people that has been denied the right to marry or have a recognized family. To what extent do you feel that this restriction would affect your approach to life? For example, do you feel that you would be drawn more to short-term relationships—as Sullivan suggests is true of some young gays? To what extent do you feel that the lack of these rights would adversely affect your life?

4. Sullivan writes: "[G]iving [homosexuals] an equal right to affirm their commitment doesn't reduce the incentive for heterosexuals to do the same." However, many antigay marriage activists make precisely that argument—that gay marriage "devalues" heterosexual marriage, by implication making it less attractive to men and women. To what degree

does the value you place on marriage depend on its being an institution reserved for a heterosexual man and woman?

5. Sullivan writes that marriage provides a bulwark against the "maelstrom of sex and relationships to which we are all prone." Do you agree that people who have undertaken the public commitment of marriage are less likely to yield to temptation than, say, people who have made a private commitment that has not been publicly recognized? If so, describe what it is about the public nature of the commitment that would tend to encourage fidelity.

6. Noting that "it is difficult to argue with a definition," Sullivan bypasses the argument that marriage is by definition between a man and a woman. Instead, he insists on articulating for the sake of his argument a broader and more complex definition of the nature of marriage: as a public contract that has, at its center, an "emotional, financial, and psychological bond between two people." However, since other relationships—such as that between a father and son—are often characterized by emotional, financial, and psychological bonds, clearly more is needed before this definition could be called comprehensive. In a sentence beginning "Marriage is . . . ," craft your own comprehensive definition of marriage, one that reflects your own beliefs.

Against Gay Marriage
William J. Bennett

In the following selection, William J. Bennett, a prominent cultural conservative, explains why he thinks that allowing gays to marry would damage the institution of marriage. Note that Bennett attempts to rebut Andrew Sullivan's pro-gay marriage arguments. Bennett served as chairman of the National Endowment for the Humanities (1981–85) and secretary of education (1985–88) under President Ronald Reagan, and as President George H. W. Bush's "drug czar" (1989–90). His writings on cultural issues in America include The Book of Virtues *(1997) and* The Broken Hearth: Reversing the Moral Collapse of the American Family *(2001). He has served as senior editor of the conservative journal* National Review *and is codirector of Empower America, a conservative advocacy organization. This piece first appeared as an op-ed column in the* Washington Post *on May 21, 1996.*

1   We are engaged in a debate which, in a less confused time, would be considered pointless and even oxymoronic: the question of same-sex marriage.

2   But we are where we are. The Hawaii Supreme Court has discovered a new state constitutional "right"—the legal union of same-sex couples. Unless a "compelling state interest" can be shown against them, Hawaii will become the first state to sanction such unions. And if Hawaii legalizes same-sex marriages, other states might well have to recognize them because of the Constitution's Full Faith and Credit Clause. Some in Congress recently introduced legislation to prevent this from happening.

3   Now, anyone who has known someone who has struggled with his homosexuality can appreciate the poignancy, human pain and sense of exclusion that are often involved. One can therefore understand the effort to achieve for homosexual unions both legal recognition and social acceptance. Advocates of homosexual marriages even make what appears to be a sound conservative argument: Allow marriage in order to promote faithfulness and monogamy. This is an intelligent and politically shrewd argument. One can even concede that it might benefit some people. But I believe that overall, allowing same-sex marriages would do significant, long-term social damage.

4   Recognizing the legal union of gay and lesbian couples would represent a profound change in the meaning and definition of marriage. Indeed, it would be the most radical step ever taken in the deconstruction of society's most important institution. It is not a step we ought to take.

5   The function of marriage is not elastic; the institution is already fragile enough. Broadening its definition to include same-sex marriages would stretch it almost beyond recognition—and new attempts to broaden the definition still further would surely follow. On what principled grounds could the advocates of same-sex marriage oppose the marriage of two consenting brothers? How could they explain why we ought to deny a marriage license to a bisexual who wants to marry two people? After all, doing so would be a denial of that person's sexuality. In our time, there are more (not fewer) reasons than ever to preserve the essence of marriage.

6   Marriage is not an arbitrary construct; it is an "honorable estate" based on the different, complementary nature of men and women—and how they refine, support, encourage and complete one another. To insist that we maintain this traditional understanding of marriage is not an attempt to put others down. It is simply an acknowledgment and celebration of our most precious and important social act.

7   Nor is this view arbitrary or idiosyncratic. It mirrors the accumulated wisdom of millennia and the teaching of every major religion. Among worldwide cultures, where there are so few common threads, it is not a coincidence that marriage is almost universally recognized as an act meant to unite a man and a woman.

8   To say that same-sex unions are not comparable to heterosexual marriages is not an argument for intolerance, bigotry or lack of compassion (although I am fully aware that it will be considered so by some). But it is an argument for making distinctions in law about relationships that are themselves distinct. Even Andrew Sullivan, among the most intelligent advocates of same-sex marriage, has admitted that a homosexual marriage contract will entail a greater understanding of the need for "extramarital outlets." He argues that gay male relationships are served by the "openness of the contract," and he has written that homosexuals should resist allowing their "varied and complicated lives" to be flattened into a "single, moralistic model."

9   But this "single, moralistic model" is precisely the point. The marriage commitment between a man and a woman does not—it cannot—countenance extramarital outlets. By definition it is not an open contract; its essential idea is fidelity. Obviously that is not always honored in practice. But it is normative, the ideal to which we aspire precisely because we believe some things are right

(faithfulness in marriage) and others are wrong (adultery). In insisting that marriage accommodate the less restrained sexual practices of homosexuals, Sullivan and his allies destroy the very thing that supposedly has drawn them to marriage in the first place.

10   There are other arguments to consider against same-sex marriage—for example, the signals it would send, and the impact of such signals on the shaping of human sexuality, particularly among the young. Former Harvard professor E. L. Pattullo has written that "a very substantial number of people are born with the potential to live either straight or gay lives." Societal indifference about heterosexuality and homosexuality would cause a lot of confusion. A remarkable 1993 article in *The Post* supports this point. Fifty teenagers and dozens of school counselors and parents from the local area were interviewed. According to the article, teenagers said it has become "cool" for students to proclaim they are gay or bisexual—even for some who are not. Not surprisingly, the caseload of teenagers in "sexual identity crisis" doubled in one year. "Everything is front page, gay and homosexual," according to one psychologist who works with the schools. "Kids are jumping on it . . . [counselors] are saying, 'What are we going to do with all these kids proclaiming they are bisexual or homosexual when we know they are not?' "

11   If the law recognizes homosexual marriages as the legal equivalent of heterosexual marriages, it will have enormous repercussions in many areas. Consider just two: sex education in the schools and adoption. The sex education curriculum of public schools would have to teach that heterosexual and homosexual marriage are equivalent. "Heather Has Two Mommies" would no longer be regarded as an anomaly; it would more likely become a staple of a sex education curriculum. Parents who want their children to be taught (for both moral and utilitarian reasons) the privileged status of heterosexual marriage will be portrayed as intolerant bigots; they will necessarily be at odds with the new law of matrimony and its derivative curriculum.

12   Homosexual couples will also have equal claim with heterosexual couples in adopting children, forcing us (in law at least) to deny what we know to be true: that it is far better for a child to be raised by a mother and a father than by, say, two male homosexuals.

13   The institution of marriage is already reeling because of the effects of the sexual revolution, no-fault divorce and out-of-wedlock births. We have reaped the consequences of its devaluation. It is exceedingly imprudent to conduct a radical, untested and inherently flawed social experiment on an institution that is the keystone in the arch of civilization. That we have to debate this issue at all tells us that the arch has slipped. Getting it firmly back in place is, as the lawyers say, a "compelling state interest."

Review Questions

1. What is the "intelligent and politically shrewd" conservative argument for marriage, according to Bennett?

2. What "enormous repercussion" does Bennett predict in the area of sex education, if the law recognizes homosexual marriage?

3. Summarize two of Bennett's arguments against broadening "the meaning and definition" of marriage to include same-sex marriages.

4. According to Bennett, what distinguishes the sexual behavior of heterosexuals from that of homosexuals?

Discussion and Writing Suggestions

1. Write a critique of Bennett's arguments against gay marriage. Follow the principles discussed in Chapter 2. For example, to what extent do you agree with Bennett's assertion that one argument against same-sex marriage is that it sends "the wrong signals"? Or his assertion that "it is far better for a child to be raised by a mother and a father than by, say, two male homosexuals"? You may wish to include some of Andrew Sullivan's points in your discussion.

2. Contending that homosexual relationships involve "less restrained sexual practices" than heterosexual ones, Bennett quotes Andrew Sullivan, who admits that a homosexual marriage contract will need to feature an acknowledgment of the need for "extramarital outlets." Propose a definition of marriage that allows for such outlets.

3. Imagine that you are one of the advocates of same-sex marriage to whom Bennett refers in the fifth paragraph of his op-ed column. In a brief paragraph, argue why same-sex marriages should be allowed, but not the marriage of two consenting brothers.

**Many Women at Elite Colleges
Set Career Path to Motherhood**
Louise Story

Should young mothers stay home to raise their children? Should they be encouraged to pursue their careers—putting the kids in day care, or (for those who can afford them) in the care of nannies? Since World War II, women have been entering the workforce in steadily greater numbers. In 1940, less than 10% of mothers with children under 18 worked outside the home; by 1948, that ratio had risen to about 25%. By 2003, 71% of mothers with children under 18 worked outside the home. In recent years, however, newspaper and magazine writers have coined such phrases as "the opt-out revolution" (i.e., women opting out of work) to suggest that more and more women are abandoning careers in favor of full-time motherhood. Feminists and other liberal cultural commentators often decry such reports and books on the subject, charging that the "Mommy Wars" these publications purport to describe are largely a media creation, whipped up to sell books and magazines, and perhaps to advance an antifeminist, reactionary agenda.

Louise Story's article "Many Women at Elite Colleges Set Career Path to Motherhood," published on the front page of the New York Times *on September 20, 2005, landed squarely in the middle of this dispute. The response, both in the "blogosphere" and in op-ed pieces in publications such as the online magazine* Slate *and the* Los Angeles Times, *was immediate and heated—so much so that three days later, the* New York Times *published a follow-up article by Story outlining the methodology of her survey. Louise Story was a student at the Columbia School of Journalism and an intern at the* New York Times *when she wrote the article, based on a questionnaire e-mailed to 138 Yale undergraduate women as well as interviews with undergraduate women at Yale and other universities.*

1   Cynthia Liu is precisely the kind of high achiever Yale wants: smart (1510 SAT), disciplined (4.0 grade point average), competitive (finalist in Texas oratory competition), musical (pianist), athletic (runner) and altruistic (hospital volunteer). And at the start of her sophomore year at Yale, Ms. Liu is full of ambition, planning to go to law school. So will she join the long tradition of famous Ivy League graduates? Not likely. By the time she is 30, this accomplished 19-year-old expects to be a stay-at-home mom. "My mother's always told me you can't be the best career woman and the best mother at the same time," Ms. Liu said matter-of-factly. "You always have to choose one over the other."

2   At Yale and other top colleges, women are being groomed to take their place in an ever more diverse professional elite. It is almost taken for granted that, just as they make up half the students at these institutions, they will move into leadership roles on an equal basis with their male classmates. There is just one problem with this scenario: many of these women say that is not what they want.

3   Many women at the nation's most elite colleges say they have already decided that they will put aside their careers in favor of raising children. Though some of these students are not planning to have children and some hope to have a family and work full time, many others, like Ms. Liu, say they will happily play a traditional female role, with motherhood their main commitment.

4   Much attention has been focused on career women who leave the work force to rear children. What seems to be changing is that while many women in college two or three decades ago expected to have full-time careers, their daughters, while still in college, say they have already decided to suspend or end their careers when they have children.

5   "At the height of the women's movement and shortly thereafter, women were much more firm in their expectation that they could somehow combine full-time work with child rearing," said Cynthia E. Russett, a professor of American history who has taught at Yale since 1967. "The women today are, in effect, turning realistic." Dr. Russett is among more than a dozen faculty members and administrators at the most exclusive institutions who have been on campus for decades and who said in interviews that they had noticed the changing attitude.

6   Many students say staying home is not a shocking idea among their friends. Shannon Flynn, an 18-year-old from Guilford, Conn., who is a freshman at Harvard, says many of her girlfriends do not want to work full time. "Most probably do feel like me, maybe even tending toward wanting to not work at all," said Ms. Flynn, who plans to work part time after having children, though she

is torn because she has worked so hard in school. "Men really aren't put in that position," she said.

7   Uzezi Abugo, a freshman at the University of Pennsylvania who hopes to become a lawyer, says she, too, wants to be home with her children at least until they are in school. "I've seen the difference between kids who did have their mother stay at home and kids who didn't, and it's kind of like an obvious difference when you look at it," said Ms. Abugo, whose mother, a nurse, stayed home until Ms. Abugo was in first grade.

8   While the changing attitudes are difficult to quantify, the shift emerges repeatedly in interviews with Ivy League students, including 138 freshman and senior females at Yale who replied to e-mail questions sent to members of two residential colleges over the last school year. The interviews found that 85 of the students, or roughly 60 percent, said that when they had children, they planned to cut back on work or stop working entirely. About half of those women said they planned to work part time, and about half wanted to stop work for at least a few years. Two of the women interviewed said they expected their husbands to stay home with the children while they pursued their careers. Two others said either they or their husbands would stay home, depending on whose career was furthest along. The women said that pursuing a rigorous college education was worth the time and money because it would help position them to work in meaningful part-time jobs when their children are young or to attain good jobs when their children leave home.

9   In recent years, elite colleges have emphasized the important roles they expect their alumni—both men and women—to play in society. For example, earlier this month, Shirley M. Tilghman, the president of Princeton University, welcomed new freshmen, saying: "The goal of a Princeton education is to prepare young men and women to take up positions of leadership in the 21st century. Of course, the word 'leadership' conjures up images of presidents and C.E.O.'s, but I want to stress that my idea of a leader is much broader than that." She listed education, medicine and engineering as other areas where students could become leaders. In an e-mail response to a question, Dr. Tilghman added: "There is nothing inconsistent with being a leader and a stay-at-home parent. Some women (and a handful of men) whom I have known who have done this have had a powerful impact on their communities."

10   Yet the likelihood that so many young women plan to opt out of high-powered careers presents a conundrum. "It really does raise this question for all of us and for the country: when we work so hard to open academics and other opportunities for women, what kind of return do we expect to get for that?" said Marlyn McGrath Lewis, director of undergraduate admissions at Harvard, who served as dean for coeducation in the late 1970's and early 1980's. It is a complicated issue and one that most schools have not addressed. The women they are counting on to lead society are likely to marry men who will make enough money to give them a real choice about whether to be full-time mothers, unlike those women who must work out of economic necessity.

11   It is less than clear what universities should, or could, do about it. For one, a person's expectations at age 18 are less than perfect predictors of their life choices 10 years later. And in any case, admissions officers are not likely to ask applicants whether they plan to become stay-at-home moms. University

officials said that success meant different things to different people and that universities were trying to broaden students' minds, not simply prepare them for jobs. "What does concern me," said Peter Salovey, the dean of Yale College, "is that so few students seem to be able to think outside the box; so few students seem to be able to imagine a life for themselves that isn't constructed along traditional gender roles."

12   There is, of course, nothing new about women being more likely than men to stay home to rear children. According to a 2000 survey of Yale alumni from the classes of 1979, 1984, 1989 and 1994, conducted by the Yale Office of Institutional Research, more men from each of those classes than women said that work was their primary activity—a gap that was small among alumni in their 20's but widened as women moved into their prime child-rearing years. Among the alumni surveyed who had reached their 40's, only 56 percent of the women still worked, compared with 90 percent of the men. A 2005 study of comparable Yale alumni classes found that the pattern had not changed. Among the alumnae who had reached their early 40's, just over half said work was their primary activity, compared with 90 percent of the men. Among the women who had reached their late 40's, some said they had returned to work, but the percentage of women working was still far behind the percentage of men. A 2001 survey of Harvard Business School graduates found that 31 percent of the women from the classes of 1981, 1985 and 1991 who answered the survey worked only part time or on contract, and another 31 percent did not work at all, levels strikingly similar to the percentages of the Yale students interviewed who predicted they would stay at home or work part time in their 30's and 40's.

13   What seems new is that while many of their mothers expected to have hard-charging careers, then scaled back their professional plans only after having children, the women of this generation expect their careers to take second place to child rearing. "It never occurred to me," Rebecca W. Bushnell, dean of the School of Arts and Sciences at the University of Pennsylvania, said about working versus raising children. "Thirty years ago when I was heading out, I guess I was just taking it one step at a time." Dr. Bushnell said young women today, in contrast, are thinking and talking about part-time or flexible work options for when they have children. "People have a heightened awareness of trying to get the right balance between work and family." Sarah Currie, a senior at Harvard, said many of the men in her American Family class last fall approved of women's plans to stay home with their children. "A lot of the guys were like, 'I think that's really great,'" Ms. Currie said. "One of the guys was like, 'I think that's sexy.' Staying at home with your children isn't as polarizing of an issue as I envision it is for women who are in their 30's now."

14   For most of the young women who responded to e-mail questions, a major factor shaping their attitudes seemed to be their experience with their own mothers, about three out of five of whom did not work at all, took several years off or worked only part time. "My stepmom's very proud of my choice because it makes her feel more valuable," said Kellie Zesch, a Texan who graduated from the University of North Carolina two years ago and who said that once she had children, she intended to stay home for at least five years and then consider working part time. "It justified it to her, that I don't look down on her for not having a career." Similarly, students who are committed to full-time careers,

without breaks, also cited their mothers as influences. Laura Sullivan, a sophomore at Yale who wants to be a lawyer, called her mother's choice to work full time the "greatest gift." "She showed me what it meant to be an amazing mother and maintain a career," Ms. Sullivan said.

15   Some of these women's mothers, who said they did not think about these issues so early in their lives, said they were surprised to hear that their college-age daughters had already formed their plans. Emily Lechner, one of Ms. Liu's roommates, hopes to stay home a few years, then work part time as a lawyer once her children are in school. Her mother, Carol, who once thought she would have a full-time career but gave it up when her children were born, was pleasantly surprised to hear that. "I do have this bias that the parents can do it best," she said. "I see a lot of women in their 30's who have full-time nannies, and I just question if their kids are getting the best." For many feminists, it may come as a shock to hear how unbothered many young women at the nation's top schools are by the strictures of traditional roles. "They are still thinking of this as a private issue; they're accepting it," said Laura Wexler, a professor of American studies and women's and gender studies at Yale. "Women have been given full-time working career opportunities and encouragement with no social changes to support it. "I really believed 25 years ago," Dr. Wexler added, "that this would be solved by now."

16   Angie Ku, another of Ms. Liu's roommates who had a stay-at-home mom, talks nonchalantly about attending law or business school, having perhaps a 10-year career and then staying home with her children. "Parents have such an influence on their children," Ms. Ku said. "I want to have that influence. Me!" She said she did not mind if that limited her career potential. "I'll have a career until I have two kids," she said. "It doesn't necessarily matter how far you get. It's kind of like the experience: I have tried what I wanted to do." Ms. Ku added that she did not think it was a problem that women usually do most of the work raising kids. "I accept things how they are," she said. "I don't mind the status quo. I don't see why I have to go against it." After all, she added, those roles got her where she is. "It worked so well for me," she said, "and I don't see in my life why it wouldn't work."

Review Questions

1. Of the 138 freshman and senior females at Yale who replied to the e-mail questions sent by the *New York Times,* how many indicated that when they had children, they planned to work less or stop working entirely?

2. How many of these female students said that they expected their husbands to stay home? How many said they or their husbands would stay home, "depending on whose career was furthest along"?

3. According to the 2000 survey of Yale alumnae from the classes of 1979, 1984, 1989, and 1994, what percentage of female alumnae in their

forties still worked? What percentage of male alumnae in their forties still worked?

Discussion and Writing Questions

1. Are you surprised by the results of Story's survey? Talk to some of your female classmates (in other courses, as well as in your writing course) about their marriage and career plans. To what extent does your informal survey bear out Story's conclusions?

2. Story quotes a female University of Pennsylvania student as follows: "I've seen the difference between kids who did have their mothers stay at home and kids who didn't, and it's kind of like an obvious difference when you look at it." What do you think the student means by "an obvious difference"? Have you noticed any such differences—obvious or not?

3. According to Story, "many" women at the nation's elite universities say they are not planning to work after they have children. According to the article, this conclusion is based on the responses of 138 women to an e-mailed questionnaire. In your opinion, does the number of women interviewed justify the article's use of the word "many" in that context? Explain why or why not.

4. A majority of the women interviewed for the article said that, after they had children, they planned to work less or stop working entirely. If you are a female student, briefly describe your plan for working once you have children. If you are a male student, briefly describe what kind of plan you would like your wife to have.

5. Story quotes Shirley M. Tilghman, the president of Princeton University, as follows: "The goal of a Princeton education is to prepare young men and women to take up positions of leadership in the 21st century." Imagine that you are an admissions official at Princeton, and your duty is to admit the students who you believe are best qualified to become leaders in the twenty-first century. You are trying to decide between two students, both of whom are equally qualified in all ways, except for the fact that one student has stated that she intends to pursue a full-time career, and the other has stated that she intends to work for ten years, then give up her career to raise her children. In light of the second student's stated plan, would you be more likely to admit the first student? Or would this knowledge of their goals have no bearing on your decision? Explain your reasoning.

6. According to Story, the example set by their mothers' choices regarding career versus motherhood affected many female students' values and beliefs on the subject. Describe your own mother's choices in this area. How did you feel about her choices when you were growing up, and how do you feel about them now? How likely is it that when you have

children, your mother's example will affect your own eventual decision (if you are a woman) about whether or not to work, or (if you are a man) whether or not you will want your wife to work?

What Yale Women Want, and Why It Is Misguided
Karen Stabiner

Four days after Louise Story's article appeared in the New York Times, *writer Karen Stabiner published the following response as an op-ed in the* Los Angeles Times. *Stabiner has written about health, women's and family issues for such publications as the* New Yorker, *the* New York Times *and the* Los Angeles Times. *She is the author of six books, including* My Girl: Adventures with a Teen in Training *(2005) and* The Empty Nest: 31 Writers Tell the Truth about Relationships, Love and Freedom after the Kids Fly the Coop *(2007). Stabiner lives in Santa Monica, California.*

1   If the last generation of women obsessed about cracking the glass ceiling, a new crop of college undergrads seems less interested in the professional stratosphere than in a soft—a cushy—landing.

2   The *New York Times* recently got its hands on a Yale University questionnaire in which 60 percent of the 138 female respondents said that they intend to stop working when they have children, and then to work part time, if at all, once the kids are in school. A reporter talked to students at other elite East Coast colleges who echoed the same back-to-the-future sentiment: Work is but a way-station; a woman's place is in the home.

3   The young women think they're doing the right thing for their eventual children, having watched too many of their moms' generation try to juggle career and family. And at least one male student at Harvard finds the whole lord-and-master idea "sexy." This, from excellent students who have clambered over the backs of other, merely good students to gain entry into schools that traditionally have incubated tomorrow's leaders.

4   These future moms betray a startling combination of naivete and privilege. To plot this kind of future, a woman has to have access to a pool of wealthy potential husbands, she has to stay married at a time when half of marriages end in divorce, and she has to ignore the history of the women's movement. (Homework assignment: research Betty Friedan's motivation for writing "The Feminine Mystique.") It's also helpful if she ignores the following: The number of dual-working couples is on the rise. Ditto, the number of women in the work force.

5   The one number that's dwindling? Households supported by one adult, who in the current fantasy would be the extremely well-paid husband. Fewer than 25 percent of American households survive on one paycheck, and in a few years that number will decline to fewer than 20 percent.

6   If the undergrads still believe they can beat the odds, they must've slept through statistics. Or worse, they think they're above the fray. They seem to

have learned one lesson—I'm in it for me—far too well, confusing personal comfort with social progress.

7   Laura Wexler, a Yale professor of American studies and women's and gender studies, confessed surprise that women still consider this a "private" issue, and she wondered how 25 years could pass without more social change to make women's decisions easier.

8   Her colleague, Yale College Dean Peter Salovey, expressed concern that so few students were able to think "outside the box," gender-wise.

9   And a Tiffany's box it is; every step of this retro scenario requires capital, from law school—a popular goal for most of these aspiring if temporary professionals—to the husband with bucks. The choice of law is a little chilling in its practicality: You can't take 10 years off from biomedical research or orthopedic surgery and fit right in when you choose to go back to work, but the law is more of an evergreen profession.

10   As a working mother, I have nothing but empathy for the desire to avoid what author Arlie Hochschild rightly calls the second shift—in her book of that name—the double workday that most employed mothers put in. I have nothing but anger at the proposed solution. Do we grab a private solution or address the public issue? Is a hedge-fund husband the answer, or should women smart enough to be tomorrow's leaders seek new ideas that pay more than lip-service to family values?

11   There are only two possibilities here: If these young women are right that staying home means better children, we have to come up with a way to give more parents—moms and dads—the chance to be at home more frequently during their kids' formative years. The women's movement is about choice and responsibility, not just choice, and the math here should be simple for girls who get over 700 on their math SAT: Opportunity for one coed does not equal choice for all.

12   Or they're wrong, and in their smugness have managed to insult every mother in this country who needs to work. Surely some of the mothers of these 138 young women had jobs. Are their daughters worse off than those whose mothers stayed at home? If all of the undergrads agree that some among them turned out better than others—and that's where their stay-home logic inevitably leads them—then they should step forward.

13   No consensus?

14   Class dismissed.

Discussion and Writing Questions

1. Comment on Stabiner's contention that what Yale women want (as indicated in Story's survey) is "misguided." To what extent do you agree?

2. Stabiner writes: "If the last generation of women obsessed about cracking the glass ceiling, a new crop of college undergrads seems less interested in the professional stratosphere than in a soft—and a cushy—landing." To what extent do you believe that this description fairly

characterizes the viewpoints of the Yale and other undergrads quoted and summarized in Story's article? In your answer, refer to specific parts of Story's article.

3. Stabiner faults the Yale students for, among other things, "confusing personal comfort with social progress." She cites approvingly a Yale professor quoted by Story who expresses surprise that students still consider this a "private" issue. To what extent do you believe that people who support social progress have a duty to factor this support into their own personal choices?

4. As a solution to the issues raised by the Story article, Stabiner proposes the kind of social change that would allow parents to stay at home regularly during their children's formative years. In a brief paragraph, propose how such changes might come about. Your solution may take any form—from legislative initiatives to consciousness raising—but be specific.

5. Stabiner implies that the viewpoint about suspending their careers articulated by the Yale women collapses if children of working mothers turn out to be not "worse off" than children of stay-at-home mothers. For what other reasons (besides taking care of the children) do you think a woman—or a man, for that matter—might want or need to take a break from her or his career? List some of these reasons, and explain whether or not you find each reason valid.

6. Stabiner accuses some of the students in Story's survey of managing "to insult every mother in this country who needs to work." What do you think she means by this? Is she right?

A Marriage Agreement
Alix Kates Shulman

The subject may seem mundane, but housework remains a highly contentious issue between spouses. According to the National Healthy Marriage Resource Center, the issue of "housework and childcare" was among the top five sources of conflict between couples with new babies. A recent study found that married women continued to spend more than twice as much time on household chores as their husbands. Overall, married American women perform 70–80% of the total domestic work—regardless of their employment status. This gender gap persists even in the face of a professed willingness among husbands to share the burden. One study showed that men who claimed to support feminist ideals performed an average of only four minutes more housework per day than those who professed tradi-tional beliefs. Nor does a wife's relatively high income motivate her husband to increase his level of household support. Recent research indicates that in cases where women con-tribute more than half of the family's income, the more money she makes, the more housework she does—an average of five to six hours more each week. Many married women cite a willingness to help out more around the house as the main thing they would change about their husbands. Perhaps this explains why marital researchers have found that married men who perform more housework and child-care duties have better sex lives and happier marriages than those who don't.

Alix Kates Shulman's "A Marriage Agreement" is a famous document in the history of intra-marital labor negotiations. The piece was first published in 1970 in a feminist journal and subsequently reprinted as a cover story in Life *magazine, appearing as well in* Ms., New York Magazine, *and* Redbook. *In the "Agreement," Shulman argues that men and women should share housework equally and then proposes a novel (some would say drastic) measure to ensure that they do. When first published, the "Agreement" provoked heated responses from such writers as Norman Mailer and Joan Didion. It is now featured in the standard Harvard textbook on contract law.*

1   When my husband and I were first married, a decade ago, keeping house was less a burden than a game. We both worked full-time in New York City, so our small apartment stayed empty most of the day and taking care of it was very little trouble. Twice a month we'd spend Saturday cleaning and doing our laundry at the laundromat. We shopped for food together after work, and though I usually did the cooking, my husband was happy to help. Since our meals were simple and casual, there were few dishes to wash. We occasionally had dinner out and usually ate breakfast at a diner near our offices. We spent most of our free time doing things we enjoyed together, such as taking long walks in the evenings and spending weekends in Central Park. Our domestic life was beautifully uncomplicated.

2   When our son was born, our domestic life suddenly became *quite* complicated; and two years later, when our daughter was born, it became impossible. We automatically accepted the traditional sex roles that society assigns. My husband worked all day in an office; I left my job and stayed at home, taking on almost all the burdens of housekeeping and child raising.

3   When I was working I had grown used to seeing people during the day, to having a life outside the home. But now I was restricted to the company of two demanding preschoolers and to the four walls of an apartment. It seemed unfair that while my husband's life had changed little when the children were born, domestic life had become the only life I had.

4   I tried to cope with the demands of my new situation, assuming that other women were able to handle even larger families with ease and still find time for themselves. I couldn't seem to do that.

5   We had to move to another apartment to accommodate our larger family, and because of the children, keeping it reasonably neat took several hours a day. I prepared half a dozen meals every day for from one to four people at a time—and everyone ate different food. Shopping for this brood—or even just running out for a quart of milk—meant putting on snowsuits, boots and mittens; getting strollers or carriages up and down the stairs; and scheduling the trip so it would not interfere with one of the children's feeding or nap or illness or some other domestic job. Laundry was now a daily chore. I seemed to be working every minute of the day—and still there were dishes in the sink; still there wasn't time enough to do everything.

6   Even more burdensome than the physical work of housekeeping was the relentless responsibility I had for my children. I loved them, but they seemed to be taking over my life. There was nothing I could do, or even contemplate, without first considering how they would be affected. As they grew older, just answering their constant questions ruled out even a private mental life. I had once enjoyed reading, but now if there was a moment free, instead of reading for myself, I read to them. I wanted to work on my own writing, but there simply weren't enough hours in the day. I had no time for myself; the children were always *there*.

7   As my husband's job began keeping him at work later and later—and sometimes taking him out of town—I missed his help and companionship. I wished he would come home at six o'clock and spend time with the children so they could know him better. I continued to buy food with him in mind and dutifully set his place at the table. Yet sometimes whole weeks would go by without his having dinner with us. When he did get home the children often were asleep, and we both were too tired ourselves to do anything but sleep.

8   We accepted the demands of his work as unavoidable. Like most couples, we assumed that the wife must accommodate to the husband's schedule, since it is his work that brings in the money.

9   As the children grew older I began free-lance editing at home. I felt I had to squeeze it into my "free" time and not allow it to interfere with my domestic duties or the time I owed my husband—just as he felt he had to squeeze in time for the children during weekends. We were both chronically dissatisfied, but we knew no solutions.

10   After I had been home with the children for six years I began to attend meetings of the newly formed Women's Liberation Movement in New York City. At these meetings I began to see that my situation was not uncommon; other women too felt drained and frustrated as housewives and mothers. When we started to talk about how we would have chosen to arrange our lives, most of us agreed that even though we might have preferred something different, we had never felt we had a choice in the matter. We realized that we had slipped into full domestic responsibility simply as a matter of course, and it seemed unfair.

11   When I added them up, the chores I was responsible for amounted to a hectic 6 A.M.–9 P.M. (often later) job, without salary, breaks or vacation. No employer would be able to demand these hours legally, but most mothers take them for granted—as I did until I became a feminist.

12   For years mothers like me have acquiesced to the strain of the preschool years and endless household maintenance without any real choice. Why, I asked myself, should a couple's decision to have a family mean that the woman must immerse years of her life in their children? And why should men like my husband miss caring for and knowing their children?

13   Eventually, after an arduous examination of our situation, my husband and I decided that we no longer had to accept the sex roles that had turned us into a lame family. Out of equal parts love for each other and desperation at our situation, we decided to re-examine the patterns we had been living by, and starting again from scratch, to define our roles for ourselves.

14 We began by agreeing to share completely all responsibility for raising our children (by then aged five and seven) and caring for our household. If this new arrangement meant that my husband would have to change his job or that I would have to do more free-lance work or that we would have to live on a different scale, then we would. It would be worth it if it could make us once again equal, independent and loving as we had been when we were first married.

15 Simply agreeing verbally to share domestic duties didn't work, despite our best intentions. And when we tried to divide them "spontaneously," we ended up following the traditional patterns. Our old habits were too deep-rooted. So we sat down and drew up a formal agreement, acceptable to both of us, that clearly defined the responsibilities we each had.

16 It may sound a bit formal, but it has worked for us. Here it is:

Marriage Agreement

I. Principles

17 We reject the notion that the work which brings in more money is more valuable. The ability to earn more money is a privilege which must not be compounded by enabling the larger earner to buy out of his/her duties and put the burden either on the partner who earns less or on another person hired from outside.

18 We believe that each partner has an equal right to his/her own time, work, value, choices. As long as all duties are performed, each of us may use his/her extra time any way he/she chooses. If he/she wants to use it making money, fine. If he/she wants to spend it with spouse, fine. If not, fine.

19 As parents we believe we must share all responsibility for taking care of our children and home—not only the work but also the responsibility. At least during the first year of this agreement, *sharing responsibility* shall mean dividing the *jobs* and dividing the *time*.

20 In principle, jobs should be shared equally, 50-50, but deals may be made by mutual agreement. If jobs and schedule are divided on any other than a 50-50 basis, then at any time either party may call for a re-examination and redistribution of jobs or a revision of the schedule. Any deviation from 50-50 must be for the convenience of both parties. If one party works overtime in any domestic job, he/she must be compensated by equal extra work by the other. The schedule may be flexible, but changes must be formally agreed upon. The terms of this agreement are rights and duties, not privileges and favors.

II. Job Breakdown and Schedule

(A) Children

(1) Mornings: Waking children; getting their clothes out; making their lunches; seeing that they have notes, homework, money, bus passes, books; brushing their hair; giving them breakfast (making coffee for us). Every other week each parent does all.

(2) Transportation: Getting children to and from lessons, doctors, dentists (including making appointments), friends' houses, park, parties, movies,

libraries. Parts occurring between 3 and 6 P.M. fall to wife. She must be compensated by extra work from husband (see 10 below). Husband does all weekend transportation and pick-ups after 6.

(3) Help: Helping with homework, personal problems, projects like cooking, making gifts, experiments, planting; answering questions; explaining things. Parts occurring between 3 and 6 P.M. fall to wife. After 6 P.M. husband does Tuesday, Thursday and Sunday; wife does Monday, Wednesday and Saturday. Friday is free for whoever has done extra work during the week.

(4) Nighttime (after 6 P.M.): Getting children to take baths, brush their teeth, put away their toys and clothes, go to bed; reading with them; tucking them in and having nighttime talks; handling if they wake or call in the night. Husband does Tuesday, Thursday and Sunday. Wife does Monday, Wednesday and Saturday. Friday is split according to who has done extra work during the week.

(5) Baby sitters: Getting baby sitters (which sometimes takes an hour of phoning). Baby sitters must be called by the parent the sitter is to replace. If no sitter turns up, that parent must stay home.

(6) Sick care: Calling doctors; checking symptoms; getting prescriptions filled; remembering to give medicine; taking days off to stay home with sick child; providing special activities. This must still be worked out equally, since now wife seems to do it all. (The same goes for the now frequently declared school closings for so-called political protests, whereby the mayor gets credit at the expense of the mothers of young children. The mayor closes only the schools, not the places of business or the government offices.) In any case, wife must be compensated (see 10 below).

(7) Weekends: All usual child care, plus special activities (beach, park, zoo). Split equally. Husband is free all Saturday, wife is free all Sunday.

(B) Housework

(8) Cooking: Breakfast; dinner (children, parents, guests). Breakfasts during the week are divided equally; husband does all weekend breakfasts (including shopping for them and dishes). Wife does all dinners except Sunday nights. Husband does Sunday dinner and any other dinners on his nights of responsibility if wife isn't home. Whoever invites guests does shopping, cooking and dishes; if both invite them, split work.

(9) Shopping: Food for all meals, housewares, clothing and supplies for children. Divide by convenience. Generally, wife does local daily food shopping; husband does special shopping for supplies and children's things.

(10) Cleaning: Dishes daily; apartment weekly, biweekly or monthly. Husband does dishes Tuesday, Thursday and Sunday. Wife does Monday, Wednesday and Saturday. Friday is split according to who has done

extra work during week. Husband does all the house cleaning in exchange for wife's extra child care (3 to 6 daily) and sick care.

(11) Laundry: Home laundry, making beds, dry cleaning (take and pick up). Wife does home laundry. Husband does dry-cleaning delivery and pickup. Wife strips beds, husband remakes them.

21   Our agreement changed our lives. Surprisingly, once we had written it down, we had to refer to it only two or three times. But we still had to work to keep the old habits from intruding. If it was my husband's night to take care of the children, I had to be careful not to check up on how he was managing. And if the baby sitter didn't show up for him, I would have to remember it was *his* problem.

22   Eventually the agreement entered our heads, and now, after two successful years of following it, we find that our new roles come to us as readily as the old ones had. I willingly help my husband clean the apartment (knowing it is his responsibility) and he often helps me with the laundry or the meals. We work together and trade off duties with ease now that the responsibilities are truly shared. We each have less work, more hours together and less resentment.

23   Before we made our agreement I had never been able to find the time to finish even one book. Over the past two years I've written three children's books, a biography and a novel and edited a collection of writings (all will have been published by spring of 1972). Without our agreement I would never have been able to do this.

24   At present my husband works a regular 40-hour week, and I write at home during the six hours the children are in school. He earns more money now than I do, so his salary covers more of our expenses than the money I make with my free-lance work. But if either of us should change jobs, working hours or income, we would probably adjust our agreement.

25   Perhaps the best testimonial of all to our marriage agreement is the change that has taken place in our family life. One day after it had been in effect for only four months our daughter said to my husband, "You know, Daddy, I used to love Mommy more than you, but now I love you both the same."

Review Questions

1. What "notion" does the "Agreement," in its first paragraph, explicitly reject? What does the "Agreement" call the "ability to earn more money"?

2. According to the "Agreement," what does shared responsibility mean, in terms of taking care of the children and the home?

3. If one party works overtime in any domestic job, according to the "Agreement," what must the other party do?

4. Who is responsible for all of the housecleaning, according to the "Agreement"? What reason is given for this provision?

Discussion and Writing Suggestions

1. In an article published in *The Atlantic Monthly*, Caitlin Flanagan writes that Shulman's "marriage agreement virtually demanded to be ridiculed." Do you agree? For example, is the agreement itself a ridiculous idea, or are some of its specific provisions ridiculous? Explain your responses.

2. Describe your own reaction upon reading the paragraph beginning, "Even more burdensome than the physical work of housekeeping was the relentless responsibility I had for my children."

3. The "Agreement" states that the larger earner in a family is not entitled to "buy out" of the housework duties. Describe your reaction to the priorities implied by this statement. To what extent do you believe that earning money can or should be separated from household duties?

4. Describing how she and her husband had to "keep the old habits from intruding," Shulman writes that she had to be careful not to check up on him to see how he was managing, and to remember that if the sitter didn't show up, it was his problem. To what "old habit" do you think she is referring? Why do you think Shulman uses the word "habit," rather than, for example, *trait?*

5. In her article "How Serfdom Saved the Women's Movement," Caitlin Flanagan describes the circumstances surrounding "A Marriage Agreement": Shulman's marriage was troubled and eventually ended in divorce. To what extent does this knowledge change your perception of "A Marriage Agreement"?

6. Write an "Agreement" that explicitly regulates your relationship with another person (or persons) in your life. This may be a personal, business, or educational relationship. What would be the advantages and disadvantages of having such an agreement govern the relationship?

7. Note that the "Agreement" provides for the husband and wife to alternate days on which each is responsible for helping their children with "personal problems." Try the following creative writing exercise: In a brief paragraph, write from the point of view of a 7-year-old child living in such a family. Describe what it is like to have parents who have made such an arrangement and your feelings about the "Agreement."

**The Myth of Co-Parenting:
How It Was Supposed to Be. How It Was.**
Hope Edelman

The previous selections in the chapter (Hekker excepted) have dealt with issues of modern marriage from a journalistic, scholarly, or activist viewpoint. In the following two essays, two professional writers—a woman and a man—offer personal perspectives on their own marriages. You are already familiar with some of the issues they will discuss. What is distinctive about these selections is their tone: The writing is by turns raw, wounded, angry, and defensive and offers an unflinchingly honest, if brutal, assessment of each writer's marriage. These essays strikingly reveal the miscommunication and resentment that can afflict even mature, thoughtful, dedicated couples. In the first, Hope Edelman describes the disillusionment and anger she felt when, after the birth of their child, her husband immersed himself in his career, leaving her to run their household alone.

Hope Edelman has written three nonfiction books, including Motherless Daughters *(1995). Her essays and articles have appeared in the* New York Times, *the* Chicago Tribune, *the* San Francisco Chronicle, *and* Seventeen *magazine. She lives with her husband and two children in Los Angeles. This essay was written for the anthology* The Bitch in the House *(2002).*

1   Throughout much of 1999 and 2000, my husband spent quite a lot of time at work. By "quite a lot" I mean the kind of time Fermilab scientists spent trying to split the atom, which is to say, every waking moment. The unofficial count one week came in at ninety-two hours, which didn't include cell phone calls answered on grocery checkout lines or middle-of-the-night brainstorms that had to be e-mailed before dawn. Often I would wake at 3:00 A.M. and find him editing a business plan down in the living room, drinking herbal tea in front of his laptop's ethereal glow. If he had been a lawyer tallying billable hours, he would have made some firm stinking rich.

2   He was launching an Internet company back then, and these were the kind of hours most people in his industry were putting in. Phrases like "window of opportunity" and "ensuring our long-term security" were bandied about our house a lot, usually during the kind of exasperating late-night conversations that began with "The red-eye to New York? *Again?*" and included "I mean, it's not like you're trying to find a cure for cancer," somewhere within. I was working nearly full-time myself, though it soon became clear this would have to end. Our daughter was a year and a half old, and the phrase "functionally orphaned" was also getting thrown around our house a lot, usually by me.

3   So as my husband's work hours exponentially increased, I started cutting back on mine. First a drop from thirty-five per week to twenty-five, and then a dwindle down to about eighteen. At first I didn't really mind. With the exception of six weeks postpartum, this was the first time since high school that I had a good excuse not to work like a maniac, and I was grateful for the break. Still, there was something more than vaguely unsettling about feeling that my choice hadn't been much of an actual choice. When one parent works ninety-two hours a week, the other one, by necessity, has to start picking up the slack. Otherwise, some fairly important things—like keeping the refrigerator stocked, or filing income taxes, or finding a reliable baby-sitter, not to mention giving a child some semblance of security and consistency around this place, for God's sake—won't get done. A lot of slack was starting to pile up around our house. And because I was the only parent spending any real time there, the primary de-slacker was me.

4   How did I feel about this? I don't mind saying. I was extremely pissed off.

5   Like virtually every woman friend I have, I entered marriage with the belief that co-parenting was an attainable goal. In truth, it was more of a vague assumption, a kind of imagined parity I had superimposed on the idea of marriage without ever really thinking it through. *If I'm going to contribute half of the income, then he'll contribute half of the housework and child care.* Like that. If you'd asked me to elaborate, I would have said something impassioned and emphatic, using terms like "shared responsibility" and "equal division of labor." The watered-down version of feminism I identified with espoused those catchphrases, and in lieu of a more sophisticated blueprint for domestic life, I co-opted the talk as my own. But really, I didn't know what I was talking about beyond the fact that I didn't want to be the dominant parent in the house.

6   When I was growing up in suburban New York, my mother seemed to do everything. *Everything.* Carpooling, haircuts, vet appointments, ice cream cakes, dinners in the Crock-Pot, book-report dioramas—the whole roll call for a housewife of the 1960s and 1970s. My father, from my child's point of view, did three things. He came home from work in time for dinner. He sat at the kitchen table once a month and paid the bills. And, on weekend trips, he drove the car. Certainly he did much more than that, including earn all of our family's income, but my mother's omnipresence in our household meant that anyone else felt, well, incidental in comparison. The morning after she died, of breast cancer at forty-two, my younger siblings and I sat at the kitchen table with our father as dawn filtered through the yellow window shades. I looked at him sitting there, in a polo shirt and baseball cap, suddenly so small beneath his collapsed shoulders. I was barely seventeen. He was fifty-one. *Huh,* I thought. *Who are you?*

7   There were no chore charts taped to the refrigerator, no family powwows, no enthusiastic TV nannies suddenly materializing outside our front door. My father taught himself to use a microwave and I started driving my siblings for their haircuts and that, as they say, was that.

8   My cousin Lorraine, a devout Baha'i, once told me it doesn't matter how many orgasms a potential husband gives you; what really matters is the kind of father he'll be. At first I thought she said this because Baha'is disavow premarital sex, but the more men I dated, the more I realized Lorraine was right. Loyalty and devotion are undoubtedly better traits to have in a spouse than those fleeting moments of passion, though I can't deny the importance of the latter. When I met John, it was like winning the boyfriend jackpot. He was beautiful and sexy, and devoted and smart, *so* smart, and he had the kindest green eyes. The first time I saw those eyes, when I was negotiating an office sublease from him in New York, he smiled right at me and it happened, just the way you dream about when you're twelve: I knew this was someone I would love. *And* he wanted children, which immediately separated him from a cool three-quarters of the men I'd dated before. I was thirty-two when we started dating, and just becoming acutely aware that I didn't have unlimited time to wait.

9   What happened next happened fast. Within two years, John and I were parents and homeowners in a canyon outside Los Angeles. By then he was deep into the process of starting his own company, which left us with barely an hour to spend together at the end of each day. And even though I so badly

wanted him to succeed, to get the acclaim a smart, hardworking, honest person deserves—and even though I was grateful that his hard, honest work earned enough to support us both—well, let me put it bluntly. Back there when I was single and imagining the perfect partnership? This wasn't what I had in mind.

10   When John became so scarce around our house, I had to compensate by being utterly present in every way: as a kisser of boo-boos; a dispenser of discipline; an employer of baby-sitters; an assembler of child furniture; a scary-monster slayer, mortgage refinancer, reseeder of dying backyards. And that's before I even opened my office door for the day. Balancing act? I was the whole damn circus, all three rings.

11   It began to make me spitting mad, the way the daily duties of parenting and home ownership started to rest entirely on me. It wasn't even the additional work I minded as much as the total responsibility for every decision made. The frustration I felt after researching and visiting six preschools during my so-called work hours, trying to do a thorough job for both of us, and then having John offhandedly say, "Just pick the one you like best." Or the irritation I felt when, after three weeks of weighing the options, I finally made the choice, and then he raised his eyebrows at the cost. *I didn't sign up for this!* I began shouting at my sister over the phone.

12   How does it happen, I wondered both then and now, that even today, in this post–second wave, post-superwoman, dual-income society we're supposed to live in, the mother nearly always becomes the primary parent, even when she, too, works full-time—the one who meets most or all of the children's and the household's minute-by-minute needs? We start out with such grand intentions for sharing the job, yet ultimately how many fathers handle the dental appointments, shop for school clothes, or shuttle pets to and from the vet? Nine times out of ten, it's still the mother who plans and emcees the birthday parties, the mother who cuts the meeting short when the school nurse calls. Women have known about this Second Shift for years, the way the workday so often starts up again for women when they walk through the door at the end of the *other* workday—a time mandated perhaps by the baby-sitter's deadline, but also by their own guilt, sense of responsibility, tendency to prioritize their husband's job first, or a combination of all three. Still, I—like many other enlightened, equality-oriented women having babies in this era—had naïvely thought that a pro-feminist partner, plus my own sheer will power, would prevent this from happening to me. I hadn't bargained for how deeply the gender roles of "nurturer" and "provider" are ingrained in us all, or—no matter how much I love being a mother to my daughter—how much I would grow to resent them.

13   When it became clear that my husband and I were not achieving the kind of co-parenting I'd so badly wanted us to achieve, I felt duped and infuriated and frustrated and, beneath it all, terribly, impossibly sad. Sad for myself, and sad for my daughter, who—just like me as a child—had so little one-on-one time with her father. No matter how sincerely John and I tried to buck convention, no matter how often I was the one who sat down at the kitchen table to pay the bills, there we were: he absorbed in his own world of work, me consumed by mine at home. My parents all over again.

14 The intensity of John's workplace was, originally, supposed to last for six months, then for another six months, then for only about three months more. But there was always some obstacle on the horizon: first-round funding, second-round funding, hirings, firings, had to train a sales force, had to meet a new goal. And meetings, all those meetings. Seven in the morning, nine at night. How were all those other dot-com wives managing?

15 There was no time together for anything other than the most pragmatic exchanges. When he walked through the door at 10:00 P.M., I'd lunge at him with paint chips to approve, or insurance forms to sign, or leaks to examine before I called the plumber first thing in the morning. Fourteen hours of conversation compressed into twenty highly utilitarian minutes before we fell, exhausted, into bed. A healthy domestic situation, it was not.

16 I was angry with the kind of anger that had nothing to do with rationality. A lot of the time, I was mad at Gloria Steinem for having raised women's expectations when I was just a toddler—but at least she lived by her principles, marrying late and never trying to raise kids; so then I got mad at Betty Friedan for having started it all with *The Feminine Mystique*, and when that wasn't satisfying enough, I got mad at all the women in my feminist criticism class in graduate school, the ones who'd sat there and so smugly claimed it was impossible for a strong-willed woman to ever have an equal partnership with a man. Because it was starting to look as if they'd been right.

17 But mostly I was mad at John, because he'd never actually sat down with me to say, "This is what starting a dot-com company will involve," or even, "I'd like to do this—what do you think?"—the way I imagine I would have with him before taking on such a demanding project (which, of course, we'd then have realized together was not feasible unless he quit his job or cut back dramatically, which—of course—was out of the question). Legitimate or not, I felt that at least partly because he was "the husband" and his earning power currently eclipsed mine, his career took precedence, and I had to pick up the household slack, to the detriment of my own waning career—or in addition to it. Before our marriage, I had never expected that. I don't remember the conversation where I asked him to support me financially in exchange for me doing everything else. In fact, I'd never wanted that and still decidedly didn't. I was not only happy to put in my portion of the income (though it would inevitably be less than usual during any year I birthed and breast-fed an infant), I expected to and *wanted* to contribute as much as I could: Part of who I was—what defined me and constituted a main source of my happiness and vitality—was my longtime writing and teaching career. I didn't want to give it up, but I also didn't want hired professionals running my household and raising my child. It felt like an impossible catch-22.

18 Face-to-face, John and I didn't give ultimatums. At first, we didn't even argue much out loud. Instead we engaged in a kind of low-level quibbling where the stakes were comfortably low. Little digs that didn't mean much in isolation but eventually started to add up. Like bickering about whose fault it was we never took vacations. (He said mine, I said his.) And whether we should buy our daughter a swing set. (I said yes, he said not now.) And about who forgot to roll the trash cans to the bottom of the driveway, again. (Usually him.)

19   I'd been through therapy. I knew the spiel. How you were supposed to say, "When you're gone all the time, it makes me feel angry and resentful and lonely," instead of, "How much longer do you realistically think I'm going to put up with this crap?" I tried that first approach, and there was something to it, I admit. John listened respectfully. He asked what he could do to improve. Then it was his turn. He told me how he'd begun to feel like a punching bag in our home. How my moods ruled our household, how sometimes he felt like wilting when he heard that sharp edge in my voice. Then he said he was sorry and I said I was sorry, and he said he'd try to be home more and I said I'd try to lighten up. And this would work, for a while. Until the night John would say he'd be home at eight to put Maya to bed but would forget to call about the last-minute staff meeting that started at six, and when he'd walk through the door at ten I'd be too pissed off to even say hello. Instead, I'd snap, "How much longer do you realistically think I'm going to put up with this crap?" And the night would devolve from there.

20   Neither of us was "wrong." Neither was completely right. The culpability was shared. Both of us were stuck together on that crazy carousel, where the more time John spent away from home, the more pissed off I got, and the more pissed off I got, the less he wanted to be around.

21 One day I said fuck it, and I took John's credit card and bought a swing set. Not one of those fancy redwood kinds that look like a piece of the Alamo, but a sturdy wood one nonetheless with a tree house at the top of the slide, and I paid for delivery and assembly, too. On the way home I stopped at one of those places that sell the fancy redwood kind and ordered a playground-quality bucket swing for another seventy bucks.

22   Fuck it.

23   There were other purchases I'd made like this, without John's involvement— the silk bedroom curtains, the Kate Spade wallet I didn't really need—each one thrilling me with a momentary, devilish glee. But the swing set: the swing set was my gutsiest act of rebellion thus far. Still, when it was fully installed on our side lawn, the cloth roof of the tree house gently flapping in the breeze, I felt oddly unfulfilled. Because, after all, what had I really achieved? My daughter had a swing set, but I was still standing on the grass by myself, furiously poking at gopher holes with my foot, thinking about whether I'd have time on Thursday to reseed the lawn alone. When what I really wanted was for my husband to say, "Honey, let me help you with that reseeding, and then we'll all three go out for dinner together." I just wanted him to come home, to share with me—and Maya—all the joys and frustrations and responsibilities of domestic life.

24   On bad days, when the baby-sitter canceled or another short-notice business trip had just been announced, he would plead with me to hire a full-time nanny—we'd cut corners elsewhere, we'd go into savings, whatever it took, he said. I didn't want to hear it. "I don't need a nanny, I need a husband!" I shouted. Didn't he understand? My plan hadn't been to hire someone to raise our child. My plan had been to do it together: two responsible parents with two fulfilling jobs, in an egalitarian marriage with a well-adjusted kid who was equally bonded to us both.

25 In writing class I tell my students there are just two basic human motivators: desire and fear. Every decision we make, every action we take, springs from this divided well. Some characters are ruled by desire. Others are ruled by fear. So what was my story during the year and a half that John spent so much time at work? He claimed that I was fear-driven, that I was threatened by the loss of control, which may in fact have been true. When I try to dissect my behavior then, reaching beneath all the months of anger and complaints, I do find fear: the fear that I'd never find a way to balance work and family life without constantly compromising one, the other, or both. But mostly what I find is desire. For my daughter to have a close relationship with her father, for my husband to have more time to spend with me, for me to find a way to have some control over my time, even with a husband and a child factored into the mix. And then there was the big one: for my husband to fulfill the promise I felt he made to me on our wedding day, which was to be my partner at home and in life. Somewhere along the way, we'd stopped feeling like a team, and I wanted that fellowship back.

26   I wish, if only to inject a flashy turning point into this story right about now, that I could say some climactic event occurred from which we emerged dazed yet transformed, or that one of us delivered an ultimatum the other couldn't ignore and our commitment to each other was then renewed. But in reality, the way we resolved all this was gradual, and—in retrospect—surprisingly simple. John got the company stabilized and, as he'd promised, finally started working fewer hours. And I, knowing he would be home that much more, slowly started adding hours to my workday. With the additional income, we hired a live-in nanny, who took over much of the housework as well. And then, a few months after Francis arrived, Maya started preschool two mornings a week. Those became blessed writing hours for me, time when I was fully released of the guilt of paying others to watch my child. Between 9:00 A.M. and 12:30 P.M. Maya was exactly where she was supposed to be and, within that time frame, so was I.

27   With Francis came an additional benefit: a baby-sitter on Friday nights. For the first time since Maya's birth, John and I had a set night each week to devote to each other, and as we split combination sushi plates and did side-by-side chatarangas in a 6:00 P.M. yoga class, we began to slowly build upon the foundation we'd laid with our marriage—and, thankfully, even in the darkest months, we'd always trusted hadn't disappeared. Yes, there were still some Friday nights when I watched TV alone because John was flying back from New York, and other Fridays when I had to sit late in front of the computer to meet a deadline. And there were some weekend days when John still had to take meetings, though they became fewer and fewer over time.

28 It has taken real effort for me to release the dream of completely equal co-parenting, or at least to accept that we may not be the family to make it real. We're still quite a distance from that goal, and even further when you factor in the amount of household support we now have. Does John do 50 percent of the remaining child care? No. But neither do I contribute 50 percent of the income, as I once did. Ours is still an imbalanced relationship in some ways, but imbalance I've learned to live with—especially after the extreme inequity we once had.

29   What really matters now—more than everything being absolutely equal, more than either my husband or me "striking it rich"—is that John is home before Maya's bedtime almost every night now to join the pileup on her bed, and that we took our first real family vacation last December. This is the essence of what I longed for during those bleak, angry months of my daughter's first two years. It was a desire almost embarrassing in its simplicity, yet one so strong that, in one of the greatest paradoxes of my marriage, it might have torn my husband and me apart: the desire to love and be loved, with reciprocity and conviction, with fairness and respect; the desire to capture that elusive animal we all grow up believing marriage is, and never stop wanting it to be.

Discussion and Writing Questions

1. Reread paragraph 5, which begins, "Like virtually every woman friend I have." To what extent does this paragraph describe your own expectations regarding coparenting with your (eventual) spouse? To what extent has reading about an experience such as Edelman's caused you to adjust these expectations? Explain.

2. In a brief paragraph, describe the parenting roles played by your own parents when you were growing up. How much of the parenting did your mother perform? Your father? What were your feelings about this parenting arrangement then, and what are your feelings now? How likely is it that your parents' example will affect your own expectations of your husband or wife, when you are married and attempting to divide household responsibilities between yourself and your spouse?

3. Edelman writes that even though she wanted her husband to succeed and was glad for the money he was making, she couldn't escape the feeling that the life she was living "wasn't what [she] had in mind" when she had been single and "imagining the perfect partnership." In a brief paragraph, describe your own "perfect partnership" with a spouse. Be sure to take into account the "reality check" that essays such as Edelman's (and Shulman's) provide—that is, it's probably unrealistic to imagine a high-earning spouse who is also able to perform at least half of the housework and child-raising duties.

4. Edelman writes, "I hadn't bargained for how deeply the gender roles of 'nurturer' and 'provider' are ingrained in us all." To what extent do you agree that the kinds of division-of-household-labor problems Edelman describes stem from ingrained gender roles? In responding, draw upon your own experiences and observations.

5. Edelman writes: "Neither of us was 'wrong.' Neither was completely right." Do you agree? Explain your response.

6. Edelman explains that her problem was eventually solved when, among other things, she and her husband hired a nanny. However, elsewhere in the essay Edelman describes her resistance to the idea of hiring professional help. Describe your reaction to her (presumed) compromise. To what extent do you feel it was a betrayal of her ideals? To what extent do you feel it was the right thing to do in her situation?

7. *For men only:* Write a response to Edelman's essay, as if you were her husband.

My Problem with Her Anger
Eric Bartels

In the previous selection, Hope Edelman describes how her husband's absence made her feel "angry and resentful and lonely." In the following essay, Eric Bartels writes about what it is like to be on the receiving end of such spousal anger. Eric Bartels is a feature writer for the Portland Tribune *in Portland, Oregon, where he lives with his wife and two children. This is a revised version of the essay by this title that appeared in* The Bastard on the Couch: 27 Men Try Really Hard to Explain Their Feelings About Love, Loss, Fatherhood, and Freedom *(2004), an anthology edited by Daniel Jones.*

1   My wife and kids were sleeping when I finished the dishes the other night, shook the water off my hands and smudged them dry with one of the grimy towels hanging on the door to the oven. I gave the kitchen floor a quick sweep, clearing it of all but the gossamer tufts of cat hair that always jet away from the broom as if under power.

2   I turned to shut the lights, but then I noticed the two metal grills I had left to soak in the basin. They're the detachable, (cast iron type) (stove-top kind) that we occasionally use to affect a kind of indoor, open-flame cooking experience. Submerging them in water for awhile makes it easier to remove the carbonized juices and bits of flesh that get welded on during use. It's a good, sensible way to save labor.

3   The problem was that they'd been in the sink for several days now. And then it occurred to me: What I was staring at was the dark heart of the divide between men and women.

4   It's unlikely I was any less harried or less tired the previous few nights as I went about my kitchen duties, a responsibility that has fallen to me more or less exclusively of late. No, my energy level is fairly constant—that is to say depleted—at that particular point of just about any day. I could, and probably should have finished the grill-cleaning project sooner. Just as I should make the bed every morning instead of occasionally. Just as I should always throw my underwear into the hamper before showering, rather than leaving them on top of it, or on the floor next to it.

5   These are the things men do that quietly annoy the living shit out of a woman. Until she becomes a mother. Then they inspire a level of fury unlike anything she has ever experienced. And that fury won't be kept secret. On the receiving end, the husband will be left to wonder why the punishment is so wildly out of line with the crime. This is the kind of vitriol that should be reserved for lying politicians, corporate greed and hitters who don't take a pitch when their team trails in the late innings—not a dedicated marriage partner with garden-variety human foibles.

6   Yet here we are, my wife and me. We're both good people. We have lots of friends. We make a decent living at relatively satisfying professional jobs: She, half-time at a small advertising firm; I, as a newspaper writer. And we're dedicated, attentive parents to a six-year old daughter and a two-year old son.

7   We don't use profanity in front of the children, unless we're arguing angrily. We don't talk to each other disrespectfully, except when arguing angrily. And we don't say bad things about each other to the kids, unless, of course, we just finished arguing angrily.

8   I know my wife's life is hard. She spends more time with the kids than I do and is almost completely responsible for running them around to day care and school. I contribute regularly and earnestly to the shopping, cooking and cleaning, but a fair amount of it still falls to her. And her job, although part-time for the last six years, presents her with Hell's own revolving door of guilt over neglecting her work for kids and vice versa.

9   I work hard to take pressure off her and have given up some freedoms myself since our first child was born: time with friends, regular pickup basketball games, beer. And I honestly don't mind living without these things. What gets me, though, is how little credit I get for the effort. My wife gets tired. She gets frustrated. She gets angry. And she seems to want to take it out on me.

10   Then logic starts moving backward in an ugly zigzag pattern. If, in her mind, my shortcomings provide the justification for her anger, then the perception of my behavior must be groomed like the playing field of a game I can't seem to win. The things I do that don't conform to my new loser image—and to think this woman once thought I was cooler than sliced bread—don't even show up on the scoreboard. Until, finally, nothing I do is right.

11   My efforts to organize the contents of the armoire one day—a project she had suggested—led to a screaming fight. The clutter I was planning to move to the basement would just create more junk down there, she said. But we hardly use the basement, I thought, and besides, why couldn't we just make another, separate project of sorting out the basement later? Doesn't it solve the more pressing armoire problem in the meantime? Isn't that logical?

12   Evidently not.

13   One night she stomped into the kitchen as I was cleaning up after a dinner that I may well have cooked and served and announced in angry tones that she needed more help getting the kids ready for bed than I had been providing, as if she had just found me drinking beer and playing video games. Isn't that something we could discuss rationally, I asked her, when we're not both right in the middle of our respective (unpleasant) (demanding) nightly routines?

14   It didn't occur to her, I guess.

15 And a few nights later, after bathing the kids in succession, putting them in their pajamas and feeding them their vitamins, I was rocking our son to sleep when I heard my wife approach. I think she had been downstairs doing laundry. She walks into the bathroom and scornfully asks no one in particular "Why is there still water in the bathtub?"

16 I missed it.

17 I make a nice dinner after a long day at work, broiled pork chops with steamed zuccini, perhaps, and she asks why I made rice instead of pasta. At the grocery store, I try to buy food that's somewhere between not entirely toxic and prohibitively expensive, but I often disappoint her. I wash clothes the wrong way, not separating them properly by color. I spend too much time rinsing off dishes before loading them into the dishwasher.

18 If this is my castle, it is under siege. From within.

19 At times, the negativity threatens to grind my spirit into dust. I make it through an arduous week, gleeful to have it behind me, only to come home to the sound of her loudly and impatiently scolding our son for standing on a chair or turning on the TV or dumping his cheese puffs on the floor, exactly the stuff two-year old boys are supposed to do. Okay, children need to learn "no," and my wife does a lot of the teaching, but I'm certain there's a gentler way to pronounce the word.

20 I try to make this point calmly, and when that doesn't work, I make it more forcefully. Then we fight, until the (shame and) futility of that leaves me feeling deflated and distant, in a place where passion of any kind has slipped into a coma. And then it's time to start all over.

21 At times I watch my wife's mercury rise steadily, predictably to that point where she lashes out, almost as if she wanted to get there. I tell her, in the quietest, most reasonable tone I can manage, to please relax. Choose: "(You, Your Daughter, Your Son) did/did not do (this, that, the other)," she replies, her ire mounting. But, I think to myself, I didn't ask her what she's angry about, I asked her to stay calm. Aren't those different things?

22 I think it's fairly well established by now that marriage is a challenge, a creaky, old institution that may not have fully adapted itself to modern life, one that now fails in this country more often than not. Put children in the picture and you have an exponentially higher degree of difficulty.

23 Motherhood asks the modern woman, who has grown up seeing professional success as hers for the taking, to add the loss of a linear career path to an already considerable burden: child rearing, body issues, a shifting self-image and a husband who fell off his white horse long, long ago. I suppose this would make anyone angry.

24 Perhaps for women of recent generations, anger has replaced the quiet desperation of the past. That seems like a healthy development to me. But that doesn't mean there aren't several good reasons why, having seen the frustrated, angry, resentful place that the demands of modern motherhood will almost certainly take them, women shouldn't take the next logical, evolutionary step.

25 It seems to me that a woman should now focus only secondarily on what the world, and more specifically, her partner can do for her during the challenging early years of child rearing. She must now truly empower herself by turning to

the more important issue: Controlling the monstrous effects that motherhood can have on her own emotional landscape.

26   In other words, buck up.

27   For better or worse, men don't experience life the way women do. Absent the degree of intuition and empathy that seem an integral (natural) part of a woman's nurturing instinct, men grow up in a simpler milieu in which challenges are to be quickly surmounted, without a great deal of fanfare. Something breaks, you fix it and move on. (But don't throw it out, it could come in handy at some point.)

28   It's not a mindset that lends itself to a great deal of introspection and deep thought. That's not to say that women can't fix things or that men are shallow-minded. These (just seem like) are philosophical tendencies propelled by disparate biological imperatives. The result in men is an inclination not to worry about things before they happen. This imbues them with a confidence that, however vexing a problem might seem, it can and will be resolved.

29   I don't think most women share this confidence. A friend of mine says that everything in a woman's world starts with fear. Everything becomes tied in some way to fears of disapproval and abandonment and loss of control and God knows what else. To make matters worse, a man's more measured response to (in) certain situations is likely to suggest to his wife that he is not sufficiently engaged. Indifferent. Oblivious.

30   Am I the only guy who feels like he forever stands accused of not understanding the pressures my wife is under? That I can't possibly fathom her frustrations? After all, what would a man know about controlling his impulses?

31   What would he know? I like that one. Remember, we're talking about men here, the people with the built-in testosterone factory. The ones whose favorite childhood entertainments run to breaking windows, starting fires and dismembering small animals. The ones who instantly want to know if their first car will do 100 mph. The ones who attend beery high school parties with the goal of getting laid, but who'll settle for a good fistfight. Women should be eager to learn what most men know about managing anger.

32   For many years, I made a living as a bartender. I was good at it and loved the challenge of having to nimbly beat back the surging, immediate gallery of tasks that a big crowd and a busy night present. But it's a job where things go wrong pretty much constantly and I would occasionally lose my cool, kicking a cooler door closed or angrily sending an empty bottle smashing into a bin with an ear-splitting explosion. I imagined I was just blowing off a little steam.

33   I didn't know what I was really doing until I was a patron at someone else's bar one night. I watched a bartender momentarily capture everyone's attention with a loud fit of pique and realized quickly that witnesses saw the whole thing as landing somewhere between laughable and pathetic. We didn't care what was bothering him. We were having drinks and a good time. Too bad he wasn't enjoying the evening himself.

34   Was the guy under a lot of pressure? Yes. Was he being vexed by all manner of impediments to his ability to do his job? Almost certainly. Did anybody care? No.

35   I did a lot less kicking doors and throwing things after that.

36   Of course I care about my wife's happiness. Whether we're bothered by the same things or react to challenges the same way is irrelevant. She is my partner and I love her. We have important things to do together. The life we've built depends heavily on her ability to find contentment.

37   But she's not the only one in the family who has tough days. I have my own stuff to deal with and so do our kids, young as they are. When my wife decides it's okay to look darkly at her self or the day she's having, she's giving herself permission to ignore what's going on in other's lives. However little she regards the obligations and pressures of my existence, the fact is that I have some less than radiant days myself.

38   Women could try to accept that it is theoretically possible for a man to be tired, feel stress and even need a bit of emotional support himself. The children can certainly provide a lift, but they are also notoriously inconsistent about refraining from imperfect, untimely behaviors: talking in loud, excited voices, soiling themselves and moving at high speed in close proximity to valued objects and unforgiving hardwood furniture.

39   An overworked wife is certainly within her rights, as ever, to express her concerns and wishes at these moments. But that is not the same as a bilious, ill-timed attack that suggests her husband, through arrogance and selfishness, knows absolutely nothing of the realities of her world. In fact, he probably has a pretty good idea. He's probably even willing to meet any reasonable request to help. He'd just like it if someone would ask him nicely.

40   I'm amazed at how willing my wife is to push my buttons sometimes. And it's not like she's unfamiliar with the instrument panel. She evidently hasn't noticed that I occasionally ignite like dry kindling.

41   I should probably admit about now that I'm not always a model of decorum. I'm a personable, intelligent guy, but I'm not one of those wise, super-evolved aliens with the massive cranium from science fiction. I've said unkind things to people. I've thrown elbows on the basketball court. Gripped by paroxysmic anger, I've sent any number of small appliances to the promised land. And I do like to win. But this is about not fighting.

42   Anyone who's ever watched a young child's face crumple in fear and bewilderment as parents unleash their anger, in any direction, knows instantly what the stakes are. Parents do not need the toxic stew of anger coursing through them while in charge of small, impressionable children. And partners who are struggling to remember what particular disease of the brain led to their union won't be helped back to the right path by the rotating wheel of frustration, resentment and blame.

43   I fear that when anger is allowed to manifest itself regularly, it becomes less and less necessary to question its origins. No need to examine it, no need to work backward in the hope of identifying and defusing the triggers to the fast-replicating chain of events. And what is the hope of altering a behavior if you don't know where it came from and never see it coming?

44   It baffles me that someone of my wife's intelligence would shout at our son to stop yelling or demand in a voice twisted with exasperation that our daughter

stop whining. Can't she see what she's doing? It's like hitting someone to curb his or her violent tendencies. Of course I understand her frustration. But to let the expression of that frustration take any form, however inappropriate or unproductive, is indefensible.

45   Anger can spread quickly and I don't want us to poison the house where our kids are growing up. I don't know for a fact that whiney, self-centered children are always the product of undisciplined, self-indulgent parents, but what reasonable person would want to take that chance? Isn't a bit of restraint a rather small price to pay?

46   Anger is not power. Managing anger is power. A good friend of many years, with whom I've had many passionate debates on all manner of issues, used to tell me how his father would sit impassively during their own lively exchanges. His father, a university department head, would never lose his temper, never so much as raise his voice. I think I dismissed it as humanly impossible. My friend said it drove him crazy. But he is now an eloquent, engaging orator who runs a weekly literary discussion group out of his home. Then again, he also has two young sons and is divorced.

47   The level of discipline my friend learned from his father doesn't generally reside where my wife grew up. Individually, my in-laws are charming, intelligent, accomplished people. But together, they struggle mightily to break old habits. You can get one or another of them to acknowledge the familiar cycle of intolerance, blame and recrimination that often cripples their dealings with each other, but no one seems to have the will to fix it. As if the patience it would require would be seen as weakness.

48   My wife is the black sheep of that family. She has a quick mind, both analytical and imaginative. She has no love for convention and looks easily through hypocrisy of all kinds. She also has big-time Type A tendencies, character traits that make her the choice for many of the organizational and administrative duties in our shared life like paying bills and scheduling the kids' activities.

49   But these proclivities also work against her. The chaotic, unpredictable reality of having two small children threatens and at times overwhelms her compulsion for order. She breaks down. Traveling, with the on-the-fly time-management it requires, makes her crazy. I watched her walk face-first into a glass door at the airport. Another time, near the baggage carousel, she distractedly pushed our son's stroller into another child. The child was seated at the time. A pointless quarrel over a trip to the Home Depot led to her backing out of the driveway and into a parked mail truck one morning.

50   My wife and I need to fix this anger thing. We knew, or should have known, what we were getting into. We signed the contract. Shook on it. Kissed, actually. But I think we missed some of the small print. We wanted kids and had a vague idea that it would involve some work. Well, I have a news flash: It can be really, really hard.

51   And that goes for guys, too. I don't recall being told about spending more money each year than I actually earn, with no exotic vacations, nice cars or fancy anything else to show for it. I wasn't informed that I would give up golf

altogether, just as I was pushing my handicap down toward single digits. And I'm certain I was not warned that sex would become a rarer commodity than at any time in the thirty years since I learned to participate in it.

52   But I've gotten used to all that. I do what most men do. I take a deep breath and push ahead, fairly confident that if I can just soldier on, the things I've sacrificed and more will be my reward down the road.

53   I suppose the anger issues in our household loom as large as they do, in part, because of my fervor to confront (defeat) them. It's been a battlefield at times. My wife and I have been mean and fought dirty and we've hurt each other. We need to recognize that and make up our minds to change, no matter how much work it requires.

54   But hey, we're still here. Our children, who we love so dearly, are growing up and every day we can count on the reassuring rhythms of life: the sun rises in the morning, a weather system slips over the Oregon Cascades and blots it out, cats barf up hairballs on the carpet. I'm optimistic. I don't think we've done any permanent damage. I don't think it's anything we can't fix.

55   But that's just me.

Discussion and Writing Questions

1. Reflecting on his wife and other working mothers, Bartels concludes: "To truly empower herself, she will need to find a way to get beyond— on her own, with help, or however—the destructive impulses that the frustrations of modern motherhood can bring out in her." Your response?

2. Bartels suggests that women "of his generation" seem more comfortable expressing anger than women of previous generations did, and he attributes this, in part, to the fact that they have been in the workforce. To what extent do you find this explanation plausible? Explain your answer.

3. Bartels describes his failure to promptly clean the indoor grill, as well as a propensity for leaving dirty underwear on the floor, as typical "domestic lapses" common to men. To what extent does this square with your own observations of male behavior? To what extent do you feel, as Bartels implies, that such behavior cannot be modified?

4. Write a critique of Bartels's argument that, for the sake of their marriage and family, his wife needs to move past her "destructive impulses." Pay particular attention to the persuasive strategies he employs to support his thesis. Now respond to his argument. With which of his points do you agree, and with which do you disagree? State your overall conclusion as to the validity of the piece. Follow the principles in Chapter 2.

5. With the goal of suggesting a possible solution to the challenges Bartels and his wife face, evaluate his marriage according to one or more of the principles you have read about in previous selections. If Bartels's grievances are to be assuaged, to what extent do he and his wife need to fundamentally reexamine their assumptions regarding, say, the household division of labor? How much of that change should be Bartels's? How much his wife's?

6. *For women only:* Write a response to Bartels, as if you were his wife.

SYNTHESIS ACTIVITIES

1. Write an explanatory synthesis focused on the development of the "love match" model of marriage. Why did it emerge? When? How does it differ from previous models? Explain the effect of the rise of the "love match" model on the institution of marriage as a whole. Focus particularly on the effect this model has had on people's expectations of marriage and on who should get married. For your sources, draw upon Graham (in Chapter 1, pages 8–11), Coontz, Popenoe and Whitehead, Schwartz and Scott, Sullivan, Edelman, and Bartels. *An option:* As part of an extended conclusion that might be as long as a third of the final paper, explore the role you expect (hope?) love to play in your own marriage. So that your conclusion remains a part of the overall synthesis, let your exploration emerge from your awareness of the historical determinants of the love match. You now know that there have been other models for marriage—the "economic" match, for instance, or the "compatibility" match. As you contemplate your own (prospective) marriage, to what extent will you insist on a love match?

2. Explain the working mother versus stay-at-home mother debate. Focus in particular on the struggles women face as they try to balance the concerns of work versus family. You may also wish to touch upon the issue of housework, as the two issues sometimes overlap. Because this is an *explanatory* synthesis, make sure that your explanation of the varying viewpoints remains objective. Draw primarily upon the selections by Hekker, Story, Stabiner, Shulman, and Edelman (as well as Bartels, if you find it relevant).

3. Argue that one parent should—or should not—stop working (at least for a time) when children are born. In formulating your argument, be sure to acknowledge the various arguments on all sides of the issue. Then assert which course of action, overall, would best benefit American families. Draw upon as many of the articles in this chapter as will support your case.

4. Devise a blueprint for contemporary wives and husbands to avoid (or at least effectively address) common marital conflicts. First explain elements of your blueprint and then argue for its viability. For example, first explain how best to take care of the children when both parents must work or prefer to work. Then argue that your plan is reasonable. You could do the same for devising a fair division of household labor. In developing this combination explanatory/argument synthesis, consult such sources as Coontz, Popenoe and Whitehead, Story, Stabiner, Shulman, Edelman, and Bartels.

5. To what extent is it a good idea for young people to delay getting married until their late twenties or beyond? In supporting your argument for earlier or later marriage, draw upon such sources as Popenoe and Whitehead, Story, Stabiner, Edelman, and Bartels.

6. Compare and contrast Terry Martin Hekker's first essay, on the satisfactions of being a stay-at-home mother, with the Edelman and Shulman selections. How does each of these women feel about her married and family lives? As points of comparison and contrast, consider their attitudes toward housework, their children, their husbands, and their desire for self-fulfillment. In writing your conclusion, consider what factors might have been responsible for these women's differing views on these matters.

7. Analyze a marital relationship—real or fictional—using one or more of the principles in articles from the chapter. (If you have read any Jane Austen novels or Leo Tolstoy's *Anna Karenina* or Gustave Flaubert's *Madame Bovary,* you may wish to use the marriages of characters in those books.) Focus on how the principle you have chosen allows one to better understand the relationship in question. Follow the general format for writing analyses discussed in Chapter 4.

8. Compare and contrast Sullivan's and Bennett's arguments on gay marriage. In particular, focus on the assumptions regarding the nature of marriage that each brings to his argument. (You may want to consider how Sullivan's argument follows from a principle found in the selection by Coontz.)

9. Discuss whether or not, as Eric Bartels writes, "marriage is a creaky, old institution that may not have fully adapted itself to modern life." In supporting your argument, draw upon Hekker, Coontz, Popenoe and Whitehead, Schwartz and Scott, Edelman, Bartels, and any of the other selections you think relevant. Follow the general format for writing argument syntheses in Chapter 3.

10. Conduct an analysis of a bridal or newlywed magazine, movie, or television show, guided by a principle you select from one or more selections in this chapter. Use this analytical principle to understand more clearly how popular culture, as expressed

in the magazine, movie, or television show you have selected, helps to form, reinforce, or (perhaps) undermine our expectations of marriage. Follow the guidelines in Chapter 4 for writing your analysis.

11. Alix Kates Shulman's "A Marriage Agreement" applies legal language to an intimate domestic issue, creating a juxtaposition that some readers find jarring. Argue that it is appropriate—or inappropriate (perhaps even wildly so)—to expect that a marriage could/should be governed by such a document. For your sources, draw upon Hekker, Edelman, and Bartels.

12. Offer—and explain—the one piece of advice that you would give to someone who is about to get married. In supporting your argument that this is the single most important advice that anybody who is getting married should follow, draw from among the following selections: Hekker, Coontz, Popenoe and Whitehead, Schwartz and Scott, Story, Stabiner, Edelman, and Bartels.

RESEARCH ACTIVITIES

1. The *New York Times* article "Many Women at Elite Colleges Set Career Path to Motherhood" inspired the response "Homeward Bound," by Linda Hirshman in *American Prospect* (December 2005). Hirshman argues that, for the good of all women and society in general, every mother should work. Compare and contrast Hirshman's article with the Story and Stabiner selections.

2. Do an Internet search, using Google or another search engine, for reaction to the Terry Martin Hekker 2006 essay "Paradise Lost (Domestic Division)." Locate mentions of the piece on blogs (try sites dealing with the "Mommy Wars," working mothers, or stay-at-home mothers), in letters to the editor of the *New York Times,* and in op-ed pieces; then synthesize some of the responses that Hekker's essay inspired.

3. Find and report on additional articles dealing with the "Mommy Wars"—the dispute over whether mothers should stay at home to take care of the children or whether they should pursue careers, leaving their children with other caregivers. To what extent has the controversy evolved over the past few years? To what extent does a critical consensus appear to be forming—perhaps by feminists, perhaps by traditionalists—over what young mothers should do? Write a synthesis explaining your findings, and, perhaps, arguing your own position.

4. What is the state of gay marriage in the United States today? How many states, for example, allow gay marriage? Prohibit gay marriage? How many recognize civil unions? What has been the position of the federal government over the past 15 years? What kinds of state and federal legislation have been passed (or debated)

in recent years, and what kinds of decisions have been made by state and federal courts in response? What do recent polls about the subject reveal? Based on your findings, do you believe that the social and political climate for gay marriage is improving or deteriorating?

5. Research arranged marriages—either in an ethnic subculture in the United States or in a foreign country. On the whole, how happy do people report being in these marriages? Provide statistical and/or anecdotal evidence concerning this rate of satisfaction. Compare this rate to that of people in nonarranged marriages, preferably in that same culture—or, if that information is not available, compare it to the rate of marital satisfaction in our country, as reported by sources such as the National Marriage Project (<http://marriage .rutgers.edu/>). If you know people who have been in an arranged marriage, ask for their views on the subject.

6. While marriage agreements such as Alix Kates Shulman's never took hold, another sort of contract regarding marriage has become commonplace—the prenuptial agreement. Research and write an overview of prenuptial contracts (including, if possible, some of the more notorious lawsuits they have engendered). Search, in particular, for pieces that express an opinion regarding their use (op-ed pieces, magazine articles, letters to the editor). You may also wish to conduct an informal poll among your friends as to whether or not they approve of their use, whether or not they might insist, before their own marriage, on a prenuptial contract, etc. Report on your findings.

7. Investigate the effect that no-fault divorce laws have had on marriage in this country. Write a synthesis summarizing the circumstances under which the states passed such laws, the effect of these laws on the national divorce rate, and a brief overview of the controversy over the laws and their effect on the institution of marriage.

8. President John Adams and First Lady Abigail Adams had one of the more famous marriages in the history of the presidency. Abigail Adams's letters to her husband, in which she counseled him on matters public and private and in which she was an early advocate for women's issues, are still widely read, and in part form the lyrics for the Broadway musical *1776*. Research John and Abigail Adams's marriage. In which ways was it typical of its time and place? In which ways was it atypical—i.e., in which ways did it seem more like a modern marriage?

9. The 1950s are often considered the "Golden Age" of marriage. When conservative commentators evoke the "good old days" of marriage, it is almost always the 1950s model they have in mind— a father with a good job, a mother who stays home and raises the children, a house in the suburbs, and an extended family that is usually located in another town or even state. Such marriages were

the basis of popular contemporary 1950s sitcoms like *Father Knows Best* and *Ozzie and Harriet,* and they were also satirized in the 1998 film *Pleasantville.*

Research the realities of marriage in the 1950s. (Stephanie Coontz has written extensively on this subject.) To what extent is the stereotype accurate? Was there a "dark side" to marriage in the 1950s? Consider the political, economic, and cultural climate of the 1950s. What effect did these factors have on marriages of the day?

10. Research the issue of day care in this country. Locate studies that have shown positive or negative consequences to putting kids in day care. Draw also upon op-ed pieces, articles, sections in books, or personal opinions you have discovered (for example, on blogs concerning motherhood, working mothers, or stay-at-home mothers), and write a synthesis reporting on your findings.

11. Marriage researcher Andrew Cherlin has noted how weddings, once events controlled by kinship groups or parents, are now increasingly controlled by the couples themselves. One result is that the wedding has become a status symbol—"an important symbol of the partners' personal achievements and a stage in their self-development." Research the wedding industry in this country, which generates over $60 billion annually. On what is all this money being spent? What kinds of services are most popular among clients—and why? Where are people getting married? Examine a bridal magazine. What do you think the industry is *really* selling? Try to find quotations from wedding industry professionals on this topic.

6 Obedience to Authority

Would you obey an order to inflict pain on another person? Most of us, if confronted with this question, would probably be quick to answer: "Never!" Yet if the conclusions of researchers are to be trusted, it is not psychopaths who kill noncombatant civilians in wartime and torture victims in prisons around the world but rather ordinary people following orders. People obey. This is a basic, necessary fact of human society. As psychologist Stanley Milgram has written, "Obedience is as basic an element in the structure of social life as one can point to. Some system of authority is a requirement of all communal living."

The question, then, is not, "Should we obey the orders of an authority figure?" but rather, "To what *extent* should we obey?" Each generation seems to give new meaning to these questions. During the Vietnam War, a number of American soldiers followed a commander's orders and murdered civilians in the hamlet of My Lai. In 1987 former White House military aide Oliver North was prosecuted for illegally diverting money raised by selling arms to Iran—considered by the U.S. government to be a terrorist state—to fund the anticommunist Contra (resistance) fighters in Nicaragua. North's attorneys claimed that he was following the orders of his superiors. And, although North was found guilty,* the judge who sentenced him to perform community service (there was no prison sentence) largely agreed with this defense when he called North a pawn in a larger game played by senior officials in the Reagan administration. In the 1990s the world was horrified by genocidal violence in Rwanda and in the former nation of Yugoslavia. These were civil wars, in which people who had been living for generations as neighbors suddenly, upon the instigation and orders of their leaders, turned upon and slaughtered one another.

Finally, in April 2004, the world (particularly, the Muslim world) was horrified by accounts—and graphic photographs—of the degrading torture and humiliation of Iraqi prisoners at the hands of American soldiers in a Baghdad prison. Among the questions raised by this incident: Were these soldiers obeying orders to "soften up" the prisoners for interrogation? Were they fulfilling the roles of prison guards they thought were expected of them? Were they abusing others because, given the circumstances, they could? President Bush asserted that this kind of abuse "does not reflect the nature of the American people." But as the Milgram and Zimbardo experiments in this chapter demonstrate, we are likely to be unpleasantly surprised by revelations of just what our "nature" really is—not only as Americans but, more fundamentally, as human beings.

---

* In July 1990, North's conviction was overturned on appeal.

In less dramatic ways, conflicts over the extent to which we obey orders surface in everyday life. At one point or another, you may face a moral dilemma at work. Perhaps it will take this form: The boss tells you to overlook File X in preparing a report for a certain client. But you're sure that File X pertains directly to the report and contains information that will alarm the client. What should you do? The dilemmas of obedience also emerge on some campuses with the rite of fraternity or sports-related hazing. Psychologists Janice Gibson and Mika Haritos-Fatouros have made the startling observation that whether the obedience in question involves a pledge's joining a fraternity or a torturer's joining an elite military corps, the *process* by which one acquiesces to a superior's order (and thereby becomes a member of the group) is remarkably the same:

> There are several ways to teach people to do the unthinkable, and we have developed a model to explain how they are used. We have also found that college fraternities, although they are far removed from the grim world of torture and violent combat, use similar methods for initiating new members, to ensure their faithfulness to the fraternity's rules and values. However, this unthinking loyalty can sometimes lead to dangerous actions: Over the past 10 years, there have been countless injuries during fraternity initiations and 39 deaths. These training techniques are designed to instill obedience in people, but they can easily be a guide for an intensive course in torture.

> 1. *Screening to find the best prospects:*
>   - Normal, well-adjusted people with the physical, intellectual, and, in some cases, political attributes necessary for the task.
> 2. *Techniques to increase binding among these prospects:*
>   - Initiation rites to isolate people from society and introduce them to a new social order, with different rules and values.
>   - Elitist attitudes and "in-group" language, which highlight the differences between the group and the rest of society.
> 3. *Techniques to reduce the strain of obedience:*
>   - Blaming and dehumanizing the victims, so it is less disturbing to harm them.
>   - Harassment, the constant physical and psychological intimidation that prevents logical thinking and promotes the instinctive responses needed for acts of inhuman cruelty.
>   - Rewards for obedience and punishments for not cooperating.
>   - Social modeling by watching other group members commit violent acts and then receive rewards.
>   - Systematic desensitization to repugnant acts by gradual exposure to them, so they appear routine and normal despite conflicts with previous moral standards.*

---

* Janice T. Gibson and Mika Haritos-Fatouros, "The Education of a Torturer," *Psychology Today* November 1986. Reprinted with permission from *Psychology Today Magazine.* Copyright 1986 Sussex Publishers, Inc.

Many of these processes appear to have been at work in the Iraqi prison scandal.

In this chapter, you will explore the dilemmas inherent in obeying the orders of an authority. First, psychologist Solomon Asch describes an experiment he devised to demonstrate the powerful influence of group pressure upon individual judgment. Psychologist Stanley Milgram then reports on his own landmark study in which he set out to determine the extent to which ordinary individuals would obey the clearly immoral orders of an authority figure. The results were shocking, not only to the psychiatrists who predicted that few people would follow such orders but also to many other social scientists—some of whom applauded Milgram for his fiendishly ingenious design, some of whom bitterly attacked him for unethical procedures. We include one of these attacks, a scathing review by psychologist Diana Baumrind.

Next, Philip Zimbardo reports on his famous—and equally controversial—Stanford Prison Experiment, in which volunteers exhibited astonishingly convincing authoritarian and obedient attitudes as they playacted at being prisoners and guards. Psychoanalyst and philosopher Erich Fromm then discusses the comforts of obedient behavior in "Disobedience as a Psychological and Moral Problem." In "Uncivil Disobedience: Violating the Rules for Breaking the Law," James J. Lopach and Jean A. Luckowski apply the standards of such famous civil disobedience practitioners as Mohandas Gandhi and Martin Luther King, Jr., to more contemporary acts of protest, including environmental activism. They conclude that many such activities fail to qualify as true civil disobedience.

Opinions and Social Pressure
Solomon E. Asch

In the early 1950s, Solomon Asch (1907–1996), a social psychologist at Rutgers University, conducted a series of simple but ingenious experiments on the influence of group pressure upon the individual. Essentially, he discovered, individuals can be influenced by groups to deny the evidence of their own senses. Together with the Milgram experiments of the next decade (see the selections that follow here), these studies provide powerful evidence of the degree to which individuals can surrender their own judgment to others, even when those others are clearly in the wrong. The results of these experiments have implications far beyond the laboratory: They can explain a good deal of the normal human behavior we see every day—at school, at work, at home.

1   That social influences shape every person's practices, judgments, and beliefs is a truism to which anyone will readily assent. A child masters his "native" dialect down to the finest nuances; a member of a tribe of cannibals accepts cannibalism as altogether fitting and proper. All the social sciences take their departure from the observation of the profound effects that groups

exert on their members. For psychologists, group pressure upon the mind of the individual raises a host of questions they would like to investigate in detail.

1   How, and to what extent, do social forces constrain people's opinions and attitudes? This question is especially pertinent in our day. The same epoch that has witnessed the unprecedented technical extension of communication has also brought into existence the deliberate manipulation of opinion and the "engineering of consent." There are many good reasons why, as citizens and as scientists, we should be concerned with studying the ways in which human beings form their opinions and the role that social conditions play.

3   Studies of these questions began with the interest in hypnosis aroused by the French physician Jean Martin Charcot (a teacher of Sigmund Freud) toward the end of the 19th century. Charcot believed that only hysterical patients could be fully hypnotized, but this view was soon challenged by two other physicians, Hyppolyte Bernheim and A. A. Liébault, who demonstrated that they could put most people under hypnotic spell. Bernheim proposed that hypnosis was but an extreme form of a normal psychological process which became known as "suggestibility." It was shown that monotonous reiteration of instructions could induce in normal persons in the waking state involuntary bodily changes such as swaying or rigidity of the arms, and sensations such as warmth and odor.

4   It was not long before social thinkers seized upon these discoveries as a basis for explaining numerous social phenomena, from the spread of opinion to the formation of crowds and the following of leaders. The sociologist Gabriel Tarde summed it all up in the aphorism: "Social man is a somnambulist."

5   When the new discipline of social psychology was born at the beginning of this century, its first experiments were essentially adaptations of the suggestion demonstration. The technique generally followed a simple plan. The subjects, usually college students, were asked to give their opinions or preferences concerning various matters; some time later they were again asked to state their choices, but now they were also informed of the opinions held by authorities or large groups of their peers on the same matters. (Often the alleged consensus was fictitious.) Most of these studies had substantially the same result: confronted with opinions contrary to their own, many subjects apparently shifted their judgments in the direction of the views of the majorities or the experts. The late psychologist Edward L. Thorndike reported that he had succeeded in modifying the esthetic preferences of adults by this procedure. Other psychologists reported that people's evaluations of the merit of a literary passage could be raised or lowered by ascribing the passage to different authors. Apparently the sheer weight of numbers or authority sufficed to change opinions, even when no arguments for the opinions themselves were provided.

6   Now the very ease of success in these experiments arouses suspicion. Did the subjects actually change their opinions, or were the experimental victories scored only on paper? On grounds of common sense, one must question whether opinions are generally as watery as these studies indicate. There is some reason to wonder whether it was not the investigators who, in their

enthusiasm for a theory, were suggestible, and whether the ostensibly gullible subjects were not providing answers which they thought good subjects were expected to give.

7   The investigations were guided by certain underlying assumptions, which today are common currency and account for much that is thought and said about the operations of propaganda and public opinion. The assumptions are that people submit uncritically and painlessly to external manipulation by suggestion or prestige, and that any given idea or value can be "sold" or "unsold" without reference to its merits. We should be skeptical, however, of the supposition that the power of social pressure necessarily implies uncritical submission to it: independence and the capacity to rise above group passion are also open to human beings. Further, one may question on psychological grounds whether it is possible as a rule to change a person's judgment of a situation or an object without first changing his knowledge or assumptions about it.

8   In what follows I shall describe some experiments in an investigation of the effects of group pressure which was carried out recently with the help of a number of my associates. The tests not only demonstrate the operations of group pressure upon individuals but also illustrate a new kind of attack on the problem and some of the more subtle questions that it raises.

9   A group of seven to nine young men, all college students, are assembled in a classroom for a "psychological experiment" in visual judgment. The experimenter informs them that they will be comparing the lengths of lines. He shows two large white cards [see Figure 1]. On one is a single vertical black line—the standard whose length is to be matched. On the other card are three vertical lines of various lengths. The subjects are to choose the one that is of the same length as the line on the other card. One of the three actually is of the same length; the other two are substantially different, the difference ranging from three quarters of an inch to an inch and three quarters.

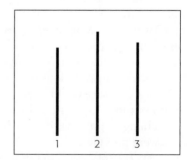

FIGURE 1 Subjects were shown two cards. One bore a standard line. The other bore three lines, one of which was the same length as the standard. The subjects were asked to choose this line.

10   The experiment opens uneventfully. The subjects announce their answers in the order in which they have been seated in the room, and on the first round every person chooses the same matching line. Then a second set of cards is exposed; again the group is unanimous. The members appear ready to endure politely another boring experiment. On the third trial there is an unexpected disturbance. One person near the end of the group disagrees with all the others in his selection of the matching line. He looks surprised, indeed incredulous, about the disagreement. On the following trial he disagrees again, while the others remain unanimous in their choice. The dissenter becomes more and more worried and hesitant as the disagreement continues in succeeding trials; he may pause before announcing his answer and speak in a low voice, or he may smile in an embarrassed way.

11   What the dissenter does not know is that all the other members of the group were instructed by the experimenter beforehand to give incorrect answers in unanimity at certain points. The single individual who is not a party to this pre-arrangement is the focal subject of our experiment. He is placed in a position in which, while he is actually giving the correct answers, he finds himself unexpectedly in a minority of one, opposed by a unanimous and arbitrary majority with respect to a clear and simple fact. Upon him we have brought to bear two opposed forces: the evidence of his senses and the unanimous opinion of a group of his peers. Also, he must declare his judgments in public, before a majority which has also stated its position publicly.

12   The instructed majority occasionally reports correctly in order to reduce the possibility that the naive subject will suspect collusion against him. (In only a few cases did the subject actually show suspicion; when this happened, the experiment was stopped and the results were not counted.) There are 18 trials in each series, and on 12 of these the majority responds erroneously.

13   How do people respond to group pressure in this situation? I shall report first the statistical results of a series in which a total of 123 subjects from three institutions of higher learning (not including my own Swarthmore College) were placed in the minority situation described above.

14   Two alternatives were open to the subject: he could act independently, repudiating the majority, or he could go along with the majority, repudiating the evidence of his senses. Of the 123 put to the test, a considerable percentage yielded to the majority. Whereas in ordinary circumstances individuals matching the lines will make mistakes less than 1 per cent of the time, under group pressure the minority subjects swung to acceptance of the misleading majority's wrong judgments in 36.8 per cent of the selections.

15   Of course individuals differed in response. At one extreme, about one quarter of the subjects were completely independent and never agreed with the erroneous judgments of the majority. At the other extreme, some individuals went with the majority nearly all the time. The performances of individuals in this experiment tend to be highly consistent. Those who strike out on the path of independence do not, as a rule, succumb to the majority even over an extended series of trials, while those who choose the path of compliance are unable to free themselves as the ordeal is prolonged.

16   The reasons for the startling individual differences have not yet been investigated in detail. At this point we can only report some tentative generalizations from talks with the subjects, each of whom was interviewed at the end of the experiment. Among the independent individuals were many who held fast because of staunch confidence in their own judgment. The most significant fact about them was not absence of responsiveness to the majority but a capacity to recover from doubt and to reestablish their equilibrium. Others who acted independently came to believe that the majority was correct in its answers, but they continued their dissent on the simple ground that it was their obligation to call the play as they saw it.

17   Among the extremely yielding persons we found a group who quickly reached the conclusion: "I am wrong, they are right." Others yielded in order "not to spoil your results." Many of the individuals who went along suspected that the majority were "sheep" following the first responder, or that the majority were victims of an optical illusion; nevertheless, these suspicions failed to free them at the moment of decision. More disquieting were the reactions of subjects who construed their difference from the majority as a sign of some general deficiency in themselves, which at all costs they must hide. On this basis they desperately tried to merge with the majority, not realizing the longer-range consequences to themselves. All the yielding subjects underestimated the frequency with which they conformed.

18   Which aspect of the influence of a majority is more important—the size of the majority or its unanimity? The experiment was modified to examine this question. In one series the size of the opposition was varied from one to 15 persons. The results showed a clear trend. When a subject was confronted with only a single individual who contradicted his answers, he was swayed little: he continued to answer independently and correctly in nearly all trials. When the opposition was increased to two, the pressure became substantial: minority subjects now accepted the wrong answer 13.6 per cent of the time. Under the pressure of a majority of three, the subjects' errors jumped to 31.8 per cent. But further increases in the size of the majority apparently did not increase the weight of the pressure substantially. Clearly the size of the opposition is important only up to a point.

19   Disturbance of the majority's unanimity had a striking effect. In this experiment the subject was given the support of a truthful partner—either another individual who did not know of the prearranged agreement among the rest of the group, or a person who was instructed to give correct answers throughout.

20   The presence of a supporting partner depleted the majority of much of its power. Its pressure on the dissenting individual was reduced to one fourth: that is, subjects answered incorrectly only one fourth as often as under the pressure of a unanimous majority. The weakest persons did not yield as readily. Most interesting were the reactions to the partner. Generally the feeling toward him was one of warmth and closeness; he was credited with inspiring confidence. However, the subjects repudiated the suggestion that the partner decided them to be independent.

21   Was the partner's effect a consequence of his dissent, or was it related to his accuracy? We now introduced into the experimental group a person who was instructed to dissent from the majority but also to disagree with the subject. In some experiments the majority was always to choose the worst of the comparison lines and the instructed dissenter to pick the line that was closer to the length of the standard one; in others the majority was consistently intermediate and the dissenter most in error. In this manner we were able to study the relative influence of "compromising" and "extremist" dissenters.

22   Again the results are clear. When a moderate dissenter is present the effect of the majority on the subject decreases by approximately one third, and extremes of yielding disappear. Moreover, most of the errors the subjects do make are moderate, rather than flagrant. In short, the dissenter largely controls the choice of errors. To this extent the subjects broke away from the majority even while bending to it.

23   On the other hand, when the dissenter always chose the line that was more flagrantly different from the standard, the results were of quite a different kind. The extremist dissenter produced a remarkable freeing of the subjects; their errors dropped to only 9 percent. Furthermore, all the errors were of the moderate variety. We were able to conclude that dissents *per se* increased independence and moderated the errors that occurred, and that the direction of dissent exerted consistent effects.

24   In all the foregoing experiments each subject was observed only in a single setting. We now turned to studying the effects upon a given individual of a change in the situation to which he was exposed. The first experiment examined the consequences of losing or gaining a partner. The instructed partner began by answering correctly on the first six trials. With his support the subject usually resisted pressure from the majority: 18 of 27 subjects were completely independent. But after six trials the partner joined the majority. As soon as he did so, there was an abrupt rise in the subjects' errors. Their submission to the majority was just about as frequent as when the minority subject was opposed by a unanimous majority throughout.

25   It was surprising to find that the experience of having had a partner and of having braved the majority opposition with him had failed to strengthen the individuals' independence. Questioning at the conclusion of the experiment suggested that we had overlooked an important circumstance; namely, the strong specific effect of "desertion" by the partner to the other side. We therefore changed the conditions so that the partner would simply leave the group at the proper point. (To allay suspicion it was announced in advance that he had an appointment with the dean.) In this form of the experiment, the partner's effect outlasted his presence. The errors increased after his departure, but less markedly than after a partner switched to the majority.

26   In a variant of this procedure the trials began with the majority unanimously giving correct answers. Then they gradually broke away until on the sixth trial the naive subject was alone and the group unanimously against him. As long as the subject had anyone on his side, he was almost invariably

independent, but as soon as he found himself alone, the tendency to conform to the majority rose abruptly.

27   As might be expected, an individual's resistance to group pressure in these experiments depends to a considerable degree on how wrong the majority was. We varied the discrepancy between the standard line and the other lines systematically, with the hope of reaching a point where the error of the majority would be so glaring that every subject would repudiate it and choose independently. In this we regretfully did not succeed. Even when the difference between the lines was seven inches, there were still some who yielded to the error of the majority.

28   The study provides clear answers to a few relatively simple questions, and it raises many others that await investigation. We would like to know the degree of consistency of persons in situations which differ in content and structure. If consistency of independence or conformity in behavior is shown to be a fact, how is it functionally related to qualities of character and personality? In what ways is independence related to sociological or cultural conditions? Are leaders more independent than other people, or are they adept at following their followers? These and many other questions may perhaps be answerable by investigations of the type described here.

29   Life in society requires consensus as an indispensable condition. But consensus, to be productive, requires that each individual contribute independently out of his experience and insight. When consensus comes under the dominance of conformity, the social process is polluted and the individual at the same time surrenders the powers on which his functioning as a feeling and thinking being depends. That we have found the tendency to conformity in our society so strong that reasonably intelligent and well-meaning young people are willing to call white black is a matter of concern. It raises questions about our ways of education and about the values that guide our conduct.

30   Yet anyone inclined to draw too pessimistic conclusions from this report would do well to remind himself that the capacities for independence are not to be underestimated. He may also draw some consolation from a further observation: those who participated in this challenging experiment agreed nearly without exception that independence was preferable to conformity.

Review Questions

1. What is "suggestibility"? How is this phenomenon related to social pressure?

2. Summarize the procedure and results of the Asch experiment. What conclusions does Asch draw from these results?

3. To what extent did varying the size of the majority and its unanimity affect the experimental results?

4. What distinction does Asch draw between consensus and conformity?

Discussion and Writing Suggestions

1. Before discussing the experiment, Asch considers how easily people's opinions or attitudes may be shaped by social pressure. To what extent do you agree with this conclusion? Write a short paper on this subject, drawing upon examples from your own experience or observation or from your reading.

2. Do the results of this experiment surprise you? Or do they confirm facts about human behavior that you had already suspected, observed, or experienced? Explain, in two or three paragraphs. Provide examples, relating these examples to features of the Asch experiment.

3. Frequently, the conclusions drawn from a researcher's experimental results are challenged on the basis that laboratory conditions do not accurately reflect the complexity of human behavior. Asch draws certain conclusions about the degree to which individuals are affected by group pressures based on an experiment involving subjects choosing matching line lengths. To what extent, if any, do you believe that these conclusions lack validity because the behavior at the heart of the experiment is too dissimilar to real-life situations of group pressure on the individual? Support your opinions with examples.

4. We are all familiar with the phenomenon of "peer pressure." To what extent do Asch's experiments demonstrate the power of peer pressure? To what extent do you think that other factors may be at work? Explain, providing examples.

5. Asch's experiments, conducted in the early 1950s, involved groups of "seven to nine young men, all college students." To what extent do you believe that the results of a similar experiment would be different today? To what extent might they be different if the subjects had included women, as well, and subjects of various ages, from children, to middle-aged people, to older people? To what extent do you believe that the social class or culture of the subjects might have an impact upon the experimental results? Support your opinions with examples and logical reasoning. (Beware, however, of overgeneralizing, based upon insufficient evidence.)

The Perils of Obedience
Stanley Milgram

In 1963, a Yale psychologist conducted one of the classic studies on obedience. Stanley Milgram designed an experiment that forced participants either to violate their conscience by obeying the immoral demands of an authority figure or to refuse those demands.

Surprisingly, Milgram found that few participants could resist the authority's orders, even when the participants knew that following these orders would result in another person's pain. Were the participants in these experiments incipient mass murderers? No, said Milgram. They were "ordinary people, simply doing their jobs." The implications of Milgram's conclusions are immense.

Consider these questions: Where does evil reside? What sort of people were responsible for the Holocaust, and for the long list of other atrocities that seem to blight the human record in every generation? Is it a lunatic fringe, a few sick but powerful people who are responsible for atrocities? If so, then we decent folk needn't ever look inside ourselves to understand evil since (by our definition) evil lurks out there, in "those sick ones." Milgram's study suggested otherwise: that under a special set of circumstances the obedience we naturally show authority figures can transform us into agents of terror.

The article that follows is one of the longest in this book, and it may help you to know in advance the author's organization. In paragraphs 1–11, Milgram discusses the larger significance and the history of dilemmas involving obedience to authority; he then summarizes his basic experimental design and follows with a report of one experiment. Milgram organizes the remainder of his article into sections, which he has subtitled "An Unexpected Outcome," "Peculiar Reactions," "The Etiquette of Submission," and "Duty Without Conflict." He begins his conclusion in paragraph 108. If you find the article too long or complex to complete in a single sitting, then plan to read sections at a time, taking notes on each until you're done. Anticipate the article that immediately follows this one: It reviews Milgram's work and largely concerns the ethics of his experimental design. Consider these ethics as you read so that you, in turn, can respond to Milgram's critics.

Stanley Milgram (1933–1984) taught and conducted research at Yale and Harvard Universities and at the Graduate Center, City University of New York. He was named Guggenheim Fellow in 1972–1973 and a year later was nominated for the National Book Award for Obedience to Authority. *His other books include* Television and Antisocial Behavior *(1973),* The City and the Self *(1974),* Human Aggression *(1976), and* The Individual in the Social World *(1977).*

1   Obedience is as basic an element in the structure of social life as one can point to. Some system of authority is a requirement of all communal living, and it is only the person dwelling in isolation who is not forced to respond, with defiance or submission, to the commands of others. For many people, obedience is a deeply ingrained behavior tendency, indeed a potent impulse overriding training in ethics, sympathy, and moral conduct.

2   The dilemma inherent in submission to authority is ancient, as old as the story of Abraham, and the question of whether one should obey when commands conflict with conscience has been argued by Plato, dramatized in *Antigone*, and treated to philosophic analysis in almost every historical epoch. Conservative philosophers argue that the very fabric of society is threatened by disobedience, while humanists stress the primacy of the individual conscience.

3   The legal and philosophic aspects of obedience are of enormous import, but they say very little about how most people behave in concrete situations. I set up a simple experiment at Yale University to test how much pain an ordinary citizen would inflict on another person simply because he was ordered to by an experimental

scientist. Stark authority was pitted against the subjects' strongest moral imperatives against hurting others, and with the subjects' ears ringing with the screams
of the victims, authority won more often than not. The extreme willingness of
adults to go to almost any lengths on the command of an authority constitutes the
chief finding of the study and the fact most urgently demanding explanation.

4   In the basic experimental design, two people come to a psychology laboratory to take part in a study of memory and learning. One of them is designated
as a "teacher" and the other a "learner." The experimenter explains that the
study is concerned with the effects of punishment on learning. The learner is
conducted into a room, seated in a kind of miniature electric chair; his arms are
strapped to prevent excessive movement, and an electrode is attached to his
wrist. He is told that he will be read lists of simple word pairs, and that he will
then be tested on his ability to remember the second word of a pair when he
hears the first one again. Whenever he makes an error, he will receive electric
shocks of increasing intensity.

5   The real focus of the experiment is the teacher. After watching the learner
being strapped into place, he is seated before an impressive shock generator. The
instrument panel consists of thirty level switches set in a horizontal line. Each
switch is clearly labeled with a voltage designation ranging from 15 to 450 volts.
The following designations are clearly indicated for groups of four switches,
going from left to right: Slight Shock, Moderate Shock, Strong Shock, Very
Strong Shock, Intense Shock, Extreme Intensity Shock, Danger: Severe Shock.
(Two switches after this last designation are simply marked XXX.)

6   When a switch is depressed, a pilot light corresponding to each switch is illu-
minated in bright red; an electric buzzing is heard; a blue light, labeled "voltage
energizer," flashes; the dial on the voltage meter swings to the right; and various relay clicks sound off.

7   The upper left-hand corner of the generator is labeled SHOCK GENERATOR,
TYPE ZLB, DYSON INSTRUMENT COMPANY, WALTHAM, MASS. OUTPUT 15 VOLTS—
450 VOLTS.

8   Each subject is given a sample 45-volt shock from the generator before his run
as teacher, and the jolt strengthens his belief in the authenticity of the machine.

9   The teacher is a genuinely naive subject who has come to the laboratory for
the experiment. The learner, or victim, is actually an actor who receives no
shock at all. The point of the experiment is to see how far a person will proceed
in a concrete and measurable situation in which he is ordered to inflict increasing pain on a protesting victim.

10   Conflict arises when the man receiving the shock begins to show that he is
experiencing discomfort. At 75 volts, he grunts; at 120 volts, he complains
loudly; at 150, he demands to be released from the experiment. As the voltage
increases, his protests become more vehement and emotional. At 285 volts, his
response can be described only as an agonized scream. Soon thereafter, he makes
no sound at all.

11   For the teacher, the situation quickly becomes one of gripping tension. It is
not a game for him; conflict is intense and obvious. The manifest suffering of
the learner presses him to quit; but each time he hesitates to administer a shock,

the experimenter orders him to continue. To extricate himself from this plight, the subject must make a clear break with authority.*

12   The subject, Gretchen Brandt,† is an attractive thirty-one-year-old medical technician who works at the Yale Medical School. She had emigrated from Germany five years before.

13   On several occasions when the learner complains, she turns to the experimenter coolly and inquires, "Shall I continue?" She promptly returns to her task when the experimenter asks her to do so. At the administration of 210 volts, she turns to the experimenter, remarking firmly, "Well, I'm sorry, I don't think we should continue."

14   EXPERIMENTER: The experiment requires that you go on until he has learned all the word pairs correctly.

15   BRANDT: He has a heart condition. I'm sorry. He told you that before.

16   EXPERIMENTER: The shocks may be painful but they are not dangerous.

17   BRANDT: Well, I'm sorry, I think when shocks continue like this, they *are* dangerous. You ask him if he wants to get out. It's his free will.

18   EXPERIMENTER: It is absolutely essential that we continue. . . .

19   BRANDT: I'd like you to ask him. We came here of our free will. If he wants to continue I'll go ahead. He told you he had a heart condition. I'm sorry. I don't want to be responsible for anything happening to him. I wouldn't like it for me either.

20   EXPERIMENTER: You have no other choice.

21   BRANDT: I think we are here on our own free will. I don't want to be responsible if anything happens to him. Please understand that.

22   She refuses to go further and the experiment is terminated.

23   The woman is firm and resolute throughout. She indicates in the interview that she was in no way tense or nervous, and this corresponds to her controlled appearance during the experiment. She feels that the last shock she administered to the learner was extremely painful and reiterates that she "did not want to be responsible for any harm to him."

24   The woman's straightforward, courteous behavior in the experiment, lack of tension, and total control of her own action seem to make disobedience a simple and rational deed. Her behavior is the very embodiment of what I envisioned would be true for almost all subjects.

An Unexpected Outcome

25 Before the experiments, I sought predictions about the outcome from various kinds of people—psychiatrists, college sophomores, middle-class adults, graduate students, and faculty in the behavioral sciences. With remarkable similarity, they predicted that virtually all subjects would refuse to obey the

---

* The ethical problems of carrying out an experiment of this sort are too complex to be dealt with here, but they receive extended treatment in the book from which this article is adapted.

† Names of subjects described in this piece have been changed.

experimenter. The psychiatrists, specifically, predicted that most subjects would not go beyond 150 volts, when the victim makes his first explicit demand to be freed. They expected that only 4 percent would reach 300 volts, and that only a pathological fringe of about one in a thousand would administer the highest shock on the board.

26 These predictions were unequivocally wrong. Of the forty subjects in the first experiment, twenty-five obeyed the orders of the experimenter to the end, punishing the victim until they reached the most potent shock available on the generator. After 450 volts were administered three times, the experimenter called a halt to the session. Many obedient subjects then heaved sighs of relief, mopped their brows, rubbed their fingers over their eyes, or nervously fumbled cigarettes. Others displayed only minimal signs of tension from beginning to end.

27 When the very first experiments were carried out, Yale undergraduates were used as subjects, and about 60 percent of them were fully obedient. A colleague of mine immediately dismissed these findings as having no relevance to "ordinary" people, asserting that Yale undergraduates are a highly aggressive, competitive bunch who step on each other's necks on the slightest provocation. He assured me that when "ordinary" people were tested, the results would be quite different. As we moved from the pilot studies to the regular experimental series, people drawn from every stratum of New Haven life came to be employed in the experiment: professionals, white-collar workers, unemployed persons, and industrial workers. *The experiment's total outcome was the same as we had observed among the students.*

28 Moreover, when the experiments were repeated in Princeton, Munich, Rome, South Africa, and Australia, the level of obedience was invariably somewhat *higher* than found in the investigation reported in this article. Thus one scientist in Munich found 85 percent of his subjects to be obedient.

29 Fred Prozi's reactions, if more dramatic than most, illuminate the conflicts experienced by others in less visible form. About fifty years old and unemployed at the time of the experiment, he has a good-natured, if slightly dissolute, appearance, and he strikes people as a rather ordinary fellow. He begins the session calmly but becomes tense as it proceeds. After delivering the 180-volt shock, he pivots around in his chair and, shaking his head, addresses the experimenter in agitated tones:

30 PROZI: I can't stand it. I'm not going to kill that man in there. You hear him hollering?

31 EXPERIMENTER: As I told you before, the shocks may be painful, but . . .

32 PROZI: But he's hollering. He can't stand it. What's going to happen to him?

33 EXPERIMENTER (*his voice patient, matter-of-fact*): The experiment requires that you continue, Teacher.

34 PROZI: Aaah, but unh, I'm not going to get that man sick in there—know what I mean?

35 EXPERIMENTER: Whether the learner likes it or not, we must go on, through all the word pairs.

36 PROZI: I refuse to take the responsibility. He's in there hollering!

37   EXPERIMENTER: It's absolutely essential that you continue, Prozi.

38   PROZI (*indicating the unused questions*): There's too many left here. I mean, Jeez, if he gets them wrong, there's too many of them left. I mean, who's going to take the responsibility if anything happens to that gentleman?

39   EXPERIMENTER: I'm responsible for anything that happens to him. Continue, please.

40   PROZI: All right. (*Consults list of words.*) The next one's "Slow—walk, truck, dance, music." Answer, please (*A buzzing sound indicates the learner has signaled his answer.*) Wrong. A hundred and ninety-five volts. "Dance." (*Zzumph!*)

41   LEARNER (*yelling*): Let me out of here! My heart's bothering me! (*Teacher looks at experimenter.*)

42   EXPERIMENTER: Continue, please.

43   LEARNER (*screaming*): Let me out of here! You have no right to keep me here! Let me out of here, my heart's bothering me, let me out!

44   PROZI (*shakes head, pats the table nervously*): You see, he's hollering. Hear that? Gee, I don't know.

45   EXPERIMENTER: The experiment requires . . .

46   PROZI (*interrupting*): I know it does, sir, but I mean—hunh! He don't know what he's getting in for. He's up to 195 volts! (*Experiment continues, through 210 volts, 225 volts, 240 volts, 255 volts, 270 volts, at which point Prozi, with evident relief, runs out of word-pair questions.*)

47   EXPERIMENTER: You'll have to go back to the beginning of that page and go through them again until he's learned them all correctly.

48   PROZI: Aw, no. I'm not going to kill that man. You mean I've got to keep going up with the scale? No sir. He's hollering in there. I'm not going to give him 450 volts.

49   EXPERIMENTER: The experiment requires that you go on.

50   LEARNER: Ohhh. I absolutely refuse to answer anymore. (*Shouting urgently now.*) Let me out of here! You can't hold me here! Get me out. Get-me-out-of-here!

51   EXPERIMENTER: Continue. The next word is "Green," please.

52   PROZI: "Green—grass, hat, ink, apple." (*Nothing happens. No answering buzz. Just gloomy silence.*)

53   PROZI: I don't think he is going to answer.

54   EXPERIMENTER: If the learner doesn't answer in a reasonable time, about four or five seconds, consider the answer wrong. And follow the same procedures you have been doing for wrong answers. Say, "Wrong," tell him the number of volts, give him the punishment, read him the correct answer. Continue, please.

55   PROZI: "Green—grass, hat, ink, apple." Answer, please. (*More silence. Subject just sits there.*)

56   EXPERIMENTER: Go on with the procedure, please.

57   PROZI: Three hundred and fifteen volts. The answer is "ink." (*Zzumph!*)

58   LEARNER: Ohh. Ooohh.

59   PROZI (*relieved to hear response*): Next one . . .

60   LEARNER: I absolutely refuse to answer.

61   PROZI: You got to. You get a shock if you don't answer. (*Experiment continues with learner refusing to answer, and finally, failing even to grunt or groan. At 375 volts, the subject stands up.*)

62   PROZI: I think something's happened to that fellow in there. I don't get no answer. He was hollering at less voltage. Can't you check in and see if he's all right, please?

63   EXPERIMENTER (*with same detached calm*): Not once we've started. Please continue, Teacher.

64   PROZI (*sits down, sighs deeply*): "Cool—day, shade, water, paint." Answer, please. Are you all right in there? Are you all right?

65   EXPERIMENTER: Please continue, Teacher. Continue, please. (*Subject pushes lever. Zzumph!*)

66   PROZI (*swiveling around in his chair*): Something's happened to that man in there. (*Swiveling back.*) Next one. "Low—dollar, necklace, moon, paint." (*Turning around again.*) Something's happened to that man in there. You better check on him, sir. He won't answer or nothing.

67   EXPERIMENTER: Continue. Go on, please.

68   PROZI: You accept all responsibility?

69   EXPERIMENTER: The responsibility is mine. Correct. Please go on. (*Subject returns to his list, starts running through words as rapidly as he can read them, works through to 450 volts.*)

70   PROZI: That's that.

71   EXPERIMENTER: Continue using the 450 switch for each wrong answer. Continue, please.

72   PROZI: But I don't get anything!

73   EXPERIMENTER: Please continue. The next word is "white."

74   PROZI: Don't you think you should look in on him, please?

75   EXPERIMENTER: Not once we've started the experiment.

76   PROZI: What if he's dead in there? (*Gestures toward the room with the electric chair.*) I mean, he told me he can't stand the shock, sir. I don't mean to be rude, but I think you should look in on him. All you have to do is look in on him. All you have to do is look in the door. I don't get no answer, no noise. Something might have happened to the gentleman in there, sir.

77   EXPERIMENTER: We must continue. Go on, please.

78   PROZI: You mean keep giving him what? Four-hundred-fifty volts, what he's got now?

79   EXPERIMENTER: That's correct. Continue. The next word is "white."

80   PROZI (*now at a furious pace*): "White—cloud, horse, rock, house." Answer, please. The answer is "horse." Four hundred and fifty volts. (*Zzumph!*) Next word, "Bag—paint, music, clown, girl." The answer is "paint." Four hundred and fifty volts. (*Zzumph!*) Next word is "Short—sentence, movie . . . "

81   EXPERIMENTER: Excuse me, Teacher. We'll have to discontinue the experiment.

Peculiar Reactions

82 Morris Braverman, another subject, is a thirty-nine-year-old social worker. He looks older than his years because of his bald head and serious demeanor. His

brow is furrowed, as if all the world's burdens were carried on his face. He appears intelligent and concerned.

83   When the learner refuses to answer and the experimenter instructs Braverman to treat the absence of an answer as equivalent to a wrong answer, he takes his instruction to heart. Before administering 300 volts he asserts officiously to the victim, "Mr. Wallace, your silence has to be considered as a wrong answer." Then he administers the shock. He offers half-heartedly to change places with the learner, then asks the experimenter, "Do I have to follow these instructions literally?" He is satisfied with the experimenter's answer that he does. His very refined and authoritative manner of speaking is increasingly broken up by wheezing laughter.

84   The experimenter's notes on Mr. Braverman at the last few shocks are:

> Almost breaking up now each time gives shock. Rubbing face to hide laughter. Squinting, trying to hide face with hand, still laughing. Cannot control his laughter at this point no matter what he does. Clenching fist, pushing it onto table.

85   In an interview after the session, Mr. Braverman summarizes the experiment with impressive fluency and intelligence. He feels the experiment may have been designed also to "test the effects on the teacher of being in an essentially sadistic role, as well as the reactions of a student to a learning situation that was authoritative and punitive." When asked how painful the last few shocks administered to the learner were, he indicates that the most extreme category on the scale is not adequate (it read EXTREMELY PAINFUL) and places his mark at the edge of the scale with an arrow carrying it beyond the scale.

86   It is almost impossible to convey the greatly relaxed, sedate quality of his conversation in the interview. In the most relaxed terms, he speaks about his severe inner tension.

87   EXPERIMENTER: At what point were you most tense or nervous?

88   MR. BRAVERMAN: Well, when he first began to cry out in pain, and I realized this was hurting him. This got worse when he just blocked and refused to answer. There was I. I'm a nice person, I think, hurting somebody, and caught up in what seemed a mad situation . . . and in the interest of science, one goes through with it.

89   When the interviewer pursues the general question of tension, Mr. Braverman spontaneously mentions his laughter.

90   "My reactions were awfully peculiar. I don't know if you were watching me, but my reactions were giggly, and trying to stifle laughter. This isn't the way I usually am. This was a sheer reaction to a totally impossible situation. And my reaction was to the situation of having to hurt somebody. And being totally helpless and caught up in a set of circumstances where I just couldn't deviate and I couldn't try to help. This is what got me."

91   Mr. Braverman, like all subjects, was told the actual nature and purpose of the experiment, and a year later he affirmed in a questionnaire that he had learned something of personal importance: "What appalled me was that I could possess this capacity for obedience and compliance to a central idea, i.e., the

value of a memory experiment, even after it became clear that continued adherence to this value was at the expense of violation of another value, i.e., don't hurt someone who is helpless and not hurting you. As my wife said, 'You can call yourself Eichmann.'* I hope I deal more effectively with any future conflicts of values I encounter."

The Etiquette of Submission

92 One theoretical interpretation of this behavior holds that all people harbor deeply aggressive instincts continually pressing for expression, and that the experiment provides institutional justification for the release of these impulses. According to this view, if a person is placed in a situation in which he has complete power over another individual, whom he may punish as much as he likes, all that is sadistic and bestial in man comes to the fore. The impulse to shock the victim is seen to flow from the potent aggressive tendencies, which are part of the motivational life of the individual, and the experiment, because it provides social legitimacy, simply opens the door to their expression.

93 It becomes vital, therefore, to compare the subject's performance when he is under orders and when he is allowed to choose the shock level.

94 The procedure was identical to our standard experiment, except that the teacher was told that he was free to select any shock level on any of the trials. (The experimenter took pains to point out that the teacher could use the highest levels on the generator, the lowest, any in between, or any combination of levels.) Each subject proceeded for thirty critical trials. The learner's protests were coordinated to standard shock levels, his first grunt coming at 75 volts, his first vehement protest at 150 volts.

95 The average shock used during the thirty critical trials was less than 60 volts—lower than the point at which the victim showed the first signs of discomfort. Three of the forty subjects did not go beyond the very lowest level on the board, twenty-eight went no higher than 75 volts, and thirty-eight did not go beyond the first loud protest at 150 volts. Two subjects provided the exception, administering up to 325 and 450 volts, but the overall result was that the great majority of people delivered very low, usually painless, shocks when the choice was explicitly up to them.

96 This condition of the experiment undermines another commonly offered explanation of the subjects' behavior—that those who shocked the victim at the most severe levels came only from the sadistic fringe of society. If one considers that almost two-thirds of the participants fall into the category of "obedient" subjects, and that they represented ordinary people drawn from working, managerial, and professional classes, the argument becomes very shaky. Indeed, it is highly reminiscent of the issue that arose in connection with Hannah Arendt's 1963 book, *Eichmann in Jerusalem*. Arendt contended that the prosecution's efforts to depict Eichmann as a sadistic monster was fundamentally wrong, that he came

---

* *Adolf Eichmann* (1906–1962), the Nazi official responsible for implementing Hitler's "Final Solution" to exterminate the Jews, escaped to Argentina after World War II. In 1960, Israeli agents captured him and brought him to Israel, where he was tried as a war criminal and sentenced to death. At his trial, Eichmann maintained that he was merely following orders in arranging murders of his victims.

closer to being an uninspired bureaucrat who simply sat at his desk and did his job. For asserting her views, Arendt became the object of considerable scorn, even calumny. Somehow, it was felt that the monstrous deeds carried out by Eichmann required a brutal, twisted personality, evil incarnate. After witnessing hundreds of ordinary persons submit to the authority in our own experiments, I must conclude that Arendt's conception of the banality of evil comes closer to the truth than one might dare imagine. The ordinary person who shocked the victim did so out of a sense of obligation—an impression of his duties as a subject—and not from any peculiarly aggressive tendencies.

97   This is, perhaps, the most fundamental lesson of our study: ordinary people, simply doing their jobs, and without any particular hostility on their part, can become agents in a terrible destructive process. Moreover, even when the destructive effects of their work become patently clear, and they are asked to carry out actions incompatible with fundamental standards of morality, relatively few people have the resources needed to resist authority.

98   Many of the people were in some sense against what they did to the learner, and many protested even while they obeyed. Some were totally convinced of the wrongness of their actions but could not bring themselves to make an open break with authority. They often derived satisfaction from their thoughts and felt that—within themselves, at least—they had been on the side of the angels. They tried to reduce strain by obeying the experimenter but "only slightly," encouraging the learner, touching the generator switches gingerly. When interviewed, such a subject would stress that he had "asserted my humanity" by administering the briefest shock possible. Handling the conflict in this manner was easier than defiance.

99   The situation is constructed so that there is no way the subject can stop shocking the learner without violating the experimenter's definitions of his own competence. The subject fears that he will appear arrogant, untoward, and rude if he breaks off. Although these inhibiting emotions appear small in scope alongside the violence being done to the learner, they suffuse the mind and feelings of the subject, who is miserable at the prospect of having to repudiate the authority to his face. (When the experiment was altered so that the experimenter gave his instructions by telephone instead of in person, only a third as many people were fully obedient through 450 volts.) It is a curious thing that a measure of compassion on the part of the subject—an unwillingness to "hurt" the experimenter's feelings—is part of those binding forces inhibiting his disobedience. The withdrawal of such deference may be as painful to the subject as to the authority he defies.

Duty Without Conflict

100   The subjects do not derive satisfaction from inflicting pain, but they often like the feeling they get from pleasing the experimenter. They are proud of doing a good job, obeying the experimenter under difficult circumstances. While the subjects administered only mild shocks on their own initiative, one experimental variation showed that, under orders, 30 percent of them were willing to deliver 450 volts even when they had to forcibly push the learner's hand down on the electrode.

101   Bruno Batta is a thirty-seven-year-old welder who took part in the variation requiring the use of force. He was born in New Haven, his parents in Italy. He has a rough-hewn face that conveys a conspicuous lack of alertness. He has some difficulty in mastering the experimental procedure and needs to be corrected by the experimenter several times. He shows appreciation for the help and willingness to do what is required. After the 150-volt level, Batta has to force the learner's hand down on the shock plate, since the learner himself refuses to touch it.

102   When the learner first complains, Mr. Batta pays no attention to him. His face remains impassive, as if to dissociate himself from the learner's disruptive behavior. When the experimenter instructs him to force the learner's hand down, he adopts a rigid, mechanical procedure. He tests the generator switch. When it fails to function, he immediately forces the learner's hand onto the shock plate. All the while he maintains the same rigid mask. The learner, seated alongside him, begs him to stop, but with robotic impassivity he continues the procedure.

103   What is extraordinary is his apparent total indifference to the learner; he hardly takes cognizance of him as a human being. Meanwhile, he relates to the experimenter in a submissive and courteous fashion.

104   At the 330-volt level, the learner refuses not only to touch the shock plate but also to provide any answers. Annoyed, Batta turns to him, and chastises him: "You better answer and get it over with. We can't stay here all night." These are the only words he directs to the learner in the course of an hour. Never again does he speak to him. The scene is brutal and depressing, his hard, impassive face showing total indifference as he subdues the screaming learner and gives him shocks. He seems to derive no pleasure from the act itself, only quiet satisfaction at doing his job properly.

105   When he administers 450 volts, he turns to the experimenter and asks, "Where do we go from here, Professor?" His tone is deferential and expresses his willingness to be a cooperative subject, in contrast to the learner's obstinacy.

106   At the end of the session he tells the experimenter how honored he has been to help him, and in a moment of contrition, remarks, "Sir, sorry it couldn't have been a full experiment."

107   He has done his honest best. It is only the deficient behavior of the learner that has denied the experimenter full satisfaction.

108   The essence of obedience is that a person comes to view himself as the instrument for carrying out another person's wishes, and he therefore no longer regards himself as responsible for his actions. Once this critical shift of viewpoint has occurred, all of the essential features of obedience follow. The most far-reaching consequence is that the person feels responsible *to* the authority directing him but feels no responsibility *for* the content of the actions that the authority prescribes. Morality does not disappear—it acquires a radically different focus: the subordinate person feels shame or pride depending on how adequately he has performed the actions called for by authority.

109   Language provides numerous terms to pinpoint this type of morality: *loyalty, duty, discipline* all are terms heavily saturated with moral meaning and refer to the degree to which a person fulfills his obligations to authority. They refer not to the "goodness" of the person per se but to the adequacy with which a subordinate fulfills his socially defined role. The most frequent defense of the individual who has performed a heinous act under command of authority is that

he has simply done his duty. In asserting this defense, the individual is not introducing an alibi concocted for the moment but is reporting honestly on the psychological attitude induced by submission to authority.

110 For a person to feel responsible for his actions, he must sense that the behavior has flowed from "the self." In the situation we have studied, subjects have precisely the opposite view of their actions—namely, they see them as originating in the motives of some other person. Subjects in the experiment frequently said, "If it were up to me, I would not have administered shocks to the learner."

111 Once authority has been isolated as the cause of the subject's behavior, it is legitimate to inquire into the necessary elements of authority and how it must be perceived in order to gain compliance. We conducted some investigations into the kinds of changes that would cause the experimenter to lose his power and to be disobeyed by the subject. Some of the variations revealed that:

- *The experimenter's physical presence has a marked impact on his authority.* As cited earlier, obedience dropped off sharply when orders were given by telephone. The experimenter could often induce a disobedient subject to go on by returning to the laboratory.
- *Conflicting authority severely paralyzes action.* When two experimenters of equal status, both seated at the command desk, gave incompatible orders, no shocks were delivered past the point of their disagreement.
- *The rebellious action of others severely undermines authority.* In one variation, three teachers (two actors and a real subject) administered a test and shocks. When the two actors disobeyed the experimenter and refused to go beyond a certain shock level, thirty-six of the forty subjects joined their disobedient peers and refused as well.

112 Although the experimenter's authority was fragile in some respects, it is also true that he had almost none of the tools used in ordinary command structures. For example, the experimenter did not threaten the subjects with punishment—such as loss of income, community ostracism, or jail—for failure to obey. Neither could he offer incentives. Indeed, we should expect the experimenter's authority to be much less than that of someone like a general, since the experimenter has no power to enforce his imperatives, and since participation in a psychological experiment scarcely evokes the sense of urgency and dedication found in warfare. Despite these limitations, he still managed to command a dismaying degree of obedience.

113 I will cite one final variation of the experiment that depicts a dilemma that is more common in everyday life. The subject was not ordered to pull the lever that shocked the victim, but merely to perform a subsidiary task (administering the word-pair test) while another person administered the shock. In this situation, thirty-seven of forty adults continued to the highest level on the shock generator. Predictably, they excused their behavior by saying that the responsibility belonged to the man who actually pulled the switch. This may illustrate a dangerously typical arrangement in a complex society: it is easy to ignore responsibility when one is only an intermediate link in a chain of action.

114   The problem of obedience is not wholly psychological. The form and shape of society and the way it is developing have much to do with it. There was a time, perhaps, when people were able to give a fully human response to any situation because they were fully absorbed in it as human beings. But as soon as there was a division of labor things changed. Beyond a certain point, the breaking up of society into people carrying out narrow and very special jobs takes away from the human quality of work and life. A person does not get to see the whole situation but only a small part of it, and is thus unable to act without some kind of overall direction. He yields to authority but in doing so is alienated from his own actions.

115   Even Eichmann was sickened when he toured the concentration camps, but he had only to sit at a desk and shuffle papers. At the same time the man in the camp who actually dropped Cyclon-b into the gas chambers was able to justify *his* behavior on the ground that he was only following orders from above. Thus there is a fragmentation of the total human act; no one is confronted with the consequences of his decision to carry out the evil act. The person who assumes responsibility has evaporated. Perhaps this is the most common characteristic of socially organized evil in modern society.

Review Questions

1. Milgram states that obedience is a basic element in the structure of social life. How so?

2. What is the dilemma inherent in obedience to authority?

3. Summarize the obedience experiments.

4. What predictions did experts and laypeople make about the experiments before they were conducted? How did these predictions compare with the experimental results?

5. What are Milgram's views regarding the two assumptions bearing on his experiment that (1) people are naturally aggressive and (2) a lunatic, sadistic fringe is responsible for shocking learners to the maximum limit?

6. How do Milgram's findings corroborate Hannah Arendt's thesis about the "banality of evil"?

7. What, according to Milgram, is the "essence of obedience"?

8. How did being an intermediate link in a chain of action affect a subject's willingness to continue with the experiment?

9. In the article's final two paragraphs, Milgram speaks of a "fragmentation of the total human act." To what is he referring?

Discussion and Writing Suggestions

1. Milgram writes (paragraph 2): "Conservative philosophers argue that the very fabric of society is threatened by disobedience, while humanists

stress the primacy of the individual conscience." Develop the arguments of both the conservative and the humanist regarding obedience to authority. Be prepared to debate the ethics of obedience by defending one position or the other.

2. Would you have been glad to have participated in the Milgram experiments? Why or why not?

3. The ethics of Milgram's experimental design came under sharp attack. Diana Baumrind's review of the experiment typifies the criticism; but before you read her work, try to anticipate the objections she raises.

4. Given the general outcome of the experiments, why do you suppose Milgram gives as his first example of a subject's response the German émigré's refusal to continue the electrical shocks?

5. Does the outcome of the experiment upset you in any way? Do you feel the experiment teaches us anything new about human nature?

6. Comment on Milgram's skill as a writer of description. How effectively does he portray his subjects when introducing them? When re-creating their tension in the experiment?

7. Mrs. Braverman said to her husband: "You can call yourself Eichmann." Do you agree with her? Explain.

8. Reread paragraphs 29 through 81, the transcript of the experiment in which Mr. Prozi participated. Appreciating that Prozi was debriefed—that is, was assured that no harm came to the learner—imagine what Prozi might have been thinking as he drove home after the experiment. Develop your thoughts into a monologue, written in the first person, with Prozi at the wheel of his car.

Review of Stanley Milgram's Experiments on Obedience
Diana Baumrind

Many of Milgram's colleagues saluted him for providing that "hard information" about human nature. Others attacked him for violating the rights of his subjects. Still others faulted his experimental design and claimed he could not, with any validity, speculate on life outside the laboratory based on the behavior of his subjects within.

In the following excerpted review, psychologist Diana Baumrind excoriates Milgram for "entrapping" his subjects and potentially harming their "self-image or ability to trust adult authorities in the future." In a footnote at the end of this selection (page 231), we summarize Milgram's response to Baumrind's critique.

Diana Baumrind is a psychologist who, when writing this review, worked at the Institute of Human Development, University of California, Berkeley. The review appeared in American Psychologist *shortly after Milgram published the results of his first experiments in 1963.*

1 ... The dependent, obedient attitude assumed by most subjects in the experimental setting is appropriate to that situation. The "game" is defined by the experimenter and he makes the rules. By volunteering, the subject agrees implicitly to assume a posture of trust and obedience. While the experimental conditions leave him exposed, the subject has the right to assume that his security and self-esteem will be protected.

2   There are other professional situations in which one member—the patient or client—expects help and protection from the other—the physician or psychologist. But the interpersonal relationship between experimenter and subject additionally has unique features which are likely to provoke initial anxiety in the subject. The laboratory is unfamiliar as a setting and the rules of behavior ambiguous compared to a clinician's office. Because of the anxiety and passivity generated by the setting, the subject is more prone to behave in an obedient, suggestible manner in the laboratory than elsewhere. Therefore, the laboratory is not the place to study degree of obedience or suggestibility, as a function of a particular experimental condition, since the base line for these phenomena as found in the laboratory is probably much higher than in most other settings. Thus experiments in which the relationship to the experimenter as an authority is used as an independent condition are imperfectly designed for the same reason that they are prone to injure the subjects involved. They disregard the special quality of trust and obedience with which the subject appropriately regards the experimenter.

3   Other phenomena which present ethical decisions, unlike those mentioned above, *can* be reproduced successfully in the laboratory. Failure experience, conformity to peer judgment, and isolation are among such phenomena. In these cases we can expect the experimenter to take whatever measures are necessary to prevent the subject from leaving the laboratory more humiliated, insecure, alienated, or hostile than when he arrived. To guarantee that an especially sensitive subject leaves a stressful experimental experience in the proper state sometimes requires special clinical training. But usually an attitude of compassion, respect, gratitude, and common sense will suffice, and no amount of clinical training will substitute. The subject has the right to expect that the psychologist with whom he is interacting has some concern for his welfare, and the personal attributes and professional skill to express his good will effectively.

4   Unfortunately, the subject is not always treated with the respect he deserves. It has become more commonplace in sociopsychological laboratory studies to manipulate, embarrass, and discomfort subjects. At times the insult to the subject's sensibilities extends to the journal reader when the results are reported. Milgram's (1963) study is a case in point. The following is Milgram's abstract of his experiment:

> This article describes a procedure for the study of destructive obedience in the laboratory. It consists of ordering a naive S to administer increasingly

more severe punishment to a victim in the context of a learning experiment.* Punishment is administered by means of a shock generator with 30 graded switches ranging from Slight Shock to Danger: Severe Shock. The victim is a confederate of E. The primary dependent variable is the maximum shock the S is willing to administer before he refuses to continue further.† 26 Ss obeyed the experimental commands fully, and administered the highest shock on the generator. 14 Ss broke off the experiment at some point after the victim protested and refused to provide further answers. The procedure created extreme levels of nervous tension in some Ss. Profuse sweating, trembling, and stuttering were typical expressions of this emotional disturbance. One unexpected sign of tension—yet to be explained— was the regular occurrence of nervous laughter, which in some Ss developed into uncontrollable seizures. The variety of interesting behavioral dynamics observed in the experiment, the reality of the situation for the S, and the possibility of parametric variations‡ within the framework of the procedure point to the fruitfulness of further study [p. 371].

5   The detached, objective manner in which Milgram reports the emotional disturbance suffered by his subjects contrasts sharply with his graphic account of that disturbance. Following are two other quotes describing the effects on his subjects of the experimental conditions:

I observed a mature and initially poised businessman enter the laboratory smiling and confident. Within 20 minutes he was reduced to a twitching, stuttering wreck, who was rapidly approaching a point of nervous collapse. He constantly pulled on his earlobe, and twisted his hands. At one point he pushed his fist into his forehead and muttered: "Oh God, let's stop it." And yet he continued to respond to every word of the experimenter, and obeyed to the end [p. 377].

In a large number of cases the degree of tension reached extremes that are rarely seen in sociopsychological laboratory studies. Subjects were observed to sweat, tremble, stutter, bite their lips, groan, and dig their fingernails into their flesh. These were characteristic rather than exceptional responses to the experiment.

One sign of tension was the regular occurrence of nervous laughing fits. Fourteen of the 40 subjects showed definite signs of nervous laughter and smiling. The laughter seemed entirely out of place, even bizarre. Full-blown, uncontrollable seizures were observed for 3 subjects. On one occasion we observed a seizure so violently convulsive that it was necessary to call a halt to the experiment. . . [p. 375].

---

* In psychological experiments, *S* is an abbreviation for *subject*; *E* is an abbreviation for *experimenter*.

† In the context of a psychological experiment, a *dependent variable* is a behavior that is expected to change as a result of changes in the experimental procedure.

‡ *Parametric variation* is a statistical term that describes the degree to which information based on data for one experiment can be applied to data for a slightly different experiment.

Milgram does state that,

> After the interview, procedures were undertaken to assure that the subject
> would leave the laboratory in a state of well being. A friendly reconciliation
> was arranged between the subject and the victim, and an effort was made to
> reduce any tensions that arose as a result of the experiment [p. 374].

It would be interesting to know what sort of procedures could dissipate the type
of emotional disturbance just described. In view of the effects on subjects, trau-
matic to a degree which Milgram himself considers nearly unprecedented in
sociopsychological experiments, his casual assurance that these tensions were
dissipated before the subject left the laboratory is unconvincing.

6   What could be the rational basis for such a posture of indifference? Perhaps
Milgram supplies the answer himself when he partially explains the subject's
destructive obedience as follows, "Thus they assume that the discomfort caused
the victim is momentary, while the scientific gains resulting from the experiment are enduring" [p. 378]. Indeed such a rationale might suffice to justify the
means used to achieve his end if that end were of inestimable value to humanity or were not itself transformed by the means by which it was attained.

7   The behavioral psychologist is not in as good a position to objectify his faith
in the significance of his work as medical colleagues at points of breakthrough.
His experimental situations are not sufficiently accurate models of real-life experience; his sampling techniques are seldom of a scope which would justify the
meaning with which he would like to endow his results; and these results are
hard to reproduce by colleagues with opposing theoretical views. Unlike the
Sabin vaccine,* for example, the concrete benefit to humanity of his particular
piece of work, no matter how competently handled, cannot justify the risk that
real harm will be done to the subject. I am not speaking of physical discomfort,
inconvenience, or experimental deception per se, but of permanent harm, however slight. I do regard the emotional disturbance described by Milgram as
potentially harmful because it could easily effect an alteration in the subject's
self-image or ability to trust adult authorities in the future. It is potentially harmful to a subject to commit, in the course of an experiment, acts which he himself considers unworthy, particularly when he has been entrapped into
committing such acts by an individual he has reason to trust. The subject's personal responsibility for his actions is not erased because the experimenter reveals
to him the means which he used to stimulate these actions. The subject realizes
that he would have hurt the victim if the current were on. The realization that
he also made a fool of himself by accepting the experimental set results in additional loss of self-esteem. Moreover, the subject finds it difficult to express his
anger outwardly after the experimenter in a self-acceptant but friendly manner
reveals the hoax.

8   A fairly intense corrective interpersonal experience is indicated wherein the
subject admits and accepts his responsibility for his own actions, and at the same
time gives vent to his hurt and anger at being fooled. Perhaps an experience as

---

* The Sabin vaccine provides immunization against polio.

distressing as the one described by Milgram can be integrated by the subject, provided that careful thought is given to the matter. The propriety of such experimentation is still in question even if such a reparational experience were forthcoming. Without it I would expect a naive, sensitive subject to remain deeply hurt and anxious for some time, and a sophisticated, cynical subject to become even more alienated and distrustful.

9   In addition the experimental procedure used by Milgram does not appear suited to the objectives of the study because it does not take into account the special quality of the set which the subject has in the experimental situation. Milgram is concerned with a very important problem, namely, the social consequences of destructive obedience. He says,

> Gas chambers were built, death camps were guarded, daily quotas of corpses were produced with the same efficiency as the manufacture of appliances. These inhumane policies may have originated in the mind of a single person, but they could only be carried out on a massive scale if a very large number of persons obeyed orders [p. 371].

But the parallel between authority-subordinate relationships in Hitler's Germany and in Milgram's laboratory is unclear. In the former situation the SS man or member of the German Officer Corps, when obeying orders to slaughter, had no reason to think of his superior officer as benignly disposed towards himself or their victims. The victims were perceived as subhuman and not worthy of consideration. The subordinate officer was an agent in a great cause. He did not need to feel guilt or conflict because within his frame of reference he was acting rightly.

10   It is obvious from Milgram's own description that most of his subjects were concerned about their victims and did trust the experimenter, and that their distressful conflict was generated in part by the consequences of these two disparate but appropriate attitudes. Their distress may have resulted from shock at what the experimenter was doing to them as well as from what they thought they were doing to their victims. In any case there is not a convincing parallel between the phenomena studied by Milgram and destructive obedience as the concept would apply to the subordinate-authority relationship demonstrated in Hitler's Germany. If the experiments were conducted "outside of New Haven and without any visible ties to the university," I would still question their validity on similar although not identical grounds. In addition, I would question the representativeness of a sample of subjects who would voluntarily participate within a noninstitutional setting.

11   In summary, the experimental objectives of the psychologist are seldom incompatible with the subject's ongoing state of well being, provided that the experimenter is willing to take the subject's motives and interests into consideration when planning his methods and correctives. Section 4b in *Ethical Standards of Psychologists* (APA, undated) reads in part:

> Only when a problem is significant and can be investigated in no other way is the psychologist justified in exposing human subjects to emotional stress

or other possible harm. In conducting such research, the psychologist must seriously consider the possibility of harmful aftereffects, and should be prepared to remove them as soon as permitted by the design of the experiment. Where the danger of serious aftereffects exists, research should be conducted only when the subjects or their responsible agents are fully informed of this possibility and volunteer nevertheless [p. 12].

From the subject's point of view procedures which involve loss of dignity, self-esteem and trust in rational authority are probably most harmful in the long run and require the most thoughtfully planned reparations, if engaged in at all. The public image of psychology as a profession is highly related to our own actions, and some of these actions are changeworthy. It is important that as research psychologists we protect our ethical sensibilities rather than adapt our personal standards to include as appropriate the kind of indignities to which Milgram's subjects were exposed. I would not like to see experiments such as Milgram's proceed unless the subjects were fully informed of the dangers of serious aftereffects and his correctives were clearly shown to be effective in restoring their state of well being.*

References

American Psychological Association (n.d.). *Ethical standards of psychologists: A summary of ethical principles.* Washington, DC: APA.

Milgram, S. (1963). Behavioral study of obedience. *Journal of Abnormal and Social Psychology. 67,* 371–378.

---

* Stanley Milgram replied to Baumrind's critique in a lengthy critique of his own [From Stanley Milgram, "Issues in the Study of Obedience: A Reply to Baumrind," *American Psychologist* 19, 1964, pp. 848–851]. Following are his principal points:

• Milgram believed that the experimental findings were in large part responsible for Baumrind's criticism. He writes:

Is not Baumrind's criticism based as much on the unanticipated findings as on the method? The findings were that some subjects performed in what appeared to be a shockingly immoral way. If, instead, every one of the subjects had broken off at "slight shock," or at the first sign of the learner's discomfort, the results would have been pleasant, and reassuring, and who would protest?

• Milgram objected to Baumrind's assertion that those who participated in the experiment would have trouble justifying their behavior. Milgram conducted follow-up questionnaires. The results, summarized in Table 1, indicate that 84 percent of the subjects claimed they were pleased to have been a part of the experiment.

• Baumrind objected that studies of obedience cannot meaningfully be carried out in a laboratory setting, since the obedience occurred in a context where it was appropriate. Milgram's response: "I reject Baumrind's argument that the observed obedience does not count because it occurred where it is appropriate. That is precisely why it *does* count. A soldier's obedience is no less meaningful because it occurs in a pertinent military context." (Footnote continued on next page.)

Review Questions

1. Why might a subject volunteer for an experiment? Why do subjects typi-cally assume a dependent, obedient attitude?

2. Why is a laboratory not a suitable setting for a study of obedience?

3. For what reasons does Baumrind feel that the Milgram experiment was potentially harmful?

4. For what reasons does Baumrind question the relationship between Milgram's findings and the obedient behavior of subordinates in Nazi Germany?

Discussion and Writing Suggestions

1. Baumrind contends that the Milgram experiment is imperfectly designed for two reasons: (1) The laboratory is not the place to test obedience; (2) Milgram disregarded the trust that subjects usually show an experimenter. To what extent do you agree with Baumrind's objec-tions? Do you find them all equally valid?

2. Baumrind states that the ethical procedures of the experiment keep it from having significant value. Do you agree?

3. Do you agree with Baumrind that the subjects were "entrapped" into committing unworthy acts?

4. Assume the identity of a participant in Milgram's experiment who obeyed the experimenter by shocking the learner with the maximum voltage. You have just returned from the lab, and your spouse asks you about your day. Compose the conversation that follows.

• Milgram concludes his critique in this way: "If there is a moral to be learned from the obedience study, it is that every man must be responsible for his own actions. This author accepts full responsibility for the design and execution of the study. Some people may feel it should not have been done. I dis-agree and accept the burden of their judgment."

TABLE 1   Excerpt from Questionnaire Used in a Follow-up Study of the Obedience Research

Now That I Have Read the Report, and All Things Considered . . .	Defiant	Obedient	All
1. I am very glad to have been in the experiment	40.0%	47.8%	43.5%
2. I am glad to have been in the experiment	43.8%	35.7%	40.2%
3. I am neither sorry nor glad to have been in the experiment	15.3%	14.8%	15.1%
4. I am sorry to have been in the experiment	0.8%	0.7%	0.8%
5. I am very sorry to have been in the experiment	0.0%	1.0%	0.5%

Note—Ninety-two percent of the subjects returned the questionnaire. The characteristics of the nonrespondents were checked against the respondents. They differed from the respondents only with regard to age; younger people were overrepresented in the nonresponding group.

The Stanford Prison Experiment
Philip G. Zimbardo

As well known—and as controversial—as the Milgram obedience experiments, the Stanford Prison Experiment (1973) raises troubling questions about the ability of individuals to resist authoritarian or obedient roles, if the social setting requires these roles. Philip G. Zimbardo, professor of psychology at Stanford University, set out to study the process by which prisoners and guards "learn" to become compliant and authoritarian, respectively. To find subjects for the experiment, Zimbardo placed an advertisement in a local newspaper:

> Male college students needed for psychological study of prison life. $15 per day for 1–2 weeks beginning Aug. 14. For further information & applications, come to Room 248, Jordan Hall, Stanford U.

The ad drew 75 responses. From these Zimbardo and his colleagues selected 21 college-age men, half of whom would become "prisoners" in the experiment, the other half "guards." The elaborate role-playing scenario, planned for two weeks, had to be cut short due to the intensity of subjects' responses. This article first appeared in the New York Times Magazine *on April 8, 1973.*

> *In prison, those things withheld from and denied to the prisoner become precisely what he wants most of all.*
> —Eldridge Cleaver, "Soul on Ice"

> *Our sense of power is more vivid when we break a man's spirit than when we win his heart.*
> —Eric Hoffer, "The Passionate State of Mind"

> *Every prison that men build / Is built with bricks of shame, / And bound with bars lest Christ should see / How men their brothers maim.*
> —Oscar Wilde, "The Ballad of Reading Gaol"

> *Wherever anyone is against his will that is to him a prison.*
> —Epictetus, "Discourses"

1   The quiet of a summer morning in Palo Alto, Calif., was shattered by a screeching squad car siren as police swept through the city picking up college students in a surprise mass arrest. Each suspect was charged with a felony, warned of his constitutional rights, spread-eagled against the car, searched, handcuffed, and carted off in the back seat of the squad car to the police station for booking.

2   After fingerprinting and the preparation of identification forms for his "jacket" (central information file), each prisoner was left isolated in a detention cell to wonder what he had done to get himself into this mess. After a while, he

"The Mind Is a Formidable Jailer" ["The Stanford Prison Experiment"] by Philip G. Zimbardo as published in the *New York Times Magazine*, 8 April 1973. Copyright © 1973 by the New York Times. Reprinted with permission from the New York Times.

was blindfolded and transported to the "Stanford County Prison." Here he began the process of becoming a prisoner—stripped naked, skin-searched, deloused, and issued a uniform, bedding, soap, and towel.

3   The warden offered an impromptu welcome:

4   "As you probably know, I'm your warden. All of you have shown that you are unable to function outside in the real world for one reason or another—that somehow you lack the responsibility of good citizens of this great country. We of this prison, your correctional staff, are going to help you learn what your responsibilities as citizens of this country are. Here are the rules. Sometime in the near future there will be a copy of the rules posted in each of the cells. We expect you to know them and to be able to recite them by number. If you follow all of these rules and keep your hands clean, repent for your misdeeds, and show a proper attitude of penitence, you and I will get along just fine."

5   There followed a reading of the 16 basic rules of prisoner conduct, "Rule Number One: Prisoners must remain silent during rest periods, after lights are out, during meals, and whenever they are outside the prison yard. Two: Prisoners must eat at mealtimes and only at mealtimes. Three: Prisoners must not move, tamper, deface, or damage walls, ceilings, windows, doors, or other prison property. . . . Seven: Prisoners must address each other by their ID number only. Eight: Prisoners must address the guards as 'Mr. Correctional Officer.' . . . Sixteen: Failure to obey any of the above rules may result in punishment."

6   By late afternoon these youthful "first offenders" sat in dazed silence on the cots in their barren cells trying to make sense of the events that had transformed their lives so dramatically.

7   If the police arrests and processing were executed with customary detachment, however, there were some things that didn't fit. For these men were now part of a very unusual kind of prison, an experimental mock prison, created by social psychologists to study the effects of imprisonment upon volunteer research subjects. When we planned our two-week-long simulation of prison life, we sought to understand more about the process by which people called "prisoners" lose their liberty, civil rights, independence, and privacy, while those called "guards" gain social power by accepting the responsibility for controlling and managing the lives of their dependent charges.

8   Why didn't we pursue this research in a real prison? First, prison systems are fortresses of secrecy, closed to impartial observation, and thereby immune to critical analysis from anyone not already part of the correctional authority. Second, in any real prison, it is impossible to separate what each individual brings into the prison from what the prison brings out in each person.

9   We populated our mock prison with a homogeneous group of people who could be considered "normal-average" on the basis of clinical interviews and personality tests. Our participants (10 prisoners and 11 guards) were selected from more than 75 volunteers recruited through ads in the city and campus newspapers. The applicants were mostly college students from all over the United States and Canada who happened to be in the Stanford area during the summer and were attracted by the lure of earning $15 a day for participating in a study of prison life. We selected only those judged to be emotionally stable, physically healthy, mature, law-abiding citizens.

10   The sample of average, middle-class, Caucasian, college-age males (plus one Oriental student) was arbitrarily divided by the flip of a coin. Half were randomly assigned to play the role of guards, the others of prisoners. There were no measurable differences between the guards and the prisoners at the start of the experiment. Although initially warned that as prisoners their privacy and other civil rights would be violated and that they might be subjected to harassment, every subject was completely confident of his ability to endure whatever the prison had to offer for the full two-week experimental period. Each subject unhesitatingly agreed to give his "informed consent" to participate.

11   The prison was constructed in the basement of Stanford University's psychology building, which was deserted after the end of the summer-school session. A long corridor was converted into the prison "yard" by partitioning off both ends. Three small laboratory rooms opening onto this corridor were made into cells by installing metal barred doors and replacing existing furniture with cots, three to a cell. Adjacent offices were refurnished as guards' quarters, interview-testing rooms, and bedrooms for the "warden" (Jaffe) and the "superintendent" (Zimbardo). A concealed video camera and hidden microphones recorded much of the activity and conversation of guards and prisoners. The physical environment was one in which prisoners could always be observed by the staff, the only exception being when they were secluded in solitary confinement (a small, dark storage closet, labeled "The Hole").

12   Our mock prison represented an attempt to simulate the psychological state of imprisonment in certain ways. We based our experiment on an in-depth analysis of the prison situation, developed after hundreds of hours of discussion with Carlo Prescott (our ex-con consultant), parole officers, and correctional personnel, and after reviewing much of the existing literature on prisons and concentration camps.

13   "Real" prisoners typically report feeling powerless, arbitrarily controlled, dependent, frustrated, hopeless, anonymous, dehumanized, and emasculated. It was not possible, pragmatically or ethically, to create such chronic states in volunteer subjects who realize that they are in an experiment for only a short time. Racism, physical brutality, indefinite confinement, and enforced homosexuality were not features of our mock prison. But we did try to reproduce those elements of the prison experience that seemed most fundamental.

14   We promoted anonymity by seeking to minimize each prisoner's sense of uniqueness and prior identity. The prisoners wore smocks and nylon stocking caps; they had to use their ID numbers; their personal effects were removed and they were housed in barren cells. All of this made them appear similar to each other and indistinguishable to observers. Their smocks, which were like dresses, were worn without undergarments, causing the prisoners to be restrained in their physical actions and to move in ways that were more feminine than masculine. The prisoners were forced to obtain permission from the guard for routine and simple activities such as writing letters, smoking a cigarette, or even going to the toilet; this elicited from them a childlike dependency.

15   Their quarters, though clean and neat, were small, stark, and without esthetic appeal. The lack of windows resulted in poor air circulation, and persistent odors arose from the unwashed bodies of the prisoners. After 10 P.M.

lockup, toilet privileges were denied, so prisoners who had to relieve themselves would have to urinate and defecate in buckets provided by the guards. Sometimes the guards refused permission to have them cleaned out, and this made the prison smell.

16   Above all, "real" prisons are machines for playing tricks with the human conception of time. In our windowless prison, the prisoners often did not even know whether it was day or night. A few hours after falling asleep, they were roused by shrill whistles for their "count." The ostensible purpose of the count was to provide a public test of the prisoners' knowledge of the rules and of their ID numbers. But more important, the count, which occurred at least once on each of the three different guard shifts, provided a regular occasion for the guards to relate to the prisoners. Over the course of the study, the duration of the counts was spontaneously increased by the guards from their initial perfunctory 10 minutes to a seemingly interminable several hours. During these confrontations, guards who were bored could find ways to amuse themselves, ridiculing recalcitrant prisoners, enforcing arbitrary rules, and openly exaggerating any dissension among the prisoners.

17   The guards were also "deindividualized": They wore identical khaki uniforms and silver reflector sunglasses that made eye contact with them impossible. Their symbols of power were billy clubs, whistles, handcuffs, and the keys to the cells and the "main gate." Although our guards received no formal training from us in how to be guards, for the most part they moved with apparent ease into their roles. The media had already provided them with ample models of prison guards to emulate.

18   Because we were as interested in the guards' behavior as in the prisoners', they were given considerable latitude to improvise and to develop strategies and tactics of prisoner management. Our guards were told that they must maintain "law and order" in this prison, that they were responsible for handling any trouble that might break out, and they were cautioned about the seriousness and potential dangers of the situation they were about to enter. Surprisingly, in most prison systems, "real" guards are not given much more psychological preparation or adequate training than this for what is one of the most complex, demanding, and dangerous jobs our society has to offer. They are expected to learn how to adjust to their new employment mostly from on-the-job experience, and from contacts with the "old bulls" during a survival-of-the-fittest orientation period. According to an orientation manual for correctional officers at San Quentin, "the only way you really get to know San Quentin is through experience and time. Some of us take more time and must go through more experiences than others to accomplish this; some really never do get there."

19   You cannot be a prisoner if no one will be your guard, and you cannot be a prison guard if no one takes you or your prison seriously. Therefore, over time a perverted symbiotic relationship developed. As the guards became more aggressive, prisoners became more passive; assertion by the guards led to dependency in the prisoners; self-aggrandizement was met with self-deprecation, authority with helplessness, and the counterpart of the guards' sense of mastery and control was the depression and hopelessness witnessed in the

prisoners. As these differences in behavior, mood, and perception became more evident to all, the need for the now "righteously" powerful guards to rule the obviously inferior and powerless inmates became a sufficient reason to support almost any further indignity of man against man:

20   Guard K: "During the inspection, I went to cell 2 to mess up a bed which the prisoner had made and he grabbed me, screaming that he had just made it, and he wasn't going to let me mess it up. He grabbed my throat, and although he was laughing I was pretty scared. . . . I lashed out with my stick and hit him in the chin (although not very hard), and when I freed myself I became angry. I wanted to get back in the cell and have a go with him, since he attacked me when I was not ready."

21   Guard M: "I was surprised at myself . . . I made them call each other names and clean the toilets out with their bare hands. I practically considered the prisoners cattle, and I kept thinking: 'I have to watch out for them in case they try something.'"

22   Guard A: "I was tired of seeing the prisoners in their rags and smelling the strong odors of their bodies that filled the cells. I watched them tear at each other on orders given by us. They didn't see it as an experiment. It was real and they were fighting to keep their identity. But we were always there to show them who was boss."

23   Because the first day passed without incident, we were surprised and totally unprepared for the rebellion that broke out on the morning of the second day. The prisoners removed their stocking caps, ripped off their numbers, and barricaded themselves inside the cells by putting their beds against the doors. What should we do? The guards were very much upset because the prisoners also began to taunt and curse them to their faces. When the morning shift of guards came on, they were upset at the night shift who, they felt, must have been too permissive and too lenient. The guards had to handle the rebellion themselves, and what they did was startling to behold.

24   At first they insisted that reinforcements be called in. The two guards who were waiting on stand-by call at home came in, and the night shift of guards voluntarily remained on duty (without extra pay) to bolster the morning shift. The guards met and decided to treat force with force. They got a fire extinguisher that shot a stream of skin-chilling carbon dioxide and forced the prisoners away from the doors; they broke into each cell, stripped the prisoners naked, took the beds out, forced the prisoners who were the ringleaders into solitary confinement, and generally began to harass and intimidate the prisoners.

25   After crushing the riot, the guards decided to head off further unrest by creating a privileged cell for those who were "good prisoners" and then, without explanation, switching some of the troublemakers into it and some of the good prisoners out into the other cells. The prisoner ringleaders could not trust these new cellmates because they had not joined in the riot and might even be "snitches." The prisoners never again acted in unity against the system. One of the leaders of the prisoner revolt later confided:

26   "If we had gotten together then, I think we could have taken over the place. But when I saw the revolt wasn't working, I decided to toe the line. Everyone settled into the same pattern. From then on, we were really controlled by the guards."

27   It was after this episode that the guards really began to demonstrate their inventiveness in the application of arbitrary power. They made the prisoners obey petty, meaningless, and often inconsistent rules, forced them to engage in tedious, useless work, such as moving cartons back and forth between closets and picking thorns out of their blankets for hours on end. (The guards had previously dragged the blankets through thorny bushes to create this disagreeable task.) Not only did the prisoners have to sing songs or laugh or refrain from smiling on command; they were also encouraged to curse and vilify each other publicly during some of the counts. They sounded off their numbers endlessly and were repeatedly made to do pushups, on occasion with a guard stepping on them or a prisoner sitting on them.

28   Slowly the prisoners became resigned to their fate and even behaved in ways that actually helped to justify their dehumanizing treatment at the hands of the guards. Analysis of the tape-recorded private conversations between prisoners and of remarks made by them to interviewers revealed that fully half could be classified as nonsupportive of other prisoners. More dramatic, 85 percent of the evaluative statements by prisoners about their fellow prisoners were uncomplimentary and deprecating.

29   This should be taken in the context of an even more surprising result. What do you imagine the prisoners talked about when they were alone in their cells with each other, given a temporary respite from the continual harassment and surveillance by the guards? Girl friends, career plans, hobbies or politics?

30   No, their concerns were almost exclusively riveted to prison topics. Their monitored conversations revealed that only 10 percent of the time was devoted to "outside" topics, while 90 percent of the time they discussed escape plans, the awful food, grievances or ingratiating tactics to use with specific guards in order to get a cigarette, permission to go to the toilet, or some other favor. Their obsession with these immediate survival concerns made talk about the past and future an idle luxury.

31   And this was not a minor point. So long as the prisoners did not get to know each other as people, they only extended the oppressiveness and reality of their life as prisoners. For the most part, each prisoner observed his fellow prisoners allowing the guards to humiliate them, acting like compliant sheep, carrying out mindless orders with total obedience, and even being cursed by fellow prisoners (at a guard's command). Under such circumstances, how could a prisoner have respect for his fellows, or any self-respect for what *he* obviously was becoming in the eyes of all those evaluating him?

32   The combination of realism and symbolism in this experiment had fused to create a vivid illusion of imprisonment. The illusion merged inextricably with reality for at least some of the time for every individual in the situation. It was remarkable how readily we all slipped into our roles, temporarily gave up our identities, and allowed these assigned roles and the social forces in the situation to guide, shape, and eventually to control our freedom of thought and action.

33   But precisely where does one's "identity" end and one's "role" begin? When the private self and the public role behavior clash, what direction will attempts to impose consistency take? Consider the reactions of the parents, relatives, and friends of the prisoners who visited their forlorn sons, brothers, and lovers during

two scheduled visitors' hours. They were taught in short order that they were our guests, allowed the privilege of visiting only by complying with the regulations of the institution. They had to register, were made to wait half an hour, were told that only two visitors could see any one prisoner; the total visiting time was cut from an hour to only 10 minutes, they had to be under the surveillance of a guard, and before any parents could enter the visiting area, they had to discuss their son's case with the warden. Of course they complained about these arbitrary rules, but their conditioned, middle-class reaction was to work within the system to appeal privately to the superintendent to make conditions better for their prisoners.

34   In less than 36 hours, we were forced to release prisoner 8612 because of extreme depression, disorganized thinking, uncontrollable crying, and fits of rage. We did so reluctantly because we believed he was trying to "con" us—it was unimaginable that a volunteer prisoner in a mock prison could legitimately be suffering and disturbed to that extent. But then on each of the next three days another prisoner reacted with similar anxiety symptoms, and we were forced to terminate them, too. In a fifth case, a prisoner was released after developing a psychosomatic rash over his entire body (triggered by rejection of his parole appeal by the mock parole board). These men were simply unable to make an adequate adjustment to prison life. Those who endured the prison experience to the end could be distinguished from those who broke down and were released early in only one dimension—authoritarianism. On a psychological test designed to reveal a person's authoritarianism, those prisoners who had the highest scores were best able to function in this authoritarian prison environment.

35   If the authoritarian situation became a serious matter for the prisoners, it became even more serious—and sinister—for the guards. Typically, the guards insulted the prisoners, threatened them, were physically aggressive, used instruments (night sticks, fire extinguishers, etc.) to keep the prisoners in line, and referred to them in impersonal, anonymous, deprecating ways: "Hey, you," or "You [obscenity], 5401, come here." From the first to the last day, there was a significant increase in the guards' use of most of these domineering, abusive tactics.

36   Everyone and everything in the prison was defined by power. To be a guard who did not take advantage of this institutionally sanctioned use of power was to appear "weak," "out of it," "wired up by the prisoners," or simply a deviant from the established norms of appropriate guard behavior. Using Erich Fromm's definition of sadism, as "the wish for absolute control over another living being," all of the mock guards at one time or another during this study behaved sadistically toward the prisoners. Many of them reported—in their diaries, on critical-incident report forms, and during post-experimental interviews—being delighted in the new-found power and control they exercised and sorry to see it relinquished at the end of the study.

37   Some of the guards reacted to the situation in the extreme and behaved with great hostility and cruelty in the forms of degradation they invented for the prisoners. But others were kinder; they occasionally did little favors for the prisoners, were reluctant to punish them, and avoided situations where prisoners were being harassed. The torment experienced by one of these good

guards is obvious in his perceptive analysis of what it felt like to be responded to as a "guard":

38   "What made the experience most depressing for me was the fact that we were continually called upon to act in a way that just was contrary to what I really feel inside. I don't feel like I'm the type of person that would be a guard, just constantly giving out [orders] . . . and forcing people to do things, and pushing and lying—it just didn't seem like me, and to continually keep up and put on a face like that is just really one of the most oppressive things you can do. It's almost like a prison that you create yourself—you get into it, and it becomes almost the definition you make of yourself, it almost becomes like walls, and you want to break out and you want just to be able to tell everyone that 'this isn't really me at all, and I'm not the person that's confined in there—I'm a person who wants to get out and show you that I am free, and I do have my own will, and I'm not the sadistic type of person that enjoys this kind of thing.'"

39   Still, the behavior of these good guards seemed more motivated by a desire to be liked by everyone in the system than by a concern for the inmates' welfare. No guard ever intervened in any direct way on behalf of the prisoners, ever interfered with the orders of the cruelest guards, or ever openly complained about the subhuman quality of life that characterized this prison.

40   Perhaps the most devastating impact of the more hostile guards was their creation of a capricious, arbitrary environment. Over time the prisoners began to react passively. When our mock prisoners asked questions, they got answers about half the time, but the rest of the time they were insulted and punished—and it was not possible for them to predict which would be the outcome. As they began to "toe the line," they stopped resisting, questioning and, indeed, almost ceased responding altogether. There was a general decrease in all categories of response as they learned the safest strategy to use in an unpredictable, threatening environment from which there is no physical escape—do nothing, except what is required. Act not, want not, feel not, and you will not get into trouble in prisonlike situations.

41   Can it really be, you wonder, that intelligent, educated volunteers could have lost sight of the reality that they were merely acting a part in an elaborate game that would eventually end? There are many indications not only that they did, but that, in addition, so did we and so did other apparently sensible, responsible adults.

42   Prisoner 819, who had gone into an uncontrollable crying fit, was about to be prematurely released from the prison when a guard lined up the prisoners and had them chant in unison, "819 is a bad prisoner. Because of what 819 did to prison property we all must suffer. 819 is a bad prisoner." Over and over again. When we realized 819 might be overhearing this, we rushed into the room where 819 was supposed to be resting, only to find him in tears, prepared to go back into the prison because he could not leave as long as the others thought he was a "bad prisoner." Sick as he felt, he had to prove to them he was not a "bad" prisoner. He had to be persuaded that he was not a prisoner at all, that the others were also just students, that this was just an experiment and not a prison and the prison staff were only research psychologists. A report from the warden notes, "While I believe that it was necessary for *staff* [me] to enact the warden role, at least some of the time, I am startled by the ease with which I could turn off my sensitivity and concern for others for 'a good cause.'"

43   Consider our overreaction to the rumor of a mass escape plot that one of the guards claimed to have overheard. It went as follows: Prisoner 8612, previously released for emotional disturbance, was only faking. He was going to round up a bunch of his friends, and they would storm the prison right after visiting hours. Instead of collecting data on the pattern of rumor transmission, we made plans to maintain the security of our institution. After putting a confederate informer into the cell 8612 had occupied to get specific information about the escape plans, the superintendent went back to the Palo Alto Police Department to request transfer of our prisoners to the old city jail. His impassioned plea was only turned down at the last minute when the problem of insurance and city liability for our prisoners was raised by a city official. Angered at this lack of cooperation, the staff formulated another plan. Our jail was dismantled, the prisoners, chained and blindfolded, were carted off to a remote storage room. When the conspirators arrived, they would be told the study was over, their friends had been sent home, there was nothing left to liberate. After they left, we would redouble the security features of our prison making any future escape attempts futile. We even planned to lure ex-prisoner 8612 back on some pretext and imprison him again, because he had been released on false pretenses! The rumor turned out to be just that—a full day had passed in which we collected little or no data, worked incredibly hard to tear down and then rebuild our prison. Our reaction, however, was as much one of relief and joy as of exhaustion and frustration.

44   When a former prison chaplain was invited to talk with the prisoners (the grievance committee had requested church services), he puzzled everyone by disparaging each inmate for not having taken any constructive action in order to get released. "Don't you know you must have a lawyer in order to get bail, or to appeal the charges against you?" Several of them accepted his invitation to contact their parents in order to secure the services of an attorney. The next night one of the parents stopped at the superintendent's office before visiting time and handed him the name and phone number of her cousin who was a public defender. She said that a priest had called her and suggested the need for a lawyer's services! We called the lawyer. He came, interviewed the prisoners, discussed sources of bail money, and promised to return again after the weekend.

45   But perhaps the most telling account of the insidious development of this new reality, of the gradual Kafkaesque metamorphosis of good into evil, appears in excerpts from the diary of one of the guards, Guard A:

46   *Prior to start of experiment:* "As I am a pacifist and nonaggressive individual. I cannot see a time when I might guard and/or maltreat other living things."

47   *After an orientation meeting:* "Buying uniforms at the end of the meeting confirms the gamelike atmosphere of this thing. I doubt whether many of us share the expectations of 'seriousness' that the experimenters seem to have."

48   *First Day:* "Feel sure that the prisoners will make fun of my appearance and I evolve my first basic strategy—mainly not to smile at anything they say or do which would be admitting it's all only a game. . . . At cell 3 I stop and setting my voice hard and low say to 5486, 'What are you smiling at?' 'Nothing, Mr. Correctional Officer.' 'Well, see that you don't.' (As I walk off I feel stupid.)"

49   *Second Day:* "5704 asked for a cigarette and I ignored him—because I am a non-smoker and could not empathize. . . . Meanwhile since I was feeling empathetic towards 1037, I determined not to talk with him. . . . After we had count and lights out [Guard D] and I held a loud conversation about going home to our girl friends and what we were going to do to them."

50   *Third Day (preparing for the first visitors' night):* "After warning the prisoners not to make any complaints unless they wanted the visit terminated fast, we finally brought in the first parents. I made sure I was one of the guards on the yard, because this was my first chance for the type of manipulative power that I really like—being a very noticed figure with almost complete control over what is said or not. While the parents and prisoners sat in chairs, I sat on the end of the table dangling my feet and contradicting anything I felt like. This was the first part of the experiment I was really enjoying. . . . 817 is being obnoxious and bears watching."

51   *Fourth Day:* ". . . The psychologist rebukes me for handcuffing and blindfolding a prisoner before leaving the [counseling] office, and I resentfully reply that it is both necessary security and my business anyway."

52   *Fifth Day:* "I harass 'Sarge' who continues to stubbornly overrespond to all commands. I have singled him out for the special abuse both because he begs for it and because I simply don't like him. The real trouble starts at dinner. The new prisoner (416) refuses to eat his sausage . . . we throw him into the Hole ordering him to hold sausages in each hand. We have a crisis of authority; this rebellious conduct potentially undermines the complete control we have over the others. We decide to play upon prisoner solidarity and tell the new one that all the others will be deprived of visitors if he does not eat his dinner. . . . I walk by and slam my stick into the Hole door. . . . I am very angry at this prisoner for causing discomfort and trouble for the others. I decided to force-feed him, but he wouldn't eat. I let the food slide down his face. I didn't believe it was me doing it. I hated myself for making him eat but I hated him more for not eating."

53   *Sixth Day:* "The experiment is over. I feel elated but am shocked to find some other guards disappointed somewhat because of the loss of money and some because they are enjoying themselves."

54   We were no longer dealing with an intellectual exercise in which a hypothesis was being evaluated in the dispassionate manner dictated by the canons of the scientific method. We were caught up in the passion of the present, the suffering, the need to control people, not variables, the escalation of power, and all the unexpected things that were erupting around and within us. We had to end this experiment: So our planned two-week simulation was aborted after only six (was it only six?) days and nights.

55   Was it worth all the suffering just to prove what everybody knows—that some people are sadistic, others weak, and prisons are not beds of roses? If that is all we demonstrated in this research, then it was certainly not worth the anguish. We believe there are many significant implications to be derived from this experience, only a few of which can be suggested here.

56   The potential social value of this study derives precisely from the fact that normal, healthy, educated young men could be so radically transformed under the institutional pressures of a "prison environment." If this could happen in

so short a time, without the excesses that are possible in real prisons, and if it could happen to the "cream-of-the-crop of American youth," then one can only shudder to imagine what society is doing both to the actual guards and prisoners who are at this very moment participating in that unnatural "social experiment."

57   The pathology observed in this study cannot be reasonably attributed in pre-existing personality differences of the subjects, that option being eliminated by our selection procedures and random assignment. Rather, the subjects' abnormal social and personal reactions are best seen as a product of their transaction with an environment that supported the behavior that would be pathological in other settings, but was "appropriate" in this prison. Had we observed comparable reactions in a real prison, the psychiatrist undoubtedly would have been able to attribute any prisoner's behavior to character defects or personality maladjustment, while critics of the prison system would have been quick to label the guards as "psychopathic." This tendency to locate the source of behavior disorders inside a particular person or group underestimates the power of situational forces.

58   Our colleague, David Rosenhan, has very convincingly shown that once a sane person (pretending to be insane) gets labeled as insane and committed to a mental hospital, it is the label that is the reality which is treated and not the person. This dehumanizing tendency to respond to other people according to socially determined labels and often arbitrarily assigned roles is also apparent in a recent "mock hospital" study designed by Norma Jean Orlando to extend the ideas in our research.

59   Personnel from the staff of Elgin State Hospital in Illinois role-played either mental patients or staff in a weekend simulation on a ward in the hospital. The mock mental patients soon displayed behavior indistinguishable from that we usually associate with the chronic pathological syndromes of acute mental patients: Incessant pacing, uncontrollable weeping, depression, hostility, fights, stealing from each other, complaining. Many of the "mock staff" took advantage of their power to act in ways comparable to our mock guards by dehumanizing their powerless victims.

60   During a series of encounter debriefing sessions immediately after our experiment, we all had an opportunity to vent our strong feelings and to reflect upon the moral and ethical issues each of us faced, and we considered how we might react more morally in future "real-life" analogues to this situation. Year-long follow-ups with our subjects via questionnaires, personal interviews, and group reunions indicate that their mental anguish was transient and situationally specific, but the self-knowledge gained has persisted.

61   By far the most disturbing implication of our research comes from the parallels between what occurred in that basement mock prison and daily experiences in our own lives—and we presume yours. The physical institution of prison is but a concrete and steel metaphor for the existence of more pervasive, albeit less obvious, prisons of the mind that all of us daily create, populate, and perpetuate. We speak here of the prisons of racism, sexism, despair, shyness, "neurotic hang-ups," and the like. The social convention of marriage, as one example, becomes for many couples a state of imprisonment in which one

partner agrees to be prisoner or guard, forcing or allowing the other to play the reciprocal role—invariably without making the contract explicit.

62   To what extent do we allow ourselves to become imprisoned by docilely accepting the roles others assign us or, indeed, choose to remain prisoners because being passive and dependent frees us from the need to act and be responsible for our actions? The prison of fear constructed in the delusions of the paranoid is no less confining or less real than the cell that every shy person erects to limit his own freedom in anxious anticipation of being ridiculed and rejected by his guards—often guards of his own making.

Review Questions

1. What was Zimbardo's primary goal in undertaking the prison experiment?

2. What was the profile of the subjects in the experiment? Why is this profile significant?

3. Zimbardo claims that there is a "process" (paragraphs 2, 7) of becoming a prisoner. What is this process?

4. What inverse psychological relationships developed between prisoners and guards?

5. What was the result of the prison "riot"?

6. Why did prisoners have no respect for each other or for themselves?

7. How does the journal of Guard A illustrate what Zimbardo calls the "gradual Kafkaesque metamorphosis of good into evil"? (See paragraphs 45–54.)

8. What are the reasons people would voluntarily become prisoners?

9. How can the mind keep people in jail?

Discussion and Writing Suggestions

1. Reread the four epigraphs to this article. Write a paragraph of response to any one of them, in light of Zimbardo's discussion of the prison experiment.

2. You may have thought, before reading this article, that being a prisoner is a physical fact, not a psychological state. What are the differences between these two views?

3. In paragraph 8, Zimbardo explains his reasons for not pursuing his research in a real prison. He writes that "it is impossible to separate what each individual brings into the prison from what the prison brings out in each person." What does he mean? And how does this distinction prove important later in the article? (See paragraph 58.)

4. Zimbardo reports that at the beginning of the experiment each of the "prisoner" subjects "was completely confident of his ability to endure whatever the prison had to offer for the full two-week experimental period" (paragraph 10). Had you been a subject, would you have been so confident, prior to the experiment? Given what you've learned of the experiment, do you think you would have psychologically "become" a prisoner or guard if you had been selected for these roles? (And if not, what makes you so sure?)

5. Identify two passages in this article: one that surprised you relating to the prisoners and one that surprised you relating to the guards. Write a paragraph explaining your response to each. Now read the two passages in light of each other. Do you see any patterns underlying your responses?

6. Zimbardo claims that the implications of his research matter deeply— that the mock prison he created is a metaphor for prisons of the mind "that all of us daily create, populate, and perpetuate" (paragraph 61). Zimbardo mentions the prisons of "racism, sexism, despair, [and] shyness." Choose any one of these and discuss how it might be viewed as a mental prison.

7. Reread paragraphs 61 and 62. Zimbardo makes a metaphorical jump from his experiment to the psychological realities of your daily life. Prisons—the artificial one he created and actual prisons—stand for something: social systems in which there are those who give orders and those who obey. All metaphors break down at some point. Where does this one break down?

8. Zimbardo suggests that we might "choose to remain prisoners because being passive and dependent frees us from the need to act and be responsible for our actions" (paragraph 62). Do you agree? What are the burdens of being disobedient?

Disobedience as a Psychological and Moral Problem
Erich Fromm

Erich Fromm (1900–1980) was one of the twentieth century's distinguished writers and thinkers. Psychoanalyst and philosopher, historian and sociologist, he ranged widely in his interests and defied easy characterization. Fromm studied the works of Freud and Marx closely, and published on them both, but he was not aligned strictly with either. In much of his voluminous writing, he struggled to articulate a view that could help bridge ideological and personal conflicts and bring dignity to those who struggled with isolation in the industrial world. Author of more than 30 books and contributor to numerous edited collections and journals, Fromm is best known for Escape from Freedom *(1941),* The Art of Loving *(1956), and* To Have or To Be? *(1976).*

In the essay that follows, first published in 1963, Fromm discusses the seductive comforts of obedience, and he makes distinctions among varieties of obedience, some of which he believes are destructive, and others, life affirming. His thoughts on nuclear annihilation may seem dated in these days of post–Cold War cooperation, but it is worth remembering that Fromm wrote his essay just after the Cuban missile crisis, when fears of a third world war ran high. (We might note that despite the welcome reductions of nuclear stockpiles, the United States and Russia still possess, and retain battle plans for, thousands of warheads.) And in the wake of the 9/11 attacks, the threat of terrorists acquiring and using nuclear weapons against the United States seems very real. On the major points of his essay, concerning the psychological and moral problems of obedience, Fromm remains as pertinent today as when he wrote more than 40 years ago.

1   For centuries kings, priests, feudal lords, industrial bosses, and parents have insisted that *obedience is a virtue* and that *disobedience is a vice.* In order to introduce another point of view, let us set against this position the following statement: *human history began with an act of disobedience, and it is not unlikely that it will be terminated by an act of obedience.*

2   Human history was ushered in by an act of disobedience according to the Hebrew and Greek myths. Adam and Eve, living in the Garden of Eden, were part of nature; they were in harmony with it, yet did not transcend it. They were in nature as the fetus is in the womb of the mother. They were human, and at the same time not yet human. All this changed when they disobeyed an order. By breaking the ties with earth and mother, by cutting the umbilical cord, man emerged from a prehuman harmony and was able to take the first step into independence and freedom. The act of disobedience set Adam and Eve free and opened their eyes. They recognized each other as strangers and the world outside them as strange and even hostile. Their act of disobedience broke the primary bond with nature and made them individuals. "Original sin," far from corrupting man, set him free; it was the beginning of history. Man had to leave the Garden of Eden in order to learn to rely on his own powers and to become fully human.

3   The prophets, in their messianic concept, confirmed the idea that man had been right in disobeying; that he had not been corrupted by his "sin," but freed from the fetters of pre-human harmony. For the prophets, *history* is the place where man becomes human; during its unfolding he develops his powers of reason and of love until he creates a new harmony between himself, his fellow man, and nature. This new harmony is described as "the end of days," that period of history in which there is peace between man and man, between man and nature. It is a "new" paradise created by man himself, and one which he alone could create because he was forced to leave the "old" paradise as a result of his disobedience.

4   Just as the Hebrew myth of Adam and Eve, so the Greek myth of Prometheus sees all human civilization based on an act of disobedience. Prometheus, in stealing the fire from the gods, lays the foundation for the evolution of man.

There would be no human history were it not for Prometheus' "crime." He, like Adam and Eve, is punished for his disobedience. But he does not repent and ask for forgiveness. On the contrary, he proudly says: "I would rather be chained to this rock than be the obedient servant of the gods."

5   Man has continued to evolve by acts of disobedience. Not only was his spiritual development possible only because there were men who dared to say no to the powers that be in the name of their conscience or their faith, but also his intellectual development was dependent on the capacity for being disobedient—disobedient to authorities who tried to muzzle new thoughts and to the authority of long-established opinions which declared a change to be nonsense.

6   If the capacity for disobedience constituted the beginning of human history, obedience might very well, as I have said, cause the end of human history. I am not speaking symbolically or poetically. There is the possibility, or even the probability, that the human race will destroy civilization and even all life upon earth within the next five to ten years. There is no rationality or sense in it. But the fact is that, while we are living technically in the Atomic Age, the majority of men—including most of those who are in power—still live emotionally in the Stone Age; that while our mathematics, astronomy, and the natural sciences are of the twentieth century, most of our ideas about politics, the state, and society lag far behind the age of science. If mankind commits suicide it will be because people will obey those who command them to push the deadly buttons; because they will obey the archaic passions of fear, hate, and greed; because they will obey obsolete clichés of State sovereignty and national honor. The Soviet leaders talk much about revolutions, and we in the "free world" talk much about freedom. Yet they and we discourage disobedience—in the Soviet Union explicitly and by force, in the free world implicitly and by the more subtle methods of persuasion.

7   But I do not mean to say that all disobedience is a virtue and all obedience is a vice. Such a view would ignore the dialectical relationship between obedience and disobedience. Whenever the principles which are obeyed and those which are disobeyed are irreconcilable, an act of obedience to one principle is necessarily an act of disobedience to its counterpart and vice versa. Antigone is the classic example of this dichotomy. By obeying the inhuman laws of the State, Antigone necessarily would disobey the laws of humanity. By obeying the latter, she must disobey the former. All martyrs of religious faiths, of freedom, and of science have had to disobey those who wanted to muzzle them in order to obey their own consciences, the laws of humanity, and of reason. If a man can only obey and not disobey, he is a slave; if he can only disobey and not obey, he is a rebel (not a revolutionary); he acts out of anger, disappointment, resentment, yet not in the name of a conviction or a principle.

8   However, in order to prevent a confusion of terms an important qualification must be made. Obedience to a person, institution, or power (heteronomous obedience) is submission; it implies the abdication of my autonomy and the acceptance of a foreign will or judgment in place of my own. Obedience to my own reason or conviction (autonomous obedience) is not an act of submission but one of affirmation. My conviction and my judgment, if authentically mine,

are part of me. If I follow them rather than the judgment of others, I am being myself; hence the word *obey* can be applied only in a metaphorical sense and with a meaning which is fundamentally different from the one in the case of "heteronomous obedience."

9   But this distinction still needs two further qualifications, one with regard to the concept of conscience and the other with regard to the concept of authority.

10   The word *conscience* is used to express two phenomena which are quite distinct from each other. One is the "authoritarian conscience" which is the internalized voice of an authority whom we are eager to please and afraid of displeasing. This authoritarian conscience is what most people experience when they obey their conscience. It is also the conscience which Freud speaks of, and which he called "Super-Ego." This Super-Ego represents the internalized commands and prohibitions of father, accepted by the son out of fear. Different from the authoritarian conscience is the "humanistic conscience"; this is the voice present in every human being and independent from external sanctions and rewards. Humanistic conscience is based on the fact that as human beings we have an intuitive knowledge of what is human and inhuman, what is conducive of life and what is destructive of life. This conscience serves our functioning as human beings. It is the voice which calls us back to ourselves, to our humanity.

11   Authoritarian conscience (Super-Ego) is still obedience to a power outside of myself, even though this power has been internalized. Consciously I believe that I am following *my* conscience; in effect, however, I have swallowed the principles of *power;* just because of the illusion that humanistic conscience and Super-Ego are identical, internalized authority is so much more effective than the authority which is clearly experienced as not being part of me. Obedience to the "authoritarian conscience," like all obedience to outside thoughts and power, tends to debilitate "humanistic conscience," the ability to be and to judge oneself.

12   The statement, on the other hand, that obedience to another person is *ipso facto* submission needs also to be qualified by distinguishing "irrational" from "rational" authority. An example of rational authority is to be found in the relationship between student and teacher; one of irrational authority in the relationship between slave and master. Both relationships are based on the fact that the authority of the person in command is accepted. Dynamically, however, they are of a different nature. The interests of the teacher and the student, in the ideal case, lie in the same direction. The teacher is satisfied if he succeeds in furthering the student; if he has failed to do so, the failure is his and the student's. The slave owner, on the other hand, wants to exploit the slave as much as possible. The more he gets out of him the more satisfied he is. At the same time, the slave tries to defend as best he can his claims for a minimum of happiness. The interests of slave and master are antagonistic, because what is advantageous to the one is detrimental to the other. The superiority of the one over the other has a different function in each case; in the first it is the condition for the furtherance of the person subjected to the authority, and in the second it is the condition for his exploitation. Another distinction runs parallel to this: rational authority is rational because the authority, whether it is held by a teacher or a captain of a ship giving orders in an emergency, acts in the name of reason

which, being universal, I can accept without submitting. Irrational authority has to use force or suggestion, because no one would let himself be exploited if he were free to prevent it.

13   Why is man so prone to obey and why is it so difficult for him to disobey? As long as I am obedient to the power of the State, the Church, or public opinion, I feel safe and protected. In fact it makes little difference what power it is that I am obedient to. It is always an institution, or men, who use force in one form or another and who fraudulently claim omniscience and omnipotence. My obedience makes me part of the power I worship, and hence I feel strong. I can make no error, since it decides for me; I cannot be alone, because it watches over me; I cannot commit a sin, because it does not let me do so, and even if I do sin, the punishment is only the way of returning to the almighty power.

14   In order to disobey, one must have the courage to be alone, to err, and to sin. But courage is not enough. The capacity for courage depends on a person's state of development. Only if a person has emerged from mother's lap and father's commands, only if he has emerged as a fully developed individual and thus has acquired the capacity to think and feel for himself, only then can he have the courage to say "no" to power, to disobey.

15   A person can become free through acts of disobedience by learning to say no to power. But not only is the capacity for disobedience the condition for freedom; freedom is also the condition for disobedience. If I am afraid of freedom, I cannot dare to say "no," I cannot have the courage to be disobedient. Indeed, freedom and the capacity for disobedience are inseparable; hence any social, political, and religious system which proclaims freedom, yet stamps out disobedience, cannot speak the truth.

16   There is another reason why it is so difficult to dare to disobey, to say "no" to power. During most of human history obedience has been identified with virtue and disobedience with sin. The reason is simple: thus far throughout most of history a minority has ruled over the majority. This rule was made necessary by the fact that there was only enough of the good things of life for the few, and only the crumbs remained for the many. If the few wanted to enjoy the good things and, beyond that, to have the many serve them and work for them, one condition was necessary: the many had to learn obedience. To be sure, obedience can be established by sheer force. But this method has many disadvantages. It constitutes a constant threat that one day the many might have the means to overthrow the few by force; furthermore there are many kinds of work which cannot be done properly if nothing but fear is behind the obedience. Hence the obedience which is only rooted in the fear of force must be transformed into one rooted in man's heart. Man must want and even need to obey, instead of only fearing to disobey. If this is to be achieved, power must assume the qualities of the All Good, of the All Wise; it must become All Knowing. If this happens, power can proclaim that disobedience is sin and obedience virtue; and once this has been proclaimed, the many can accept obedience because it is good and detest disobedience because it is bad, rather than to detest themselves for being cowards. From Luther to the nineteenth century one was concerned with overt and explicit authorities. Luther, the pope, the princes, wanted to uphold it; the middle class, the workers, the

philosophers, tried to uproot it. The fight against authority in the State as well as in the family was often the very basis for the development of an independent and daring person. The fight against authority was inseparable from the intellectual mood which characterized the philosophers of the enlightenment and the scientists. This "critical mood" was one of faith in reason, and at the same time of doubt in everything which is said or thought, inasmuch as it is based on tradition, superstition, custom, power. The principles *sapere aude* and *de omnibus est dubitandum*—"dare to be wise" and "of all one must doubt"— were characteristic of the attitude which permitted and furthered the capacity to say "no."

17   The case of Adolf Eichmann [see note, page 221] is symbolic of our situation and has a significance far beyond the one in which his accusers in the courtroom in Jerusalem were concerned with. Eichmann is a symbol of the organization man, of the alienated bureaucrat for whom men, women and children have become numbers. He is a symbol of all of us. We can see ourselves in Eichmann. But the most frightening thing about him is that after the entire story was told in terms of his own admissions, he was able in perfect good faith to plead his innocence. It is clear that if he were once more in the same situation he would do it again. And so would we—and so do we.

18   The organization man has lost the capacity to disobey, he is not even aware of the fact that he obeys. At this point in history the capacity to doubt, to criticize, and to disobey may be all that stands between a future for mankind and the end of civilization.

Review Questions

1. What does Fromm mean when he writes that disobedience is "the first step into independence and freedom"?

2. Fromm writes that history began with an act of disobedience and will likely end with an act of obedience. What does he mean?

3. What is the difference between "heteronomous obedience" and "autonomous obedience"?

4. How does Fromm distinguish between "authoritarian conscience" and "humanistic conscience"?

5. When is obedience to another person *not* submission?

6. What are the psychological comforts of obedience, and why would authorities rather have people obey out of love than out of fear?

Discussion and Writing Suggestions

1. Fromm suggests that scientifically we live in the modern world but that politically and emotionally we live in the Stone Age. As you observe events in the world, both near and far, would you agree? Why?

2. Fromm writes: "If a man can only obey and not disobey, he is a slave; if he can only disobey and not obey, he is a rebel (not a revolutionary)" (paragraph 7). Explain Fromm's meaning here. Explain, as well, the implication that to be fully human one must have the freedom to both obey and disobey.

3. Fromm writes that "obedience makes me part of the power I worship, and hence I feel strong" (paragraph 13). Does this statement ring true for you? Discuss, in writing, an occasion in which you felt powerful because you obeyed a group norm.

4. In paragraphs 15 and 16, Fromm equates obedience with cowardice. Can you identify a situation in which you were obedient but, now that you reflect on it, were also cowardly? That is, can you recall a time when you caved in to a group but now wish you hadn't? Explain.

5. Fromm says that we can see ourselves in Adolf Eichmann—that as an organization man he "has lost the capacity to disobey, he is not even aware of the fact that he obeys." To what extent do you recognize yourself in this portrait?

Uncivil Disobedience: Violating the Rules for Breaking the Law
James J. Lopach and Jean A. Luckowski

Most of the readings in this chapter have illustrated the dangers of unthinking obedience to either individual or group authority. But we don't mean to suggest that disobedience is always the best, the wisest, the most moral, or the most logical choice. As even Stanley Milgram acknowledged at the beginning of his article, "Some system of authority is a requirement of all communal living, and it is only the person dwelling in isolation who is not forced to respond, with defiance or submission, to the commands of others" (page 214). Many believe that even in cases of civil disobedience, when people break laws they consider to be unjust, they should base their actions on respect for fundamental principles, rather than on personal preferences.

In the following article, James J. Lopach and Jean A. Luckowski consider the circumstances under which acts of civil disobedience are justified—and, particularly, whether or not they follow the precepts of such honored practitioners as Socrates, Mohandas Gandhi, and Martin Luther King, Jr. The authors urge teachers and students to find a reasonable balance between the two poles of authority and anarchy.

James J. Lopach is a professor in the department of political science at the University of Montana, where he teaches American government and public law. Jean A. Luckowski is a professor in the department of curriculum and instruction at the University of Montana, where she teaches social studies methods and professional ethics. This article was originally published in Education Next, *Spring 2005.*

1   A new kind of civil disobedience came to Missoula, Montana, recently. On a bridge over the Clark Fork River, a group from Wild Rockies Earth First! blocked a truck carrying logs from the Bitterroot Forest. Two of the protesters tied ropes to the rig, lowered themselves and their sign, "Globalization Kills Our Forests," to within a few feet of the torrent below, and refused to cooperate with rescuers who were dispatched from local fire stations to "rescue" them. The Earth Firsters were eventually coaxed to safety and charged with felony criminal endangerment. At their arraignment they denied that they had put the firefighters at risk, demanded to be set free, and ridiculed the conditions of their release on bail. One defendant brandished what a local newspaper called her "flame-and-monkey-wrench tattoos," an emblem, apparently, of her willingness to wreck rather than to respect government.

2   Earth First's brand of civil disobedience—frequently ill-tempered, not always nonviolent, and often coolly self-righteous—seems to be increasingly popular these days. Groups as diverse as ACT UP (gay rights), Critical Mass (environmental bicyclists), even the archconservative Catholic League are getting on the civil disobedience bandwagon. After the Ninth Circuit Court upheld a ban on "under God" in the Pledge of Allegiance in 2003, the League's president wrote, "It is up to the teachers in the nine western states affected by this decision to break the law. They should instruct their students on the meaning of civil disobedience and then practice it." Some of the new breed of lawbreakers lay claim to the traditions of civil disobedience. ACT UP, for instance, says its "fusion of organized mass struggle and nonviolence . . . originated largely with Mohandas Gandhi." Appreciation of that past seems to be shockingly selective, however. Indeed, as even the Catholic League president insinuated, our schools, incubators of civic culture, play a significant role in instructing students about civil disobedience. But are American schools teaching the fundamentals of the social contract? Do our teachers appreciate that there is more to civil disobedience than mere self-expression or simple claims on conscience?

Not Your Father's Disobedience

3   Traditional civil disobedience has usually combined deep spiritual beliefs with intense political ones. And while appreciating the differences in the two worlds—render unto Caesar what is Caesar's and to God what is God's—practitioners respected both. Gandhi, for instance, while leading a massive populist movement against British occupation of India (in the 1930s and 1940s), grew distrustful of mass demonstrations because participants were unwilling to go through the difficult process of purifying their actions; that is, grounding their activism in religious faith and human dignity. Martin Luther King, who warned that civil disobedience risked anarchy, went to jail "openly, lovingly, and with a willingness to accept the penalty."

4   While sometimes willful and defiant and sometimes passive to the point of self-extinction (Socrates did not protest his punishment), the heroes of civil disobedience believed in the need to obey a higher authority and to be cleansed of self-interestedness. For instance, King's words from an Alabama jail cell in 1963 (where he was being punished for marching in defiance of a court order): "A just law is a man-made code that squares with the moral law or the law of God. . . .

An unjust law is a human law that is not rooted in eternal law and natural law." Compare those sentiments with the words written 40 years later by Craig Marshall, an Earth Liberation Front activist, from his Oregon jail cell (where he was serving a five-year term for setting fire to logging trucks): "There are necessary evils if we want to be effective in our struggles, such as the use of petro-fuels in igniting huge bonfires in which we can watch corporations go bankrupt. . . . I hope I don't sound as if I'm condemning these activities—by all means, burn the [expletive deleted] to the ground."

5 Compare the reasoning of Gandhi and King, who presume harmony between a moral order and a rightly formed conscience, to the rationalizing of Earth First! and its political cousin the Earth Liberation Front (ELF). For Earth First! an ethic of "Deep Ecology" justifies "using all the tools in the tool box—ranging from grassroots organizing [to] monkey wrenching [which includes] ecotage, ecodefense, billboard bandits, desurveying, road reclamation, tree spiking."

6 Similarly, the Earth Liberation Front argues that "dependence on the substances in the natural environment" justifies "more and more step[ping] outside of this societal law to enforce natural law" and boasts that since late 1997 "there have been over two dozen major actions performed by the ELF in North America alone resulting in nearly $40 million in damage."

7 In many respects Martin Luther King would seem to have more in common with the Supreme Court, which dismissed his Birmingham appeal, than with modern protesters. "In fair administration of justice no man can be judge in his own case," the Court wrote in 1967, "however exalted his station, however righteous his motives, and irrespective of his race, color, politics, or religion. . . . Respect for judicial process is a small price to pay for the civilizing hand of law, which alone can give abiding meaning to constitutional freedom."

Then and Now—and Then Again

8 In 1972, when the United States was experiencing race riots, war protests, and campus violence, Harvard political scientist Edward C. Banfield penned an essay, "How Many, and Who, Should Be Set at Liberty?" describing an American society spinning out of control. Banfield sounded an alarm that should resonate for teachers, administrators, and curriculum committees today as they consider their civic education duties. Banfield quoted John Locke grouching about youth's innate "inability to control impulses and to take the future into account." He went on to warn that society would only prolong this adolescent predisposition if it instructed the individual "that he must be his own ultimate judge of what is right and wrong and that the 'moral censure' of anyone claiming authority over him is mere opinion." Quoting another political philosopher, John Stuart Mill, Banfield notes that no society can reasonably expect a liberated individual to naturally "accept and act upon certain indispensable social rules," and so society must transmit the wisdom and authority of "received opinion" to its young lest they remain mere children.

9 Unfortunately, contemporary social studies practice runs the risk of increasing, more than decreasing, the likelihood that students leave schools as mere children. Even aside from the question of whether schools are adequately exposing students to ideas of political theorists like Locke and Mill (much less to

those of Plato, Jean-Jacques Rousseau, or Thomas Jefferson), the learning theory known as "constructivism"* has encouraged the ahistorical trend. Now widely accepted among educators, constructivism has, inadvertently perhaps, undermined a sense of responsibility to the larger community by, as Diane Ravitch has observed, encouraging students to "construct . . . their own knowledge through their own discoveries."

10   When viewed simply as a student-centered methodology and poorly applied, constructivism can—and does—lead to inadequate teacher-led explanations of complex ideas like that of the "unjust law." And by emphasizing that children are their own measure of things, teachers shirk their responsibility as subject-matter experts. Students with a faulty moral compass and nothing but half-baked opinions come away from the classroom thinking that laws are simply inconvenient obstacles to achieving personal goals.

What's Taught—What's Not

11 In fact, there are civil disobedience lesson plans, but most are based on poorly applied constructivist theory. One developed by Gallaudet University, for instance, invites high school students to compare the Underground Railroad with some other act of civil disobedience in U.S. history, but offers no basic definition of the concept and instead simplistically asks students "when they might consider breaking the law because it is unjust." Typical of these lesson plans, it is thin on substance, leaves the students to teach themselves about civil disobedience, and does not help teachers whose own knowledge of civil disobedience is weak.

12   Even the best of social studies materials can set students on the wrong track. A PBS lesson plan on civil disobedience, packaged with the video, "A Force More Powerful: A Century of Nonviolent Conflict," says that Gandhi's method of nonviolence had three parts: "identify an unjust law . . . , refuse to obey it, and accept the consequences." While more substantive than many such materials, the PBS lesson still leaves out the critical Gandhian step of self-purification. According to Gandhi, who was also known as Mahatma, or "Great Soul," this is the time when practitioners must make a "total moral commitment," that is, commit themselves to "a living faith in a living God" and not to a "useful political strategy in a specific situation." This is no small matter in the civil disobedience tradition—and it could be considered a major omission from the PBS lesson. King, too, urged his followers to steel themselves to passive nonviolence

---

* **Constructivism:** According to the Southwest Educational Development Laboratory (a nonprofit educational development corporation based in Austin, Texas, <http://www.sedl.org/scimath/compass/v0ln03/>), constructivism is a method for "constructing knowledge in the classroom." The child learns

by gathering information and experiencing the world around her. Such learning exemplifies constructivism—an idea that has caused much excitement and interest among educators. Constructivism emphasizes the importance of the knowledge, beliefs, and skills an individual brings to the experience of learning. It recognizes the construction of new understanding as a combination of prior learning, new information, and readiness to learn. Individuals make choices about what new ideas to accept and how to fit them into their established views of the world.

—*Classroom Compass*, Winter 1994 (1:3)

in the manner of Jesus Christ. For Gandhi and King, law-breaking is justified only when it respects authority and recognizes the opponent's human dignity.

13   Another PBS lesson plan on civil disobedience asks students to identify "issues of concern" (such as school uniforms or a tax exemption for a business that pollutes), "brainstorm different ways people make their opinions known about issues of concern," "discuss which of these methods are 'acceptable' means of protest to them," and "identify possible negative consequences of activism to individuals engaged in these activities." Missing from the plan is a definition of civil disobedience or mention of the four essential components of civil disobedience— or even the three components that they had identified in the earlier lesson. Nor does the lesson discuss the difference between a fundamental principle and a personal desire or between legal protest, civil disobedience, and purely criminal activity, much less the threats that each poses to a democratic society. In these and other lessons, the teacher is directed to place the burden on the student to "construct" his or her own understanding of civil disobedience—a notion that contradicts the beliefs of the most profound protesters.

14   In matters of civil disobedience such constructivism only pushes students toward a naive belief in the primacy of conscience (which can easily become a synonym for self-centeredness). Even the Center for Civic Education, a 40-year-old nonprofit organization whose National Advisory Committee reads like a Who's Who of democratic values and traditions (including a dozen current and former members of Congress and a couple of Supreme Court justices), does not explain in its curriculum standards that civil disobedience is rooted in fundamental principles as opposed to personal preferences.

A Defective Canon

15   It is not surprising, then, that history and government textbooks, increasingly shaped by loose standards, incomplete assessments, and a generation of constructivist pedagogy, poorly serve the teacher's critical need for solid information about civil disobedience. Many U.S. history textbooks make only superficial mention of civil disobedience, generally in relation to the modern civil-rights movement. One widely used 8th-grade text, *American Odyssey*, by Gary Nash, contends that King followed the "Gandhian strategy of nonviolence . . . investigation, negotiation, publicity, and demonstration," but omits mention of self-purification and the need to accept the consequences of one's actions.

16   Twelfth-grade American government texts, where a political theory perspective is expected, routinely say almost nothing about civil disobedience. The Center for Civic Education's secondary-level *We the People* ignores the acceptance of consequences in its answer to the question, "Must you obey bad rules?" Another senior government text (*American Government*, by Steven Kelman) implies that all peaceful protest is legal protest and describes King's nonviolent activities without explaining civil disobedience. Though these texts do not specifically condone civil disobedience, neither do they encourage students to consider the wisdom of the past while making their own judgments.

17   To provide some perspective on the question of what is not taught in most civics texts, we look at *American Civics* by William Hartley and William

Vincent. They provide one of the more succinct definitions of civil disobedience offered to high schoolers: "The right of all Americans to express their dissent against laws in these and many other ways is protected by the Constitution. People do not have the right, however, to break the laws while expressing their dissent. . . . During the civil-rights movement, and at other times in the past, some Americans have shown their dissent by intentionally disobeying laws they believed to be wrong. This practice is called civil disobedience. As you know, people who disobey a law must face the consequences." This kind of treatment is needed for students who should be wrestling with fundamental concepts of government rather than their personal feelings about it.

Do as I Say—Or as I Do?

18 A student's inclination to cross the line of legality under the guise of self-expression can also be abetted by imprudent teachers. According to a 2003 report in a Maryland newspaper, a local high school English teacher, as part of a lesson on Henry David Thoreau, urged his students to perform a "nonconformist act." Two young women were suspended from school after they stood on top of a cafeteria table, staged a long kiss, and shouted "End homophobia now!" What lessons the teacher drew from this event we do not know. But such pedagogy merely trivializes civil disobedience and panders to students' desires to be outrageous and to make adults uncomfortable.

19   A Kentucky high school teacher took negative role modeling further, getting convicted for trespassing on the U.S. government's Western Hemisphere Institute for Security Cooperation at Fort Benning, Georgia, and then fired for missing class while serving her 90-day jail sentence. While she complained, according to *Education Week,* that the school district should have granted her a leave of absence, a letter writer to the newspaper reminded the teacher of her history: "While civil disobedience and legal protest have long been used as ways of attracting attention to a cause, civil disobedience is unique because it has always carried with it the obvious risk of arrest and possible imprisonment."

20   Though the trespassing teacher is surely an anomaly, her apparent failure to appreciate the important nuances in balancing liberty and authority is an all-too-common failing of the new civil disobedience. Coming to the correct balance means neither empowering political majorities to regulate liberty in new ways nor excusing individuals from the consequences of their actions. Getting the balance right means thwarting the present trend toward teaching the tenets of personal autonomy and ignoring the history that has already taught us much about the need for—and limits of—legitimate government. The forces that shape civics education—teachers, standards, methods, and materials—have important roles to play. But they must state clearly that civil disobedience differs from peaceful and legal protest; that civil disobedience involves violating a law that a rightly formed conscience determines to be in conflict with a fundamental principle of human dignity; and that civil disobedience is circumscribed by the practitioner's obligation to honor legitimate government by accepting punishment openly and respectfully. Without this tilt toward authority and away from anarchy, individual liberty will be endangered.

Review Questions

1. In what ways do the tactics of organizations like Earth First! and the Earth Liberation Front violate the central tenets of civil disobedience, as practiced by Mohandas Gandhi and Martin Luther King, according to Lopach and Luckowski?

2. What are the "four essential components of civil disobedience," according to the authors?

3. How has the teaching of civil disobedience been "defective," according to the authors?

Discussion and Writing Suggestions

1. The authors begin with an example of civil disobedience practiced by the environmental group Earth First! What do you think of the goals and tactics of such environmental groups? Before responding, you may want to conduct a preliminary Web search for information about Earth First!

2. Lopach and Luckowski draw a distinction between the kinds of civil disobedience practiced by Socrates, Gandhi, and King and the kind practiced by contemporary groups such as Earth First! and other practioners of "constructivisim." They also draw a distinction between disobedience "rooted in fundamental principles as opposed to [disobedience rooted in] personal preferences." To what extent do you understand and accept these differences? Who should be the arbiter of such distinctions? To what extent might members of Earth First! or the Earth Liberation Front accept or reject these distinctions or argue that they are indeed acting in support of "fundamental principles"?

3. The authors blame many social science and civics textbooks of the last 30 years, as well as teachers, for presenting inaccurate or incomplete accounts of civil disobedience. In some cases, "such pedagogy merely trivializes civil disobedience and panders to students' desires to be outrageous and to make adults uncomfortable." They also assert (provocatively) that "[s]tudents with a faulty moral compass and nothing but half-baked opinions come away from the classroom thinking that laws are simply inconvenient obstacles to achieving personal goals." Consider your own education in civil disobedience, both from textbooks and from teachers. To what extent do Lopach and Luckowski appear justified in their critique? For example, does your understanding of civil disobedience include the willingness to go to jail, or to face other legal penalties, as a consequence of disobeying what you consider unjust laws?

4. Lopach and Luckowski argue that teachers should emphasize that "civil disobedience involves violating a law that a rightly formed conscience determines to be in conflict with a fundamental principle of human dignity. . . . " (See also paragraph 5.) What do they mean by a "rightly formed conscience"? What do *you* think a "rightly formed conscience"

means? For example, does it mean a state of mind that impels you to do whatever you would prefer to do (and what duly constituted authority—whether parents, teachers, or government—prohibits you from doing), consistent with your own general principles of morality? To what extent could the standard of a "rightly formed conscience" be used to justify *any* behavior?

SYNTHESIS ACTIVITIES

1. Compare and contrast the Asch and the Milgram experiments, considering their separate (1) objectives, (2) experimental designs and procedures, (3) results, and (4) conclusions. To what extent do the findings of these two experiments reinforce one another? To what extent do they highlight different, if related, social phenomena? To what extent do their results reinforce those of Zimbardo's prison experiment?

2. Milgram writes that "perhaps the most fundamental lesson of our study [is that] ordinary people, simply doing their jobs, and without any particular hostility on their part, can become agents in a terrible destructive process." Using this statement as a principle, analyze several situations recounted in this chapter, and perhaps some outside this chapter, of which you are aware because of your studies, your reading, and possibly even your own experience. Draw upon not only Milgram himself, but also Asch, Zimbardo, and Fromm.

3. The writer Doris Lessing has argued that children need to be taught how to disobey so they can recognize and avoid situations that give rise to harmful obedience. If you were the curriculum coordinator for your local school system, how would you teach children to disobey responsibly? What would be your curriculum? What homework would you assign? What class projects? What field trips? One complicated part of your job would be to train children to understand the difference between *responsible* disobedience and anarchy. What is the difference?

   Take up these questions in a paper that draws on both your experiences as a student and your understanding of the selections in this chapter. Points that you might want to consider in developing the paper: defining overly obedient children; appropriate classroom behavior for responsibly disobedient children (as opposed to inappropriate behavior); reading lists; homework assignments; field trips; class projects.

4. A certain amount of obedience is a given in society. Stanley Milgram and others observe that social order, civilization itself, would not be possible unless individuals were willing to surrender a portion of their autonomy to the state. Allowing that we all are obedient (we must be), define the point at which obedience to a figure of authority becomes dangerous.

As you develop your definition, consider the ways you might use the work of authors in this chapter and their definitions of acceptable and unacceptable levels of obedience. Do you agree with the ways in which others have drawn the line between reasonable and dangerous obedience? What examples from current stories in the news or from your own experience can you draw on to test various definitions?

5. Describe a situation in which you were faced with a moral dilemma of whether or not to obey a figure of authority. After describing the situation and the action you took (or didn't take), analyze your behavior in light of any two readings in this chapter. You might consider a straightforward, four-part structure for your paper: (1) your description; (2) your discussion, in light of source A; (3) your discussion, in light of source B; and (4) your conclusion— an overall appraisal of your behavior.

6. Erich Fromm equates disobedience with courage: "In order to disobey, one must have the courage to be alone, to err, and to sin." Novelist Doris Lessing makes much the same statement by equating obedience with shame: "among our most shameful memories is this, how often we said black was white because other people were saying it." Using such statements as principles for analysis, examine an act of obedience or disobedience in your own life and determine the extent to which, following Fromm or Lessing, you now consider it courageous or shameful. Having completed this part of your analysis, conclude by reassessing your behavior. Write one or more paragraphs on whether or not you would behave similarly if given a second chance in the same situation.

7. Discuss the critical reaction to the Milgram experiments. Draw upon Baumrind, as well as Milgram himself, in summarizing both the ethical and procedural objections to the experiments. Following these summaries, develop your own critique, positive or negative, bringing in Milgram himself, where appropriate.

8. In his response to Diana Baumrind, Stanley Milgram makes a point of insisting that follow-up interviews with subjects in his experiments show that a large majority were pleased, in the long run, to have participated. (See Table 1 in the footnote to Baumrind, pages 231–232.) Writing on his own postexperiment surveys and interviews, Philip Zimbardo writes that his subjects believed their "mental anguish was transient and situationally specific, but the self-knowledge gained has persisted" (paragraph 60). Why might they *and* the experimenters nonetheless have been eager to accept a positive, final judgment of the experiments? Develop a paper in response to this question, drawing on the selections by Milgram, Zimbardo, and Baumrind.

9. Develop a synthesis in which you extend Baumrind's critique of Milgram to the Stanford Prison Experiment. This assignment

requires that you understand the core elements of Baumrind's critique; that you have a clear understanding of Zimbardo's experiment; and that you systematically apply elements of the critique, as you see fit, to Zimbardo's work. In your conclusion, offer your overall assessment of the Stanford Prison Experiment. To do this, you might answer Zimbardo's own question in paragraph 55: "Was [the experiment] worth all the suffering?" Or you might respond to another question: Do you agree that Zimbardo is warranted in extending the conclusions of his experiment to the general population?

10. In response to the question "Why is man so prone to obey and why is it so difficult for him to disobey?" Erich Fromm suggests that obedience lets people identify with the powerful and invites feelings of safety. Disobedience is psychologically more difficult and requires an act of courage (see paragraphs 13 and 14). Solomon Asch notes that the tendency to conformity is generally stronger than the tendency to independence. And in his final paragraph, Philip Zimbardo writes that a "prison of fear" keeps people compliant and frees them of the need to take responsibility for their own actions. In a synthesis that draws on these three sources, explore the interplay of *fear* and its opposite, *courage,* in relation to obedience. To prevent the paper from becoming too abstract, direct your attention repeatedly to a single case, the details of which will help to keep your focus. This case may be based upon a particular event from your own life or the life of someone you know.

11. For purposes of evaluating the moral aspects of acts of obedience and disobedience, Erich Fromm posits two kinds of obedience: "heteronomous" and "autonomous." The first, which is an act of submission, is obedience "to a person, institution, or power." The second is obedience "to my own reason or conviction," and so is not submission, but rather affirmation. Fromm makes further distinctions, such as that between the "authoritarian conscience" and the "humanistic conscience" and between submission to "rational authority" and submission to "irrational authority." Compare and contrast some of Lopach and Luckowski's distinctions (such as the distinction between "fundamental principles" and "personal preferences") with Fromm's distinctions. Evaluate some of the acts of obedience (for example, by radical environmental groups) discussed by Lopach and Luckowski in light of some of Fromm's categories.

RESEARCH ACTIVITIES

1. When Milgram's results were first published in book form in 1974, they generated heated controversy. The reaction by Baumrind reprinted here represents only a very small portion of that

controversy. Research other reactions to the Milgram experiments and discuss your findings. Begin with the reviews listed and excerpted in the *Book Review Digest;* also use the *Social Science Index,* the *Readers' Guide to Periodical Literature,* and newspaper indexes to locate articles, editorials, and letters to the editor on the experiments. (Note that editorials and letters are not always indexed. Letters appear within two to four weeks of the weekly magazine articles to which they refer, and within one to two weeks of newspaper articles.) What were the chief types of reactions? To what extent were the reactions favorable?

2. Milgram begins his book *Obedience to Authority* with a reference to Nazi Germany. The purpose of his experiment, in fact, was to help throw light on how the Nazi atrocities could have happened. Research the Nuremberg war crimes tribunals following World War II. Drawing specifically on the statements of those who testified at Nuremberg, as well as those who have written about it, show how Milgram's experiments do help explain the Holocaust and other Nazi crimes. In addition to relevant articles, see Telford Taylor, *Nuremberg and Vietnam: An American Tragedy* (1970); Hannah Arendt, *Eichmann in Jerusalem: A Report on the Banality of Evil* (1963); Richard A. Falk, Gabriel Kolko, and Robert J. Lifton (eds.), *Crimes of War* (1971).

3. Obtain a copy of the transcript of the trial of Adolf Eichmann—the Nazi official who carried out Hitler's "final solution" for the extermination of the Jews. Read also Hannah Arendt's *Eichmann in Jerusalem: A Report on the Banality of Evil,* along with the reviews of this book. Write a critique both of Arendt's book and of the reviews it received.

4. The My Lai massacre in Vietnam in 1969 was a particularly egregious case of overobedience to military authority in wartime. Show the connections between this event and Milgram's experiments. Note that Milgram himself treated the My Lai massacre in the epilogue to his *Obedience to Authority: An Experimental View* (1974).

5. Investigate the court-martial of Lt. William Calley, convicted for his role in the My Lai massacre. Discuss whether President Nixon was justified in commuting his sentence. Examine in detail the dilemmas the jury must have faced when presented with Calley's defense that he was only following orders.

6. Research the Watergate break-in of 1972 and the subsequent cover-up by Richard Nixon and members of his administration, as an example of overobedience to authority. Focus on one particular aspect of Watergate (e.g., the role of the counsel to the president, John Dean, or why the crisis was allowed to proceed to the point where it actually toppled a presidency). In addition to relevant articles, see Robert Woodward and Carl Bernstein, *All the President's Men* (1974); Leon Jaworski, *The Right and the Power: The Prosecution of Watergate* (1976); *RN: The Memoirs of Richard Nixon* (1978); John

Dean, *Blind Ambition* (1976); John Sirica, *To Set the Record Straight: The Break-in, the Tapes, the Conspirators, the Pardon* (1979); Sam Ervin, *The Whole Truth: The Watergate Conspiracy* (1980); John Ehrlichman, *Witness to Power: The Nixon Years* (1982).

7. In April 2004, news broke of the systematic abuse, including beatings and sexual humiliation, by American military police, of Iraqi "detainees" at Baghdad's Abu Ghraib prison. The scandal was intensified—as was outrage in the Muslim world—by graphic photographs that the soldiers had taken of these activities. A high-level American inquiry uncovered some of the following abuses:

> Punching, slapping, and kicking detainees; jumping on their naked feet . . . positioning a naked detainee on a MRE Box, with a sandbag on his head, and attaching wires to his fingers, toes, and penis to simulate electric torture . . . having sex with a female detainee. . . . Using military working dogs (without muzzles) to intimidate and frighten detainees, and in at least one case biting and severely injuring a detainee. . . . Breaking chemical lights and pouring the phosphoric liquid on detainees. . . . Beating detainees with a broom handle and a chair. . . . Sodomizing a detainee with a chemical light and perhaps a broom stick.

In the days following, many commentators noted the similarities between the Abu Ghraib guards' behavior and the behavior of some of the subjects in the Milgram and Zimbardo experiments. Zimbardo himself, in an op-ed piece in the *Boston Globe*, wrote:

> The terrible things my guards [at Stanford] did to their prisoners were comparable to the horrors inflicted on the Iraqi detainees. My guards repeatedly stripped their prisoners naked, hooded them, chained them, denied them food or bedding privileges, put them into solitary confinement, and made them clean toilet bowls with their bare hands. . . . Over time, these amusements took a sexual turn, such as having the prisoners simulate sodomy on each other. . . . Human behavior is much more under the control of situational forces than most of us recognize or want to acknowledge. In a situation that implicitly gives permission for suspending moral values, many of us can be morphed into creatures alien to our usual natures.

Research the Abu Ghraib scandal; then write a paper comparing and contrasting what happened in the Baghdad prison with what happened in Zimbardo's Stanford Prison Experiment—and possibly also in Milgram's electric shock experiments. Focus not only on what happened, but also on *why* it may have happened.

8. Examine conformity as a social phenomenon (and a particular manifestation of obedience to group authority) in some particular area. For example, you may choose to study conformity as it exists among schoolchildren, adolescent peer groups, social clubs or associations, or businesspeople. You may want to draw upon your

sociology or social psychology textbooks and such classic studies as William H. Whyte's *The Organization Man* (1956) or David Riesman's *The Lonely Crowd* (1950), or focus upon more recent books and articles, such as Rosabeth Moss Kantor's *A Tale of "O": On Being Different in an Organization* (1980) and John Goldhammer's 1996 book *Under the Influence: The Destructive Effects of Group Dynamics* (1996). You may also find enlightening some fictional treatments of conformity, such as Sinclair Lewis's *Babbitt* (1922), Sloan Wilson's *The Man in the Gray Flannel Suit* (1950), and Herman Wouk's *The Caine Mutiny: A Novel of World War II* (1951). What are the main factors creating the urge to conform among the particular group you are examining? What kinds of forces may be able to counteract conformity?

9. At the outset of his article, Stanley Milgram refers to imaginative works revolving around the issue of obedience to authority: the story of Abraham and Isaac; three of Plato's dialogues, "Apology," "Crito," and "Phaedo"; and the story of Antigone (dramatized by both the fifth-century B.C. Athenian Sophocles and the twentieth-century Frenchman Jean Anouilh). Many other fictional works deal with obedience to authority—for example, George Orwell's *1984* (1949), Herman Wouk's novel *The Caine Mutiny* (and his subsequent play *The Caine Mutiny Court Martial*), and Shirley Jackson's "The Lottery." Check with your instructor, with a librarian, and with such sources as the *Short Story Index* to locate other imaginative works on this theme. Write a paper discussing the various ways in which the subject has been treated in fiction and drama. To ensure coherence, draw comparisons and contrasts among works showing the connections and the variations on the theme of obedience to authority.

7 What's Happening at the Mall?

Perhaps you think the answer to this chapter's opening question is obvious. After all, we Americans frequent shopping centers more than we do houses of worship. Each month, nearly 200 million of us shop at a mall and buy fully one-half of the nation's consumer goods (excluding cars and car parts), some $1.8 trillion worth. So what's happening at the mall? We shop, which is hardly news. Yet if leading scholars and cultural critics can be believed, we do much, much more, often unaware of a larger drama being staged in which we play a significant part. As the historian and American studies scholar James J. Farrell observes:

> Shopping centers are constructed of steel and concrete, bricks and mortar, but they are also made of culture. Indeed, culture is about the only thing they *can* be made of. . . . They're a place where we answer important questions: What does it mean to be human? What are people for? What is the meaning of things? Why do we work? What do we work for? And what, in fact, are we shopping for? Like colleges and churches, malls provide answers to these critical questions.

So we may go to malls to buy designer jeans or the latest electronic gear. But because malls are where we also go to see and be seen, to judge, to learn, and to buy both what we want as well as what we need, in visiting the mall we are participating in a larger cultural phenomenon—likely without realizing it.

Geographers describe shopping centers as "built environments" in which the engine of mass production capitalism meets you, the end-consumer. Consider the matchup: On entering the mall, you come face-to-face with billions of dollars invested in product design, manufacturing, advertising, and distribution—not to mention additional millions devoted to making the mall itself an appealing space in which to shop. Management knows that, on average, you will spend $71.04 on your 3.2 visits per month and devotes considerable effort to liberating you from your money. From employing broad strategies like corridor designs that direct pedestrian flow past the maximum number of stores, to narrow ones like selecting background music to create just the right ambience for your visit, mall owners strive to provide a satisfying, stimulating experience—and they employ retail science to aid the process: Have you ever considered why the metal chairs in most food courts lack padding? Management has. Comfortable chairs encourage leisurely meals and discourage shopping. Make chairs *un*comfortable and customers will return to the stores more quickly. Whether or not you recognize these strategies, they exist and management employs them.

The shopping mall has become so commonplace a fixture on the retail landscape that we overlook its relatively new arrival as a building type. In the post–World War II years, the Eisenhower administration initiated the construction of thousands of miles of highways to promote interstate commerce just as automobiles became widely available. By the millions, Americans followed the highways out of town, abandoning the city and its problems for homes in the safer, cleaner, less expensive suburbs. Visionary architect Victor Gruen understood that the rapidly expanding suburbs lacked not only opportunities for shopping but also spaces that fostered the spirited give and take of community life. A carefully designed structure might achieve both, Gruen reasoned, a place in which to meet, stroll, and talk—as people had in markets for thousands of years—as well as a place in which to shop. Gruen set to work. Mindful of the way that automobiles choked traditional shopping districts, he relegated cars to parking lots, away from the stores, thereby creating inside his shopping centers pedestrian promenades reminiscent of the grand arcades of nineteenth-century Europe. He also improved the shopping experience by carefully controlling the mix of retail tenants. Because the center was (and continues to be) private property, management could exclude bars and pool halls and other businesses that, in its view, detracted from its image of upbeat consumerism. Gone, too, were vagrants and political protesters, who may have enjoyed constitutional protections on Main Street but who were considered trespassers at the mall. And finally, implementing a technical solution that had been impractical before the 1950s, Gruen enclosed his centers to protect shoppers from the elements. His centrally heated and cooled buildings created a spring-like shopping environment, year-round.

One-half of Gruen's vision proved prophetic. In the 50 years following the debut of his innovative Southdale Center in Edina, Minnesota, developers opened 45,000 other centers across the country (the number includes open-air, enclosed, and strip malls). However, developers eventually abandoned Gruen's call to merge community and commercial functions in a single, town-like shopping environment. If the appearance of community could enhance sales, mall management would offer community services. But if the noisy and sometimes rude exercise of community threatened business, management would protect its profits by barring, for example, picketers. Court cases followed that raised questions of how free free-speech ought to be in America's new public (though legally private) gathering places. Thus the mall emerged on the American scene with a mixed identity as both a commercial and a community space, an identity that remains fractured to this day. Victor Gruen lived long enough to see the profit motive overtake the needs of community in the design and management of shopping centers, and he left America for Europe deeply disappointed.

Meanwhile malls have grown ever larger and more extravagant, with especially ambitious ones offering lavish entertainment. Restaurants, movie theaters, amusement parks, and water parks attract and *keep* crowds for extended periods. As a building type, the mall became so dominant that public venues began to incorporate mall-like features. Attend a special exhibit at your local museum and the exit will likely funnel you into a gift shop. Catch a plane to visit a friend, and you will find the airport looking every bit like a mall, with wide pedestrian boulevards opening onto storefronts. Malls, and elements of mall design, are everywhere.

Historians, geographers, religious studies experts, architects, psychologists, anthropologists, sociologists, and cultural critics all study what goes on (and does not go on) in shopping centers, and all have something to say about their significance in our lives. In reading the 10 selections that follow, you will learn more about these perspectives. And because you have almost certainly shopped in malls, you will bring direct experience to your reading and writing on the topic. The chapter opens with a selection from *One Nation Under Goods,* in which American studies scholar James J. Farrell asks, "Why should we think about malls?" The next three selections set the emergence of shopping centers in a broad context. Kenneth T. Jackson provides a brief history of shopping malls from ancient times to the present. Victor Gruen, one of the most influential shopping mall developers of the twentieth century, offers his vision for shopping centers that would provide "in modern community life [what] the ancient Greek Agora, the Medieval Market Place and our own Town Squares provided in the past."Geographer Richard Francaviglia then suggests the ways in which Walt Disney's Main Street USA, his idealized re-creation of late nineteenth- and early twentieth-century small-town Main Streets, became a prototype for modern mall design.

Writing on the opening of the Mall of America, the nation's largest, David Guterson suggests that malls offer "only a desolate substitute for the rich, communal lifeblood of the traditional marketplace." Theologian Jon Pahl regards malls as "sacred spaces," and libertarian commentator Virginia Postrel finds reason to be heartened that actual, authentic life can be found at malls.

The chapter ends with sociological, historical, and psychological analyses. Sociologist George Lewis, writing in the *Journal of Popular Culture,* claims that management may publicly promote the *idea* of the mall as a community space but privately discourages the emergence of real communities. Even so, authentic communities of elders and teens manage to form at the mall, their priority being to socialize, not shop. Historian Lizabeth Cohen explores the ways in which mall development has perpetuated America's class and racial divisions. In recounting the battles of developers to exclude undesirable elements (for example, political protesters and the homeless) from malls, Cohen finds a threat to the "shared public sphere upon which our democracy depends." Finally, in a chapter from his classic book *The Malling of America,* William Kowinski writes humorously but pointedly on "mallaise," a zombie-like mental state that can overtake unwary shoppers.

Some authors in this chapter indict mall culture; others celebrate it. Your goal in reading and writing on this topic will be to challenge and clarify your own thinking. And you may, after working with this material, come to regard the most ordinary of activities, shopping at the mall, in a strange, new light.

Shopping for American Culture
James J. Farrell

Our discussion of malls and their place in American culture opens with "Shopping for American Culture," the introduction to James J. Farrell's One Nation Under Goods: Malls and the Seductions of American Shopping *(Smithsonian Books, 2003). Farrell, a historian, directs the American Studies program at St. Olaf College. Unapologetic in his enjoyment of malls (unlike several others in the chapter), he writes: "I love malls. I love them for all the obvious reasons. I love the color and the crowds. . . . I love people watching: seeing the wonder of children's eyes and the animated conversations of teenagers." If we want to understand American culture, says Farrell, we must study life at America's shopping malls, for malls express our consumer culture, revealing us to ourselves.*

1   Malls are an American cultural phenomenon. The United States now has more shopping centers than high schools, and in the last forty years, shopping center space has increased by a factor of twelve. By 2000, there were more than forty-five thousand shopping malls with 5.47 billion square feet of gross leasable space in the United States. Currently, America's shopping centers (most of which are strip malls) generate more than a trillion dollars in annual sales. Not counting sales of cars and gasoline, that's slightly more than half of the nation's retail activity. The International Council of Shopping Centers (ICSC) reported that in 2000, America's shopping centers served 196 million Americans a month and employed more than 10.6 million workers, about 8 percent of the nonfarm workforce in the country. We go to malls 3.2 times a month and spend an average of $71.04 each time (a one-third increase in spending from 1995 to 2000). Shopping centers also support our state and city governments, generating $46.6 billion in sales taxes, almost half of all state tax revenue (see Table 7.1).[1]

2   Shopping is such a common part of America's pursuit of happiness that we usually take shopping centers for granted. But although malls are usually places of consumer forgetfulness, they can inspire a sense of thoughtfulness. It's no particular problem if we come back from the mall empty-handed, but it should be a deep disappointment if we come back empty-headed.[2]

3   But why should we think about malls?

4   Quite simply, because Americans go to malls. We may not like the malling of America, but if we want to understand Americans, we have to look for them where they are, not where we think they ought to be. We need to follow Americans to the mall and see what they're doing because shopping centers can

TABLE 7.1 Shopping Centers in the United States				
	1970	1980	1990	2000
Number of shopping centers	11,000	22,100	36,500	45,000
Total leasable sales area (billions of square feet)	1.49	2.96	4.39	5.57
Retail sales in shopping centers (billions of dollars)	82.0	305.4	681.4	1,136.0
Employment in shopping centers (millions of people)	2.49	5.28	8.60	10.69

Source: Data from ICSC, *Scope.* (*Scope* is a publication of the International Council of Shopping Centers, Inc., New York, N.Y.; reprinted by permission.)

reveal cultural patterns that we don't usually see. In some ways, culture is what happens when we are not paying attention. When we are fully conscious of our choices, they are likely to express our individual values and preferences, but when we're going about our daily business with little thought about what we're doing, we act according to the habits of our hearts, and those habits are shaped as much by culture as by character.[3]

5   Malls are a great place for the pleasures of shopping, but they're an even better place for the pleasures of thinking, in part because they help us think about the cultural contours of shopping. Shopping is, etymologically, the process of going to shops to purchase goods and services. According to Webster, a shop is a small retail store; the word comes from a root that denoted the booths or stalls of the marketplace. The verb *to shop* appeared in the late eighteenth century; by the late twentieth century, shopping had become a way of life. Measured in constant dollars, the average American of today consumes twice as many goods and services as the average American of 1950 and ten times as much as a counterpart from 1928. On average, we each consume more than one hundred pounds of materials a day. Shopping, it seems, might be more American than apple pie.[4]

6   Sometimes shopping is a utilitarian act. We need a shirt or a suitcase, and we go to the mall to get it. Sometimes, though, shopping is intrinsically pleasurable, and we go to the mall to just do it. Shopping itself can be therapeutic, even fun, whether or not anything ends up in the shopping bag. So an exploration of malls can help us think about what we have in mind—as well as what we don't have in mind—when we are shopping.[5]

7   When we get home from the mall, we tell the family, "I was shopping." It sounds simple. Yet shopping is a complex act, or, more precisely, a complex interaction. It's not just a matter of choosing items and paying for them, it's an act of desire that is shaped individually and culturally, an interaction with shops and with a complex infrastructure of production and distribution. It's an act of conscience in which our own values interact with commercial and cultural values. Shopping requires a biological being to enter an architectural space outfitted with commercial art and designed to sell artifacts manufactured and distributed in a market economy. Shopping centers are

built of solid materials, but the spaces are also socially constructed and regulated by political entities. Our malls reflect and affect personal perceptions, social norms, religious beliefs, ethical values, cultural geography, domestic architecture, foreign policy, and social psychology. And the artifacts within shopping centers are equally complex, synthesizing material form and symbolic meaning. Shopping is no simple task.

8   Malls are a good place to think about retailing and retail culture, an important subset of American commercial culture. Because we are consumers, we think we know how consumption works, but we don't usually pay attention to how consumption is *produced*. In malls of America, consumption is not just happenstance. It's carefully planned and programmed. To be informed consumers, therefore, we need information not just about the products we buy but also about the spaces—architectural and social—where we buy them.

9   Malls are America's public architecture, a primary form of public space, the town halls of the twentieth and twenty-first centuries. Sociologist Mark Gottdiener contends that the mall "has become the most successful form of environmental design in contemporary settlement space." The late nineteenth century was known for its train stations and department stores. In the early twentieth century it was skyscrapers and subways. Mid-twentieth-century Americans created suburban forms, including subdivisions, malls, and office parks. The late twentieth century was an era of malls and airports, and the airports increasingly looked like malls.[6]

10   Malls are also art galleries, carefully crafted collections of commercial art. To the connoisseur, they offer an unending display of artful design, including product design, package design, retail design, visual merchandising, sculpture, and architecture. The artists we find in museums often challenge our conceptions of ourselves and unsettle our sense of society. The artists who exhibit their skills in the museums we call malls, on the other hand, tend to reinforce our sense of ourselves, producing a commercial art that makes malls more popular than museums in American culture. But even people who have taken courses in art appreciation don't always take time to appreciate the creativity of commercial art.

11   Malls are also outstanding museums of contemporary American material culture. In them, we find a huge collection of the artifacts that help us make sense of our world. And as in most museums, reading these artifacts can help us read the culture.

12   Indeed, as cultural institutions, malls perform what Paul Lauter calls "cultural work," a term that describes "the ways in which a book or other kind of 'text'— a movie, a Supreme Court decision, an advertisement, an anthology, an international treaty, a material object—helps construct the frameworks, fashion the metaphors, create the very language by which people comprehend their experience and think about their world." In short, malls help teach us the common sense of our culture. If we look closely at malls, we will soon be looking inside our own heads. So it is partly the purpose of this book to explain this social construction of common sense—the way we teach each other, both explicitly and implicitly, the common sense of our culture.[7]

13   Understanding a single act of shopping means understanding the culture in which it occurs. When we go to the mall looking for jeans, we find ourselves

embedded in a cultural fabric that fits us like a pair of jeans. Shopping centers are constructed of steel and concrete, bricks and mortar, but they are also made of culture. Indeed, culture is about the only thing they *can* be made of. Retailers routinely use our cultural values to stimulate sales. Shopping centers reinforce these values even as they distract us from other American values—justice, equality, democracy, and spirituality—that might also animate our lives.[8]

14   As this suggests, malls are a manifestation of popular philosophy. They're a place where we answer important questions: What does it mean to be human? What are people for? What is the meaning of things? Why do we work? What do we work for? And what, in fact, are we shopping for? Like colleges and churches, malls provide answers to these critical questions. Like colleges, malls are places where we make statements about the good, the true, and the beautiful. Like churches, they are places where we decide what is ultimately valuable and how we will value it. And malls are places where we act out, and institutionalize, our values.[9]

15   As the local outlet of the new world order, malls can teach us a great deal about the central institutions of our American lives. Malls are the intersection of manufacturing and merchandising, nature and culture, home and away, love and money. At the mall, we can see the market at work, and we can contemplate what it means to live in a society shaped by the powerful institutions of commercial capitalism. American individualism often makes it hard for Americans to understand institutions and the prescriptions and patterns that structure our lives. We forget that when we walk into a mall, we walk into a market full of *cultural* questions and controversies. Anthropologists Mary Douglas and Baron Isherwood contend that "consumption is the very arena in which culture is fought over and licked into shape." Malls, therefore, are one place where we make significant decisions both as individuals and as a society.[10]

16   Yet if we want to understand malls, we must examine them within a broader framework. The mall makes sense in the flow of our whole lives, as we compare and contrast it to what we experience every day. The mall, for example, tells us immediately that it's not home and it's not work. It's an architecture of pleasure, not of comfort or efficiency. Shopping is what academics would call an "intertextual experience," an activity that only makes sense if we know how to read many different cultural "texts": ads, stores, mannequins, clothes, logos, race, class, gender, and sexuality. And the mall's complexities are multiplied by its customers.

17   There are many malls in America, and each mall is many things to many people. Architecturally, a mall is singular, but sociologically, psychologically, and culturally, it's plural. Each store is a variety store, not just because it sells a variety of products but because it evokes different responses from a variety of people. Each of us brings our own cognitive map to the mall, so it's a different place to a mother and her child, to a mall worker and a mall walker. It's different if we're different in any way—and we all are. Malls mean different things to women and men, to blacks and whites, to gay people and their heterosexual friends, to teenagers and senior citizens. The mall looks and feels different to poor people than it does to the affluent. Although the mall may try to be all things to all people, it succeeds mainly by being different things to different

people. It's possible to speak truthfully about an American consumer culture, but if we look closely, we'll see that we are a consumption society with many different and interconnected consumer cultures.[11]

. . .

18   . . . We often go to malls to buy things we don't have—a pair of pants, a toaster, a new lamp, a book, or a CD. Yet we also go to buy more important things—an identity, a secure sense of self, a set of social relationships, a deeper sense of community, an expression of who we are and who we would like to be. We go to shopping centers with the unfulfilled needs of our American lives, so the mall's attractions are one way of studying the deficiencies of American life. We can use the things we carry *at* the mall to help us understand the things we carry *to* the mall. We can use the mall to make sense of our everyday life.

19   This book is the story of the stories we tell at the mall. Whatever else they may be, shopping centers are places where we tell stories about ourselves—about who we are and what we value. In the plot to separate us from our money, malls are also plotted. They tell stories—about business, about shoppers, about work and leisure, about good and evil, about American culture(s). Stores, and not just bookstores, are full of stories. Victoria's Secret is a romance novel about sex, seduction, and desire, about bodies and beauty, about femininity and masculinity. Sportsmart is the sports page of the mall, telling stories about striving and success. Abercrombie & Fitch combines adventure stories with coming-of-age stories. The Gap started by telling stories about the generation gap, but now their stories are about "cool" characters and their "casual" lives. The stories of progress at Radio Shack are often futuristic fantasies, and Hot Topic tells stories about individualism and conformity, dissent and deviance. The Rainforest Café spins adventure yarns and nature stories. The department stores tell stories about abundance and choice. All of the retailers tell stories about "the good life" and about America. All of the *things* in the mall also have a story. Each artifact is a story of nature becoming culture, of raw material (com)modified to make it meaningful to Americans. At the mall, it's always story time, and, at least according to the publicity, there's almost always a happy ending.

20   This book is the story of all those stories. It's a storybook.

21   It's also my story. It's a story by me, of course, but it's also a story about me, because I'm one of the people I'm writing about. I'm not a power shopper, but I love malls. I love them for all the obvious reasons. I love the color and the crowds. I love looking at commercial art, because it is, in fact, beautiful. I love people watching: seeing the wonder of children's eyes and the animated conversations of teenagers. I like the oasis of pedestrianism in a car culture: I like walking, and I like to walk in malls. But I also love malls because in them, as geographer Jon Goss says, "I have learned a great deal about myself: about my humanity, the values and beliefs of 'my' culture, and my intimate desires."[12]

22   I appreciate malls more now than I did at the beginning of my research. When you look closely at their complexity, especially the intricate coordination needed to produce each day's consumption, it's a miracle that they work as well

as they do. I have come to understand that shopping centers are part of a huge conspiracy, a conspiracy of customer satisfaction. The people who work in malls genuinely want to please the people who shop in malls. So I appreciate the ways that shopping center professionals study Americans to see just what, in fact, will please us, and I appreciate the many pleasures that are to be found at the mall, whether or not we ever buy anything.

23   But I also appreciate the ways that a shopping center can be a "social trap," an institution in which the sum total of perfectly good behavior is not so good. Still, my main complaint is not primarily with malls but with a larger commercial culture that characterizes us mainly as consumers. My main argument is with an America that sells itself short by buying into the cluster of values expressed so powerfully in our malls.[13]

Notes

1. International Council of Shopping Centers (ICSC), "Scope USA," at the ICSC web site, www.icsc.org; John Fetto, "Mall Rats," *American Demographics* 24 (March 2002): 10; Judith Ann Coady, "The Concrete Dream: A Sociological Look at the Shopping Mall" (Ph.D. diss., Boston University, 1987), 720; Ira G. Zepp Jr., *The New Religious Image of Urban America: The Shopping Mall as Ceremonial Center*, 2d ed. (Niwot: University Press of Colorado, 1997), 10.

2. As my colleague Eric Nelson says, malls "are the last place anyone would go to think seriously. There is nothing, however, that demands more serious thought." Eric Nelson, *Mall of America: Reflections of a Virtual Community* (Lakeville, Minn.: Galde Press, 1998), 152.

3. Zepp, *New Religious Image*, 10.

4. John C. Ryan and Alan Durning, *Stuff: The Secret Lives of Everyday Things* (Seattle: Northwest Environment Watch, 1997), 4–5.

5. Barry J. Babin, William R. Darden, and Mitch Griffin, "Work and/or Fun: Measuring Hedonic and Utilitarian Shopping Value," *Journal of Consumer Research* 20 (March 1994): 646–47.

6. Mark Gottdiener, "Recapturing the Center: A Semiotic Analysis of Shopping Malls," in *The City and the Sign: An Introduction to Urban Semiotics*, ed. Mark Gottdiener and Alexandros Ph. Lagopoulos (New York: Columbia University Press, 1986), 291.

7. Paul Lauter, *From Walden Pond to Jurassic Park: Activism, Culture, and American Studies* (Durham N.C.: Duke University Press, 2001), 11.

8. Leon G. Schiffman and Leslie Lazar Kanuk, *Consumer Behavior*, 5th ed. (Englewood Cliffs, N.J.: Prentice Hall, 1994), 437.

9. Jon Goss, "Once-upon-a-Time in the Commodity World: An Unofficial Guide to Mall of America," *Annals of the Association of American Geographers* 89 (March 1999): 47.

10. Mary Douglas and Baron Isherwood, *The World of Goods* (New York: Basic Books, 1979), 57.

11. Elizabeth Chin, *Purchasing Power: Black Kids and American Consumer Culture* (Minneapolis: University of Minnesota Press, 2001), 12–13.

12. Goss, "Once-upon-a-Time," 49.

13. David Orr, *Ecological Literacy: Education and the Transition to a Postmodern World* (Albany: State University of New York Press, 1992), 5.

Review Questions

1. According to Farrell, why should anyone think seriously about shopping centers?

2. In what ways can malls be understood as "cultural institutions"?

3. Farrell claims that the mall is "a place where we answer important questions." What are these questions?

4. How do shopping malls "tell stories"?

5. Why does Farrell appreciate malls?

Discussion and Writing Suggestions

1. Of the statistics concerning shopping centers that Farrell cites in paragraph 1 and Table 7.1, which do you find most striking? Why?

2. In paragraph 7 Farrell makes a series of provocative claims in developing the assertion that "shopping is a complex act, or, more precisely, a complex interaction." Choose any of the sentences in paragraph 7 that follow this assertion and then write for five minutes in response. Share your insights with others who have read the selection.

3. Reread paragraph 14 and select one of the questions that Farrell claims is raised by mall culture. Write two paragraphs in response: First, explain what you think Farrell means in posing the question. (For example, explain how malls help us to investigate "What does it mean to be human?") Second, discuss the validity of the question in relation to malls. (For instance, discuss how reasonable it seems to contemplate what it means to be human in a shopping mall.)

4. Farrell writes (paragraph 14): "Like churches, [malls] are places where we decide what is ultimately valuable and how we will value it." Your comments?

5. Farrell suggests (in paragraph 16) that elements of shopping malls can be "read" like a "text" for meaning. How can one find clues to understanding American culture in advertisements? Store layouts? Mannequins? Clothes? Logos?

6. Do you agree with Farrell (paragraph 18) that we go to malls in search of "an identity, a secure sense of self, a set of social relationships, a deeper sense of community, an expression of who we are and who we would like to be"? How can these things be bought?

A Brief History of Malls
Kenneth T. Jackson

Plato may not have shopped at "The Mall of Ancient Greece," but enclosed shopping areas have been around longer than you might imagine. This first section of a longer article in the American Historical Review *(October 1996) provides a brief history of shopping malls. Kenneth T. Jackson is Jacques Barzun Professor of History and the Social Sciences at Columbia University. He is widely noted for his work in American social and urban history. His publications include* Cities in American History *(1972) and* Crabgrass Frontier: The Suburbanization of the United States *(1985). He serves as editor of* The Encyclopedia of New York City *(1995).*

1   The Egyptians have pyramids, the Chinese have a great wall, the British have immaculate lawns, the Germans have castles, the Dutch have canals, the Italians have grand churches. And Americans have shopping centers. They are the common denominator of our national life, the best symbols of our abundance. By 1992, there were 38,966 operating shopping centers in the United States, 1,835 of them large, regional malls, and increasingly they were featuring the same products, the same stores, and the same antiseptic environment. They have been called "the perfect fusion of the profit motive and the egalitarian ideal," and one wag has remarked, only partially in jest, that either America is a shopping center or the one shopping center in existence is moving about the country at the speed of light.[1]

2   To be sure, the shopping center and even the shopping mall are not entirely American innovations. Merchandising outside city walls began in the Middle Ages, when traders often established markets or "fairs" beyond the gates to avoid the taxes and congestion of the urban core. For this privilege, they typically paid a fee to the lord or feudal authority who commanded the walls above the field. Similarly, enclosed shopping spaces have also existed for centuries, from the agora of ancient Greece to the Palais Royal of prerevolutionary Paris. The Jerusalem bazaar has been providing a covered shopping experience for 2,000 years, while Istanbul's Grand Bazaar was doing the same when sultans ruled the Ottoman Empire from the nearby Topkapi Palace. In England, Chester has been famous for centuries for interconnected second-story shops, protected wonderfully from the wind and the rain, which stretch for blocks at the center of town. London's Burlington Arcade, completed in 1819, was one of the world's earliest retail shopping arcades, while the Crystal Palace Exhibition of 1851, which featured a nineteen-acre building that was entirely walled and roofed in panels

---

[1] On the number of shopping centers, see Witold Rybczynski, "The New Downtowns," *Atlantic Monthly* 271 (May 1993): 98. See also William Severini Kowinski, *The Malling of America: An Inside Look at the Great Consumer Paradise* (New York, 1985); Howard Gillette, Jr., "The Evolution of the Planned Shopping Center in Suburb and City," *Journal of the American Planning Association* 51 (Autumn 1985): 449–60; George Sternlieb and James W. Hughes, eds., *Shopping Centers, USA* (Piscataway, N.J., 1981); William H. Whyte, *The City: Rediscovering the Center* (New York, 1988); and William Glaberson, "The Heart of the City Now Beats in the Mall," *New York Times* (March 27, 1992): A1, B4.

of dazzling "crystal" glass, had many characteristics of the modern mall. Its designers brought the outdoors inside and made the "palace" into a giant garden, complete with an elaborate fountain and several full-grown trees. Within the mammoth structure, crowds from many nations and social classes jostled through long aisles, entertained as much by the passing parade and the spectacle as by the official displays.

3   The most famous pre-twentieth-century enclosed retail space is the Galleria Vittorio Emanuele II in Milan, which was built to commemorate the 1859 victory of the French and Sardinians (led by King Victor Emmanuel) over Austria at the Battle of Magenta. Located near the Duomo and opened to the public in 1867, it is really a prolongation of the public street. It houses scores of separate merchants, with a glass vault on top rather than a single, enclosed building (there are no doors). Cruciform in shape, it has a four-story interior façade that stretches 645 feet in one direction and 345 feet in the other, bordered by shops, cafés, and restaurants at the ground level and mezzanine. Despite its age, the Galleria looks and feels like a modern mall, and it remains at the center of political and commercial life in Milan.[2]

4   At the end of the twentieth century, the shopping mall has become a global phenomenon. Hong Kong has as many modern malls as any metropolitan region in the United States, and tourists in Kowloon might easily imagine that they are in Orlando or Spokane. In France, the Parly II Center opened outside Paris and near Versailles in 1968. It includes all-weather air-conditioning, fountains, marble floors, sculptured plaster ceilings, and scores of shops on two floors. Singapore, Taipei, Sydney, Melbourne, Hamburg, and a hundred other cities have similarly elaborate edifices; the Kaisergalerie in Berlin and GUM in Moscow are particularly notable. Even England, ever protective of its countryside, is falling victim to regional malls and the acres of parking lots that surround them. For example, seventeen miles east of central London, set among the rolling hills of Essex, is the Lakeside Centre, a 1.35 million square-foot clone of suburban America, complete with two McDonalds, a Sam Goody, and a Gap. Since the mid-1980s, a half-dozen other regional malls, as well as 250 smaller regional clusters, have gone up among the shires and sleepy hamlets of Shakespeare's scepter'd isle. By 1993, these new shopping and exurban centers were claiming more than 17 percent of the British retail market, a three-fold increase in less than fifteen years.[3]

5   Below-ground shopping malls have also proliferated. Since 1962, for example, Montrealers have been able to survive their harsh winters by working, shopping, and living, often for months at a time, underground—or at least inside glass and concrete. Large parts of the core city are now linked by miles of subterranean walkways, all lined with shops, restaurants, snack bars, and theaters. In posh Westmount Square, tenants in high-rise apartment buildings

---

[2] A good overview of the early development of the arcade idea is Alexander Garvin, *The American City: What Works, What Doesn't* (New York, 1996), 101–20. See also Johann Friedrich Geist, *Arcades: The History of a Building Type* (Cambridge, Mass., 1982).

[3] *New York Times* (May 9, 1993): E16.

have only to take an elevator to find a supermarket, a bookstore, a bank, a movie theater, a bar and restaurant, or such expensive specialty shops as Givenchy and Pierre Cardin.[4] Similarly, in Osaka, the buried-mall concept is now almost a third of a century old. There, more than a million people per day file over the lighted signs in the floor or past the giant wall maps of the connecting Umeda and Hankyu malls to buy food, clothes, toys, and even lizards and seaweed, or to pay for overseas trips. Hawkers banging tambourines urge passers-by to sample their restaurants. Even pornography shops flourish.

6   But, as was the case with the automobile, which also was invented in Europe, it is in the United States that the shopping center and the shopping mall have found especially fertile ground. In the North American republic, large-scale retailing, once associated almost exclusively with central business districts, began moving away from the urban cores between the world wars. Baltimore's Roland Park Shopping Center (1896) is often cited as the first of the modern genus, but Country Club Plaza in Kansas City, begun in 1923, was more influential and was the first automobile-oriented shopping center. Featuring extensive parking lots behind ornamented, Old California–style brick walls, it was the effort of a single entrepreneur, Jesse Clyde Nichols, who put together a concentration of retail stores and used leasing policy to determine the composition of stores in the concentration. By doing that, Nichols created the idea of the planned regional shopping center. At the same time, he understood, as no one had before him, that customers for the 100 shops would arrive by car. Free parking was not an afterthought; it was part of the original conception. And as Country Club Plaza expanded over the decades to encompass 978,000 square feet of retail space, the number of parking spaces multiplied as well, until by 1990 there were more than 5,000 spaces for the ubiquitous motorcar.[5]

7   By the mid-1930s, the concept of the planned shopping center, as a collection of businesses under one management and with convenient parking facilities, was well known and was recognized as the best method of serving the growing market of drive-in customers. But the Great Depression and World War II had a chilling effect on private construction, and as late as 1946 there were only eight shopping centers in the United States. They included Upper Darby Center in West Philadelphia (1927), Suburban Square in Ardmore, Pennsylvania (1928), Highland Park Shopping Village outside Dallas (1931), River Oaks in Houston (1937), Hampton Village in St. Louis (1941), Colony in Toledo (1944), Shirlington in Arlington, Virginia (1944), and Belleview Square in Seattle (1946).[6]

---

[4] The Montreal complex was designed by Vincent Ponte, a native of Boston, as a way of reducing congestion on downtown streets. *New York Times*, December 17, 1976.

[5] This paragraph summarizes material in Kenneth T. Jackson, *Crabgrass Frontier: The Suburbanization of the United States* (New York, 1985), 257–61. See also William S. Worley, *J. C. Nichols and the Shaping of Kansas City* (Columbia, Mo., 1990), 10–28; Rybczynski, "New Downtowns," 98–100; S. R. De Boer, *Shopping Districts* (Washington, D.C., 1937); and Yehoshua S. Cohen, *Diffusion of an Innovation in an Urban System: The Spread of Planned Regional Shopping Centers in the United States, 1949–1968* (Chicago, 1972).

[6] John B. Rae, *The Road and the Car in American Life* (Cambridge, Mass., 1971), 230. New York City department stores began to decentralize rather early, beginning in the late 1920s. Regional Plan Association, *Suburban Branch Stores in the New York Metropolitan Region* (New York, 1951).

8   The first major planned retail shopping center in the world went up in Raleigh, North Carolina, in 1949, the brainchild of Homer Hoyt, a well-known author and demographer best remembered for his sector model of urban growth. Another early prototype was Northgate, which opened on the outskirts of Seattle in 1950. Designed by architect John Graham, Jr., it featured a long, open-air pedestrian way lined with a number of small specialty shops and ending with a department store. The idea was that the "anchor" facility would attract people, who would then shop their way to their destination. Predictably, it went up next to a highway and provided a free 4,000-space parking lot.

9   The enclosed, climate-controlled indoor mall was introduced by Victor Gruen (see following selection), an Austrian refugee from the Nazis, at the Southdale Shopping Center in Edina, Minnesota, a suburb of Minneapolis, in 1956. From the beginning, the 679,000 square-foot complex (later expanded to 1.35 million square feet) included two department stores, 139 shops, parking for 5,200 cars, and a two-story, sky-lit pedestrian walkway. Gruen had been inspired by Milan's Galleria and also by the markets of the Austrian and Swiss towns he had visited on bicycle as a young man. In America, ironically, he wanted to stop suburban sprawl, and he thought the shopping mall would do the trick. Because Minneapolis was so often cold, Gruen advertised that "in Southdale Center every day will be a perfect shopping day." The concept proved wildly popular, and it demonstrated that climate-controlled shopping arcades were likely to be more profitable than open-air shopping centers. Indoor malls proliferated, slowly at first but with increasing frequency, and within fifteen years anything that was not enclosed came to be considered second-rate.[7]

10   A few of the indoor behemoths, such as Midtown Plaza in Rochester and Chapel Square Mall in New Haven, were located downtown, but more typical were Paramus Park and Bergen Mall in New Jersey, Woodfield Mall in Schaumburg outside Chicago, King's Plaza outside Manhattan, Tyson's Corner outside Washington, and Raleigh Mall in Memphis—all of which were located on outlying highways and all of which attracted shoppers from trading areas of a hundred square miles and more. Within a mere quarter-century, they transformed the way Americans lived and worked. Indeed, reports were commonplace by the 1970s that the typical American was spending more time at the mall than at any other place other than home or work. And the shopping mall had become, along with the tract house, the freeway, and the backyard barbecue, the most distinctive product of the American postwar years.[8]

---

[7] T. R. Reid, "The Magic of Malls," *Washington Post*, September 16, 1985. Late in life, after thirty years in the United States, Gruen argued that the shopping-center idea that he pioneered had been subverted and that the country was mindlessly subsidizing suburban sprawl. He retired in frustration to Vienna, Austria. Among his many writings on the subject, see especially Victor Gruen, *The Heart of Our Cities: Diagnosis and Cure* (New York, 1964).

[8] William Severini Kowinski, "The Malling of America," *New Times* 10 (May 1, 1978); 31–55.

Review Questions

1. What were some of the precursors of the modern shopping mall?
2. In what ways was Country Club Plaza of Kansas City a prototype, in 1923, of the modern regional shopping center?
3. What was the Crystal Palace of 1851, and what was its significance?
4. Shopping malls have gone global. How so?
5. What was distinctive about the Southdale Shopping Center of Edina, Minnesota? Why do histories of shopping centers, like Jackson's, reference it today?

Discussion and Writing Suggestions

1. By "the 1970s . . . the typical American was spending more time at the mall than at any other place other than home or work." Based on personal observations, do you think this continues to be the case? What is your reaction to this news?

2. The Crystal Palace of 1851 afforded the opportunity for "crowds from many . . . social classes . . . [to be] entertained as much by the passing parade and the spectacle as by the official displays." In what ways does this report of the Crystal Palace remind you of the modern shopping mall? (Note that Jackson's reference to "the passing parade" is not to a formal parade but to a steady stream of people.)

3. Have you ever visited a mall outside the United States? In what ways was that mall similar to those in this country? Different? To what extent, when you were in a foreign mall, did you continue to feel as though you were in a foreign country? For that matter, how different is the experience of a mall in Chicago from the experience of a mall in Atlanta or Portland? Do you expect differences, even in a foreign country, or is this not a factor when visiting a mall?

4. What does Jackson mean when he refers to shopping malls as "the perfect fusion of the profit motive and the egalitarian ideal"? What has egalitarianism to do with shopping and, particularly, with malls?

5. "[A]s was the case with the automobile, which also was invented in Europe, it is in the United States that the shopping center and the shopping mall have found especially fertile ground." Why do you think this might be?

The Mall as Civic/Cultural Center
Victor Gruen and Larry Smith

Victor Gruen (born Viktor Grüenbaum, 1903–1980) is the American architect credited with creating the modern shopping mall. Born and trained in Vienna, he fled the Nazi occupation and moved to New York in 1938, where he worked as an architect before opening his own firm in 1951 in Los Angeles. Gruen believed that shopping centers would promote the interests not only of businesses but also of suburbanites, who lived in vast, culturally isolated developments that lacked the community focus of urban neighborhoods. Shopping centers could become community centers, argued Gruen, and in the process promote American values. Gruen is credited with building the first fully enclosed, air-conditioned shopping mall in Edina, Minnesota, in 1956. Ultimately, he returned to Europe, disappointed that other mall developers pursued profits more than they did community development. The following selection, in which Gruen articulates his vision for shopping centers, appears as part of the "Prologue" in Shopping Towns USA *(Reinhold Publishing, 1960).*

1   No democratic society can flourish without law and order which, when applied to the physical environment, necessitates planning. In a complex and highly mechanized society environmental planning safeguards the basic human rights. By providing the best conditions for physical and mental health, it protects *life*. By establishing barriers against anarchy and the infringements of hostile natural and man-made forces, it protects *liberty*. By the creation of a humane environment it invites and encourages the *pursuit of happiness*.

2   When environmental planning is applied to the designing of new commercial facilities, many conditions must be analyzed, criteria weighed, requirements met, and problems solved. These all involve in various ways and to varying degrees the needs and desires of the shopper. It is deeply significant that the term is "shopping center," not "selling center." This indicates clearly that the wishes and desires of the shopper take priority over those of the seller. (An earlier term, "parking center," failed to catch on.)

3   The basic need of the suburban shopper is for a conveniently accessible, amply stocked shopping area with plentiful and free parking. This is the purely practical need for which the shopping center was originally conceived and which many centers most adequately fulfill. Good planning, however, will create additional attractions for shoppers by meeting other needs which are inherent in the psychological climate peculiar to suburbia. By affording opportunities for social life and recreation in a protected pedestrian environment, by incorporating civic and educational facilities, shopping centers can fill an existing void. They can provide the needed place and opportunity for participation in modern community life that the ancient Greek *Agora*, the Medieval Market Place and our own Town Squares provided in the past.

4   That the shopping center can fulfill this perhaps subconscious but nonetheless urgent need of suburbanites for the amenities of urban living, is convincingly proved in a large number of centers. In such centers, pedestrian areas are filled with teeming life not only during normal shopping hours, but on Sundays

and holidays when people windowshop, promenade, relax in the garden courts, view exhibits and patronize the restaurants.

5   All age groups are provided for. Auditoriums are booked to capacity. Meeting rooms are busy with civic and cultural affairs. Dance schools, music schools, and ice skating rinks attract teen-agers; amusement centers are popular with children.

6   Such a planning concept also results in an upgrading of the residential area surrounding the center. It not only protects surrounding communities from blight but actually raises their desirability and consequently their property values.

7   If the shopping center becomes a place that not only provides suburbanites with their physical living requirements, but simultaneously serves their civic, cultural and social community needs, it will make a most significant contribution to the enrichment of our lives.

Discussion and Writing Suggestions

1. In paragraph 1, Gruen offers a vigorous defense of centrally planned shopping centers, arguing that retail development, just like democracy, demands law and order. We gain the free exercise of life, liberty, and happiness, he suggests, through maintaining order. How convinced are you by Gruen's defense of centralized shopping center design?

2. Gruen states (in paragraph 4) that "the shopping center can fulfill [a] subconscious but nonetheless urgent need of suburbanites for the amenities of urban living." What are these needs? To what extent do you believe that people living in the suburbs have them?

3. Reread the final paragraph of this selection. Gruen was a visionary who believed that shopping centers could meet "civic, cultural, and social community needs," as well as the commercial needs of suburbanites. Are you sympathetic to this vision? In your experience, to what extent do shopping centers today meet his standards?

The Mall as Disneyland
Richard Francaviglia

What models did developers turn to when creating the modern American shopping mall? In this next selection, Richard Francaviglia argues that Walt Disney played a key role. His romanticized "Main Street USA," a re-creation of small-town America's shopping district for his new theme park, Disneyland, set the standard for carefully designed and managed shopping environments. Main Street USA, moved indoors to a climate-controlled environment, became the modern shopping mall. A geographer and historian, Francaviglia directs the Center for Greater Southwestern Studies and the History of Cartography at the University of Texas, Arlington. This selection appeared in his book Main Street Revisited: Time, Space, and Image-Building in Small-Town America *(University of Iowa Press, 1996), which won the J. B. Jackson Prize for conveying "the insights of professional geography in language that is interesting and attractive to a lay audience."*

1   Main Street USA . . . fits into the genre of intensely designed and orchestrated space/place. On every inch of Disney's Main Street USA, from the public square to the Plaza, architecture, street furniture, and all aspects of the streetscape are historically themed and carefully engineered. It is this sense of "history" that nearly overwhelms the visitor. All of the street lights are patterned after the "whiteway" lights that lined Main Streets in the early twentieth century. The park benches, wrought iron railings, plantings—everything on Main Street is carefully designed to convey a feeling of the late Victorian period. Even the trees and bushes are carefully sculpted and tended. On Main Street USA, most visitors imbibe the ambience of the past, but they are in fact participating in something far more elementary; their attitudes and perceptions are being shaped through a type of social engineering. This leads to the fourteenth axiom of Main Street development.* *Main Street is essentially a stage upon which several types of human dramas are performed simultaneously, each character or actor in the drama having a designated role that is dependent on his or her relationship to the "set."* Whether one stands behind the counter or in front of a store window brings with it different expectations. Disney was the ultimate merchant on Main Street, and visitors to Main Street USA are the ultimate customers.

2   In Disney's Main Street USA, architecture becomes the façade that creates the impression that all was right with the world in the small town at the turn of the century; it implies that commerce (and merchants) thrive along Main Street, and that society and a community are working together in harmony. Of course, Disney's Main Street does not feature those inevitable services that indicate the other, or darker, side of life. There are no funeral parlors, pool halls, or bars. It should come as no surprise that Disney created small-town America as it *should* have been. His Main Street mirrors a pre-adolescent period free from the change and turmoil that characterizes much of life. . . .

3   What concerns, even infuriates, historians and scholars most about Walt Disney is that he created an abstracted image that it is so tempting to confuse with reality. Disney masterfully abstracted his experiences in [one of his hometowns] *Marceline* and worked with his designers to capture the essences of other towns to produce a small-town image that has nearly universal appeal. In so doing, Disney intuitively knew that *all* planned townscapes—including those Main Streets created in the eighteenth and nineteenth centuries—were in a sense engineered to create effects. Even the vistas down Main Street USA were carefully designed to have significant features (the Railroad Station and Sleeping Beauty's Castle), or, as Disney himself is reported to have said, there should be a "wienie at the end of every street.". . .

---

* Throughout the book from which this selection was taken, Francaviglia draws broad lessons, what he sees as fundamental truths, about the evolution of Main Streets across America during the nineteenth and twentieth centuries. Main Street's being a "stage upon which . . . human dramas are performed" is one such axiom. You will notice that James Farrell, earlier in the chapter, uses much the same language to discuss what goes on in shopping malls.

4   At symbolic levels, Disney's engineering of the small-town environment in Main Street USA is revealing because he so beautifully captured the essence of the romanticism of the small town. Disney himself was moved by the originals, and shaped them into an icon that affects the way we will view its "real" counterparts. To the general public, Main Street USA in Disneyland was very credible in that it featured towers and architectural turrets where they seemed logical, and even though the trim was fairly lavish, it was subdued enough to remind one of Main Streets in the relatively prosperous period during the "McKinley Era"* at about the turn of the century.

5   Students of urban design know that Disney possessed an element of genius in that he carefully designed this Main Street to have an intersection about halfway between the public square and the plaza. That intersection provides a node of activity where merchants have materials on display outside and where towers can form visual exclamation points for the architecture. Looking down one of these side streets, one sees trees that convey the feeling that the commercial streetscape is yielding to a residential area. But in reality, the trees seen behind that intersection on Main Street are the trees of Jungleland, so close is the juxtaposition between one "world" of Disneyland and another. The entire Disneyland theme park is magnificently engineered into only about ninety-six acres of space, which is smaller than the area encompassed within the city limits of most American towns! In world history, few places this small have had such a powerful effect on so many people.

6   In keeping with his ability to create magic through place, Disney used night to his advantage. Because Main Street USA is experienced at night as well as during the daytime, Disney provided marvelous rim-lighting on the buildings. Incandescent bulbs were strung along all of the cornices to convey a very stylized and ornate appearance, enabling the architecture and the streetscape to "shine" at night as well as in the daytime. The Main Street electrical parade runs through the area at night, and Main Street at night provides a kind of visual excitement that was rarely, perhaps never, actually seen in the small towns of America. Rim-lighting of this kind was, however, common in pavilions and the grand buildings of expositions. Like many of Disney's creations, rim-lighting in this context brings a touch of the exotic or even whimsical to Main Street, rather reminding one more of the festive environments of parks and fairs than the Main Street of the typical American small town. Historian and social critic Jon Weiner recently noted that "Disneyland's Main Street is a fiction; the real Main Streets of real small towns at the turn of the century were not so nice"[1]—an understatement borne out by architectural historians and historical geographers. And yet, as architect Paul Goldberger accurately noted, Disney produced "a kind of universally true Main Street— it's better than the real Main Street of the turn of the century ever could be."[2] That Disney's Main Street seems so universally beautiful comes as less of a surprise when one realizes that Walt Disney was rather sophisticated and widely travelled: in fact, Tivoli Gardens in Copenhagen, Denmark, was said

---

* William McKinley (1843–1901), the twenty-fifth President of the United States (1897–1901), was assassinated while in office.

to have greatly impressed Walt Disney in 1952—a seminal year in the early designs of Disneyland.[3] Disney and his designers reportedly were impressed by an exhibit called "Yesteryear's Main Street" at the Museum of Science and Industry in Chicago, which was sponsored by General Motors.[4] Disney's Main Street, which, according to WED (which stands for Walter Elias Disney) imagineering historian David Mumford, "is actually a typical representation of a Walt Disney imagineering project, since it represents a collaborative effort by many creative people,"[5] was thus inspired by many places. . . .

7   If this description of [Main Street USA] sounds familiar, and it should indeed, that is because it has in fact become the model of the typical American shopping mall, where the visitor or shopper leaves the car in the parking lot and enters an environment that is climatically controlled, and where the real world is left outside. In malls, as in Disney's Main Streets, every aspect of design and circulation is carefully orchestrated (Figure 1). This should come as no surprise, for

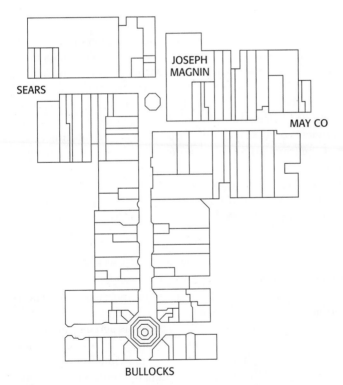

FIGURE 1   The Mall as Main Street. This diagram of the South Coast Plaza Shopping Center, a mall in Costa Mesa, California, reveals many of the same design elements seen in Disneyland's Main Street USA—notably an important intersection of four radiating axes (bottom) and a linear thoroughfare running into another point of decision-making where a carousel is positioned (upper center). The similarities are more than coincidental, as many shopping center designers have studied Disney's Main Street. Computer graphic based on a 1975 map in a kiosk at the mall.

many of the designers of shopping centers and malls in the United States have visited Disney's parks in order to develop a much better understanding of how people move through, appreciate, and patronize a retail environment.[6]

8   It is ironic that Walt Disney, who was politically conservative and espoused rugged individualism, actually produced an environment that embodies such nearly total social engineering and control. According to architectural critic Jane Holtz Kay, Disney's Main Street and shopping malls embody both "public persona" and "private autocracy."[7] The autocratic control of theme parks, of course, is linked to safety and security, and is perhaps one reason why shopping centers are highly successful, and highly criticized by those who feel that such places are "contrived." Malls, too, are able to control behavior using their "private" status. As William Kowinski succinctly stated in his classic article entitled "The Malling of America":

> Malls are designed for Disney's children. Stores are pressed close together; they have small low façades. In fact, everything about malls is minimized . . . the mall is laid out with few corners and no unused space along store rows so that there are no decisions to make—you just flow on.[8] *

9   Few can deny the attractiveness of mall environments to a generation of retail shoppers drawn to the relative serenity and the climate control of the shopping center. That such malls are a current incarnation of Main Street is borne out by the flourishing social life and the persistence of marketing and craft fairs within today's shopping centers. The relative visual uniformity of shopping centers from coast to coast should not be particularly surprising; they, like Disney's Main Street, are archetypal environments of popular culture. This has caused architectural critics to blast the lack of "imagination" of their creators while, ironically, reflecting nostalgically on the days of the *real* American town in, perhaps, the 1880s when, critics contend, there was far greater "individuality."

10   In reality, of course, this was not the case; as we have seen, by the 1880s Victorian-era Main Streets had developed into highly standardized forms. Their major architectural components could—like McDonald's—be found from coast to coast. That scholars lament the standardization of the mall while praising the architectural integrity of historic Main Streets reveals the power of nostalgia in affecting even the most educated of our citizens. Whatever else one may say about the typical shopping center, it is an abstracted reincarnation of Main Street, where pedestrians have the right of way over vehicular traffic, where *all* store façades are attractive and where all of the merchants agree to maintain regular hours and carefully control their signage and sales pitches—techniques which avoid the appearance of haphazard or eccentric individualism.

11   Sociologists have long known that people visit shopping centers for far more than commercial reasons. More than twenty years ago, when Edward Tauber insightfully stated that "not all shopping motives, by any means, are even related to the product,"[9] he introduced the concept of "sociorecreational shopping." Several very revealing articles over the last dozen or more years have shown that

---

* A selection from Kowinski's *Malling of America* appears later in this chapter.

shopping centers are important places of social interaction where people may wind up meeting future spouses and friends; where families go simply to stroll, to see people and to be seen by them; where young people go to "hang out" and socialize. Whereas academicians may condemn this type of behavior as manipulated or inauthentic, it is in fact one of the major reasons why commercial and marketing towns have existed for centuries. This may be stated as the fifteenth axiom of Main Street development: *Despite its market-driven businesses, Main Street is primarily a social environment.* Main Street is an integral element in the "collective consciousness," as geographer Alan Baker used the term, to refer to landscape creation and perception that is linked to a national identity.[10]

Notes

1. Jon Weiner, "Tall Tales and True," *Nation* 258, no. 4: 134.
2. Paul Goldberger, in Judith Adams, *The American Amusement Park Industry*: 98.
3. Arline Chambers, "The Architecture of Reassurance: Designing the Disney Theme Parks," "Disney Chronology" (unpublished paper), p. 5.
4. Andrew Lainsbury, personal communication with author, July 13, 1995.
5. Letter from David Mumford to Jack and Leon Janzen, November 13, 1992, reproduced in Jack E. Janzen, "MAIN STREET . . . Walt's Perfect Introduction to Disneyland": 30.
6. Richard Francaviglia, "Main Street Revisited."
7. Jane Holtz Kay, "When You Stimulate a Star," *Landscape Architecture*, June 1990: 54.
8. *New Times*, May 1, 1978: 33.
9. Edward Tauber, "Sociorecreational Shopping," *Human Behavior* 2, no. 4; reproduced in *Intellectual Digest* 4, no. 3 (November 1973): 38.
10. Alan R. H. Baker, "Collective Consciousness and the Last Landscape: National Ideology and the Commune Council of Mesland (Loir-et-Cher) as Landscape Architect during the 19th Century," chapter 12 in *Ideology and Landscape in Historical Perspective*, edited by Alan Baker and Gideon Biger: 255–88.

Review Questions

1. Describe the ways in which Disney's Main Street USA is a carefully controlled environment.
2. What impression does Disney's street create for the visitor, according to Francaviglia?
3. What is the critics' chief complaint about this street?
4. In what ways does mall design borrow from Disney's Main Street USA?
5. Why is the placement of an intersection important to the success of Main Street USA as well as to the typical shopping mall?

Discussion and Writing Suggestions

1. If you have visited Disneyland or Disneyworld, describe your experiences on Main Street USA. Did the street impress you as it did Francaviglia? To what extent do you find shopping mall design similar in key respects to the design of Main Street USA?

2. "Whatever else one may say about the typical shopping center, it is an abstracted reincarnation of Main Street, where pedestrians have the right of way over vehicular traffic, where *all* store facades are attractive and where all of the merchants agree to maintain regular hours and carefully control their signage and sales pitches—techniques which avoid the appearance of haphazard or eccentric individualism" (paragraph 10). To what extent do you agree that these aims are desirable?

3. In paragraph 11, quoting another author, Francaviglia introduces the term "sociorecreational shopping." Define the term and relate it to your own experiences as a mall shopper.

4. This selection is excerpted from a book-length study of America's Main Streets. Throughout the longer work, Francaviglia offers a number of "axioms" regarding his subject. You find two of these axioms in this selection. See paragraph 1: "Main Street is essentially a stage upon which several types of human dramas are performed simultaneously." An *axiom* is a statement that is universally recognized as true. Do you agree that Francaviglia's statement is beyond dispute?

5. Following question 4, Francaviglia offers a second axiom in this selection. See paragraph 11: "Despite its market-driven businesses, Main Street is primarily a social environment." Do you agree that Francaviglia's statement is beyond dispute?

The Mall as Prison
David Guterson

In 1993 journalist and novelist David Guterson, on assignment for Harper's *magazine, spent a week in the recently opened Mall of America. As you will discover, Guterson approached the mall with a skeptical eye, both fascinated with and wary of its massive scale. Guterson agrees with James Farrell that one can take the pulse of American culture by spending time in malls. But what Guterson sees is cause for alarm. A contributing editor to* Harper's, *Guterson has most notably written a collection of short stories,* The Country Ahead of Us, the Country Behind *(Vintage, 1996) and the novel* Snow Falling on Cedars, *which won the 1995 PEN/Faulkner Award.*

1　Last April, on a visit to the new Mall of America near Minneapolis, I carried with me the public-relations press kit provided for the benefit of reporters. It included an assortment of "fun facts" about the mall: 140,000 hot dogs sold each week, 10,000 permanent jobs, 44 escalators and 17 elevators, 12,750 parking places, 13,300 short tons of steel, $1 million in cash disbursed weekly from 8 automatic-teller machines. Opened in the summer of 1992, the mall was built on the 78-acre site of the former Metropolitan Stadium, a five-minute drive from the Minneapolis–St. Paul International Airport. With 4.2 million square feet of floor space—including twenty-two times the retail footage of the average American shopping center—the Mall of America was "the largest fully enclosed combination retail and family entertainment complex in the United States."

2   Eleven thousand articles, the press kit warned me, had already been written on the mall. Four hundred trees had been planted in its gardens, $625 million had been spent to build it, 350 stores had been leased. Three thousand bus tours were anticipated each year along with a half-million Canadian visitors and 200,000 Japanese tourists. Sales were projected at $650 million for 1993 and at $1 billion for 1996. Donny and Marie Osmond had visited the mall, as had Janet Jackson and Sally Jesse Raphael, Arnold Schwarzenegger, and the 1994 Winter Olympic Committee.* The mall was five times larger than Red Square[†] and twenty times larger than St. Peter's Basilica;[‡] it incorporated 2.3 miles of hallways and almost twice as much steel as the Eiffel Tower. It was also home to the nation's largest indoor theme park, a place called Knott's Camp Snoopy.

3   On the night I arrived, a Saturday, the mall was spotlit dramatically in the manner of a Las Vegas casino. It resembled, from the outside, a castle or fort, the Emerald City or Never-Never Land,[§] impossibly large and vaguely unreal, an unbroken, windowless multi-storied edifice the size of an airport terminal. Surrounded by parking lots and new freeway ramps, monolithic and imposing in the manner of a walled city, it loomed brightly against the Minnesota night sky with the disturbing magnetism of a mirage.

4   I knew already that the Mall of America had been imagined by its creators not merely as a marketplace but as a national tourist attraction, an immense zone of entertainments. Such a conceit raised provocative questions, for our architecture testifies to our view of ourselves and to the condition of our souls. Large buildings stand as markers in the lives of nations and in the stream of a people's history. Thus I could only ask myself: Here was a new structure that had cost more than half a billion dollars to erect—what might it tell us about ourselves? If the Mall of America was part of America, what was that going to mean?

---

* Celebrities Donnie and Marie Osmond, part of a Salt Lake City–based family entertainment team, were best known for three television variety shows that aired on prime time between 1976 and 1981. Sally Jesse Raphael is a talk show host whose programs aired between 1985 and 2002. Arnold Schwarzenegger needs no introduction.

† Red Square is the central square in the ancient center of Moscow, near the Kremlin, where during the Communist Soviet era military parades were held on May 1st.

‡ Built in the sixteenth century in the Italian Renaissance style, St. Peter's Basilica is the great church of Vatican City.

§ The Emerald City and Never-Never Land are the exotic, imaginary destinations featured in *The Wizard of Oz* and *Peter Pan,* respectively.

5   I passed through one of the mall's enormous entranceways and took myself inside. Although from a distance the Mall of America had appeared menacing—exuding the ambience of a monstrous hallucination—within it turned out to be simply a shopping mall, certainly more vast than other malls but in tone and aspect, design and feel, not readily distinguishable from them. Its nuances were instantly familiar as the generic features of the American shopping mall at the tail end of the twentieth century: polished stone, polished tile, shiny chrome and brass, terrazzo floors, gazebos. From third-floor vistas, across vaulted spaces, the Mall of America felt endlessly textured—glass-enclosed elevators, neon-tube lighting, bridges, balconies, gas lamps, vaulted skylights—and densely crowded with hordes of people circumambulating in an endless promenade. Yet despite the mall's expansiveness, it elicited claustrophobia, sensory deprivation, and an unnerving disorientation. Everywhere I went I spied other pilgrims who had found, like me, that the straight way was lost and that the YOU ARE HERE landmarks on the map kiosks referred to nothing in particular.

6   Getting lost, feeling lost, being lost—these states of mind are intentional features of the mall's psychological terrain. There are, one notices, no clocks or windows, nothing to distract the shopper's psyche from the alternate reality the mall conjures. Here we are free to wander endlessly and to furtively watch our fellow wanderers, thousands upon thousands of milling strangers who have come with the intent of losing themselves in the mall's grand, stimulating design. For a few hours we share some common ground—a fantasy of infinite commodities and comforts—and then we drift apart forever. The mall exploits our acquisitive instincts without honoring our communal requirements, our eternal desire for discourse and intimacy, needs that until the twentieth century were traditionally met in our marketplaces but that are not met at all in giant shopping malls.

7 On this evening a few thousand young people had descended on the mall in pursuit of alcohol and entertainment. They had come to Gators, Hooters, and Knuckleheads, Puzzles, Fat Tuesday, and Ltl Ditty's. At Players, a sports bar, the woman beside me introduced herself as "the pregnant wife of an Iowa pig farmer" and explained that she had driven five hours with friends to "do the mall party scene together." She left and was replaced by Kathleen from Minnetonka, who claimed to have "a real shopping thing—I can't go a week without buying new clothes. I'm not fulfilled until I buy something."

8   Later a woman named Laura arrived, with whom Kathleen was acquainted. "I *am* the mall," she announced ecstatically upon discovering I was a reporter. "I'd move in here if I could bring my dog," she added. "This place is heaven, it's a *mecca*."

9   "We egg each other on," explained Kathleen, calmly puffing on a cigarette. "It's like, sort of, an addiction."

10   "You want the truth?" Laura asked. "I'm constantly suffering from megamall withdrawal. I come here all the time."

11   Kathleen: "It's a sickness. It's like cocaine or something; it's a drug."

12   Laura: "Kathleen's got this thing about buying, but I just need to *be* here. If I buy something it's an added bonus."

13   Kathleen: "She buys stuff all the time; don't listen."

14   Laura: "Seriously, I feel sorry for other malls. They're so small and *boring*."

15   Kathleen seemed to think about this: "Richdale Mall," she blurted finally. She rolled her eyes and gestured with her cigarette. "Oh, my God, Laura. Why did we even *go* there?"

16   There is, of course, nothing naturally abhorrent in the human impulse to dwell in marketplaces or the urge to buy, sell, and trade. Rural Americans traditionally looked forward to the excitement and sensuality of market day; Native Americans traveled long distances to barter and trade at sprawling, festive encampments. In Persian bazaars and in the ancient Greek agoras the very soul of the community was preserved and could be seen, felt, heard, and smelled as it might be nowhere else. All over the planet the humblest of people have always gone to market with hope in their hearts and in expectation of something beyond mere goods—seeking a place where humanity is temporarily in ascendance, a palette for the senses, one another.

17   But the illicit possibilities of the marketplace also have long been acknowledged. The Persian bazaar was closed at sundown; the Greek agora was off-limits to those who had been charged with certain crimes. One myth of the Old West we still carry with us is that market day presupposes danger; the faithful were advised to make purchases quickly and repair without delay to the farm, lest their attraction to the pleasures of the marketplace erode their purity of spirit.

18   In our collective discourse the shopping mall appears with the tract house, the freeway, and the backyard barbecue as a product of the American postwar years, a testament to contemporary necessities and desires and an invention not only peculiarly American but peculiarly of our own era too. Yet the mall's varied and far-flung predecessors—the covered bazaars of the Middle East, the stately arcades of Victorian England, Italy's vaulted and skylit gallerias, Asia's monsoon-protected urban markets—all suggest that the rituals of indoor shopping, although in their nuances not often like our own, are nevertheless broadly known. The late twentieth-century American contribution has been to transform the enclosed bazaar into an economic institution that is vastly profitable yet socially enervated, one that redefines in fundamental ways the human relationship to the marketplace. At the Mall of America—an extreme example—we discover ourselves thoroughly lost among strangers in a marketplace intentionally designed to serve no community needs.

19   In the strict sense the Mall of America is not a marketplace at all—the soul of a community expressed as a *place*—but rather a tourist attraction. Its promoters have peddled it to the world at large as something more profound than a local marketplace and as a destination with deep implications. "I believe we can make Mall of America stand for all of America," asserted the mall's general manager, John Wheeler, in a promotional video entitled *There's a Place for Fun in Your Life*. "I believe there's a shopper in all of us," added the director of marketing, Maureen Hooley. The mall has memorialized its opening-day proceedings by producing a celebratory videotape: Ray Charles singing "America the Beautiful," a laser show followed by fireworks, "The Star-Spangled Banner" and "The Stars and Stripes Forever," the Gatlin Brothers, and Peter Graves. "Mall of

America . . . ," its narrator intoned. "The name alone conjures up images of greatness, of a retail complex so magnificent it could only happen in America."

20   Indeed, on the day the mall opened, Miss America visited. The mall's logo—a red, white, and blue star bisected by a red, white, and blue ribbon—decorated everything from the mall itself to coffee mugs and the flanks of buses. The idea, director of tourism Colleen Hayes told me, was to position America's largest mall as an institution on the scale of Disneyland or the Grand Canyon, a place simultaneously iconic and totemic, a revered symbol of the United States and a mecca to which the faithful would flock in pursuit of all things purchasable.

21 On Sunday I wandered the hallways of the pleasure dome with the sensation that I had entered an M.C. Escher drawing*—there was no such thing as up or down, and the escalators all ran backward. A 1993 Ford Probe GT was displayed as if popping out of a giant packing box; a full-size home, complete with artificial lawn, had been built in the mall's rotunda. At the Michael Ricker Pewter Gallery I came across a miniature tableau of a pewter dog peeing on a pewter man's leg; at Hologram Land I pondered 3-D hallucinations of the Medusa and Marilyn Monroe. I passed a kiosk called The Sportsman's Wife; I stood beside a life-size statue of the Hamm's Bear, carved out of pine and available for $1,395 at a store called Minnesot-ah! At Pueblo Spirit I examined a "dream catcher"—a small hoop made from deer sinew and willow twigs and designed to be hung over its owner's bed as a tactic for filtering bad dreams. For a while I sat in front of Glamour Shots and watched while women were groomed and brushed for photo sessions yielding high-fashion self-portraits at $34.95 each. There was no stopping, no slowing down. I passed Mug Me, Queen for a Day, and Barnyard Buddies, and stood in the Brookstone store examining a catalogue: a gopher "eliminator" for $40 (it's a vibrating, anodized-aluminum stake), a "no-stoop" shoehorn for $10, a nose-hair trimmer for $18. At the arcade inside Knott's Camp Snoopy I watched while teenagers played Guardians of the 'Hood, Total Carnage, Final Fight, and Varth Operation Thunderstorm; a small crowd of them had gathered around a lean, cool character who stood calmly shooting video cowpokes in a game called Mad Dog McCree. Left thumb on his silver belt buckle, biceps pulsing, he banged away without remorse while dozens of his enemies crumpled and died in alleyways and dusty streets.

22   At Amazing Pictures a teenage boy had his photograph taken as a body-builder—his face smoothly grafted onto a rippling body—then proceeded to purchase this pleasing image on a poster, a sweatshirt, and a coffee mug. At Painted Tipi there was wild rice for sale, hand-harvested from Leech Lake, Minnesota. At Animalia I came across a polyresin figurine of a turtle retailing for $3,200. At Bloomingdale's I pondered a denim shirt with its sleeves ripped away, the sort of thing available at used-clothing stores (the "grunge look," a Bloomingdale's employee explained), on sale for $125. Finally, at a gift shop in

---

* M.C. Escher (1898–1972) was a printmaker famous for images that confused viewers' perceptions of geometric space, making (for instance) finite walkways into infinite loops from which people could never exit. For examples of his work, go to <http://www.mcescher.com/> and select "Gallery."

Knott's Camp Snoopy, I came across a game called Electronic Mall Madness, put out by Milton Bradley. On the box, three twelve-year-old girls with good features happily vied to beat one another to the game-board mall's best sales.

23   At last I achieved an enforced self-arrest, anchoring myself against a bench while the mall tilted on its axis. Two pubescent girls in retainers and braces sat beside me sipping coffees topped with whipped cream and chocolate sprinkles, their shopping bags gathered tightly around their legs, their eyes fixed on the passing crowds. They came, they said, from Shakopee—"It's nowhere," one of them explained. The megamall, she added, was "a buzz at first, but now it seems pretty normal. 'Cept my parents are like Twenty Questions every time I want to come here. 'Specially since the shooting."

24   On a Sunday night, she elaborated, three people had been wounded when shots were fired in a dispute over a San Jose Sharks jacket. "In the *mall*," her friend reminded me. "Right here at megamall. A shooting."

25   "It's like nowhere's safe," the first added.

26   They sipped their coffees and explicated for me the plot of a film they saw as relevant, a horror movie called *Dawn of the Dead*, which they had each viewed a half-dozen times. In the film, they explained, apocalypse had come, and the survivors had repaired to a shopping mall as the most likely place to make their last stand in a poisoned, impossible world. And this would have been perfectly all right, they insisted, except that the place had also attracted hordes of the infamous living dead—sentient corpses who had not relinquished their attraction to indoor shopping.

27   I moved on and contemplated a computerized cash register in the infant's section of the Nordstrom store: "The Answer Is Yes!!!" its monitor reminded clerks. "Customer Service Is Our Number One Priority!" Then back at Bloomingdale's I contemplated a bank of televisions playing incessantly an advertisement for Egoïste, a men's cologne from Chanel. In the ad a woman on a wrought-iron balcony tossed her black hair about and screamed long and passionately; then there were many women screaming passionately, too, and throwing balcony shutters open and closed, and this was all followed by a bottle of the cologne displayed where I could get a good look at it. The brief, strange drama repeated itself until I could no longer stand it.

· · ·

28 On Valentine's Day last February—cashing in on the promotional scheme of a local radio station—ninety-two couples were married en masse in a ceremony at the Mall of America. They rode the roller coaster and the Screaming Yellow Eagle and were photographed beside a frolicking Snoopy, who wore an immaculate tuxedo. "As we stand here together at the Mall of America," presiding district judge Richard Spicer declared, "we are reminded that there is a place for fun in your life and you have found it in each other." Six months earlier, the Reverend Leith Anderson of the Wooddale Church in Eden Prairie conducted services in the mall's rotunda. Six thousand people had congregated by 10:00 A.M., and Reverend Anderson delivered a sermon entitled "The Unknown God of the Mall." Characterizing the mall as a "direct descendant" of the ancient Greek agoras, the reverend pointed out that, like the Greeks before us, we Americans have many gods. Afterward, of course, the

flock went shopping, much to the chagrin of Reverend Delton Krueger, president of the Mall Area Religious Council, who told the *Minneapolis Star Tribune* that as a site for church services, the mall may trivialize religion. "A good many people in the churches," said Krueger, "feel a lot of the trouble in the world is because of materialism."

29 But a good many people in the mall business today apparently think the trouble lies elsewhere. They are moving forward aggressively on the premise that the dawning era of electronic shopping does not preclude the building of shopping-and-pleasure palaces all around the globe. Japanese developers, in a joint venture with the [developers of Canada's West Edmonton Mall], are planning a $400 million Mall of Japan, with an ice rink, a water park, a fantasy-theme hotel, three breweries, waterfalls, and a sports center. We might shortly predict, too, a Mall of Europe, a Mall of New England, a Mall of California, and perhaps even a Mall of the World. The concept of shopping in a frivolous atmosphere, concocted to loosen consumers' wallets, is poised to proliferate globally. We will soon see monster malls everywhere, rooted in the soil of every nation and offering a preposterous, impossible variety of commodities and entertainments.

30   The new malls will be planets unto themselves, closed off from this world in the manner of space stations or of science fiction's underground cities. Like the Mall of America and West Edmonton Mall—prototypes for a new generation of shopping centers—they will project a separate and distinct reality in which an "outdoor café" is not outdoors, a "bubbling brook" is a concrete watercourse, and a "serpentine street" is a hallway. Safe, surreal, and outside of time and space, they will offer the mind a potent dreamscape from which there is no present waking. This carefully controlled fantasy—now operable in Minnesota—is so powerful as to inspire psychological addiction or to elicit in visitors a catatonic obsession with the mall's various hallucinations. The new malls will be theatrical, high-tech illusions capable of attracting enormous crowds from distant points and foreign ports. Their psychology has not yet been tried pervasively on the scale of the Mall of America, nor has it been perfected. But in time our marketplaces, all over the world, will be in essential ways interchangeable, so thoroughly divorced from the communities in which they sit that they will appear to rest like permanently docked spaceships against the landscape, windowless and turned in upon their own affairs. The affluent will travel as tourists to each, visiting the holy sites and taking photographs in the catacombs of far-flung temples.

31   Just as Victorian England is acutely revealed beneath the grandiose domes of its overwrought train stations, so is contemporary America well understood from the upper vistas of its shopping malls, places without either windows or clocks where the temperature is forever seventy degrees. It is facile to believe, from this vantage point, that the endless circumambulations of tens of thousands of strangers—all loaded down with the detritus of commerce—resemble anything akin to community. The shopping mall is not, as the architecture critic Witold Rybczynski has concluded, "poised to become a real urban place" with "a variety of commercial and noncommercial functions." On the contrary, it is poised to multiply around the world as an institution offering only a desolate substitute

for the rich, communal lifeblood of the traditional marketplace, which will not survive its onslaught.

32   Standing on the Mall of America's roof, where I had ventured to inspect its massive ventilation units, I finally achieved a full sense of its vastness, of how it overwhelmed the surrounding terrain—the last sheep farm in sight, the Mississippi River incidental in the distance. Then I peered through the skylights down into Camp Snoopy, where throngs of my fellow citizens caroused happily in the vast entrails of the beast.

Review Questions

1. According to Guterson, what is one key difference between shopping places of old and modern malls?

2. What is the difference between a marketplace and a tourist attraction?

3. What has been America's "contribution" to the closed bazaar, according to Guterson?

4. Reread paragraphs 7–15, in which Guterson reports on an interview he conducted with several mall patrons. Characterize these interviewees. Why does Guterson include these conversations in the article? What point is he making (indirectly)?

5. Reread paragraphs 21–22, in which Guterson relates his experiences wandering "the hallways of the pleasure dome." By the end of paragraph 22, what impression has he created?

6. What predictions does Guterson make concerning modern megamalls?

Discussion and Writing Suggestions

1. Guterson opens this article by citing some of the Mall of America's vital statistics. What effect do these statistics have on you?

2. Guterson makes a judgment in this selection about the Mall of America and, more broadly, about American culture. What is this judgment? As evidence for your answer, cite three or four sentences.

3. In paragraph 4, Guterson writes that the building of the Mall of America as a tourist attraction "raise[s] provocative questions, for our architecture testifies to our view of ourselves and to the condition of our souls." In paragraph 31 he makes a similar point, referring to Victorian England's nineteenth-century train stations. Explain the connection Guterson makes between architecture and the broader culture.

4. In paragraph 5, Guterson refers to fellow shoppers at the Mall of America as "other pilgrims." Speculate on his use of "pilgrims." Why does he not simply refer to these people as "shoppers"?

5. In paragraph 16, Guterson writes: "All over the planet the humblest of people have always gone to market with hope in their hearts and in expectation of something beyond mere goods—seeking a place where humanity is temporarily in ascendance." What does he mean? Is this your hope in going to the mall?

6. Guterson devotes paragraph 26 to a summary of the movie *Dawn of the Dead*. Speculate on his reasons for including the summary in this article.

The Mall as Sacred Space
Jon Pahl

The American shopping mall as "sacred" space? A number of serious theologians consider the idea quite plausible. Jon Pahl (who received his PhD from the University of Chicago Divinity School) is professor of the history of Christianity in North America at the Lutheran Theological Seminary at Philadelphia. At the seminary, Pahl's teaching interests include "History of Christian Thought," "Religions in North America," and "American Sacred Places," the course description for which reads as follows: "From the Mall of America to Walt Disney World, Niagara Falls to the Alamo, Americans have made pilgrimages to some interesting places. At the same time, more traditional sanctuaries or shrines dot the historical landscape of the U.S. What does this fascination with making places sacred mean, and what do places (both built and culturally-constructed) reveal about particular historical communities and individuals?" Such questions inform the following selection, which first appeared in Pahl's Shopping Malls and Other Sacred Spaces: Putting God in Place *(2003).*

1 Thankfully, I'm not the only one to see shopping malls as sacred places. Ira G. Zepp, a professor of religious studies at Western Maryland College, has suggested in a brief book, *The New Religious Image of Urban America*, that any large shopping center functions "interchangeably and simultaneously [as] a ceremonial center, an alternative community, a carnival, and a secular cathedral."[1] More specifically, Zepp contends that malls "as we experience them cannot be reduced to commercial and financial enterprises. They are far more than places of business." It is this "more" about malls that Zepp finds particularly interesting. People don't just visit malls to shop, he points out. Pilgrims go to malls to hang out, to exercise, to pray, even to get married. This latter function should not be surprising, since malls are designed to be like temples. Zepp quotes approvingly James Rouse, an architect responsible for over sixty malls, including many of the earliest and most famous in the United States.

According to Rouse, "it is in the marketplace that all people come together—rich and poor, old and young, black and white. It is the democratic, unifying, universal place which gives spirit and personality to the city."[2] Such faith in the "spirit" and "unifying" potential of the marketplace led Rouse to design malls in ways that drew upon common symbols from the Protestant faith he practiced his entire life. According to Rouse, businesspeople were the clergy of a new religion that transcended the parochial boundaries of creed and cult. The shopping mall, then, was to be the cathedral in this new religion, the sacred space for a "universal" faith with a distinct spirit.[3]

2   Just how successful Rouse was in realizing his dream can be verified easily enough. Visit a mall, as I did at Southlake Mall in Merrillville, Indiana, one afternoon with a group of students, and observe and ask questions. Expect resistance. You'll be trampling on some folks' sacred compulsions, sort of like violating the taboo against swearing in church or talking about religion at a private party. If you want to be legitimate, make your first stop the management offices. You will probably not get any further. My students, typically not concerned with either ritual or legitimacy, simply started interviewing people with my video camera: "So," they asked, "do you think the mall is a sacred place?" They made it through about a dozen interviews with bewildered or amused shopper/pilgrims before the security guards found them and shut them down. "You can't ask people questions in here," the guards said. Indeed, questions might make people think about why they are there, thereby disrupting the process of disorientation and reorientation by means of which the place induces us to buy. People expect a mall to be a public place. Of course, it's not. It's a privately owned enterprise that can establish its own rules about who is in, who is not, and on what terms.

3   Malls communicate the "spirit" of the market through a common formula. They *disorient* us, by using natural and religious symbols and spatial patterns in an enclosed indoor setting, and then *reorient* us toward one or another of the purveyors of goods. During my young adulthood, I would get a headache after more than a half-hour in a mall. Without some critical distance from the place, my brain couldn't take the constant stimuli that sought to persuade me that my salvation depended upon this or that acquisition. Surely, the mall is a sensual feast, if not an assault. For within the labyrinth of the typical mall, we experience water, light, trees, words, food, music, and bodies, the combined effect of which is to make us feel entranced, dazed, disoriented, and, finally, lacking something. Thus vulnerable, the soul can sell itself to the nearest, if not always the lowest, bidder. To feel lost is the customary, indeed intended, feeling. Fully 40 percent of visitors to the mall do not intend to purchase anything. Only 10 percent get out without lighter purses or wallets.[4]

4   Water, for instance, is used in almost every mall to prepare one to "go with the flow" of shopping. Water dissolves boundaries and is a widespread religious symbol. . . . Among the religious meanings of water, of course, is purification: malls use fountains, waterfalls, and reflecting pools symbolically to cleanse shoppers of any filthiness all the lucre involved in the place might suggest. Zepp points out that at many malls you might bathe symbolically in a fountain, be

refreshed by the sound of a mock waterfall, or even be baptized symbolically beside mini-flowers of water—as I pointed out to my students at Southlake Mall. In short, water initiates the visitor into an experience that is designed to be "more" than a shopping trip. As Zepp argues, "mall developers have attempted ingeniously to satisfy [the] human longing to be near water. . . . We consider water a gift."[5] But of course, this "gift" is one we will, ordinarily, feel compelled to pay for. Furthermore, we will be happy to do so, for the water in malls is "safe" water, controlled water. There is never a need for an ark in a mall. Water in malls has no utilitarian purpose—it's not necessary. It does have a poetic, and a political, function, and more than one pilgrim has gotten soaked in the process.

5   Just as malls use water to appear to be something "more" than an ordinary place, so too do malls abound with light, yet another vital religious symbol. . . . Light of many kinds is featured in shopping malls, but each light is strategically placed to draw the senses in and toward one attraction or another. Neon light is used to beckon with its peculiar glow, especially in the signs above the entries to mall attractions, casting an aura that entices with its soft yet vibrant colors. Natural light is also a prominent feature of most mall designs. At the center of most malls, as Zepp notes: "You can usually find . . . a huge skylight or a colorful and often circular series of lamps shedding such bright light . . . that you know you are in a space set apart."[6] Light, of course, is our primary experience of energy. Thus, Zepp concludes, "malls, at their centers, strive to be places of vitality and energy."[7] That they succeed admirably in drawing visitors like moths to a candle is evident in the fact that the largest one, the "Mall of America," welcomes 35 to 40 million guests annually. That's some serious energy.

6   Along with water and light, the powerful symbols of the tree and vegetation are commonly employed in mall design. Growing things are held sacred in almost every religion, and many traditions have stories or myths about trees of life or gardens of human delight. . . . The inclusion of growing things in shopping malls is, again, more than a utilitarian decision by mall developers to help keep interior air clean. For, significantly, none of the trees in the mall ever die. The trees in malls are all evergreens, even if they are deciduous. Life—abundant, even eternal—is the message. Malls thus play upon the human desire to experience growth and new life, even while juxtaposing such symbolism with profit-making that clearly tries to sap (sorry) as much life from visitors as possible. Still, the symbolism is powerful and effective: life is growth, offers this gospel, in exactly the terms that we want it. This is the Garden of Eden without the fall; the resurrection without the cross; spring and summer without fall or winter. That this growth in fact comes at a price is constantly masked or obscured by the clever design that entices us to imagine that we're inhabiting a garden of free delight. The constantly green trees whisper to us just that message, if we only have ears to hear: "Don't count the cost."

7   More directly, malls advertise themselves in words that promise us unity, devotion, love, happiness, and other phenomena that were once the benefits of traditional religious practices. Zepp catalogs dozens of advertising slogans

and catchphrases that clarify the point. He admits being surprised by the use of religious language in advertising, and in fact, most of us rarely pay attention to the words used in malls. We're too busy being disoriented or distracted by the water, light, trees, or music. Yet the words are there, with unmistakable religious meanings when we start to think about them. Thus the mall offers community: "You're a part of us," one intimates. And the mall promises us devotion. It's a place "devoted to eating, shopping, and the pursuit of happiness," offers another. The words cascade together in a barrage of religious meanings: "You are going to *love* the experience." "We want to touch your life!" "We can identify with all your needs!"[8] Really? Of course not. There is no "we" there. But clothed in such promises, and covered up by soothing music, the naked reality of the mall as a place to turn a profit is concealed, and we are enticed to partake in the sacred rites. The mall cloaks its profit-driven purpose in a poetics of promise.

8   Now, I move here into an area that risks offending some readers, but it seems obvious to me that until very recently malls primarily targeted women, and their bodies, with their messages of salvation. Like other images that encourage consumption—notably those on television—malls are filled with mannequins, posters, and other props that promote an image of an ideal female body—always young, always slim, and always "beautiful," in a stereotypical kind of way. Such images, of course, seek to reduce the identity of women to their desires for the commodities that can help them "match" the ideal. As the poster in one shop window put it, "When French women want it, they put it on The Card." This is a fascinating assertion. Of course women, and not only French ones, "want it." But if what they want can be put "on the card," or charged on a piece of plastic, then the body becomes nothing more than a naked place on which to hang commodities, or "it." In the mall, the body then becomes nothing more than a whirl of atoms: a place without soul, consciousness, or orientation. All places are equal; desire has no bounds, as long as "it" can be put on "the card." Thus vacated, the body can be possessed—so to speak—by any number of spirits of the place, attached to any number of illusions that guarantee the body some "it"—something "new" or "improved" or "bigger" or "better" or "more." People have often been possessed by such promises.

9   Men, of course, experience the consequences of this system differently—but in no less damaging ways. "Real" men, for instance, are supposed to disdain the mall. Many have confided in me, after reading drafts of this chapter or hearing me speak about it: "I hate the mall, too. I guess it's a guy thing." As I've reflected on this comment, it amuses me and makes me sad. As it happens, I don't hate malls, and in fact I have learned to enjoy them quite a bit—while simply recognizing them for what they are. As I've put it before, malls have lots of cool stuff, and the best ones have manifold delights for the senses. We can smell perfumes and colognes, eat lunch, a snack, or an entire dinner, listen to music or scan books for hours on end, and revel in displays of human craftsmanship, ingenuity, and diversity. My sons, and many young people, have taught me to appreciate my experience of the mall without having to buy into the sacred promises. When guys tell me, then, that they "hate the mall, too," it suggests that men can't take pleasure in the carnivalesque atmosphere

of the mall or in the sensual or aesthetic pleasures the places convey. And the fact is that most men in America aren't terribly attuned to this level of experience. By being unable to appreciate the obvious delights of such a place, men ironically "buy into" the flip side of the gender stereotypes that oppress women, although men's bodies, too, increasingly are subject to pressures to conform to stereotypical ideals of beauty.

10   I'm glad, then, that my children and other young people have taught me how to appreciate malls without getting a headache in them. In fact, I can even admire inveterate mall pilgrims, especially the numerous senior citizens who exercise in them, or who otherwise find malls sanctuaries of civility in an otherwise uncivil society.[9] I've come to understand, in fact, that malls may be functioning better as "churches" than are many buildings bearing the name. As Ira Zepp concludes: "The shopping mall, open almost every day from 10 A.M. to 9 P.M. . . . is a more inclusive and egalitarian center [than] most churches."[10] That he is right is a sign of just how disoriented believers in God have become in America. If churches aren't connecting people to true happiness, how can we blame people for seeking happiness in a place that promises it to them accompanied by powerful experiences of water, light, trees, and bodies? Zepp again: "Malls are contemporary versions of that age-old combination of commerce and community. They will continue to fill the void created by our social institutions' failure in providing centers of ritual and meaning."[11] Malls have become sacred places because traditional churches, synagogues, temples, and mosques have failed.

11   Finally, however, even though traditional religious communities often fail to fulfill their own promises, I also have to say a gentle but clear "no" to the promises of the mall. For the success of the mall's offer of salvation depends upon my coming to feel a fabricated sense that somehow I lack something that only the mall, as a cathedral of the market, can provide. And, frankly, the most serious absences in my life have not been due to my failure to acquire a particular commodity, but can be traced directly to my own poor choices or uncertain will. Sin, to use an old-fashioned word for that lack, is a little deeper than my failure to acquire a wide-screen TV, and surely human suffering is more serious than not having the latest style of tennis shoes. Still, we all can get trapped in the false logic, because we do not want to have to confront our deepest personal, moral, or political failings. It's much easier to have to "confront" only the absences that the images of the mall make us feel. Indeed, malls exist to mask true absences, deny them, or make us forget them. All the mall can give us are very finite experiences of consuming whatever commodity happens to strike our current fancy, in exchange for our cash. The promises of "unity" and "happiness" and "love" are lies. This stairway to heaven is, then, really nothing new in history; it's as old as humanity. It's the same system rejected in the *Bhagavad Gita,* the same system that the Buddha saw through as he sat under the Bo tree, and the same system that Luther protested in the Reformation, in which people were offered salvation for dropping a few coins in an indulgence coffer. But today the system is packaged in such a way that souls continue to climb this stairway to heaven, when it is really an escalator, leading nowhere.

Notes

1. Ira G. Zepp, *The New Religious Image of Urban America: The Shopping Mall as Ceremonial Center* (Westminster, Md.: Christian Classics: 1986), 15.

2. James Rouse, "The Regional Shopping Center: Its Role in the Community It Serves," unpublished lecture at Harvard Graduate School of Design, April 26, 1963, as cited in Zepp, *New Religious Image*, 31.

3. Scholars have recently turned from disdain for malls to appreciation for their "hip" character or at least have tried to present a more balanced account of the commodification of the world. See, for a relatively tame example, Leigh Eric Schmidt, *Consumer Rites: The Buying and Selling of American Holidays* (Princeton, N.J.: Princeton University Press, 1995). As a historian, Schmidt tries to "put balance before judgment" (p. 7). That this is, in effect, a judgment itself seems to elude Schmidt, although he offers belated "confessions" of his own "slippery positioning" on "ongoing cultural contests" at the end of the work.

4. Zepp, *New Religious Image*, 15.

5. Ibid., 58–9.

6. Ibid., 56.

7. Ibid., 37.

8. Ibid., 6–8, 12–13.

9. See on this theme Witold Rybczynski, *City Life: Urban Expectations in a New World* (New York: Scribner, 1996).

10. Zepp, *New Religious Image*, 80.

11. Ibid., 150.

Review Questions

1. How are shoppers like pilgrims? What do they seek at the mall?
2. In what ways do shopping malls purposefully disorient and reorient us?
3. What is the significance of water, light, and vegetation in shopping malls, according to Pahl?
4. In what ways can women be "possessed" at shopping malls?
5. Pahl ultimately says "a gentle but clear 'no' to the promises of the mall." Why?

Discussion and Writing Suggestions

1. A famous designer of malls, James Rouse, writes, "It is in the marketplace that all people come together—rich and poor, old and young, black and white. It is the democratic, unifying, universal place which gives spirit and personality to the city." Your response?

2. Evaluate the logic of *one* of Pahl's paragraphs (4–6) in which he argues for the sacred significance of light, water, and vegetation in shopping

malls. Do you accept his argument? Follow the guidelines for writing critiques on page 41.

3. In paragraph 3 Pahl writes that as a young man he would get headaches at shopping malls before he was able to gain "some critical distance from the place." What is this "critical distance"? Distance from what? In responding to the question, see paragraph 9, where Pahl writes: "I don't hate malls, and in fact I have learned to enjoy them quite a bit—while simply recognizing them for what they are." How does "critical distance" play a role in Pahl's "recognizing" meaning in malls?

4. Following up on Discussion and Writing Suggestion #3 above, what do you suppose are the dangers of entering a mall without "critical distance"?

5. Pahl argues that malls incorporate the symbols of sacred spaces into their design through the use of lighting, water, vegetation, and dramatic architecture. Does the use of such symbols, alone, make a place sacred? In your view, what requirements of a space, aside from the appearance of certain symbols, make it sacred?

6. Pahl concludes that the mall's "promises of 'unity' and 'happiness' and 'love' are lies." Does his rejection of the mall as a place that can address "our deepest personal, moral, or political failings" invalidate his thesis that the shopping mall can be viewed as a sacred space?

The Mall as Setting for Authentic Life
Virginia Postrel

Critics like David Guterson slam shopping malls for being cookie-cutter replications, a national embarrassment, and a symbol of all that is basely profit driven and inauthentic in American life. Cultural commentator Virginia Postrel takes a different view: The mall, "exuberantly fake" by design, provides a comfortable, safe place for people to meet and interact. Postrel has served as editor of Reason *magazine, writes for several news outlets as well as a column for* The Atlantic, *and has authored two books:* The Future and Its Enemies *(1998) and* The Substance of Style *(2003), the opening pages of which appear below.*

1 As soon as the Taliban fell, Afghan men lined up at barbershops to have their beards shaved off. Women painted their nails with once-forbidden polish. Formerly clandestine beauty salons opened in prominent locations. Men traded postcards of beautiful Indian movie stars, and thronged to buy imported TVs, VCRs, and videotapes. Even burka merchants diversified their wares, adding colors like brown, peach, and green to the blue and off-white dictated by the Taliban's whip-wielding virtue police. Freed to travel to city markets, village women demanded better fabric, finer embroidery, and more variety in their traditional garments.

2   When a Michigan hairdresser went to Kabul with a group of doctors, nurses, dentists, and social workers, she intended to serve as an all-purpose assistant to the relief mission's professionals. Instead, she found her own services every bit as popular as the serious business of health and welfare. "When word got out there was a hairdresser in the country, it just got crazy," she said. "I was doing haircuts every fifteen minutes."

3   Liberation is supposed to be about grave matters: elections, education, a free press. But Afghans acted as though superficial things were just as important. As a political commentator noted, "The right to shave may be found in no international treaty or covenant, but it has, in Afghanistan, become one of the first freedoms to which claim is being laid."

4   That reaction challenged many widely held assumptions about the nature of aesthetic value. While they cherish artworks like the giant Bamiyan Buddhas leveled by the Taliban, social critics generally take a different view of the frivolous, consumerist impulses expressed in more mundane aesthetic pleasures. "How depressing was it to see Afghan citizens celebrating the end of tyranny by buying consumer electronics?" wrote Anna Quindlen in a 2001 Christmas column berating Americans for "uncontrollable consumerism."

5   Respectable opinion holds that our persistent interest in variety, adornment, and new sensory pleasures is created by advertising, which generates "the desire for products consumers [don't] need at all," as Quindlen put it, declaring that "I do not need an alpaca swing coat, a tourmaline brooch, a mixer with a dough hook, a CD player that works in the shower, another pair of boot-cut black pants, lavender bath salts, vanilla candles or a KateSpadeGucciPradaCoach bag."

6   What's true for New Yorkers should be true for Afghans as well. Why buy a green burka when you're a poor peasant and already have two blue ones? Why paint your nails red if you're a destitute widow begging on the streets? These indulgences seem wasteful and irrational, just the sort of false needs encouraged by commercial manipulation. Yet liberated Kabul had no ubiquitous advertising or elaborate marketing campaigns. Maybe our desires for impractical decoration and meaningless fashion don't come from Madison Avenue after all. Maybe our relation to aesthetic value is too fundamental to be explained by commercial mind control.

7   Human beings know the world, and each other, through our senses. From our earliest moments, the look and feel of our surroundings tell us who and where we are. But as we grow, we imbibe a different lesson: that appearances are not just potentially deceiving but frivolous and unimportant—that aesthetic value is not real except in those rare instances when it transcends the quotidian to become high art. We learn to contrast surface to substance, to believe that our real selves and the real world exist beyond the superficiality of sensation.

8   We have good cause, of course, to doubt the simple evidence of our senses. The sun does not go around the earth. Lines of the same length can look longer or shorter depending on how you place arrows on their ends. Beautiful people are not necessarily good, nor are good people necessarily beautiful. We're wise to maintain reasonable doubts.

9   But rejecting our sensory natures has problems of its own. When we declare that mere surface cannot possibly have legitimate value, we deny human experience and ignore human behavior. We set ourselves up to be fooled again and again, and we make ourselves a little crazy. We veer madly between overvaluing and undervaluing the importance of aesthetics. Instead of upholding rationality against mere sensuality, we tangle ourselves in contradictions.

10   This book [*The Substance of Style*] seeks to untangle those confusions, by examining afresh the nature of aesthetic value and its relation to our personal, economic, and social lives. It's important to do so now, because sensory appeals are becoming ever more prominent in our culture. To maintain a healthy balance between substance and surface, we can no longer simply pretend that surfaces don't matter. Experience suggests that the comfortable old slogans, and the theories behind them, are wrong.

11   Afghanistan is not the only place where human behavior confounds conventional assumptions, raising questions about the sources of aesthetic value. Consider "authenticity," which aesthetic authorities consider a prime measure of worth. Here, too, experience suggests a more complex standard, or perhaps a more subjective definition of what's authentic, than intellectual discourse usually provides.

12   Built atop one of the hills that divide the San Fernando Valley from the core of Los Angeles, Universal CityWalk is deliberately fake. Its architect calls the open-air shopping mall "a great simulacrum of what L.A. should do. This isn't the L.A. we did get, but it's the L.A. we could have gotten—the quintessential, idealized L.A."

13   Like the rest of Los Angeles, CityWalk's buildings are mostly stucco boxes. Their aesthetic energy comes from their façades, which are adorned with bright signs, colorful tiles, video screens, murals, and such playful accessories as a giant King Kong. Unlike the typical shopping center, CityWalk has encouraged its tenants to let their decorative imaginations run wild. The place has a tiny artificial beach and, of course, palm trees. A fountain shoots water up through the sidewalk. A fictional radio station sells hamburgers, and a real museum displays vintage neon signs. The three blocks of city "street" are off-limits to vehicles.

14   When City Walk opened in 1993, it was roundly condemned as an inauthentic facsimile of real city life. Intellectuals saw only a fortress, a phony refuge from the diversity and conflict of a city recently torn by riots. A conservative journalist called it "Exhibit A in a hot new trend among the beleaguered middle classes: bunkering," while a liberal social critic said CityWalk "has something of the relationship to the real city that a petting zoo has to nature."

15   The public reacted differently. Almost immediately, CityWalk became not a bunker but a grand mixing zone. "Suddenly CityWalk was full of people. And they were all grinning," wrote a delighted veteran of European cafés shortly after the new mall opened. He predicted that the artificial city street would soon become a beloved hangout, that locals would never want to leave. He was right.

A decade later, CityWalk may be "the most vital public space in Los Angeles," declares a magazine report. On a Saturday night,

> People from all across L.A. have gathered here in one great undifferentiated mass, as they rarely do in the city itself. Toddlers are tearing across CityWalk's sidewalk fountain. Salvadoran, Armenian, Korean, black, and white, they squeal as the hidden water jets erupt, soaking their overalls. Hundreds of teenagers who have made CityWalk their hangout are picking each other up and sucking down frozen mochas. Families from Encino to East L.A. are laughing, stuffing their faces, gawking at the bright spires of light.

16   So much for the assumption that artifice and interaction are contradictory, that the only experience a "simulacrum" can produce is inauthentic. By offering a place of shared aesthetic pleasures, CityWalk has created not an isolated enclave but a space where people from many different backgrounds can enjoy themselves together.

17   Half a world away is an even more artificial environment, where not only the street but the sky itself is fake. The social results are similar. "It's a very special building, very different, very beautiful," says a black South African of Johannesburg's Montecasino, a casino that replicates a Tuscan village, right down to imported cobblestones and an old Fiat accumulating parking tickets by the side of the make-believe road. Unlike many places in Johannesburg, Montecasino attracts a racially mixed crowd, including unemployed black men who chat beneath its artificial trees and watch the gamblers at play. Like CityWalk, the casino offers its aesthetic pleasures to all comers. Its deracinated design is central to its appeal.

18   "Montecasino imposes nothing on anyone. It is completely, exuberantly fake," writes a Togo-based critic. "And, as in Las Vegas, it is this fakeness that ensures its egalitarian popularity. Blacks and whites feel equally at home in this reassuringly bogus Tuscany. The price of democracy, it would seem, is inauthenticity." Or maybe something is wrong with aesthetic standards that would deny people pleasures that don't conform to their particular era or ethnicity. Maybe we've misunderstood the meaning and value of authenticity.

Review Questions

1. How does Postrel characterize Anna Quindlen's reaction to Afghans rushing to purchase consumer electronics after being liberated?

2. What distinction do people sometimes make between "substance" and "surface"? How does Postrel object to this distinction? (In answering, you may want to use the statement quoted for Discussion and Writing Suggestion #3.)

3. Postrel says that CityWalk and other "exuberantly fake" places like Las Vegas surprise critics. How so? What have the similarities of such places to do with Postrel's exploration of substance and surface?

Discussion and Writing Suggestions

1. "Liberation is supposed to be about grave matters: elections, education, a free press. But Afghans acted as though superficial things [like shaving or getting nails polished] were just as important." Your comments?

2. Have you ever been to a place like CityWalk or Las Vegas, so obvious in its fakeness, its *in*authenticity, that you find yourself relaxing and having a good time? In what ways does the very inauthenticity of the setting lend itself to a kind of intimacy? Perhaps this was not your experience, and the fakeness of the setting offended (or amused) you—as the Mall of America offended David Guterson (see pages 286–293). If so, explain that reaction.

3. "The price of democracy, it would seem, is inauthenticity." Postrel quotes a Togo-based critic here (see paragraph 18) who is referring to the success of a Johannesburg casino fashioned after a Tuscan village. What is the special appeal of such a purposely fake place? What is it about a place like Las Vegas that "ensures its egalitarian popularity"?

The Mall as Refuge
George Lewis

In this article, which first appeared in the Journal of Popular Culture *(Fall 1990), George Lewis investigates the extent to which shopping malls "really act as [a] social magnet, bringing people together in a true sense of community." Through public service programs and promotions, mall management would have us believe that its facilities function as town centers in the spirit that Victor Gruen had envisioned. But Lewis, a sociologist at the University of the Pacific, challenges that view, concluding that the groups that congregate in malls "seldom share the common ties and engage in the sort of social interactions necessary to forge a sense of 'we-ness.'" Lewis bases his insights on a study of two groups—elders and teenagers—at a New England shopping center.*

1   Everyday life in America, in the past three decades, has been critically affected by the evolution and spread of the shopping mall as the central concept in American retailing. These economic monoliths, evolving from the earlier retail form of the suburban shopping center, are now about far more than just shopping. People go to the modern mall for professional services, such as legal, medical or optical aid. There are fashion shows, art shows and musical performances in these climate controlled, air conditioned spaces. Restaurants, video arcades, movie theatres and even ice skating rinks and sand beaches with tanning lights focused upon them are found in the contemporary enclosed mall. In a word, the regional shopping mall has become a kind of civic center, a point of attraction for millions of Americans, whether they choose to buy something there regularly or not.

· · ·

Community in the Mall: Manufactured Illusion or Social Reality?

2 With all its promotions and public service programs, does the mall really act as this sort of social magnet, bringing people together in a true sense of community? The answer, if one is to define community as more than just the bringing together of demographically similar persons in one locale, is more apt to be negative than it is positive. Malls can, and do, lure and assemble *collectivities* and *crowds* of shoppers, but these groups seldom share the common ties and engage in the sort of social interactions necessary to forge a sense of "we-ness"—of community—from the raw social material of a crowd.

3   Jessie Bernard makes a crucial conceptual distinction here between "the community," which emphasizes *locale* as its most important and fundamental criterion, and "community," which emphasizes *common ties* and *interaction* as significant criteria in its conceptualization. "Community," then, is characterized not by locale, but by the *gemeinschaften* spirit of communal and primary relationships in which intimacy, sentiment, and a sense of belonging exist among individuals.[1]

4   Thomas Bender agrees, further defining community as characterized by close, usually face to face relationships. "Individuals are bound together by affective or emotional ties rather than by a perception of individual self-interest. There is a 'we-ness' in a community; one is a member."[2]

5   If this is the sort of social relationship one means by community, then it is difficult to find among customers at most shopping malls. Physically, malls are geared for high turnover. Chairs and benches in rest areas and food courts are unpadded in the seat—designed to be uncomfortable if sat in too long. The architecture of the mall itself, behind the colorful neon store logos and displays, is anonymous, uniform, predictable and plain. The corridors are wide and filled with hurrying customers. Security guards discourage loiterers and help to move foot traffic along. The muzak, if it exists, reinforces the image of the mall as a public space—a place where strangers encounter one another en route to their desired locations.

6   Most shoppers who frequent the mall, even if lured there by some promotional scheme, come alone or in small groups of two or three.[3] They are intent upon their business, focusing upon shopping and not upon interaction with other mall customers. For the most part, they do not know each other and they don't come to the mall on any regular, day-to-day basis. In short, the high turnover, volume of persons, and transiency that is a designed part of most malls works *against* the development and emergence of community within their walls.

7   This is understood by mall managers and developers. As one put it: "Having the *perception* of a community feeling does not mean that it actually exists. It is not the same thing. Perception is not necessarily reality."[4] So the important thing, from a marketing perspective, is to create the warm *illusion* of community, while at the same time quietly stacking the deck against its actual development. "We don't want the mall to be a community in any real sense, because we'll attract people we don't want to. People who are not here to shop but are coming

for some other purpose. It would upset our tenants who want to make money. We don't want anything to upset our tenants."

8   And yet, within this illusion, this false setting of community, the seeds of community have been planted. Ironically, among the very sorts of persons the managers and developers do not want to see attracted to the mall—the non-shoppers—have arisen fledgling forms of community, characterized by primary ties, face to face interaction, daily meeting and the development of social networks. These developing communities, or social worlds—one comprised mainly of retired persons and others over 65, and the other of teenagers—are the empirical focus of this paper. The data presented here were collected in June and July of 1988 in a series of unstructured interviews conducted in a large shopping center in New England. The interviews, which total over 200 hours of material, are one portion of a research effort undertaken by the Salt Center For Cultural Studies, in examining various facets of the impact of popular and mass culture on regional cultural forms.[5]

· · ·

The Elderly

9   The mall is a central life setting for many elderly persons who frequent it on a regular basis. They walk back and forth, up and down the common area of the older wing of the mall (the "old mall"), greeting friends and acquaintances and sitting with them, visiting, in the sunken circular seating areas they have named the "north hole," "south hole," or "center hole." Some visit the mall every day, arriving when the doors are opened in the morning. Many stay all day, leaving in mid to late afternoon. A few will have a light dinner at one of the mall eateries before going home for the evening.

10   Many of these persons are retired, many widowed. They feel they have little else to fill their days. Their time in the mall usually conforms to set routines. They will be found in a specific seating area at a regular time, have coffee at the same restaurant at the same time, and leave the mall each day within 15 or 20 minutes of their leaving time the day before. This patterning of behavior is pervasive among the elderly and characterizes the nature of their social interaction at the mall.

11   Bert, for example, a 78-year-old retiree, comes to the mall every day of the week. "I come here at quarter of eleven and I leave at twenty minutes past one," he says matter-of-factly, as he sneaks a glance at his watch. "I do this every day. Every day except. . . ."

12   His two companions finish for him; "Five days a week. He's missed one day this year."

13   Bert resumes his own account. "And I have my lunch here at noontime." This is Bert's eleven o'clock stop, outside of Porteous, one of the large department-style anchor stores of the mall. He won't be here at eleven-thirty.

14   "I move every half hour. I go from here down to where the clock is. Then where the clock is, I go down in front of Woolworth's, then I come back again and go up there and take my bus by the front of JC Penney."

15   Linda, a mall custodian, noted that the elderly "would rather be at the mall than anywhere else. They probably know more about the place

than I do. Probably know more than security does, too. I know 'cause my father-in-law is one of 'em. He comes in twice a day, every day. Ya, he sets over in the old mall, then he comes down and sets by Porteous for a while, then over by McDonalds."

16   The controlled environment of the mall offers another benefit to the elderly—it is a safe and comfortable place to walk for exercise. As Jacobs has pointed[6] out, many malls have instituted some form of walking program for the elderly—though the impetus for these programs usually comes from outside the mall itself, as the elderly are most often perceived by mall management as a group who does very little, if any, buying and thus contributes quite minimally in proportion to their presence, to the economic life of the mall.

17   "We really don't want them to come here if they're not going to shop," a mall manager remarked. "They take up seats we would like to have available for shoppers." However, from a public relations standpoint, it is difficult for mall management to overtly discourage the elderly from using the mall for their own purposes. Conversely, management can sometimes be talked into the minimal support of programs such as walking-for-health, in hopes it shows off to the community of shoppers they do want to attract, the degree of social consciousness and responsibility they supposedly feel.

18   The mall studied here is no exception to this pattern. A local doctor and the YMCA spearheaded the senior walking program, which opened in the spring of 1987 and which is now jointly sponsored by the doctor, the Y and the mall. The program encourages the elderly to walk laps and to record their own progress. To date, there are over 300 walkers signed into this program.

19   For those participating, entrance to the mall can be as early as 6:00 a.m., when security unlocks the doors—a full 3 or 4 hours prior to the opening of most commercial establishments inside the mall.

20   Pat, a regular "miler" in the program, usually arrives by car a few minutes before six and waits until the glass doors are unlocked.

21   "Age first," Pat insists as he holds a door for his two companions. Inside the mall, silent mannequins observe the three men begin their daily laps. Pat, now eighty years old, decides to take a short cut.

22   "You cheated," accuses the security guard.

23   "No, *you're* cheatin'," Pat accuses. "You're supposed to unlock all these doors and you're talkin' instead. I gotta bum hip, and when you get to my age, you won't be walkin'!" He smiles and disappears down the corridor. Two women call out to him in disbelief.

24   "You were here before us!"

25   "That's right," Pat laughs. "You're gettin' lazy."

26   After his five miles of walking laps, Pat sits down at his favorite restaurant, just now opening for business. Coming to the mall, he says, "gets me out of the house. I wish they opened at five. Pretty soon I'll be meeting six or seven fellas I know. We talk, shoot the breeze. I just come out here to kill a little time, that's all. What am I going to do at home?"

27   He leans back to prop his elbow on the back of his chair. His eyes follow a woman in red high heels taking choppy steps past a boutique. "I was in business

65 years. Was in the meat business. Gave it to my son, my son gave it to his son. I don't know whether you ever heard of it—Pat's Meat Mart?"

28   Two elderly ladies in cotton skirts and sneakers walk past and wave to Pat. "Morning," he answers. These women he identifies as past customers of his, as he jokes with them. "I have a lot of customers, really I do . . . people know us, ya know."

29   He looks down and then away, as if he doesn't want to talk anymore. Then: "I was going to show you my darlin's picture." He pulls out his wallet and unfolds a fragile, yellowed newspaper clipping. "She was the nicest. Everybody loved her. They only make one like her. . . . I miss this one, I tell ya. I do, I really do. Oh, we were inseparable. I had her for 34 years. She died when she was 51, so— God wanted her. There's nothing I could do, ya know. That's the story of my life." A tight little smile.

30   "Where do ya want me to send the bill?" he asks, snapping back to the present.

31   Retired and living alone, many of these elderly seek the mall as a safe and neutral ground to keep up old job contacts—not just the more surface relationships with old customers, but more primary ties with workmates themselves. George, who worked for a large electrical plant until they "closed out" in 1983 and forced him into retirement, meets his work buddies every Friday in the mall for lunch. Over the five years he has done this, he notes, fewer and fewer are alive to attend. "Every month," he says, "the faces we used to see, they're thinnin' out, . . . thinnin' out. . . ."

32   Charlie comes to the mall to meet people and to avoid heat in the summer and cold in the winter. "Some people I meet here," he says, "I've known for forty years." The elderly congregate in knots and clusters, laughing and joking among themselves. Charlie flags down Bob and Irene in the crowd and gives them two coupons from the previous day's paper, good for money off at a mall fast food stand.

33   Connie complains of telephone sales people to the group—especially a seller of cemetery plots. "I told him I have my plot all picked out. I'm just sitting here waiting to go. He didn't call back." She continues, "Here (in the mall) we sit and talk about our illnesses, medications, diets. We have a lot of fun."

34   More than most social worlds, the world of the elderly in the mall takes its shape and character from the face to face relationships of the people who regularly are a part of it. For these elderly—most of whom are retired, who live alone, and are most probably widowed—there is now little or no need to expend energy, concern and time in the areas of career, job development, self-improvement, spousal relations, or even in family and community activities. Cut off from these concerns and ties, their status and power position in the larger society lowered, they find meaning in the construction and maintenance of networks of personal relationships with others like themselves.[7] These "personal communities," then, are not defined by a bounded area so much as they are a web-like network of personal relationships in which each person is selectively attached to a definite number of discrete persons. At the edges of this network are those persons, such as the servers in the restaurants, the custodians, and the security personnel, with whom relationships are affectively neutral, of a surface level, and usually joking in nature.

35   Harry sums it up. "It's hard being a senior citizen. Very hard. It's a monotonous life. You know, when you're constructive for a good many years and then you have to relax and do nothing—and you're alone—that's worse."

36   Tom, sitting beside Harry, points out that he has some pretty good friends at the mall. He continues; "Girls down in the food court. They all look for us. We don't come in, they ask everybody where we are. They think we're sick, or something."

37   Harry and Bert tip their heads in agreement. "They look out for us. We kid a lot with them and everything."

38   Harry takes it from there. "Well, you're seeing a face, you know. If you stayed at home and you're alone, you see nothing. No matter where you'd live, you'd see a car go by. But people, you don't see." Silence. Then, "So you come out here to see the living, more or less." He looks to his friends for reinforcement. "Am I right? I think so."

39   Tom jumps in. "But you make everything sound so *sad*, Harry. My Lord, it's not *that* bad. I come out here to see my friends. To get out of the house. That's all."

The Teens

40   Teenagers visit the mall on an almost daily basis. They arrive in groups or individually to meet their friends. A number work in the mall, usually at minimum wage, in the fast food establishments located, for the most part, in the "new wing" of the mall, built just three years ago. When they are off work, they "hang out" with other youths, who use the mall as a place for social gathering.

41   The mall is one of the few places teenagers can go in this society where they are—albeit reluctantly—allowed to stay without being asked to leave.[8] Many who frequent the mall don't go to school. Some also try to stay away from their homes, but they really don't have anywhere else they can be on their own. As Millison concluded, malls are much the suburban equivalent to the urban street corners where inner city kids congregate.[9] Suburban kids come to malls to look around, meet and make friends, stay away from home, and hang out—because there is nowhere else to go.

42   Paul, a security guard, explains. "We aren't allowed to harass the kids, and I know they gotta hang out somewhere. But we tell them to keep moving, especially around the seats and tables in the food service area. They know they have to keep moving. If they get too loud, or talk back, or are creating any kind of disturbance like that, then we clear them out. Troublemakers we identify, and we don't let them back in."

43   Calling themselves "mall rats" (males) and "mall bunnies" (females), the teens congregate in the new wing of the mall, the largest number of them arriving in the late afternoon. They wander around the different shops, playing video games in the arcade, smoking cigarettes, showing off their latest hair, makeup and clothing styles, and waiting for something, anything, to happen. Most of them will stay until nine-thirty or ten, when the stores close and the mall shuts down.

44   Derick, 15, his hands jammed into the pockets of his frayed cutoff jean shorts, admits that the mall is "a place to go before I have to go to work. I only work right across the street. I have nowhere else to hang out. Most of my friends hang out here."

45   Looking at the arcade in the adjacent wing of the mall, he gestures towards it with a quick nod of his head. "Go over there to play video games. Spend all my money. I don't like spending all my money, but it's there." He shrugs. "Fuck it."

46   Standing near Derick in the small knot of teenagers, Ed, 16, takes a long, slow drag off his cigarette and exhales out the corner of his mouth. "I just started coming on almost a daily basis last year, because it was something to do," he says. "You can come here anytime. It's pretty good, but if we didn't have anything, you'd probably get in more trouble than we would if we came here, so it kinda works out, you know. It's something to do and it kinda keeps you outa trouble."

47   As he says this, he scans the familiar row of neon lit food stalls. Shoppers rush by, but he appears calm and undisturbed, like his four friends standing nearby. They chatter noisily among themselves, making jokes, and playfully pushing each other around, only half aware, seemingly, of the bustle and motion of other people.

48   Nodding toward his friends, Ed goes on to explain the social networking that takes place in the mall. "I met all these people here. I've met lots of other people, too. One place where you can always find someone. If you know somebody, they know somebody else, they'll probably see 'em here, and you'll know them, then they'll know someone who is walking around and you know that person. So when you come here, you kinda build on people."

49   Some teens spend a great deal of time networking in the mall. For them, it is practically a second home. Tammy, age 14, says, "I used to come here every Saturday from eleven o'clock to nine-thirty, and just walk around with my friends, like Gina here, just walk around and check out the guys."

50   When roaming from shop to shop, playing video games, or cruising the strip becomes tiresome, teens usually migrate to the food court. Here they sit, talk, bum change, smoke cigarettes and try to avoid the attention of the security people, even as most of the activities they are engaged in will inevitably attract it.

51   The group gathers around a table, some standing, others sitting and talking. One of the girls breaks from her conversation to announce that Bob is coming. Bob has been kicked out of the mall for boisterous behavior and is not allowed in for another two months.

52   "Just about all of us have gotten kicked out at one time or another," Tony says in a matter of fact manner. "I was sitting down without anything to eat once, and like I didn't know the policy and he said, 'Move,' and I go, 'Why?' I ran my mouth a little too much. What I basically did was stand up for myself, but he didn't like that, so he just booted me for a couple months."

53   "Actually, I'm not supposed to even be in here. He said he's kicked me out forever, but I mean like I changed my hair style so he doesn't recognize me anymore."

54   Ed nods. "I changed mine and I changed my jacket. I used to wear a big leather jacket. I used to wear that all the time. That gave me away. But I've started wearing this jacket now with all my KISS pins on. And as long as I don't act up or do anything, they don't really care. See, I like it here so much I hafta come back."

55   Liz, 15, discusses relationships with the security guards in general. "Some days they can really get on us and other days they just won't come and like we'll be

sitting down at the table and on busy days or on days they're not in a really good mood, they'll come over and tell us to move."

56 "They have no respect for mall rats," a boy standing on the edge of the group adds. "It's just days like that they can be real dinks."

57 And yet the mild harassment of the security guards is easily borne, especially when changing one's costume or haircut can many times be enough to erase identity in their eyes. Indeed, such treatment is better, for most, than the treatment they can expect elsewhere. And this relatively light scrutiny given them by the security guards also allows some teens to get away with minor interpersonal drug transactions, especially when the mall is crowded and busy.

58 "Other than The Beach, which is just like, 'deal it out on the streets,' I mean ya can get just about anything out here—pot, acid, hash, right here on Saturdays, when it is crowded."

59 "If you know the right people, you can pick up anything."

60 "And we pretty much know everybody here."

61 For some teens, the mall—with or without drugs—is an escape from home or school. Heather, 16, explains that she comes here "to get away from home, get away from problems 'cause I can't stay at home. Because of my nephew and my sister. They bother me. So I come to the mall." Slouching in her seat, she flips open the top of her red Marlboro box and counts her cigarettes. "School is no better. I go through a year of school, and they still put me through the next grade even if I'm failing. I like it, but it's not gonna get me through college if I do that. I don't care about partying. I just wanna get through school."

62 For Tiffany the mall has become a second home of sorts. At the age of thirteen she lives with Tony, another of the mall rats, and one other mall friend. "My mom kicked me out when I was eleven," she says with an edge of anger in her voice. "She's a bitch. I call her every day and she's just. . . ." Tiffany stops short as she shakes her head and rolls her eyes.

63 "I started going to foster homes and everything and I just quit. Now, I'm in State custody and I just. . . ." She stops again and laughs nervously and blushes. "Sorry about that," she says, apologizing to her friends, seeming to imply that she has become too personal, too emotional. Abruptly, she continues, "I don't do anything that they want me to do." She lets out a quick triumphant laugh.

64 "I swear to God if they came up to me and dragged me where I didn't want to go, I'd beat the crap right out of them. I would kill 'em. I got 'em twisted around my little finger. They don't mess with me." She growls, as she clenches her teeth and curls her small fist, pounding it lightly on the table.

65 Tony leans back and shakes his head slightly to part his long hair from his face. "I left home and I quit school and moved from, like, hotel to hotel for awhile with a Navy buddy and that wasn't a really good situation, 'cause we were getting kicked outta hotels and motels. We didn't have anywhere to go. So we went up to The Beach and when I went up there it's like there's a Burger King and an auto parts store and a Shop and Save and it's like . . . there was no mall. I was real glad to get back down here, 'cause it was, like, up there, it was boring the hell out of me."

66 The social world of these teens revolves around their contacts and time at the mall. Indeed, this world of the teenager is, in its larger sense, one of segregation

from adults and the assumption of adult sexual, economic, and social roles. This segregation, and the relative lack of any clearly defined and socially supported roles for youth, help define the mall community of "rats and bunnies," especially those who have opted out, or been driven from, socially acceptable school and family settings.

67   These youths, disallowed entrance into the social world of adulthood, are attempting to forge meaning and community from their shifting networks of face to face peer relationships in the mall. And yet, unlike the elderly, theirs is a relatively unstable social system. Teens come and go and, more importantly, they do grow up. As a consequence, relationships rest almost entirely in present time and revolve around present circumstances. The past is seldom spoken of, or shared. "Best friends" at the mall may part ways next month, and not see each other again. This fluidity and change in social relationships is a socially uncertain part of the teen years which, for mall rats and bunnies, is also characterized by a lingering malaise concerning the world outside their fragile community—a malaise in which jealousy, mistrust and despair are prominent features. As Tony says:

68   "We are the mall rats. We are the mall. What the fuck else can I say?"

Conclusion: Community in the Mall

69 The American shopping mall has been bemoaned by critics for its impersonality, its uniformity, its total focus on meaningful interaction as rational and economic in nature. Where are the primary relations, the face to face interactions, the social networks that exist along with the economic transactions of the traditional marketplace, the local community, or even the urban village? This case study of one American mall suggests that, for shoppers in the mall, one does indeed need to look elsewhere for the primary interactive ties of community, no matter how cleverly mall management creates the *illusion* of community at the mall. In the end, it seems, this is a shared illusion—neither management nor shoppers are fooled by it, but both can *pretend* that they are creating or engaging in the meaningful and socially necessary relations of community.

70   Ironically, then, the real community ties that do exist in the mall have little to do with its economic function. The elder and the teen spend very little money there and do not frequent the mall for economic reasons. They are there, each day, to greet friends, to create and strengthen their meaningful, face to face primary relationships, to define themselves as a social world, whether it be one of "milers" or of "mall rats"—a community of kind to which they can give emotional support and from which they can draw a sense of self and group identity.

71   Mall management does not like to see such groups develop. They use mall space for other than economic purposes. These warm knots of community can and do disrupt the cool smooth flow of economic transaction. Group members take seats designed for shoppers. They create a focus in the mall that is not economic in nature.

72   Politically, however, it is hard—especially with the elderly—to ban, or even to overtly discourage their presence. But it can be contained and monitored by security personnel. And, especially with the teens, if it becomes too socially visible and disruptive, some members of the group can be ejected.

73   Why, then, under these less than ideal circumstances, do the elderly and teenagers use the mall as their locus of community? It seems likely there are at least five general social reasons for this choice. First, and probably most important, elders and teens both represent social groupings for whom our society provides little social space. The elderly, once they are retired especially, are cut off from the familiar and fulfilling world of work. Their income drops sharply. They are likely to be treated more and more as children by both their families and their non-elderly acquaintances. If they are widowed and live at home, they have lost most of the primary face to face support they have relied on for most of their adult lives.[10]

74   Consequently, they have a need to seek out others in similar situations. The mall is a central, safe place to get to, and there is usually regularly scheduled mass transportation available for the benefit of the shoppers (when it most likely would *not* be available on any regular basis for, say, transport to a non-economically oriented center or meeting place, such as a park or activities center).

75   For the teens, caught as they are between the statuses of childhood and adulthood, there are few social spaces or physical places open where they can congregate and develop their own contacts and social networks.[11] Most often, their activity is too closely defined, monitored, and circumscribed for them to see it as their own (in institutions such as the family and the school). Or, if they do find a niche of their own—such as cruising Main Street or hanging out in a park or fast food parking lot—they are usually dispersed by the authorities, or caught in curfews, or both.

76   And when school and family settings become nonviable alternatives, teens really have very few places to go. Once again, the mall offers its lure. It is centrally located, easy to get to for those with or without their own transportation, seen as a "safe" place by parents, and may, for some, also be the location of their full- or part-time job (usually for minimum wage—but that is another bit of discrimination teens have to bear).

77   Second, the elderly and teens are, to a great extent, faceless persons to adult American society. They are categorized as "old people" or "kids," and, because of the unimportance of their marginal status, they tend to be overlooked as individuals, though they are stereotypically reacted to as members of groups. For both of these groups, this social reaction increases their need to affirm identity and to create meaningful community for themselves.[12]

78   It also means that, in the mall setting, the elderly are usually overlooked, are nearly invisible to the shoppers hurrying on their way. Being socially invisible, the elderly cannot get much in the way of shoppers and thus their presence, as disruption, is less likely to be an issue requiring action on the part of mall management.

79   For the teens, even the security guards who keep them under surveillance can easily be fooled by a simple change of hair style or jacket. The boisterous teen who is ejected from the mall easily "slips out" of his or her public identity and is back the next day or week, a unique *person* returning to his or her community, invisible in return even to the watching security guards.

80   Third, as alluded to in point one above, the mall is centrally located, easy to get to, safe and climate controlled. The amenities that exist there for the shoppers—

restaurants, rest rooms, benches and seats—can also be used by the non-shopper, as long as mall management does not actively discourage such usage.

81   Fourth, for the elderly, discouragement could be dangerous, in a public relations sense. Conversely, the elderly can be used to advantage to further the mall's illusion of community by publicizing their support of community programs such as that of walking-for-health. For the teens, many of them work in the fast food stores and do leave money in the video arcade and the record stores. Therefore they do have some economic links to some of the businesses operating in the mall. The mall rats and bunnies also provide a visually exciting and socially validating backdrop for these youth oriented businesses, for other youths and young adults who come to shop.

82   Finally, these communities seem, in general, to police themselves quite well. They are aware of their status in the eyes of mall management and attempt, each in their own distinctive way, to keep a low enough profile so their presence is tolerated.[13]

83   Ironically, then, and for these reasons, deep within the impersonal and concrete structure of the mall, cultural chains of belonging seem to have been forged. The sense of community, to such an extent denied these groupings of the elderly and the young, in the larger society, is being created and shared in the mall, while shoppers rush blindly past under lights of cold neon, across the polished sheen of endless tiled floors.

Notes

1. Jessie Bernard, *The Sociology of Community* (Glenview, Ill: Scott, Foresman, 1973), p. 3.

2. Thomas Bender, *Community and Social Change in America* (Baltimore: Johns Hopkins University Press, 1978), p. 7.

3. Chain Store Age Executive, "Why They Shop Some Centers," 1987, 54, 33.

4. Interview with mall marketing director, 1986.

5. The author served as Director of Research for this study. Interviews quoted in this paper were conducted by himself, SALT staff members Pamela Wood and Hugh French, and students Brett Jenks, Edite Pedrosa, Amy Rowe, Julie Maurer, Peter Lancia, Harry Brown, Amy Schnerr and Lou Brown. Original tapes and transcripts are on file at SALT CENTER, Kennebunkport, ME 04609.

6. Jerry Jacobs, *The Mall: An Attempted Escape From Every Day Life* (Prospect Heights, Ill: Waveland Press, 1984), pp. 27–32.

7. Robert Atchley, *Social Forces and Aging* (Belmont, CA: Wadsworth, 1985), pp. 56–58.

8. Bob Greene, "Fifteen: Young Men Cruising Shopping Malls," *Esquire*, 1982, 98, pp. 17–18; Kowinski, *op. cit.*, pp. 68–73.

9. Martin Millison, *Teenage Behavior In Shopping Centers*, International Council of Shopping Centers, 1976, p. 11.

10. Peggy Eastman, "Elders Under Siege," *Psychology Today*, 1984, January, p. 30.

11. Richard Flacks, *Youth and Social Change* (Chicago: Markham, 1971), p. 17.

12. *Loc. cit.*, p. 223.

13. This includes relations between the two groups. The elderly mainly frequent the old wing of the mall, while the teens frequent the new wing. The elderly arrive very early and usually leave by late afternoon. The teens usually arrive in mid to late afternoon and stay until the mall closes.

Review Questions

1. In what sense have modern malls become "civic centers"?

2. What are the differences between "the community" and "community," according to Lewis? Why does he introduce this distinction early in the article?

3. What conditions at malls inhibit the growth of community?

4. For what reasons do elders come to the mall? How does mall management react to their presence?

5. Why do teenagers visit the mall?

6. What characteristics do the teenage community and the elderly community share when at the mall?

7. In what sense is the world of the mall a "shared illusion," according to Lewis?

8. What five reasons does Lewis give for teens and elders seeking out the mall as a place to build their communities?

Discussion and Writing Suggestions

1. Lewis quotes a mall manager saying: "Having the *perception* of a community feeling does not mean that it actually exists. It is not the same thing." Why would mall managers take the trouble to create an illusion that malls encourage community ties?

2. Why is it "ironic," according the Lewis, that malls have become the meeting place for actual communities?

3. In shopping malls you have visited, what evidence do you find of an elders' community similar to the one Lewis describes?

4. Read the account of Pat, a mall regular (paragraphs 20–29). What is your response to Pat's story?

5. Reread paragraphs 43–57. Based on your experience, how accurate is Lewis's description of what teenagers do at the mall?

6. One of the key investigative tools for a sociologist like Lewis is the personal interview. Reread those portions of the article devoted to interviews of the elderly and teenagers. How important are these interviews to the success of Lewis's argument? What, in your view, do they add to the selection?

7. Write several paragraphs describing one of your experiences as a "mall rat" or "mall bunny." Include an account of the teenagers who gather at the mall as well as a description of the mall itself (for example, discuss its location, its appearance, the type of customers it attracts). In a final paragraph describe the extent to which you think the people you have described form a community.

The Mall as Threat to Democratic Values
Lizabeth Cohen

In the following article, which appeared in the American Historical Review *(October 1996), Lizabeth Cohen traces the "restructuring of the consumer marketplace" that followed America's population shift to the suburbs after World War II. Millions of people who had lived in the cities, walking to the corner store, faced an entirely new experience as shoppers once they moved to the suburbs. In their new homes, a trip to the store meant a ride in the car, likely to a shopping center where relations between store owner and customer had fundamentally changed. Cohen, a professor of history at New York University, studies the effects that the new mass-consumption society had on America. You will see that she identifies two developments, relating to segregation and free speech, that threaten our general welfare.*

1 Whereas, at first, developers had sought to legitimize the new shopping centers by arguing for their centrality to both commerce and community, over time they discovered that those two commitments could be in conflict. The rights of free speech and assembly traditionally safeguarded in the public forums of democratic communities were not always good for business, and they could conflict with the rights of private property owners—the shopping centers—to control entry to their land. Beginning in the 1960s, American courts all the way up to the Supreme Court struggled with the political consequences of having moved public life off the street and into the privately owned shopping center. Shopping centers, in turn, began to reconsider the desirable balance between commerce and community in what had become the major sites where suburbanites congregated.[1]

2   Once regional shopping centers like the Paramus malls had opened in the 1950s, people began to recognize them as public spaces and to use them to reach out to the community. When the Red Cross held blood drives, when labor unions picketed stores in organizing campaigns, when political candidates campaigned for office, when anti-war and anti-nuclear activists gathered signatures for petitions, they all viewed the shopping center as the obvious place to reach masses of people. Although shopping centers varied in their responses—from

tolerating political activists to monitoring their actions to prohibiting them outright—in general, they were wary of any activity that might offend customers. A long, complex series of court tests resulted, culminating in several key Supreme Court decisions that sought to sort out the conflict between two basic rights in a free society: free speech and private property. Not surprisingly, the cases hinged on arguments about the extent to which the shopping center had displaced the traditional "town square" as a legitimate public forum.[2]

3   The first ruling by the Supreme Court was *Amalgamated Food Employees Union Local 590 vs. Logan Valley Plaza, Inc.* (1968), in which Justice Thurgood Marshall, writing for the majority, argued that refusing to let union members picket the Weis Markets in the Logan Valley Plaza in Altoona, Pennsylvania, violated the workers' First Amendment rights, since shopping centers had become the "functional equivalent" of a sidewalk in a public business district. Because peaceful picketing and leaflet distribution on "streets, sidewalks, parks, and other similar public places are so historically associated with the exercise of First Amendment rights," he wrote, it should also be protected in the public thoroughfare of a shopping center, even if privately owned. The Logan Valley Plaza decision likened the shopping center to a company town, which had been the subject of an important Supreme Court decision in *Marsh vs. Alabama* (1946), upholding the First Amendment rights of a Jehovah's Witness to proselytize in the company town of Chickasaw, Alabama, despite the fact that the Gulf Shipbuilding Corporation owned all the property in town. The "Marsh Doctrine" affirmed First Amendment rights over private property rights when an owner opened up his or her property for use by the public.[3] The stance taken in Logan Valley began to unravel, however, as the Supreme Court became more conservative under President Richard Nixon's appointees. In *Lloyd Corp. vs. Tanner* (1972), Justice Lewis F. Powell, Jr., wrote for the majority that allowing anti-war advocates to pass out leaflets at the Lloyd Center in Portland, Oregon, would be an unwarranted infringement of property rights "without significantly enhancing the asserted right of free speech." Anti-war leaflets, he argued, could be effectively distributed elsewhere, without undermining the shopping center's appeal to customers with litter and distraction.[4]

4   The reigning Supreme Court decision today is *PruneYard Shopping Center vs. Robbins* (1980). The Supreme Court upheld a California State Supreme Court ruling that the state constitution granted a group of high school students the right to gather petitions against the U.N. resolution "Zionism Is Racism." The court decided that this action did not violate the San Jose mall owner's rights under the U.S. Constitution. But, at the same time, the court reaffirmed its earlier decisions in *Lloyd vs. Tanner* and *Scott Hudgens vs. National Labor Relations Board* (1976) that the First Amendment did not guarantee access to shopping malls, and it left it to the states to decide for themselves whether their own constitutions protected such access.

5   Since *PruneYard*, state appellate courts have been struggling with the issue, and mall owners have been winning in many more states than they have lost. Only in six states, California, Oregon, Massachusetts, Colorado, Washington, and most recently New Jersey, have state supreme courts protected citizens' right of free speech in privately owned shopping centers. In New Jersey, the courts have been

involved for some time in adjudicating free speech in shopping centers. In 1983, the Bergen Mall was the setting of a suit between its owners and a political candidate who wanted to distribute campaign materials there. When a Paramus Municipal Court judge ruled in favor of the mall, the candidate's attorney successfully appealed on the familiar grounds that "there is no real downtown Paramus. Areas of the mall outside the stores are the town's public sidewalks." He further noted that the mall hosted community events and contained a meeting hall, post office, and Roman Catholic chapel. In this case, and in another one the following year over the right of nuclear-freeze advocates to distribute literature at the Bergen Mall, free speech was protected on the grounds that the mall was equivalent to a town center.[5]

6   Such suits should be unnecessary (at least for a while) in New Jersey, because in a historic decision in December 1994 the New Jersey Supreme Court affirmed that the state constitution guaranteed free speech to opponents of the Persian Gulf War who wanted to distribute leaflets at ten regional malls throughout the state. Writing for the majority, Chief Justice Robert N. Wilentz confirmed how extensively public space has been transformed in postwar New Jersey:

> The economic lifeblood once found downtown has moved to suburban shopping centers, which have substantially displaced the downtown business districts as the centers of commercial and social activity. . . . Found at these malls are most of the uses and activities citizens engage in outside their homes. . . . This is the new, the improved, the more attractive downtown business district—the new community—and no use is more closely associated with the old downtown than leafletting. Defendants have taken that old downtown away from its former home and moved all of it, except free speech, to the suburbs.

Despite the New Jersey Supreme Court's commitment to free speech, it nonetheless put limits on it, reaffirming the regional mall owners' property rights. Its ruling allowed only the distribution of leaflets—no speeches, bullhorns, pickets, parades, demonstrations, or solicitation of funds. Moreover, the court granted owners broad powers to regulate leaflet distribution by specifying days, hours, and areas in or outside the mall permissible for political activity. Thus, although shopping centers in New Jersey and five other states have been forced to accommodate some political activity, they have retained authority to regulate it and are even finding ways of preventing legal leafletters from exercising their constitutional rights, such as by requiring them to have million-dollar liability policies, which are often unobtainable or prohibitively expensive. In many other states, shopping centers have been able to prohibit political action outright, much as they control the economic and social behavior of shoppers and store owners.[6]

7   An unintended consequence of the American shift in orientation from public town center to private shopping center, then, has been the narrowing of the ground where constitutionally protected free speech and free assembly can legally take place.

. . .

8   Mass consumption in postwar America created a new landscape, where public space was more commercialized [and] more privatized within the regional shopping center than it had been in the traditional downtown center. This is not to romanticize the city and its central business district. Certainly, urban commercial property owners pursued their own economic interests, [and] political activity in public spaces was sometimes limited. . . . Nonetheless, the legal distinction between public and private space remained significant; urban loitering and vagrancy laws directed against undesirables in public places have repeatedly been struck down by the courts, while privately owned shopping centers have been able to enforce trespassing laws.[7] Overall, an important shift from one kind of social order to another took place between 1950 and 1980, with major consequences for Americans. A free commercial market attached to a relatively free public sphere (for whites) underwent a transformation to a more regulated commercial marketplace (where mall management controlled access, favoring chains over local independents, for example) and a more circumscribed public sphere of limited rights. Economic and social liberalism went hand in hand and declined together.

9   Not by accident, public space was restructured and segmented by class and race in New Jersey, as in the nation, just as African Americans gained new protections for their right of equal access to public accommodations. Although civil rights laws had been on the books in New Jersey since the late nineteenth century, comprehensive legislation with mechanisms for enforcement did not pass until the 1940s. With the "Freeman Bill" of 1949, African Americans were finally guaranteed equal access to schools, restaurants, taverns, retail stores, hotels, public transportation, and facilities of commercial leisure such as movie theaters, skating rinks, amusement parks, swimming pools, and beaches, with violators subject to fines and jail terms. Throughout the 1940s and 1950s, African-American citizens of New Jersey—and other northern states—vigilantly challenged discrimination by private property owners. Yet larger structural changes in community marketplaces were under way, financed by private commercial interests committed to socioeconomic and racial segmentation. While African Americans and their supporters were prodding courts and legislatures to eliminate legal segregation in public places, real-estate developers, retailers, and consumers were collaborating to shift economic resources to new kinds of segregated spaces.[8]

10   The landscape of mass consumption created a metropolitan society in which people were no longer brought together in central marketplaces and the parks, streets, and public buildings that surrounded them but, rather, were separated by class and race in differentiated commercial sub-centers. Moreover, all commercial sub-centers were not created equal. Over time, shopping centers became increasingly class stratified, with some like the Bergen Mall marketing themselves to the lower middle class, while others like the Garden State Plaza went upscale to attract upper middle-class consumers. If tied to international capital, some central business districts—such as New York and San Francisco— have prospered, although they have not been left unscarred from recent retail mergers and leveraged buy-outs. Other downtowns, such as Hackensack and Elizabeth, New Jersey, have become "Cheap John Bargain Centers" serving

customers too poor and deprived of transportation to shop at malls. Even in larger American cities, poor urban populations shop downtown on weekends while the white-collar workers who commute in to offices during the week patronize the suburban malls closer to where they live. Some commercial districts have been taken over by enterprising, often newly arrived, ethnic groups, who have breathed new life into what would otherwise have been in decay, but they nonetheless serve a segmented market. Worst off are cities like Newark, once the largest shopping district in the state, which saw every one of its major department stores close between 1964 and 1992 and much of its retail space remain abandoned, leaving residents such as Raymond Mungin to wonder, "I don't have a car to drive out to the malls. What can I do?" Mass consumption was supposed to bring standardization in merchandise and consumption patterns. Instead, diverse social groups are no longer integrated into central consumer marketplaces but rather are consigned to differentiated retail institutions, segmented markets, and new hierarchies.[9]

11   Finally, the dependence on private spaces for public activity and the more recent privatization of public space gravely threaten the government's constitutional obligations to its citizens. Not only freedom of speech and public assembly in shopping centers are at issue. Just recently, Amtrak's Pennsylvania Station in New York City tried to stave off two suits requiring it to respect constitutional rights guaranteed in public places: an effort by artist Michael Lebron to display a political message on the gigantic curved and lighted billboard that he had rented for two months, and a case brought by the Center for Constitutional Rights to force Amtrak to stop ejecting people from the station because they are homeless. When Jürgen Habermas theorized about the rise and fall of a rational public sphere, he recognized the centrality in the eighteenth and nineteenth centuries of accessible urban places—cafés, taverns, coffeehouses, clubs, meeting houses, concert and lecture halls, theaters, and museums—to the emergence and maintenance of a democratic political culture. Over the last half-century, transformations in America's economy and metropolitan landscape have expanded the ability of many people to participate in the mass market. But the commercializing, privatizing, and segmenting of physical gathering places that has accompanied mass consumption has made more precarious the shared public sphere upon which our democracy depends.[10]

Notes

1. Shopping centers retreated from promoting themselves as central squares and street corners not only because of the free speech issue but also to limit the loitering of young people. *New York Times:* "Supermarkets Hub of Suburbs," February 7, 1971: 58; "Coping with Shopping-Center Crises, Dilemma: How Tough to Get If Young Are Unruly," March 7, 1971: sect. 3, p. 1; "Shopping Centers Change and Grow," May 23, 1971: sect. 7, p. 1.

2. For a useful summary of the relevant court cases and legal issues involved, see Curtis J. Berger, "*PruneYard* Revisited: Political Activity on Private Lands," *New York University Law Review* 66 (June 1991): 633–94; also "Shopping Centers Change and Grow," *New York Times* (May 23, 1971): sect. 7, p. 1. The corporate

shopping center's antagonism to free political expression and social action is discussed in Herbert I. Schiller, *Culture Inc.: The Corporate Takeover of Public Expression* (New York, 1989), 98–101.

3. On *Amalgamated vs. Logan Valley Plaza*, see "Property Rights vs. Free Speech," *New York Times* (July 9, 1972): sect. 7, p. 9; "Amalgamated Food Employees Union Local 590 v. Logan Valley Plaza," 88 S.Ct. 1601 (1968), *Supreme Court Reporter*, 1601–20; 391 US 308, U.S. Supreme Court Recording Briefs 1967, No. 478, microfiche; "Free Speech: Peaceful Picketing on Quasi-Public Property," *Minnesota Law Review* 53 (March 1969): 873–82. On *Marsh vs. State of Alabama*, see 66 S.Ct. 276, *Supreme Court Reporter*, 276–84. Other relevant cases between *Marsh vs. Alabama* and *Amalgamated vs. Logan Valley Plaza* are *Nahas vs. Local 905, Retail Clerks International Assoc.* (1956), *Amalgamated Clothing Workers of America vs. Wonderland Shopping Center, Inc.* (1963), *Schwartz-Torrance Investment Corp. vs. Bakery and Confectionary Workers' Union, Local No. 31* (1964); with each case, the Warren court was moving closer to a recognition that the shopping center was becoming a new kind of public forum.

4. "4 Nixon Appointees End Court's School Unanimity, Shopping Centers' Right to Ban Pamphleteering Is Upheld, 5 to 4," *New York Times* (June 23, 1972): 1; "Shopping-Center Industry Hails Court," *New York Times* (July 2, 1972): sect. 3, p. 7; "Lloyd Corporation, Ltd. v. Donald M. Tanner (1972)," 92 S.Ct. 2219 (1972), *Supreme Court Reporter*, 2219–37. The American Civil Liberties Union brief went to great lengths to document the extent to which shopping centers have replaced traditional business districts; see "Brief for Respondents," U.S. Supreme Court Record, microfiche, 20–29. See also People's Lobby Brief, U.S. Supreme Court Record, microfiche, 5.

   The Supreme Court majority wanted to make it clear that in finding in favor of the Lloyd Center, it was not reversing the Logan Valley decision, arguing for a distinction based on the fact that anti-war leafletting was "unrelated" to the shopping center, while the labor union was picketing an employer. The four dissenting justices, however, were less sure that the distinction was valid and that the Logan Valley decision was not seriously weakened by Lloyd. The important court cases between *Amalgamated vs. Logan Valley Plaza* and *Lloyd vs. Tanner* included *Blue Ridge Shopping Center vs. Schleininger* (1968), *Sutherland vs. Southcenter Shopping Center* (1971), and *Diamond vs. Bland* (1970, 1974).

5. Berger, "*PruneYard* Revisited"; Kowinski, *Malling of America*, 196–202, 355–59; "Shopping Malls Protest Intrusion by Protesters," *New York Times* (July 19, 1983): B1; "Opening of Malls Fought," *New York Times* (May 13, 1984): sect. 11 (New Jersey), 7; "Michael Robins v. PruneYard Shopping Center (1979)," 592 P. 2nd 341, *Pacific Reporter*, 341–51; "PruneYard Shopping Center v. Michael Robins," 100 S.Ct. 2035 (1980), *Supreme Court Reporter*, 2035–51; U.S. Supreme Court Record, *PruneYard Shopping Center vs. Robins* (1980), microfiche. The most important Supreme Court case between *Lloyd vs. Tanner* and *PruneYard* was *Scott Hudgens vs. National Labor Relations Board* (1976), where the majority decision backed further away from Logan Valley Plaza and refused to see the mall as the functional equivalent of downtown. "Scott Hudgens v. National Labor Relations Board," 96 S.Ct. 1029 (1976), *Supreme Court Reporter*, 1029–47.

6. "Court Protects Speech in Malls," *New York Times* (December 21, 1994): A1; "Big Malls Ordered to Allow Leafletting," *Star-Ledger* (December 21, 1994): 1; "Now, Public Rights in Private Domains," *New York Times* (December 25, 1994): E3; "Free Speech in the Mall," *New York Times* (December 26, 1994): 38; Frank Askin, "Shopping for Free Speech at the Malls," 1995, unpublished ms. in possession of the author.

7. "Amtrak Is Ordered Not to Eject the Homeless from Penn Station," *New York Times* (February 22, 1995): A1.

8. Article on passage of New Jersey Civil Rights Bill, *New York Times*, March 24, 1949; Marion Thompson Wright, "Extending Civil Rights in New Jersey through the Division Against Discrimination," *Journal of Negro History* 38 (1953): 96–107; State of New Jersey, Governor's Committee on Civil Liberties, "Memorandum on Behalf of Joint Council for Civil Rights in Support of a Proposed Comprehensive Civil Rights Act for New Jersey," 1948, II, B 8, Folder "Civil Rights, New Jersey, 1941–48," NAACP Papers, Library of Congress, Washington, D.C.; "Report of Legislative Committee, NJ State Conference of NAACP Branches," March 26, 1949, II, B 8, Folder "Civil Rights, New Jersey, 1941–48," NAACP Papers. Other NAACP files on discrimination document the actual experiences of African Americans in New Jersey during the 1940s and 1950s.

9. "Closing of 'Last' Department Store Stirs Debate on Downtown Trenton," *Star-Ledger*, June 5, 1983; "Urban Areas Crave Return of Big Markets," *Star-Ledger*, July 17, 1984; "Elizabeth Clothier Mourns Demise of Century-Old Customized Service," *Sunday Star-Ledger*, January 10, 1988; "President's Report to the Annual Meeting Passaic Valley Citizens Planning Association." Box A, Folder 3.

10. Jürgen Habermas, *The Structural Transformation of the Public Sphere: An Inquiry into a Category of Bourgeois Society*, Thomas Burger trans., with Frederick Lawrence (Cambridge, Mass., 1989); Geoff Eley, "Nations, Publics, and Political Cultures: Placing Habermas in the Nineteenth Century," in Nicholas B. Dirks, Geoff Eley, and Sherry B. Ortner, eds., *Culture/Power/History: A Reader in Contemporary Social Theory* (Princeton, N.J., 1994), 297–335.

Review Questions

1. In what sense was suburbanization a new form of racial segregation, according to Cohen?

2. Explain the legal battles that arose in connection with shopping centers.

3. The rise of the shopping center over the last 50 years has given many people access to the mass market, says Cohen. But this access has come at a price. What is that price?

Discussion and Writing Suggestions

1. Cohen argues that shopping centers gave rise to a new form of racial segregation in this country. In your own experience, have you observed or experienced segregation at a shopping center?

2. Reread paragraph 9 and comment on this passage: "While African Americans and their supporters were prodding courts and legislatures to eliminate legal segregation in public places, real-estate developers, retailers, and consumers were collaborating to shift economic resources to new kinds of segregated spaces." To what extent do you agree that suburban shopping malls constitute "segregated spaces"?

3. What evidence do you find from your own experience that shopping centers are "class stratified"—that is, some centers cater to the upper-middle class, some to the lower-middle class?

4. Have you seen any evidence that political activity (for instance, protesting or gathering of signatures for petitions) is any less welcome in a shopping center than it is on a city street? Write a descriptive paragraph or two describing the experience.

5. Interview an older acquaintance or relative, perhaps a grandparent, on how shopping has changed over the years. Does this person recall a time before the rise of shopping centers? What was better about shopping in the middle of the twentieth century versus shopping at the beginning of the twenty-first? What was worse?

Mallaise: How to Know If You Have It
William Kowinski

William Kowinski's The Malling of America: An Inside Look at the Great Consumer Paradise *(William Morrow, 1985) has become a classic in the literature on the cultural impact of shopping centers. The following selection, which forms a chapter in* Malling, *is representative of Kowinski's tone throughout: ironic, playful, and pointed in its critique of malls and their effects. "Mallaise" is his attempt to name the disease that some people feel on being absorbed by the totality of the mall's environment. Perhaps you will recognize one or more of the symptoms.*

1   Malls make some people sick. Literally, sometimes. They feel feverish, their eyes glaze, their stomachs tumble, they fall down, they throw up.

2   Some people are just annoyed by one or another aspect of a mall, or a nonspecific quality of a particular mall, or malls in general. "That mall makes me *sick!*" they say. Or "I don't like malls—I *hate* them." Malls make people angry. Some of these people are shoppers, but some are people who work in malls or even own mall stores.

3   Malls affect people. They're designed to. But in some ways, either by their nature or by a side effect caused by their main ingredients, they do things to people that people are unaware of or don't understand, but if they knew or understood, they probably wouldn't like it.

4   There are other more obvious things that happen to people in malls that they don't or wouldn't like. Crime, for instance.

5   This section of *The Malling of America* is about some of the negative aspects of malls that affect people and that people perceive. Does the mall make you tired? Set your nerves on edge? Do you find it difficult to concentrate? Do you feel the absence of certain phenomena—weather, for example, or civil liberties? Do you sometimes wonder if you are really as safe as mall management would like you to believe?

6   If you're a parent, do you fear for your children's ability to survive outside comfort control because they spend so much time in the mall? And if you're an adolescent, do you feel your horizons becoming limited to a hundred chain store-outlets and three anchor department stores? Or are you worried that this is precisely the world your parents do live in, and where they want you always to remain?

7   These are some of the symptoms of mallaise. Perhaps you have one or two, or know someone who does, or perhaps you want to be prepared, just in case. Then perhaps you should read on.

8   I had my first attack of *mal de mall* in Columbia, Maryland. I was in a restaurant in the Columbia Mall having coffee. The attack was characterized by feverishness, sudden fatigue, and high anxiety, all recurring whenever I glanced out at the mall itself. The thought of going out there again made me sweat and swoon, and I had to fight the hallucinatory certainty that when I left the restaurant I would be in Greengate mall, or maybe Woodfield, or Tysons Corner. Or *all* of them.

9   *Mal de mall*, or mall sickness, is one of the classifications of mallaise, the general term for physical and psychological disturbances caused by mall contact. I know because I made them all up. Among the symptoms I have personally observed or heard about from their victims are these:

10   *Dismallcumbobulation:* "I don't like to go to malls because I always get lost," a woman told me, "and that's embarrassing. I feel stupid. It makes me mad." The hyped-up overabundance of similar products plus the bland sameness of many mall environments make people feel lost even when they aren't. Even familiar malls relocate stores and reconfigure themselves, which adds to the feeling of a continuous featureless space. And the similarity of one mall to another is disorienting. You walk out of the Stuft Potato and you not only don't remember which way your car is, you might not remember what mall this is. There are other kinds of dismallcumbobulation: the loss of a sense of time as well as place, and forgetting one's purpose in coming to the mall—all of which can lead to apathy and hopelessness, loss of consciousness, or fainting. Some victims recommend deep-breathing exercises every fifteen minutes while at the mall.

11   *Inability to Relate to Others:* "It's impossible to talk to someone when you're shopping at the mall," a friend told me, explaining why she prefers to shop alone. "I notice it at the mall all the time—you see two people together but they aren't really talking to each other. They're talking, but they're staring off in different directions, and pretty soon they just wander away from each other." Among the possible effects of this symptom are disenchantment and divorce.

12   *Plastiphobia,* or the fear of being enclosed in a cocoon of blandness. "Suddenly I just stood still and looked around," a young man said. "I saw all the people and what we were all doing there, what we were spending our day doing, and I suddenly just couldn't wait to get out. I was in a plastic place with plastic people buying plastic products with plastic charge cards. I had to escape." Sometimes this reaction is accompanied by severe anxiety, alienation from the human race, and in at least one very severe case I know of, by all the usual manifestations of a drug overdose.

13   All of these, and their variations, are unfortunate side effects (or perhaps just extreme cases) of the main psychological effects that the mall intends.

Excitement may become overstimulation; relaxation may drift into confusion and torpor. The combination is what I call the Zombie Effect.

14   There is, in fact, a fine line between the ideal mall shopper and the dismayed mall shopper, between mall bliss and mallaise, between the captivated shopper and the Zombie Effect. The best description of the Zombie Effect I've heard was Barbara Lambert's, which she imparted while we toured the malls of Chicagoland.

15   It hits you, Barbara said, when you're standing there naked, looking in the mirror of the dressing room. Your clothes are in a pile on the floor or draped over a chair. Maybe it's just a little cubicle with a curtain, and you can still hear the hum and buzz of the mall and the tinny timbres of Muzak. You're about to try something on, in an effortless repetition of what you've been doing since you came to the mall. And suddenly you realize *you've been here all day.* Time has in fact been passing while you've been gliding through store after store in a tender fuzz of soft lights and soft music. The plash of fountains, the glow of people, but almost no intrusive sound has broken your floating— no telephone, no demands, nothing to dodge or particularly watch out for. Just a gentle visual parade of clothes, fabric tags, and washing instructions. Racks, displays, cosmetics, brisk signs, flowing greenery, and spasms of color in the dream light. An ice-cream cone, a cup of coffee. Other figures have glided by: walking models of the mall's products, or walking models of the weird. An old man who reminds you of your grandfather, sitting on a blond-wood bench under a potted palm. A woman who may or may not have been your best friend's other best friend in high school, striding by on strange shoes—or maybe that's a new style and yours are strange? You're looking at your naked image in a bare little room, and a little breeze touches you. Whatever you actually came here for is in the distant past. You've been floating here . . . for hours.

16   But that's the whole idea of this psychological structure: to turn off your mind and let you float; to create a direct and unfettered connection between eyeing and buying; and the more you do, the easier it becomes. Malls make for great eye/hand-on-credit-card co-ordination.

17   The way it's done is with a combination of peacefulness and stimulation. The environment bathes you in sweet neutrality with soft light, candied music, and all the amenities that reassure and please without grabbing too much individual attention. At the same time, the stores and products dance for you with friendly smiles and colorful costumes. The sheer number of products and experiences you pay for and their apparent variety are in themselves factors that excite and focus.

18   Once again, it's all a lot like television. TV lulls and stimulates simultaneously. The medium itself is familiar and comfortable and friendly; the programs can be interesting but it is not really by accident that they are not as compact, colorful, dramatic, or insistent as the commercials. Watching television we are everywhere and nowhere in particular, just as at the mall. Suddenly you might realize that you've been watching it all day, just floating for hours. And if you look at people watching television—especially their eyes—they look pretty much like mall shoppers: the Zombie Effect.

19   But these effects are all supposed to be pleasant and unconscious. When either the lulling or stimulating quality—or especially the combination and conflict between them—is strongly felt, then it's no longer pleasant. Overstimulation causes anxiety, and sometimes an intense focus on heavy-duty, no-nonsense, get-out-of-my-way shopping, or else a frenzied need to get out of there, fast and forever. The lulling and sense deprivation cause listlessness and confusion, and occasionally rebellion at being Muzaked into implacable mushy madness. The conflict of both going on at the same time can cause the sense of dislocation and exhaustion that is the clearest indicator of the Zombie Effect. The victim shuffles and mumbles, is distant or unduly preoccupied, doesn't listen, acts automatically, and not only can't remember where the car is parked but often doesn't care.

20   There are ancilliary symptoms and causes as well: headaches caused by guilt at buying too much; depression at not being able to buy everything; the walking emptiness caused by consistently emphasized, endless greed.

21   The cure for all forms of mallaise is theoretically simple: The victim leaves the mall. There are no laws requiring people to stay in the mall, or even to go there in the first place. It isn't anyone's civic, moral, spiritual, or intellectual duty. The mall may be the best place—or even the only place—to shop for certain products, but that doesn't mean the shopper has to stay there for hours. Nevertheless, it isn't always easy to leave.

22   For that is another aspect of the Zombie Effect: Victims stay for no good or apparent reason, and even beyond their conscious desire to be there. Shoppers mallinger partly because of the mall's psychological apparatus, its implicit promise of safety, sanctuary, and salvation. Of Nirvana! The Crystal City! A New Heaven on a New Earth! The mall hasn't become the most successful artificial environment in America for nothing.

23   With its real walls and psychological illusions, the mall protects against so many hazards and uncertainties that the mallaise sufferer may well mallinger a little longer to ponder the consequences of walking out. Such a person may fear trading the malladies of the Zombie Effect for the perils of mall withdrawal, which is characterized by shaking in downtown areas, fear of crossing streets, inordinate terror in the presence of rain or sunshine, confusion when actual travel is required between purchases, and the feeling of estrangement when wearing a coat.

24   I wish I could say that medical science is on top of this new set of malladies, but the truth is that it is scandalously behind the times. Right now, there may be many thousands of Zombie Effect sufferers, untreated and undiagnosed. If you find this hard to believe—well, have you been to the mall lately?

25   There is one more form of mallaise that is especially frustrating because it is not so simply cured, even theoretically. It is the state of being malcontented with what the mall offers and how it offers it. Sufferers will rail on about the same limited clothing styles reproduced in a hundred mall shops, or the same five movies shown in two dozen mall theaters—the only cinemas around. They will complain endlessly about fast-print outlets masquerading as bookstores, where clerks don't know anything more about books than what appears on the

computer stock list. They will raise angry fists against the screening boxes calling themselves cinemas, with their dark and blurry unwatchable images on the screen, and cold and tinny sound.

26   These unfortunate mallcontents really have a problem, because in many places they don't have any alternative: If they want to shop for clothes, see a first-run movie, buy a new book or record, it's the mall or nothing.

27   They flail away at the promises the mall implies but does not keep. They are in a sense prisoners of the mall, if only because the mall's predominance has destroyed the alternatives they miss, even the imaginary ones.

Discussion and Writing Suggestions

1. At what point in this selection did you realize that Kowinski has a sense of humor? Work through the piece and mark what in your view are the funniest lines.

2. Through humor, Kowinski makes a number of penetrating observations about mall culture. Of the various maladies he catalogs (with tongue in cheek), which one seems the most insightful? Why?

3. Have you observed in yourself, a friend, or family member any symptoms of *mal de mall?* Describe your experience.

4. Kowinski compares mall shopping to television watching (see paragraph 18). Is the comparison apt, in your view?

5. In paragraph 16, Kowinski writes that the "whole idea of [the mall's] psychological structure [is] to turn off your mind and let you float; to create a direct and unfettered connection between eyeing and buying." Have you ever noticed that malls are designed to have a "psychological structure"? Explain.

6. In introducing the Zombie Effect (see paragraph 18), Kowinski writes: "Watching television we are everywhere and nowhere in particular, just as at the mall." Do you agree?

7. Kowinski gives the feeling of being lost in a mall a funny name: *dismallcumbobulation.* But he is making a serious point in noting the essential sameness of malls. Have you noticed how one mall often looks like others—with the same chain stores and repeating architectural features? One could shop at a mall in Louisville or in Buffalo and not be able to tell them apart. How do you respond to these similarities? Have you ever been dismallcumbobulated?

8. In paragraph 25, Kowinski may come closest to expressing his underlying view of malls than at any other point in the selection. Reread the paragraph and summarize what you take to be his general attitude toward malls.

SYNTHESIS ACTIVITIES

1. In an explanatory paper that draws on several selections in this chapter, explain to a time traveler from the sixteenth century, or a visitor from the remotest regions on present-day Earth, the phenomenon of shopping malls. Answer basic questions, such as: What is a mall? When did malls appear? Why? How are malls organized and managed? Discuss important factors that gave rise to malls: weather; transportation (development of cars and highways); and the growth of suburbs. Finally, without taking sides, explain the controversies sparked by malls.

2. In an exploratory paper, one in which you speculate more than argue, attempt to define the deep-seated appeal that shopping centers hold for many people. The selections by Pahl, Postrel, and Francaviglia should be helpful. Working with these and one or two other authors in this chapter, explore the psychological (and if Pahl is to be believed, even spiritual) changes that can come over shoppers as they enter a mall.

3. James Farrell (paragraph 14) writes: "Like churches, [malls] are places where we decide what is ultimately valuable and how we will value it." Jon Pahl devotes considerable effort to understanding malls as sacred spaces. Working with these authors and any others in the chapter who can contribute to the discussion, write an argument on the spiritual or religious dimensions of shopping malls. In this argument, you could discount the connection entirely, accept it, or accept it in part.

4. Lizabeth Cohen argues that malls built in the suburbs effectively shut out people who lived in the city and who could not afford a car—a development Cohen regards as a new expression of an old problem: racial and economic segregation. In your experience with shopping malls, what evidence do you find of either or both types of segregation? In developing a response, draw on the selection by Farrell (and his notion that malls tell "stories"). Descriptions of your own experiences in malls could figure heavily into your paper.

5. Richard Francaviglia writes that "Sociologists have long known that people visit shopping centers for far more than commercial reasons" (paragraph 11). In a paper that draws on the work of Francaviglia, Gruen, Pahl, Postrel, and Lewis as well as on your own experience, explain these noncommercial reasons for going to the mall.

6. Francaviglia characterizes mall management as "autocratic." In a paper that draws on Francaviglia and also on Cohen and Guterson, answer this question: For customers, store owners, and mall management, what is gained and what is lost in rigorously controlling activities at the mall?

7. Several authors in this chapter write on the layout of malls. Kowinski relates the experience of getting lost. Francaviglia writes on the importance of intersections. For Guterson, the mall feels like a giant prison. Given the work of these authors and your experience at malls, write a paper examining the importance of mall design.

8. Use William Kowinski's concept of "mallaise" to analyze one or more of your visits to a mall. As independent evidence for mallaise, you might refer to the selections by Guterson (especially paragraph 5) and Pahl (especially paragraph 3). The test of your analysis will be how successfully Kowinski's vocabulary helps you to see your shopping experience(s) in new and interesting ways.

9. Jackson (paragraph 2) and Guterson (paragraphs 6, 16–18) recall the bazaars and marketplaces of old in which people came not only to buy but also to engage in the give and take of community life. Guterson (see especially paragraph 31) and Lewis (see paragraphs 1–7), particularly, claim that authentic community is difficult to find in modern shopping centers. Postrel, by contrast, argues that authentic communication is possible in malls. What is your sense of shopping malls as a center of community life? Drawing on the views of authors in this chapter, develop your answer into an argument.

10. Guterson, Kowinski, Cohen, Lewis, and Pahl have criticized shopping malls. By contrast, Farrell, Postrel, Francaviglia, and Gruen find much to recommend in malls. Given your experiences in malls, with which set of authors do you tend to agree? Do malls please you more than they disturb you, or vice versa? Draw on the authors in this chapter as you develop your answer in an argument.

11. In *Shopping Towns USA*, Victor Gruen envisioned shopping centers becoming the hub of suburban life. Centers would combine commercial space with public, civic space into "crystallization points" that would free suburbanites from traveling to the city to make major purchases. Moreover, shopping centers with their tightly controlled programs for design and management would make rational the previously haphazard method of locating stores in suburbia. Gruen did not live to see his vision fulfilled. Was his plan naive? Do you think the community function of shopping centers could coexist with the commercial function? Is there still hope for such a combination, or is the mall's effort best left to making money?

12. In the introduction to this chapter you will find a block quotation from James J. Farrell's book *One Nation Under Goods*. Farrell claims that shopping centers are places where the culture answers fundamental questions about itself, such as: "What does it mean to be human? What are people for?" Reread the full list of questions, select *one,* and write a synthesis in which you argue that it is possible, or impossible, to

answer such a question by studying shopping centers. In addition to using Farrell's selection, you might draw on the work of Francaviglia, Gruen, Lewis, Pahl, and Cohen.

13. Relate an experience you've had in a shopping center and analyze it in light of any of the reading selections in this chapter. How can the insights of one (or more) of the chapter's authors help you to understand your experience?

RESEARCH ACTIVITIES

1. Devote some time to viewing movies that are set, at least partially, in malls: You might consider the horror classic George Romero's *Dawn of the Dead* (a sequel to *Night of the Living Dead*), *Mall Rats*, *Scenes from a Mall*, and *Fast Times at Ridgemont High*. Watch one or more of the movies several times, and then write a paper in which you "read" the director's vision of modern American life as it is expressed in shopping malls. As part of your research, you might draw on movie reviews. More ambitious projects will involve a comparative treatment of two or more movies.

2. Investigate and report on the types of data that social scientists collect in their efforts to help store owners boost sales. You might begin with a book like *Why We Buy: The Science of Shopping*, in which Paco Underhill (an anthropologist) relates how he conducts field studies of shoppers in the act of shopping. Others who investigate the purchasing habits of shoppers include sociologists, psychologists, and economists. The general topic, the "science of shopping," is very broad, and you will want to narrow the focus. Some possibilities: the design of store displays, the training of sales staff, the choice of background music, or the routing of customers through a retail space. This assignment stresses information, so you will be writing an explanatory synthesis.

3. Read William Kowinski's *Malling of America*, from which one selection in this chapter ("Mallaise") was excerpted. *Malling* has become something of a classic. After you read it, gather book reviews from around the country (check the *Book Review Digest*) and report on the book's reception.

4. Identify one shopping mall project about which you would like to learn more. The project may be a national destination mall, like the Mall of America, or a regional mall near your home. Based on newspaper and magazine articles, trace for readers the mall's progress from the permit process to the opening. How involved was the community in the process? Were there protests? Did the town or city government provide incentives for mall development? Did the developers rely on union labor? These are just of a few of the many questions you might explore in your research. Your goal is to tell the mall's story, from conception to design to building to occupancy.

5. Research the phenomenon of "dead" or "ghost" malls: facilities that are 20 years or older that have been left vacant. What are the forces that drive malls to failure? (Possibilities: population trends; an anchor store's not renewing its lease; competition from new or neighboring malls.) How great a problem are vacant malls? How have communities repurposed them? In writing your paper, gather enough research to point out broad, industrywide trends and then, as a case study, illustrate these trends by relating the demise of a *particular* shopping mall.

6. Choose a shopping mall to visit three or four times over the course of several weeks. On your first visit, spend one hour watching people shop, and take notes. Later, review your notes and decide on a particular question you would like to explore on return visits. Pose that question as precisely as possible: It may concern a particular population at the mall (seniors, mothers with kids, fathers with kids, couples, teens, etc.); a particular aspect of mall management (perhaps security, janitorial, or food services); mall architecture; traffic flow. Any of the readings in this chapter will help you to identify a particular question to pursue. Having framed the question, return to the mall for a series of one-hour visits in which you make and record observations. (Avoid shopping! Your focus is on gathering information.) Write a paper in which you report on your research. Include a description of the mall studied, a context for your question (a discussion of why the question is interesting), data that you recorded (albeit informally), and a discussion of what you discovered.

7. Research one of the predecessors of the modern mall. You might research the Greek stoa, the Roman Forum, the Middle Eastern bazaar or souk, the Grand Bazaar of Constantinople, the Royal Exchange (London), the Palais Royal (Paris), or the arcades of London or Milan. The research paper that you write will be explanatory in nature. Assume that your audience is familiar with shopping malls but unfamiliar with the shopping venues throughout history that preceded the mall.

8. Reread paragraphs 1–7 in Lizabeth Cohen's article "The Mall as Threat to Democratic Values," and select for further research one of the Supreme Court cases she discusses concerning the limits to free speech in privately owned shopping centers. Locate the Supreme Court opinion and summarize it. Re-create for readers the conflict that led to the court case, and discuss (after your summary) the implications of the Court's decision on future protests at shopping centers. You might try conducting your research on the Internet, particularly if you have access to the LexisNexis database. Select "Federal Case Law" and, within this area, "Supreme Court" cases. Choose "Guided Search," as opposed to "Basic Search," so that you can use more keywords and combinations of keywords. Try such keywords as "free speech" OR "freedom of speech" AND "mall"

OR "privately owned shopping center" and other such terms; and search for "all available dates." If you have the citation number for a case (like "485 U.S. 112"), you can directly input the citation (without the need for keywords) to retrieve the case.

9. Research differences in shopping patterns between men and women. You might focus on one or more of the following questions: Do men and women shop with different expectations about the speed of making purchases? Do either tend to shop for the sake of (that is, the pleasure of) shopping? Do women "look" more than men? Do either tend to regard shopping more as a social as opposed to functional, or necessary, activity? Do men more than women tend to be impulse shoppers? Locate carefully controlled studies when conducting your research.

To Sleep

8

Every night nearly every person on the planet undergoes an astounding metamorphosis. As the sun sets, a delicate timing device at the base of our brain sends a chemical signal throughout our body, and the gradual slide toward sleep begins. Our body becomes inert, and our lidded eyes roll slowly from side to side. Later, the eyes begin the rapid eye movements that accompany dreams, and our mind enters a highly active state where vivid dreams trace our deepest emotions. Throughout the night we traverse a broad landscape of dreaming and nondreaming realms, wholly unaware of the world outside. Hours later, as the sun rises, we are transported back to our bodies and to waking consciousness.

And we remember almost nothing.

So begins *The Promise of Sleep* by researcher and sleep pioneer William Dement, who for 50 years has investigated what happens each night after we close our eyes. Later in this chapter you will hear more from Dement; but for the moment, let his sense of wonder about what another author in this chapter calls that "state so familiar yet so strange" spark your own interest in sleep, a behavior that will occupy one-third of your life.

Not until 1929 did Johannes Berger use a new device called the electroencephalogram (EEG) to confirm that far from shutting down while asleep, our brains remain highly active. With the insight that sleep is not merely the absence of wakefulness, and the subsequent discovery that each night's sleep unfolds in five classifiable stages, sleep research accelerated in the twentieth century. Yet for thousands of years sleep (and its frustrating absence) has sparked the inquiries of physicians, scientists, and philosophers. As early as 1300 BCE, the Egyptians used opium as a medication to treat insomnia. Nearly a thousand years later, Aristotle framed his inquiry into sleep with questions that occupy us still:

> With regard to sleep and waking, we must consider what they are: whether they are peculiar to soul or to body, or common to both; and if common, to what part of soul or body they appertain: further, from what cause it arises that they are attributes of animals, and whether all animals share in them both. . . .
>
> —"On Sleep and Sleeplessness"

Allowing for the fact that modern sleep researchers do not investigate the "soul," per se, they nevertheless retain a high level of interest in the nature of consciousness and what happens to it when we sleep. The ancients thought of sleep as a daily, metaphorical death. If sleep is not a death, then what precisely *is* it? Does sleep repair the body? Does it consolidate the day's learning? Is it a strategy for keeping the sleeper safe? Does it aid in development and maintenance of the central nervous system? Researchers have investigated each of these questions but have found no definitive answers. Theoretical explanations of sleep aside, at the clinical level specialists cannot yet remedy all 84 known sleep disorders, which rob sufferers of needed rest and keep them, according to the famous insomniac poet and critic Samuel Taylor Coleridge, in "anguish and in agony." The investigations, therefore, continue.

Up to 40 million Americans suffer from sleep disruptions that for some trigger serious health risks, including cardiovascular disease, obesity, and depression. Sleep loss leads to measurable cognitive and physical deficits comparable to those observed in people impaired by alcohol. The sleep that *we don't* get each day adds up to a cumulative debt that we must "repay" in order to function at full capacity, say sleep specialists. Failure to sleep enough (eight hours is the norm, though individual requirements vary) leads to quantifiable costs:

- Americans spend $15 billion per year in direct health care costs related to problems with sleeping.
- The U.S. economy loses $50 billion per year in diminished productivity due to problems with sleeping.
- The National Highway Traffic and Safety Administration estimates that sleep-deprived drivers cause 100,000 accidents each year, resulting in 1,500 fatalities and 71,000 injuries.

The literature of sleep research is vast. Investigators study the sleep of insects, fish, amphibians, birds, and mammals (including humans) with the tools of biology, neurology, chemistry, psychology, and a host of other disciplines. This chapter brings the study of sleep to a focus very close to home for readers of this book: the sleep of adolescents, one of the many subspecialties of sleep medicine. You may know that the sleep of infants and toddlers merits special attention from specialists since, when children don't sleep well, few others in the home do, either. And you may be aware that the sleep of older people, which can grow troubled due to both physiological and psychological changes, has been the subject of intense study. An equally active area among researchers is the sleep of 10- to 19-year-olds, who require one hour more of sleep each night (due to rapidly maturing bodies) than do adults or children who no longer nap—and this at a time in life when the scheduling demands of school and work tend to decrease the amount of sleep available to adolescents.

If you find yourself at the threshold of late adolescence and early adulthood, or are otherwise connected to an adolescent who is a sibling or friend, you will discover much of interest in this chapter on the "strange state" of sleep. We begin with an overview of the subject, "A Third of Life" by Paul Martin, in which you will learn (among other things) that certain dolphins put one-half of their brains to sleep at a time so that the other half can keep them swimming—and surfacing for air. "Improving Sleep" edited by Lawrence Epstein, MD, reviews the fundamentals of sleep medicine, including REM (rapid eye movement) and non-REM sleep. We move next to a news release on the troubled state of adolescent sleep, based on a poll conducted by the National Sleep Foundation. Researcher Mary A. Carskadon then explains how the biological, behavioral, and social worlds converge to make sleeping so difficult for many adolescents. William C. Dement and Christopher Vaughan follow with "Sleep Debt and the Mortgaged Mind," an inquiry into what happens to a body deprived of sleep.

So that you can assess the current state of your own sleep, we offer the Pittsburgh Sleep Quality Index, a self-scoring assessment used in many sleep studies. Use the PSQI to rate your sleep along seven dimensions and determine your overall sleep score. In "How Sleep Debt Hurts College Students," June J. Pilcher and Amy S. Walters deprive students of a night's sleep and test their cognitive functioning the next day. (The news is not good for those who pull "all-nighters.") Finally, "Starting Time and School Life" reports on the progress of the first major experiment in the United States to align the starting time of high school with the sleep/wake cycles of adolescents.

The National Institutes of Health distributes $200 million a year for sleep research, with some of that money reserved for new curricula that alert science students to the importance of good sleep hygiene. In effect, this chapter offers such a curriculum. In reading the selections that follow, not only will you gain an opportunity to practice the skills of summary, synthesis, critique, and analysis; you will also gain information that can help you feel and function better in your daily life.

A Third of Life
Paul Martin

In our chapter opening, Paul Martin, who holds a PhD in behavioral biology from Cambridge University, provides an overview of sleep and its place in both human and animal evolution. Martin introduces the concept of sleep debt and its consequences—a principal focus of this chapter—and then reviews the behavioral characteristics of sleep. The present selection forms the first chapter of Martin's Counting Sheep: The Science and Pleasures of Sleep and Dreams *(2002).*

Man . . . consumes more than one third of his life in this his irrational situation.
Erasmus Darwin, *Zoonomia* (1801)

1   Sleep: a state so familiar yet so strange. It is the single most common form of human behaviour and you will spend a third of your life doing it—25 years or more, all being well. When you die, a bigger slice of your existence will have passed in that state than in making love, raising children, eating, playing

games, listening to music, or any of those other activities that humanity values so highly.

2   Sleep *is* a form of behaviour, just as eating or socialising or fighting or copulating are forms of behaviour, even if it is not the most gripping to observe. Most of the action goes on inside the brain. It is also a uniquely private experience, even when sharing a bed. When we are awake we all inhabit a common world, but when we sleep each of us occupies a world of our own. Most of us, however, have precious little awareness of what we experience in that state. Our memories of sleeping and dreaming mostly evaporate when we awake, erasing the record every morning.

3   Many of us do not get enough sleep and we suffer the consequences, often without realising what we are doing to ourselves. The demands of the 24-hour society are marginalising sleep, yet it is not an optional activity. Nature imposes it upon us. We can survive for longer without food. When our sleep falls short in quantity or quality we pay a heavy price in depressed mood, impaired performance, damaged social relationships and poorer health. But we usually blame something else.

4   Sleep is an active state, generated within the brain, not a mere absence of consciousness. You are physiologically capable of sleeping with your eyelids held open by sticking plaster, bright lights flashing in your eyes and loud music playing in your ears. We shall later see how science has revealed the ferment of electrical and chemical activity that goes on inside the brain during sleep, and how the sleeping brain operates in a quite different mode from waking consciousness. We shall see too how lack of sleep erodes our quality of life and performance while simultaneously making us more vulnerable to injuries and illness. Science amply supports William Shakespeare's view that sleep is the 'chief nourisher in life's feast'.

5   What is sleep and what is it for? Why do so many people have such problems with it? Why do we dream? Although sleep forms a central strand of human and animal life it is still poorly understood and widely neglected. It is an inglorious example of familiarity breeding contempt. Sleep is so much a part of our everyday existence that we take it for granted. We are ignorant even of our ignorance. In 1758, Doctor Samuel Johnson summed it up like this:

> Among the innumerable mortifications that waylay human arrogance on every side may well be reckoned our ignorance of the most common objects and effects . . . Vulgar and inactive minds confound familiarity with knowledge, and conceive themselves informed of the whole nature of things when they are shown their form or told their use . . . Sleep is a state in which a great part of every life is passed. No animal has been yet discovered whose existence is not varied with intervals of insensibility. Yet of this change so frequent, so great, so general, and so necessary, no searcher has yet found either the efficient or final cause; or can tell by what power the mind and body are thus chained down in irresistible stupefaction; or what benefits the animal receives from this alternate suspension of its active powers.

The scientists who do know something about sleep often bemoan society's ignorance of it. They point to the vast gap between current scientific understanding of sleep, patchy though it is, and the practical benefits it could bring if that knowledge were absorbed and acted upon by society. Our collective indifference towards sleep has enormous and largely avoidable costs.

A sleep-sick society?

> The mere presence of an alarm clock implies sleep deprivation, and what bedroom lacks an alarm clock?
>
> James Gleick, *Faster* (1999)

6   All is not well with the state of sleep. Many of us depend on an alarm clock to prise us out of bed each morning, and children's bedrooms increasingly resemble places of entertainment rather than places of sleep. When given the opportunity, we sleep in at the weekends and feel only half awake when we do get up. On that long-awaited holiday we find the change of scenery (or is it the air?) makes us even sleepier. We are told that lying around and sleeping too much will only make us sleepier. But in truth we feel sleepy at weekends and on holidays not because we are sleeping too much, but because we have slept too little the rest of the time.

7   A century ago the majority toiled long hours while the affluent few idled away their time. Today, however, the more conventionally successful you are, the less free time you will probably have. Having nothing to do is seen as a sign of worthlessness, while ceaseless activity signifies status and success. Supposedly unproductive activities are deprioritised or delegated. And according to prevailing cultural attitudes, sleeping is one of the least productive of all human activities. . . . In their ceaseless pursuit of work and pleasure the cash-rich buy time from others, hiring them to clean their houses, look after their children and cook their food. But one of the activities you simply cannot delegate to anyone else is sleeping.

8   Evolution equipped humans, in common with all other animals, with biological mechanisms to make us sleep at roughly the same time every day. However, those mechanisms evolved to cope with a pre-industrial world that was vastly different from the one we now inhabit.

9   Our daily cycles of sleep and activity are no longer driven by dawn and dusk, but by clocks, electric lighting and work schedules. Sleep has become increasingly devalued in the 24-hour society. Many regard sleep as wasted time and would prefer to sacrifice less of their busy lives to it. We live in a world where there are too many tired, sleep-deprived people. Think of those pinched, yawning faces you can see every day on the trains and in buses and in cars crawling through jams. They look as if they have been brainwashed, but they are just tired.

10   We pay a steep price for neglecting sleep, in our ignorance and indifference. The scientific evidence tells us that far too many people in industrialised societies

are chronically sleep-deprived, with damaging consequences for their mental and physical health, performance at work, quality of life and personal relationships. William Dement, a pioneering scientist in the field, believes that we now live in a 'sleep-sick society'. Scientists have not yet reached a consensus about the precise extent of sleep deprivation in society, but they do all agree that sleepiness is a major cause of accidents and injuries. In fact, sleepiness is responsible for far more deaths on the roads than alcohol or drugs.

11   Everyone has heard about the need for a balanced diet and physical exercise, even if many of us fail to follow the advice. But sleep is lost in a deep well of ignorance and apathy. Even the medical profession pays it scant regard. Sleep and its disorders barely feature in the teaching of medicine, and few physicians are fully equipped to deal with the sleep problems they regularly encounter. When researchers from Oxford University investigated British medical education in the late 1990s, they discovered that the average amount of time devoted to sleep and sleep disorders in undergraduate teaching was five minutes, rising to a princely peak of 15 minutes in preclinical training. Your doctor is therefore unlikely to be an expert on the subject.

12   The general public and the medical profession are not the only ones to display a remarkable indifference to sleep. So too do most contemporary writers. Considering that sleep accounts for a third of human existence, it features remarkably rarely in novels, biographies, social histories or learned texts on neurobiology, psychology and medicine. And the few accounts that have made it into print are mostly concerned with what happens when it goes wrong. Insomnia and nightmares loom large in the tiny literature of sleep.

13   Few biographies mention the sleep behaviour or dreams of their subjects. That part of their story is almost invariably missing, as if somehow we all cease to exist at night. And most of those scholarly books that set out to explain how the human mind works say little or nothing about what goes on during the several hours of every day when the mind is sleeping and dreaming. They are really just books about how the brain works when it is awake. Our neglect of sleep is underlined by its absence from our literature.

14   Vladimir Nabokov once said that all the great writers have good eyes. What has happened to the eyes of writers as far as sleep and dreams are concerned? It was not always so. Older literature is distinctly richer in references to sleeping and dreaming, perhaps because darkness and sleep and dreams were much more prominent aspects of everyday life before the invention of the electric light bulb and the advent of the 24-hour society. Shakespeare's works are thick with allusions to sleep and dreams, as are Dickens's. We shall encounter some of them later. Meanwhile, to set the right tone, here is Sancho Panza's eulogy to sleep from *Don Quixote*:

> God bless the inventor of sleep, the cloak that covers all man's thoughts, the food that cures all hunger, the water that quenches all thirst, the fire that warms the cold, the cold that cools the heat; the common coin, in short, that can purchase all things, the balancing weight that levels the shepherd with the king and the simple with the wise.

The universal imperative

> Almost all other animals are observed to partake of sleep, aquatic, winged, and terrestrial creatures alike. For every kind of fish and the soft-shelled species have been seen sleeping, as has every other creature that has eyes.
>
> Aristotle (384–322 B.C.), *On Sleep and Waking*

15 Sleep is a universal human characteristic, like eating and drinking. Absolutely everybody does it. Sleep occupies about one third of each human life, and up to two thirds of a baby's time. (According to Groucho Marx, the proportion rises to three thirds if you live in Peoria.) It is a common bond that ties us all together. We have no choice: the longer we go without sleep, the stronger our desire for it grows. Tiredness, like hunger and thirst, will eventually force us to do the right thing whether we want to or not.

16   The dreams that accompany sleep are equally ubiquitous features of human life, even if many of us retain little memory of them after we awake. Dreaming is a classless activity that unites monarchs and paupers, a thought that Charles Dickens mused upon in one of his essays:

> Here, for example, is her Majesty Queen Victoria in her palace, this present blessed night, and here is Winking Charley, a sturdy vagrant, in one of her Majesty's jails . . . It is probable that we have all three committed murders and hidden bodies. It is pretty certain that we have all desperately wanted to cry out, and have had no voice; that we have all gone to the play and not been able to get in; that we have all dreamed much more of our youth than of our later lives.

Sleep is not a specifically human trait, of course. On the contrary, it is a universal characteristic of complex living organisms, as Aristotle deduced more than 23 centuries ago. Sleep is observed in animals of every sort, including insects, molluscs, fish, amphibians, birds and mammals. Within the animal world, sleep does vary enormously in quantity, quality and timing, accounting for anything up to 80 per cent of some animals' lifespans. But they all do it, one way or another. Some species, especially predators, spend more of their lives asleep than they do awake, a fact that TV documentaries and natural-history books seldom mention.

17   How do we know that an animal is sleeping? It is hard enough sometimes to be sure that a human is asleep, let alone a fish or a fly. The ultimate indicator of whether an animal or person is asleep is the distinctive pattern of electrical activity in its brain. During deep sleep the billions of individual nerve cells in the brain synchronise their electrical activity to some extent, generating characteristic waves of tiny voltage changes that can be detected by electrodes placed on the scalp. We shall be exploring the nature and internal structure of sleep later. The easiest way to recognise sleep, however, is from overt behaviour.

18   Sleep has several rather obvious distinguishing characteristics. A sleeping person or animal will generally remain in the same place for a prolonged period, perhaps several hours. There will be a certain amount of twitching, shifting of

posture and fidgeting. Young animals will suckle while they sleep and ruminants will carry on chewing the cud. But sleepers normally do not get up and change their location. (When they do, we recognise it as a curious phenomenon and call it sleepwalking.)

19   Sleeping organisms also adopt a characteristic posture. Sloths and bats, for example, sleep hanging upside down from a branch. The Mediterranean flour moth sleeps with its antennae swivelled backwards and the tips tucked under its wings. If you are careful, you can gently lift the sleeping moth's wing without disturbing it—a trick that will definitely not work when it is awake. A lizard will settle on a branch during the hours before sunset, curl up its tail, close its eyelids, retract its eyeballs and remain in that distinctly sleep-like posture all night unless it is disturbed. A partridge, like many birds, will rest its weight on one leg while it sleeps. It is said that some gourmets can tell *which* leg, from its taste.

20   Monkeys and apes, including humans, usually sleep lying down. Indeed, we are built in such a way that we find it difficult to sleep properly unless we are lying down. People can and sometimes do sleep after a fashion while sitting, notably in aeroplanes, business meetings and school classrooms. If you are really exhausted, you might even manage to snatch some sleep standing up. But sleep taken while standing or sitting upright is generally fitful, shallow and unrefreshing. The non-horizontal sleeper may repeatedly nod off, but as soon as they descend beyond the shallowest stages of sleep their muscles relax, they begin to sway and their brain wakes them up again. That is why we 'nod off'. If you travel frequently on trains or buses, you might have had the dubious pleasure of sitting next to a weary commuter who has nodded off all over your shoulder. Recordings of brain-wave patterns show that people sleeping in an upright sitting position achieve only the initial stages of light sleep, not the sustained, deep sleep we require to wake up feeling truly refreshed. The reason is simple. Our muscles relax when we are fully asleep and we would fall over if we were not already lying down. Our brains therefore do not permit us to enter sustained, deep sleep unless we are in a physically stable, horizontal (or near-horizontal) posture.

21   Despite the virtual impossibility of sleeping deeply while sitting upright, we are sometimes forced to try. In *Down and Out in Paris and London*, George Orwell describes a particularly unwelcoming form of overnight accommodation that was known to the homeless of prewar London as the Twopenny Hangover. At the Twopenny Hangover the night's residents would sit in a row along a bench. In front of them was a rope, and the would-be sleepers would lean on this rope as though leaning over a fence. In that posture they were supposed to sleep. At five o'clock the next morning an official, wittily known as the valet, would cut the rope so that the residents could begin another day of wandering the streets.

22   Nowadays, tourist-class airline passengers travelling long distances can enjoy an experience similar to the Twopenny Hangover, albeit at vastly greater expense. George Orwell's autobiographical account of grinding poverty in the late 1920s is also a sharp reminder that lack of money is often accompanied by lack of decent sleep. Rough sleepers rarely get a good night's sleep.

23   Sleep has several other distinctive characteristics besides immobility and posture. In many species, including humans, individuals return to the same place each night (or each day, if they are nocturnal) in order to sleep. More generally, all members of a given species will tend to choose the same sorts of sleeping places. The distinctive feature of those places is often their security. Birds usually sleep on inaccessible branches or ledges. Many small mammals sleep in underground burrows where they are safer from predators. Fishes lie on the bottom, or wedge themselves into a crevice or against the underside of a rock. We humans prefer to sleep in relatively private and secure places. Given the choice, we rarely opt to sleep on busy streets or in crowded restaurants.

24   One obvious feature of sleep is a marked reduction in responsiveness to sights, sounds and other sensory stimuli. To provoke a response from a sleeping organism, stimuli have to be more intense or more relevant to the individual. For example, the reef fish known as the slippery dick sleeps during the hours of darkness, partly buried in the sand. While it is in this state, the sleeping slippery dick can be gently lifted to the surface by hand without it waking up and swimming off.

25   A sort of perceptual wall is erected during sleep, insulating the mind from the outside world. You would still be able to sleep if you had no eyelids, because your sleeping brain would not register what your eyes could see. This sensory isolation is highly selective, however. You can sleep through relatively loud noises from traffic or a radio, but a quiet mention of your name can rouse you immediately. Your brain is not simply blocked off during sleep. Moreover, this reduced responsiveness is rapidly reversible—a characteristic that distinguishes sleep from states such as unconsciousness, coma, anaesthesia and hibernation. A suitable stimulus, particularly one signifying immediate danger, can snap a sleeping person into staring-eyed alertness in an instant.

26   Another diagnostic feature of sleep is its regular cycle of waxing and waning. Living organisms sleep and wake according to a regular 24-hour cycle, or circadian rhythm. All members of a given species tend to sleep during the same part of the 24-hour cycle, when their environment is least favourable for other activities such as looking for food. For most species this means sleeping during the hours of darkness, but some species do the reverse. Many small mammals, which would be more vulnerable to predators during daylight, sleep by day and forage at night. Aside from a few nocturnal specialists such as owls, birds cannot easily fly in the dark, and most reptiles find it hard to maintain a sufficiently high body temperature to be active during the cool of night. Most birds and reptiles therefore sleep at night. Predators tend to sleep when their prey are asleep and hunt when their prey are up and about.

27   Sleep, then, is characterised by a special sleeping place and posture, prolonged immobility, a selective and rapidly reversible reduction in responsiveness to stimuli, and a 24-hour cycle. According to these and other criteria, all mammals, birds, fish, amphibians, reptiles and insects that have been inspected have been found to sleep.

· · ·

Half asleep

> And the small fowl are making melody
> That sleep away the night with open eye

> Geoffrey Chaucer, A *Prologue to The Canterbury Tales* (c. 1387)

28 Sleep is such an overriding biological imperative that evolution has found ingenious ways of enabling animals to do it in the face of formidable obstacles. Nature, it seems, will do almost anything to ensure that animals sleep.

29   Consider dolphins, for example. They are air-breathing mammals like us, so they must swim to the surface each time they want to take a breath. They would drown if they fell into deep sleep while deep underwater. One possible solution to this biological design conundrum would be to wake up each time a breath of air was required. However, evolution has produced a more elegant solution: only one half of the dolphin's brain goes to sleep at a time.

30   Dolphins are capable of what is known as unihemispheric sleep, in which one hemisphere of the brain submerges into deep sleep while the other hemisphere remains awake. The two halves of the brain take it in turns to sleep, swapping at intervals of between one and three hours. This cerebral juggling trick enables dolphins to sleep underwater without drowning, which is just as well considering that they spend a good third of their lives asleep. Unihemispheric sleep has been recorded in several species of dolphins, porpoises and whales, including bottlenosed and Amazonian dolphins, Black Sea porpoises and white whales.

31   Despite the apparent convenience of being able to sleep and stay awake simultaneously, very few mammals are capable of unihemispheric sleep. The biological benefits of sleeping with only half of the brain at a time presumably outweigh the disadvantages only under unusual conditions, such as those encountered by air-breathing mammals living in the deep oceans.

32   Unihemispheric sleep is widespread in birds, however. They do it for a different biological reason. Sleeping with half the brain awake and one eye open allows them to sleep while simultaneously remaining vigilant for predators. In birds, each eye exclusively feeds the visual processing areas in the opposite half of the brain: thus, all the nerve fibres coming from the right eye connect to the left hemisphere of the brain and vice versa. When a bird is in unihemispheric sleep its open eye is the one corresponding to the waking half of the brain, while the closed eye is connected to the sleeping half. If a bird feels relatively safe, it closes both eyes, and both sides of its brain go to sleep.

33   An experiment with mallard ducks demonstrated how unihemispheric sleep helps birds to stay safe from predators. Four ducks were placed in a row along a perch, the idea being that the ducks at either end of the row would feel more vulnerable to predators than the two in the middle. In the natural world it is generally a bad idea to be on the edge of a group if you might end up as some other animal's dinner. As predicted, video recordings showed that the outer two birds were much more likely to sleep with one eye open than the two on the inside; their unihemispheric sleep increased by 150 per cent. The amount of unihemispheric sleep rose further when the ducks were shown frightening video images of an approaching predator.

34   The relationship between unihemispheric sleep and vigilance was finely controlled. The exposed birds on the ends of the row preferentially opened their

outward-facing eye—the one directed towards potential danger. From time to time, a bird would turn round and switch eyes, so that the open eye was still the one facing out. Simultaneous recordings of brain activity confirmed that the brain hemisphere corresponding to the open eye was always awake, while the hemisphere corresponding to the closed eye was the one in deep sleep.

35   The one-eyed tactic was effective: when an attacking predator was simulated on a video screen, the birds sleeping with one eye open were able to react in a fraction of a second—far faster than if they had been in deep sleep with both eyes shut.

36   Humans are not capable of unihemispheric sleep, although at least one writer has played with the fantasy. Damon Runyon wrote of how he once played cards with a fading champion card player who now lacked the stamina to stay awake during marathon games of gin rummy lasting eight or ten hours. When the man lost a game after making a bad play, the punters betting on him to win clamoured to remove their bets from the next game, on the grounds that he was asleep. Then someone pointed out that the allegedly sleeping player's eyes were open, so he must be awake. 'The one on your side is', retorted one of the backers, 'but the one on the other side is closed. He is sleeping one-eye.'

Review Questions

1. What are some of the qualities of sleep that make it "so strange," in Martin's view?

2. Cite some signs of sleep deprivation, and indicate some aspects of modern life that lead to lack of sleep.

3. What are the distinguishing characteristics of sleep, and which species have been observed to sleep?

4. What is unihemispheric sleep, and why is it a characteristic of some marine mammals and birds?

Discussion and Writing Suggestions

1. Before reading Martin's article, to what extent did you consider sleep a "behavior"? How did you think of it, if not as a behavior? Explain.

2. What accounts for the relatively scant attention sleep has received in popular culture? In developing your answer, read what Samuel Johnson said on the matter in 1758 (see paragraph 5). To what extent does his response answer this question today?

3. What single observation about sleep stands out for you from this article? Explain your fascination.

4. Martin writes that "[e]volution equipped humans . . . to . . . sleep at roughly the same time every day . . . to cope with a pre-industrial world that was vastly different from the one we now inhabit" (paragraph 8). Imagine the world before the invention of electric or gas lighting.

(If you go camping, you have direct experience with this world.) In what ways do you think that modern life is working at odds with bodily rhythms that evolved over tens of thousands of years?

5. Do you consider yourself sleep deprived? Several other authors in this chapter will address the issue; but based on the signs of sleep deprivation that Martin reviews, how serious is your sleep debt? Write about one incident that prompted you to consider getting more sleep.

Improving Sleep*
Lawrence Epstein, MD, Editor

Of the hundreds of introductions to the physiology of sleep, this selection appearing in a *Harvard Special Health Report* edited by Lawrence Epstein, MD is among the clearest for audiences without a formal background in medicine. We excerpt the opening sections of the larger report: overviews of sleep mechanics, sleep throughout life, and consequences of sleep deprivation.

1   Some nights, sleep comes easily, and you sail through the night in a satisfying slumber. Waking up after a night of good sleep feels wonderful—you're refreshed, energized, and ready to take on the world. Other nights, sleep comes slowly or not until the wee hours. Or you may fall asleep, only to awaken throughout the night.

2   If you have trouble sleeping, you're not alone. Almost everyone occasionally suffers from short-term insomnia. According to the National Institutes of Health, about 60 million Americans a year have insomnia frequently or for extended periods of time. About half of all people over 65 have frequent sleeping problems, and an estimated 40 million Americans have a chronic sleep disorder such as sleep apnea, restless legs syndrome, or narcolepsy. We pay a high price for all the sleep deprivation caused by sleep problems. For example:

- Insufficient sleep is directly linked to poor health, with new research suggesting it increases the risk of diabetes, heart disease, obesity, and even premature death. Even a few nights of bad sleep can be detrimental.
- The combination of sleep deprivation and driving can have deadly consequences. A 2006 review by the Institute of Medicine of the National Academy of Sciences found that almost 20% of all serious car accidents and 57% of fatal accidents are associated with driver sleepiness.
- Sleep deprivation played a role in catastrophes such as the Exxon Valdez oil spill off the coast of Alaska, the space shuttle Challenger explosion, and the nuclear accident at Three Mile Island.

3   Sleep problems affect virtually every aspect of day-to-day living, including mood, mental alertness, work performance, and energy level. Yet few Americans

seek treatment for their sleep problems. If you aren't getting your share of sleep, you needn't fumble about in a fog of fatigue. This report describes the complex nature of sleep, the latest in sleep research, the factors that can disturb sleep, and, most importantly, what you can do to get the sleep you need for optimal health, safety, and well-being.

Sleep Mechanics

4   For centuries, scientists scrutinized minute aspects of human activity, but showed little interest in the time that people spent in sleep. Sleep seemed inaccessible to medical probing and was perceived as an unvarying period of inactivity—a subject best suited to poets and dream interpreters who could conjure meaning out of the void. All that changed in the 1930s, when scientists learned to place sensitive electrodes on the scalp and record the signals produced by electrical activity in the brain. These brain waves can be seen on an electroencephalogram, or EEG (see Figure 1), which today is captured on a computer screen. Since then,

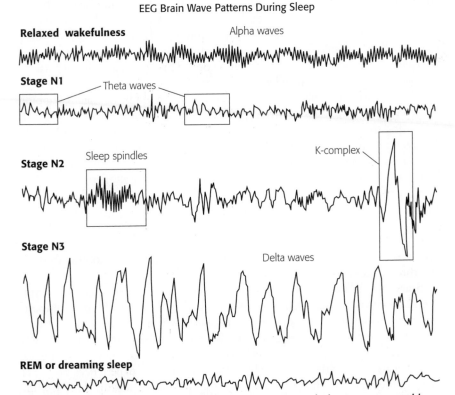

EEG Brain Wave Patterns During Sleep

Relaxed wakefulness   Alpha waves

Stage N1   Theta waves

Stage N2   Sleep spindles   K-complex

Stage N3   Delta waves

REM or dreaming sleep

FIGURE 1   These brain waves, taken by electroencephalogram, are used by sleep experts to identify the stages of sleep. Close your eyes and your brain waves will look like the first band, "relaxed wakefulness." Theta waves indicate Stage N1 sleep. (The "N" designates non-REM sleep.) Stage N2 sleep shows brief bursts of activity as sleep spindles and K-complex waves. Deep sleep is represented by large, slow delta waves (Stage N3).

researchers gradually came to appreciate that sleep is a highly complex activity. Using electrodes to monitor sleepers' eye movements, muscle tone, and brain wave patterns, they identified several discrete stages of sleep. And today, researchers continue to learn how certain stages of sleep help to maintain health, growth, and functioning.

5   Scientists divide sleep into two major types: rapid eye movement (REM) sleep or dreaming sleep, and non-REM or quiet sleep. Surprisingly, they are as different from one another as sleeping is from waking.

Quiet Sleep

6   Sleep specialists have called non-REM or quiet sleep "an idling brain in a movable body." During this phase, thinking and most physiological activities slow down, but movement can still occur, and a person often shifts position while sinking into progressively deeper stages of sleep.

7   To an extent, the convention of describing people "dropping" into sleep actually parallels changes in brain wave patterns at the onset of non-REM sleep. When you are awake, billions of brain cells receive and analyze sensory information, coordinate behavior, and maintain bodily functions by sending electrical impulses to one another. If you're fully awake, the EEG will record a messy, irregular scribble of activity. Once your eyes are closed and your nerve cells no longer receive visual input, brain waves settle into a steady and rhythmic pattern of about 10 cycles per second. This is the alpha-wave pattern, characteristic of calm, relaxed wakefulness.

8   The transition to quiet sleep is a quick one that might be likened to flipping a switch—that is, you are either awake (switch on) or asleep (switch off), according to recent research. Some brain centers and pathways stimulate the entire brain to wakefulness; others promote falling asleep. One chemical, hypocretin, seems to play an important role in regulating when the flip between states occurs and keeping you in the new state. Interestingly, people with narcolepsy often lack hypocretin, and they consequently flip back and forth between sleep and wakefulness frequently.

Three Stages of Quiet Sleep

9   Unless something disturbs the process, you will soon proceed smoothly through the three stages of quiet sleep.

10   **Stage N1.** In making the transition from wakefulness into light sleep, you spend about five minutes in Stage N1 sleep. On the EEG, the predominant brain waves slow to four to seven cycles per second, a pattern called theta waves. Body temperature begins to drop, muscles relax, and eyes often move slowly from side to side. People in Stage N1 sleep lose awareness of their surroundings, but they are easily jarred awake. However, not everyone experiences Stage N1 sleep in the same way: If awakened, one person might recall being drowsy, while another might describe having been asleep.

11   **Stage N2.** This first stage of true sleep lasts 10 to 25 minutes. Your eyes are still, and your heart rate and breathing are slower than when awake. Your brain's electrical activity is irregular. Large, slow waves intermingle with brief bursts of activity called sleep spindles, when brain waves speed up for roughly half a

second or longer. About every two minutes, EEG tracings show a pattern called a K-complex, which scientists think represents a sort of built-in vigilance system that keeps you poised to awaken if necessary. K-complexes can also be provoked by certain sounds or other external or internal stimuli. Whisper someone's name during Stage N2 sleep, and a K-complex will appear on the EEG. You spend about half the night in Stage N2 sleep, which leaves you moderately refreshed.

12   **Stage N3.** Eventually, large slow brain waves called delta waves become a major feature on the EEG. This is Stage N3, known as deep sleep or slow-wave sleep. During this stage, breathing becomes more regular. Blood pressure falls, and pulse rate slows to about 20% to 30% below the waking rate. The brain becomes less responsive to external stimuli, making it difficult to wake the sleeper.

13   Slow-wave sleep seems to be a time for your body to renew and repair itself. Blood flow is directed less toward your brain, which cools measurably. At the beginning of this stage, the pituitary gland releases a pulse of growth hormone that stimulates tissue growth and muscle repair. Researchers have also detected increased blood levels of substances that activate your immune system, raising the possibility that slow-wave sleep helps the body defend itself against infection.

14   Normally, young people spend about 20% of their sleep time in stretches of slow-wave sleep lasting up to half an hour, but slow-wave sleep is nearly absent in most people over age 65. Someone whose slow-wave sleep is restricted will wake up feeling unrefreshed, no matter how long he or she has been in bed. When a sleep-deprived person gets some sleep, he or she will pass quickly through the lighter sleep stages into the deeper stages and spend a greater proportion of sleep time there, suggesting that slow-wave sleep fills an essential need.

Dreaming (REM) Sleep

15 Dreaming occurs during REM sleep, which has been described as an "active brain in a paralyzed body." Your brain races, thinking and dreaming, as your eyes dart back and forth rapidly behind closed lids. Your body temperature rises. Your blood pressure increases, and your heart rate and breathing speed up to daytime levels. The sympathetic nervous system, which creates the fight-or-flight response, is twice as active as when you're awake. Despite all this activity, your body hardly moves, except for intermittent twitches; muscles not needed for breathing or eye movement are quiet.

16   Just as slow-wave sleep restores your body, scientists believe that REM or dreaming sleep restores your mind, perhaps in part by helping clear out irrelevant information. Recent studies of students' ability to solve a complex puzzle involving abstract shapes suggest the brain processes information overnight; students who got a good night's sleep after seeing the puzzle fared much better than those asked to solve the puzzle immediately. Earlier studies found that REM sleep facilitates learning and memory. People tested to measure how well they had learned a new task improved their scores after a night's sleep. If they were roused from REM sleep, the improvements were lost. On the other hand, if they were awakened an equal number of times from slow-wave sleep, the

improvements in the scores were unaffected. These findings may help explain why students who stay up all night cramming for an examination generally retain less information than classmates who get some sleep.

17   About three to five times a night, or about every 90 minutes, a sleeper enters REM sleep. The first such episode usually lasts only for a few minutes, but REM time increases progressively over the course of the night. The final period of REM sleep may last a half-hour. Altogether, REM sleep makes up about 25% of total sleep in young adults. If someone who has been deprived of REM sleep is left undisturbed for a night, he or she enters this stage earlier and spends a higher proportion of sleep time in it—a phenomenon called REM rebound.

Sleep Architecture

18 During the night, a normal sleeper moves between different sleep stages in a fairly predictable pattern, alternating between REM and non-REM sleep. When these stages are charted on a diagram, called a hypnogram (see Figure 2), the different levels resemble a drawing of a city skyline. Sleep experts call this pattern sleep architecture.

19   In a young adult, normal sleep architecture usually consists of four or five alternating non-REM and REM periods. Most deep sleep occurs in the first half of the night. As the night progresses, periods of REM sleep get longer and alternate with Stage N2 sleep. Later in life, the sleep skyline will change, with less Stage N3 sleep, more Stage N1 sleep, and more awakenings.

Your Internal Clock

20 Scientists have discovered that certain brain structures and chemicals produce the states of sleeping and waking.

21   A pacemaker-like mechanism in the brain regulates the circadian rhythm of sleeping and waking. ("Circadian" means "about a day.") This internal clock,

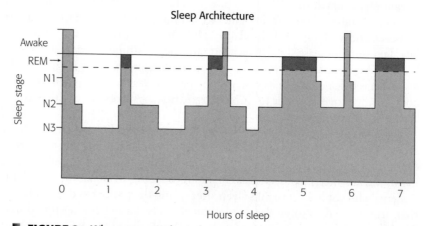

FIGURE 2   When experts chart sleep stages on a hypnogram, the different levels resemble a drawing of a city skyline. This pattern is known as sleep architecture. The hypnogram above shows a typical night's sleep of a healthy young adult.

which gradually becomes established during the first months of life, controls the daily ups and downs of biological patterns, including body temperature, blood pressure, and the release of hormones.

22 The circadian rhythm makes people's desire for sleep strongest between midnight and dawn, and to a lesser extent in midafternoon. In one study, researchers instructed a group of people to try to stay awake for 24 hours. Not surprisingly, many slipped into naps despite their best efforts not to. When the investigators plotted the times when the unplanned naps occurred, they found peaks between 2 a.m. and 4 a.m. and between 2 p.m. and 3 p.m.

23 Most Americans sleep during the night as dictated by their circadian rhythms, although many nap in the afternoon on the weekends. In societies where taking a siesta is the norm, people can respond to their bodies' daily dips in alertness with a one- to two-hour afternoon nap during the workday and a correspondingly shorter sleep at night.

Mechanisms of Your "Sleep Clock"

24 In the 1970s, studies in rats identified the suprachiasmatic nucleus as the location of the internal clock. This cluster of cells is part of the hypothalamus, the brain center that regulates appetite and other biological states (see Figure 3). When this tiny area was damaged, the sleep/wake rhythm disappeared and the rats no longer slept on a normal schedule. Although the clock is largely self-regulating, its location allows it to respond to several types of external cues to keep it set at 24 hours. Scientists call these cues "zeitgebers," a German word meaning "time givers."

25 **Light.** Light striking your eyes is the most influential zeitgeber. When researchers invited volunteers into the laboratory and exposed them to light at intervals that were at odds with the outside world, the participants

The Sleep Wake Control Center

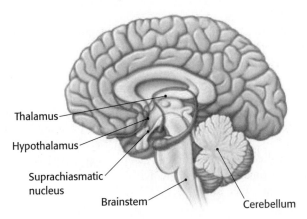

Thalamus

Hypothalamus

Suprachiasmatic nucleus

Brainstem

Cerebellum

FIGURE 3 The pacemaker-like mechanism in your brain that regulates the circadian rhythm of sleeping and waking is thought to be located in the suprachiasmatic nucleus. This cluster of cells is part of the hypothalamus, the brain center that regulates appetite, body temperature, and other biological states.

unconsciously reset their biological clocks to match the new light input. The circadian rhythm disturbances and sleep problems that affect up to 90% of blind people demonstrate the importance of light to sleep/wake patterns.

26   **Time.** As a person reads clocks, follows work and train schedules, and demands that the body remain alert for certain tasks and social events, there is cognitive pressure to stay on schedule.

27   **Melatonin.** Cells in the suprachiasmatic nucleus contain receptors for melatonin, a hormone produced in a predictable daily rhythm by the pineal gland, which is located deep in the brain between the two hemispheres. Levels of melatonin begin climbing after dark and ebb after dawn. The hormone induces drowsiness in some people, and scientists believe its daily light-sensitive cycles help keep the sleep/wake cycle on track.

Your Clock's Hour Hand

28 As the circadian rhythm counts off the days, another part of the brain acts like the hour hand on a watch. This timekeeper resides in a nugget of nerve cells within the brain stem, the area that controls breathing, blood pressure, and heartbeat. Fluctuating activity in the nerve cells and the chemical messengers they produce seem to coordinate the timing of wakefulness, arousal, and the 90-minute changeover between REM and non-REM sleep.

29   Several neurotransmitters (brain chemicals that neurons release to communicate with adjacent cells) play a role in arousal. Their actions help explain why medications that mimic or counteract their effects can influence sleep. Adenosine and gamma-aminobutyric acid (GABA) are believed to promote sleep. Acetylcholine regulates REM sleep. Norepinephrine, epinephrine, dopamine, and the recently discovered hypocretin stimulate wakefulness. Individuals vary greatly in their natural levels of neurotransmitters and in their sensitivity to these chemicals.

Sleep Throughout Life

30 To a certain extent, heredity determines how people sleep throughout their lives. Identical twins, for example, have much more similar sleep patterns than nonidentical twins or other siblings. Differences in sleeping and waking seem to be inborn. There are night owls and early-morning larks, sound sleepers and light ones, people who are perky after five hours of sleep and others who are groggy if they log less than nine hours. Nevertheless, many factors can affect how a person sleeps. Aging is the most important influence on basic sleep rhythms—from age 20 on, it takes longer to fall asleep [a period of time called *sleep latency*], you sleep less at night, Stages N1 and N2 sleep increase, Stage N3 sleep and REM sleep decrease, and nighttime awakenings increase (see Table 1).

Childhood

31 For an adult to sleep like a baby is not only unrealistic but also undesirable. A newborn may sleep eight times a day, accumulating 18 hours of sleep and spending about half of it in REM sleep. The REM to non-REM cycle is shorter, usually lasting less than an hour.

TABLE 1   Sleep Changes During Adulthood

As people age, it takes longer to fall asleep (increased sleep latency). And sleep efficiency—or the percentage of time spent asleep while in bed—decreases as people grow older.

	Age 20	Age 40	Age 60	Age 70	Age 80
Sleep latency	16 minutes	17 minutes	18 minutes	18.5 minutes	19 minutes
Total sleep time	7.5 hours	7 hours	6.2 hours	6 hours	5.8 hours
% of time in Stage N2 sleep	47%	51%	53%	55%	57%
% of time in Stage N3 sleep	20%	15%	10%	9%	7.5%
% of time in REM sleep	22%	21%	20%	19%	17%
Sleep efficiency	95%	88%	84%	82%	79%

Source: Ohayon MM, et al. "Meta-analysis of quantitative sleep parameters from childhood to old age in healthy individuals; Developing normative sleep values across the human lifespan," *Sleep* (2004), Vol. 27, No. 7, pp. 1255-73.

---

32   At about the age of 4 weeks, a newborn's sleep periods get longer. By 6 months, infants spend longer and more regular periods in non-REM sleep; most begin sleeping through the night and taking naps in the morning and afternoon. During the preschool years, daytime naps gradually shorten, until by age 6 most children are awake all day and sleep for about 10 hours a night.

33   Between age 7 and puberty, nocturnal melatonin production is at its lifetime peak, and sleep at this age is deep and restorative. At this age, if a child is sleepy during the day, parents should be concerned.

Adolescence

34   In contrast, adolescents are noted for their daytime drowsiness. Except for infancy, adolescence is the most rapid period of body growth and development. Although teenagers need about an hour more sleep each day than they did as young children, most of them actually sleep an hour or so less. Parents usually blame teenagers' busy schedule of activities for their grogginess and difficulty awakening in the morning. However, the problem may also be biological. One study indicated that some adolescents might have delayed sleep phase syndrome, where they are not sleepy until well after the usual bedtime and cannot wake at the time required for school, producing conflicts between parents and sleepy teenagers as well as with secondary schools, which usually open earlier than elementary schools. It is unknown whether this phase shift occurs primarily as a physiological event or as a response to abnormal light exposure.

Adulthood

35   During young adulthood, sleep patterns usually seem stable but in fact are slowly evolving. Between age 20 and age 30, the amount of slow-wave sleep drops by about half, and nighttime awakenings double. By age 40, slow-wave sleep is markedly reduced.

36   Women's reproductive cycles can greatly influence sleep. During the first trimester of pregnancy, many women are sleepy all the time and may log an

extra two hours a night if their schedules permit. As pregnancy continues, hormonal and anatomical changes reduce sleep efficiency so that less of a woman's time in bed is actually spent sleeping. As a result, fatigue increases. The postpartum period usually brings dramatic sleepiness and fatigue—because the mother's ability to sleep efficiently has not returned to normal, because she is at the mercy of her newborn's rapidly cycling shifts between sleeping and waking, and because breast-feeding promotes sleepiness. Researchers are probing whether sleep disturbances during pregnancy may contribute to postpartum depression and compromise the general physical and mental well-being of new mothers.

37   Women who aren't pregnant may experience monthly shifts in sleep habits. During the second phase of the menstrual cycle, between ovulation and the next menses, some women fall asleep and enter REM sleep more quickly than usual. A few experience extreme sleepiness. Investigators are studying the relationship between such sleep alterations, cyclic changes in body temperature, and levels of the hormone progesterone to see whether these physiologic patterns also correlate with premenstrual mood changes.

Middle Age

38 When men and women enter middle age, slow-wave sleep continues to diminish. Nighttime awakenings become more frequent and last longer. Waking after about three hours of sleep is particularly common. During menopause, many women experience hot flashes that can interrupt sleep and lead to chronic insomnia. Obese people are more prone to nocturnal breathing problems, which often start during middle age. Men and women who are physically fit sleep more soundly as they grow older, compared with their sedentary peers.

The Later Years

39 Like younger people, older adults still spend about 20% of sleep time in REM sleep, but other than that, they sleep differently. Slow-wave sleep accounts for less than 5% of sleep time, and in some people it is completely absent. Falling asleep takes longer, and the shallow quality of sleep results in dozens of awakenings during the night. Doctors used to reassure older people that they needed less sleep than younger ones to function well, but sleep experts now know that isn't true. At any age, most adults need seven and a half to eight hours of sleep to function at their best. Since older people often have trouble attaining this much sleep at night, they often supplement nighttime sleep with daytime naps. This can be a successful strategy for accumulating sufficient total sleep over a 24-hour period. However, if you find that you need a nap, it's best to take one midday nap, rather than several brief ones scattered throughout the day and evening.

40   Sleep disturbances in elderly people, particularly in those who have Alzheimer's disease or other forms of dementia, are very disruptive for caregivers. In one study, 70% of caregivers cited these problems as the decisive factor in seeking nursing home placement for a loved one.

Consequences of Sleep Deprivation

41 Many people don't realize that lack of sufficient sleep can lead to a range of ill effects, triggering mild to potentially life-threatening consequences. There are

several different types of sleep deprivation that vary in duration and severity. These can be broadly categorized as complete or partial sleep deprivation.

Complete Sleep Deprivation

42   Normally, you go about 16 or 17 hours between sleep sessions. Complete sleep deprivation happens as the hours extend beyond this point. First you feel tired, then exhausted. By 2 or 3 a.m., many people have a hard time keeping their eyes open, but the effects extend throughout the body. Simple tasks that you would normally have no trouble accomplishing start to become difficult.

43   In fact, a number of studies of hand-eye coordination and reaction time have shown that such sleep deprivation can be as debilitating as being intoxicated. In one study, volunteers stayed awake for 28 hours, beginning at 8 a.m., and periodically took driving simulation tests. At a different time, the volunteers' driving ability was tested after drinking 10 to 15 grams of alcohol at 30-minute intervals until their blood alcohol content (BAC) level reached 0.10. The study concluded that 24 hours of wakefulness had the same deleterious effect on driving ability as that of a BAC of 0.10—enough to be charged with driving while intoxicated in most states.

44   Sleep deprivation also leaves you prone to two potentially dangerous phenomena, microsleeps and automatic behavior (page 354), which play a role in thousands of transportation accidents each year. When complete sleep deprivation extends for two or three days, people have difficulty completing tasks demanding a high attention level and often experience mood swings, depression, and increased feelings of tension.

45   Performance is also highly influenced by fluctuations in circadian rhythms. For example, sleep-deprived people may still function fairly well during the morning and evening. But during the peaks of sleepiness in the afternoon and overnight hours, people often literally cannot stay awake and may fall asleep while standing, sitting, or even while talking on the telephone, working on the computer, or eating. A small percentage experience paranoia and hallucinations.

Partial Sleep Deprivation

46 Partial sleep deprivation occurs when you get some sleep, but not 100% of what you need. Experts refer to this as building up a sleep debt. An example would be when a person who needs 7.5 hours of sleep a night hits a stretch of several days in a row in which he or she only gets four to six hours.

47   After a single night of short sleep, most people function at or near their normal level. They may not feel great, but they can usually get through the day without others noticing that anything is amiss. After two or more nights of short sleep, people usually show signs of irritability and sleepiness. Work performance begins to suffer—particularly on complicated tasks—and people are more likely to complain of headaches, stomach problems, and sore joints. In addition, people face a far higher risk of falling asleep on the job and while driving.

48   Long-term partial sleep deprivation occurs when someone gets less than the optimal amount of sleep for months or years on end—a common scenario for insomniacs and people with sleep disorders. But even healthy people who can't resist the round-the-clock commerce, communication, and entertainment opportunities our 24/7 society now offers may fall prey to this problem.

MICROSLEEPS AND AUTOMATIC BEHAVIOR

Microsleeps are brief episodes that occur in the midst of ongoing wakeful activity. They usually last a few seconds but can go on for 10 or 15 seconds. Brain wave monitoring by EEG of someone experiencing microsleeps shows brief periods of Stage N1 sleep intruding into wakefulness. During this time, the brain does not respond to noise or other sensory inputs and you don't react to things happening around you. "Noding off" can be the result of a microsleep.

Automatic behavior refers to a period of several minutes or more during which a person is awake and performing routine duties but not attending to his or her surroundings or responding to changes in the environment. Examples include a driver who keeps his car on the road but misses his intended exit and a train engineer who can continue pressing a lever at regular intervals but doesn't notice an obstruction on the track.

---

49   A growing number of studies have linked long-term sleep deficits with significant health problems.

50   **Obesity.** A 2006 study found that over 16 years, middle-aged women who reported sleeping five hours or less per night were 32% more likely to gain 33 pounds or more than women who slept seven hours or more. Another study found that men limited to four hours of sleep for two consecutive nights experienced hormonal changes that made them feel hungry and crave carbohydrate-rich foods such as cakes, candy, ice cream, and pasta.

51   **Heart health.** Middle-aged people who sleep five hours or less a night have a greater risk of developing high blood pressure, compared with people who sleep seven to nine hours a night. Women who averaged five hours of sleep a night were 39% more likely to develop heart disease than women who slept eight hours.

52   **Mental health.** A number of studies have found that persistent insomnia raises the risk for anxiety, depression, and other mood disorders.

53   **Mortality.** A study of almost a million people over age 30 found that men who reported usually sleeping less than four hours a day were nearly three times as likely to die within six years as men who said they averaged seven or eight hours of sleep.

Sleep as Part of a Healthy Lifestyle

54 Clearly, getting enough sleep is just as important as other vital elements of good health, such as eating a healthy diet, getting regular exercise, and practicing good dental hygiene. In short, sleep is not a luxury but a basic component of a healthy lifestyle.

55   Just like purchasing healthy foods, taking an after-dinner walk, or flossing your teeth, getting adequate sleep requires time and discipline. Mentally block off certain hours for sleep and then follow through on your intention, avoid building up a sleep debt, and take steps to set up an ideal sleep environment. Seek a doctor's help if conventional steps toward good sleep don't work.

56   This doesn't mean that you can't have any fun, or that you need to beat yourself up if you don't get eight hours of sleep 365 days a year. Just as an occasional ice cream sundae won't make you obese, staying up a few extra hours for a party or to meet a deadline is perfectly acceptable—as long as you make plans to compensate the next day by sleeping in, taking a short afternoon nap, or going to bed earlier. If you have to get up at 7 a.m. to be at work by 9, you'd best forgo late-night talk shows—or record them to watch the next evening. If you don't get to bed until 2 a.m. one night, allow time over the next day or two to catch up on lost sleep. But over the long haul, you need to make sure you consistently get enough sleep.

57   Sleep decisions are a quality-of-life issue. Whatever your interests and goals, getting enough sleep puts you in a better position to enjoy and achieve them.

Review Questions

1. What are the costs of disturbed sleep?

2. Explain why sleep is an active, not a passive, state. In your answer, refer to REM and non-REM sleep.

3. Studies suggest that "students who stay up all night cramming for an examination generally retain less information than classmates who get some sleep." Why?

4. To what does the term "sleep architecture" refer? What pattern does a normal sleeper's sleep architecture follow?

5. What is "circadian rhythm"? For what is it responsible and what part of the body controls it?

6. What habits affect sleep quality? How so?

7. How does sleep architecture change throughout a person's life?

Discussion and Writing Suggestions

1. Based on personal observation, what direct evidence do you have that people in different stages of life, from infants to elders, have different sleep patterns?

2. Study Figure 2, "Sleep Architecture." In a paragraph, describe the hypnogram's presentation of a "a typical night's sleep of a healthy young adult." Describe transitions through stages of sleep, and REM and non-REM sleep. In a second paragraph, discuss your reactions upon learning of the complex architecture of sleep.

3. "Parents usually blame teenagers' busy schedule of activities for their grogginess and difficulty awakening in the morning. However, the problem may also be biological," according to the *Harvard Special Health Report.* Recall any battles you had in your adolescent past over your "grogginess." Would it have changed anyone's reactions to know that your developing body (as opposed to your work, party, or TV schedule) was to blame?

4. Have you ever suffered through a period of disrupted sleep? Describe the experience in two paragraphs—the first written in the first person (the "I" perspective), the second written in the third person (the "he" or "she" perspective). Compare paragraphs. Which do you prefer? Why?

America's Sleep-Deprived Teens
Nodding Off at School, Behind the Wheel
National Sleep Foundation

The National Sleep Foundation (NSF), according to its Web site, "is an independent nonprofit organization dedicated to improving public health and safety by achieving understanding of sleep and sleep disorders, and by supporting sleep-related education, research, and advocacy." (See <http://www.sleepfoundation.org/>.) The NSF periodically issues news releases on studies its member physicians conduct. The following release, dated March 28, 2006, helped focus national attention on the dangers of adolescent sleep debt.

1 Many of the nation's adolescents are falling asleep in class, arriving late to school, feeling down and driving drowsy because of a lack of sleep that gets worse as they get older, according to a new poll released today by the National Sleep Foundation (NSF).

2 In a national survey on the sleep patterns of U.S. adolescents (ages 11–17), NSF's 2006 *Sleep in America* poll finds that only 20% of adolescents get the recommended nine hours of sleep on school nights, and nearly one-half (45%) sleep less than eight hours on school nights.

3 What's more, the poll finds that parents are mostly in the dark about their adolescents' sleep. While most students know they're not getting the sleep they need, 90% of parents polled believe that their adolescent is getting enough sleep at least a few nights during the school week.

4 The poll indicates that the consequences of insufficient sleep affect nearly every aspect of teenage life. Among the most important findings:

- At least once a week, more than one-quarter (28%) of high school students fall asleep in school, 22% fall asleep doing homework, and 14% arrive late or miss school because they oversleep.
- Adolescents who get insufficient amounts of sleep are more likely than their peers to get lower grades, while 80% of adolescents who get an optimal amount of sleep say they're achieving As and Bs in school.
- More than one-half (51%) of adolescent drivers have driven drowsy during the past year. In fact, 15% of drivers in 10th to 12th grades drive drowsy at least once a week.
- Among those adolescents who report being unhappy, tense and nervous, 73% feel they don't get enough sleep at night and 59% are excessively sleepy during the day.
- More than one-quarter (28%) of adolescents say they're too tired to exercise.

5   The poll also finds that the amount of sleep declines as adolescents get older. The survey classifies nine or more hours a night as an optimal amount of sleep in line with sleep experts' recommendations for this age group, with less than eight hours classified as insufficient. Sixth-graders report they sleep an average of 8.4 hours on school nights, while 12th-graders sleep just 6.9 hours—1.5 hours less than their younger peers and two hours less than recommended. In fact, by the time adolescents become high school seniors, they're missing out on nearly 12 hours (11.7) of needed sleep each week.

6   "This poll identifies a serious reduction in adolescents' sleep as students transition from middle school to high school. This is particularly troubling as adolescence is a critical period of development and growth—academically, emotionally and physically," says Richard L. Gelula, NSF's chief executive officer. "At a time of heightened concerns about the quality of this next generation's health and education, our nation is ignoring a basic necessity for success in these areas: adequate sleep. We call on parents, educators and teenagers themselves to take an active role in making sleep a priority."

Awareness gap between parents and teens about sleep

7   While nine out of ten parents state their adolescent is getting enough sleep at least a few nights during the school week, more than one-half (56%) of adolescents say they get less sleep than they think they need to feel their best. And, 51% say they feel too tired or sleepy during the day.

8   Also at issue is the quality of sleep once an adolescent goes to bed. Only 41% of adolescents say they get a good night's sleep every night or most nights. One in 10 teens reports that he/she rarely or never gets a good night's sleep.

9   Overall, 7% of parents think their adolescent may have a sleep problem, whereas 16% of adolescents think they have or may have one. Many adolescents (31%) who think they have a sleep problem have not told anyone about it.

Everyday pressures + nature = less sleep

10 As children reach adolescence, their circadian rhythms—or internal clocks—tend to shift, causing teens to naturally feel more alert later at night and wake up later in the morning. A trick of nature, this "phase delay" can make it difficult for them to fall asleep before 11:00 p.m.; more than one-half (54%) of high school seniors go to bed at 11:00 p.m. or later on school nights. However, the survey finds that on a typical school day, adolescents wake up around 6:30 a.m. in order to go to school, leaving many without the sleep they need.

11   "In the competition between the natural tendency to stay up late and early school start times, a teen's sleep is what loses out," notes Jodi A. Mindell, PhD, co-chair of the poll task force and an NSF vice chair. "Sending students to school without enough sleep is like sending them to school without breakfast. Sleep serves not only a restorative function for adolescents' bodies and brains, but it is also a key time when they process what they've learned during the day." Dr. Mindell is the director of the Graduate Program in Psychology at Saint Joseph's University and associate director of the Sleep Center at The Children's Hospital of Philadelphia.

12   It is also important for teens, like all people, to maintain a consistent sleep schedule across the entire week. Poll respondents overwhelmingly go to bed and

get up later and sleep longer on non-school nights. However, teens rarely make up for the sleep that they lose during the school week. Overall, adolescents get an average of 8.9 hours of sleep on a non-school night, about equal to the optimal amount recommended per night. Again, the poll finds this amount trends downward as adolescents get older.

13   Survey results also show that sleepy adolescents are more likely to rely on naps, which sleep experts point out should not be a substitute for, but rather complement, a good night's sleep. About one-third (31%) of adolescents take naps regularly, and these nappers are more likely than non-nappers to say they feel cranky or irritable, too tired during the day, and fall asleep in school—all signs of insufficient sleep. And, their naps average 1.2 hours, well beyond the 45-minute maximum recommended by sleep experts so that naps do not interfere with nighttime sleep.

14   "Irregular sleep patterns that include long naps and sleeping in on the weekend negatively impact adolescents' biological clocks and sleep quality—which in turn affects their abilities and mood," says Mary Carskadon, PhD, who chairs the 2006 poll task force. "This rollercoaster system should be minimized. When students' schedules are more consistent and provide for plenty of sleep, they are better prepared to take on their busy days." Dr. Carskadon is the director of the E.P. Bradley Hospital Sleep and Chronobiology Research Lab at Brown University.

15   In terms of overall demographics, there are more similarities than differences among adolescents' responses to sleep-related questions. Boys and girls have similar sleep patterns. In terms of racial/ethnic comparisons, African-American adolescents report getting 7.2 hours of sleep on school nights, as compared to 7.6 hours reported by Hispanic adolescents, 7.4 hours by other minorities and 7.7 hours by White adolescents.

Other factors affecting adolescent sleep

16 Caffeine plays a prominent role in the life of today's adolescent. Three-quarters of those polled drink at least one caffeinated beverage every day, and nearly one-third (31%) consume two or more such drinks each day. Adolescents who drink two or more caffeinated beverages daily are more likely to get an insufficient amount of sleep on school nights and think they have a sleep problem.

17   Technology may also be encroaching on a good night's sleep. The poll finds that adolescents aren't heeding expert advice to engage in relaxing activities in the hour before bedtime or to keep the bedroom free from sleep distractions:

- Watching television is the most popular activity (76%) for adolescents in the hour before bedtime, while surfing the internet/instant-messaging (44%) and talking on the phone (40%) are close behind.
- Boys are more likely than girls to play electronic video games (40% vs. 12%) and/or exercise (37% vs. 27%) in the hour prior to bedtime; girls are more likely than boys to talk on the phone (51% vs. 29%) and/or do homework/study (70% vs. 60%) in that time.
- Nearly all adolescents (97%) have at least one electronic item—such as a television, computer, phone or music device—in their bedroom. On average, 6th-graders have more than two of these items in their bedroom, while 12th-graders have about four.

TIPS FOR TEENS

1. Sleep is food for the brain. Lack of sleep can make you look tired and feel depressed, irritable or angry. Even mild sleepiness can hurt your performance—from taking school exams to playing sports or video games. Learn how much sleep you need to function at your best—most adolescents need between 8.5 and 9.25 hours of sleep each night—and strive to get it every night. You should awaken refreshed, not tired.
2. Keep consistency in mind: establish a regular bedtime and waketime schedule, and maintain this schedule during weekends and school (or work) vacations. Don't stray from your schedule frequently, and never do so for two or more consecutive nights. If you must go off schedule, avoid delaying your bedtime by more than one hour. Awaken the next day within two hours of your regular schedule, and, if you are sleepy during the day, take an early afternoon nap.
3. Get into bright light as soon as possible in the morning, but avoid it in the evening. The light helps to signal to the brain when it should wake up and when it should prepare to sleep.
4. Understand your circadian rhythms. Then you can try to maximize your schedule throughout the day according to your internal clock. For example, to compensate for your "slump (sleepy) times," participate in stimulating activities or classes that are interactive. Try to avoid lecture classes and potentially unsafe activities, including driv-ing.
5. After lunch (or after noon), stay away from caffeinated coffee and colas as well as nicotine, which are all stimulants. Also avoid alcohol, which disrupts sleep.
6. Relax before going to bed. Avoid heavy reading, studying and computer games within one hour of going to bed. Don't fall asleep with the television on—flickering light and stimulating content can inhibit restful sleep.

- Adolescents with four or more such items in their bedrooms are much more likely than their peers to get an insufficient amount of sleep at night and almost twice as likely to fall asleep in school and while doing homework.

18   "Many teens have a technological playground in their bedrooms that offers a variety of ways to stay stimulated and delay sleep. Ramping down from the day's activities with a warm bath and a good book are much better ways to transition to bedtime," notes Dr. Carskadon. "The brain learns when it's time to sleep from the lessons it receives. Teens need to give the brain better signals about when nighttime starts . . . turning off the lights—computer screens and TV, too—is the very best signal."

- **Be a bed head, not a dead head.** Understand the dangers of insufficient sleep—and avoid them! Encourage your friends to do the same. Ask others how much sleep they've had lately before you let them drive you somewhere. Remember: friends don't let friends drive drowsy.
- **Brag about your bedtime.** Tell your friends how good you feel after getting more than 8 hours of sleep!
- **Do you study with a buddy?** If you're getting together after school, tell your pal you need to catch a nap first, or take a nap break if needed. (Taking a nap in the evening may make it harder for you to sleep at night, however.)
- **Steer clear of raves and say no to all-nighters.** Staying up late can cause chaos in your sleep patterns and your ability to be alert the next day . . . and beyond. Remember, the best thing you can do to prepare for a test is to get plenty of sleep. All-nighters or late-night study sessions might seem to give you more time to cram for your exam, but they are also likely to drain your brainpower.

How parents can help teens get more sleep

19 Dr. Mindell notes that "the poll data suggest that parents may be missing red flags that their teenager is not getting the sleep that he or she desperately needs. Simply asking teens if they get enough sleep to feel their best is a good way for parents to begin a valuable conversation about sleep's importance."

20   Some warning signs that your child may not be getting the sleep he/she needs:

- Do you have to wake your child for school? And, is it difficult to do so?
- Has a teacher mentioned that your child is sleepy or tired during the day?
- Do you find your child falling asleep while doing homework?
- Is your child sleeping two hours later or more on weekends than on school nights?
- Is your child's behavior different on days that he/she gets a good night's sleep vs. days that he/she doesn't?
- Does he/she rely on a caffeinated drink in the morning to wake up? And/or drink two or more caffeinated drinks a day?
- Does he/she routinely nap for more than 45 minutes?

21   Parents can play a key role in helping their adolescents develop and maintain healthy sleep habits. In general, it is important for parents and adolescents to talk about sleep—including the natural phase delay—and learn more about good sleep habits in order to manage teens' busy schedules. What's more, teens often mirror their parents' habits, so adults are encouraged to be good role models by getting a full night's sleep themselves.

22   And, there are ways to make it easier for an adolescent to get more sleep and a better night's sleep:

- Set a consistent bedtime and waketime (even on weekends) that allows for the recommended nine or more hours of sleep every night.
- Have a relaxing bedtime routine, such as reading for fun or taking a warm bath or shower.
- Keep the bedroom comfortable, dark, cool and quiet.
- Get into bright light as soon as possible in the morning, but avoid it in the evening.
- Create a sleep-friendly environment by removing TVs and other distractions from the bedroom and setting limits on usage before bedtime.
- Avoid caffeine after lunchtime.

23   NSF released the poll findings as part of its 9th annual National Sleep Awareness Week® campaign, held March 27–April 2, 2006. For more sleep tips for parents and adolescents, as well as the Summary of Findings for the 2006 *Sleep in America* poll, visit NSF's website at <www.sleepfoundation.org>.

Methodology

24   The 2006 *Sleep in America* poll was conducted for the National Sleep Foundation by WB&A Market Research. Telephone interviews were conducted between September 19 and November 29, 2005, with a targeted random sample of 1,602 caregivers and, separately, their adolescent children ages 11–17 in grades 6–12. Using the targeted random sample, quotas were established by grade and race/ethnicity, with minority respondents being over-sampled to reflect equal proportions of respondents by grade, as well as the actual distribution of race/ethnicity based on the U.S. census. The poll's margin of error is plus or minus 2.4%; the response rate for the survey was 27%.

Review Questions

1. What is the recommended amount of sleep for a teenager? What percentage of American teenagers get this much sleep? How knowledgeable are their parents about their sleep?

2. How much sleep debt do high school seniors typically accumulate in a week? Cite some of the consequences of getting insufficient sleep as a teenager, according to the poll results.

3. Why is a lack of sleep in the teenage years particularly harmful, according to experts?

4. What is a "phase delay" and how does it contribute to an adolescent's sleep debt?

5. What percentage of adolescents take regular naps? Optimally, how should naps be used? What is the recommended amount of daytime napping? What is the danger of especially long naps?

6. What is "rollercoaster" sleep and why is it not healthy?

7. How do consumer electronics affect adolescent sleep?

Discussion and Writing Suggestions

1. According to the survey results, once a week roughly one-quarter of high school students fall asleep in class, 22% fall asleep doing homework, and 14% are late to or miss school because of insufficient sleep. Are/were you one of these students? Do you know these students? Why are America's teenagers not getting sufficient sleep, in your view?

2. How does the amount and quality of your sleep compare to that of teenagers who responded to the National Sleep Foundation survey?

3. To what extent do you believe that consumer electronics in your bedroom (or dorm room) affect the quality of your sleep? How do you respond to the finding that with four or more such items, you are more likely to suffer a sleep deficit? Can you explain the correlation?

4. At the end of this article, the NSF offers several recommendations for helping adolescents get more sleep. How realistic do you find these recommendations? Cite some factors in the lives of active adolescents that make it problematic to get the recommended nine hours of sleep each night.

When Worlds Collide: Adolescent Need for Sleep Versus Societal Demands
Mary A. Carskadon

Consult the reference list of any scientific article on adolescent sleep, or type the words "adolescent" and "sleep" into any search engine, and the name "Mary Carskadon" will stand out, as if in relief. A professor of psychiatry and human behavior at Brown University School of Medicine and director of sleep and chronobiology research at E.P. Bradley Hospital in Rhode Island, Carskadon has authored widely cited, foundational studies on the sleep of adolescents. In the present selection, which first appeared as a chapter in Adolescent Sleep Needs and School Starting Times *(1999), Carskadon reviews the biological, behavioral, and social forces that converge to make getting an adequate night's sleep such a challenge for so many teenagers.*

1   Our understanding of the development of sleep patterns in adolescents has advanced considerably in the last 20 years. Along the way, theoretical models of the processes underlying the biological regulation of sleep have improved, and certain assumptions and dogmas have been examined and found wanting. Although the full characterization of teen sleep regulation remains to be accomplished, our current understanding poses a number of challenges for the education system.

2   The early 1970s found us with a growing awareness that sleep patterns change fundamentally at the transition to adolescence—a phenomenon that is widely acknowledged today. Survey studies clearly showed then and continue to show that the reported timing of sleep begins to shift in early adolescence, with bedtime

and rising time both occurring at later hours. This delayed sleep pattern is particularly evident on nonschool nights and days, though the evening delay is obvious on school nights as well. Associated with the delay of sleep is a decline in the amount of sleep obtained and an increase in the discrepancy between school nights and weekend nights. Although the nonschool-night "oversleeping" was acknowledged as recovery from insufficient sleep during the school week, we initially assumed that the amount of sleep required declines with age. This was axiomatic: the older you are, the less sleep you need.

Assessing the Need for Sleep in the Second Decade

3   A longitudinal study begun in 1976 at the Stanford University summer sleep camp attempted to examine this axiom.[1] Boys and girls enrolled in this research project at ages 10, 11, or 12 and came to the lab for a 72-hour assessment each year for five or six years. They were asked to keep a fixed schedule, sleeping 10 hours a night for the week before the study, and their sleep was recorded on three consecutive nights from 10 p.m. to 8 a.m. Our hypothesis was that the reduced need for sleep in older children would manifest itself through less sleep within this 10-hour nocturnal window. This hypothesis was *not* confirmed. In fact, regardless of age or developmental stage, the children all slept about 9¼ of the 10 hours. Furthermore, delays in sleep resulted in a reduced likelihood of spontaneous waking before 8 a.m. for all but the youngest participants. One conclusion, therefore, was that the need for sleep does not change across adolescent development.

4   This study also showed an interesting pattern with respect to waking alertness, which was assessed using a technique called the Multiple Sleep Latency Test (MSLT). The MSLT measures the speed of falling asleep across repeated 20-minute trials in standard conditions. Thus a child who stays awake 20 minutes can be considered alert, faster sleep onsets are a sign of reduced alertness, and a child who falls asleep in five minutes or less is excessively sleepy.[2] The longitudinal study demonstrated that—even though the total amount of sleep was unchanged—alertness declined in association with pubertal development.[3] Figure 1 illustrates the MSLT patterns: under these experimental conditions, more mature adolescents showed signs of reduced alertness even though they slept an equivalent amount at night. One interpretation of these data is that older teenagers may need *more* sleep than when they were younger. On the other hand, the pattern of sleep tendency showing a midafternoon dip may reflect maturation of a regulated behavioral pattern favoring an afternoon nap or siesta.

Behavioral Factors

5   The principle that adolescents sleep later and less because of a panoply of psychosocial factors was also axiomatic during the 1970s and the 1980s. The evidence for this included a change in parental involvement in youngsters' sleep schedules as the children age. Thus, until about ages 11 or 12, more children than not reported that they woke spontaneously in the morning and that parents set their bedtimes. Fewer children in their early teens reported that parents still set their bedtimes, and most said that they required an alarm clock or a parent to assist them in waking up.[4]

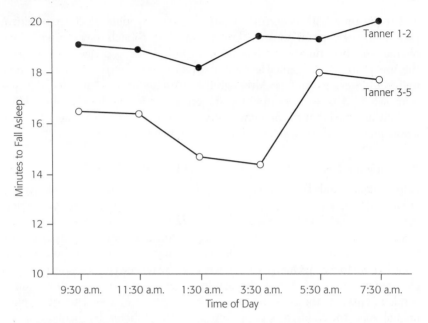

FIGURE 1 Developmental Change in Daytime Alertness Under Conditions of 'Optimal' Sleep*

The upper line, labeled Tanner 1-2, shows that pre- and early-pubescent boys and girls with a 10-hour sleep opportunity are not at all sleepy. The lower line, labeled Tanner 3-5, shows that more physically mature youngsters are sleepier, even though they have the same sleep opportunity.

6   Other behavioral factors contributing to the changing sleep patterns with age include increased social opportunities and growing academic demands. Another major contributor to changing adolescent sleep patterns is employment. One survey of youngsters in New England in the late 1980s found that two-thirds of high school students had jobs and that nearly 30% worked 20 or more hours in a typical school week.[5] Those high school students who worked 20 hours or more reported later bedtimes, shorter sleep times, more frequent episodes of falling asleep in school, and more frequent oversleeping and arriving late at school.

7   In addition to changing parental involvement, increasing school and social obligations, and greater participation in the work force, there are a myriad of other phenomena that have not been well explored. Access in the bedroom to computers, televisions, telephones, and so forth probably contributes to the delay of and reduction in sleep.

8   Another factor that has a major influence on adolescent sleep is the school schedule. The starting time of school puts limits on the time available for sleep. This is a nonnegotiable limit established largely without concern for sleep. Most school districts set the earliest starting time for older adolescents and the latest

---

* The "Tanner Scale" measures sexual maturity. The higher the scale number, the more sexually mature the person.

starting time for younger children. District officials commonly acknowledge that the school schedule is determined by the availability of school buses, along with such other factors as time of local sunrise, sports teams' schedules, and so forth. . . . [C]oncerns about the impact of school schedules on sleep patterns (as well as concerns about after-school teen delinquency) have sparked a reexamination in a number of districts. Our studies indicate that such a reexamination is merited by the difficulties many teenagers experience.

Biological Factors

9   As findings of the tendency for adolescent sleep patterns to be delayed were reported not only in North America but also in South America, Asia, Australia, and Europe, a sense arose that intrinsic developmental changes may also play a role in this phenomenon.[6] At the same time, conceptual models of the underlying internal mechanisms that control the length and timing of sleep began to take shape.

10   Current models posit three factors that control human sleep patterns. One of these factors is behavior and includes external factors such as those discussed above. The intrinsic factors have been called "sleep/wake homeostasis" and the "circadian timing system," or "process S" and "process C" in one model.[7] Sleep/wake homeostasis more simply stated is that sleep favors wake and wake favors sleep. All other things being equal, therefore, the longer one is awake, the greater the pressure for sleep to occur. Conversely, the closer one is to having slept, the less pressure there is to sleep. This process accounts for the increased need for sleep after staying awake all night and the difficulty of staying awake in general when faced with a chronic pattern of insufficient sleep. Process S can be examined using measures of sleep tendency, such as the MSLT, or measures of EEG (electroencephalogram) slow wave activity (SWA) during sleep. Sleep tendency and SWA increase with insufficient sleep. Both factors also show changes across adolescent development that may be related to the timing of sleep.

11   Under conditions of optimal sleep, such as those described in the longitudinal study of sleep, slow wave sleep declines by 40% from early to late adolescence. This decline may indicate a reduced pressure for sleep with greater maturation. One interpretation of this finding is that the reduced pressure for sleep makes staying up late an easier task for older adolescents. Others have interpreted this finding as marking a structural change in the brain (thinning of cortical synaptic density) that is unrelated to sleep/wake homeostasis. The change in sleep tendency—that is, the appearance of a midday trough at midpuberty (Figure 1)—may indicate a reorganization of the sleep/wake homeostatic mechanism to favor daytime napping and an extended late-day waking period, again favoring a later bedtime. These hypotheses are speculative and require additional study.

12   Much of the contemporary excitement about adolescent sleep comes from studies of the circadian timing mechanism, which independently and interactively exerts influences on sleep through processes that favor or inhibit sleep according to the dictates of an internal biological "clock." Several features of the human circadian timing system and its interactions with sleep and wakefulness are relevant here.

- Circadian rhythms are biological oscillations with periods of about 24 hours.
- Circadian rhythms are synchronized to the 24-hour day chiefly by light signals.
- The chief circadian oscillator in mammals is located deep within the brain in the suprachiasmatic nuclei (SCN) of the hypothalamus.
- Circadian rhythms can be assessed by measuring the timing of biological events. . . .
- Circadian rhythms control the timing of REM (rapid eye movement) sleep within the sleep period.

13   A first attempt to examine whether the circadian timing system undergoes developmental changes during adolescent maturation involved a survey of sixth-grade girls. In this survey, one series of questions allowed us to estimate physical development and another series gave a measure of circadian phase preference. Phase preference refers to an individual's tendency to favor activities in the morning or evening, i.e., morningness/eveningness. In these 275 sixth-grade girls, the puberty score and circadian phase preference score showed a significant relationship: less mature girls favored earlier hours, and more mature girls favored later hours.[8] These data were the first to implicate a biological process in the later timing of adolescent sleep.

. . .

14   One other important finding from our studies is that the circadian timing system can be reset if light exposure is carefully controlled. In many of our studies, we require adolescents to keep a specific sleep schedule (for example, 10 p.m. to 8 a.m.) and to wear eyeshades to exclude light during these hours. In fact, we pay adolescents to keep this schedule! When we measure melatonin secretion* before the students go on the new schedule (when they are still on their self-selected routine) and again after 10 or 11 nights on the new schedule, we find that the melatonin secretion has moved significantly toward a common time: those who were early melatonin secretors move to a later time, and those who were late secretors move earlier.[9] Thus we know that the system is not immutable; with time, effort, *and* money, we can get adolescents to realign their rhythms!

15   Let us summarize what we now know about the developmental trends in adolescent sleep behavior and adolescents' sleep/wake and circadian systems.

- As they mature, adolescents tend to go to bed later and to wake up later (given the opportunity).
- Adolescents also tend to sleep less as they mature.
- The difference between the amount and timing of sleep on weekend nights versus school nights grows during adolescence.
- These trends are apparent in adolescents both in North America and in industrialized countries on other continents.

---

* [O]ne of the best ways to identify time in the intrinsic biological clock in humans is to examine melatonin secretion. Melatonin is a hormone that is produced by the pineal gland and regulated by the circadian timing system. Melatonin secretion occurs during nocturnal hours in both day-active species, like humans, and night-active species. Melatonin can be measured from saliva samples collected in dim lighting conditions.

- Sleep requirements do not decline during adolescent development.
- Daytime sleep tendency is augmented during puberty.
- The timing of events controlled by the circadian timing system is delayed during puberty.

16   We propose that the delay of sleep during adolescent development is favored by behavioral and intrinsic processes and that the reduction of sleep experienced by adolescents is largely driven by a collision between the intrinsic processes and the expectations and demands of the adult world. The study described in the following section illustrates this point.

School Transition Project

17 Our school transition project took a look at what happened to sleep and circadian rhythms in a group of youngsters for whom the transition from junior high school to senior high school required a change in the starting time for school from 8:25 a.m. to 7:20 a.m. Twenty-five youngsters completed our study at two time points, in the spring of the ninth grade and in the autumn of the 10th grade.[10] These boys and girls were all well beyond the beginning changes of puberty; some were physically mature. They were enrolled in the study with instructions simply to keep their usual schedules, to wear small activity monitors on their wrists, and to keep diaries of their activities and sleep schedule for two consecutive weeks. At the end of the two weeks, participants came to the sleep laboratory for assessment of the onset phase of melatonin secretion, overnight sleep study, and daytime testing with the MSLT. The laboratory sleep schedule was fixed to each student's average school-night schedule based on the data from the wrist monitor (actigraph).

18   As predicted, the actigraph data showed that students woke up earlier when confronted with the 7:20 a.m. start time, although rising time was on average only about 25 minutes earlier (6:26 a.m. to 6:01 a.m.), not the 65 minutes represented by the school schedule change. Sleep onset times did not change, averaging about 10:40 p.m. in both grades. The average amount of sleep on school nights fell from seven hours and nine minutes to six hours and 50 minutes, a statistically significant amount and probably a meaningful amount when considered as producing an ever cumulating sleep deficit.

19   The amount of sleep these students obtained in ninth grade was below the amount we feel is required for optimal alertness, and the further decline in 10th grade had added impact. One way to examine the impact is to look at the MSLT data from tests that occurred at 9:30 a.m., 10:30 a.m., 12:30 p.m., and 2:30 p.m. If we look at comparable MSLT data from Figure 1, we find an average score of 18.9 minutes for the early pubertal children and 15.5 minutes for the mid- to late pubertal adolescents sleeping on the optimizing 10-hour schedule. The ninth-grade students in this more naturalistic study, by contrast, had an average MSLT speed of falling asleep of 11.4 minutes, and in 10th grade the sleep score was 8.5 minutes. In clinical terms, these students were in a borderline zone for daytime sleepiness, well below the alert range and below the "normal" range, yet not in the "pathological" range.

20   A closer look at the MSLT test results shows that the students in 10th grade were in the pathological range when tested at 8:30 a.m. (MSLT score = 5.1 minutes). Furthermore, nearly 50% of these 10th-graders showed a reversed sleep pattern on the morning MSLT tests that is similar to the pattern seen in patients with the sleep disorder called narcolepsy—that is, REM sleep occurs before non-REM sleep. The 12 students who showed this "narcoleptic" pattern fell asleep in an average of 3.4 minutes when tested at 8:30 a.m. These students did not have narcolepsy; what they did have was a significant mismatch between their circadian rhythms and the necessity to get up and go to school. The evidence for this mismatch was a later time for the onset of melatonin secretion compared with those who did not have the "narcoleptic" pattern: 9:46 p.m. versus 8:36 p.m. This marker of the circadian timing system indicates that 1) the students' natural time to fall asleep is about 11 p.m. or later (on average) and 2) the abnormally short time to sleep onset on the 8:30 a.m. MSLT and the abnormal occurrence of REM sleep took place because the students were tested at the very nadir of their circadian day. In other words, at 8:30 a.m., these students' brains were far better suited to be asleep than awake!

21   Why were these 12 students so different from the others? We were unable to identify a specific cause. None of the 25 students made an optimal adjustment to the new schedule; none was sleeping even as much as 8¼ hours on school nights, a value we suggest elsewhere might be adequate if not optimal for high school students.[11] A few students maintained a "normal" level of alertness, others were borderline, and still others were in the pathological range. The 12 students whose circadian timing systems moved to a much later timing in 10th grade, however, showed signs associated with marked impairment, particularly in the morning hours.

Consequences, Concerns, and Countermeasures

22   Among the known consequences of insufficient sleep are memory lapses, attentional deficits, depressed mood, and slowed reaction time. Sleep deprivation studies have shown that divergent thinking suffers with inadequate sleep. A few surveys have noted poorer grades in students with inadequate sleep. Many important issues have not yet been well studied. For example, little is known about the consequences of insufficient sleep for relationship formation and maintenance, emotion regulation, delinquency, drug use, and violent behavior. Long-term consequences of insufficient sleep—particularly at critical developmental stages—are utterly unknown.

23   The problem of inadequate sleep affects more segments of our society than adolescents; however, adolescents appear to be particularly vulnerable and face difficult challenges for obtaining sufficient sleep. Even without the pressure of biological changes, if we combine an early school starting time—say 7:30 a.m., which, with a modest commute, makes 6:15 a.m. a viable rising time—with our knowledge that optimal sleep need is 9¼ hours, we are asking that 16-year-olds go to bed at 9 p.m. Rare is the teenager of the 1990s who will keep such a schedule. School work, sports practices, clubs, volunteer work, and paid employment take precedence. When biological changes are factored in, the

ability even to have merely "adequate" sleep is lost. As a consequence, sleepy teens demand that parents provide an extreme form of reveille, challenge teachers to offer maximal classroom entertainment and creativity just to keep them awake, and suffer the consequences of disaffection from school and dissatisfaction with themselves.

24   Can these problems be solved by delaying the starting time for school as adolescents move into the pubertal years? Not entirely. Moving the opening bell to a later time may help many teens with the mismatch between biological time and scholastic time, but it will not provide more hours in the day. It is not difficult to project that a large number of students see a later starting time as permission to stay up later at night studying, working, surfing the net, watching television, and so forth. Today's teens know little about their sleep needs or about the biological timing system. Interestingly, students do know they are sleepy, but they do not have skills to cope with the issue, and many assume— just as adults do—that they are expected to function with an inadequate amount of sleep. This assumption is a physiological fallacy: sleep is not optional. Sleep is biologically obligatory. If students learn about sleep, they have a basis to use a changed school starting time to best advantage. Adding information about sleep to the school curriculum can certainly help.

25   As with other fields of scientific investigation, the knowledge base, the scientific opportunities, and the level of pure excitement in sleep and biological rhythms research have never been greater. This knowledge and excitement can be shared with students at every academic level. Furthermore, sleep and biological rhythms are natural gateways to learning because students are drawn to the topics. Thus, as grammar school students learn about the nutrition pyramid, so too could they learn about the body's sleep requirements and how the biological timing system makes humans day-active rather than night-active. (Did you know that, if you put your hamster in a box with lights that turn on at night and off in the daytime, it will start running on its wheel during the day?)

26   As middle school students are learning about comparative biology, they can be sharing in the excitement of where, when, and how animals sleep. (Did you know that certain dolphins can be half asleep . . . literally? One half of the brain sleeps while the other half is awake! Did you know that mammals stop regulating body temperature in REM sleep? Did you know that you are paralyzed in REM sleep?)

27   High school students can share the excitement in the discoveries about genes that control the biological clock, about the brain mechanisms that control dreaming, about the way sleep creates breathing problems, and about sleep disorders that may affect their family members. (Did you know that snoring may be a sign of a serious sleep disorder afflicting as many as 5% of adults? Did you know that some people act out their dreams at night? Did you know that genes controlling the biological clock in mice and fruit flies are nearly identical?)

Challenges and an Opportunity

28 The challenges are great, and solutions do not come easily. School scheduling is incredibly complex, and accounting for youngsters' sleep needs and biological propensities adds to the complexity. Yet we cannot assume that the system is immutable. Given that the primary focus of education is to maximize human

potential, then a new task before us is to ensure that the conditions in which learning takes place address the very biology of our learners.

Notes

1. Mary A. Carskadon, "Determinants of Daytime Sleepiness: Adolescent Development, Extended and Restricted Nocturnal Sleep" (Doctoral dissertation, Stanford University, 1979); idem, "The Second Decade," in Christian Guilleminault, ed., *Sleeping and Waking Disorders: Indications and Techniques* (Menlo Park, Calif.: Addison Wesley, 1982), pp. 99–125; and Mary A. Carskadon, E. John Orav, and William C. Dement, "Evolution of Sleep and Daytime Sleepiness in Adolescents," in Christian Guilleminault and Elio Lugaresi, eds., *Sleep/Wake Disorders: Natural History, Epidemiology, and Long-Term Evolution* (New York: Raven Press, 1983), pp. 201–16.

2. Mary A. Carskadon and William C. Dement, "The Multiple Sleep Latency Test: What Does It Measure?" *Sleep*, vol. 5, 1982, pp. 67–72.

3. Mary A. Carskadon et al., "Pubertal Changes in Daytime Sleepiness," *Sleep*, vol. 2, 1980, pp. 453–60.

4. Carskadon, "Determinants of Daytime Sleepiness."

5. Mary A. Carskadon, "Patterns of Sleep and Sleepiness in Adolescents," *Pediatrician*, vol. 17, 1990, pp. 5–12.

6. Mirian M. M. Andrade and Luiz Menna-Barreto, "Sleep Patterns of High School Students Living in São Paulo, Brazil," in Mary A. Carskadon, ed., *Adolescent Sleep Patterns: Biological, Social, and Psychological Influences* (New York: Cambridge University Press, forthcoming); Kaneyoshi Ishihara, Yukako Honma, and Susumu Miyake, "Investigation of the Children's Version of the Morningness-Eveningness Questionnaire with Primary and Junior High School Pupils in Japan," *Perceptual and Motor Skills*, vol. 71, 1990, pp. 1353–54; Helen M. Bearpark and Patricia T. Michie, "Prevalence of Sleep/Wake Disturbances in Sidney Adolescents," *Sleep Research*, vol. 16, 1987, p. 304; and Inge Strauch and Barbara Meier, "Sleep Need in Adolescents: A Longitudinal Approach," *Sleep*, vol. 11, 1988, pp. 378–86.

7. Alexander A. Borbély, "A Two Process Model of Sleep Regulation," *Human Neurobiology*, vol. 1, 1982, pp. 195–204.

8. Mary A. Carskadon, Cecilia Vieira, and Christine Acebo, "Association Between Puberty and Delayed Phase Preference," *Sleep*, vol. 16, 1993, pp. 258–62.

9. Carskadon et al., "An Approach to Studying Circadian Rhythms."

10. Mary A. Carskadon et al., "Adolescent Sleep Patterns, Circadian Timing, and Sleepiness at a Transition to Early School Days," *Sleep*, in press.

11. Amy R. Wolfson and Mary A. Carskadon, "Sleep Schedules and Daytime Functioning in Adolescents," *Child Development*, vol. 69, 1998, pp. 875–87.

Review Questions

1. What fundamental shift in sleep patterns occurs in the transition to adolescence, and what problems does this shift cause?

2. What did investigators discover when they examined the "axiom" that "the older you are, the less sleep you need"?

3. What behavioral and social factors can affect adolescent sleep?

4. Carskadon presents two "conceptual models of the underlying internal mechanisms that control the length and timing of sleep." What are they and how can they be measured?

5. What, exactly, are the colliding worlds of Carskadon's title?

Discussion and Writing Suggestions

1. Carskadon describes the results of a study measuring the sleepiness of students transitioning to high school (see paragraphs 17–21). For the 12 students who "were far better suited to be asleep than awake," the typical school start time of 8:30 a.m. represented "the very nadir of their circadian day." In a paragraph of (vivid) description, corroborate this insight from personal experience.

2. Is there any sense in which you feel vindicated in your early morning sleepiness by Carskadon's article? Throughout adolescence, adults may have blamed your sleepiness on character flaws—laziness, perhaps. Does the science behind Carskadon's article help you to feel any better about yourself? Write a letter to one such adult accuser explaining why you were not a lazy-good-for-nothing after all!

3. In matters relating to sleepiness/wakefulness, in what ways has your world "collided" with the world of "societal demands"? Collisions often produce casualties. Have there been casualties in your case?

4. Carskadon calls our attention to the problems adolescents may face when their sleep schedules conflict with the scheduling demands of the broader world. She points, as well, to the seemingly intractable causes of this conflict. (See especially paragraphs 22–23.) What do you think of her proposals to minimize, if not avoid, this conflict? Can you offer any proposals of your own?

Sleep Debt and the Mortgaged Mind
William C. Dement and Christopher Vaughan

William Dement, MD, PhD, is one of the founders of modern sleep medicine, universally acknowledged as a pioneer (along with Mary Carskadon, whose work appears earlier in this chapter). A professor and researcher at Stanford University, Dement has authored numerous articles, books, and book chapters on sleep. His particular interest has been the topic of sleep "debt," the focus of the following selection, which appeared originally as a chapter in The Promise of Sleep *(1999), cowritten with Christopher Vaughan.*

1   The night of March 24, 1989, was cold and calm, the air crystalline, as the giant *Exxon Valdez* oil tanker pulled out of Valdez, Alaska, into the tranquil waters of

Prince William Sound. In these clearest of possible conditions the ship made a planned turn out of the shipping channel and didn't turn back in time. The huge tanker ran aground, spilling millions of gallons of crude oil into the sound. The cost of the cleanup effort was over $2 billion. The ultimate cost of continuing environmental damage is incalculable. Furthermore, when the civil trial was finally over in the summer of 1995, the Exxon Corporation was assessed an additional $5 billion in punitive damages. Everyone I query in my travels vividly recalls the accident, and most have the impression that it had something to do with the master's alcohol consumption. No one is aware of the true cause of the tragedy. In its final report, the National Transportation Safety Board (NTSB) found that sleep deprivation and sleep debt were direct causes of the accident. This stunning result got a brief mention in the back pages of the newspapers.

2 Out of the vast ocean of knowledge about sleep, there are a few facts that are so important that I will try to burn them into your brain forever. None is more important than the topic of sleep debt. If we can learn to understand sleep indebtedness and manage it, we can improve everyday life as well as avoid many injuries, horribly diminished lives, and premature deaths.

3 The *Exxon Valdez* disaster offers a good example of how sleep debt can create a tragedy and how the true villain—sleep indebtedness—remains concealed. I am sure that I was just as shocked as anyone when I learned about America's worst oil spill. The TV coverage of the dead birds and seals filled me with outrage over the environmental devastation. One of my friends went to Alaska and participated in the cleanup. He brought back photos and a big jar of crude oil. If you haven't been exposed to crude oil, keep away from it. It isn't the purified stuff that goes into your car. It's awful. It stinks to high heaven. You want to vomit.

4 I was among the millions who were following the news, but I had no idea that it would have a special meaning for me a year later. The National Commission on Sleep Disorders Research finally mandated by Congress was convened for the first time in March 1990, and 20 commissioners were assembled in Washington, D.C. After the first meeting I decided to visit a friend, Dr. John Lauber, who had been confirmed by the Senate as one of five members of the National Transportation Safety Board. He told me that the board would very likely identify sleep deprivation as the "direct cause" of the grounding of the *Exxon Valdez*.

5 I had worked with John a few years earlier on a study of the layover sleep of pilots on intercontinental airlines. He was head of human factors research at NASA-Ames and at the beginning of the layover study knew little about "sleep debt." At the end of the study, he was one of the few real experts in the world. Two months after the visit with John he sent me the NTSB's final report.

6 The report noted that on the March night when the *Exxon Valdez* steamed out of Valdez there were ice floes across part of the shipping lane, forcing the ship to turn to avoid them. The captain determined that this maneuver could be done safely if the ship was steered back to the main channel when it was abeam of a well-known landmark, Busby Island. With this plan established, he turned over command to the third mate and left the bridge. Although news reports linked much of what happened next to the captain's alcohol consumption, the captain was off the bridge well before the accident. The direct cause of

America's worst oil spill was the behavior of the third mate, who had slept only 6 hours in the previous 48 and was severely sleep deprived.

7   As the *Exxon Valdez* passed Busby Island, the third mate ordered the helm to starboard, but he didn't notice that the autopilot was still on and the ship did not turn. Instead it plowed farther out of the channel. Twice lookouts warned the third mate about the position of lights marking the reef, but he didn't change or check his previous orders. His brain was not interpreting the danger in what they said. Finally he noticed that he was far outside the channel, turned off the autopilot, and tried hard to get the great ship pointed back to safety—too late.

8   For several years I would ask every audience that I addressed if there was anyone in the audience who had not heard the words *"Exxon Valdez."* A hand was never raised. Then I would say, "Who knows what caused the grounding?" Many hands would be raised, and the answer would always be "alcohol." Thus I could never exploit the potential impact of this catastrophe in getting knowledge about sleep into the mainstream, because of the media emphasis on the captain's drinking. When the report finally came out, there was no real interest. Even at the trial, in the summer of 1995, the true cause of the accident received little attention. What everyone ought to be talking about is how to deal with sleep deprivation and how to avoid it in the transportation industry and throughout all components of society, saying over and over again "Look what it caused." But instead, the poor captain has been hounded for nearly a decade.

9   An even more dramatic tragedy was the explosion of the space shuttle *Challenger*. After a year-long investigation, the Rogers Commission declared that in the absence of adequate data on O-ring function at low temperatures the decision to launch the rocket was an error. Those of us who saw this catastrophic event on television over and over and over know the ghastly consequences of that error. But not well known at all is the fact that the Human Factors Subcommittee attributed the error to the severe sleep deprivation of the NASA managers. This conclusion was only included in the committee's final report, which only noted that top managers in such situations are generally the ones who sacrifice the most sleep.

10   Was this the most costly case of sleepiness in history? The parents of any teenager who has died while asleep at the wheel might not agree. Even the most careful drivers are at risk, because we simply do not tell people—not even young people in the driver-training courses required in many states—how to recognize signs of dangerous sleepiness.

11   Of course, even children are at risk. For example in the past several years I have received many reports of school bus accidents where the driver fell asleep. Unfortunately, it may take another *Exxon Valdez* or *Challenger* before the sleep community can mobilize public opinion to do something about this issue. Thus, I find myself in the bizarre circumstance of simultaneously fearing and at the same time hoping for another highly visible disaster.

12   Just last year I stepped up to the podium to make the danger absolutely clear to my Stanford students. Drowsiness, that feeling when the eyelids are trying to close and we cannot seem to keep them open, is the last step before we fall asleep, not the first. If at this moment we let sleep come, it will arrive instantly. When driving a car, or in any hazardous situation, the first wave of drowsiness should be

a dramatic warning. Get out of harm's way instantly! My message to the students is "Drowsiness is red alert!" I delivered and explained this message over and over in my 1997 undergraduate course "Sleep and Dreams," and the students got it. I am confident few will ever drive while drowsy.

13   Everyone can recall a jolt of heart-stopping panic in the face of peril—when we realize a cab seems about to jump the curb we're standing on, or when we lose track of a child in a crowd. The response is instantaneous. We act. We should have a similar response the instant we feel drowsy at the wheel.

Ignorance About Sleepiness

14 . . . I now think of the continuum of sleepiness and alertness as the state upon which all human behavior is acted out. Today we can claim with confidence that where we are on this continuum, from the high peak of optimal alertness to the deep trough of extreme drowsiness, is the single most important determinant of how well we perform. Accordingly, the total absence of this subject from psychology textbooks or any other educational materials is incomprehensible. Although the scientific knowledge has been available for more than two decades, students are still not acquiring crucial knowledge about sleepiness, sleep debt, and sleep deprivation in any of our educational institutions. . . .

15   The feeling of being tired and needing sleep is a basic drive of nature, like hunger. If you don't eat enough, you are driven to eat. If you go long enough without food, you can think of nothing else. Once you get food, you eat until you feel full and then you stop. Thus, the subjective responses of hunger and satiation ensure that you fulfill your overall daily requirement for calories. In essentially the same way, your sleep drive keeps an exact tally of accumulated waking hours. Like bricks in a backpack, accumulated sleep drive is a burden that weighs down on you. Every hour that you are awake adds another brick to the backpack: The brain's sleep load increases until you go to sleep, when the load starts to lighten.

16   In a very real sense all wakefulness is sleep deprivation. As soon as you wake up, the meter starts ticking, calculating how many hours of sleep you will need to pay off that night. Or, to continue the load metaphor, it tallies how many bricks you will have to shed to get back to zero. Generally people need to sleep one hour for every two hours awake, which means that most need around eight hours of sleep a night. Of course, some people need more and some need less, and a few people seem to need a great deal more or less. From the work we have done, we must conclude that each person has his or her own specific daily sleep requirement. The brain tries to hit this mark, and the further you are from getting the number of hours of sleep you need, the harder your brain tries to force you to get that sleep.

. . .

Sleep Debt: Nature's Loan Shark

17 . . . The brain keeps an exact accounting of how much sleep it is owed. In our first study, we restricted the sleep of 10 volunteers to exactly 5 hours each night for 7 nights and observed that the tendency to fall asleep increased progressively each successive day. For the first time in the history of sleep research, we discovered that the effect of each successive night of partial sleep loss carried over, and the effect appeared to accumulate in a precisely additive fashion. In other words, the

strength of the tendency to fall asleep was progressively greater during each successive day with exactly the same amount of sleep each night. For some time Mary [Carskadon] and I referred to this as an increased sleep tendency, and it was clear that the increase did not dissipate without additional rest. How people recover from various levels of sleep deprivation after getting sleep has not been well studied. However, current evidence suggests that the accumulated lost sleep must be paid back at some time, perhaps even hour for hour.

18   We use the term "sleep debt" because accumulated lost sleep is like a monetary debt: It must be paid back. Regardless of how rapidly it can be paid back, the important thing is that the size of the sleep debt and its dangerous effects are definitely directly related to the amount of lost sleep. My guess is that after a period of substantial sleep loss, we can pay back a little and feel a lot better, although the remaining sleep debt is still large. The danger of an unintended sleep episode is still there. Until proven otherwise, it is reasonable and certainly safer to assume that accumulated lost sleep must be paid back hour for hour. Therefore, if you miss 3 hours one night, you must sleep 11 hours the next night (3 plus your normal 8) in order to feel alert throughout the day.

19   Your sleep debt may have accumulated in small increments over many days. For example, during a five-day work week where you needed 8 hours each night and instead got 6, you would build up a sleep debt of 10 hours (5 times 2). From this perspective, sleeping in until noon on Saturday is not enough to pay back the 10 lost hours plus your nightly requirement of 8; you would have to sleep until about 5:00 P.M. to balance the sleep ledger. Of course, most people won't sleep that long, and in fact it is difficult to do because of the alerting process of the biological clock. . . . More likely, you will sleep in an extra hour or two and get up feeling better. But the debt is still there, demanding to be paid. Later that day you'll start feeling the effects of the sleep debt again. And if you borrow more sleep time over subsequent nights, you won't just stay sleepy, you'll get even sleepier. As your debt grows, your energy, mood, and cognition will be undermined.

20   There is another important way that sleep deprivation can occur and sleep debt can accumulate. . . . [S]everal sleep disorders are characterized by very severe and impairing daytime sleepiness. In such patients we typically see hundreds of brief interruptions of sleep in a single night. In spite of this, careful tabulation of the intervening short periods of sleep can add up to what ought to be a satisfactory amount of total sleep.

21   Several groups of sleep researchers have carried out studies on normal volunteers which have clarified this situation. In these studies, subjects were awakened every minute or so throughout entire nights, and the next day's alertness was evaluated using the [Multiple Sleep Latency Test, which measures sleepiness, the speed with which subjects fall asleep]. The nocturnal awakenings were brief, 5 to 10 seconds, and subjects usually returned to sleep immediately. Although there were usually several hundred interruptions, the cumulative total sleep can add up to normal amounts. Nevertheless, daytime sleepiness is markedly increased, as if there had been no sleep at all, or very little.

22   Interrupting sleep every minute or so all night long is a heroic experimental manipulation. I am happy to report that the results of these particular experiments have been very consistent. Accordingly, we may conclude that the restorative

value of sleep is severely curtailed if sleep periods are not allowed to continue for at least several minutes. If 10 to 15 minutes of sleep are allowed to occur before an interruption, this effect is greatly lessened. These studies have led to the concept that there are minimal units of restorative sleep. In other words, it is as if the bank that keeps track of sleep debt doesn't accept small deposits.

23   In one of our first studies we evaluated the clinical usefulness of the MSLT by comparing narcoleptics and normal sleepers. The results were fabulous. The MSLT sharply distinguished patients and normals. However, the MSLT scores of a few normal volunteers were in the pathologically sleepy range (1 to 5 minutes). This latter group tended to be college students. For a while we thought that these younger "normals" were in the early stages of the narcoleptic sleep disorder, not yet manifesting the other symptoms. But it was hard to imagine why Stanford University would attract so many budding narcoleptics. We tested a few more students, allowing a baseline normal amount of sleep (8 hours a day) and carefully measuring their sleep tendency day to day with the MSLT. Nearly all of the students appeared to be pathologically sleepy! I should not have been so surprised, because I have been watching students fall asleep in class ever since I was a college student myself.

24   The obvious explanation finally occurred to Mary and me: The students needed more sleep. To prove this we did studies where we extended their nightly hours in bed to 10, and over several days, the MSLT score steadily improved. Now that we know about sleep debt, we can only imagine how many thousands of observations on human behavior have been made over the decades on chronically sleep-deprived subjects whom researchers thought were "normal." Since people are so severely affected by a large sleep debt, its presence can potentially alter the results of almost all research measures, from I.Q. tests to observations of drug side effects. The baseline studies of all human research, regardless of their nature, now must include measures of daytime sleep tendency, so that the variable degree of chronic sleep loss does not contaminate every study.

25   Despite the fact that "sleep debt" has entered common parlance (some researchers also call it "sleep load" or "sleep tendency"), many people don't fully understand the concept. Again and again I hear people complain that they sleep a full night, even an extra hour or so, and still feel just as sleepy or even sleepier than before. "Well," they think, "I must be sleepy because I am sleeping too much." The fact is that you don't work off a large sleep debt, which is what most of us have, by getting one good night's sleep.

. . .

Driving Under the Influence of Sleep Debt

26 People *must* learn to pay attention to their own sleep debt and how it is affecting them. Not doing so, and misunderstanding the rules of sleep debt and arousal, can be extremely dangerous. A friend of mine, also a Stanford professor, once participated in a bicycle race that lasted several days and included a number of laps around Lake Tahoe. He got very little sleep at night during the period of the race, but then he slept about nine hours a night for the two nights he stayed at the lake after the race. He woke up on Sunday morning feeling

rested, ready to pack up and drive home. But as he was coming down the winding mountain road he began to yawn and his eyelids felt heavy. He told me that he was a little surprised because he thought he had gotten plenty of sleep. If someone had been with him, he probably would have traded places, but it did not occur to him to pull over and take a nap. As he drove on, it became harder and harder to keep his eyes open, and he began to be concerned. At that moment he saw a sign for a restaurant only several miles farther down the road. "Good," he thought, "I'll be able to get some coffee." Right after that he fell asleep, just for a moment, and awoke with a terrible start to find that he had drifted into the oncoming lane. He jerked the wheel to the right, but the road curved to the left, and the car went over a 30-foot ledge. The next thing he knew he was upside down, suspended by his seat belt, the car impaled on a jagged rock that had sliced through the roof and into the empty passenger seat next to him. He sustained serious cuts and bruises, and his right arm was completely paralyzed, but miraculously he was alive.

27   When he told me the story later, he still didn't understand how he could have been so sleepy. "But Bill, I got two full nights of sleep before I left Tahoe." Not knowing about sleep debt, he could not know that a few hours of extra sleep does not alleviate the sleep debt accumulated over the preceding nights or weeks. He was driving alone without the stimulation of conversation, along a route he knew fairly well. In short, there was little to act as a dike against the sea of sleep debt that he had built up. Ironically, his awareness of how terribly drowsy he was feeling may have forestalled sleep in the minutes before the crash. When he saw the sign for the restaurant up ahead and knew that he would soon get coffee, he relaxed and let that worry go. A few moments later he was hurtling off the mountain road. If the idea that drowsiness is supremely dangerous had been burned into his brain, he would have stopped driving no matter how difficult or inconvenient.

Fatal Fatigue: Alcohol and Sleep Debt

28 . . . [O]lder children never feel sleepy during the day. They were the only group we studied in the Stanford Summer Sleep Camp who never fell asleep in the 20 minutes allotted for the individual sleep latency tests. And of course, children are usually not sleep deprived. Putting all our results together, we can state with confidence that if you feel sleepy or drowsy in the daytime, then you must have a sizable sleep debt. Sleep debt is the physical side of the coin, and the feelings of sleepiness or drowsiness are the psychological side. As an analogy, dehydration is the physical side of the coin and the feeling of being thirsty is the psychological side. To carry the analogy a little further, if we have thoroughly quenched our thirst, we cannot immediately feel thirsty. But if we are becoming dehydrated, the desire to drink may be diminished if we are involved in something very interesting or demanding. At some point, of course, thirst becomes overwhelming. Likewise, we cannot feel sleepy in the daytime if we do not have a sleep debt, but we may not feel sleepy if we are doing something that excites us. If we have a very strong tendency to fall asleep and we reduce the stimuli that are keeping us awake, we will very soon begin to feel sleepy and will inevitably fall asleep, intentionally or otherwise.

29   But all those interested in traffic safety and all those who wish to have a long life as well must take note. When a crash is attributed to alcohol, the real culprit, or at least a coconspirator, is often sleep deprivation. In studies that are second to none in importance, the powerful interaction between sleep and alcohol was revealed by the outstanding sleep research team at Henry Ford Hospital Sleep Disorders Center. A group of volunteers slept 10 hours a night for one week, 8 hours a night during a separate week, and on a third schedule simulated a social weekend by getting 5 hours of sleep for 2 nights. In the morning after completing each schedule, all of the volunteers were given either a low dose of alcohol or a placebo. Then their degree of impaired alertness was evaluated utilizing the MSLT and performance tests. When the subjects were given the low dose of alcohol after the 8-hour schedule, they became slightly more sleepy than when given placebo. After the schedule of 2 nights with little sleep, the exact same dose of alcohol the next morning made them severely sleepy, barely able to stay awake. However, the exact same dose of alcohol after 10 hours of sleep every night for a week had no discernible effect. In other words, alcohol may not be a potent sedative by itself, but it becomes very sedating when paired with sleep debt. It is tempting to speculate that all sedatives, particularly sleeping pills, interact with sleep debt. This area deserves much more research. . . .

30   The implications of this are far-reaching. People are well aware of the dangers of drinking and driving, but they don't know that a large sleep debt and even a small amount of alcohol can create a "fatal fatigue." People can be just fine driving after a single drink one day (when they have little sleep debt), yet be a hazard to themselves and others if they have that same drink on a day in which they have a large sleep debt. A fact little known by the public at large is that in nearly every accident linked to alcohol consumption, sleep debt almost certainly plays a major role.

31   In one state traffic agency, researchers are trying very hard to understand traffic accidents designated as alcohol related even though the alcohol in the tissue is far below any level thought to be impairing.

. . .

32   [E]xperiments demonstrate that individuals thought to be completely normal can be carrying a sizable sleep debt, which impairs their mood, energy, and performance. If you haven't already done so, I think it's worthwhile to ask yourself how your sleep debt is affecting you. How often do you think about taking a quick snooze? How often do you rub your eyes and yawn during the day? How often do you feel like you really need some coffee? Each of these is a warning of a sleep debt that you ignore at your peril. I can't overemphasize the dangers of unintended sleep episodes or severe drowsiness. I hope this information can save your life.

33   I know that people often are driven to stay up late and get up early, that the demands of modern life push us to stay up past our biological bedtime. But I also know it's not too onerous to avoid accumulating sleep debt. . . . Studies suggest the likelihood that people can avoid dangerously high sleep debt by adding a relatively small amount of sleep to their normal sleep schedule. People who have lowered their sleep debt usually report that they gain a new sense of well-being.

That may just mean not watching the news at night, or putting off some other nonessential pleasure, like the bedtime crossword puzzle. I bet most people would give up many late-night diversions if they could feel truly awake throughout the day—fresh and full of hope, senses wide open, the mind receptive to people and ideas.

Review Questions

1. What was the actual, though little reported, cause of the *Exxon Valdez* disaster?

2. Dement asserts that "Drowsiness is red alert!" What does he mean?

3. What is the "continuum of sleepiness and alertness"? What is its significance?

4. How is sleeping like eating and drinking?

5. What is sleep debt? How is it "carried over"? How is the amount of sleep debt correlated with the dangers posed by sleep debt?

6. Why may a person feel sleepy even after getting a full night's sleep?

7. In what way is sleep debt often a "co-conspirator" in alcohol-related crashes?

Discussion and Writing Suggestions

1. Consider your own sleep habits. Given what you've read in this article, are you currently sleep deprived? Have you ever been? Have you ever noticed in your daily performance of a task the kinds of impairments due to sleep debt that Dement discusses?

2. In the title and throughout the article, Dement uses a metaphor from the banking industry—mortgage—to discuss sleep debt. (This term is sometimes useful to politicians and social commentators—who speak of "mortgaging" our future.) Cite several instances of the use of this metaphor and comment on its effectiveness. To what extent does the metaphor help to convey Dement's central message? In your answer, discuss how a mind can be "mortgaged."

3. Have you ever experienced the sensation of driving drowsy—which Dement says should be a "red alert" to stop your car and rest? In a paragraph, describe the scene: the sensation of drowsiness, the conversation you have with yourself to stay awake, the efforts to fight off sleep (e.g., turning on the radio, opening a window, slapping your face)—and then the nodding head and the startled waking.

4. Do you respond to Dement's raising a "red alert" (paragraph 12) about driving and drowsiness any differently than you would if a parent raised the same alert? Why?

The Pittsburgh Sleep Quality Index
Daniel Buysse

In light of William Dement's cautions on the dangers of sleep debt—and also Mary Carskadon's review of the biological, behavioral, and social forces that converge to rob adolescents of sleep—we offer a tool to assess the quality of your own sleep: the Pittsburgh Sleep Quality Index, or PSQI. Because the test can be self-scored, you can get a numerical indicator of the quality of your own sleep. Daniel J. Buysse, MD, is medical director of the Sleep Evaluation Center in the department of psychiatry at the University of Pittsburgh. A past president of the American Academy of Sleep Medicine, Buysse developed the PSQI with Charles F. Reynolds, III, MD; Timothy H. Monk, PhD; Susan R. Berman; and David J. Kupfer, MD. The authors first presented the PSQI in Psychiatry Research *(May 1989) as a tool "specifically designed to measure sleep quality in clinical populations." Today, the PSQI is a widely used instrument in sleep research.*

Pittsburgh Sleep Quality Index (PSQI)

Name _____ ID # _____ Date _____ Age _____

Instructions:

The following questions relate to your usual sleep habits during the past month *only*. Your answers should indicate the most accurate reply for the *majority* of days and nights in the past month. Please answer all questions.

1. During the past month, when have you usually gone to bed at night?

                    USUAL BED TIME _____

2. During the past month, how long (in minutes) has it usually taken you to fall asleep each night?

                    NUMBER OF MINUTES _____

3. During the past month, when have you usually gotten up in the morning?

                    USUAL GETTING UP TIME _____

4. During the past month, how many hours of *actual sleep* did you get at night? (This may be different than the number of hours you spend in bed.)

                    HOURS OF SLEEP PER NIGHT _____

For each of the remaining questions, check the one best response. Please answer *all* questions.

5. During the past month, how often have you had trouble sleeping because you . . .

(a) Cannot get to sleep within 30 minutes

| Not during the past month _____ | Less than once a week _____ | Once or twice a week _____ | Three or more times a week _____ |

(b) Wake up in the middle of the night or early morning

| Not during the past month _____ | Less than once a week _____ | Once or twice a week _____ | Three or more times a week _____ |

(c) Have to get up to use the bathroom

| Not during the past month _____ | Less than once a week _____ | Once or twice a week _____ | Three or more times a week _____ |

(d) Cannot breathe comfortably

| Not during the past month _____ | Less than once a week _____ | Once or twice a week _____ | Three or more times a week _____ |

(e) Cough or snore loudly

| Not during the past month _____ | Less than once a week _____ | Once or twice a week _____ | Three or more times a week _____ |

(f) Feel too cold

Not during the past month _____	Less than once a week _____	Once or twice a week _____	Three or more times a week _____

(g) Feel too hot

Not during the past month _____	Less than once a week _____	Once or twice a week _____	Three or more times a week _____

(h) Had bad dreams

Not during the past month _____	Less than once a week _____	Once or twice a week _____	Three or more times a week _____

(i) Have pain

Not during the past month _____	Less than once a week _____	Once or twice a week _____	Three or more times a week _____

(j) Other reason(s), please describe _____

_____

How often during the past month have you had trouble sleeping because of this?

Not during the past month _____	Less than once a week _____	Once or twice a week _____	Three or more times a week _____

6. During the past month, how would you rate your sleep quality overall?

        Very good _____
        Fairly good _____
        Fairly bad _____
        Very bad _____

7. During the past month, how often have you taken medicine (prescribed or "over the counter") to help you sleep?

Not during the past month _____	Less than once a week _____	Once or twice a week _____	Three or more times a week _____

8. During the past month, how often have you had trouble staying awake while driving, eating meals, or engaging in social activity?

Not during the past month _____	Less than once a week _____	Once or twice a week _____	Three or more times a week _____

9. During the past month, how much of a problem has it been for you to keep up enough enthusiasm to get things done?

        No problem at all _____
        Only a very slight problem _____
        Somewhat of a problem _____
        A very big problem _____

10. Do you have a bed partner or roommate?

        No bed partner or roommate _____
        Partner/roommate in other room _____
        Partner in same room, but not same bed _____
        Partner in same bed _____

If you have a roommate or bed partner, ask him/her how often in the past month you have had . . .

(a) Loud snoring

Not during the past month _____	Less than once a week _____	Once or twice a week _____	Three or more times a week _____

(b) Long pauses between breaths while asleep

Not during the past month _____	Less than once a week _____	Once or twice a week _____	Three or more times a week _____

(c) Legs twitching or jerking while you sleep

Not during the past month _____	Less than once a week _____	Once or twice a week _____	Three or more times a week _____

(d) Episodes of disorientation or confusion during sleep

| Not during the past month _____ | Less than once a week _____ | Once or twice a week _____ | Three or more times a week _____ |

(e) Other restlessness while you sleep; please describe _____

_____

| Not during the past month _____ | Less than once a week _____ | Once or twice a week _____ | Three or more times a week _____ |

Scoring Instructions for the Pittsburgh Sleep Quality Index

The Pittsburgh Sleep Quality Index (PSQI) contains 19 self-rated questions and 5 questions rated by the bed partner or roommate (if one is available). Only self-rated questions are included in the scoring. The 19 self-rated items are combined to form seven "component" scores, each of which has a range of 0–3 points. In all cases, a score of "0" indicates no difficulty, while a score of "3" indicates severe difficulty. The seven component scores are then added to yield one "global" score, with a range of 0–21 points, "0" indicating no difficulty and "21" indicating severe difficulties in all areas.

Scoring proceeds as follows:

Component 1: Subjective sleep quality

Examine question #6, and assign scores as follows:

Response	Component 1 score
"Very good"	0
"Fairly good"	1
"Fairly bad"	2
"Very bad"	3

Component 1 score: _____

Component 2: Sleep latency [amount of time needed to fall asleep]

1. Examine question #2, and assign scores as follows:

Response	Score
≤ 15 minutes	0
16–30 minutes	1
31–60 minutes	2
> 60 minutes	3

Question #2 score: _____

2. Examine question #5a, and assign scores as follows:

Response	Score
Not during the past month	0
Less than once a week	1
Once or twice a week	2
Three or more times a week	3

Question #5a score: _____

3. Add #2 score and #5a score

Sum of #2 and #5a: _____

4. Assign component 2 score as follows:

Sum of #2 and #5a	Component 2 score
0	0
1–2	1
3–4	2
5–6	3

Component 2 score: _____

Component 3 Sleep duration

Examine question #4, and assign scores as follows:

Response	Component 3 score
≥ 7 hours	0
≥ 6 < 7 hours	1
≥ 5 < 6 hours	2
< 5 hours	3

Component 3 score: _____

Component 4: Habitual sleep efficiency

(1) Write the number of hours slept (question #4) here: _____
(2) Calculate the number of hours spent in bed:
         Getting up time (question #3): _____
         − Bedtime (question #1):   _____

         Number of hours spent in bed: _____
(3) Calculate habitual sleep efficiency as follows:
         (Number of hours slept/Number of hours spent in bed) × 100 = Habitual sleep efficiency (%)
              (_____/_____) × 100 = _____%
(4) Assign component 4 score as follows:

Habitual sleep efficiency %	Component 4 score
>85%	0
75–84%	1
65–74%	2
<65%	3

Component 4 score: _____

Component 5: Sleep disturbances

(1) Examine questions #5b–5j, and assign scores for *each* question as follows:

Response	Score
Not during the past month	0
Less than once a week	1
Once or twice a week	2
Three or more times a week	3

#5b score _____
c score _____
d score _____
e score _____
f score _____
g score _____
h score _____
i score _____
j score _____

(2) Add the scores for questions #5b–5j:
              Sum of #5b–5j: _____
(3) Assign component 5 score as follows:

Sum of #5b–5j	Component 5 score
0	0
1–9	1
10–18	2
19–27	3

Component 5 score: _____

Component 6: Use of sleeping medication

Examine question #7 and assign scores as follows:

Response	Component 6 score
Not during the past month	0
Less than once a week	1
Once or twice a week	2
Three or more times a week	3

Component 6 score: _____

Component 7: Daytime dysfunction

(1) Examine question #8, and assign scores as follows:

Response	Score
Never	0
Once or twice	1
Once or twice each week	2
Three or more times each week	3

Question #8 score: _____

(2) Examine question #9, and assign scores as follows:

Response	Score
No problem at all	0
Only a very slight problem	1
Somewhat of a problem	2
A very big problem	3

Question #9 score: _____

(3) Add the scores for question #8 and #9:

Sum of #8 and #9: _____

(4) Assign component 7 score as follows:

Sum of #8 and #9	Component 7 score
0	0
1–2	1
3–4	2
5–6	3

Component 7 score: _____

Global PSQI Score

Add the seven component scores together:

Global PSQI Score: _____

Discussion and Writing Suggestions

1. Complete the Pittsburgh Sleep Quality Index and compute your score, which will fall in a scale from 0 to 21 points. The higher your score, the greater your sleep difficulties. Where do you fall in the range?

2. Examine your seven "component" scores, which you will have calculated in computing your overall score. ("Sleep Latency" refers to the ease with which you fall asleep. The other six components are self-explanatory.) Which component(s) does the PSQI indicate are your strongest? Your weakest? Based on your subjective assessment of your own sleep, is the scoring accurate?

3. Did you need a formal test to determine how well you are sleeping? Were you aware that the quality of your sleep could be assessed along seven dimensions?

4. How useful do you find a numerical sleep score, as compared to an impressionistic assessment, such as "I sleep well" or "I'm a poor sleeper"? Why might sleep researchers develop an instrument that yields numerical scores?

5. If you are interested in seeing how an instrument such as the PSQI is created and clinically tested for accuracy, see the article that introduced it to the world in *Psychiatry Research* (Volume 28, No. 2, May 1989). You should be able to locate the article in your school library's electronic database—or via electronic interlibrary loan.

6. If your PSQI score suggests that you have difficulties sleeping, do you see any need to take action—especially in light of the preceding selection by William Dement? What action(s) (if any) might be appropriate?

How Sleep Debt Hurts College Students
June J. Pilcher and Amy S. Walters

The "all-nighter" is a rite of passage among many college students, who—pressed by competing schedules (and, let's be honest, the desire to have fun)—sometimes ignore the need to sleep, for 24 hours or more, in order to study for an exam or meet a paper deadline. Propped up by caffeinated beverages the next day, the student may even boast: "It was hard, but I got it done. I aced that exam." Perhaps not. Sleep researchers June Pilcher, who holds a PhD in biopsychology and teaches at Clemson University, and Amy Walters, MA, of Bradley University (when this article was published), report on an experiment that deprived students of a night's sleep and tested their cognitive functioning the next day. Both the results of these tests and the students' estimates of their performance may surprise (and deflate) you. This selection first appeared in the Journal of American College Health *(November 1997).*

A note on the specialized language of statistics: You should be able to understand this article whether or not you are familiar with the terms standard deviation, mean, *or* probability *(e.g., p <.05). Like all researchers who collect numerical information, Pilcher and Walters run their data through statistical analyses to determine if their results are significant. For a useful guide to definitions of statistical terms, see the online "Statistics Glossary," by Valerie J. Easton and John H. McColl, <http://www.stats.gla.ac.uk/steps/glossary/index.html>. Consult their "Alphabetical index of all entries."*

Abstract. The effects of sleep deprivation on cognitive performance and on psychological variables related to cognitive performance were studied in 44 college students. Participants completed the Watson-Glaser Critical Thinking Appraisal after either 24 hours of sleep deprivation or approximately 8 hours of sleep. After completing the cognitive task, the participants completed 2 questionnaires, one assessing self-reported effort, concentration, and estimated performance, the other assessing off-task cognitions. As expected, sleep-deprived participants performed significantly worse than the nondeprived participants on the cognitive task. However, the sleep-deprived participants rated their concentration and effort higher than the nondeprived participants did. In addition, the sleep-deprived participants rated their estimated performance significantly higher than the nondeprived participants did. The findings indicate that college students are not aware of the extent to which sleep deprivation negatively affects their ability to complete cognitive tasks.

1   Voluntary sleep deprivation is a common occurrence for many college students, who often partially deprive themselves of sleep during the week and compensate by increasing their sleep time over the weekend.(n1) This pattern of sleep deprivation and rebound becomes more pronounced around examination periods, sometimes resulting in 24 to 48 hours of total sleep deprivation. By depriving themselves of sleep, college students are not only increasing their feelings of sleepiness during the day, thus decreasing their ability to pay attention in class, but are also negatively affecting their ability to perform on exams.

2   It is well established that sleep deprivation of 24 hours or more leads to noticeable decrements in performance levels.(n2, n3) The psychological variables behind these decrements, however, are less clear. One theory states that decreases in performance are attributable to a decrease in the ability of the sleep-deprived person to focus the attention and effort necessary to complete the task successfully.(n4, n5) Similarly, a number of early sleep-deprivation studies concluded that the detrimental effects of sleep loss on performance result from periods of inattention called lapses.(n6-n8) Moreover, one early study specifically concluded that sleep loss leads to a decrease in attention to external stimuli.(n9) None of the earlier studies, however, attempted to assess self-reported variables that reflect changes in psychological events or thoughts that may be associated with the observed decrements in performance.

3   The effect of sleep deprivation on psychological variables associated with performance, such as self-reported estimates of attention, effort, and performance, have not been thoroughly investigated. Few studies have examined perceived effort and performance,(n11-n15) and the results from those studies have often been contradictory. For example, some researchers have suggested that sleep deprivation may affect the willingness of the individual to put forth the effort to perform well on a task more than the actual ability of the individual to perform.(n11, n12)

4   By contrast, other researchers have concluded that participants may recognize their decreased performance levels following sleep deprivation and attempt to overcome this decrease by increasing their effort.(n15) However, other studies have shown that a perceived increase in effort does not appear to overcome the detrimental effects of sleep deprivation. In one study,(n13) the participants were given a reward for better performance, which resulted in an increase in perceived effort but no change in actual performance. In addition, studies have shown that increasing amounts of sleep loss do not have a detrimental effect on participants' self-reported motivation levels.(n14, n15) As these results show,

the relationships between sleep deprivation and psychological variables associated with performance are not clearly understood.

5   Another method of examining psychological variables that may be associated with the decrease in performance following sleep deprivation is assessment of off-task cognitions. Off-task cognitions are thoughts that are not directed to the completion of the task at hand but that intrude upon concentration. These cognitions can include negative evaluations of one's performance on the task, such as "I don't know how to do this," or completely unrelated thoughts, such as "I wonder what I should have for lunch today." Only one study to date has investigated the effect of sleep deprivation on off-task cognitions,(n10) but the participants in that study were specifically selected for their high baseline levels of off-task cognitions. Conclusions, therefore, could not be drawn about the effect of sleep deprivation on off-task cognitions independent of baseline levels.

6   Sleep-deprived participants' current mood state may provide additional information about the ability of the individual to perform following sleep deprivation. One of the best documented effects of sleep deprivation and one that would be expected to decrease complex task-solving ability is an increase in self-reported sleepiness and fatigue.(n14, n16, n17)

7   Other specific mood states could also influence successful task completion. For example, if sleep deprivation has a consistent negative effect on tension or anxiety, sleep-deprived participants would be expected to have more difficulty than nondeprived participants in maintaining the necessary attention and effort to complete a complex cognitive task. Although several studies have reported that sleep deprivation decreases positive mood states and increases negative mood states,(n3, n14, n18, n19) relatively few studies have examined the effect of sleep deprivation on specific mood states.

8   Another important consideration is the effect of sleep deprivation on an individual's ability to accurately assess psychological variables, such as concentration, effort, and estimated performance. Research findings have shown that the accuracy of self-reports varies, depending upon experimental characteristics surrounding the task. For example, Johnson and colleagues(n20) found that participants' self-reports of the amount of effort they put into a task corresponded better with performance on a difficult task than on a very easy task. The researchers also found that the amount of reported effort, but not necessarily actual performance, could be increased by giving an external incentive.

9   In addition, Beyer(n21) noted that self-evaluations of performance on longer tasks are more accurate than self-evaluations of performance on shorter tasks. Self-report estimates of performance have also been shown to be altered by feedback on the accuracy of actual performance as the person completes the task.(n22) These findings indicate that self-report data on psychological variables can be manipulated by a variety of experimental conditions. One experimental condition that has not been thoroughly investigated is sleep deprivation.

10   In sum, our current study addressed three specific issues. First, does sleep loss lead to changes in self-reported levels of psychological variables related to actual performance? As measures of psychological variables, we examined self-reported levels of concentration, effort, and estimated performance and self-reported off-task cognitions while the participant completed a complex cognitive task. Because sleep

deprivation increases feelings of sleepiness and fatigue, we expected the sleep-deprived individuals to report lower levels of concentration, effort, and estimated performance and higher levels of off-task cognitions if they were capable of accurately assessing these psychological variables.

11   The second aim of our study was to determine whether sleep deprivation significantly alters mood states that may be related to performance. As specific measures of mood, we assessed feelings of tension, depression, anger, vigor, fatigue, and confusion. On the basis of a previous study that used the same mood measures,(n23) we expected sleep-deprived participants to report increased fatigue, confusion, and tension and decreased vigor.

12   The final purpose of our current study was to determine whether sleep deprivation alters people's ability to make an accurate assessment of their concentration, effort, and estimated performance. To investigate this aspect of sleep deprivation, we compared self-reported assessments with actual performance levels.

Method

Participants

13 We solicited study participants from five psychology classes, two 100-level courses, one 200-level course, and two 400-level courses. Of the original 65 volunteers, 44 (26 women and 18 men) completed the study. The mean age of the respondents, who were given extra credit points as an incentive to participate, was 20.5 years (SD = 4.37).

Materials

14 We used the Watson-Glaser Critical Thinking Appraisal (WG; The Psychological Corporation, San Antonio, TX) to measure cognitive performance. We chose the WG because it would be cognitively challenging and similar to normal testing conditions for college students in that it is a linguistic task that requires mental but no physical effort. The WG contains three portions: inference, recognition of assumptions, and deduction. To increase the similarity of the task to normal testing conditions for college students, we administered the test with a 40-minute time limit.

15   We used self-report scales to measure mood, off-task cognitions, effort, concentration, and estimated performance. To assess current mood, we used the Profile of Mood States (POMS; Educational and Industrial Testing Service, San Diego, CA). The POMS scale provides a list of 65 words describing current mood states (see Table 1). The student participants rated each word based on their current mood.

16   We assessed the number of off-task cognitions while the participant completed the WG task, using the Cognitive Interference Questionnaire (CIQ).(n24) The CIQ provides a list of types of thoughts. The participants respond by stating how often they experienced those thoughts while completing the WG task. We developed a short psychological variables questionnaire, using Likert-type scales (1 to 7), to measure self-reported estimates of effort, concentration, and estimated performance. In the written instructions for the questionnaire, participants were told to respond to the questions in relation to the WG task. A complete copy of the psychological variables questionnaire is available from

TABLE 1 Examples of Self-Report Scale Used in Study of Sleep Deprivation	
Test/question	Response/scale
Profile of Mood Status	
1. Friendly	Not at all (0) to extremely (4)
2. Tense	Not at all (0) to extremely (4)
3. Angry	Not at all (0) to extremely (4)
Cognitive Interference Questionnaire	
1. I thought about how poorly I was doing.	Never (1) to very often (5)
2. I thought about what the experimenter would think of me.	Never (1) to very often (5)
3. I thought about other activities (eg, assignments, work).	Never (1) to very often (5)
Psychological Variables Questionnaire	
1. How well were you able to concentrate on the task?	Not at all (1) to extremely (well) (7)
2. How well do you think you performed on this task?	Poorly (1) to extremely well (7)
3. How much effort did this task take?	Very little (1) to very much (7)

Note. These are examples of the types of questions to which participants were asked to respond.

the author on request. Higher numbers on each of the self-report variables represent a greater frequency of that variable. For example, higher numbers on the estimated performance scale indicate a higher level of estimated performance.

Procedures

17 The experiment began at 10 PM on a Friday night and concluded at 11 AM the next morning. Approximately 8 participants were tested each Friday night. All participants were requested in advance not to drink alcoholic beverages or take nonprescription drugs from 10 PM on Thursday night until the conclusion of the experiment. In addition, we asked all participants to get out of bed between 7 AM and 9 AM on Friday morning and not to nap during the day.

18 The experiment commenced with all participants reporting to the sleep laboratory at 10 PM on Friday night. At that time, the students were randomly assigned in a block fashion to either a sleep-deprived (n = 23) or a nondeprived group (n = 21), were given the final set of instructions for the experiment, and signed consent forms. In an effort to create realistic sleep loss and nonsleep loss conditions for college students, we chose to limit the length of sleep deprivation to 24 hours for the sleep-deprived group and to allow the nondeprived group to sleep in their own beds under normal sleeping conditions for approximately 8 hours.

19 After the meeting at the sleep laboratory on the Friday night of the experiment, the members of the nondeprived group were told to go home and sleep approximately 8 hours. They were instructed to go to bed between 11 PM and 1 AM and to get out of bed between 7 AM and 9 AM on Saturday morning. The nondeprived participants were called at 9 AM on Saturday morning to ensure that they were awake, and they were encouraged to eat breakfast before reporting to the testing site at 10 AM.

20 The sleep-deprived group remained awake under the supervision of two research assistants in the sleep laboratory. Participants interacted with each

other and with the research assistants, watched movies, played video and board games, or worked on personal projects during the night. They were allowed to bring food to eat during the night, but were asked to limit caffeinated beverages and sugary snacks to two of each. Sleep-deprived participants were escorted to a restaurant for breakfast at about 8 AM on Saturday morning. After breakfast, they were escorted to the testing area at 10:00 AM.

21   Testing took place at the university library in an isolated room of study cubicles, with one person per cubicle. To assess their compliance with instructions, we asked the participants to complete a short questionnaire that included questions on sleep times and items consumed since Thursday night. All participants then completed the POMS scale, followed by the WG. After finishing the WG, all of the participants completed the questionnaire assessing self-reported effort, concentration, and estimated performance in relation to the WG. The last 18 participants in each of the groups also filled out the CIQ. The entire testing period took less than 1 hour.

Data Analyses

22 The data from the POMS, WG, and CIQ were initially scored according to the directions given for each measure. We calculated six POMS scores (tension-anxiety, depression-dejection, anger-hostility, vigor, fatigue, and confusion-bewilderment), one WG score representing the performance percentile of the individual in relation to other college students, and three CIQ scores (off-task cognitions relevant to task, off-task cognitions irrelevant to task, and general mind wandering). We derived self-reported effort, concentration, and estimated performance from the questions on the psychological variables questionnaire. We averaged self-reported sleep data for the sleep-deprived and the nondeprived groups separately, by group, for Thursday and Friday nights.

23   All statistical analyses were completed on SAS (SAS Institute, Cary, NC). To assess whether sleep deprivation had an effect on actual performance and self-reported estimates of psychological variables and mood states, we performed multiple analysis of variance (MANOVA), by sleep condition, on all variables.

Results

24 All of the student participants reported that they slept approximately 8 hours on Thursday night. The sleep-deprived participants reported sleeping an average of 7.91 hours (SD = 1.26), whereas nondeprived participants reported sleeping an average of 7.79 hours (SD = 0.69). The wake-up times on Friday morning were very similar for both groups. The deprived group reported a mean time of getting out of bed of 8:55 AM (SD = 1.22 hours), and the nondeprived group reported a mean time of getting out of bed time of 8:30 AM (SD = 1.10 hours).

25   On Friday night, nondeprived participants reported sleeping an average of 7.92 hours (SD = 0.51 hours) and a mean time of getting out of bed on Saturday morning of 8:40 AM (SD = 0.73 hours). Two participants, one in each sleep condition, reported taking a nap of less than 30 minutes on Friday. We analyzed the data both with and without the two napping participants

	Sleep-deprived		Nondeprived	
Variables	M	SD	M	SD
Watson-Glaser	24.52	21.29	38.71	25.63[*]
Cognitive Interference Questionnaire				
Distracting task-relevant thoughts	2.36	0.62	2.22	0.53
Distracting task-irrelevant thoughts	1.59	0.70	1.58	0.58
General mind wandering	4.17	1.92	3.72	1.60
Estimated effort	4.03	1.00	3.41	0.70 [*]
Estimated concentration	4.30	1.66	3.28	1.31 [*]
Estimated performance	4.54	1.36	3.36	0.84 [***]
Profile of Mood States				
Tension/anxiety	14.22	7.30	11.19	8.05
Depression/dejection	11.96	12.08	9.86	10.22
Anger/hostility	11.65	9.00	8.00	7.46
Vigor	16.87	6.90	17.86	6.06
Fatigue	12.35	6.80	7.95	5.88 [*]
Confusion/bewilderment	10.65	5.22	5.95	4.10 [**]

TABLE 2   Means and Standard Deviations of Sleep- and Nondeprived Participant Groups

Note. Significant differences between groups: [*] $p < .05$; [**] $p < .01$; [***] $p < .001$.

included. Because the results from the two analyses were very similar, we report the results from all participants. None of the participants reported using alcohol or nonprescription drugs (except for acetaminophen) between 10 PM on Thursday and 10 AM on Saturday.

26   For means and standard deviations on the WG and the self-report tasks, see Table 2. As expected, the sleep-deprived participants performed significantly worse on the WG than the nondeprived participants did, $F(1,42) = 4.02$, $p < .05$.

27   Although we expected that sleep-deprived participants would have more difficulty concentrating on the task and, thus, would show an increase in off-task cognitions, none of the CIQ scales was significantly increased in the sleep-deprived group. Furthermore, instead of the expected decrease in self-reported concentration, as measured by the psychological variables questionnaire, the sleep-deprived participants reported higher subjective levels of concentration while completing the task than the nondeprived participants did, $F(1,42) = 5.03$, $p < .05$.

28   The sleep-deprived participants also estimated that they expended significantly more effort to complete the task than did the nondeprived participants, $F(1,42) = 5.49$, $p < .05$. Interestingly, although sleep-deprived participants actually performed worse on the WG than the nondeprived participants, the students deprived of sleep reported significantly higher levels of estimated performance than the nondeprived participants did, $F(1,42) = 11.79$, $p < .001$.

29   The sleep-deprived participants reported higher levels on five of the six POMS scales, but only the increases in the fatigue and confusion scales were significant: fatigue, $F(1,42) = 5.21$, $p < .05$; confusion, $F(1,42) = 10.88$, $p < .01$.

Discussion

30 As we expected, the results from our current study indicated that participants who were deprived of sleep for 24 hours performed significantly worse on a complex cognitive task than nondeprived participants. Although they actually performed worse, the sleep-deprived participants reported significantly higher levels of estimated performance, as well as more effort expended on the cognitive task, than the nondeprived participants did. In addition, sleep-deprived participants reported a significantly higher level of self-rated concentration than nondeprived participants did. We found no significant differences in levels of off-task cognitions between the sleep-deprived and nondeprived groups.

31 The apparent contradiction between the self-reported data on effort, concentration, and estimated performance and the actual performance level of sleep-deprived participants is somewhat surprising. It is unlikely that the disagreement between the self-reported variables and actual performance was a result of the type of task used. The Watson-Glaser task should have provided a suitable scenario for accurately assessing psychological variables because more difficult and longer tasks have been shown to result in more accurate self-estimates of both effort and performance.(n20, n21)

32 Several explanations for the disagreement between the self-report data and the actual performance levels are possible. Sleep-deprived participants may have expended more effort to complete the task, but the effort was not sufficient to overcome the performance decrements caused by being deprived of sleep. Furthermore, the increase in effort could have led the sleep-deprived participants to believe that they were performing better and concentrating more than they actually were.

33 An alternative explanation is that sleep deprivation may have negatively affected the degree to which participants recognized internal effort. In turn, this could have led the sleep-deprived participants to believe that they were expending more effort than they actually were, which may also have led to increases in estimated performance and self-rated concentration. Regardless of the mechanism behind the self-report data, the results indicated that our sleep-deprived participants did not realize the extent to which their own performances were affected by sleep loss, and they appeared to be making incorrect assumptions about their ability to concentrate and to provide the necessary effort to complete the task.

34 Interestingly, sleep deprivation did not result in the expected change in reporting off-task cognitions. Although a previous study(n10) found that participants who habitually reported distracting thoughts were more likely to do so when deprived of sleep, it appears that the effect of sleep deprivation on off-task cognitions depends on whether the sleep-deprived person regularly experiences high levels of off-task cognitions. Therefore, reporting off-task cognitions does not appear to be specifically affected by sleep deprivation, independent of baseline levels.

35 A second major finding of this research is that sleep deprivation differentially affected mood states in these college students. The current findings indicate that sleep deprivation significantly affected only the fatigue and confusion subscales on the POMS. The reported increase in fatigue and confusion could have contributed to the significant decrease in actual performance that we observed in the sleep-deprived student participants. It is interesting to note that none of the remaining

POMS subscales changed significantly in the sleep-deprived participants, indicating that some mood changes commonly ascribed to sleep deprivation, such as anger, irritability, and anxiety, were not necessarily products of 24 hours of sleep loss.

36   The current findings on mood states are very similar to those reported by Dinges and colleagues.(n23) Sleep-deprived participants in both studies reported significantly more fatigue and confusion than nondeprived participants. Dinges and colleagues reported significantly more tension and significantly less vigor in sleep-deprived participants.

37   Similarly, we noted a trend for more tension and less vigor in the sleep-deprived participants in our study. The most likely reason for the small differences between the two studies is that Dinges and colleagues collected mood data every 2 hours for a 64-hour sleep-deprivation period, whereas we collected mood data only once—immediately before the students' completion of the cognitive task. Furthermore, neither study reported a significant increase in angry or depressed feelings following sleep deprivation, indicating that sleep deprivation does not necessarily increase reports of anger and depression, as is commonly believed.

38   In sum, our findings suggest that college students are not aware of the extent to which sleep deprivation impairs their ability to complete cognitive tasks successfully because they consistently overrate their concentration and effort, as well as their estimated performance. In addition, the current data suggest that 24 hours of sleep deprivation significantly affects only fatigue and confusion and does not have a more general effect on positive or negative mood states. The practical implication of these findings is that many college students are unknowingly sabotaging their own performance by choosing to deprive themselves of sleep [while] they complete complex cognitive tasks.

References

(n1.) Hawkins J, Shaw P. Self-reported sleep quality in college students: A repeated measures approach. Sleep. 1992;15(6):545–549.

(n2.) Dinges DE. The nature of sleepiness: Causes, contexts, and consequences. In: Eating, Sleeping, and Sex. Stunkard A, Baum A, eds. Hillsdale, NJ: Erlbaum; 1988.

(n3.) Pilcher JJ, Huffcutt AI. Effects of sleep deprivation on performance: A meta-analysis. Sleep. 1996;19(4):318–326.

(n4.) Johnson LC. Sleep deprivation and performance. In: Webb WW, ed. Biological Rhythms, Sleep, and Performance. New York: Wiley; 1982.

(n5.) Meddis R. Cognitive dysfunction following loss of sleep. In: Burton E, ed. The Pathology and Psychology of Cognition. London: Methuen; 1982.

(n6.) Williams HL, Lubin A. Speeded addition and sleep loss. J EXP Psychol. 1967;73:313–317.

(n7.) Elkin AL, Murray DJ. The effects of sleep loss on short-term recognition memory. Can J Psychol. 1974;28:192–198.

(n8.) Polzella DJ. Effects of sleep-deprivation on short-term memory and recognition. J Exp Psychol. 1975;104:194–200.

(n9.) Hockey GRJ. Changes in attention allocation in a multicomponent task under loss of sleep. Br J Psychol. 1970;61(4):473–480.

(n10.) Mikulincer M, Babkoff H, Caspy T, Weiss H. The impact of cognitive interference on performance during prolonged sleep loss. Psychol Res. 1990;52:80–86.

(n11.) Kjellberg A. Sleep deprivation and some aspects of performance. Waking Sleeping. 1977;1:139–154.

(n12.) Horne JA. Why We Sleep. New York: Oxford University Press; 1988.

(n13.) Horne JA, Pettitt AN. High incentive effects on vigilance performance during 72 hours of total sleep deprivation. Acta Psychologica. 1985;58:123–139.

(n14.) Mikulincer M, Babkoff H, Caspy T, Sing H. The effects of 72 hours of sleep loss on psychological variables. Br J Psychol. 1989;80:145–162.

(n15.) Dinges DF, Kribbs NB, Steinberg KN, Powell JW. Do we lose the willingness to perform during sleep deprivation? Sleep Res. 1992;21:318.

(n16.) Angus RG, Heslegrave RJ. Effects of sleep loss on sustained cognitive performance during a command and control simulation. Behav Res Methods Instruments Computers. 1985;17:55–67.

(n17.) Linde L, Bergstrom M. The effect of one night without sleep on problem-solving and immediate recall. Psychol Res. 1992;54:127–136.

(n18.) Brendel DH, Reynolds CF III, Jennings JR, et al. Sleep stage physiology, mood, and vigilance responses to total sleep deprivation in healthy 80-year-olds and 20-year-olds. Psychophysiology. 1990;27:677–686.

(n19.) Leung L, Becker CE. Sleep deprivation and house staff performance: Update. J Occup Med. 1992;34:1153–1160.

(n20.) Johnson NE, Saccuzzo DP, Larson GE. Self-reported effort versus actual performance in information processing paradigms. J Gen Psychol. 1995;122(2):195–210.

(n21.) Beyer S. Gender differences in the accuracy of self-evaluations of performance. J Pers Soc Psychol. 1990;59(5):960–970.

(n22.) Critchfield TS. Bias in self-evaluation: Signal probability effects. J Exp Anal Behav. 1994;62:235–250.

(n23.) Dinges DF, Gillen KA, Powell JW, et al. Mood reports during total and partial sleep deprivation: Is anger inevitable? Sleep Res. 1995;24:441.

(n24.) Sarason IG, Sarason B, Keefe D, Hayes B, Shearin EN. Cognitive interference: Situational determinants and traitlike characteristics. J Pers Soc Psychol. 1986;51:215–226.

Discussion and Writing Suggestions

1. Have you ever stayed awake all night to complete schoolwork? How many college students of your acquaintance (or, perhaps, you yourself) believe that it is possible to "pull an all-nighter" without degrading your performance the next day? Does the study by Pilcher and Walters change your opinion? Explain your response.

2. The authors conclude that "college students are not aware of the extent to which sleep deprivation impairs their ability to complete cognitive tasks successfully because they consistently overrate their concentration and effort, as well as their estimated performance. . . . [M]any college

students are unknowingly sabotaging their own performance by choosing to deprive themselves of sleep [while] they complete complex cognitive tasks." To what extent do these conclusions describe you?

3. In paragraphs 32–33, the authors present several explanations to account for the discrepancy between students' "self-report data and [their] actual performance levels" on the cognitive task in the experiment. Which of these explanations seems most plausible? Why?

4. How convincing do you find the results of this study? Can you refute them? Do you find yourself *wanting* to refute them? To the extent that you are convinced, what are the odds you will stop staying awake all night to study for exams or to write papers?

5. Carefully review paragraphs 1–12 to understand how the authors justify the need to conduct their present research. Summarize how they go about making this justification. Focus on how they make their argument, not on the content of their argument.

6. Why does the experimental method lend itself to studying questions related to sleep deprivation and self-reports of concentration, effort, etc.?

7. Would you volunteer for an experiment similar to the one Pilcher and Walters conducted? Why or why not?

Starting Time and School Life
Patricia K. Kubow, Kyla L. Wahlstrom, and Amy Bemis

The Minneapolis Public School system was the first major system in the country to change school starting times to accommodate the sleep needs of adolescents. The effort represents an attempt at social engineering, the use of the best scientific evidence available (in this case, on the phase-delayed sleep of adolescents) to effect a desired change: specifically, better sleep and improved learning for students. As you might imagine, altering the start times of an entire school district was a tremendous logistical undertaking, and inevitable conflicts emerged. In the selection that follows, Patricia Kubow of Bowling Green University and Kyla Wahlstrom of the University of Minnesota Center for Applied Research and Educational Improvement report on some of the birth pangs of the Minneapolis initiative. You might read with a question in mind: Would sleep-deprived students at your former high school have benefited from a delayed start time?

Reflections from Educators and Students

1 With the 1997–98 school year in the Minneapolis Public Schools (MPS) came a change in the starting time for most of the schools in the district. It appears that Minneapolis may be the first major metropolitan school district in the

United States to undertake systemwide changes in school starting time based on the current research about adolescents and their sleep needs. The seven high schools changed from a 7:15 a.m. to an 8:40 a.m. start. . . .

2   A study is being conducted by the Center for Applied Research and Educational Improvement (CAREI) at the University of Minnesota in conjunction with the MPS to ascertain the impact of changing school starting times on the educational endeavor and on the community. The findings reveal that the changes affect the various stakeholders differently and are acutely felt at the personal level.

. . .

Findings from the High Schools

3   The focus group data from the high schools revealed that there were three main areas of concern regarding the change in starting time: its impact on students, its impact on teachers' instructional endeavors, and its impact on teachers' personal lives. Thus we developed a survey questionnaire that sought to gauge the magnitude of concern among teachers about those three areas.

Impact on students as perceived by teachers.

4   Fifty-seven percent of the teachers responding to the written survey reported that a greater number of students were more alert during the first two periods of the day than had been the case with the earlier starting time. In fact, this item generated the most agreement of any question on the survey. Sixteen percent were neutral in their answers, and 27% disagreed. Slightly more than half (51%) of the teachers also agreed or strongly agreed that they saw fewer students sleeping at their desks. Interestingly, the respondents were evenly divided (33% agreed or strongly agreed, 32% neither agreed nor disagreed, 35% disagreed or strongly disagreed) regarding the statement "I see improved student behavior in general." This finding contrasts with the findings from Edina that reported markedly improved student behavior, as evidenced by quieter behavior in the hallways between classes and less lunchroom misbehavior.

5   Teachers were evenly divided in reporting the nature of the comments (positive versus negative) they had heard from students and from parents regarding the later starting time. Twenty-five percent said that they had heard neither positive nor negative comments from students, and 40% said that no comment had been heard from parents. Although practices, extended-day programs, and rehearsals were shortened, students still arrived home at a later hour than they had the previous year, fostering parental concerns about safety and somewhat reducing student participation in after-school activities.

6   Difficulties with students' work schedules were noted by several MPS respondents, who wrote that these teenagers had less time to work or had to work later in the day in order to put in as many hours as they once had. In the study by Wahlstrom and Freeman, 15 employers of suburban high school students were asked about the impact of the later start on their businesses. Fourteen of the 15 employers agreed that there had been no negative impact from the later dismissal, because their businesses did not need the extra help until the schools

were dismissed. Minneapolis teachers observed that there appeared to be less involvement in extracurricular activities; Edina teachers did not notice any appreciable decrease in student involvement in after-school activities. Finally, both suburban and city teachers noted that some students seemed more tired at the end of the day, now that class extended an hour later into the afternoon. Additional parent feedback will be gathered in order to more fully understand the impact of the later start on students and families.

Impact on students as reported by students.

7   Minneapolis high school students in the focus groups reported general dissatisfaction with the later start's impact on after-school activities and their own schedules. The data suggest some differentiation between grade levels, with ninth-graders consistently more negative about the later start than older students. Because the after-school schedule was pushed later in the day, students reported that they were more tired, had less time to study and do homework, and had shorter practices or practices at odd hours. For example, a lack of facilities and field lights necessitated morning practices; consequently, some students had to forgo the morning sleep that was to be a benefit of the later school starting time. Moreover, there were often conflicts in the scheduling of activities, forcing students to make tough decisions about which activity to choose and reducing their opportunities to participate in more than one.

8   As did the high school staff members, students expressed concern about having to leave school during the last period to attend practices and games and about middle-schoolers' being unable to participate in senior high athletics. Students explained that the later school starting time sometimes limited the number of hours they could work, reduced their income, and affected the types of jobs available to them. The schedule changes affected not only work, sports, and studying but also opportunities for relaxation and socialization. The good news is that several students reported that they were more alert and efficient during the day, and this enabled them to complete more of their homework at school.

9   Student focus groups in the suburban high school revealed a very different, and generally positive, picture. As in Minneapolis, some students mentioned that athletic practices were moved to an early morning time, which seemed to them to negate the beneficial effects of having a later start. However, the majority of students in the suburban focus groups said that they felt less tired at the end of the day when they did their homework and that the later dismissal had not negatively affected their involvement in after-school activities. Nearly all the students in the focus groups noted that they were feeling more rested and alert for the first hour of class and that they were generally going to bed at the same time as they had been when the starting time was an hour earlier—thus they were, indeed, getting about one hour more of sleep each school night.

Impact on instructional endeavors.

10 By a slight majority, teachers reported that the later start enabled students to come to school more rested and therefore more ready for learning. The tradeoff, however, was that at the end of the day many student athletes needed to be excused from their last hour of class to get to an athletic event on time. One teacher wrote,

"Now, I lose one-half of my sixth-hour International Baccalaureate class in the fall to sports' start times." The dilemma was felt by the coaches as well as the classroom teachers: "As a teacher and a coach, I was extremely troubled that I had to excuse my student athletes from class 13 times this spring for track meets. Many of us coaches were very distressed about this situation because it goes against everything we stand for as educators." The majority sentiment about students' missing class because of sports was summed up in this comment: "Please keep in mind that the primary purpose of schools is to educate, not to run extracurricular sports programs. The coaches will have to adapt." Clearly, this is a critical issue to resolve if the later starting time is to remain in place and benefit all students, not just those who are not involved in athletics.

11   During the focus groups with teachers, the participants noted that fewer students were seeking academic help before and after school. This concern was substantiated by the written survey, in which 50% of the teachers disagreed or strongly disagreed that more students were seeking academic help before school and 60% disagreed or strongly disagreed that more students were seeking academic help after school. Again, this was in direct contrast to the finding in Edina, where teachers reported that with the later start many more students came to school early to get additional help from teachers with their homework or to prepare for a quiz. Whether these findings are related to economics and having access to a car instead of having to rely on a school bus needs to be studied further.

12   During the focus groups, the high school teachers generally agreed that the 8:40 start had a negative impact on the end of the school day, defined as the time period right after lunch through the last academic hour. Because of early dismissals for activities, sports practices, and personal appointments, many students missed the last period. As a result, teachers were unable to cover the desired amount of curriculum, and students missed class discussions, labs, and required assignments. Some students even chose electives rather than required courses because they had to miss their last class so often. This, in turn, created a high demand for certain classes during fifth hour and small classes during sixth hour.

13   The impact of the late starting time on transportation issues and on learning appeared to be vastly different between the city high schools and the suburban high school. Being in the "second tier" of the MPS's three-tiered busing schedule meant that buses arrived late much more often. This was usually because of delays that occurred during the first run for the elementary schools that started at 7:40. One teacher noted, "Tardies are still a problem with the 8:40 start time, with many students late because of late buses. This is very frustrating—almost impossible to teach when you have a continuous stream of late students." Late buses were never mentioned by teachers as an ongoing problem in the suburban district of Edina, whose high school is also in the second tier of a three-tiered transportation schedule. However, it is very important to note that the suburb is about one-seventh the size of the city in terms of square miles, and it was easier to make up time with shorter distances between neighborhoods and schools.

14   Finally, many teachers in the high schools with a later starting time commented on the positive effect the change had had on their own preparation for the instructional day. Faculty or department meetings were being held before school instead of after school, and teachers found that they were fresher for

thinking through difficult curriculum issues and had greater energy to be engaged in professional discussions. Two suburban teachers noted that they had time to incorporate the most recent world events into their daily social studies and economics lessons because they had time to go to the Internet each morning before classes began. Will the overall effect of a later start be to improve instruction and student achievement? That question is being studied at this time, and we may have some answers within the next year.

Impact on teachers' personal lives.

15 The professional and personal lives of teachers are unquestionably interdependent, and the findings from the focus groups highlighted the need to ask more definitively about teachers' personal lives on the written questionnaire. Fifty-one percent of the respondents agreed or strongly agreed with the statement "I have found that the later start time has had a positive impact on my personal schedule before school." Thirty-four percent disagreed or strongly disagreed, and only 14% were neutral. By contrast, 68% disagreed or strongly disagreed with the statement "I have found that the later start time has had a positive impact on my personal schedule after school" (with 49% of that total at the strongly disagree level). Sixteen percent were neutral, and 16% agreed or strongly agreed.

16   Those teachers who experienced a positive personal outcome from the later start cited improved health, more personal family time in the morning, greater alertness in the morning, and time to exercise in the morning before going to work. The fact that they were getting more sleep and were better rested was brought up by 16% of the teachers. One stated, "I did not get more and more exhausted as the year progressed as I formerly did," while another reflected, "I realized in May that in years past I've been totally sleep deprived and acted as such!"

17   The negative outcomes from the later start were a strong theme in the focus groups and were even slightly more prevalent on the written questionnaire. The most often mentioned personal reason for disliking the later starting time was that it resulted in having to drive in heavier traffic both to and from school. Teachers also reported being more tired at the end of the day than in previous years. The combination of personal obligations and teacher fatigue was perceived by Minneapolis faculty members as having decreased teacher supervision of after-school activities.

Overall view of the high school changes.

18 The teachers were asked to complete the statement "My feelings, overall, about the later start are . . . " with one of the following responses: "Hate it," "Don't like it," "Neutral," "Like it," or "Love it." Only slightly more respondents (45%) chose "like it" or "love it" than chose "don't like it" or "hate it" (44%). Only 11% felt neutral. As for the strongest responses, 23% chose "love it," and 15% chose "hate it."

19   Finally, the following question was asked: What would be the ideal starting time for school? Although 44% of respondents had said that they either hated or did not like the new starting time, the responses to this question made it clear that very few (3.5%) wanted to return to the previous starting time of 7:15 a.m.

The most popular time for Minneapolis high schools to start, according to these teachers, was 8 a.m. . . . Indeed, almost three-quarters of the teachers surveyed (72.7%) chose a starting time of 8 a.m. or later.

. . .

Conclusion

20 The findings of [this] study raise questions about whether a universal starting time or a flexible one is best for students. It is unlikely that any one schedule could accommodate the needs of all stakeholders. Given this fact, the district could investigate the possibility of creating flexible schedules so as to offer viable options for students, families, and school personnel. Several respondents to the high school teachers' questionnaire spontaneously made such suggestions.

- "I would rather restructure the school day and schedule. Provide more learning (not just credit makeup or remediation) for students after 2 p.m.—especially courses that are interdisciplinary."
- "Flexible starts/endings would be ideal."
- "At the high school, flexible starting time should be an option. Athletes need the early time. Students who work need the early start, morning people like the early start, but others benefit from the later start."
- "I think we should have an early start and a late start. Have school start at 7:15 for those who want to come then and another start at 9:15 for those who like it late. Everyone goes a full six periods, but the early ones get out two hours sooner (or take an extra class). There certainly are enough students and staff who would like both start times."

21 One teacher noted, "The 7:15 a.m. starting time was a death knell for period 1 (and often period 2)." The research on adolescent sleep patterns is indicating that some change in school starting times may be beneficial. . . .

22 Educators who have experienced the change to a later start as positive speak forcefully about its impact. "Even though the change in starting time has affected after-school activities, I feel that the benefits—of having school hours more tuned in to 'teenage clocks'—are significant," said one teacher. Another commented, "If you are involved in any kind of after-school activity, it can be difficult to take care of personal business, but the positives for the kids outweigh this single personal consideration." And finally, a word of caution from a teacher about hasty decisions in any direction: "This change has been a long time in coming—please give it a long trial before making a judgment." The effects on teaching and learning are only beginning to emerge. If we are to know anything of substance, the medical and educational research into this issue and its outcomes must continue for several years to come.

Discussion and Writing Suggestions

1. The experiment in the Minneapolis Public Schools "to undertake systemwide changes in school starting time based on the current research about adolescents and their sleep needs" is an example of

social engineering: changes in public policy based on the desire to bring about a particular effect. Based on your reading of this report, what factors make social engineering a highly complex effort? What aspects of real social settings make unintended consequences likely?

2. There are many stakeholders in the experiment on delayed start times in the Minneapolis Public Schools: students, parents, teachers, administrators, coaches, staff (cafeteria workers, for instance), bus drivers, and others. With so many people affected by *whatever* time school is set to begin, how would you, as a superintendent of schools in your hometown, weigh the competing needs of stakeholders and select an optimal start time? How would you define "optimal"? Whose needs would be paramount? Why?

3. Earlier in this chapter, the noted adolescent sleep researcher Mary Carskadon writes: "Can these problems [associated with sleep-deprived adolescents] be solved by delaying the starting time for school as adolescents move into the pubertal years? Not entirely. Moving the opening bell to a later time may help many teens with the mismatch between biological time and scholastic time, but it will not provide more hours in the day." Your comments? To what extent are their days so crammed with activities that high school students will be left sleep deprived *regardless* of start times?

4. Would a delayed start time have addressed any significant problems at your high school? How might teachers have responded to the later start time? Students? Coaches? Parents?

5. Several of those interviewed in the Minneapolis study supported a "flexible starting time" for high schools. Colleges have essentially adopted this approach by scheduling classes throughout the day (as opposed to having all students begin at a fixed time each morning). Given their flexible schedules, do you think college students are any less sleep deprived than high school students? What implications does your answer hold for the Minnesota experiment and others like it?

6. The authors of this article based their research report on surveys and focus groups, a very different strategy from the lab-based research of Pilcher and Walters (see pages 385–394). Consider both types of research. What can researchers do in a lab that they cannot do in field research via surveys or focus groups? And, vice versa, what is possible with a broad survey approach that is not possible in a lab?

Synthesis Activities

1. Explain the fundamentals of sleep for an audience (perhaps someone like yourself before reading this chapter) who regards sleep as a passive state characterized by the absence of wakefulness. Make clear that sleep is ubiquitous (fruit flies, fish, cats, alligators, and humans all

sleep); is an active, not a passive behavior; has an "architecture" that changes over one's life; can be especially troubling for adolescents; and can be delayed or otherwise disrupted in ways that cause sleep debt and associated problems. Refer to the *Harvard Special Health Report* ("Improving Sleep") and to the selections by the National Sleep Foundation, Dement, Carskadon, and Pilcher and Walters.

2. Use one or more of the selections in this chapter to analyze the quality of your sleep in a typical week. As part of your analysis, be sure to take (and score) the Pittsburgh Sleep Quality Index. Recall that the purpose of any analysis is to increase understanding of a little-understood phenomenon—in this case, *your* sleep patterns. What principle(s) or definition(s) will you use from the chapter readings to guide your analysis? Follow the general format for writing analyses on page 111.

3. Three selections in this chapter first appeared in journals or books intended for professionals interested in sleep: those by Pilcher and Walters; Carskadon; and Kubow, Wahlstrom, and Bemis. Using standards of good writing established by your composition instructor and textbooks, evaluate the presentation of one of these three selections. In your critique, focus on the author's or authors' success at communicating a key idea. What are your standards for evaluation: a writer's ability to organize at the global, section, or paragraph level? Sentence style? Word choice? Conciseness? Tone? How many criteria will you use in making your overall assessment? Follow the general format for writing critiques on page 41.

4. In an explanatory synthesis, discuss phase-delayed sleep: whom it affects; its biological, behaviorial, and social causes; its related problems; and its remedies (to the extent they exist). Refer to chapter selections as needed, but be sure to reference Dement; Carskadon; and Kubow, Wahlstrom, and Bemis. Follow the general format for writing syntheses on pages 58–59.

5. Discuss why cramming for an examination (staying awake all night to study or to write a paper) can be a mistake. Your discussion should include an account of sleep debt and its consequences. Refer to chapter selections as needed, but be sure to reference Dement, Carskadon, and Pilcher and Walters. Follow the general format for writing syntheses on pages 58–59.

6. Draw upon the selections in this chapter to create an advertising campaign aimed at promoting good sleep hygiene among college students. The campaign might take the form of a brochure, a poster, a series of e-mails, or a Web site. In your campaign, explain the importance of sleep, particularly for adolescents. Create a separate Works Cited page for the sources you reference in your campaign.

7. Argue for or against the proposition that the health office at your college should set up an educational program to promote good

sleep hygiene among students. In developing your argument, refer to the scientific evidence on adolescent sleep needs and sleep debt and its consequences. Among the selections you refer to should be those by the National Sleep Foundation, Dement, Carskadon, and Pilcher and Walters.

8. Argue for or against the proposition that the start time of the high school you attended should be later than it currently is. In your argument, consider the scientific evidence relating to problems associated with phase-delayed sleep. Consider also the complications of coordinating schedules among the various stakeholders in any change of start time: for instance, among students, teachers, parents, coaches, and staff. In your paper, refer to the selections by the National Sleep Foundation, Dement, Carskadon, and Kubow, Wahlstrom, and Bemis.

9. Explain your reactions to the reading selections in this chapter. What you have learned about sleep will inevitably find its way into this paper. But keep the focus on your *reactions* to learning about one or more of the following: sleep debt and cramming for exams; sleep debt and the dangers of drowsiness while driving; the problems caused when adolescent sleep patterns collide with the scheduling demands of the business and scholastic worlds; the rise in use of sleep medications among adolescents and young adults. Let your interest in the topic dictate the specific focus of your explanation.

RESEARCH ACTIVITIES

1. Sleep specialists do not agree on the purpose of sleep. Investigate theories of why we—as well as other creatures—sleep. The oldest theories—based largely on speculation—date to the times of Aristotle and earlier. In recent decades biologists and physicians have proposed theories based on current scientific research.

2. Research "unihemispheric sleep," the phenomenon that allows certain species (of dolphins and birds, for instance) to put one half of their brain to sleep at a time. Which species exhibit this behavior? Why? What are the mechanisms involved?

3. Discuss references to sleep in one or more artistic works. Macbeth's and Lady Macbeth's troubled sleep following their murder of King Duncan comes to mind. You might consider "The Pains of Sleep" (<http://etext.virginia.edu/stc/ Coleridge/poems/ Pains_of_Sleep.html>), the work of the famous insomniac Samuel Taylor Coleridge. You might consider, as well, cinematic works like the Al Pacino film *Insomnia* (2002), directed by Christopher Nolan, or the unusual dreamlike visions of Richard Linklater in films like *Waking Life* (2001) and *A Scanner Darkly* (2006).

4. Research and write an overview of sleep disorders (there are 84, divided into four general classifications). If you find yourself especially intrigued by one disorder—for instance, sleep apnea, restless leg syndrome, or night terrors—focus your research on that.

5. Investigate sleep specialists' use of the polysomnograph to monitor body functions as patients sleep in a laboratory. What does the polysomnograph measure? How is the patient monitored? How is the polysomnograph read and interpreted? What role does it play in the diagnosis and treatment of sleep disorders?

6. Several authors in this chapter discuss circadian rhythm. Conduct more research into the "internal clock" that determines for us (and other creatures) patterns of wakefulness and sleep. What is this clock? Where is it located? When, in response to what, and how did it evolve?

7. Investigate NASA's interest in the sleep problems of astronauts, a select group whose accelerated daily exposure to patterns of light and dark plays havoc with their sleep. What, precisely, are the problems? What solutions is NASA devising? (You might also want to investigate the sleep challenges that NASA anticipates for long-distance missions to Mars and beyond.)

8. Investigate sleep researchers' inquiries into sleep deprivation. Begin with a close reading of Pilcher and Walters in this chapter. Consult their reference list, and see especially the pioneering work of William Dement, whose scholarship is also represented in this chapter.

9. Investigate the history or promotion of sleeping aids—medicinal (for instance, opiates, melatonin, and the new prescription drugs), behavioral (what's "counting sheep" all about?), and mechanical (white noise machines, etc.). If one particular area of this research captures your attention (for example, the business aspects of sleeping aids, or the social consequences), pursue that area, rather than preparing a broad overview.

10. The inventor of psychoanalysis, Sigmund Freud, initially made his reputation with his startling theories about the interpretation of dreams. (In Freud's theories, people and objects occurring in dreams were frequently symbolic.) Investigate one or more current theories on the content of the dreams that occur during REM sleep, as discussed, for example, in the *Harvard Health Letter*. How does the content of dreams correlate with the dreamer's life?

11. Several authors in this chapter discuss the sometimes catastrophic consequences (such as the *Exxon Valdez* disaster) of sleep deprivation. In some cases, insufficient sleep time is built into the job—for example, the duty schedules of some airline flight crews, long-distance truck drivers, or medical interns. Select one such

job area, and discuss the particular problems caused by enforced (or voluntary) sleep deprivation. Or discuss recent attempts to address such long-standing problems with policies designed to ensure that people get sufficient sleep so as not to pose a danger to themselves or others.

9 New and Improved: Six Decades of Advertising

Possibly the most memorable ad campaign of the twentieth century (dating from the late 1920s) takes the form of a comic strip. A bully kicks sand into the face of a skinny man relaxing on the beach with his girlfriend. Humiliated, the skinny man vows to get even. "Don't bother, little boy!" huffs the scornful girlfriend, who promptly dumps him. At home, the skinny man kicks a chair in frustration, declares that he's sick of being a scarecrow, and says that if Charles Atlas (once a "97-lb. weakling" himself) can give him a "real body," he'll send for his FREE book. In the next frame, the once-skinny man, now transformed into a hunk, thanks to Atlas's "Dynamic Tension" fitness program, admires himself in front of the mirror: "Boy, it didn't take Atlas long to do this for me. Look, how those muscles bulge! . . . That big stiff won't dare insult me now!" Back on the beach, the bully is decked by the once-skinny man, as his adoring girlfriend looks on: "Oh Mac! You are a real man after all!"

Crude? Undoubtedly. But variations of this ad, which made Atlas a multimillionaire, ran for decades (his company is still in business). Like other successful ads, it draws its power from skillful appeals to almost primitive urges—in this particular case, the urge to gain dominance over a rival for the attention of the opposite sex. Of course, effective ads don't always work on such a primal level. Another famous ad of the 1920s appeals to our need to gain respect from others for higher accomplishments than punching out opponents. Headlined "They Laughed When I Sat Down at the Piano—But When I Started to Play. . . !" the text offers a first-person account of a man who sits down to play the piano at a party. As he does so, the guests make good-natured fun of him; but once he began to play, "a tense silence fell on the guests. The laughter died on their lips as if by magic. I played through the first bars of Liszt's immortal 'Liebenstraum.' I heard gasps of amazement. My friends sat breathless—spellbound." For 16 additional paragraphs, the writer goes on to detail the effect of his playing upon the guests and to explain how "You, too, can now *teach yourself* to be an accomplished musician—right at home," by purchasing the program of the U.S. School of Music. Again, the reader is encouraged to send for the free booklet. And by the way, "Forget the old-fashioned idea that you need 'special talent'" to play an instrument.

The ubiquity of advertising is a fact of modern life. In fact, advertising can be traced as far back as ancient Roman times when pictures were inscribed on walls to promote gladiatorial contests. In those days, however, the illiteracy of most of the population and the fact that goods were made by hand and could not be mass produced limited the need for more widespread advertising. One of the first American advertisers was Benjamin Franklin, who pioneered the use of large headlines and made strategic use of white space. But advertising as the mass phenomenon we know is a product of the twentieth century, when the United States became an industrial nation—and particularly of the post–World War II period, when a prosperous economy created our modern consumer society, marked by the middle-class acquisition of goods, the symbols of status, success, style, and social acceptance. Today, we are surrounded not only by a familiar array of billboards, print ads, and broadcast ads, but also by the Internet, which has given us "spam," the generic name for an entire category of digital pitches for debt reduction, low mortgage rates, and enhanced body parts—compared to which the average Buick ad in a glossy magazine reads like great literature.

Advertisements are more than just appeals to buy; they are windows into our psyches and our culture. They reveal our values, our (not-so-hidden) desires, our yearnings for a different lifestyle. For example, the Marlboro man, that quintessence of taciturn cowboy masculinity, at home only in the wide open spaces of Marlboro Country, is a mid-twentieth-century American tribute to (what is perceived as) nineteenth-century American values, popularized in hundreds of westerns. According to James Twitchell, a professor of English and advertising at the University of Florida, "He is what we have for royalty, distilled manhood. . . . The Marlboro Man needs to tell you nothing. He carries no scepter, no gun. He never even speaks. Doesn't need to." He is also the product of a bolt of advertising inspiration: Previously, Marlboro had been marketed—unsuccessfully—as a woman's cigarette. Another example of how ads reveal culture is the memorable campaign for the Volkswagen Beetle in the 1960s. That campaign spoke to the counterculture mentality of the day: Instead of appealing to the traditional automobile customer's desire for luxury, beauty, size, power, and comfort, Volkswagen emphasized how small, funny-looking, bare-bones—but economical and sensible—their cars were. On the other hand, snob appeal—at an affordable price, of course—has generally been a winning strategy. In the 1980s and 1990s Grey Poupon mustard ran a successful campaign of TV commercials featuring one Rolls-Royce pulling up alongside another. A voice from one vehicle asks, "Pardon me; do you have any Grey Poupon?" "But of course!" replies a voice in the other car; and a hand with a jar of mustard reaches out from the window of the second car to pass to the unseen occupant of the first car. This campaign is a perfect illustration of what University of California at Davis history professor Roland Marchand calls the appeal of the democracy of goods: "the wonders of modern mass production and distribution enable . . . everyone to enjoy society's most desirable pleasures, conveniences, or benefits."

So pervasive and influential has advertising become that it has created a significant backlash among social critics. Among the most familiar charges against advertising: It fosters materialism, it psychologically manipulates people to buy things they don't need, it perpetuates gender and racial stereotypes (particularly in its illustrations), it is deceptive, it is offensive, it debases the language, and it is omnipresent—we cannot escape it. Although arguing the truth or falsity of these assertions makes for lively debate, our focus in this chapter is not on the ethics of advertising, but rather on how it works. What makes for successful advertising? How do advertisers—and by advertisers we mean not only manufacturers but also the agencies they hire to produce their advertisements—pull our psychological levers to influence us to buy (or think favorably of) their products? What are the textual and graphic components of an effective advertisement—of an effective advertising campaign? How—if at all—has advertising evolved over the past several decades?

Advertising has seen significant changes in the six decades since the end of World War II. It is unlikely that the comic strip Charles Atlas ad or the verbose "They Laughed When I Sat Down at the Piano" ad would succeed today. Both seem extremely dated. More representative of today's advertising style is the successful milk campaign; each ad features a celebrity such as Bernie Mac or Lauren Bacall with a milk mustache, a headline that says simply "got milk?", and a few short words of text supposedly spoken by the pictured celebrity. But the changes in advertising during the six decades covered in this chapter are more of style than of substance. On the whole, the similarities between an ad produced in the 1950s and one produced today are more significant than the differences. Of course, hair and clothing styles change with the times, message length recedes, and both text and graphics assume a lesser degree of apple-pie social consensus on values. But on the whole, the same psychological appeals, the same principles of headline and graphic design that worked 60 years ago, continue to work today. We choose one automobile over another, for instance, less because our vehicle of choice gets us from point A to point B, than because we invest it— or the advertiser does—with rich psychological and cultural values. In 1957 the French anthropologist and philosopher Roland Barthes wrote (in a review of a French automobile, the Citroën DS), "I think that cars today are almost the exact equivalent of the great Gothic cathedrals: I mean the supreme creation of an era, conceived with passion by unknown artists, and consumed in image if not in usage by a whole population which appropriates them as a purely magical object." It's not known whether Barthes ever considered a career as an advertising copywriter; but he probably would have been a good one.

How advertising works, then, is the subject of the present chapter. By applying a variety of theoretical and practical perspectives to a gallery of six decades of advertisements (and to other ads of your own choosing), you'll be able to practice your analytical skills upon one of the more fascinating areas of American mass culture. The main subjects of your analyses are represented later in this chapter by a portfolio of 42 advertisements that originally appeared in such magazines as *Time, Newsweek, U.S. News and World Report,* and *Sunset.* For ease of comparison and contrast, most of the ads can be classified into a relatively few categories: cigarettes, alcohol, automobiles, and food, with a number of other ads in the "miscellaneous" category. These ads have been selected for their inherent interest, as well as for the variety of tools that have been employed to communicate the message, what some advertisers call the USP—the Unique Selling Proposition.

The first part of the chapter, however, consists of a number of articles or passages from books, each representing an analytical tool, a particular perspective from which one can view individual advertisements. In the first selection, "Advertising's Fifteen Basic Appeals," Jib Fowles offers a psychological perspective. Fowles identifies and discusses the most common needs to which advertisers attempt to appeal. Among these are the need for sex, the need for affiliation with other people, the need for dominance, and the need for autonomy. In "Making the Pitch in Print Advertising," Courtland L. Bovée et al. outline the key elements of the textual component of advertising—including headlines, subheadlines, and body text. In "Elements of Effective Layout," Dorothy Cohen discusses the key components of advertising graphics: balance, proportion, movement, unity, clarity and simplicity, and emphasis.

Finally, as indicated above, the chapter continues and concludes with "A Portfolio of Advertisements: 1945–2003," a collection of 42 ads for various products published in popular magazines in the United States and Great Britain during the last 60 years.

Charles O'Neill, an independent marketing consultant, has written, "Perhaps, by learning how advertising works, we can become better equipped to sort out content from hype, product values from emotions, and salesmanship from propaganda." We hope that the selections in this chapter will allow you to do just that, as well as to develop a greater understanding of one of the most pervasive components of American mass culture.

Advertising's Fifteen Basic Appeals
Jib Fowles

Our first selection provides what you will likely find the single most useful analytical tool for studying advertisements. Drawing upon studies of numerous ads and upon interviews with subjects conducted by Harvard psychologist Henry A. Murray, Fowles developed a set of 15 basic appeals he believes to be at the heart of American advertising. These appeals, according to Fowles and to Murray, are directed primarily to the "lower brain," to those "unfulfilled urges and motives swirling in the bottom half of [our] minds," rather than to the part of the brain that processes our more rational thoughts and impulses. As you read Fowles's article and his descriptions of the individual appeals, other examples from contemporary print and broadcast ads may occur to you. You may find it useful to jot down these examples for later incorporation into your responses to the discussion and synthesis questions that follow.

Jib Fowles has written numerous articles and books on the popular media, including Mass Advertising as Social Forecast: A Method for Futures Research *(1976),* Why Viewers Watch: A Reappraisal of Television's Effects *(1992),* Advertising and Popular Culture *(1996), and* The Case for Television Violence *(1999). This selection first appeared in* Etc. *39:3 (1982) and was reprinted in* Advertising and Popular Culture.

Emotional Appeals

1   The nature of effective advertisements was recognized full well by the late media philosopher Marshall McLuhan. In his *Understanding Media,* the first sentence of the section on advertising reads, "The continuous pressure is to create ads more and more in the image of audience motives and desires."

2   By giving form to people's deep-lying desires, and picturing states of being that individuals privately yearn for, advertisers have the best chance of arresting attention and affecting communication. And that is the immediate goal of advertising: to tug at our psychological shirtsleeves and slow us down long enough for a word or two about whatever is being sold. We glance at a picture of a solitary rancher at work, and "Marlboro" slips into our minds.

3   Advertisers (I'm using the term as a shorthand for both the products' manufacturers, who bring the ambition and money to the process, and the advertising agencies, who supply the know-how) are ever more compelled to invoke consumers' drives and longings; this is the "continuous pressure" McLuhan refers to. Over the past century, the American marketplace has grown increasingly congested as more and more products have entered into the frenzied competition after the public's dollars. The economies of other nations are quieter than ours since the volume of goods being hawked does not so greatly exceed demand. In some economies, consumer wares are scarce enough that no advertising at all is necessary. But in the United States, we go to the other extreme. In order to stay in business, an advertiser must strive to cut through the considerable commercial hub-bub by any means available—including the emotional appeals that some observers have held to be abhorrent and underhanded.

4   The use of subconscious appeals is a comment not only on conditions among sellers. As time has gone by, buyers have become stoutly resistant to advertisements. We live in a blizzard of these messages and have learned to turn up our collars and ward off most of them. A study done a few years ago at Harvard University's Graduate School of Business Administration ventured that the average American is exposed to some 500 ads daily from television, newspapers, magazines, radio, billboards, direct mail, and so on. If for no other reason than to preserve one's sanity, a filter must be developed in every mind to lower the number of ads a person is actually aware of—a number this particular study estimated at about seventy-five ads per day. (Of these, only twelve typically produced a reaction—nine positive and three negative, on the average.) To be among the few messages that do manage to gain access to minds, advertisers must be strategic, perhaps even a little underhanded at times.

5   There are assumptions about personality underlying advertisers' efforts to communicate via emotional appeals, and while these assumptions have stood the test of time, they still deserve to be aired. Human beings, it is presumed, walk around with a variety of unfulfilled urges and motives swirling in the

bottom half of their minds. Lusts, ambitions, tendernesses, vulnerabilities—they are constantly bubbling up, seeking resolution. These mental forces energize people, but they are too crude and irregular to be given excessive play in the real world. They must be capped with the competent, sensible behavior that permits individuals to get along well in society. However, this upper layer of mental activity, shot through with caution and rationality, is not receptive to advertising's pitches. Advertisers want to circumvent this shell of consciousness if they can, and latch on to one of the lurching, subconscious drives.

6   In effect, advertisers over the years have blindly felt their way around the underside of the American psyche, and by trial and error have discovered the softest points of entree, the places where their messages have the greatest likelihood of getting by consumers' defenses. As McLuhan says elsewhere, "Gouging away at the surface of public sales resistance, the ad men are constantly breaking through into the *Alice in Wonderland* territory behind the looking glass, which is the world of subrational impulses and appetites."

7   An advertisement communicates by making use of a specially selected image (of a supine female, say, or a curly-haired child, or a celebrity) which is designed to stimulate "subrational impulses and desires" even when they are at ebb, even if they are unacknowledged by their possessor. Some few ads have their emotional appeal in the text, but for the greater number by far the appeal is contained in the artwork. This makes sense, since visual communication better suits more primal levels of the brain. If the viewer of an advertisement actually has the importuned motive, and if the appeal is sufficiently well fashioned to call it up, then the person can be hooked. The product in the ad may then appear to take on the semblance of gratification for the summoned motive. Many ads seem to be saying, "If you have this need, then this product will help satisfy it." It is a primitive equation, but not an ineffective one for selling.

8   Thus, most advertisements appearing in national media can be understood as having two orders of content. The first is the appeal to deep-running drives in the minds of consumers. The second is information regarding the good[s] or service being sold: its name, its manufacturer, its picture, its packaging, its objective attributes, its functions. For example, the reader of a brassiere advertisement sees a partially undraped but blandly unperturbed woman standing in an otherwise commonplace public setting, and may experience certain sensations; the reader also sees the name "Maidenform," a particular brassiere style, and, in tiny print, words about the material, colors, price. Or, the viewer of a television commercial sees a demonstration with four small boxes labeled 650, 650, 650, and 800; something in the viewer's mind catches hold of this, as trivial as thoughtful consideration might reveal it to be. The viewer is also exposed to the name "Anacin," its bottle, and its purpose.

9   Sometimes there is an apparently logical link between an ad's emotional appeal and its product information. It does not violate common sense that Cadillac automobiles be photographed at country clubs, or that Japan Air Lines be associated with Orientalia. But there is no real need for the linkage to have a bit of reason behind it. Is there anything inherent to the connection between Salem cigarettes and mountains, Coke and a smile, Miller Beer and comradeship? The link being forged in minds between product and appeal is a pre-logical one.

10   People involved in the advertising industry do not necessarily talk in the terms being used here. They are stationed at the sending end of this communications channel, and may think they are up to any number of things—Unique Selling Propositions, explosive copywriting, the optimal use of demographics or psychographics, ideal media buys, high recall ratings, or whatever. But when attention shifts to the receiving end of the channel, and focuses on the instant of reception, then commentary becomes much more elemental: an advertising message contains something primary and primitive, an emotional appeal, that in effect is the thin end of the wedge, trying to find its way into a mind. Should this occur, the product information comes along behind.

11   When enough advertisements are examined in this light, it becomes clear that the emotional appeals fall into several distinguishable categories, and that every ad is a variation on one of a limited number of basic appeals. While there may be several ways of classifying these appeals, one particular list of fifteen has proven to be especially valuable.

Advertisements can appeal to:

1. The need for sex
2. The need for affiliation
3. The need to nurture
4. The need for guidance
5. The need to aggress
6. The need to achieve
7. The need to dominate
8. The need for prominence
9. The need for attention
10. The need for autonomy
11. The need to escape
12. The need to feel safe
13. The need for aesthetic sensations
14. The need to satisfy curiosity
15. Physiological needs: food, drink, sleep, etc.

Murray's List

12 Where does this list of advertising's fifteen basic appeals come from? Several years ago, I was involved in a research project which was to have as one segment an objective analysis of the changing appeals made in post-World War II American advertising. A sample of magazine ads would have their appeals coded into the categories of psychological needs they seemed aimed at. For this content analysis to happen, a complete roster of human motives would have to be found.

13   The first thing that came to mind was Abraham Maslow's famous four-part hierarchy of needs. But the briefest look at the range of appeals made in advertising was enough to reveal that they are more varied, and more profane, than Maslow had cared to account for. The search led on to the work of psychologist Henry A. Murray, who together with his colleagues at the Harvard Psychological Clinic has constructed a full taxonomy of needs. As described in *Explorations in*

Personality, Murray's team had conducted a lengthy series of in-depth interviews with a number of subjects in order to derive from scratch what they felt to be the essential variables of personality. Forty-four variables were distinguished by the Harvard group, of which twenty were motives. The need for achievement ("to overcome obstacles and obtain a high standard") was one, for instance; the need to defer was another; the need to aggress was a third; and so forth.

14   Murray's list had served as the groundwork for a number of subsequent projects. Perhaps the best-known of these was David C. McClelland's extensive study of the need for achievement, reported in his *The Achieving Society*. In the process of demonstrating that a people's high need for achievement is predictive of later economic growth, McClelland coded achievement imagery and references out of a nation's folklore, songs, legends, and children's tales.

15   Following McClelland, I too wanted to cull the motivational appeals from a culture's imaginative product—in this case, advertising. To develop categories expressly for this purpose, I took Murray's twenty motives and added to them others he had mentioned in passing in *Explorations in Personality* but not included on the final list. The extended list was tried out on a sample of advertisements, and motives which never seemed to be invoked were dropped. I ended up with eighteen of Murrays' motives, into which 770 print ads were coded. The resulting distribution is included in the 1976 book *Mass Advertising as Social Forecast*.

16   Since that time, the list of appeals has undergone refinements as a result of using it to analyze television commercials. A few more adjustments stemmed from the efforts of students in my advertising classes to decode appeals; tens of term papers surveying thousands of advertisements have caused some inconsistencies in the list to be hammered out. Fundamentally, though, the list remains the creation of Henry Murray. In developing a comprehensive, parsimonious inventory of human motives, he pinpointed the subsurface mental forces that are the least quiescent and most susceptible to advertising's entreaties.

Fifteen Appeals

17   **1. Need for Sex.**   Let's start with sex, because this is the appeal which seems to pop up first whenever the topic of advertising is raised. Whole books have been written about this one alone, to find a large audience of mildly titillated readers. Lately, due to campaigns to sell blue jeans, concern with sex in ads has redoubled.

18   The fascinating thing is not how much sex there is in advertising, but how little. Contrary to impressions, unambiguous sex is rare in these messages. Some of this surprising observation may be a matter of definition: the Jordache ads with the lithe, blouse-less female astride a similarly clad male is clearly an appeal to the audience's sexual drives, but the same cannot be said about Brooke Shields* in the Calvin Klein commercials. Directed at young women and their credit-card carrying mothers, the image of Miss Shields instead invokes the need

---

* Brooke Shields (b. 1965) is a model (at age 3 she was the Ivory Snow baby), as well as a stage (*Grease*), TV, and film actress; her most well-known films are *Pretty Baby* (1978) and *Blue Lagoon* (1980).

to be looked at. Buy Calvins and you'll be the center of much attention, just as Brooke is, the ads imply; they do not primarily inveigle their target audience's need for sexual intercourse.

19   In the content analysis reported in *Mass Advertising as Social Forecast* only two percent of ads were found to pander to this motive. Even *Playboy* ads shy away from sexual appeals: a recent issue contained eighty-three full-page ads, and just four of them (or less than five percent) could be said to have sex on their minds.

20   The reason this appeal is so little used is that it is too blaring and tends to obliterate the product information. Nudity in advertising has the effect of reducing brand recall. The people who do remember the product may do so because they have been made indignant by the ad; this is not the response most advertisers seek.

21   To the extent that sexual imagery is used, it conventionally works better on men than women; typically a female figure is offered up to the male reader. A Black Velvet liquor advertisement displays an attractive woman wearing a tight black outfit, recumbent under the legend, "Feel the Velvet." The figure does not have to be horizontal, however, for the appeal to be present as National Airlines revealed in its "Fly me" campaign. Indeed, there does not even have to be a female in the ad; "Flick my Bic"* was sufficient to convey the idea to many.

22   As a rule, though, advertisers have found sex to be a tricky appeal, to be used sparingly. Less controversial and equally fetching are the appeals to our need for affectionate human contact.

23   **2. Need for Affiliation.**   American mythology upholds autonomous individuals, and social statistics suggest that people are ever more going it alone in their lives, yet the high frequency of affiliative appeals in ads belies this. Or maybe it does not: maybe all the images of companionship are compensation for what Americans privately lack. In any case, the need to associate with others is widely invoked in advertising and is probably the most prevalent appeal. All sorts of goods and services are sold by linking them to our unfulfilled desires to be in good company.

24   According to Henry Murray, the need for affiliation consists of desires "to draw near and enjoyably cooperate or reciprocate with another; to please and win affection of another; to adhere and remain loyal to a friend." The manifestations of this motive can be segmented into several different types of affiliation, beginning with romance.

25   Courtship may be swifter nowadays, but the desire for pair-bonding is far from satiated. Ads reaching for this need commonly depict a youngish male and female engrossed in each other. The head of the male is usually higher than the female's, even at this late date; she may be sitting or leaning while he is standing. They are not touching in the Smirnoff vodka ads, but obviously there is an intimacy, sometimes frolicsome, between them. The couple does touch for

---

* "Flick my Bic" became a famous and successful slogan in advertisements for Bic cigarette lighters during the late 1970s and 1980s. Fowles hints at the not-too-subtle sexual implications of the line.

Martell Cognac when "The moment was Martell." For Wind Song perfume they have touched, and "Your Wind Song stays on his mind."

26 Depending on the audience, the pair does not absolutely have to be young—just together. He gives her a DeBeers diamond, and there is a tear in her laugh lines. She takes Geritol* and preserves herself for him. And numbers of consumers, wanting affection too, follow suit.

27 Warm family feelings are fanned in ads when another generation is added to the pair. Hallmark Cards brings grandparents into the picture, and Johnson and Johnson Baby Powder has Dad, Mom, and baby, all fresh from the bath, encircled in arms and emblazoned with "Share the Feeling." A talc has been fused to familial love.

28 Friendship is yet another form of affiliation pursued by advertisers. Two women confide and drink Maxwell House coffee together; two men walk through the woods smoking Salem cigarettes. Miller Beer promises that afternoon "Miller Time" will be staffed with three or four good buddies. Drink Dr. Pepper, as Mickey Rooney is coaxed to do, and join in with all the other Peppers. Coca-Cola does not even need to portray the friendliness; it has reduced this appeal to "a Coke and a smile."

29 The warmth can be toned down and disguised, but it is the same affiliative need that is being fished for. The blonde has a direct gaze and her friends are firm businessmen in appearance, but with a glass of Old Bushmill you can sit down and fit right in. Or, for something more upbeat, sing along with the Pontiac choirboys.

30 As well as presenting positive images, advertisers can play to the need for affiliation in negative ways, by invoking the fear of rejection. If we don't use Scope, we'll have the "Ugh! Morning Breath" that causes the male and female models to avert their faces. Unless we apply Ultra Brite or Close-Up to our teeth, it's good-bye romance. Our family will be cursed with "House-a-tosis" if we don't take care. Without Dr. Scholl's antiperspirant foot spray, the bowling team will keel over. There go all the guests when the supply of Dorito's nacho cheese chips is exhausted. Still more rejection if our shirts have ring-around-the-collar, if our car needs to be Midasized. But make a few purchases, and we are back in the bosom of human contact.

31 As self-directed as Americans pretend to be, in the last analysis we remain social animals, hungering for the positive, endorsing feelings that only those around us can supply. Advertisers respond, urging us to "Reach out and touch someone," in the hopes our monthly [phone] bills will rise.

32 **3. Need to Nurture.** Akin to affiliative needs is the need to take care of small, defenseless creatures—children and pets, largely. Reciprocity is of less consequence here, though; it is the giving that counts. Murray uses synonyms like "to feed, help, support, console, protect, comfort, nurse, heal." A strong need it is,

---

* The original Geritol (a combination of the words "geriatric" and "tolerance") was an iron tonic and vitamin supplement marketed to people over 40 between 1950 and 1979 with the slogan, "Do you have iron poor, tired blood?" Though today Geritol is the label on a group of health-related products, the name became famous—and, to some extent, funny—as a means of restoring energy and youthful vigor to middle-age and elderly people.

woven deep into our genetic fabric, for if it did not exist we could not successfully raise up our replacements. When advertisers put forth the image of something diminutive and furry, something that elicits the word "cute" or "precious," then they are trying to trigger this motive. We listen to the childish voice singing the Oscar Mayer wiener song, and our next hot-dog purchase is prescribed. Aren't those darling kittens something, and how did this Meow Mix get into our shopping cart?

33   This pitch is often directed at women, as Mother Nature's chief nurturers. "Make me some Kraft macaroni and cheese, please," says the elfin preschooler just in from the snowstorm, and mothers' hearts go out, and Kraft's sales go up. "We're cold, wet, and hungry," whine the husband and kids, and the little woman gets the Manwiches ready. A facsimile of this need can be hit without children or pets: the husband is ill and sleepless in the television commercial, and the wife grudgingly fetches the NyQuil.

34   But it is not women alone who can be touched by this appeal. The father nurses his son Eddie through adolescence while the John Deere lawn tractor survives the years. Another father counts pennies with his young son as the subject of New York Life Insurance comes up. And all over America are businessmen who don't know why they dial Qantas Airlines* when they have to take a trans-Pacific trip; the koala bear knows.

35   **4. Need for Guidance.**   The opposite of the need to nurture is the need to be nurtured: to be protected, shielded, guided. We may be loath to admit it, but the child lingers on inside every adult—and a good thing it does, or we would not be instructable in our advancing years. Who wants a nation of nothing but flinty personalities?

36   Parent-like figures can successfully call up this need. Robert Young[†] recommends Sanka coffee, and since we have experienced him for twenty-five years as television father and doctor, we take his word for it. Florence Henderson[‡] as the expert mom knows a lot about the advantages of Wesson oil.

37   The parent-ness of the spokesperson need not be so salient; sometimes pure authoritativeness is better. When Orson Welles[§] scowls and intones, "Paul Masson will sell no wine before its time," we may not know exactly what he means, but we still take direction from him. There is little maternal about

---

* Qantas Airlines is an Australian airline whose ads during the 1980s and 1990s featured a cuddly koala bear standing in for both the airline and the exotic delights of Australia.

[†] Robert Young (1907–1988) acted in movies (including Alfred Hitchcock's *Secret Agent* (1936) and *Crossfire* (1947) and TV (starring in the long-running 1950s series *Father Knows Best* and the 1960s series *Marcus Welby, M.D.*). A classic father figure, in his later career he appeared in ads for Sanka coffee.

[‡] Florence Henderson (b. 1934), acted on Broadway and TV (primarily, in musical and comedy roles). Her most famous TV show was *The Brady Bunch* (1968–74), where she played a mother of three daughters who married a man with three sons.

[§] Orson Welles (1915–1985) was a major American filmmaker and actor whose films include *Citizen Kane* (1941—generally considered the greatest American film of all time), *The Magnificent Ambersons* (1942), *The Lady from Shanghai* (1947), *Macbeth* (1948), and *Touch of Evil* (1958). Toward the end of his life—to the dismay of many who revered him—the magisterial but financially depleted Welles became a spokesman for Paul Masson wines.

Brenda Vaccaro* when she speaks up for Tampax, but there is a certainty to her that many accept.

38   A celebrity is not a necessity in making a pitch to the need for guidance, since a fantasy figure can serve just as well. People accede to the Green Giant, or Betty Crocker, or Mr. Goodwrench.† Some advertisers can get by with no figure at all: "When E. F. Hutton‡ talks, people listen."

39   Often it is tradition or custom that advertisers point to and consumers take guidance from. Bits and pieces of American history are used to sell whiskeys like Old Crow, Southern Comfort, Jack Daniel's. We conform to traditional male/female roles and age-old social norms when we purchase Barclay cigarettes, which informs us "The pleasure is back."

40   The product itself, if it has been around for a long time, can constitute a tradition. All those old labels in the ad for Morton salt convince us that we should continue to buy it. Kool-Aid says "You loved it as a kid. You trust it as a mother," hoping to get yet more consumers to go along.

41   Even when the product has no history at all, our need to conform to tradition and to be guided are strong enough that they can be invoked through bogus nostalgia and older actors. Country-Time lemonade sells because consumers want to believe it has a past they can defer to.

42   So far the needs and the ways they can be invoked which have been looked at are largely warm and affiliative; they stand in contrast to the next set of needs, which are much more egoistic and assertive.

43   **5. Need to Aggress.**   The pressures of the real world create strong retaliatory feelings in every functioning human being. Since these impulses can come forth as bursts of anger and violence, their display is normally tabooed. Existing as harbored energy, aggressive drives present a large, tempting target for advertisers. It is not a target to be aimed at thoughtlessly, though, for few manufacturers want their products associated with destructive motives. There is always the danger that, as in the case of sex, if the appeal is too blatant, public opinion will turn against what is being sold.

44   Jack-in-the-Box sought to abruptly alter its marketing by going after older customers and forgetting the younger ones. Their television commercials had a seventy-ish lady command, "Waste him," and the Jack-in-the-Box clown exploded before our eyes. So did public reaction until the commercials were toned down. Print ads for Club cocktails carried the faces of octogenarians under the headline, "Hit me with a Club"; response was contrary enough to bring the campaign to a stop.

---

* Brenda Vaccaro (b. 1939) is a stage, TV, and film actress; her films include *Midnight Cowboy* (1969), *Airport '77* (1977), *Supergirl* (1984), and *The Mirror Has Two Faces* (1996).

† Mr. Goodwrench (and the slogan "Looking for Mr. Goodwrench"), personified as an engaging and highly capable auto mechanic, is a product of the General Motors marketing department.

‡ E. F. Hutton (named after its founder, Edward Francis Hutton) was a major brokerage firm that was brought down in the 1980s by corporate misconduct. Its most famous TV ad portrayed, typically, two well-dressed businesspeople in conversation in a crowded dining room or club room. The first man says to the other, "My broker says. . . . " The second man listens politely and responds, "Well, my broker is E. F. Hutton, and *he* says . . . ," and everyone else in the room strains to overhear the conversation. The tag line: "When E. F. Hutton talks, people listen."

45   Better disguised aggressive appeals are less likely to backfire: Triumph cigarettes has models making a lewd gesture with their uplifted cigarettes, but the
individuals are often laughing and usually in close company of others. When
Exxon said, "There's a Tiger in your tank," the implausibility of it concealed the
invocation of aggressive feelings.

46   Depicted arguments are a common way for advertisers to tap the audience's
needs to aggress. Don Rickles* and Lynda Carter† trade gibes, and consumers
take sides as the name of Seven-Up is stitched on minds. The Parkay
[margarine] tub has a difference of opinion with the user; who can forget it, or
who (or what) got the last word in?

47   **6. Need to Achieve.**   This is the drive that energizes people, causing them
to strive in their lives and careers. According to Murray, the need for achievement is signalled by the desires "to accomplish something difficult. To overcome
obstacles and attain a high standard. To excel one's self. To rival and surpass
others." A prominent American trait, it is one that advertisers like to hook on
to because it identifies their product with winning and success.

48   The Cutty Sark ad does not disclose that Ted Turner failed at his latest attempt
at yachting's America Cup; here he is represented as a champion on the water as
well as off in his television enterprises. If we drink this whiskey, we will be
victorious alongside Turner. We can also succeed with O. J. Simpson‡ by renting
Hertz cars, or with Reggie Jackson§ by bringing home some Panasonic equipment.
Cathy Rigby‖ and Stayfree maxipads will put people out front.

49   Sports heroes are the most convenient means to snare consumers' needs to
achieve, but they are not the only one. Role models can be established, ones
which invite emulation, as with the profiles put forth by Dewar's scotch.
Successful, tweedy individuals relate they have "graduated to the flavor of Myer's
rum." Or the advertiser can establish a prize: two neighbors play one-on-one

---

* Don Rickles (b. 1926) is a night-club comedian (who has also appeared in TV and films) famous
for his caustic wit and for humorously insulting people in the audience.

† Lynda Carter (b. 1951) is an actress whose most famous role was the heroine of the 1976 TV series
Wonder Woman.

‡ O. J. Simpson (b. 1957) is a famous football player–turned film actor (*The Naked Gun*) and defendant in a notorious murder trial in the 1990s. In a highly controversial decision, Simpson was acquitted
of killing his ex-wife Nicole Simpson and her friend Ron Goldman; but in a subsequent civil trial he was
found liable for the two deaths. Before the trial, Simpson was well-known for his TV commercials for
Hertz rental cars, featuring him sprinting through airports to get to the gate to demonstrate what you
wouldn't have to do if you rented a car through Hertz.

§ Reggie Jackson (b. 1946), a member of the Baseball Hall of Fame, played as an outfielder between
1967 and 1987. Known as "Mr. October" for his dramatic game-winning at-bats during post-season play,
he had more strikeouts (2,597) than any other player. He was the first baseball player to have a candy
bar (the "Reggie Bar") named after him, and toward the end of his career was a pitchman for Panasonic
televisions.

‖ Cathy Rigby, an Olympian, was the first American gymnast to win a medal (in 1970) at the World
Championships. She went on to star in a Broadway revival of the musical *Peter Pan* (surpassing Mary
Martin for the greatest number of performances). Subsequently, she became a sportscaster for ABC
Sports.

basketball for a Michelob beer in a television commercial, while in a print ad a bottle of Johnnie Walker Black Label has been gilded like a trophy.

50   Any product that advertises itself in superlatives—the best, the first, the finest—is trying to make contact with our needs to succeed. For many consumers, sales and bargains belong in this category of appeals, too; the person who manages to buy something at fifty percent off is seizing an opportunity and coming out ahead of others.

51   **7. Need to Dominate.**   This fundamental need is the craving to be powerful— perhaps omnipotent, as in the Xerox ad where Brother Dominic exhibits heavenly powers and creates miraculous copies. Most of us will settle for being just a regular potentate, though. We drink Budweiser because it is the King of Beers, and here comes the powerful Clydesdales to prove it. A taste of Wolfschmidt vodka and "The spirit of the Czar lives on."

52   The need to dominate and control one's environment is often thought of as being masculine, but as close students of human nature, advertisers know it is not so circumscribed. Women's aspirations for control are suggested in the campaign theme, "I like my men in English Leather, or nothing at all." The females in the Chanel No. 19 ads are "outspoken" and wrestle their men around.

53   Male and female, what we long for is clout; what we get in its place is Mastercard.

54   **8. Need for Prominence.**   Here comes the need to be admired and respected, to enjoy prestige and high social status. These times, it appears, are not so egalitarian after all. Many ads picture the trappings of high position; the Oldsmobile stands before a manorial doorway, the Volvo is parked beside a steeple-chase. A book-lined study is the setting for Dewar's 12, and Lenox China is displayed in a dining room chock full of antiques.

55   Beefeater gin represents itself as "The Crown Jewel of England" and uses no illustrations of jewels or things British, for the words are sufficient indicators of distinction. Buy that gin and you will rise up the prestige hierarchy, or achieve the same effect on yourself with Seagram's 7 Crown, which ambiguously describes itself as "classy."

56   Being respected does not have to entail the usual accoutrements of wealth: "Do you know who I am?" the commercials ask, and we learn that the prominent person is not so prominent without his American Express card.

57   **9. Need for Attention.**   The previous need involved being *looked up to*, while this is the need to be *looked at*. The desire to exhibit ourselves in such a way as to make others look at us is a primitive, insuppressible instinct. The clothing and cosmetic industries exist just to serve this need, and this is the way they pitch their wares. Some of this effort is aimed at males, as the ads for Hathaway shirts and Jockey underclothes. But the greater bulk of such appeals is targeted singlemindedly at women.

58   To come back to Brooke Shields: this is where she fits into American marketing. If I buy Calvin Klein jeans, consumers infer, I'll be the object of fascination. The desire for exhibition has been most strikingly played to in a print campaign of many years' duration, that of Maidenform lingerie. The woman exposes herself, and sales surge. "Gentlemen prefer Hanes" the ads dissemble, and women who want eyes upon them know what they should do.

Peggy Fleming* flutters her legs for L'eggs, encouraging females who want to be the star in their own lives to purchase this product.

59   The same appeal works for cosmetics and lotions. For years, the little girl with the exposed backside sold gobs of Coppertone, but now the company has picked up the pace a little: as a female, you are supposed to "Flash 'em a Coppertone tan." Food can be sold the same way, especially to the diet-conscious; Angie Dickinson poses for California avocados and says, "Would this body lie to you?" Our eyes are too fixed on her for us to think to ask if she got that way by eating mounds of guacomole.

60   **10. Need for Autonomy.**   There are several ways to sell credit card services, as has been noted: Mastercard appeals to the need to dominate, and American Express to the need for prominence. When Visa claims, "You can have it the way you want it," yet another primary motive is being beckoned forward—the need to endorse the self. The focus here is upon the independence and integrity of the individual; this need is the antithesis of the need for guidance and is unlike any of the social needs. "If running with the herd isn't your style, try ours," says Rotan-Mosle, and many Americans feel they have finally found the right brokerage firm.

61   The photo is of a red-coated Mountie on his horse, posed on a snow-covered ledge; the copy reads, "Windsor—One Canadian stands alone." This epitome of the solitary and proud individual may work best with male customers, as may Winston's man in the red cap. But one-figure advertisements also strike the strong need for autonomy among American women. As Shelly Hack[†] strides for Charlie perfume, females respond to her obvious pride and flair; she is her own person. The Virginia Slims tale is of people who have come a long way from subservience to independence. Cachet perfume feels it does not need a solo figure to work this appeal, and uses three different faces in its ads; it insists, though, "It's different on every woman who wears it."

62   Like many psychological needs, this one can also be appealed to in a negative fashion, by invoking the loss of independence or self-regard. Guilt and regrets can be stimulated: "Gee, I could have had a V-8." Next time, get one and be good to yourself.

63   **11. Need to Escape.**   An appeal to the need for autonomy often co-occurs with one for the need to escape, since the desire to duck out of our social obligations, to seek rest or adventure, frequently takes the form of one-person flight. The dashing image of a pilot, in fact, is a standard way of quickening this need to get away from it all.

64   Freedom is the pitch here, the freedom that every individual yearns for whenever life becomes too oppressive. Many advertisers like appealing to the need for escape because the sensation of pleasure often accompanies escape, and what nicer emotional nimbus could there be for a product? "You deserve a break today," says McDonald's, and Stouffer's frozen foods chime in, "Set yourself free."

65   For decades men have imaginatively bonded themselves to the Marlboro cowboy who dwells untarnished and unencumbered in Marlboro Country some

---

* Peggy Fleming (b. 1948), an Olympic figure skater, and Gold Medal winner (1968), later became a TV sports commentator and a representative for UNICEF (the United Nations Children's Emergency Fund).

[†] Shelly Hack (b. 1952) portrayed Tiffany Welles in the 1970s TV show *Charlie's Angels*.

distance from modern life; smokers' aching needs for autonomy and escape are personified by that cowpoke. Many women can identify with the lady ambling through the woods behind the words, "Benson and Hedges and mornings and me."

66   But escape does not have to be solitary. Other Benson and Hedges ads, part of the same campaign, contain two strolling figures. In Salem cigarette advertisements, it can be several people who escape together into the mountaintops. A commercial for Levi's pictured a cloudbank above a city through which ran a whole chain of young people.

67   There are varieties of escape, some wistful like the Boeing "Someday" campaign of dream vacations, some kinetic like the play and parties in soft drink ads. But in every instance, the consumer exposed to the advertisement is invited to momentarily depart his everyday life for a more carefree experience, preferably with the product in hand.

68   **12. Need to Feel Safe.**   Nobody in their right mind wants to be intimidated, menaced, battered, poisoned. We naturally want to do whatever it takes to stave off threats to our well-being, and to our families'. It is the instinct of self-preservation that makes us responsive to the ad of the St. Bernard with the keg of Chivas Regal. We pay attention to the stern talk of Karl Malden* and the plight of the vacationing couples who have lost all their funds in the American Express travelers cheques commercials. We want the omnipresent stag from Hartford Insurance to watch over us too.

69   In the interest of keeping failure and calamity from our lives, we like to see the durability of products demonstrated. Can we ever forget that Timex takes a licking and keeps on ticking? When the American Tourister suitcase bounces all over the highway and the egg inside doesn't break, the need to feel safe has been adroitly plucked.

70   We take precautions to diminish future threats. We buy Volkswagen Rabbits for the extraordinary mileage, and MONY insurance policies to avoid the tragedies depicted in their black-and-white ads of widows and orphans.

71   We are careful about our health. We consume Mazola margarine because it has "corn goodness" backed by the natural food traditions of the American Indians. In the medicine cabinet is Alka-Seltzer, the "home remedy"; having it, we are snug in our little cottage.

72   We want to be safe and secure; buy these products, advertisers are saying, and you'll be safer than you are without them.

73   **13. Need for Aesthetic Sensations.**   There is an undeniable aesthetic component to virtually every ad run in the national media: the photography or filming or drawing is near-perfect, the type style is well chosen, the layout could scarcely be improved upon. Advertisers know there is little chance of good

---

* Karl Malden (b. 1912), with his familiar craggy face and outsized nose, was a stage and later a film actor. He was the original Mitch in the Broadway production of Tennessee Williams's *Streetcar Named Desire,* a role he reprised in the 1951 movie version. His films include *On the Waterfront* (1954), *Cheyenne Autumn* (1964), and *Patton* (1970), and he starred in the 1972 TV series *Streets of San Francisco.* Malden became famous to a later generation of viewers as a pitchman for the American Express card, with the slogan, "Don't leave home without it!"

communication occurring if an ad is not visually pleasing. Consumers may not be aware of the extent of their own sensitivity to artwork, but it is undeniably large.

74   Sometimes the aesthetic element is expanded and made into an ad's primary appeal. Charles Jordan shoes may or may not appear in the accompanying avant-grade photographs; Kohler plumbing fixtures catch attention through the high style of their desert settings. Beneath the slightly out of focus photograph, languid and sensuous in tone, General Electric feels called upon to explain, "This is an ad for the hair dryer."

75   This appeal is not limited to female consumers: J&B scotch says "It whispers" and shows a bucolic scene of lake and castle.

76   **14. Need to Satisfy Curiosity.**   It may seem odd to list a need for information among basic motives, but this need can be as primal and compelling as any of the others. Human beings are curious by nature, interested in the world around them, and intrigued by tidbits of knowledge and new developments. Trivia, percentages, observations counter to conventional wisdom—these items all help sell products. Any advertisement in a question-and-answer format is strumming this need.

77   A dog groomer has a question about long distance rates, and Bell Telephone has a chart with all the figures. An ad for Porsche 911 is replete with diagrams and schematics, numbers and arrows. Lo and behold, Anacin pills have 150 more milligrams than its competitors; should we wonder if this is better or worse for us?

78   **15. Physiological Needs.**   To the extent that sex is solely a biological need, we are now coming around full circle, back toward the start of the list. In this final category are clustered appeals to sleeping, eating, drinking. The art of photographing food and drink is so advanced, sometimes these temptations are wondrously caught in the camera's lens: the crab meat in the Red Lobster restaurant ads can start us salivating, the Quarterpounder can almost be smelled, the liquor in the glass glows invitingly. Imbibe, these ads scream.

Styles

79 Some common ingredients of advertisements were not singled out for separate mention in the list of fifteen because they are not appeals in and of themselves. They are stylistic features, influencing the way a basic appeal is presented. The use of humor is one, and the use of celebrities is another. A third is time imagery, past and future, which goes to several purposes.

80   For all of its employment in advertising, humor can be treacherous, because it can get out of hand and smother the product information. Supposedly, this is what Alka-Seltzer discovered with its comic commercials of the late sixties; "I can't believe I ate the whole thing," the sad-faced husband lamented, and the audience cackled so much it forgot the antacid. Or, did not take it seriously.

81   But used carefully, humor can punctuate some of the softer appeals and soften some of the harsher ones. When Emma says to the Fruit-of-the-Loom fruits, "Hi, cuties. Whatcha doing in my laundry basket?" we smile as our curiosity is assuaged along with hers. Bill Cosby gets consumers tickled about the children in his Jell-O commercials, and strokes the need to nurture.

82   An insurance company wants to invoke the need to feel safe, but does not want to leave readers with an unpleasant aftertaste; cartoonist Rowland Wilson creates an avalanche about to crush a gentleman who is saying to another, "My insurance company? New England Life, of course. Why?" The same tactic of humor undercutting threat is used in the cartoon commercials for Safeco when the Pink Panther wanders from one disaster to another. Often humor masks aggression: comedian Bob Hope in the outfit of a boxer promises to knock out the knock-knocks with Texaco; Rodney Dangerfield, who "can't get no respect," invites aggression as the comic relief in Miller Lite commercials.

83   Roughly fifteen percent of all advertisements incorporate a celebrity, almost always from the fields of entertainment or sports. The approach can also prove troublesome for advertisers, for celebrities are human beings too, and fully capable of the most remarkable behavior. If anything distasteful about them emerges, it is likely to reflect on the product. The advertisers making use of Anita Bryant* and Billy Jean King[†] suffered several anxious moments. An untimely death can also react poorly on a product. But advertisers are willing to take risks because celebrities can be such a good link between producers and consumers, performing the social role of introducer.

84   There are several psychological needs these middlemen can play upon. Let's take the product class of cameras and see how different celebrities can hit different needs. The need for guidance can be invoked by Michael Landon, who plays such a wonderful dad on "Little House on the Prairie"; when he says to buy Kodak equipment, many people listen. James Garner for Polaroid cameras is put in a similar authoritative role, so defined by a mocking spouse. The need to achieve is summoned up by Tracy Austin and other tennis stars for Canon AE-1; the advertiser first makes sure we see these athletes playing to win. When Cheryl Tiegs[‡] speaks up for Olympus cameras, it is the need for attention that is being targeted.

85   The past and future, being outside our grasp, are exploited by advertisers as locales for the projection of needs. History can offer up heroes (and call up the need to achieve) or traditions (need for guidance) as well as art objects (need for aesthetic sensations). Nostalgia is a kindly version of personal history and

---

* Anita Bryant (b. 1940), a singer and entertainer (and as Miss Oklahoma, runner-up in the 1958 Miss America competition), became controversial during the late 1970s with her campaigns against homosexuality and AIDS. At the time, she was making ads and TV commercials for Florida orange juice, but was dropped by the sponsor after boycotts by activists.

[†] Billy Jean King (b. 1943) was a championship tennis player in the late 1960s and 1970s. In 1973 she was named *Sports Illustrated*'s "Sportsperson of the Year," the first woman to win this honor. She won four U.S. championships and six Wimbledon's single championships. In 1973, in a much publicized "Battle of the Sexes" match, King won all three sets against the 55-year-old Bobby Riggs (once ranked as the best tennis player in the world), who had claimed that "any half-decent male player could defeat even the best female players."

[‡] Cheryl Tiegs (b. 1947) is a supermodel perhaps best known for her affiliation with the *Sports Illustrated Annual Swimsuit Issue*. A 1978 poster of Tiegs in a pink swimsuit became a cultural icon. Recently, she has entered the business world with an accessory and wig line for Revlon.

is deployed by advertisers to rouse needs for affiliation and for guidance; the need to escape can come in here, too. The same need to escape is sometimes the point of futuristic appeals but picturing the avant-garde can also be a way to get at the need to achieve.

Analyzing Advertisements

86 When analyzing ads yourself for their emotional appeals, it takes a bit of practice to learn to ignore the product information (as well as one's own experience and feelings about the product). But that skill comes soon enough, as does the ability to quickly sort out from all the non-product aspects of an ad the chief element which is the most striking, the most likely to snag attention first and penetrate brains farthest. The key to the appeal, this element usually presents itself centrally and forwardly to the reader or viewer.

87   Another clue: the viewing angle which the audience has on the ad's subjects is informative. If the subjects are photographed or filmed from below and thus are looking down at you much as the Green Giant does, then the need to be guided is a good candidate for the ad's emotional appeal. If, on the other hand, the subjects are shot from above and appear deferential, as is often the case with children or female models, then other needs are being appealed to.

88   To figure out an ad's emotional appeal, it is wise to know (or have a good hunch about) who the targeted consumers are; this can often be inferred from the magazine or television show it appears in. This piece of information is a great help in determining the appeal and in deciding between two different interpretations. For example, if an ad features a partially undressed female, this would typically signal one appeal for readers of *Penthouse* (need for sex) and another for readers of *Cosmopolitan* (need for attention).

89   It would be convenient if every ad made just one appeal, were aimed at just one need. Unfortunately, things are often not that simple. A cigarette ad with a couple at the edge of a polo field is trying to hit both the need for affiliation and the need for prominence; depending on the attitude of the male, dominance could also be an ingredient in this. An ad for Chimere perfume incorporates two photos: in the top one the lady is being commanding at a business luncheon (need to dominate), but in the lower one she is being bussed (need for affiliation). Better ads, however, seem to avoid being too diffused; in the study of post-World War II advertising described earlier, appeals grew more focused as the decades passed. As a rule of thumb, [only twenty percent of ads have one primary appeal,] about sixty percent have two conspicuous appeals; the last twenty percent have three or more. Rather than looking for the greatest number of appeals, decoding ads is most productive when the loudest one or two appeals are discerned, since those are the appeals with the best chance of grabbing people's attention.

90   Finally, analyzing ads does not have to be a solo activity and probably should not be. The greater number of people there are involved, the better chance there is of transcending individual biases and discerning the essential emotional lure built into an advertisement.

Do They or Don't They?

91 Do the emotional appeals made in advertisements add up to the sinister manipulation of consumers?

92   It is clear that these ads work. Attention is caught, communication occurs between producers and consumers, and sales result. It turns out to be difficult to detail the exact relationship between a specific ad and a specific purchase, or even between a campaign and subsequent sales figures, because advertising is only one of a host of influences upon consumption. Yet no one is fooled by this lack of perfect proof; everyone knows that advertising sells. If this were not the case, then tight-fisted American businesses would not spend a total of fifty billion dollars annually on these messages.

93   But before anyone despairs that advertisers have our number to the extent that they can marshal us at will and march us like automatons to the check-out counters, we should recall the resiliency and obduracy of the American consumer. Advertisers may have uncovered the softest spots in minds, but that does not mean they have found truly gaping apertures. There is no evidence that advertising can get people to do things contrary to their self-interests. Despite all the finesse of advertisements, and all the subtle emotional tugs, the public resists the vast majority of the petitions. According to the marketing division of the A. C. Nielsen Company, a whopping seventy-five percent of all new products die within a year in the marketplace, the victims of consumer disinterest which no amount of advertising could overcome. The appeals in advertising may be the most captivating there are to be had, but they are not enough to entrap the wily consumer.

94   The key to understanding the discrepancy between, on the one hand, the fact that advertising truly works, and, on the other, the fact that it hardly works, is to take into account the enormous numbers of people exposed to an ad. Modern-day communications permit an ad to be displayed to millions upon millions of individuals; if the smallest fraction of that audience can be moved to buy the product, then the ad has been successful. When one percent of the people exposed to a television advertising campaign reach for their wallets, that could be one million sales, which may be enough to keep the product in production and the advertisements coming.

95   In arriving at an evenhanded judgment about advertisements and their emotional appeals, it is good to keep in mind that many of the purchases which might be credited to these ads are experienced as genuinely gratifying to the consumer. We sincerely like the goods or service we have bought, and we may even like some of the emotional drapery that an ad suggests comes with it. It has sometimes been noted that the most avid students of advertisements are the people who have just bought the product; they want to steep themselves in the associated imagery. This may be the reason that Americans, when polled, are not negative about advertising and do not disclose any sense of being misused. The volume of advertising may be an irritant, but the product information as well as the imaginative material in ads are partial compensation.

96   A productive understanding is that advertising messages involve costs and benefits at both ends of the communications channel. For those few ads which

do make contact, the consumer surrenders a moment of time, has the lower brain curried, and receives notice of a product; the advertiser has given up money and has increased the chance of sales. In this sort of communications activity, neither party can be said to be the loser.

Review Questions

1. Why is advertising more common in highly industrialized countries like the United States than in countries with "quieter" economies?
2. How are advertisers' attempts to communicate their messages, and to break through customer resistance, keyed to their conception of human psychology, according to Fowles?
3. What are the "two orders of content" of most advertisements, according to Fowles?
4. How is Fowles indebted to Henry Murray?
5. Why must appeals to our need for sex and our need to aggress be handled carefully, according to Fowles?
6. How does the use of humor or the use of celebrities fit into Fowles's scheme?

Discussion and Writing Suggestions

1. In paragraph 4 Fowles cites a study indicating that only a fraction of the advertisements bombarding consumers every day are even noticed, much less acted upon. How do the results of this study square with your own experience? About how many of the commercial messages that you view and hear every day do you actually pay attention to? What kinds of messages draw your attention? What elicits positive reactions? Negative reactions? What kinds of appeals are most successful in making you want to actually purchase the advertised product?

2. What do you think of Fowles's analysis of "advertising's fifteen basic appeals"? Does this classification seem an accurate and useful way of accounting for how most advertising works upon us? Would you drop any of his categories, or perhaps incorporate one set into another set? Has Fowles neglected to consider other appeals that you believe to be equally important? If so, can you think of one or more advertisements that employ such appeals omitted by Fowles?

3. Categorize several of the ads in the ad portfolio later in the chapter (pages 437–483) using Fowles's schema. Explain how the headlines, body text, and graphics support your categorization choices.

4. Fowles asserts that "[c]ontrary to impressions, unambiguous sex is rare in [advertising] messages." This article first appeared in 1982. Does Fowles's statement still seem true today? To what extent do you believe that advertisers in recent years have increased their reliance on overt sexual appeals? Cite examples.

5. Fowles believes that "the need to associate with others [affiliation] . . . is probably the most prevalent appeal" in advertising. To what extent do you agree with this statement? Locate or cite print or broadcast ads that rely on the need for affiliation. How do the graphics and text of these ads work on what Fowles calls "the deep running drives" of our psyches or "the lower brain"?

6. Locate ads that rely upon the converse appeals to nurture and to guidance. Explain how the graphics and text in these ads work upon our human motivations. If possible, further categorize the appeal: for example, are we provided with guidance from a parent figure, some other authority figure, or from the force of tradition?

7. Conduct (perhaps with one or more classmates) your own analysis of a set of contemporary advertisements. Select a single issue of a particular magazine, such as *Time* or the *New Yorker.* Review all of the full-page ads, classifying each according to Fowles's categories. An ad may make more than one appeal (as Fowles points out in paragraph 89), but generally one will be primary. What do your findings show? Which appeals are the most frequent? The least frequent? Which are most effective? Why? You may find it interesting to compare the appeals of advertising in different magazines aimed at different audiences—for example, a general-interest magazine, such as *Newsweek,* compared with a more specialized magazine, such as the *New Republic,* or *People,* or *Glamour,* or *Guns and Ammo.* To what extent do the types of appeals shift with the gender or interests of the target audience?

Making the Pitch in Print Advertising
Courtland L. Bovée, John V. Thill, George P. Dovel, and Marian Burk Wood

No two ads are identical, but the vast majority employ a common set of textual features: headlines, body copy, and slogans. In the following selection, the authors discuss each of these features in turn, explaining their importance in attracting the potential customer's attention and selling the virtues of the product or service offered. You will find this discussion useful in making your own analyses of advertisements.

Courtland L. Bovée is the C. Allen Paul Distinguished Chair at Grossmont College. John V. Thill is CEO of Communication Specialists of America. George P. Dovel is president of the Dovel Group. Marian Burk Wood is president of Wood and Wood Advertising. This passage originally appeared in the authors' textbook Advertising Excellence *(McGraw-Hill, 1995).*

Copywriters and Copywriting

1 Given the importance of copy, it comes as no surprise that copywriters are key players in the advertising process. In fact, many of the most notable leaders and voices in the industry began their careers as copywriters, including Jane Maas, David Ogilvy, Rosser Reeves, Leo Burnett, and William Bernbach. As a profession, copywriting is somewhat unusual because so many of its top practitioners have been in their jobs for years, even decades (rather than moving up the management ranks as is usual in many professions). Copywriters can either work for agencies or set themselves up as free-lancers, selling their services to agencies and advertisers. Because it presents endless opportunities to be creative, copywriting is one of those rare jobs that can be fresh and challenging year after year.

2 Although successful copywriters share a love of language with novelists, poets, and other writers, copywriting is first and foremost a business function, not an artistic endeavor. The challenge isn't to create works of literary merit, but to meet advertising objectives. This doesn't mean that copywriting isn't an art, however; it's simply art in pursuit of a business goal. Nor is it easy. Such noted literary writers as Stephen Vincent Benét, George Bernard Shaw, and Ernest Hemingway tried to write ad copy and found themselves unable to do it effectively. It's the combined requirements of language skills, business acumen, and an ability to create under the pressure of tight deadlines and format restrictions (such as the limited number of words you have to work with) that make copywriting so challenging—and so endlessly rewarding.

3 Copywriters have many styles and approaches to writing, but most agree on one thing: copywriting is hard work. It can involve a great deal of planning and coordinating with clients, legal staffers, account executives, researchers, and art directors. In addition, it usually entails hammering away at your copy until it's as good as it can be. David Ogilvy talked about doing 19 drafts of a single piece of copy and writing 37 headlines for a Sears ad in order to get 3 possibilities to show to the client. Actually, the chance to write and rewrite that many times is a luxury that most copywriters don't have; they often must produce copy on tight schedules with unforgiving deadlines (such as magazine publication deadlines).

4 The task of copywriting is most often associated with the headlines and copy you see in an ad, but copywriters actually develop a wide variety of other materials, from posters to catalogs to press releases, as well as the words you hear in radio and television commercials.

Print Copy

5 Copywriters are responsible for every word you see in print ads, whether the words are in a catchy headline or in the fine print at the bottom of the page. The three major categories of copy are headlines, body copy, and slogans.

Headlines

6   The *headline*, also called a *heading* or a *head*, constitutes the dominant line or lines of copy in an ad. Headlines are typically set in larger type and appear at the top of the ad, although there are no hard-and-fast rules on headline layout. *Subheads* are secondary headlines, often written to move the reader from the main headline to the body copy. Even if there is a pageful of body copy and only a few words in the headline, the headline is the most important piece of copy for two reasons: First, it serves as the "come-on" to get people to stop turning the page and check out your ad. Second, as much as 80 percent of your audience may not bother to read the body copy, so whatever message these nonreaders carry away from the ad will have to come from the headline.

7   Copywriters can choose from a variety of headline types, each of which performs a particular function.

- *News headlines*. News headlines present information that's new to the audience, such as announcing a new store location, a new product, or lower prices. This approach is common because potential customers are often looking for new solutions, lower prices, and other relevant changes in the marketplace. For example, a newspaper ad from the Silo home electronics chain announced a recent sale using a news headline: "Everything on Sale! 4 Days Only! 5–20% Off Everything!" Headlines like this are typical in local newspaper advertising.
- *Emotional headlines*. The emotional appeal . . . is represented by emotional headlines. The quotation headline "I'm sick of her ruining our lives" was used in an ad for the American Mental Health Fund to echo the frustration some parents feel when they can't understand their teenagers' behavior. Combined with a photo of a sad and withdrawn teenage girl, the headline grabs any parent who has felt such frustration, and the body copy goes on to explain that families shouldn't get mad at people with mental illnesses but should help them get treatment for their conditions.
- *Benefit headlines*. The benefit headline is a statement of the key customer benefit. An ad for Quicken personal finance software used the question-form headline: "How do you know exactly where your money goes and how much you have?" followed by "It's this simple" above a photograph of the product package. The customer benefit is keeping better track of your money, and Quicken is the solution offered.
- *Directive headlines*. Headlines that direct the reader to do something, or at least suggest the reader do something, can motivate consumer action. Such headlines can be a hard sell, such as "Come in now and save," or they can be something more subtle, such as "Just feel the color in these black and whites," the headline in an ad for Ensoniq keyboards.
- *Offbeat and curiosity headlines*. Humor, wordplay, and mystery can be effective ways to draw readers into an ad. An ad promoting vacation travel to Spain used the headline "Si in the dark," with a photo of a lively nighttime scene. The word *Si* is catchy because it first looks like an error, until the reader reads the body copy to learn that the ad is talking about Spain (*si* is Spanish for "yes").

- *Hornblowing headlines.* The hornblowing headline, called "Brag and Boast" heads by the Gallup & Robinson research organization, should be used with care. Customers have seen it all and heard it all, and "We're the greatest" headlines tend to sound arrogant and self-centered. This isn't to say that you can't stress superiority; you just need to do it in a way that takes the customer's needs into account, and the headline must be honest. The headline "Neuberger & Berman Guardian Fund" followed by the subhead "#1 Performing Growth and Income Fund" blows the company's own horn but also conveys an important product benefit. Since investors look for top-performing mutual funds, the information about being number one is relevant.
- *Slogan, label, or logo headlines.* Some headlines show a company's slogan, a product label, or the organization's logo. Powerful slogans like Hallmark's "When you care enough to send the very best" can make great headlines because they click with the reader's emotions. Label and logo headlines can build product and company awareness, but they must be used with care. If the label or logo doesn't make some emotional or logical connection with the reader, the ad probably won't succeed.

8 Headlines often have maximum impact when coupled with a well-chosen graphic element, rather than trying to carry the message with words alone. In fact, the careful combination of the two can increase the audience's involvement with the ad, especially if one of the two says something ironic or unexpected that has to be resolved by considering the other element. A magazine ad for Easter Seals had the headline "After all we did for Pete, he walked out on us." At first, you think the birth-defects organization is complaining. Then

---

CHECKLIST FOR PRODUCING EXCELLENT COPY

❏ A. Avoid clichés.
  - Create fresh, original phrases that vividly convey your message.
  - Remember that clever wordplay based on clichés can be quite effective.

❏ B. Watch out for borrowed interest.
  - Make sure you don't use inappropriate copy or graphics since they can steal the show from your basic sales message.
  - Be sure nothing draws attention from the message.

❏ C. Don't boast.
  - Be sure the ad's purpose isn't merely to pat the advertiser on the back.
  - Tout success when you must convince nonbuyers that lots of people just like them have purchased your product; this isn't the same as shouting "We're the best!"

❏ D. Make it personal, informal, and relevant.
- • Connect with the audience in a way that is personal and comfortable. Pompous, stiff, and overly "businesslike" tends to turn people away.
- • Avoid copy that sounds like it belongs in an ad, with too many overblown adjectives and unsupported claims of superiority.

❏ E. Keep it simple, specific, and concise.
- • Make your case quickly and stick to the point. This will help you get past all the barriers and filters that people put up to help them select which things they'll pay attention to and which they'll ignore.
- • Avoid copy that's confusing, meandering, too long, or too detailed.

❏ F. Give the audience a reason to read, listen, or watch.
- • Offer a solution to your audience's problems.
- • Entertain your audience.
- • Consider any means possible to get your audience to pay attention long enough to get your sales message across.

you see a photo of Pete with new artificial legs, walking away from a medical facility. It's a powerful combination that makes the reader feel good about the things Easter Seals can do for people.

Body Copy

9   The second major category of copy is the *body copy*, which constitutes the words in the main body of the ad, apart from headlines, photo captions, and other blocks of text. The importance of body copy varies from ad to ad, and some ads have little or no body copy. Ads for easy-to-understand products, for instance, often rely on the headline and a visual such as a photograph to get their point across. In contrast, when the selling message needs a lot of supporting detail to be convincing, an ad can be packed full of body copy. Some advertisers have the impression that long body copy should be avoided, but that isn't always the case. The rule to apply here is to use the "right" number of words. You might not need many words in a perfume ad, but you might need a page or two to cover a complex industrial product.

10   As with headlines, body copy can be built around several different formats. *Straight-line copy* is copy that takes off from the headline and develops the selling points for the product. *Narrative copy*, in contrast, tells a story as it persuades; the same selling points may be covered, but in a different context. *Dialog/monolog copy* lets one or two characters in the ad do the selling through what they are saying. *Picture-and-caption copy* relies on photographs or illustrations to tell the story, with support from their accompanying captions.

Slogans

11 The third major category of copy includes *slogans*, or *tag lines*, memorable sayings that convey a selling message. Over the years, Coca-Cola has used such slogans as "Coke is it," "It's the real thing," and "Always Coca-Cola." Slogans are sometimes used as headlines, but not always. Their importance lies in the fact they often become the most memorable result of an advertising campaign. You've probably got a few slogans stuck in your head. Ever heard of "Quality is job number 1," "Don't leave home without it," or "Melts in your mouth, not in your hand"?

12   The Korean automaker Hyundai recently switched back to the slogan "Cars that make sense," which is a great way of expressing its desired positioning as a lower-cost but still reliable alternative to Japanese and U.S. cars. For several years, the company had used "Hyundai. Yes, Hyundai," but "Cars that make sense" has proved to be a much more effective way to define the value it offers consumers.

Review Questions

1. What are the particular challenges of copywriting, as opposed to other types of writing?
2. How do the authors classify the main types of ad headlines?
3. What are the main types of body copy styles, according to the authors?

Discussion and Writing Suggestions

1. Apply the authors' criteria for effective headlines to three or four of the ads in the portfolio (pages 437–483)—or to three or four ads of your own choosing. To what extent do these headlines succeed in attracting attention, engaging the audience, and fulfilling the other requirements of effective headlines?

2. Imagine that you are a copywriter who has been assigned the account for a particular product (your choice). Develop three possible headlines for an advertisement for this product. Incorporate as many as possible of the criteria for effective headlines discussed by the authors (paragraphs 6–8).

3. Classify the *types* of headlines in a given product category in the ad portfolio (pages 437–483). Or classify the types of headlines in full-page ads in a single current magazine. Which type of headline appears to be the most common? Which type appears to be the most effective in gaining your attention and making you want to read the body copy?

4. Classify the *types* of body copy styles in a given product category in the ad portfolio. Or classify the types of body copy styles in full-page ads in

a single current magazine. How effective is the copy in selling the virtues of the product or the institution or organization behind the product?

5. Assess the effectiveness of a given ad either in the ad portfolio or in a recent magazine or newspaper. Apply the criteria discussed by the authors in the box labeled "Checklist for Producing Excellent Copy." For example, to what extent is the copy fresh and original? To what extent does the copy make the message "personal, informal, and relevant" to the target audience? To what extent is the message "simple, specific, and concise"?

6. Write your own ad for a product that you like and use frequently. In composing the ad, apply the principles of effective headlines, sub-heads, body copy, and slogans discussed by the authors. Apply also the principles of "Checklist for Producing Excellent Copy." You will also need to think of (though not necessarily create) an effective graphic for the ad.

Elements of Effective Layout
Dorothy Cohen

In the previous selection, Courtland L. Bovée et al. discuss the chief textual features of print advertising. In the following passage Dorothy Cohen reviews the equally important (and perhaps more important, in terms of seizing the reader's attention) graphic components. Chief among these are balance, proportion, movement, unity, clarity and simplicity, *and* emphasis. *After reading Cohen, you should be well equipped to work on the analysis assignments in this chapter and, more generally, to assess the graphic quality of the ads you regularly encounter in magazines and newspapers.*

This selection originally appeared in Dorothy Cohen's textbook Advertising *(1988).*

1 Fundamentally a good layout should attract attention and interest and should provide some control over the manner in which the advertisement is read. The message to be communicated may be sincere, relevant, and important to the consumer, but because of the competitive "noise" in the communication channel, the opportunity to be heard may depend on the effectiveness of the layout. In addition to attracting attention, the most important requisites for an effective layout are balance, proportion, movement, unity, clarity and simplicity, and emphasis.

Balance

2 Balance is a fundamental law in nature and its application to layout design formulates one of the basic principles of this process. Balance is a matter of weight distribution; in layout it is keyed to the *optical center* of an

advertisement, the point which the reader's eye designates as the center of an area. In an advertisement a vertical line which divides the area into right and left halves contains the center; however the optical center is between one-tenth and one-third the distance above the mathematical horizontal center line. . . .

3   In order to provide good artistic composition, the elements in the layout must be in equilibrium. Equilibrium can be achieved through balance, and this process may be likened to the balancing of a seesaw. The optical center of the advertisement serves as the fulcrum or balancing point, and the elements may be balanced on both sides of this fulcrum through considerations of their size and tonal quality.

4   The simplest way to ensure *formal balance* between the elements to the right and left of the vertical line is to have all masses in the left duplicated on the right in size, weight, and distance from the center. . . . Formal balance imparts feelings of dignity, solidity, refinement, and reserve. It has been used for institutional advertising and suggests conservatism on the part of the advertiser. Its major deficiency is that it may present a static and somewhat unexciting appearance; however, formal balance presents material in an easy-to-follow order and works well for many ads.

5   To understand *informal balance*, think of children of unequal weight balanced on a seesaw; to ensure equilibrium it is necessary to place the smaller child far from the center and the larger child closer to the fulcrum. In informal balance the elements are balanced, but not evenly, because of different sizes and color contrast. This type of a symmetric balance requires care so that the various elements do not create a lopsided or top-heavy appearance. A knowledge or a sense of the composition can help create the feeling of symmetry in what is essentially asymmetric balance.

6   Informal balance presents a fresh, untraditional approach. It creates excitement, a sense of originality, forcefulness, and, to some extent, the element of surprise. Whereas formal balance may depend on the high interest value of the illustration to attract the reader, informal balance may attract attention through the design of the layout. . . .

Proportion

7   Proportion helps develop order and creates a pleasing impression. It is related to balance but is concerned primarily with the division of the space and the emphasis to be accorded each element. Proportion, to the advertising designer, is the relationship between the size of one element in the ad to another, the amount of space between elements, as well as the width of the total ad to its depth. Proportion also involves the tone of the ad: the amount of light area in relation to dark area and the amount of color and noncolor.

8   As a general rule unequal dimensions and distances make the most lively design in advertising. The designer also places the elements on the page so that each element is given space and position in proportion to its importance in the total advertisement and does not look like it stands alone.

Movement

9 If an advertisement is to appear dynamic rather than static, it must contain some movement. *Movement* (also called *sequence*) provides the directional flow for the advertisement, gives it its follow-through, and provides coherence. It guides the reader's eye from one element to another and makes sure he or she does not miss anything.

10 Motion in layout is generally from left to right and from top to bottom—the direction established through the reading habits of speakers of Western language. The directional impetus should not disturb the natural visual flow but should favor the elements to be stressed, while care should be taken not to direct the reader's eye out of the advertisement. This can be done by the following:

- *Gaze motion* directs the reader's attention by directing the looks of the people or animals in an ad. If a subject is gazing at a unit in the layout, the natural tendency is for the reader to follow the direction of that gaze; if someone is looking directly out of the advertisement, the reader may stop to see who's staring.
- *Structural motion* incorporates the lines of direction and patterns of movement by mechanical means. An obvious way is to use an arrow or a pointed finger. . . .

Unity

11 Another important design principle is the unification of the layout. Although an advertisement is made up of many elements, all of these should be welded into a compact composition. Unity is achieved when the elements tie into one another by using the same basic shapes, sizes, textures, colors, and mood. In addition, the type should have the same character as the art.

12 A *border* surrounding an ad provides a method of achieving unity. Sets of borders may occur within an ad, and, when they are similar in thickness and tone, they provide a sense of unity.

13 Effective use of white space can help to establish unity. . . . *White space* is defined as that part of the advertising space which is not occupied by any other elements; in this definition, white space is not always white in color. White space may be used to feature an important element by setting it off, or to imply luxury and prestige by preventing a crowded appearance. It may be used to direct and control the reader's attention by tying elements together. If white space is used incorrectly, it may cause separation of the elements and create difficulty in viewing the advertisement as a whole.

Clarity and Simplicity

14 The good art director does not permit a layout to become too complicated or tricky. An advertisement should retain its clarity and be easy to read and easy to understand. The reader tends to see the total image of an advertisement; thus it should not appear fussy, contrived, or confusing. Color contrasts, including tones of gray, should be strong enough to be easily deciphered, and the various units should be clear and easy to understand. Type size and design should be

selected for ease of reading, and lines of type should be a comfortable reading length. Too many units in an advertisement are distracting; therefore, any elements that can be eliminated without destroying the message should be. One way in which clarity can be achieved is by combining the logo, trademark, tag line, and company name into one compact group.

Emphasis

15 Although varying degrees of emphasis may be given to different elements, one unit should dominate. It is the designer's responsibility to determine how much emphasis is necessary, as well as how it is to be achieved. The important element may be placed in the optical center or removed from the clutter of other elements. Emphasis may also be achieved by contrasts in size, shape, and color, or the use of white space.

Review Questions

1. How does balance in an ad differ from proportion?
2. What two possible types of movement can be incorporated into an advertisement?
3. Cite some of the chief ways of achieving unity in an ad.

Discussion and Writing Suggestions

1. Select an advertisement either in the ad portfolio (pages 437–483) or in a current magazine or newspaper. Analyze the ad in terms of Cohen's discussion of effective layout. How well does the ad employ *balance, proportion, movement, unity, clarity and simplicity,* and *emphasis* to sell the product or communicate the main idea? Which of these elements are most important in accomplishing the task?

2. Cohen writes that "balance is a fundamental law in nature." What do you think she means by this? What natural examples of balance occur to you?

3. Select two ads, one demonstrating what Cohen calls "formal balance," one demonstrating "informal balance." Cohen writes that formal balance "imparts feelings of dignity, solidity, refinement, and reserve" and that it suggests "conservatism on the part of the advertiser." Informal balance, on the other hand, "presents a fresh, untraditional approach" and "creates a sense of originality, forcefulness, and, to some extent, the element of surprise." To what degree do the ads you have selected demonstrate the truth of Cohen's assertions?

4. Find an ad demonstrating unusual use of proportion among its graphic elements. How does the distinctive proportionality help communicate the advertiser's message?

5. Find an ad demonstrating striking use of movement, clarity and simplicity, or emphasis. How does the element you have chosen work to help communicate the ad's message?

6. Find an ad that violates one or more of the graphic principles that Cohen discusses. To what extent do such violations hurt (or even destroy) the ad's effectiveness? How would you fix the problem?

A Portfolio of Advertisements: 1945–2003

The following portfolio offers for your consideration and analysis a selection of 42 full-page advertisements that appeared in American and British magazines between 1945 (shortly after the end of World War II) and 2003. In terms of products represented, the ads fall into several categories—cigarettes, alcohol (beer and liquor), automobiles, food and drink, household cleaners, lotions, and perfumes. The portfolio also includes a few miscellaneous ads for such diverse products as men's hats, telephones, and airlines. These ads originally appeared in such magazines as Time, Newsweek, U.S. News and World Report, Sports Illustrated, Ladies Home Journal, Ebony, and Ms. A number of the ads were researched in the Advertising Archive, an online (and subscription) collection maintained by The Picture Desk <www.picture-desk.com>.

The advertisements in this portfolio are not representative of all ads that appeared during the last 60 years. We made our selection largely on the basis of how interesting, striking, provocative, and unusual these particular ads appeared to us. Admittedly, the selection process was biased. That said, the ads in this portfolio offer rich possibilities for analysis. With practice, and by applying principles for analysis that you will find in the earlier selections in this chapter, you will be able to "read" into these ads numerous messages about cultural attitudes toward gender relations, romance, smoking, and automobiles. The ads will prompt you to consider why we buy products that we may not need or why we prefer one product over another when the two products are essentially identical. Each advertisement is a window into the culture. Through careful analysis, you will gain insights not only into the era in which the ads were produced but also into shifting cultural attitudes over the last 60 years.

Following the portfolio, we provide two or three specific questions for each ad (pages 484–493), questions designed to stimulate your thinking about the particular ways that the graphics and text are intended to work. As you review the ads, however, you may want to think about the more general questions about advertisements raised by the readings in this chapter:

1. What appears to be the target audience for the ad? If this ad was produced more than two decades ago, does its same target audience exist today? If so, how would this audience likely react today to the ad?

2. What is the primary appeal made by the ad, in terms of Fowles's categories? What, if any, are the secondary appeals?

3. What assumptions do the ad's sponsors make about such matters as (1) commonly accepted roles of women and men; (2) the relationship between the sexes; (3) the priorities of men and women?

4. *What is the chief attention-getting device in the ad?*
5. *How does the headline and body text communicate the ad's essential appeals?*
6. *How do the ad's graphics communicate the ad's essential appeals?*
7. *How do the expressions, clothing, and postures of the models, as well as the physical objects in the illustration, help communicate the ad's message?*
8. *How do the graphic qualities of balance, proportion, movement, unity, clarity and simplicity, and emphasis help communicate the ad's message?*

According to a recent nationwide survey:

MORE DOCTORS SMOKE CAMELS
THAN ANY OTHER CIGARETTE

YOUR "T-ZONE" WILL TELL YOU...

T for Taste...
T for Throat...

that's your proving ground for any cigarette. See if Camels don't suit your "T-Zone" to a "T."

R. J. Reynolds Tobacco Co.
Winston-Salem, N. C.

● Not a single branch of medicine was overlooked in this nationwide survey made by three leading independent research organizations. To 113,597 doctors from Canada to Mexico, from the Atlantic to the Pacific went the query — *What cigarette do you smoke, Doctor?*

The brand named most was Camel.

Like anyone else, a doctor smokes for pleasure. He appreciates rich, full flavor and cool mildness just as any other smoker. If you don't happen to be a Camel smoker now, try Camels. Let your "T-Zone" give you the answer.

Camels *Costlier Tobaccos*

Camels, 1947

The Christmas Gift
for Important Men

DS. BY N.W. AYER

• Websters are being specially boxed and Christmas wrapped this year. Boxes of 25, as low as $3.75. Give Websters by the box. A luxurious gift to yourself and to men who are used to the best.

• There are five different sizes of Websters. Each is made of 100% long Havana, bound in top-quality Broadleaf and wrapped in finest Connecticut Shadegrown. Boxes of 25 and 50 in all sizes. Wherever fine cigars are smoked.

WEBSTER CIGARS
EXECUTIVE AMERICA'S TOP CIGAR

Golden Wedding, 15c	Chico, 15c	Queens, 18c	Fancy Tales, 25c	Directors, 35c
Box of 25—$3.75	Box of 25—$3.75	Box of 25—$4.50	Box of 25—$6.25	Box of 25—$8.75

A PRODUCT OF THE WEBSTER TOBACCO COMPANY, INC., NEW YORK

Webster Cigars, 1945

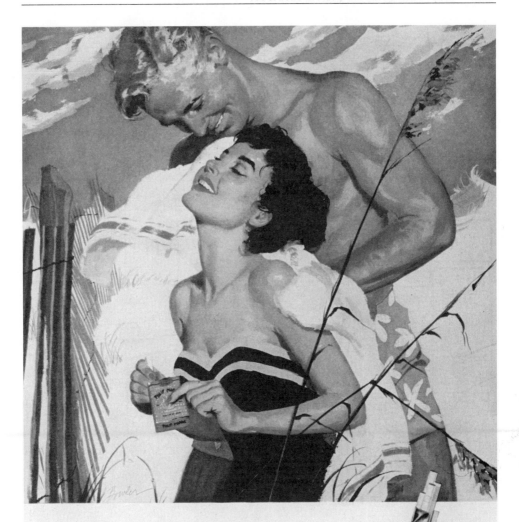

Gently Does It

GENTLENESS makes good friends in fun-making . . . and in a cigarette, where gentleness is one of the greatest requirements of modern taste. That's why today's Philip Morris, born gentle, refined to special gentleness in the making, makes so many friends among our young smokers. Enjoy the gentle pleasure, the fresh unfiltered flavor, of today's Philip Morris. In the convenient snap-open pack, regular or smart king-size.

. . . *gentle for modern taste*

Philip Morris, 1950s

Marlboro, 1970s

Camels, 1979

Can you spot the Camel Filters smoker?

©1972 R. J. Reynolds Tobacco Company, Winston-Salem, N. C.

In this picture everybody has a gimmick... almost everybody. Try picking the one who doesn't go along.

1. Nope. He's Lance Boyle. Gimmick: brags about wars he was never in. Yells "bombs away" as he flicks his French cigarette. **2.** Sorry. He's Harvey Dibble. His restaurant specializes in dried prunes. Gimmick: smokes wheat germ cigarettes. **3.** Eunice Trace, Starlet. Gimmick: restoring wholesomeness to movies. (Last film review: "At last, a movie the entire family can walk out on.") **4.** Smokey Stanhope, accountant. Gimmick: a guitar. Unfortunately makes the mistake of playing it. **5.** Right. He's just himself. And he sees through all the gimmicks. That's why he wants an honest, no-nonsense cigarette. Camel Filters. Easy and good tasting. Made from fine tobacco. **6.** Calls himself "Killer." Gimmick: thinks soccer uniform enhances his image. When he puffs out his chest, his pants fall down.

Camel Filters.
They're not for everybody
(but they could be for you).

CAMEL
FILTER CIGARETTES

Famous Camel Quality

20 mg. "tar," 1.4 mg. nicotine av. per cigarette, FTC Report AUG.'72.

Camel Filters, 1970s

"We're More satisfied."

More. For that extra measure of satisfaction.

21 mg. "tar", 1.8 mg. nicotine av. per cigarette by FTC method.

Warning: The Surgeon General Has Determined That Cigarette Smoking Is Dangerous to Your Health.

More, 1980s

Camel Lights, 1992

Camels, 2000s

Pabst Blue Ribbon, 1940s

America is returning to the genuine—in foods, fashions and tastes. Today's trend to Ballantine light Ale fits right into this modern picture. In all the world, no other beverage brewed has such extra excellence brewed into it. And "Brewer's Gold" is one big reason for Ballantine Ale's deep, rich, genuine flavor.

They all ask for ale **Ballantine** LIGHT **Ale** !

Ballantine Ale, 1950s

ERNEST HEMINGWAY, who has been called the greatest living American writer, is also internationally famous as a deep-sea fisherman. Since publication of *The Sun Also Rises* in 1926, his novels and short stories have enriched the literature of the English language consistently, year after year. His newest book is *The Old Man and the Sea*.

Ballantine Ale, 1953

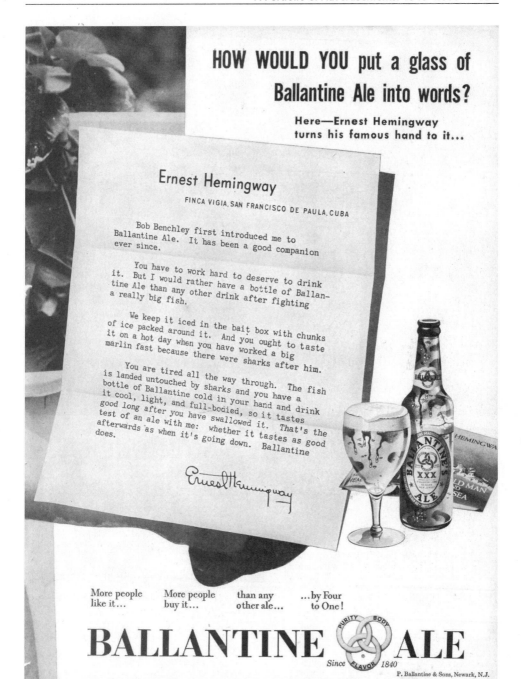

HOW WOULD YOU put a glass of Ballantine Ale into words?

Here—Ernest Hemingway
turns his famous hand to it...

Ernest Hemingway

FINCA VIGIA, SAN FRANCISCO DE PAULA, CUBA

Bob Benchley first introduced me to Ballantine Ale. It has been a good companion ever since.

You have to work hard to deserve to drink it. But I would rather have a bottle of Ballantine Ale than any other drink after fighting a really big fish.

We keep it iced in the bait box with chunks of ice packed around it. And you ought to taste it on a hot day when you have worked a big marlin fast because there were sharks after him.

You are tired all the way through. The fish is landed untouched by sharks and you have a bottle of Ballantine cold in your hand and drink it cool, light, and full-bodied, so it tastes good long after you have swallowed it. That's the test of an ale with me: whether it tastes as good afterwards as when it's going down. Ballantine does.

Ernest Hemingway

More people like it... More people buy it... than any other ale... ...by Four to One!

BALLANTINE ALE

PURITY BODY FLAVOR

Since 1840

P. Ballantine & Sons, Newark, N.J.

BACARDI® rum is so "mixable"... It's a one-brand bar.

Big, bold highballs, sassy Daiquiris, cool tonics and colas—Bacardi rum is enjoyable always and *all* ways. Extra Special: our man Fernando is pouring very rare Bacardi Añejo rum (Ahn-YAY-ho), one of the fine rums from Bacardi. So incredibly smooth he enjoys it even in a snifter. Try it, too!

*BACARDI IMPORTS, INC., MIAMI, FLA. RUM, 80 PROOF.

Bacardi Rum, 1960s

AT THE PULITZER FOUNTAIN, N.Y.C.

In Fine Whiskey...

FLEISCHMANN'S
is the **BIG** buy!

The First Taste will tell you why!

Established 1870

BLENDED WHISKEY • 86 AND 90 PROOF • 65% GRAIN NEUTRAL SPIRITS
THE FLEISCHMANN DISTILLING CORPORATION, NEW YORK CITY

Fleischmann's Whiskey, 1964

"I'll have a Hennessy Very Superior Old Pale Reserve Cognac, thank you."

The Taste of Success

Every drop of Hennessy V.S.O.P. Reserve is Grande Fine Champagne Cognac.
It's made solely from grapes grown in La Grande Champagne—the small district in
the Cognac region which is the source of the very greatest Cognac.
What's more, Hennessy is selected from the largest reserves of aged Cognacs in existence.
Enjoy a taste of success today...

Hennessy V.S.O.P. Reserve Cognac

 Hennessy V.S.O.P. Grande Fine Champagne Cognac. 80 Proof. ©Schieffelin & Co., N.Y.

Hennessy Cognac, 1968

Smirnoff Vodka, 1970s

Cossack Vodka, 1970s

Miller Beer, 1979

Bring out your best.

All they needed was an inch.

You had to stop them. So you built a wall. A determined wall made of you and the rest of the line.

And when the play unfolded, when they came at you with their cunning, they ran into your wall of strength.

They just couldn't move you an inch.

Standing your ground takes more than raw strength. It takes fierce determination. A strong sense of pride. And the very best a man has to give. At Anheuser-Busch we understand that. Which is why we brew a light beer with a clean, distinctive taste. Budweiser Light.

We know the best never comes easy. That's why there's nothing else like it.

Budweiser Beer, 1990s

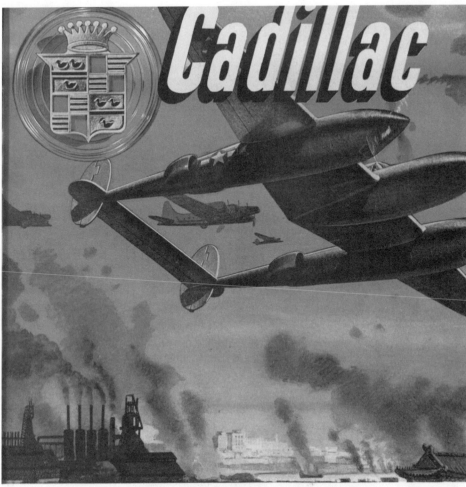

Pay-off for Pearl Harbor!

Three years ago, the sneak attack on Pearl Harbor found America unprepared to defend its rights. Yet, even at that early date, Cadillac was in its third year of building aircraft engine parts for military use. Today are look hopefully forward to the time when this important contribution to America's air power will pay off in such a scene as that illustrated above.

For more than five years we have been working toward that end. Back in 1939, we started building precision parts for Allison—America's famous liquid-cooled aircraft engine—used to power such potent fighters as the Lightning, the Warhawk, the Mustang, the Airacobra and the new Kingcobra.

In addition to our work for Allison, which has included more than 57,000,000 man-hours of precision production—we assisted Army Ordnance Engineers in designing the M-5 Light Tank and the M-8 Howitzer motor carriage, and have produced them in quantities. Both are powered by Cadillac engin equipped with Hydra-Matic transmissio

We are now building other weapons whi utilize some of our Cadillac peacetime pro ucts. We can't talk about all of them yet—t we are confident they will prove significa additions to Allied armor.

Every Sunday Afternoon . . . GENERAL MOTORS SYMPHONY OF THE AIR—NBC Network

CADILLAC MOTOR CAR DIVISION 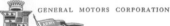 GENERAL MOTORS CORPORATION

LET'S ALL
BACK THE ATTACK
BUY WAR BONDS

Cadillac, 1945

Of all the De Soto cars ever built, 7 out of 10 are still running

8 out of 10 owners say, "De Soto is the most satisfactory car I ever owned"*

*FROM A MAIL SURVEY AMONG THOUSANDS OF OWNERS
OF 1941 AND 1942 DE SOTO CARS

DE SOTO DIVISION OF CHRYSLER CORPORATION

De Soto, 1947

"Ford's out Front from a Woman's Angle"

1. **"I don't know** synthetic enamel from a box of my children's paints... but if synthetic enamel is what it takes to make that beautiful, shiny Ford finish, I'm all for it!

2. **"My husband says the brakes** are self-centering and hydraulic—whatever that means! All I know is they're so easy that I can taxi the children all day without tiring out!

3. **"Peter, he's my teen-age son,** tells me that 'Ford is the only car in its price class with a choice of a 100-horsepower V-8 engine or a brilliant new Six.' He says no matter which engine people pick, they're out front with Ford!

6. **"Now here's another thing** women like and that's a blissfully comfortable ride—one that isn't bumpity-bump even on some of our completely forgotten roads."

Listen to the Ford Show starring Dinah Shore on Columbia Network Stations Wednesday Evenings.

4. **"The interior of our Ford is** strictly my department! It's tailored with the dreamiest broadcloth. Such a perfect fit! Mary Jane says women help design Ford interiors. There's certainly a woman's touch there!

5. **"Do you like** lovely silver, beautifully simple and chaste looking? That's what I always think of when I touch those smart Ford door handles and window openers.

There's a **Ford** in your future

Ford, 1947

Worth Its Price

If a motorist wanted to make the move to Cadillac solely for the car's prestige—he would most certainly be justified in doing so. For the Cadillac car has never stood so high in public esteem as it does today—and the rewards which grow out of this unprecedented acceptance comprise the rarest and greatest satisfactions in all motordom.

There is, for instance, *the inescapable feeling of pride* that comes with ownership of so distinguished and beloved a possession . . . the wonderful *sense of well-being* that comes from having reached a point of achievement where you can enjoy one of the world's most sought-after manufactured products . . . and the *marvelous feeling of confidence and self-esteem* that is found

CADILLAC   MOTOR   CAR   DIVISION

Cadillac, 1954

in PRESTIGE !

in the respect and admiration universally accorded the owner of a Cadillac car. Those who presently enjoy these unique Cadillac virtues will tell you that they are, in themselves, worth the car's whole purchase price.

Of course, most motorists would hesitate to take such a step purely for their personal edification. But in Cadillac's case, this wonderful prestige is actually a "bonus", so to speak—an extra dividend that comes with every Cadillac car, in addition to its breath-taking styling, its magnificent performance, its superlative luxury and its remarkable economy.

Have you seen and driven the 1954 Cadillac? If you haven't, then you've a truly wonderful adventure awaiting you—and one that you should postpone no longer.

GENERAL MOTORS CORPORATION

This is your reward for the great Dodge advance—the daring new, dramatic new '56 Dodge.

The Magic Touch of Tomorrow!

The *look* of success! The *feel* of success! The *power* of success!
They come to you in a dramatically beautiful, dynamically powered
new Dodge that introduces the ease and safety of push-button driving
–the Magic Touch of Tomorrow! It is a truly great value.

New '56 DODGE

Dodge, 1955

Drive a Riviera home tonight. Who cares if people
think you're younger, richer and more romantic than you really are?

A Riviera has a strange effect on people. Simply looking at one makes your mouth water, your eyes
open wider and your heart beat faster. You grin admiringly when you notice the headlights, tucked
behind shields that open with the touch of the headlight switch. You breathe harder when you
turn loose some of those 325 horsepower. And that's just what happens to the driver. Wait till you see the
awe a Riviera inspires in passersby! Amazing. Also attainable, for considerably less than
you might suspect. (Before you fall headlong for a Riviera, ask yourself if a firmer suspension and
assorted other sporting touches give you a twinge of anticipation. Yes? Ask your dealer about
our new Riviera Gran Sport. The name alone is a hint of what's in it for you.) Check with your Buick dealer
soon. He may convince you you're younger, richer and more romantic than you thought you were.

Wouldn't you really rather have a Buick?

Buick, 1965

Corvette Sting Ray Sport Coupe with eight standard safety features, including outside rearview mirror. Use it always before passing.

The day she flew the coupe

What manner of woman is this, you ask, who stands in the midst of a mountain stream eating a peach?

Actually she's a normal everyday girl except that she and her husband own the Corvette Coupe in the background. (He's at work right now, wondering where he misplaced his car keys.)

The temptation, you see, was over-powering. They'd had the car a whole week now, and not once had he offered to let her drive. His excuse was that this, uh, was a big hairy sports car. Too much for a woman to handle: the trigger-quick steering, the independent rear suspension, the disc brakes—plus the 4-speed transmission and that 425-hp engine they had ordered—egad! He would

teach her to drive it some weekend. So he said.

That's why she hid the keys, forcing him to seek public transportation. Sure of his departure, she went to the garage, started the Corvette, and was off for the hills, soon upshifting and downshifting as smoothly as he. His car. Hard to drive. What propaganda!

'66 CORVETTE BY CHEVROLET
Chevrolet Division of General Motors, Detroit, Michigan

Corvette, 1966

Jeep vehicle, 2003

The Turbo engine with the Family Pack.

The Diesel engine with

VOLVO GIVE THEIR BLESSING

When it comes to marriages Volvo like to put on a big spread.

That's why, with the 400 series, we're giving you a wider choice than any other manufacturer. You can pick a bigger engine with standard specification or a smaller engine with the luxury package.

In fact, with a total of five different engine sizes and six different interior packages on offer, you can mix and match as much as you like.

You could for instance, unite the 1.6 engine with the Luxury Pack, which features air-conditioning and leather upholstery.

With other manufacturers however, you don't get such a happy coupling. You'll find that the luxury package for example, only comes with the larger engine.

Volvo, 1990s

the Business Pack.

The 1.6 engine with the Leather Interior.

TO ALL SORTS OF MARRIAGES.

Volvo's approach (which applies to the 440 hatchback and 460 saloon) means you not only get the car that suits your exact needs, but you decide exactly where your money goes.

And you don't have to wait any longer for

delivery of your specially built car. For information pack call 0800 400 430.

The Volvo 400 series. From £11,175 (w ribbons not included).

THE VOLVO 400 SERIES. A CAR YOU CAN BELIE

ROAD FUND LICENCE £96.00. ALL PRICES AND PRODUCT INFORMATION CORRECT AT TIME OF GOING TO PRESS. *EXCLUDING TURBO DIESEL AND LUXURY PACK COMBINATION.

Good School Day Lunches

make healthier, brighter youngsters

Many children do not get adequate lunches! And yet upon proper food depends not only their future health, but today's well-being, cheerfulness—and even report cards!

Lunch should include a hot dish, and be substantial but easy to digest. Good nourishing soup is a big help—and Campbell's Vegetable Soup is just right! Children love it, and it brings them all the sturdy goodness of 15 different garden vegetables combined with a rich, invigorating beef stock. No wonder mothers everywhere agree "It's almost a meal in itself!"

Campbell's VEGETABLE SOUP

IOK FOR THE RED-AND-WHITE LABEL

A WEEK'S SCHOOL LUNCHES

MONDAY
Campbell's Vegetable Soup
Peanut Butter Sandwich
Orange   Baked Custard   Celery
                               Graham Crackers

TUESDAY
Campbell's Tomato Soup
Cottage Cheese and Orange Marmalade Sandwich
Banana   Carrot Sticks
                               Molasses Cookies

WEDNESDAY
Campbell's Scotch Broth
Lettuce and Hard-Cooked Egg Salad
Fresh Pear   Toasted Raisin Bread
                               Cocoa

THURSDAY
Campbell's Vegetable Soup
Cold Roast Veal Sandwich
Baked Apple   Celery
                               Milk

FRIDAY
Campbell's Cream of Spinach Soup
Toasted Tuna Fish Salad Sandwich
Stewed Peaches Sliced Tomatoes
                               Chocolate Milk

Campbell's, 1945

Coca-Cola, 1945

What's for dinner, Duchess?

Prediction: The new wives of 1947 are going to have more fun in the kitchen.

Previous cooking experience is desirable, perhaps, but not essential. There are so many new easy-to-use foods, so many new ways to prepare foods, so many interesting ways to serve foods, cooking will be a novel and exciting adventure.

Further prediction: Cheese dishes will be featured more often on their menus. They'll know that cheese gives tastiness and variety to meals. And cheese, like milk (nature's most nearly perfect food), is rich in protein, calcium, phosphorus, in vitamins A and G.

Yes, we have a personal interest in cheese. For Kraft, pioneer in cheese, is a unit of National Dairy. And what we've said about housewives using more cheese is entirely true.

It's also true that they're learning more about the whys and wherefores of food each year — just as the scientists in our laboratories are learning more about better ways to process, improve and supply it.

These men are backed by the resources of a great organization. They explore every field of dairy products, discover new ones. And the health of America benefits constantly by this National Dairy research.

Dedicated to the wider use and better understanding of dairy products as human food . . . as a base for the development of new products and materials . . . as a source of health and enduring progress on the farms and in the towns and cities of America.

NATIONAL DAIRY
PRODUCTS CORPORATION
AND AFFILIATED COMPANIES

National Dairy Products Corporation, 1947

MAY: # Heavens, Ann —
wish I could clean up quick as that!

ANN: You could, hon! Just use a cleanser that doesn't leave dirt-catching scratches.

MAY: Goodness! What in the world do scratches have to do with it?

ANN: A lot, silly! Those tiny scratches you get from gritty cleansers hold onto dirt and double your cleaning time.

MAY: Well, you old smartie! I'd never thought of *that* before.

ANN: I hadn't thought of it either—till I discovered Bon Ami! See how fine-textured and white it is. It just *slides* di:t off—and when you rinse it away, it doesn't leave any of that horrid grit in the tub.

MAY: Say no more, darling! From now on there's going to be a new cleaning team in our house —me and Bon Ami!

EASY ON YOUR HANDS, Bon Ami *Powder* is the ideal cleanser for kitchen sinks, as well as bathtubs. Also try Bon Ami *Cake* for cleaner windows, mirrors and windshields.

Bon Ami

THE **SPEEDY** CLEANSER *that*
"hasn't scratched yet!"

Bon Ami, 1947

This is the story of Annie...

NOW ANNIE WAS...

AS BEAUTIFUL A GIRL...

AS EVER WAS PUT TOGETHER!

WHY, WHEN ANNIE WALKED DOWN THE STREET...
WOW!

YET ANNIE HAD HER BAD MOMENTS...LIKE ANY OTHER GAL.

AND YOU WANT TO KNOW WHY? ANNIE'S HANDS WERE A MESS, ALWAYS ROUGH AND DRY, LIKE SANDPAPER.

AND WHEN A MAN WANTS TO HOLD A GIRL'S HANDS... EVEN A GIRL LIKE ANNIE ...HE DOESN'T WANT TO WEAR GLOVES...

THEN, LUCKILY, FANNIE TOLD ANNIE ABOUT AN ENTIRELY NEW AND DIFFERENT HAND LOTION! THE **BEFOREHAND** LOTION...**TRUSHAY!**

SO ANNIE SMOOTHED CREAMY, FRAGRANT **TRUSHAY** ON HER HANDS <u>BEFORE</u> SHE DID DISHES...BECAUSE **TRUSHAY** GUARDS HANDS <u>EVEN</u> IN HOT, SOAPY WATER!

AND ANNIE PUT **TRUSHAY** ON HER HANDS <u>BEFORE</u> SHE TUBBED HER UNDIES...SO **TRUSHAY'S** SPECIAL "OIL-RICHNESS" COULD HELP PREVENT DRYNESS AND ROUGHNESS.

SO NOW ANNIE IS ABLE TO KEEP HER HANDS SOFT AND SMOOTH AND HOLDABLE... THANKS TO **TRUSHAY'S** WONDERFUL SOFTENING HELP.

TRUSHAY

The "Beforehand" Lotion

PRODUCT OF BRISTOL-MYERS

P. S. Trushay's grand for softening hands at *any* time. Wonderful, too, for rough, dry elbows and heels...as a powder base...before and after exposure to weather. Trushay contains no alcohol, is not sticky. Begin today to use Trushay.

Trushay, 1947

Mrs. Dorian Mehle of Morrisville, Pa., is all three: a housewife, a mother, and a very lovely lady.

"I wash 22,000 dishes a year... but I'm proud of my pretty hands!"

You and Dorian Mehle have something in common. Every year, you wash a stack of dishes a quarter-mile high!

Detergents make your job so much easier. They cut right into grease and grime. They get you through dishwashing in much less time, but while they dissolve grease, they also take away the natural oils and youthful softness of your hands!

Although Dorian hasn't given up detergents her hands are as soft, as smooth, as young-looking as a teenager's. Her secret is no secret at all. It's the world's best-known beauty routine. It's pure, white Jergens Lotion, after every chore.

When you smooth on Jergens Lotion, this liquid formula doesn't just "coat" your hands. It penetrates right away, to help *replace* that softening moisture your skin needs.

Jergens Lotion has two ingredients doctors recommend for softening. Women must be recommending it, too, for more women use it than any other hand care in the world. Dorian's husband is the best testimonial to Jergens Lotion care. Even after years of married life, he still loves to hold her pretty hands!

Use Jergens Lotion like a prescription: three times a day, after every meal!

Use JERGENS LOTION—avoid detergent hands

Now—lotion dispenser FREE of extra cost with $1.00 size. Supply limited.

Jergens Lotion, 1954

President Lee A. Potter Jr., *of the Young Presidents Organization Inc. and Forman, Ford & Co. "To be successful, look the part. That certain look of success attracts the confidence of important men."*

A man's hat speaks eloquently of his personal measure of authority. That's why Disney hats are so often considered part of a businessman's equipment. The rare skill of their handcraftsmanship, the executive character of their styling reflect the critical judgment and taste of the wearer.* Disney's uniquely impressive effect has made these hats the choice of prominent men for 65 years.

*Case in point, THE DISNEY CAPELLO. This marvelously light hat, styled with flattering tapered crown and narrow brim, is fashion at its finest. At fine stores, $20. Many other Disney hats from $10 to $40.
Free! Handsome booklet containing helpful hints by American business leaders. Ask your Disney dealer for "Guide Quotes to Success."

Disney

The Hat of Presidents

Disney Hats, 1954

Madam! Suppose you traded jobs with your husband?

You can just bet the first thing he'd ask for would be a telephone in the kitchen.

You wouldn't catch him dashing to another room every time the telephone rang, or he had to make a call.

He doesn't have to do it in his office in town. It would be mighty helpful if you didn't have to do it in your "office" at home.

That's in the kitchen where you do so much of your work. And it's right there that an additional telephone comes in so handy for so many things.

Along with a lot of convenience is that nice feeling of pride in having the best of everything—especially if it is one of those attractive new telephones in color.

 P.S. *Additional telephones in kitchen, bedroom and other convenient places around the house cost little. The service charge is just pennies a day.*

Bell Telephone System

Bell Telephone, 1956

Bell Telephone, 1974

Think of her as your mother.

She only wants what's best for you.
A cool drink. A good dinner. A soft pillow and a warm blanket.
This is not just maternal instinct. It's the result of the longest
Stewardess training in the industry.
Training in service, not just a beauty course.
Service, after all, is what makes professional travelers prefer American.
And makes new travelers want to keep on flying with us.
So we see that every passenger gets the same professional treatment.
That's the American Way.

Fly the American Way
American Airlines.

American Airlines, 1968

Charlie, 1988

Shineaway 17 Lotion, 1980s

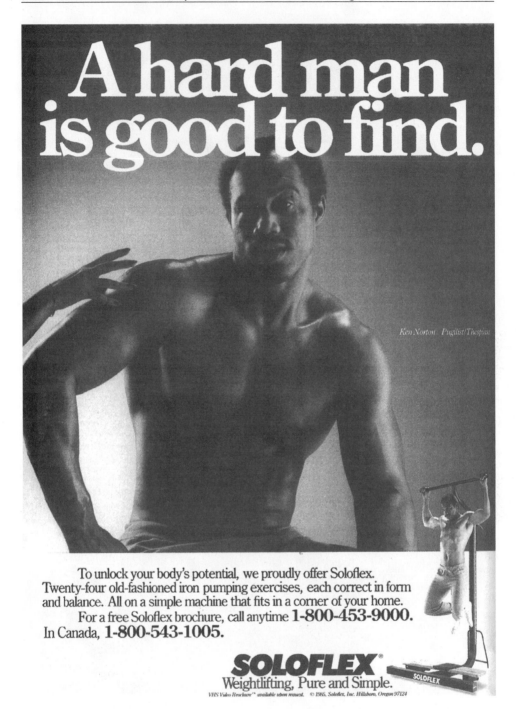

Soloflex, 1985

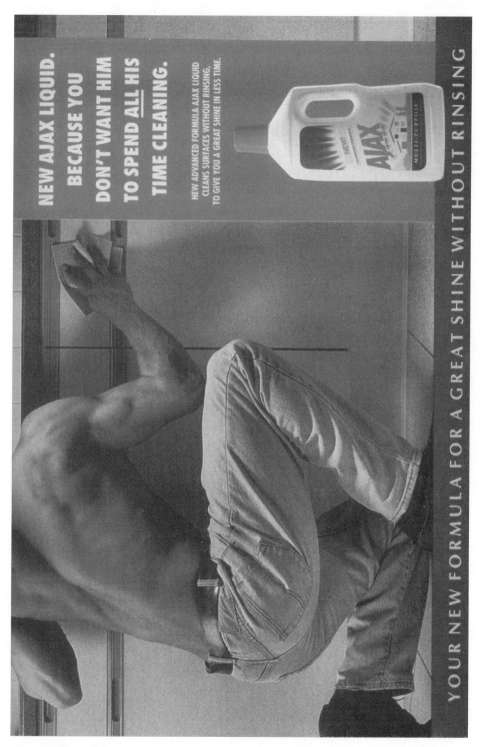

Ajax, 1990s

Discussion and Writing Suggestions

TOBACCO

Camels, 1947 (p. 439)

1. How does the intended appeal of this ad differ most dramatically from a comparable ad today?

2. What kind of psychological appeals are made by the picture in the top half of this ad and the text accompanying it? How does the image of a doctor out on a night call tie in, for selling purposes, with the ad's headline?

Webster Cigars, 1945 (p. 440)

1. How does the dress and general appearance of the people in the ad, as well as the setting depicted, communicate meaning, particularly as it applies to the appeal of the product?

2. To whom is this advertisement addressed? Cite headline and body text, as well as graphics, that support your response. What kind of ads today are addressed to a similar audience?

Philip Morris, 1950s (p. 441)

1. How do the placement, posture, and dress of the models in the ad help create its essential psychological appeal? Why do you suppose (in relation to the selling of cigarettes) the models' eyes are closed?

2. Discuss some of the messages communicated both by the graphic and the text of this ad. Focus in particular on the quality of "gentleness" emphasized in the ad.

Marlboro, 1970s (p. 442)

1. The Marlboro Man has become one of the most famous—and successful—icons of American advertising. What elements of the Marlboro Man (and his setting, Marlboro Country) do you notice, and what role do these elements play in the appeal being made by this ad?

2. This ad appeared during the 1970s. (The popularity of the Marlboro Man extended into the 1980s, however.) To what extent do you think it would have the same appeal today?

3. Comment on the elements of graphic design (balance, proportion, movement, unity, clarity and simplicity, emphasis) that help make this ad effective. Focus particularly on the element of movement.

Camels, 1979 (p. 443)

1. What do the relative positions and postures of the man and the woman in the ad indicate about the ad's basic appeal?

2. What roles do the props—particularly, the motorcycle and the models' outfits—and the setting play in helping to sell the product?

3. How do the design elements in the ad emphasize the product?

4. Compare the graphic elements of this ad to those of the Fleischmann's Whiskey ad (page 453).

Camel Filters, 1970s (p. 444)

1. How do the contrasts in appearance (including posture and facial expressions) between the Camel Filters smoker and the others in the graphic support the essential appeal made by this ad?

2. How does the body text—particularly the thumbnail descriptions of each of the six candidates for Camel Filters smoker—reinforce the ad's intended meaning?

More, 1980s (p. 445)

1. What qualities are conveyed by the couple depicted in the ad? Focus on their dress, posture, and facial expressions. How do these qualities contribute to the appeal of the product?

2. Compare and contrast the effect of this ad with earlier ads depicted for this product (Webster Cigars, Philip Morris) that also show two or more people enjoying tobacco products.

3. Comment on the effectiveness of the graphic elements of this advertisement.

Camel Lights, 1992 (p. 446)

1. During the early 1990s, Joe Camel (depicted here, shooting pool) became one of the most popular and recognized icons of contemporary marketing. The cartoon figure appeared not only on billboards and magazine ads, but also on T-shirts and baseball caps. Joe Camel's appeal, particularly to teenagers, was deemed so pernicious that a group of state attorneys general joined forces in 1997 to force R. J. Reynolds, manufacturer of Camels, to retire the offending dromedary. (The Marlboro Man was targeted in the same settlement, though one of the first models for the Marlboro Man had already died—of lung cancer.) Based on this advertisement, what appears to be the essential elements of Joe Camel's appeal?

2. Contrast this ad with the earlier Camels ads (the man on the motorcycle, the "Can you spot the Camels Filters smoker?" query), as well as the earlier ads for tobacco products, such as Webster Cigars, Philip Morris, and Marlboro. How does the appearance of Joe Camel indicate a major shift of cultural attitudes?

Camels, 2000s (p. 447)

1. This is an example of retro appeal. What elements make it so? What elements mark the ad, on the other hand, as a contemporary one? How does the combination of retro and contemporary elements (including, for example, the posture and attitude of the model) contribute to create a particular type of appeal?

2. Compare and contrast the five Camels ads presented in this section of the portfolio. Focus on the psychological appeals, the cultural values implied in the ads, and the graphic and textual means used to persuade the buyer to smoke Camels.

BEER AND LIQUOR
Pabst Blue Ribbon, 1940s (p. 448)

1. Ads in the 1940s often took comic book form. (See also the 1947 Trushay ad later in this portfolio, page 474.) To what kind of audience is this format most likely to appeal? What are some of the advantages and disadvantages of the comic book format?

2. The problem/solution structure of the narrative in this ad is one of the oldest and still most frequently employed (particularly in TV commercials) in marketing. To what extent does it seem appropriate for the selling of beer? To what extent is it appropriate for other products and services? (Cite examples from contemporary or recent ads.)

3. To what extent do you find examples of outdated social attitudes in this ad?

Ballantine Ale, 1950s (p. 449)

1. This illustration, reminiscent of some of Norman Rockwell's paintings, is typical of many beer and ale ads in the 1950s, which depict a group of well-dressed young adults enjoying their brew at a social event. Comment on the distinctive graphic elements in this ad and speculate as to why these elements are seldom employed in contemporary advertisements for beer and ale. Why, in other words, does this ad seem old-fashioned?

2. Contrast the appeal and graphics of this ad with the ads for Miller and Budweiser later in this portfolio.

3. Identify the adjectives in the body text and attempt to correlate them to the graphic in helping to construct the message of the ad.

Ballantine Ale, 1953 (pp. 450–451)

1. You may be surprised to find Ernest Hemingway selling ale. To what extent do you find celebrity endorsements an effective method of marketing? Why do you think that the creators of this ad might have believed that Hemingway (as opposed, say, to a professional athlete)

might be an effective promoter of (or is qualified to address the need for guidance on) Ballantine Ale?

2. Comment on the apparent strategy behind the graphic and textual elements in this ad—particularly, the setting, Hemingway's posture, and his letter.

3. If you are familiar with any of Hemingway's stories or novels, do you notice any similarity of style or subject matter between what you have previously read and Hemingway's testimonial letter to Ballantine Ale?

Bacardi Rum, 1960s (p. 452)

1. What meaning is conveyed by the placement, posture, and expressions of the four models in this ad? How do you think this meaning is intended to help sell the product? (Does the picture remind you of a particular movie hero?)

2. Comment on the significance of the props in the photo.

3. How does the text ("Big, bold highballs, sassy Daiquiris, cool tonics . . . ") help reinforce the meaning created by the picture?

Fleischmann's Whiskey, 1964 (p. 453)

1. Comment on (1) the significance of the extra-large bottle of whiskey; (2) the stances of the two models in the ad; (3) the way the headline contributes to the ad's meaning.

2. Compare and contrast the graphic in this ad with that of the 1979 Camels ad earlier in this portfolio (the man on the motorcycle).

Hennessy Cognac, 1968 (p. 454)

1. What is the primary appeal of this ad? How do the woman, the horse, and the headline work to create and reinforce this appeal?

2. Compare and contrast this ad to the Webster Cigars ad in terms of their appeal and their graphics.

Smirnoff Vodka, 1970s (p. 455)

1. What meaning is conveyed by the two figures in this ad? How do the models' postures and the props help reinforce this meaning?

2. How do you interpret the headline? How does the headline—and the subheadline ("You drink it for what it is")—tie in to the meaning created by the photo?

Cossack Vodka, 1970s (p. 456)

1. What is the essential appeal behind this ad?

2. The comic book style of the drawing is reminiscent of the work of Roy Lichtenstein (1923–1997), an American painter who drew inspiration from advertisements and romance magazines, as well as comic books,

to depict and parody artifacts of pop culture. What is the effect of this particular style on creating—and perhaps commenting upon—the message in the text balloon and in the ad in which it appears?

3. How does the text at the bottom of the ad reinforce the message created by the graphic? In particular, how is this message intended to sell the product?

Miller Beer, 1979 (p. 457)

1. To what extent does this 1979 ad embody marketing techniques for beer that are still employed today?

2. Comment on the posture and expressions of the three models depicted in the ad. How do these elements help create the ad's essential appeal?

3. Compare and contrast this ad with the 1950s Ballantine Ale ad earlier in this portfolio (page 449).

Budweiser Beer, 1990s (p. 458)

1. To what extent is this ad based on a similar appeal as the preceding Miller ad? To what extent is it based on other appeals?

2. What's the advantage (in terms of effectiveness of appeal) of using the second person—"you"—in the body text? How does the text attempt to make the connection between the product advertised and the activities of the football players? To what extent do you think that this is an effective ad?

3. Comment on the workings and effectiveness of the graphic design elements in this ad.

AUTOMOBILES

Cadillac, 1945 (p. 459)

1. What is the essential strategy behind portraying a group of military aircraft on a bombing raid in an automobile ad? What, exactly, is this ad selling?

2. Explain how the graphic elements of this ad—and the interplay between the elements of the graphic and the text (headline and body text)—reinforce the ad's basic appeal.

De Soto, 1947 (p. 460)

1. How does the scene portrayed in the illustration help create the basic appeal of this ad? Focus on as many significant individual elements of the illustration as you can.

2. To what extent does the caption (in the illustration) and the headline support the message communicated by the graphic?

3. Explain why both this ad and the preceding Cadillac ad are products of their particular times.

Ford, 1947 (p. 461)

1. Cite and discuss those textual elements in the ad that reflect a traditional conception of the American woman.

2. How do the visual elements of the ad reinforce the assumptions about traditional gender roles reflected in the ad?

Cadillac, 1954 (pp. 462–463)

1. What is the particular marketing strategy behind this ad? Based on the ad's text, compose a memo from the head of marketing to the chief copywriter proposing this particular ad and focusing on the strategy. The memo doesn't have to be cynical or to insult the prospective Cadillac buyers; it should just be straightforward and direct.

2. How do the ad's graphics reinforce the message in the text?

Dodge, 1955 (p. 464)

1. Discuss the multiple appeals of this ad. How are these appeals reflected in the ad's text and graphics? For instance, discuss the angle from which the automobile is photographed.

2. Both this ad and the 1947 Ford ad (page 461) feature one or more women in the graphic. Compare and contrast the use of women in the two ads.

Buick, 1965 (p. 465)

1. Compare and contrast the appeal made in this ad to the appeal made in either the 1947 Ford ad (page 461) or the 1954 Cadillac ad (pages 462–463). Cite particular aspects of the text and graphics to support your comparison.

2. The text of the ad discusses two categories of the "people" mentioned in the first sentence. Discuss how the ad makes different, if related, appeals to these two categories of "people."

3. Discuss, in terms of their overall effect, the placement of the automobile and the woman in the ad, as well as the perspective from which both are viewed.

Corvette, 1966 (p. 466)

1. How do the graphic elements reinforce the message developed in the text of this ad?

2. Comment on the dress and the posture of the model, as these relate to the ad's essential appeal. What's the significance of the woman eating a peach in a mountain stream?

3. The body text in this ad tells a story. What kind of husband-wife dynamic is implied by this story? To what extent do you find similarities

between the implied gender roles in this ad and those in the 1947 Ford ad ("Ford's out Front from a Woman's Angle," page 461)? To what extent do you find differences, ones that may be attributable to the 20 years between the two ads?

Jeep vehicle, 2003 (p. 467)

1. Explain the meaning of the ad's headline.
2. Discuss the graphic, in terms of the ad's headline. Consider the significance of the viewing angle.

Volvo, 1990s (pp. 468–469)

1. What cultural phenomenon is being addressed in the graphic and the headline of this ad? To what extent do you believe that associating Volvo with this phenomenon is an effective way to market this particular automobile?
2. What is the connection between the three apparently ill-matched couples in the illustration and the ad's basic message and appeal?
3. How is humor used to enhance the ad's (and the message's) appeal? That is, how are the couples in the illustration presented as incongruous (if happy)?

FOOD, CLEANSERS, BEAUTY PRODUCTS, AND OTHER

Campbell's, 1945 (p. 470)

1. What kind of appeal is being made in the first two sentences of the body text? How does the graphic in the top half of the ad support this appeal?
2. What kind of marketing strategy is behind the menu in the lower-right portion of the ad?

Coca-Cola, 1945 (p. 471)

1. This ad appeared shortly after the conclusion of World War II. How do the text and the graphics of the ad take advantage of the international mood at the time? Comment on the appearance and arrangement of the men portrayed in the ad.
2. Compare the strategy of this Coca-Cola ad (text and graphics) with that of the 1950s Ballantine ad (page 449).

National Dairy Products Corporation, 1947 (p. 472)

1. How does the couple pictured in the ad illustrate gender expectations of the period? Comment on the dress, postures, and expressions of the models.
2. What, exactly, is this ad *selling*? (It is presented more as a news-magazine article than as a conventional advertisement.) How is the

appeal tied to contemporary developments by "scientists" and their "research," particularly as these relate to "the new wives of 1947"?

3. What does the text of this ad imply about the situation of young married couples in postwar households?

Bon Ami, 1947 (p. 473)

1. How do the text and graphics of this ad illustrate a bygone cultural attitude toward gender roles? Notice, in particular, the dress, postures, and expressions of the women pictured, as well as the style of the illustration. Focus also on the wording of the text.

2. In terms of Jib Fowles's categories, what kind of appeal is being made by the Bon Ami ad?

Trushay, 1947 (p. 474)

1. Retell the "story of Annie" in narrative form, in a paragraph. What does Annie's story tell us about gender relations in the 1940s? To what extent have gender relations changed on the particular issue covered by Annie's story?

2. Ads that resembled comic strips were not uncommon 60 years ago. Based on the impact made by this ad today, why do you think the comic strip format might have gone out of fashion?

3. Suppose you are a contemporary copywriter for a hand lotion product. Develop some ideas for an ad or a campaign that might be effective for today's potential customers.

Jergens Lotion, 1954 (p. 475)

1. Compare and contrast the appeals and the strategies of this Jergens Lotion ad and the Trushay ad preceding it. Are the ads intended to appeal to the same target audiences? To what extent are the psychological appeals of the two ads similar? Compare the illustrations of the two ads. How do they differ in basic strategy?

2. The model in the Jergens Lotion ad is immaculately dressed and groomed, and she is sitting among stacks of fine china (as opposed to everyday dishware). What do you think is the marketing strategy behind these graphic choices?

Disney Hats, 1954 (p. 476)

1. Point out specific language in the headline and body that helps create the basic appeal of this ad for Disney hats. How does the illustration—both the man in the hat and the background against which he is posed—reinforce this appeal?

2. Comment on how the connotations and significance of men's head-wear have changed—and not changed—over the years or how they help support the appeal of the product advertised. (Notice, for example, the

hat-wearing models in the 1947 Camels ad, the 1954 Cadillac ad, the 1970s Marlboro ad, and the 1992 Camel Lights ad.)

Bell Telephone, 1956 (p. 477)

1. Discuss the attitude toward gender roles implicit in the 1956 Bell ad. How do the graphics, the headline, and the body text reinforce this attitude? What is the significance of the quotation marks around "office" in the final sentence of the third paragraph?

2. Notice that the woman at the desk seems a lot more comfortable and at ease than the man holding the crying baby and the dishes. What does this fact tell us about the attitudes toward gender roles of those who created this ad?

Bell Telephone, 1974 (p. 478)

1. Compare and contrast the 1956 Bell ad with the 1974 Bell ad, in terms of their attitudes toward gender roles. How do the text and graphics reinforce the essential differences?

2. The 1956 Bell ad pictures a woman at a desk (a white-collar job); the 1974 ad pictures a woman working at a telephone pole (a blue-collar job). Would the 1974 ad have the same impact if "Alana MacFarlane" had, like her 1956 counterpart, been pictured at a desk?

3. Like the 1954 Cadillac ad (pages 462–463), the 1974 Bell ad seems more of a public service announcement than a conventional advertisement. Compare and contrast these ads in terms of their messages to readers.

American Airlines, 1968 (p. 479)

1. Discuss the mixed messages (in terms of appeal) being transmitted by the American Airlines ad. To what extent do you think the apparently conflicting appeals make for an effective ad?

2. Comment on the dress, pose, and expression of the model in the ad, which appeared in *Ebony* magazine. How do these create a different impact than would an illustration, say, of a flight attendant serving a drink or giving a pillow to an airline passenger?

Charlie, 1988 (p. 480)

1. Notice the woman's outfit, as well as her briefcase, in the Charlie ad. How is the appearance of this woman as significant as the appearance of the woman in the Smirnoff Vodka ad (page 455) for the ad's basic message?

2. The Charlie ad and the 1974 Bell ad (page 478) are as different as can be imagined from the Trushay ad. Yet, the Bell and the Charlie ads make quite different appeals. Explain. Consider, for example, how a

woman—or a man—of the late 1940s might respond to the Bell ad, on the one hand, and the Charlie ad, on the other.

Shineaway 17 Lotion, 1980s (p. 481)

1. Account for the postures of the man and the woman, in terms of the essential message and appeal of this ad.
2. Both this and the preceding Charlie ad rely to some extent on sex appeal. Compare and contrast other aspects of these two ads.

Soloflex, 1985 (p. 482)

1. How does the illustration in this ad reinforce the basic appeal of the headline?
2. Ads are frequently criticized for the incongruity between illustration and product being advertised—for example, a scantily clad woman posed provocatively in front of a pickup truck. To what extent does the Soloflex ad present an appropriate fit between graphic and product advertised?

Ajax, 1990s (p. 483)

1. Why do you suppose the model's head is not pictured?
2. How does this ad play off shifting cultural attitudes toward gender roles? Would the ad be more objectionable if it pictured a female in a comparable state of undress?
3. Compare and contrast this ad to earlier ads for cleaners and cleansing lotions, such as Bon Ami and Jergens Lotion.

SYNTHESIS ACTIVITIES

1. Select one *category* of advertisements (cigarettes, alcohol, etc.) represented in the ad portfolio. Compare and contrast the types of appeals underlying these ads, as discussed by Fowles. To what extent do you notice significant shifts of appeal from the 1940s to the present? Which types of appeal seem to you most effective with particular product categories? Is it more likely, for example, that people will buy cigarettes because they want to feel autonomous or because the cigarettes will make them more attractive to the opposite sex?

2. Select a series of ads in different product categories that all appear to rely on the same primary appeal—perhaps the appeal to sex or the appeal to affiliation. Compare and contrast the overall strategies of these ads. Draw upon Fowles and other authors represented in this chapter to develop your ideas. To what extent do your analyses support arguments often made by social critics (and advertising people) that what people are really buying is the image, rather than the product?

3. Discuss how a selection of ads reveals shifting cultural attitudes over the past six decades toward either (a) gender relations; (b) romance between men and women; (c) smoking; (d) automobiles. In the case of (a) or (b) above, the ads don't have to be for the same category of product. In terms of their underlying appeal, in terms of the implicit or explicit messages embodied both in the text and the graphics, how and to what extent do the ads reveal that attitudes of the target audiences have changed over the years?

4. Select a TV commercial or a TV ad campaign (for example, for Sprint phone service) and analyze the commercial(s) in terms of Fowles's categories, as well as the discussions of some of the authors in this chapter. To what extent do the principles discussed by these authors apply to broadcast, as well as to print ads? What are the special requirements of TV advertising?

5. Find a small group of ads that rely upon little or no body copy—just a graphic, perhaps a headline, and the product name. What common features underlie the marketing strategies of such ads? What kinds of appeals do they make? How do their graphic aspects compare? What makes the need for text superfluous?

6. As indicated in the introduction to this chapter, social critics have charged advertising with numerous offenses: "It fosters materialism, it psychologically manipulates people to buy things they don't need, it perpetuates gender and racial stereotypes (particularly in its illustrations), it is deceptive, it is offensive, it debases the language." To what extent do some of the advertisements presented in the ad portfolio (and perhaps others of your own choosing) demonstrate the truth of one or more of these charges? In developing your response, draw upon some of the ads in the portfolio (or elsewhere).

7. Read the textual content (headlines and body text) of several ads *without* paying attention (if possible) to the graphics. Compare the effectiveness of the headline and body text by themselves with the effectiveness of the ads, *including* the graphic elements. Focusing on a group of related ads (related by product category, by appeal, by decade, etc.), devise an explanation of how graphics work to effectively communicate the appeal and meaning of the products advertised.

8. Many ads employ humor—in the graphics, in the body copy, or both—to sell a product. Examine a group of advertisements that rely on humor to make their appeal and explain how they work. For example, do they play off an incongruity between one element of the ad and another (such as between the headline and the graphic), or between one element of the ad (or the basic message of the ad) and what we know or assume to be the case in the "real world"? Do they employ wordplay or irony? Do they picture people doing funny things (funny because inappropriate or

unrealistic)? What appeal underlines the humor? Aggression? Sex? Nurturing? Based on your examination and analyses, what appear to be some of the more effective ways of employing humor?

9. Think of a new product that you have just invented. This product, in your opinion, will revolutionize the world of (fill in the blank). Devise an advertisement to announce this product to the world. Consider (or reject) using a celebrity to help sell your product. Select the basic appeal of your product (see Fowles). Then, applying concepts and principles discussed by other authors in this chapter, write the headline, subhead, and body copy for the product. Sketch out (or at least describe) the graphic that will accompany the text. Show your proposed ad to one or more of your classmates, get reactions, and then revise the ad, taking into account your market feedback.

10. Imagine that you own a small business—perhaps an independent coffee shop (not Starbucks, Peet's, or Coffee Bean), a videogame company, or a pedicab service that conveys tourists around a chic beach town. Devise an ad that announces your services and extols its benefits. Apply the principles discussed by Fowles and other writers in this chapter.

11. Write a parody ad—one that would never ordinarily be written—applying the selling principles discussed by Fowles and other authors in this chapter. For example, imagine you are the manager of the Globe Theatre in Elizabethan England and want to sell season tickets to this season's plays, including a couple of new tragedies by your playwright-in-residence, Will Shakespeare. Or imagine that you are trying to sell Remington typewriters in the age of computers (no software glitches!). Or—as long as people are selling bottled water—you have found a way to package and sell air. Advertisers can reportedly sell anything with the right message. Give it your best shot.

12. Based on the reading you have done in this chapter, discuss the extent to which you believe advertisements create needs in consumers, reflect existing needs, or some combination of both. In developing your paper, draw on both particular advertisements and on the more theoretical overviews of advertising developed in the chapter.

13. Select one advertisement and conduct two analyses of it, using two different analytical principles: perhaps one from Fowles's list of 15 emotional appeals and one from Cohen's principles of effective layout. Having conducted your analyses and developed your insights, compare and contrast the strengths and weaknesses of the analytical principles you've employed. Conclude more broadly with a discussion of how a single analytical principle can close down, as well as open up, understanding of an object under study.

14. As you have seen, advertisements change over time, both across product categories and within categories. And yet the advertisements remain a constant, their presence built on the assumption that consumers can be swayed both overtly and covertly in making purchasing decisions. In a paper drawing on the selections in this chapter, develop a theory on why ads change over time. Is it because people's needs have changed and, therefore, new ads are required? (Do the older ads appeal to the same needs as newer ads?) In developing your discussion, you might track the changes over time in one product category.

RESEARCH ACTIVITIES

1. Drawing upon contemporary magazines (or magazines from a given period), select a set of advertisements in a particular product category. Analyze these advertisements according to Fowles's categories, and assess their effectiveness in terms of the discussions of other authors in this chapter.

2. Select a particular product that has been selling for at least 25 years (e.g., Bayer aspirin, Tide detergent, IBM computers, Oldsmobile—as in "This is not your father's Oldsmobile") and trace the history of print advertising for this product over the years. To what extent has the advertising changed over the years? To what extent has the essential sales appeal remained the same? In addition to examining the ads themselves, you may want to research the company and its marketing practices. You will find two business databases particularly useful: ABI/INFORM and the academic version of LexisNexis.

3. One of the landmark campaigns in American advertising was Doyle, Dane, Bernbach's series of ads for the Volkswagen Beetle in the 1960s. In effect a rebellion against standard auto advertising, the VW ads' Unique Selling Proposition was that ugly is beautiful—an appeal that was overwhelmingly successful. Research the VW ad campaign for this period, setting it in the context of the agency's overall marketing strategy.

4. Among the great marketing debacles of recent decades was Coca-Cola's development in 1985 of a new formula for its soft drink that (at least temporarily) replaced the much-beloved old formula. Research this major development in soft drink history, focusing on the marketing of New Coke and the attempt of the Atlanta-based Coca-Coca company to deal with the public reception of its new product.

5. Advertising agencies are hired not only by manufacturers and by service industries; they are also hired by political candidates. In fact, one of the common complaints about American politics is that

candidates for public office are marketed just as if they were bars of soap. Select a particular presidential or gubernatorial election and research the print and broadcast advertising used by the rival candidates. You may want to examine the ads not only of the candidates of the major parties but also the candidates of the smaller parties, such as the Green and the Libertarian parties. How do the appeals and strategies used by product ads compare and contrast with those used in ads for political candidates?

6. Public service ads comprise another major category of advertising (in addition to product and service advertising and political advertising). Such ads have been used to recruit people to military service, to get citizens to buy war bonds, to contribute to charitable causes, to get people to support or oppose strikes, to persuade people to stop using (or not to start using) drugs, to prevent drunk driving, etc. Locate a group of public service ads, describe them, and assess their effectiveness. Draw upon Fowles, Bovée et al., and Cohen in developing your conclusions.

7. Research advertising in American magazines and newspapers before World War II. Focus on a limited number of product lines— for example, soft drinks, soap and beauty products, health-related products. What kind of differences do you see between ads in the first part of the twentieth century and more recent or contemporary advertising for the same types of products? In general, how have the predominant types of appeal used to sell products in the past changed (if they have) with the times? How are the graphics of early ads different from preferred graphics today? How has the body copy changed? (Hint: You may want to be on the alert for ads that make primarily negative appeals—i.e., what may happen to you if you don't use the product advertised.)

Appendix: A Guide to Avoiding Plagiarism

Plagiarism is using someone else's work—words, ideas, or illustrations, published or unpublished—without giving the creator of that work sufficient credit. A serious breach of scholarly ethics, plagiarism can have severe consequences. Students risk a failing grade or disciplinary action ranging from suspension to expulsion. A record of such action can adversely affect professional opportunities in the future as well as graduate school admission.

DOCUMENTATION: THE KEY TO AVOIDING UNINTENTIONAL PLAGIARISM

It can be difficult to tell when you have unintentionally plagiarized something. The legal doctrine of **fair use** allows writers to use a limited amount of another's work in their own papers and books. However, to make sure that they are not plagiarizing that work, writers need to take care to credit the source accurately and clearly for *every* use. **Documentation** is the method writers employ to give credit to the creators of material they use. It involves providing essential information about the source of the material, which enables readers to find the material for themselves. It requires two elements: (1) a list of sources used in the paper and (2) citations in the text to items in that list. To use documentation and avoid unintentionally plagiarizing from a source, you need to know how to

- Identify sources and information that need to be documented.
- Document sources in a Works Cited list.
- Use material gathered from sources: in summary, paraphrase, and quotation.
- Create in-text references.
- Use correct grammar and punctuation to blend quotations into a paper.

IDENTIFYING SOURCES AND INFORMATION THAT NEED TO BE DOCUMENTED

Whenever you use information from **outside sources**, you need to identify the source of that material. Major outside sources include books, newspapers, magazines, government sources, radio and television programs, material from electronic databases, correspondence, films, plays, interviews, speeches, and information from Web sites. Virtually all the information you find in outside sources requires documentation. The one major exception to this guideline is that you do not have to document common knowledge. **Common knowledge** is widely known information about current events, famous people, geographical facts, or familiar history. However, when in doubt, the safest strategy is to provide documentation.

DOCUMENTING SOURCES IN A WORKS CITED LIST

You need to choose the documentation style that is dominant in your field or required by your instructor. Take care to use only one documentation style in any one paper and to follow its documentation formats consistently. The most widely used style manuals are *MLA Handbook for Writers of Research Papers*, published by the **Modern Language Association (MLA)**, which is popular in the fields of English language and literature; the *Publication Manual of the American Psychological Association* **(APA)**, which is favored in the social sciences; and *The Chicago Manual of Style*, published by the **University of Chicago Press (CMS)**, which is preferred in other humanities and sometimes business. Other, more specialized style manuals are used in various fields. Certain information is included in citation formats in all styles:

- Author or other creative individual or entity
- Source of the work
- Relevant identifying numbers or letters
- Title of the work
- Publisher or distributor
- Relevant dates

CONSTRUCTING A WORKS CITED LIST IN MLA STYLE

As an accompaniment to your English text, this guide explores MLA style. MLA lists are alphabetized by authors' last names. When no author is given, an item can be alphabetized by title, by editor, or by the name of the sponsoring organization. MLA style spells out names in full, inverts only the first author's name, and separates elements with a period. In the MLA Works Cited list below, note the use of punctuation such as commas, colons, and angle brackets to separate and introduce material within elements.

Books

Bidart, Frank. Introduction. Collected Poems. By Robert Lowell. Ed. Frank Bidart and David Gewanter. New York: Farrar, Strauss and Giroux, 2003. vii–xvi.

Chernow, Ron. Alexander Hamilton. New York: Penguin, 2004.

Conant, Jennet. 109 East Palace: Robert Oppenheimer and the Secret City of Los Alamos. New York: Simon, 2005.

——. Tuxedo Park: A Wall Street Tycoon and the Secret Palace of Science That Changed the Course of World War II. New York: Simon, 2002.

Maupassant, Guy de. "The Necklace." Trans. Marjorie Laurie. An Introduction to Fiction. Ed. X. J. Kennedy and Dana Gioia. 7th ed. New York: Longman, 1999. 160–66.

Periodicals

"Living on Borrowed Time." Economist 25 Feb.–3 Mar. 2006: 34–37.

"Restoring the Right to Vote." Editorial. New York Times 10 Jan. 2006, late ed., sec. A: 24.

Spinello, Richard A. "The End of Privacy." America 4 Jan. 1997: 9–13.

Williams, N. R., M. Davey, and K. Klock-Powell. "Rising from the Ashes: Stories of Recovery, Adaptation, and Resiliency in Burn Survivors." Social Work Health Care 36.4 (2003): 53–77.

Zobenica, Jon. "You Might As Well Live." Rev. of A Long Way Down by Nick Hornby. Atlantic July–Aug. 2005: 148.

Electronic Sources

Glanz, William. "Colleges Offer Students Music Downloads." Washington Times 25 Aug. 2004. 17 Oct. 2004 <http://washingtontimes.com/business/20040824-103654-1570r.htm>.

Human Rights Watch. Libya: A Threat to Society? Arbitrary Detention of Women and Girls for "Social Rehabilitation." Feb. 2006. Index No. E1802. Human Rights Watch. 4 Mar. 2006 <http://hrw.org/reports/2006/libya0206/1.html#_Toc127869341>.

McNichol, Elizabeth C., and Iris J. Lav. "State Revenues and Services Remain below Pre-Recession Levels." Center on Budget Policy Priorities. 6 Dec. 2005. 10 Mar. 2006 <http://www.cbpp.org/12-6-05sfp2.html>.

Reporters Without Borders. "Worldwide Press Freedom Index 2005." Reporters Without Borders. 2005. 28 Feb. 2006 <http://www.rsf.org/article.php3?id_article=15331>.

USING MATERIAL GATHERED FROM SOURCES: SUMMARY, PARAPHRASE, QUOTATION

You can integrate material into your paper in three ways—by summarizing, paraphrasing, and quoting. A quotation, paraphrase, or summary must be used in a manner that accurately conveys the meaning of the source.

A **summary** is a brief restatement in your own words of the source's main ideas. Summary is used to convey the general meaning of the ideas in a source, without giving specific details or examples that may appear in the original. A summary is always much shorter than the work it treats. Take care to give the essential information as clearly and succinctly as possible in your own language.

Rules to Remember

1. Write the summary using your own words.
2. Indicate clearly where the summary begins and ends.
3. Use attribution and parenthetical reference to tell the reader where the material came from.
4. Make sure your summary is an accurate restatement of the source's main ideas.
5. Check that the summary is clearly separated from your own contribution.

A **paraphrase** is a restatement, in your own words and using your own sentence structure, of specific ideas or information from a source. The chief purpose of a paraphrase is *to maintain your own writing style* throughout your paper. A paraphrase can be about as long as the original passage.

Rules to Remember

1. Use your own words and sentence structure. Do not duplicate the source's words or phrases.
2. Use quotation marks within your paraphrase to indicate words and phrases you do quote.
3. Make sure your readers know where the paraphrase begins and ends.
4. Check that your paraphrase is an accurate and objective restatement of the source's specific ideas.
5. Immediately follow your paraphrase with a parenthetical reference indicating the source.

A **quotation** reproduces an actual part of a source, word for word, to support a statement or idea, to provide an example, to advance an argument, or to add interest or color to a discussion. The length of a quotation can range from a word or a phrase to several paragraphs. In general, quote the least amount possible that gets your point across to the reader.

Rules to Remember

1. Copy the words from your source to your paper exactly as they appear in the original. Do not alter the spelling, capitalization, or punctuation of the original. If a quotation contains an obvious error, you may insert [sic], which is Latin for "so" or "thus," to show that the error is in the original.

2. Enclose short quotations (four or fewer lines of text) in quotation marks, and set off longer quotations as block quotations.

3. Immediately follow each quotation with a parenthetical reference that gives the specific source information required.

CREATING IN-TEXT REFERENCES

In-text references need to supply enough information to enable a reader to find the correct source listing in the Works Cited list. To cite a source properly in the text of your report, you generally need to provide some or all of the following information for each use of the source:

- Name of the person or organization that authored the source.
- Title of the source (if there is more than one source by the same author or if no author is given).
- Page, paragraph, or line number, if the source has one.

These items can appear as an attribution in the text ("According to Smith . . .") or in a parenthetical reference placed directly after the summary, paraphrase, or quotation. The examples that follow are in MLA style.

Using an Introductory Attribution and a Parenthetical Reference

The author, the publication, or a generalized reference can introduce source material. Remaining identifiers (title, page number) can go in the parenthetical reference at the end, as in the first sentence of the example below. If a source, such as a Web site, does not have page numbers, it may be possible to put all the necessary information into the in-text attribution, as in the second sentence of the example below.

> *The Economist* noted that since 2004, "state tax revenues have come roaring back across the country" ("Living" 34). However, McNichol and Lav, writing for the Center on Budget and Policy Priorities, claim that recent gains are not sufficient to make up for the losses suffered.

Identifying Material by an Author of More Than One Work Used in Your Paper

The attribution and the parenthetical reference combined must provide the title of the work, the author, and the page number of the citation.

> Describing the testing of the first atom bomb, Jennet Conant says, "The test had originally been scheduled for 4:00 A.M. on July 16, when most of the surrounding population would be sound asleep and there would be the least number of witnesses" (<u>109 East Palace</u> 304–05).

Identifying Material That the Source Is Quoting

To use material that has been quoted in your cited source, add *qtd. in*, for "quoted in." Here, only one source by Conant is given in the Works Cited list.

> The weather was worrisome, but procrastination was even more problematic. General Groves was concerned that "every hour of delay would increase the possibility of someone's attempting to sabotage the tests" (qtd. in Conant 305).

USING CORRECT GRAMMAR AND PUNCTUATION TO BLEND QUOTATIONS INTO A PAPER

Quotations must blend seamlessly into the writer's original sentence, with the proper punctuation, so that the resulting sentence is neither ungrammatical nor awkward.

Using a Full-Sentence Quotation of Fewer Than Four Lines

A quotation of one or more complete sentences can be enclosed in double quotation marks and introduced with a verb, usually in the present tense and followed by a comma. Omit a period at the close of a quoted sentence, but keep any question mark or exclamation mark. Insert the parenthetical reference, then a period.

> One commentator asks, "What accounts for the government's ineptitude in safeguarding our privacy rights?" (Spinello 9).

> "What accounts," Spinello asks, "for the government's ineptitude in safeguarding our privacy rights?" (9).

Introducing a Quotation with a Full Sentence

Use a colon after a full sentence that introduces a quotation.

> Spinello asks an important question: "What accounts for the government's ineptitude in safeguarding our privacy rights?" (9).

Introducing a Quotation with "That"

A single complete sentence can be introduced with a *that* construction.

> Chernow suggests that "the creation of New York's first bank was a formative moment in the city's rise as a world financial center" (199–200).

Quoting Part of a Sentence

Make sure that quoted material blends grammatically into the new sentence.

> McNichol and Lav assert that during that period, state governments were helped by "an array of fiscal gimmicks."

Using a Quotation That Contains Another Quotation

Replace the internal double quotation marks with single quotation marks.

> Lowell was "famous as a 'confessional' writer, but he scorned the term," according to Bidart (vii).

Adding Information to a Quotation

Any addition for clarity or any change for grammatical reasons should be placed in square brackets.

> In 109 East Palace, Conant notes the timing of the first atom bomb test: "The test had originally been scheduled for 4:00 A.M. on July 16, [1945] when most of the surrounding population would be sound asleep" (304–05).

Omitting Information from Source Sentences

Indicate an omission with ellipsis marks (three spaced dots).

> In 109 East Palace, Conant says, "The test had originally been scheduled for 4:00 A.M. on July 16, when . . . there would be the least number of witnesses" (304–05).

Using a Quotation of More Than Four Lines

Begin a long quotation on a new line and set off the quotation by indenting it one inch from the left margin and double spacing it throughout. Do not enclose it in quotation marks. Put the parenthetical reference *after* the period at the end of the quotation.

> One international organization recently documented the repression of women's rights in Libya:
>> The government of Libya is arbitrarily detaining women and girls in "social rehabilitation" facilities, . . . locking them up indefinitely without due process. Portrayed as "protective" homes for wayward women and girls, . . . these facilities are de facto prisons . . . [where] the government routinely violates women's and girls' human rights, including those to due process, liberty, freedom of movement, personal dignity, and privacy. (Human)

IS IT PLAGIARISM? TEST YOURSELF ON IN-TEXT REFERENCES

Read the Original Source excerpt. Can you spot the plagiarism in the examples that follow it?

Original source

> To begin with, language is a system of communication. I make this rather obvious point because to some people nowadays it isn't obvious: they see language as above all a means of "self-expression." Of course, language is one way that we express our personal feelings and thoughts—but so, if it comes to that, are dancing, cooking and making music. Language does much more: it enables us to convey to others what we think, feel and want. Language-as-communication is the prime means of organizing the cooperative activities that enable us to accomplish as groups things we could not possibly do as individuals. Some other species also engage in cooperative activities, but these are either quite simple (as among baboons and wolves) or exceedingly stereotyped (as among bees, ants and termites). Not surprisingly, the communicative systems used by these animals are also simple or stereotypes. Language, our uniquely flexible and intricate system of communication, makes possible our equally flexible and intricate ways of coping with the world around us: in a very real sense, it is what makes us human. (Claiborne 8)

Works Cited entry:

Claiborne, Robert. Our Marvelous Native Tongue: The Life and Times of the English Language. New York: New York Times, 1983.

Plagiarism Example 1

> One commentator makes a distinction between language used as **a means of self-expression** and **language-as-communication**.

It is the latter that distinguishes human interaction from that of other species and allows humans to work cooperatively on complex tasks (8).

What's wrong?
The source's name is not given, and there are no quotation marks around words taken directly from the source (in **boldface** in the example).

Plagiarism Example 2

Claiborne notes that language "is the prime means of organizing the cooperative activities." Without language, we would, consequently, not have civilization.

What's wrong?
The page number of the source is missing. A parenthetical reference should immediately follow the material being quoted, paraphrased, or summarized. You may omit a parenthetical reference only if the information that you have included in your attribution is sufficient to identify the source in your Works Cited list and no page number is needed.

Plagiarism Example 3

Other animals also **engage in cooperative activities**. However, these actions are not very complex. Rather they are either the very **simple** activities of, for example, **baboons and wolves** or the **stereotyped** activities of animals such as **bees, ants and termites** (Claiborne 8).

What's wrong?
A paraphrase should capture a specific idea from a source but must not duplicate the writer's phrases and words (in **boldface** in the example). In the example, the wording and sentence structure follow the source too closely.

EVALUATING SOURCES

It's very important to evaluate critically every source you consult, especially sources on the Internet, where it can be difficult to separate reliable sources from questionable ones. Ask these questions to help evaluate your sources:

- Is the material relevant to your topic?
- Is the source well respected?
- Is the material accurate?

- Is the information current?
- Is the material from a primary source or a secondary source?

AVOIDING PLAGIARISM: NOTE-TAKING TIPS

The most effective way to avoid unintentional plagiarism is to follow a systematic method of note taking and writing.

- **Keep copies of your documentation information.** For all sources that you use, keep photocopies of the title and copyright pages and the pages with quotations you need. Highlight the relevant citation information in color. Keep these materials until you've completed your paper.
- **Quotation or paraphrase?** Assume that all the material in your notes is direct quotation unless you indicated otherwise. Double-check any paraphrase for quoted phrases, and insert the necessary quotation marks.
- **Create the Works Cited or References list** *first*. Before you start writing your paper, your list is a **working bibliography**, a list of possible sources to which you add source entries as you discover them. As you finalize your list, you can delete the items you decided not to use in your paper.

Credits

CHAPTER 1

Page 8: "The Future of Love: Kiss Romance Goodbye, It's Time for the Real Thing" by Barbara Graham, *UTNE Reader,* November/December 1996. Reprinted by permission of the author.

CHAPTER 2

Page 29: "We Are Not Created Equal in Every Way" by Joan Ryan from *San Francisco Chronicle,* December 12, 2000. Copyright © 2000 by *San Francisco Chronicle.* Reproduced with permission of *San Francisco Chronicle* via Copyright Clearance Center, Inc.

CHAPTER 3

Page 54: Excerpts from "Private Gets 3 Years for Iraq Prison Abuse" by David S. Cloud, from *The New York Times,* September 28, 2005. Copyright © 2005 by The New York Times. All rights reserved. Used by permission and protected by the Copyright Laws of the United States. The printing, copying, redistribution, or retransmission of the Material without express written permission is prohibited. **Page 55:** Excerpt from "Military Abuse," Globe Editorial, published in *The Boston Globe,* September 28, 2005. Copyright © 2005 Globe Newspaper Company, Inc. Reprinted with permission. Visit The Boston Globe online at www.bostonglobe.com. For more information about reprints, contact PARS International Corp. at 212-221-9595. **Page 63:** From "Calls for National Service" by Roger Landrum, from National Service: Social, Economic, and Military Impacts, edited by Michael W. Sherraden and Donald J. Eberly (Pergamon Press, 1982). Reprinted by permission of the author. **Page 65:** "Politics and National Service: A Virus Attacks the Volunteer Sector" by Bruce Chapman. Reprinted from National Service: Pro and Con, edited by Williamson M. Evers with the permission of the publisher, Hoover Institution Press. Copyright 1990 by the Board of Trustees of the Leland Stanford Junior University. **Page 77:** "A Time to Heed the Call" by David Gergen from *U.S. News & World Report,* December 24, 2001, p.60. Copyright © 2001 U.S. News & World Report, L.P. Reprinted with permission.

CHAPTER 4

Page 100: "Cookies or Heroin?" From *The Plug-In Drug, Revised and Updated—25th Anniversary Edition* by Marie Winn, copyright © 1977, 1985, 2002 by Marie Winn Miller. Used by permission of Viking Penguin, a division of Penguin Group (USA) Inc. **Page 102:** "The Coming Apart of a Dorm Society" by Edward Peselman. Reprinted by permission of the author.

CHAPTER 5

Page 124: "The Satisfactions of Housewifery and Motherhood in an Age of 'Do-Your-Own-Thing' " by Terry Martin Hekker, originally published in *The New York Times,* Dec. 20, 1977. Reprinted by permission of the author. **Page 126:** "Modern Love: Paradise Lost (Domestic Division)," by Terry Martin Hekker, *The New York Times,* January 1, 2006. Copyright © 2006 The New York Times. All rights reserved. Used by permission and protected by the Copyright Laws of the United States. The printing, copying, redistribution, or retransmission of the Material without express written permission is prohibited. **Page 130:** "The Radical Idea of Marrying for Love," "From Yoke Mates to Soul Mates," from *Marriage, A History* by Stephanie Coontz, copyright © 2005 by the S. J. Coontz Company. Used by permission of Viking Penguin, a division of Penguin Group (USA) Inc. **Page 143:** Excerpts from "The State of Our Unions: The Social Health of Marriage in America," by David Popenoe and Barbara Dafoe Whitehead, reprinted with permission from *USA Today Magazine,* July 2002. Copyright © 2002 by the Society for the Advancement of Education, Inc. All rights reserved; Excerpts from "The State of Our Unions: The Social Health of Marriage in America - 2005," by David Popenoe and Barbara Dafoe

Whitehead, reprinted by permission of the National Marriage Project, Rutgers University. **Page 156:** Pages 8–13 from *Marriages and Families: Diversity and Change*, 3rd Edition, by Mary Ann Schwartz and BarBara Marliene Scott, © 2000. Reprinted by permission of Pearson Education, Inc., Upper Saddle River, NJ. **Page 162:** From *Virtually Normal* by Andrew Sullivan, copyright © 1995 by Andrew Sullivan. Used by permission of Alfred A. Knopf, a division of Random House, Inc. **Page 167:** "… But Not a Very Good Idea, Either" by William J. Bennett, published in *The Washington Post*, May 21, 1996. Reprinted by permission of the author. **Page 170:** "Many Women at Elite Colleges Set Career Path to Motherhood" by Louise Story, *The New York Times*, September 20, 2005. Copyright © 2005 The New York Times. All rights reserved. Used by permission and protected by the Copyright Laws of the United States. The printing, copying, redistribution, or retransmission of the Material without express written permission is prohibited. **Page 176:** "What Yale Women Want (and Why It Is Misguided)" by Karen Stabiner, from the *Los Angeles Times*, September 24, 2005. Reprinted by permission of the author. **Page 178:** "A Marriage Agreement" by Alix Kates Shulman, first published in 1969 in *Up From Under*, and later reprinted in *Life Magazine, Redbook*, and other publications. Copyright © 1969, 1970, 1971 by Alix Kates Shulman. Reprinted by permission of the author. **Page 184:** "The Myth of Co-Parenting" by Hope Edelman from *The Bitch in the House* edited by Cathi Hanauer. Reprinted by permission of The Elizabeth Kaplan Literary Agency. **Page 192:** "My Problem with Her Anger" by Eric Bartels. Copyright © 2004 by Eric Bartels. Reprinted by permission of the author.

CHAPTER 6

Page 205: Adapted from "The Education of a Torturer" by Janice T. Gibson and Mika Haritos-Fatouros, *Psychology Today*, November, 1986. Reprinted with permission from Psychology Today Magazine. Copyright © 1986 Sussex Publishers, LLC. **Page 206:** "Opinions and Social Pressure" by Solomon Asch, *Scientific American*, November, 1955. Reprinted with permission. Copyright © 1955 by Scientific American, Inc. All rights reserved. **Page 213:** "The Perils of Obedience" abridged and adapted from *Obedience to Authority* by Stanley Milgram. Originally published in *Harper's Magazine*. Copyright © 1974 by Stanley Milgram. Reprinted by permission of HarperCollins Publishers. **Page 226:** Adapted from "Review of Stanley Milgram's Experiment on Obedience," by Diana Baumrind, from *American Psychologist*, 1964 (vol. 19 (6), pp. 421–423). Original title: "Some Thoughts on Ethics of Research: After Reading Milgram's 'Behavioral Study of Obedience'." Copyright © 1964 by the American Psychological Association. Reprinted with permission. **Page 233:** "The Stanford Prison Experiment" by Philip Zimbardo. Originally published as "The Mind is a Formidable Jailer," *The New York Times Magazine*, April 8, 1973. Copyright © 1973 by Philip G. Zimbardo. Reprinted by permission. **Page 245:** "Disobedience as a Psychological and Moral Problem," pp. 16–23, from *On Disobedience and Other Essays* by Erich From. Copyright © 1981 by the Estate of Erich Fromm. Reprinted by permission of HarperCollins Publishers. **Page 251:** "Uncivil Disobedience: Violating the Rules for Breaking the Law" from *Education Next* 5.2 (Spring 2005) by James J. Lopach and Jean A. Luckowski. Reprinted by permission of *Education Next*, Hoover Press.

CHAPTER 7

Page 267: From *One Nation Under Goods* by James J. Farrell. Copyright © 2003 Smithsonian Institution. Used by permission of the publisher. **Page 274:** From "All the World's a Mall: Reflections on the Social and Economic Consequences of the American Shopping Center," by Kenneth T. Jackson, from *The American Historical Review*, Vol. 101, No. 4, Oct. 1996. Reprinted by permission of the author. **Page 280:** Reprinted from *Main Street Revisited: Time, Space, and Image-Building in Small-Town America* by Richard Francavigli (University of Iowa Press, 1996) with the permission of the University of Iowa Press. **Page 286:** "Enclosed, Encyclopedic, Endured: One Week at the Mall of America" by David Guterson. Copyright © 1993 by David Guterson. Originally appeared in *Harper's Magazine* (Vol. 287, August 1993). Reprinted by permission of Georges Borchardt, Inc., for David Guterson. **Page 294:** "Shopping Malls as Sacred Places," from *Shopping Malls and Other Sacred Places: Putting God in Place* by Jon Pahl.

Copyright © 2003 by Jon Pahl. Published by permission of Brazos Press, a division of Baker Publishing Group. **Page 300:** Pages ix–xiii from Preface from *The Substance of Style* by Virginia Postrel. Copyright © 2003 by Virginia Postrel. Reprinted by permission of HarperCollins Publishers. **Page 304:** From "Community Through Exclusion and Illusion" by George Lewis, *Journal of Popular Culture*, Vol. 24, No. 2, Fall 1990, pp. 121–136, published by Blackwell Publishing Ltd. Reprinted by permission. **Page 316:** Excerpted from "From Town Center to Shopping Center: The Reconfiguration of Community Marketplaces in Postwar America" by Lizabeth Cohen, from *American Historical Review*, Vol. 101, No. 4, Oct. 1996, pp. 1050–1081. Reprinted by permission of the American Historical Association and the author. **Page 323:** "Mallaise: How to Know If You Have It" from *The Malling of America* by William Severini Kowinski. Copyright © 1985 by William Severini Kowinski. Reprinted by permission of the author.

CHAPTER 8

Page 335: From *Counting Sheep* by Paul Martin. Copyright © 2004 by the author and reprinted by permission of Thomas Dunne Books, an imprint of St. Martin's Press, LLC. **Page 353:** "America's Sleep Deprived Teens Nodding Off at School, Behind the Wheel, New National Sleep Foundation Poll Finds," press release from March 28, 2006, from the National Sleep Foundation. Used with permission of the National Sleep Foundation. For further information, please visit http://www.sleepfoundation.org. **Page 356:** "Tips for Teens" from *Adolescent Sleep Needs and Patterns: Research Report and Resource Guide,* National Sleep Foundation, 2000. Used with permission of the National Sleep Foundation. **Page 359:** From "When Worlds Collide: Adolescent Need for Sleep Versus Societal Demands" by Mary A. Carskadon, from *Adolescent Sleep Needs and School Starting Times* ed. by Kyla L. Wahlstrom, published by Phi Delta Kappa Educational Foundation, 1999. Reprinted by permission of the author. **Page 369:** From *The Promise of Sleep* by William C. Dement, copyright © 1999 by William C. Dement. Used by permission of Dell Publishing, a division of Random House, Inc. **Page 377:** "Appendix: Pittsburgh Sleep Quality Index (PSQI)" from "The Pittsburgh Sleep Quality Index: A New Instrument for Psychiatric Practice and Research" by Daniel J. Buysse, Charles F. Reynolds III, Timothy H. Monk, Susan R. Berman, and David J. Kupfer, from *Psychiatry Research*, Vol. 28, No. 2, May 1989. Reprinted by permission of Daniel Buysse. **Page 383:** "How Sleep Deprivation Affects Psychological Variables Related to College Students' Cognitive Performance" by June J. Pilcher and Amy S. Walters, from *Journal of American College Health*, Vol. 46, issue 3, November, 1997, pp. 121–126. Reprinted with permission of the Helen Dwight Reid Educational Foundation. Published by Heldref Publications, 1319 Eighteenth St., NW, Washington, DC 20036-1802. Copyright © 1997. **Page 393:** Excerpts from "Starting Time and School Life" by Patricia K. Kubow, Kyla L. Wahlstrom, and Amy Bemis, *Phi Delta Kappan*, Vol. 80, Issue 5, January 1999. Reprinted by permission of Patricia Kubow.

CHAPTER 9

Page 407: "Advertising's Fifteen Basic Appeals" by Jib Fowles. Originally published in *Et Cetera: A Review of General Semantics*, Vol. 39, Number 3. Copyright © 1982 Institute of General Semantics. Reprinted by permission of Institute of General Semantics (IGS), Fort Worth, Texas. **Page 431:** Pages 275–281 from *Advertising*, 1st Edition, by Dorothy Cohen, © 1988. Reprinted by permission of Pearson Education, Inc., Upper Saddle River, NJ.

Page 440: Image Courtesy of the Advertising Archives; 441: Image Courtesy of the Advertising Archives; 442: Image Courtesy of the Advertising Archives; 443: Image Courtesy of the Advertising Archives; 444: Image Courtesy of the Advertising Archives; 445: Image Courtesy of the Advertising Archives; 446: Image Courtesy of the Advertising Archives; 447: Image Courtesy of the Advertising Archives; 448: Image Courtesy of the Advertising Archives; 449: Image Courtesy of the Advertising Archives; 450-451: Image Courtesy of the Advertising Archives; 452: Image Courtesy of the Advertising Archives; 453: Image Courtesy of the Advertising Archives; 454: Image Courtesy of the Advertising Archives; 455: Image Courtesy of the Advertising Archives; 456: Image Courtesy of the Advertising Archives; 457: Image Courtesy of the Advertising Archives; 458: Image Courtesy of the Advertising Archives; 462–463: Image Courtesy of the Advertising Archives; 466: Image Courtesy of the Advertising Archives; 467: Courtesy Chrysler LLC; 468–469: Image Courtesy of the Advertising Archives; 471: Image Courtesy of the Advertising Archives; 480: Image Courtesy of the Advertising Archives; 481: Image Courtesy of the Advertising Archives; 482: Courtesy Soloflex, Inc.; 483: Image Courtesy of the Advertising Archives

Index

Quick Index: APA Documentation Basics

APA In-text Citations in Brief

Place citation information—author, publication year, passage locator (page or paragraph number)—in sentence or in parentheses.

Summary or paraphrase; refer only to the year of publication:

> Berk (2002) suggested that many researchers view punishment as a quick fix.

Direct quotation, author and publication date *not* mentioned in sentence:

> A good deal of research suggests that punishing a child "promotes only momentary compliance" (Berk, 2002, p. 383).

Direct quotation, author and publication date mentioned in sentence:

> According to Berk (2002), a good deal of research suggests that punishing a child "promotes only momentary compliance" (p. 383).

Direct quotation, Internet; provide page number, paragraph number (use the abbreviation para, or ¶ symbol), or paragraph number within a section, as available:

> Others have noted a rise in "problems that mimic the dysfunctional behaviors seen on reality television" (Spivek, 2006, Introduction section, ¶ 3).

APA References List in Brief

At the end of the paper, on a separate page titled "References" (no italics or quotation marks), alphabetize sources, providing full bibliographic information for each. The most common entry types follow; doubled entries show online equivalents of print sources.

BOOK

Basic entry

> Freud, S. (1920). *Dream psychology: Psychoanalysis for beginners* (M. D. Elder, Trans.). New York: James A. McCann.
>
> Freud, S. (1920). *Dream psychology: Psychoanalysis for beginners* (M. D. Elder, Trans.). Retrieved from http://www.gutenberg.org/ etext/15489

Selection from an edited book

> Halberstam, D. (2002). Who we are. In S. J. Gould (Ed.), *The best American essays 2002* (pp. 124–136). New York: Houghton Mifflin.

Later edition

> Samuelson, P., & Nordhaus, W. D. (2005). *Economics* (18th ed.). Boston: McGraw-Hill/Irwin.

ARTICLE FROM A MAGAZINE

>   Davison, P. (2000, May). Girl, seeming to
>   disappear. *Atlantic Monthly*, 108—111.
>   Davison. P. (2000, May). Girl, seeming to disap-
>   pear. *Atlantic Monthly*. Retrieved from
>   http://www.theatlantic.com/issues/2000/05
>   /davison.htm

[Do not include retrieval date unless the source is likely to change.]

ARTICLE FROM A JOURNAL PAGINATED CONTINUOUSLY THROUGH THE
ANNUAL VOLUME

>   Chene, C. (2005). Ads pressure Ontario to butt
>   out in retail locations. *Canadian Medical
>   Association Journal, 172*, 1544.

ARTICLE FROM A JOURNAL PAGINATED BY ISSUE

>   Ivanenko, A., & Massie, C. (2006). Assessment and
>   management of sleep disorders in children.
>   *Psychiatric Times, 23*(11), 90—95.
>   Ivanenko, A., & Massie, C. (2006). Assessment and
>   management of sleep disorders in children.
>   *Psychiatric Times, 23*(11), 90—95. Retrieved
>   from http://find.galegroup.com

[In referencing an online text available only through a subscription service,
provide the URL for the home page or menu page of the service.]

[Whether a journal article is paginated by issue or continuously through the
annual volume, include both volume and issue number (if available) when
citing the electronic version of the source.]

ARTICLE FROM A NEWSPAPER

>   Ridberg, M. (2006, May 4). Professors want their
>   classes 'unwired.' *Christian Science Monitor*,
>   p. 16.
>   Ridberg, M. (2006, May 4). Professors want their
>   classes 'unwired.' *Christian Science Monitor*.
>   Retrieved from http://www.csmonitor.com/2006
>   /0504/p16s01-legn.html

ARTICLE FROM THE INTERNET

>   Weinberg, H. (n.d.). Group psychotherapy resource
>   guide. Retrieved August 28, 2007, from
>   http://www.group-psychotherapy.com/

[If you think the online content might change, include the retrieval date.]

QUICK INDEX: MLA DOCUMENTATION BASICS

MLA In-text Citations in Brief

When referring to a source, use parentheses to enclose a page number reference to that source. Include the author's name if you do not mention it in your sentence:

> From the beginning, the AIDS antibody test has been "mired in controversy" (Bayer 101).

If you mention the author in the sentence, omit the name from your in-text citation:

> According to Bayer, from the beginning, the AIDS antibody test has been "mired in controversy" (101).

MLA Works Cited List in Brief

At the end of the paper, on a separate page titled "Works Cited," alphabetize (by author) the sources you have used. Provide full bibliographic information for each. Examples of entries follow, with doubled entries showing online equivalents of print sources.

BOOK

Basic entry

> Dickens, Charles. David Copperfield. New York: Signet, 1962.
>
> Dickens, Charles. The Personal History and Experience of David Copperfield The Younger. 2 vols. Harvard Classics Shelf of Fiction. New York: Collier, 1917. Bartleby.com. 2000. 14 Jan. 2008 <www.bartleby.com/307/>.

Selection from an edited book

> Hardy, Melissa. "The Heifer." The Best American Short Stories 2002. Ed. Sue Miller. Boston: Houghton, 2002. 97—115.

Later edition

> Whitten, Phillip. Anthropology: Contemporary Perspectives. 8th ed. Boston: Allyn, 2001.

ARTICLE FROM A MAGAZINE

> Davison, Peter. "Girl, Seeming to Disappear." Atlantic Monthly May 2000: 108—11.
>
> Davison, Peter. "Girl, Seeming to Disappear." Atlantic Online May 2000: 108—11. 18 Dec. 2007 <http://www.theatlantic.com/issues/2000/05/davison.htm>.

ARTICLE FROM A SCHOLARLY JOURNAL

For articles in journals paginated continuously through the year

    Chene, Christine. "Ads Pressure Ontario to Butt
        Out in Retail Locations." <u>Canadian Medical
        Association Journal</u> 172 (2005): 1544.

    Chene, Christine. "Ads Pressure Ontario to Butt
        Out in Retail Locations." <u>Canadian Medical
        Association Journal</u> 172 (2005): 1544. <u>Academic
        Search Premier</u>. EBSCOhost. Bentley College,
        Baker Lib. 3 Feb. 2007 <http://
        search.ebscohost.com>.

For articles in journals that paginate each issue separately

    Ivanenko, Anna, and Clifford Massie. "Assessment
        and Management of Sleep Disorders in
        Children." <u>Psychiatric Times</u> 23.11 (2006):
        90–95.

    Ivanenko, Anna, and Clifford Massie. "Assessment
        and Management of Sleep Disorders in
        Children." <u>Psychiatric Times</u> 23.11 (2006):
        90-95. <u>Academic OneFile</u>. Thomson Gale.
        Minuteman Lib. System, MA. 18 May 2007
        <http://find.galegroup.com/>.

ARTICLE FROM A NEWSPAPER

    Ridberg, Maia. "Professors Want Their Classes
        'Unwired'." <u>Christian Science Monitor</u> 4 May
        2006: 16.

    Ridberg, Maia. "Professors Want Their Classes
        'Unwired'." <u>Christian Science Monitor</u>
        4 May 2006: 16. 7 Oct. 2007 <http://
        www.csmonitor.com/2006/0504/
        p16s01-legn.html>.

ARTICLE FROM THE INTERNET

    "The 2006 National Survey of Information
        Technology in US Higher Education: Summary."
        <u>The Campus Computing Project</u>. 6 Oct. 2007
        <http://www.campuscomputing.net/>.

CHECKLIST FOR WRITING SUMMARIES

- **Read the passage carefully.** Determine its structure. Identify the author's purpose in writing.
- **Reread.** *Label* each section or stage of thought. *Highlight* key ideas and terms.
- **Write one-sentence summaries** of each stage of thought.
- **Write a thesis:** a one- or two-sentence summary of the entire passage.
- **Write the first draft** of your summary.
- **Check your summary** against the original passage.
- **Revise** your summary.

CHECKLIST FOR WRITING CRITIQUES

- **Introduce** both the passage being critiqued and the author.
- **Summarize** the author's main points, making sure to state the author's purpose for writing.
- **Evaluate** the validity of the presentation.
- **Respond** to the presentation: agree and/or disagree.
- **Conclude** with your overall assessment.